ALEXANDER ORLOV

ALEXANDER ORLOV
THE FBI'S
KGB GENERAL

EDWARD   GAZUR

CARROLL & GRAF PUBLISHERS
NEW YORK

ALEXANDER ORLOV
The FBI's KGB General

Carroll & Graf Publishers
An Imprint of Avalon Publishing Group Incorporated
161 William St., 16th Floor
New York, NY 10038

First Carroll & Graf edition 2002

Library of Congress Cataloging-in-Publication Data is available.

ISBN: 0-7867-0971-5

Printed in the United States of America
Distributed by Publishers Group West

This book is dedicated with deep affection and fond memories to my boyhood buddies from the old West 73rd Street and Clark Avenue neighbourhood in Cleveland, Ohio:

Johnnie Braat
Georgie Feldman
Raymie Gillespie and
Jackie Tischler

CONTENTS

ILLUSTRATIONS

secret revised code book from Washington DC to San Juan, September 1953.

The author about to depart on a naval reserve training cruise, pictured with Ruth, Kathryn Anne and son James.

Photo of Vera Orlov taken on her sixteenth birthday, 1 September 1939.

The Westbury Apartments, 3360 West 9th Street, Los Angeles, where Vera Orlov died on 15 July 1940 under the fictitious name of Vera Berg.

The house in Cleveland, Ohio, where Orlov gave the FBI the full details of his background (photo: Paul Snyder).

Clifton Park Apartments, Orlov's last residence (photo: George W. Arruda, FBI Special Agent).

The last photo of General Orlov taken in late summer 1972 by the author's son James (photo: Lieutenant Colonel James E. Gazur, US Air Force).

ACKNOWLEDGEMENTS

I extend my deepest love to my devoted parents Anne and Clarence W. Kilner, both deceased, who made this book possible through their lifetime support, devotion and inspiration. I will be forever grateful to my wonderful wife Ruth, who proofread every word in my manuscript without complaint and corrected many mistakes that I had overlooked. I give thanks to Gordon Brook-Shepherd, Hayden Peake and Nigel West for their helpful advice on writing and publishing. I extend my recognition to Dennis and Lilly Langtry Williams, who gave me a special insight on one of my chapters; and I give special thanks to Paul A. Willis, Director of Libraries, and Gordon E. Hogg, Special Collections and Archives, University of Kentucky, for their research efforts on my behalf. I give special recognition and gratitude to the Federal Bureau of Investigation and its dedicated men and women, who unselfishly serve our nation in war and peace. The FBI afforded me the opportunity to have a meaningful life's career without parallel, and if I were to restart my career path from the beginning, it would be at the front door of the FBI. And last but not least I give extra special thanks to General Alexander Orlov for his enduring sacrifices and deeds which may never become known but were a positive measure in defeating Communism in the days of the Cold War. Without him, this book could not possibly have been written.

Edward P. Gazur

PREFACE

by

Gordon Brook-Shepherd

In *The Storm Petrels*, the first of my books on major Soviet intelligence defectors, I described General Alexander Orlov as the 'brightest of all the trophies which Stalin's reign of terror presented to the West'. This was not just because, as a three-star KGB general, he outranked all the others. He also had a quality which none of them possessed – an insatiable curiosity about everything happening in his service, whether he was involved himself or not. He ferreted around like a conscientious newshound and the value of this to the historian I only came to realise after making contact, some twenty years later, with the last of his FBI 'minders', Edward P. Gazur.

Most of the unpublished material I originally collected on the General came from Ray Rocca, the CIA's counter-intelligence expert who debriefed him over many months (and to whom I dedicated the book under the guise of 'The Chrysanthemum Man' – his favourite flower). Rocca regarded him as 'a professional to the end of his days', who spoke only selectively on key operational matters and certainly took some secrets with him to his death in April 1973, including his suspected role as a recruiter of key Western agents in the mid-1930s.

But Orlov was also, uniquely, the defector who vanished for years on end even in his country of asylum. From 1938, when he and his wife and daughter entered America, still using his diplomatic passport, until 1953, when he emerged with the manuscript of his first book, he simply disappeared. He used a variety of aliases, moving from state to state, and was at such a low financial ebb that, by the time the book was completed (in the Public

Library of Cleveland, Ohio), food consisted of cheap breakfast cereals for every meal of the day. The publishing success of his *Secret History of Stalin's Crimes* put an end to these problems but pushed him, very reluctantly, into the limelight he had always shunned.

At this stage the FBI came on the scene. Frustrated by the fact that this 'brightest of all trophies' had successfully hidden himself away in the cupboard for fifteen years (under their very noses, as regards Cleveland), the agency at first behaved in a very boorish and overpowering fashion that alienated the General. But the General soon established his bona fides by his invaluable testimony before the Senate Internal Security Committee (revealing, among other things, that no fewer than eighteen Soviet spy rings had been established in the United States). In May 1956, he and his devoted wife Maria were granted permanent residence status by a special bill of Congress. His troubles were over.

The FBI unconsciously made up for their earlier behaviour by allotting him, for the last years of his life, Edward Gazur as his 'minder'. Edward and his wife Ruth became perhaps the only true friends the Orlovs had during their thirty years of open and covert asylum – so much so that he made Gazur his literary executor. This was how, many years after *The Storm Petrels*, I was able to discover the full historical value of Orlov's knowledge. He left, in Gazur's hands, an English-language copy of his secret masterpiece, 'March of Time', his reminiscences, over 659 pages in length, of his life and times.

Through a happy accident, I became the first 'outside eye' to study it at the Gazurs' hospitable Kentucky home. It proved invaluable in researching that first battle between the Bolshevik and Western intelligence, which I recounted in *The Iron Maze*. He had also given magnificent insights into the great Soviet deception game, the TRUST, and also into the entrapment of Sydney Reilly, Britain's overrated 'Ace of Spies'. Orlov had been personally involved in neither operation; he was just interested in both. Thank you, General.

INTRODUCTION

The first time I laid eyes on KGB General Alexander Orlov and his wife Maria was on 17 August 1971, and I last saw him alive on 6 April 1973 around midnight, within hours of his death the following morning. General Orlov was, and to this date still is, the highest-ranking Soviet intelligence officer ever to defect to the free world. When he arrived in 1938, he carried with him the most damaging evidence ever to surface regarding the tyrannical dictatorship of Josef Stalin and the Communist regime of the Soviet Union. In this respect he was cited as one of the most important witnesses ever to testify before the US Senate's Internal Security Subcommittee.

What began as an impartial and professional relationship with Orlov soon developed into a trusted and close personal friendship, to the extent that my wife and I considered him a part of our family; he in turn shared the same commitment. Between 1971 and 1973, we would meet regularly and have lengthy conversations about his life as a senior member of Soviet intelligence, his reasons for defecting, his life in hiding in the United States with his wife and daughter, and the frightening and personally tragic consequences of the regime's revenge for his eventual exposure of Stalin's crimes and the truth behind the great purges and show trials of the 1930s.

This book however is in no way an attempt to portray the definitive biography of Alexander Orlov, but rather a narrative of his life based on our conversations and the memories which were related to me directly by him. I have also relied heavily on his unpublished memoirs to refresh my own memory, inasmuch that

Orlov and I went over each chapter of his memoirs together and used them as a guide for our discussions. In addition, there were other episodes of personal and historical significance that we discussed that were not in his memoirs.

In all, our discussions were conducted in the context of an investigator interviewing a subject. In most instances, I took copious notes for clarification as well as regarding those episodes that were outside the scope of his memoirs. When I came to write this book after a twenty-six-year lapse, however, I found that certain notes were too sketchy for me to reconstruct their meaning and, as a result, some of what Orlov told me in 1972 was lost. What remains, as reflected in this book, is an accurate rendition of the facts as presented to me by the man still regarded by the KGB as its master spy. He is characterised as such in the selective and highly censored portions of his KGB dossier which were among the first to be released for publication after the Soviet collapse and the opening up of the KGB archives to rather limited external scrutiny by a select group of scholars.

I also have to venture that I never had any intention of writing a book about Orlov although I do admit that the idea crossed my mind more than once. I always felt that Orlov's odyssey, which began with a remarkable career in the KGB and ended with his defection and years of hiding, provided the material for a fascinating book. However, over twenty-three years passed after Orlov's death without me putting the first word to paper.

My thinking began to change in early 1994, when I received a telephone call from an FBI Special Agent, personally unknown to me, who knew that I had handled Orlov and, because of his interest in the case, wanted to know if I had heard of a recently published book, *Deadly Illusions* by John Costello and Oleg Tsarev, which was apparently based on Orlov's recently opened KGB file. Above the title on the book's dustjacket was the headline, 'The KGB Orlov Dossier Reveals Stalin's Master Spy', and the back cover listed some 'early praise' for the book by several respected authors. I was intrigued by the book and could hardly wait to read it.

Perhaps I would have been better off not to, for what I read about Orlov and the man I knew personally and called a close friend seemed to be two entirely different people. There is no doubt that the KGB archives were opened for an exposé on Orlov and that much of the information was authentic, but what came out was not an entirely objective rendering of the files, and by the time the information had reached the authors, the contents had been highly laundered. In my opinion, what the KGB had omitted would have been of more pertinence, value and interest than what they had actually furnished. As I read the book, I was troubled by questions in most of the chapters which would have gone unnoticed by the casual reader. What also puzzled me when I got thoroughly involved in the matter sometime later was that there were retired members of the American intelligence community and respected authors in the intelligence field who placed their trust in the KGB when it came to *Deadly Illusions*. None of them was directly involved with the Orlov case nor knew him as closely as I did.

What was of particular interest to me was a rather lengthy twenty-four-page 'Afterword' in which Costello justified why he believed he had not been duped and why the information furnished by the KGB should be believed. Although some of his argument was worthy of consideration and tended to support his convictions, in my view the final core analysis was that the material had been furnished by the KGB and that they had planted some dubious seeds.

After reading *Deadly Illusions* several times, my blood pressure had been sent somewhere into the infinity range. Still I had no intention of writing a book to counter its allegations, discussed in detail throughout this book, although I did make my views known to many of my colleagues in the intelligence field. However, after a while I decided to write to Costello and explain why I believed that Orlov had been unjustifiably maligned on the basis of KGB disinformation. It was then that I discovered that Costello had died some months previously, at an early age, and I had lost my chance to challenge him. I was also disturbed to learn from one of Costello's obituaries that he had been about to make a further revelation concerning Orlov, and this will be fully explored in the last chapter of this book.

With Costello now deceased, I had no one to address my questions and grievances to, and as there was no one else who could carry the banner on Orlov's behalf, I finally decided that I would write this memoir. I recall that when Orlov turned over the care of his own memoirs to me, he casually stated that I was now the 'Keeper of the Flame'. With this in mind, I could not let him down.

What is written herein is not a definitive historical record of the KGB's master spy but rather an insight into parts of his life and his secret odyssey through the eyes and ears of his close friend. There is no doubt that by some small measure Orlov had an impact on history, both as a high-ranking Soviet intelligence officer and as the senior personal representative of Stalin and the Politburo in Spain during the Spanish Civil War. When the definitive chapters of Orlov's life are unsealed in the future, his story will undoubtedly be rewritten many times. However, no future historian will ever be able to claim that they personally spoke with Orlov, and will therefore never have the benefit of knowing those explicit nuances that come with a personal relationship.

PART 1

A GENERAL IN THE KGB

ONE

A YOUNG INTELLIGENCE OFFICER

In order to understand the subsequent events of General Orlov's life, it is important to be aware of the background that shaped him and the progression of his career which culminated in his becoming a leading KGB officer.

Leiba (Leon, nicknamed Lev) Lazarevich Feldbin was born on 21 August 1895 in the rural town of Bobruysk, which lies in the Byelorussian district of Russia some 390 miles south-west of Moscow and 100 miles south-east of the Byelorussian capital of Minsk.

Feldbin's parents were Jewish and were both strongly dedicated to their religion. Up until the First World War, his father Lazar was engaged as a broker in the timber industry. His mother, Hannah Zaretsky, was adored and cherished by her son. Leon Lazarevich Feldbin would eventually become known to the world as Alexander Orlov, a cover name that was first used by him in 1936 when he became operational head of the NKVD in Spain at the start of the Spanish Civil War – and which we will use hereafter. Throughout his undercover career in espionage he used a long list of fictitious identities, but none would be more closely identified with him than the name of Orlov.

The fortunes of war prevailed on the Feldbin family when, early on in the Great War, the timber industry was virtually brought to a halt. Lazar decided to move his family to Moscow, where he found a secure position in the mercantile field.

Drawing on his scholastic aptitude, Orlov was admitted to Moscow's esteemed Lazarevsky Institute, which was highly regarded for its academic excellence. There he pursued courses that would lead to a civil service or diplomatic career. He graduated with honours, but having no inclination for government service, he opted to study law. In pursuit of his goal, he was accepted for admission to Moscow University's prestigious School of Law.

Orlov's tenure at the Law School was short-lived as in the autumn of 1916, on the eve of the Russian Revolution, he was drafted into the Tsar's army and served as a private with the 104th Infantry Regiment stationed in the Urals, far from the actual fighting.

Although he was well-qualified academically, possessed strong leadership qualities and, most of all, was highly motivated to become a military officer, he would not be able to do so in the army of the Tsar. Jews were not accepted for officer training nor were they ever assigned to the army's prime units; for the most part, they would find themselves in the infantry or in clerical positions, where their skills could be best utilised.

The situation did change to Orlov's benefit in early 1917, when the first phase of the Russian Revolution secured the forced abdication of Tsar Nicholas II and brought into being the Provisional Government. The interim government dictated the reform that would enable Orlov to enter the Third Moscow Military School, from where he graduated as a second lieutenant in March 1917. In May of that year, he joined the Bolshevik Party under the name of Lev Lazarevich Nikol'skiy.

The success of the October 1917 Revolution permitted Orlov to return to civilian life. That November he became Chief of the Information Section of the Revolutionary Finance Administration. Again, historical events interceded when civil war broke out in 1918 and the White Russian Armies consolidated their efforts to overthrow the Bolshevik Government and restore the monarchy. Orlov felt that he had no option but to help the cause of the Bolsheviks by re-entering the Red Army.

During the spring of 1920, Poland invaded Russia with such success that it occupied Kiev and most of the Ukraine, precipitating the Russo-Polish War. The White Russian Armies took this opportunity to consolidate their forces with the Poles so as to achieve their mutual objective: the overthrow of the Bolshevik Government. As a consequence, in September 1920 Orlov was posted to the 12th Red Army fighting along the Polish front. It was in this setting that fate intervened to change Orlov's direction in life forever and lead him to his career in the Russian intelligence service.

Orlov's first encounter with counter-intelligence and guerrilla warfare occurred when he was given command of a detachment that operated behind the Polish lines. It was in this capacity that he conceived ingenious planning strategies and personally led bold operations behind the enemy's lines. However, it was one particular incident that brought him to the attention of Felix Dzerzhinsky, the Chairman of the Cheka (the forerunner of the KGB), and which provided the impetus that would eventually bring about his long and fruitful association with the KGB. He would later remark in his twilight years that this was the most physically active phase of his life and acknowledged that this was the experience that had formulated his desire for a career in espionage.

In the same month that Orlov was posted to the 12th Red Army, he and two of his men in the guerrilla company were reconnoitring an area that had recently been taken by the Polish Army. The situation was such that the front line fluctuated daily, and in order to attack behind the enemy line a crossing-point had to be established from where entry would be relatively safe. As they approached a thicket overgrown with large white birch trees, they heard the sound of a horse neighing. Suddenly a horse appeared carrying a man in the dress of a Polish gentleman engaged in hunting. Man and horse came towards Orlov's group, and as they approached the portly gentleman raised his hands above his head in the act of surrendering. He carried no hunting arms but a small pistol was discovered hidden under his tunic. The prisoner was taken to the nearby army headquarters.

When they first encountered the man, he seemed excited and spoke in a mixture of Polish and Russian. He identified himself as Vodzinsky and claimed to be a Polish Army newspaperman and photographer. His credentials verified the name and occupation.

En route to their destination, Orlov observed the beautiful chestnut-coloured horse, which appeared to be of excellent bloodlines and which, during the war, was the type of mount that could only be in the possession of a military officer. The saddle was finely crafted out of quality leather and the workmanship clearly indicated it to be of English origin and quite expensive. Perhaps this man was more than a Polish Army newspaperman.

Vodzinsky was searched thoroughly at army headquarters and the only thing found that seemed to be out of the ordinary was an inexpensive notebook of the type used by schoolchildren in writing an assigned essay for homework. Vodzinsky spoke very little Russian and asked for an interpreter. He refused to furnish any information concerning the strength and movement of Polish troops and invoked his rights under the provisions of the Geneva Convention. All he would admit to was the fact that he had strayed into the area where he had been captured as he had been assured that Russian troops were a considerable distance away.

Vodzinsky was questioned at length about the notebook he carried. On its cover was written the name 'Senkovsky', which he claimed was his pen name. Inside were the usual pre-printed lines used to help guide a youngster in writing, and those lines that had already been used were in a rather neat handwriting in the Polish language. Vodzinsky claimed that he harboured an ambition to become a novelist after the war and that what was in the notebook was a novel he was writing under his pen name.

The notebook was translated and brought to Orlov. It was written in the first person and told the story of a Russian who has deserted his post, made his way through the front lines and surrendered to the Poles. He claims to possess vital information concerning the disposition of Russian troops and has been taken to regimental headquarters, where he has been questioned. Here he relates that he was the aide-de-camp in the Russian Staff and has deserted because he is a Polish patriot. He knows that the

Polish Army is falling into a Russian trap and had to warn the Poles of the impending disaster. However, everything he relates is contrary to what Polish intelligence believes, although he has raised some serious doubts. He is then taken to army headquarters, where he is confronted by the 'Commandant', an old man who apparently knows the hero of the story and berates him for being a Polish traitor. The narrator denies this and states that he only wants to share the fate of his countrymen. Finally, the Commandant puts his arm around the narrator's shoulders and indicates that, in spite of everything, he believes the narrator to be a true Polish hero.

Something about the prose of this so-called novel did not sit well with Orlov. The events depicted in it sounded more like reality than fiction. He believed it to be a narration of actual events in the form of a diary rather than a novel. Furthermore, at several points the narrator referred to himself as 'S', which Orlov concluded could stand for Senkovsky. Perhaps this was Vodzinsky's real name.

Orlov had Vodzinsky brought before him for interrogation. Vodzinsky continued to claim that the story was only a novel under the pen name Senkovsky and that it was only a lapse when he referred to the hero as 'S' because he had not yet named him. Orlov remained unconvinced and believed that Vodzinsky was hiding something. However, he did not reveal his suspicions to the captive as he had already formulated a plan in the event that Vodzinsky continued the pretence.

Another reason for doubting Vodzinsky's legend was that he claimed to be a photographer. However, when Orlov's staff photographer was purposely brought in contact with the captive and asked him a few casual technical questions, it was apparent that Vodzinsky knew nothing about photography.

Rather than sending Vodzinsky to a prisoner-of-war compound, he was incarcerated in a cell with three other prisoners. Two of them were planted counter-intelligence agents and the third was a legitimate Polish prisoner by the name of Captain Yanek. The Polish officer had been found on the battlefield in a shell-shocked condition along with a fellow officer by the name of Major Zembinsky. Yanek had been sent to a Russian field hospital, where he soon recovered, while the Major was taken first to Orlov's headquarters for interrogation and then to a prisoner-of-war compound. Vodzinsky and Yanek were drawn to one another and became friends. They often conversed in whispers, but Yanek was overheard by the planted spies telling Vodzinsky about his friend Zembinsky and of his great concern regarding the fate of his fellow officer.

In time, Yanek was transferred to a prisoner-of-war compound and within a week a new prisoner took his place in the cell. The new prisoner identified himself to his fellow inmates as Major Zembinsky. Vodzinsky was overjoyed at the situation and confided to the Major that Yanek had been held in the very same cell and that his fate was unknown. The new cellmate and Vodzinsky soon became friends, and before long Vodzinsky confided his fears that his captors would learn that he was actually Senkovsky. Should this happen, they would be able to determine that he had deserted from the Red Army and he would be put to death.

Vodzinsky had placed his confidence in the wrong man and his fate was now sealed, because the man who called himself Zembinsky was not the real Major but a Polish Communist working for the Russians. With this additional knowledge, it did not take long to discover that Senkovsky was a deserter from the Red Army.

When confronted with this information, Vodzinsky readily admitted his true identity. He was Colonel Senkovsky of the Polish Army and commander of all guerrilla warfare forces in the Polish Army. In some respects, this would make him the counterpart of Orlov, who at the time of the incident was the guerrilla commander of a detachment, but by the end of the Russo-Polish War was the guerrilla commander for the whole 12th Red Army.

Senkovsky no longer spoke Russian like a foreigner but like a native. He came from a mixed Russian-Polish family and had maintained his loyalty to both sides of the family. Under wartime conditions, however, he had been forced to decide where he would place his loyalty and the decision had been difficult for him. He had defected the month before from the 58th Soviet Division, where he had held the Staff position of aide-de-camp to the commander of the Division as well as head of guerrilla forces when the unit was making its way into Poland. He was in possession of information that indicated that the Poles were falling into a trap and would be routed, and he had felt compelled to pass on this information. So the story in the notebook was in fact his diary written in a somewhat veiled manner. The 'Commandant' was a reference to Józef Piłsudski, the then President of Poland, who had earned the title when he had run the Polish Socialist Party. Piłsudski had forgiven his old friend Senkovsky for going over to the other side to serve in the Red Army and had appointed him Chief of Guerrilla Operations.

Senkovsky admitted that on the day he was captured, he had been seeking a crossing-point for Polish guerrillas to make their way behind the Russian line. Orlov couldn't help thinking that the circumstances could so easily have been reversed and that he could have been Senkovsky's prisoner. The outcome would have been his interrogation by the Polish Defensiva and his own execution. Instead, it was Senkovsky's fate which was sealed and he would be executed as a traitor. His final request was a plea to receive the last rites of the Catholic Church.

During a conversation with Orlov, Senkovsky casually mentioned that he had been a boyhood friend of Felix Dzerzhinsky and his sister Altona. In their youth, the three friends had dabbled in poetry and dreamt of the future. Senkovsky related that he had always admired Dzerzhinsky and lamented the fact that, unlike his friend, he had failed along the path of life. At this time, Dzerzhinsky was probably the most powerful man in the Soviet Union, second only to Lenin.

Orlov was sceptical of Senkovsky's story, but as Dzerzhinsky's name had been brought into play, he was obliged to inform Dzerzhinsky of the situation. He immediately wired him a short summary of the facts and really expected no reply. On the second day, he was surprised to receive a communication signed by

Dzerzhinsky and Deputy War Commissar Skliansky instructing him to send Senkovsky to Moscow under guard.

A month later Orlov received a detailed intelligence report from Dzerzhinsky's office outlining Poland's guerrilla operations behind the Soviet lines and the identities of the French military attachés in Warsaw who were responsible for organising and financing Poland's guerrilla operations. The source of this valuable intelligence information was none other than Senkovsky, who had again switched sides.

Months later Orlov was in Moscow on business when he learned that Dzerzhinsky had received Senkovsky with open arms and they had had lunch together that day in the Chief's office. Dzerzhinsky had gone out of his way in the name of boyhood loyalty and spared the life of his old friend.

The Senkovsky incident was the lightning rod that first brought Orlov to the personal attention of the chief of the Soviet secret police. Dzerzhinsky was also aware of some of Orlov's daring exploits behind enemy lines and it was he who personally sponsored Orlov's candidacy into the early organisation that would become known around the world as the KGB. Orlov was particularly fond of his patron and felt that he was the best leader the KGB ever had. Dzerzhinsky ran the organisation with an iron fist and every member knew where he stood, yet this leader had compassion for everyone under him.

Orlov's description of the Senkovsky incident was seriously recounted, but when he had finished I couldn't help noticing the appearance of a grin on his face. I knew him well enough to know that he had something jocular to add. He asked if I was wondering what had happened to Senkovsky's horse and saddle. Actually, I had become so absorbed in the story that I had lost track of these minor details. He then told me that the horse and saddle were far superior to what he had been issued, so he had appropriated them both. The horse turned out to be the best mount he had ever owned and the saddle was far more than he could ever afford. When he was posted to Moscow in 1921, he had had to relinquish the horse but kept the saddle. As horseback riding was one of his passions, the saddle had stayed with him throughout the years until he had been reluctantly forced to sell it to finance his defection.

At the begining of 1921, Orlov was brought back to Moscow for a brief period and then posted to the Cheka's elite Border Guard in the northern Russian city of Archangel, where he was placed in charge of counter-intelligence. Here he married Maria Rozhnetsky on 1 April 1921.

Maria had been born in Kiev on 12 September 1903. She had joined the Bolshevik Party in 1919 and worked for the Bolshevik Government for a short period before joining the Red Army. She had been posted to the Red Army General Staff, near the Polish border, in a clerical capacity, and it was here that she first met Orlov. Orlov would later state that Maria was the most beautiful and intelligent woman he had ever met. They shared the same political ideology, and had the same interests and goals in life, and from early on he was satisfied that this was the woman with whom he wished to spend the rest of his life.

Orlov admitted that his service with the 12th Red Army and the Border Guard was one of the most fruitful periods of his career. He enjoyed the robust lifestyle of the military and, most of all, the excitement of planning and carrying out operations behind enemy lines. He also enjoyed being able to pursue his love of horses and firearms. He so strongly favoured military values that he considered making the military a career, but he was aware of the mundane nature of the day-to-day routine of military life in peacetime. At this juncture, therefore, he felt it more important to complete his law school education when hostilities ceased. What he did take from his military experience was a substantial background in guerrilla warfare and counter-intelligence that became the nucleus for his career with the KGB.

In the autumn of 1921, the Orlovs were both released from military service and returned to Moscow, where Orlov re-entered law school on a part-time basis. Maria was accepted as a medical student at the Second Moscow University.

The era following the Revolution and the Civil War were hectic and in 1921 efforts were made to establish the Soviet Supreme Court. In spite of Orlov's somewhat limited legal qualifications, he was a trusted member of the Party and was therefore appointed as an Assistant Prosecutor in the Collegium of Appeals of the Soviet Supreme Court. Here he was involved in writing the Soviet's original criminal code and is credited for this work in the 1922 and 1923 issues of the *Soviet Jurisprudence Weekly.*

On 1 September 1923, in Moscow, the Orlovs' daughter was born. She was named Veronika, but always called Vera, and was their only child. Considered their most prized and loved possession, Vera would die from a recurring illness on 15 July 1940 in Los Angeles, California.

Early in 1924, Orlov graduated from the Moscow University School of Law. His impressive record at the Collegium of Appeals had not gone unnoticed by Dzerzhinsky, and in 1924 he brought Orlov into the OGPU, the forerunner of the KGB, as a deputy in the Economic Directorate. Orlov served in Moscow for about a year and in 1925 was appointed a brigade commander of the OGPU Border Guard stationed in Tiflis, Transcaucasia. It was here that he would first come into contact with the infamous Lavrenti Beria, then Deputy Chief of the OGPU in Georgia.

Again good fortune smiled on Orlov when, in early 1926, he was recalled to Moscow to head a department in the newly organised Foreign Department (INO) of the OGPU. The INO had been formed ostensibly to control foreign trade but in reality had been put in place to propagate foreign intelligence and subversion. Here Orlov seized an opportunity for a posting to the Soviet Embassy in Paris and credits Dzerzhinsky with recommending him for his first assignment outside of the Soviet Union. He discussed the matter with his wife, and they both agreed that it would not only be a good career move but an opportunity for adventure in a Western capital.

Towards the early part of July 1926, Orlov had in hand his transfer to Paris, but within a matter of days Dzerzhinsky was dead from a heart attack. Orlov attended the funeral of his mentor, who was eulogised by both the Politburo and the common man in the street. Orlov had lost his mentor but remembered Dzerzhinsky as the man who had determined the future course of his life.

In the waning months of the summer of 1926, Orlov was dispatched to Paris under a false identity and the cover of an accredited Soviet diplomat to the Soviet Trade Delegation. In fact, he was the chief of the legal *rezidentura* at the Embassy, from where he conducted an extensive espionage network second only to the operation in Berlin, which, in the 1920s, was the spy capital of Europe. It was also the focal point of Soviet espionage on the basis of the INO's indisputable appraisal that the German Government was the archenemy of the Soviets. The INO had placed its optimal resources there, and in consideration of Orlov's proven track record in Paris he was reassigned to the Soviet Trade Delegation in Berlin in January 1928 as an accredited diplomat. There he operated under the fictitious identity of Lev Lazarevich Feldel, a name he had no problem remembering as it was so similar to his real name.

The Soviet Trade Delegation was housed in a huge, ornate commercial building on Lindenstrasse not far from the Soviet Embassy on Unter den Linden, one of the best known and fashionable avenues in Berlin. The Delegation supported a large staff of both KGB and GRU (military intelligence) personnel who did not go unnoticed by the German intelligence service (GIS). The main activities of these intelligence officers were the handling of the illegal spy networks and industrial espionage. In those tumultuous days before Adolf Hitler's rise to power, the Soviets focused on obtaining Germany's technological and industrial secrets both by legitimate means or whatever it took. If the Soviets couldn't buy or barter a secret process or means of production, they would set out to steal it. Thus Orlov's assignment in Berlin was part legitimate and part illegal.

During his assignment in Berlin, Orlov made friends with Eduard Winter, a General Motors distributor in Berlin who was anxious to sell cars to the Soviet Union. The nature of their relationship was purely business, and with Orlov's help Winter was able to sell a number of GM cars to the Soviet Union. This, of course, was the legitimate side of Orlov's assignment in Berlin.

In April 1931, Orlov was called back to Moscow, where he was appointed Chief of the Economic Department for Foreign Trade of the KGB; in reality, this was a directorate under the INO. At this time, the INO was undergoing a metamorphosis and Orlov was to become a key player because of the experience and knowledge that he had acquired during his years in Berlin. Up to this point, the KGB had relied heavily on the policy of operating their intelligence activities out of the legal *rezidenturas* within the Soviet diplomatic establishment of a particular country. This *modus operandi* did have its positive side in that, under diplomatic cover, the KGB officers enjoyed the protection of diplomatic immunity. However, the negative side came into play when the opposing intelligence service could readily identify the KGB officers within the diplomatic community and thereby minimise their effectiveness.

However, based on his experiences in Berlin, Orlov believed that a policy change was necessary in order to ensure the probability of a higher success rate for the Soviet's spying activities. As a result, the KGB Centre now recognised Orlov as the man who could transform the service.

During those tumultuous years in Berlin, Orlov had become aware of the fact that the KGB had had far more failures than successes. The GIS had been able to penetrate the Soviet spy networks operating in Germany with an uncanny success rate, and Orlov reasoned that it was because the KGB relied so heavily on the legal *rezidentura* in Berlin as its primary base of operation. Admittedly, the GIS was one of the best in Europe and its organisation proved to be very effective against the KGB. Orlov could see that the GIS focused its attention on the legal *rezidentura*, identified the KGB officers within that establishment and then focused its resources on the activities of those officers. Orlov reasoned that the KGB officers should work independently of the diplomatic establishment and maintain no connection with it whatsoever. The opposing intelligence service would thereby lose the advantage of easily identifying the KGB officers operating in its country.

Orlov had to travel frequently to the KGB Centre in Moscow to confer with his superior, Artur Artuzov, the Chief of the INO, about the activities of the legal *rezidentura* in Berlin. Over the years they had become personal friends, and Artuzov listened to what Orlov had to say. Orlov's views were well known at the Centre but not accepted by many of the department heads. After all, the proposed new method of operation might have a decided disadvantage for a KGB officer should he be apprehended as he would no longer have the protection of diplomatic immunity. By early 1931, the GIS was breathing down Orlov's neck and the KGB Centre realised that it would soon have to pull its key man out of Berlin. Artuzov took this as the opportune moment to come down on Orlov's side and selected him to reorganise and implement the INO's new foreign intelligence operational policy. Orlov did stress that the KGB always had some clandestine operations that had no overt connections with the diplomatic establishments, but the majority of their operations went through the legal *rezidenturas*. This would now change and the emphasis would be on illegal *rezidenturas*.

Orlov reported back to the KGB Centre in April 1931 and from that day forward concentrated his efforts on the new direction. First he travelled to every capital in Europe to discuss the new policy with the chiefs of the legal *rezidenturas* to gather their input. Then the details had to be worked out by Orlov's staff at the Centre and eventually put in place. New means of communication and codes between the illegal in the field and the Centre had to be worked out, and, most of all, use of dead drops had to be perfected.

Britain, France and Germany as well as Russia's long-time natural enemy Poland were the prime targets of KGB espionage and intelligence-gathering. However, following the First World War a new target emerged on the horizon, one that in 1932 was considered secondary to the prime targets yet important enough to be calculated into the KGB's future plans. This of course was the United States.

Orlov admitted that the KGB's interest and operations lagged far behind the GRU in the United States in the early 1930s because the GRU already had some of its people in place there. However, the KGB was banking on the fact that the United States would eventually recognise the USSR as a sovereign country and that the Soviet Union would then be able to establish an embassy in the US. One of the problems that would be difficult to overcome was the long line of communications between an illegal in the US and the Centre. At least a Soviet embassy would be a base of operations from where the logistics of an illegal *rezident* could be worked out. The KGB did not have long to wait because in the following year, 1933, the United States and the Soviet Union established diplomatic relations.

TWO

1932

What Orlov now felt he had to do was to visit America personally and make his own assessment as to what requirements the
KGB would need to target the United States as well as to lay
out the groundwork for a future deployment. He would have to
have a cover that would enable him to enter the US without any
suspicion on the part of the authorities and would permit him
to travel about in the US without any restriction. He decided that
the cover he had used in Berlin as a member of the Soviet Trade
Delegation would be more than adequate for this purpose. What
he did require was a US sponsor to vouch for him so that he
could obtain a visa to enter the country. He settled on his business acquaintance Eduard Winter, the General Motors representative and distributor in Berlin, because he knew that Winter would
gladly extend help to him to obtain the visa, if for no other reason
than to sell the Soviets GM cars.

Orlov decided that September 1932 would be the best time
for him to make the trip. At the beginning of the month, he
contacted Winter by telephone and informed him that he was
now connected with the headquarters of the Soviet trade missions
as an advisor to the many departments which would be buying
cars. He made it clear that his office did not make the actual
purchases but that he was in a position to advise and influence
those departments considering making a purchase. He stated that
he would like to visit GM plants in the US in order to evaluate
the product better and make his recommendations. Winter
jumped at the opportunity and agreed to contact the US Embassy
in Berlin to facilitate Orlov's request. He called Orlov back within

a few days and told him that the only formality was for Orlov to appear in person at the US Embassy with his passport in hand. Winter had already executed the necessary consular forms attesting to his sponsorship.

In the meantime, Orlov made arrangements for passage on the SS *Europa* sailing for the United States from Bremerhaven on 17 September. He arrived in Berlin on the 15th and by prearrangement met Winter on the morning of the 16th. Winter furnished Orlov with a letter of introduction to a Mr Howard, who was the manager of the General Motors Export Company in New York. Orlov related that the letter was quite flattering towards him, mentioning that he had been influential in the Soviet Government's purchase of GM cars in the past and that every courtesy should be extended to him. They proceeded to the Consular Office of the US Embassy, where Orlov presented his fraudulent passport in the name of Lev Leonedovich Nikolaev, one of the many aliases he had used in Berlin and the only one known to Winter. Orlov then signed the form which stated that Lev Leonedovich Nikolaev would be admitted entry into the US as a non-immigrant visitor under the Immigration Act of 1924. The visa notation was stamped in his passport on 16 September 1932.

The one element from that day that would come back to haunt him was his answer to the questions whether he was or ever had been a member of the Communist Party, and whether he had ever advocated the overthrow of the US Government by whatever means. He answered in the negative, as he had been instructed to do by the KGB. A more minor matter was the denial that he had relatives living in the US.

Orlov thanked Winter for his assistance and, in turn, Winter replied that he would cable General Motors Overseas Corporation and advise them of Orlov's arrival in New York. He fully expected that someone from the company would meet Orlov when the ship docked.

Orlov proceeded to Bremerhaven that afternoon and boarded the SS *Europa* that evening. The next day the ocean liner departed for the United States carrying Orlov, in his second-class cabin, to his next assignment. The trip was uneventful and the food excellent. The ship arrived in New York's harbour late in the evening of 23 September and docked the following morning. Orlov was met by a General Motors representative who spoke fluent German. At the time, Orlov spoke only rudimentary English which he had either picked up or taught himself in preparation for the assignment.

At the time of his arrival, the Soviet Union was not recognised by the US Government and Orlov was not allowed entry without more formal immigration procedures. The US Government looked with suspicion on anyone coming from the Communist Soviet Union, although Orlov didn't believe that he was singled out as some of the other passengers were also subjected to a closer examination by the immigration authorities. They were all taken to Ellis Island, where they awaited further processing.

A Special Immigration Board of Inquiry was convened on Monday morning, 26 September, to establish Orlov's eligibility for entry into the US. He was sworn in and testified under oath through an interpreter. Following a precis of his background, he was questioned about the purpose of his visit to the US. He testified that he had come to the US to inspect GM car plants and that he was authorised to negotiate for the purchase of 150 cars for various Soviet government agencies. The actual purchases would be handled by AMTORG, the New York-based Soviet trading arm in the US. Orlov was well versed on the covert operation of AMTORG, the acronym for the Soviet Trading Corporation, which dealt with industrial espionage, as prior to his assignment to Paris in 1926 he had been a member of the Economic Directorate of the KGB which oversaw AMTORG.

He also had to satisfy the Board of Inquiry that he had sufficient funds to sustain himself during his visit. He testified that he possessed funds to the amount of $3,000, from which he was authorised to withdraw his living and travel expenses. His salary would be paid directly to his wife in Moscow. He related that he would be staying in the New York City area with the exception of an inspection of a GM car plant in Detroit.

The GM official also testified under oath and corroborated the purpose of Orlov's trip to conduct business with GM and tour a GM plant. He also noted that the trip had been arranged under the auspices of GM. Then the GM official was required to post a cash bond for $500 to ensure Orlov's departure. Orlov was told that he would be allowed entry for a period of four months, and if he had not left by that time the bond would be forfeited. In addition, he would be in violation of US immigration laws. The last formality called for Orlov to surrender his Soviet passport to the immigration authorities, which would be returned to him on his departure.

Orlov related that he was a happy man when he and the GM official boarded the ferry for Manhattan. He never looked back at Ellis Island during the short voyage and could only think that he had passed one of the most crucial tests of his assignment. As for the GM official, his mind was on the 150 GM cars that Orlov was going to negotiate to buy. The GM official took Orlov directly to the New Yorker Hotel, where GM had made prior arrangements for his stay. When he signed the register and inquired about payment, he was told that GM had already taken care of the matter.

For the balance of the week Orlov met daily with James Mooney, the Vice President of General Motors responsible for overseas operations, and other GM officials at the company's office in New York. During the course of their negotiations, Orlov learned that GM had long sought to establish a GM agency in Moscow but that their efforts had been thwarted by Soviet officials who had taken an indifferent and surly attitude towards their proposal. Orlov informed them that he was unaware of these circumstances and that their previous relationship with his Government was beyond his knowledge and control. He took this as his opportunity to reject the proposed visit to a GM plant in Detroit and concluded that he would file a favourable report; in future, any dealings would be through AMTORG. Orlov confided that he had had no intention of visiting the Detroit GM plant as he considered it a waste of his time, but that he had had no idea how he would get out of making the trip. He was therefore relieved when the negotiations broke down and the visit could be cancelled.

However, he did have another agenda in connection with his feigned business meetings with GM. He had been asked by the KGB to assess the mood of the industrialists to determine if they would support the Soviet Union in their efforts to gain recognition by the US Government. There was no doubt that this issue had been brought into play at the highest levels of the Kremlin. The US was in the depths of its greatest depression and the USSR was emerging as a virile new nation willing to buy US industrial goods. Could the placing of large orders with US industrialists be a trade-off for their influence with the US Government to gain this vital recognition? The Kremlin felt that GM's reaction would be a guide to that of other giant US industrialists. Orlov found the GM executives eager to do business with the Soviets, and they expressed the opinion that commercial ties between the two countries could be facilitated by diplomatic recognition. No doubt the Kremlin was elated to receive Orlov's report that the industrialists would support their cause.

The following year the US recognised the USSR as a sovereign nation and diplomatic relations between the two countries were established. Both the Soviets and the KGB were the big winners in the end.

Having achieved his goals with GM, Orlov checked out of the New Yorker Hotel. In time, he moved to various rooming houses in Manhattan, where he was able to melt into the crowds and be less conspicuous. He first moved to Harlem, where he resided on West 144th Street and then on West 142nd Street, both in the vicinity of the New York City College. His final move was to another rooming house on West 120th Street in the midst of the city-like campus of Columbia University. He was required to report all these moves to the Immigration and Naturalisation Service (INS).

What was most obvious and troubling to Orlov was his inadequacy in the English language. There was no way he could efficiently operate in the US, or play a key supervisory role in the future at the KGB Centre, without the benefit of a solid knowledge of the language. He was therefore determined to learn as much as he could in the short time he was in the United States.

Within a matter of a few days after moving to the first of his rooming houses, he registered at Columbia University in a course for foreigners who wanted to learn English. In order to accelerate the process, he also registered a few days later with the Berlitz School of Languages on 5th Avenue near Washington Park. At both institutions he registered as 'Leo Nikoloeff', the more Americanised version of his passport name. He did not anticipate any correspondence from either of the schools, but in this manner he plausibly covered his tracks should the INS have reason to make a routine inquiry.

Orlov stated that he had many objectives to accomplish in New York before returning to the Soviet Union, but none more meaningful to him personally than learning English. By 1932, he had mastered French and German and was able to get along in Polish, but he saw the new language as a deliberate challenge. He would call this period his 'days with Hollywood' as he would take every available opportunity to visit the cinema, often sitting through a film at least twice and on some occasions three times. This was of course before the days of television and he felt that there was no better tool to learn a language than through watching movies. He claimed to have seen more films in those two months than he saw during the rest of his life. When I asked him what his favourite film was, he replied without hesitation *A Farewell to Arms* starring Gary Cooper. He recalled that he must have sat through it five times. It must have come as a surprise when he actually met Ernest Hemingway, the author of the book on which the film was based, several years later in Spain.

Orlov also read at least one of the many New York daily newspapers, but leaned towards the *New York Times* because it gave more international coverage. He would read the advertisements in the subway and, as he walked along the streets, he would look at anything in the English language including the names of streets and business establishments. Orlov estimated that he learned more English in that two-month period than he could have done by studying the language for two years at a college. By the time he left the United States, he felt that he had mastered the basics and was confident that he would have no problem speaking and understanding the language.

One of his major objectives in making the trip was to scout out prospective dead-drop sites in the New York City area for later consideration by the KGB Centre. In 1932, there was no apparent reason to investigate the area in the vicinity of Washington, the nation's capital, as there were no diplomatic relations between the US and the Soviets. Prospects for the establishment of diplomatic relations were always on the horizon but never seemed to crystallise. Orlov also reasoned that if a Soviet embassy were established in Washington, a dead drop in the New York area could easily be serviced from Washington because of the excellent transportation network between the two cities. Furthermore, the extra distance would be more than compensated by the security that a New York dead drop would provide. Although the focus of attention would now be away from KGB operations handled through the legal *rezidenturas*, there would always be a need for dead drops by both methods of operation.

Orlov travelled from one end of Manhattan to the other and around all the adjacent boroughs. He visited numerous parks, both small and large, and came to the conclusion that the area afforded a wealth of venues for dead drops. He had no system in place to rate these many facilities but in the end felt that Central Park, Fort Tryon Park and the Bronx Park afforded the maximum of security with a minimum of servicing problems. He stressed that he was not seeking specific dead-drop sites as this would be a matter handled by the illegal in the field. However, a specific site would first have to be recommended and justified by the illegal to the Centre and, in turn, the Centre would have to approve or deny the recommendation. For this to happen, the Centre would need to be conversant with the general area of the dead drop in order to render an informed decision.

There seemed to be an exception to Orlov's narrative that he was only scouting general dead-drop sites in New York City during his 1932 trip, a fact I came upon by accident (see page 588). He had also travelled to Boston over a weekend. When the KGB Centre wanted to communicate with him, they would contact him through AMTORG. He in turn would visit the AMTORG office occasionally for this purpose. On one particular visit, he received a coded message that he should seek out a possible dead-drop site in the Boston area in connection with a matter under consideration by the Centre. The INS had already been advised that he would be receiving messages through AMTORG so his contacts there would arouse no suspicion.

Therefore, he travelled to Boston over a weekend and his concluding recommendation to the Centre was that the Mount Auburn Cemetery, adjacent to Harvard University, Cambridge, was the most feasible site for a dead drop in the Boston area. He never knew for certain if the site was ever utilised by the KGB, but in the end the Mount Auburn Cemetery became the final resting place for the three members of the Orlov family.

Orlov told me a little about AMTORG that proved interesting. He related that it was actually a KGB operation, which outwardly was a legitimate Soviet trading company but which employed a cadre of Soviet intelligence personnel among the 500 or more people working there. The organisation was no more than a cover for the real work of espionage, although to a great extent it did provide an avenue of trade between the two nations. Although instigated by the KGB, the majority of intelligence activity operating through the cover of the organisation was from the GRU.

Soon after he arrived in the US, Orlov ran into an intelligence officer assigned under the guise of AMTORG whom he would have close contact with a few years later in the Spanish Civil War. Lieutenant Colonel Vladimir Gorev and Orlov became friends of the first order. Gorev was formerly a KGB officer who later went into the Red Army and graduated from the Frunze Academy of the Red Army Staff. In Spain, Orlov would learn via another colleague, General Kleber, the pseudonym for Lazar Stern, that in the early 1930s Kleber and Gorev were both in New York City working a network of spies for the GRU under the cover of AMTORG. Kleber was using the fictitious name Zilbert for this particular operation. Kleber's network had penetrated a corporation that was doing highly sensitive work for the US Navy that would have been invaluable to the Soviet Navy. Bit by bit Kleber was able to obtain plans of the naval project through their agent at the plant, but in time became suspicious that the information being passed to the GRU was 'build-up material' actually prepared by the FBI to appear legitimate but which was misleading and of little value. Kleber was not alone in this belief as the material sent on to the GRU Centre was carefully analysed by Soviet naval experts and found to be questionable. Via a coded message to AMTORG, Kleber was ordered by his superior, General Berzin, to drop everything and return to Moscow immediately as his arrest by the FBI was imminent. Kleber told Orlov that on the following day he was able to obtain passage on a French ship departing for Europe that day. He added that he could feel the breath of the FBI on his back and was more than glad to escape to Europe.

Kleber also related a humorous situation connected with his early work in New York City which could have resulted in a catastrophe. He had preceded his comrade Gorev to New York in the early 1930s and, when Gorev was dispatched to work with him, they had arranged to meet at the St George Hotel. While Kleber waited for Gorev at the St George Hotel in Brooklyn, Gorev was waiting at the St George Hotel in Manhattan. Both were furious with the other for being 'stood up', but rationalised that something out of the ordinary must have happened. These were the early days when alternative meeting sites were not the established practice, but in time they were able to connect through the good offices of AMTORG.

The one thing that bothered Orlov, and which he witnessed daily during the brief time he was in the US, was the great depression that had enveloped the nation. He could see the inordinate number of men on the streets who seemed to be loitering with no apparent place to go, although of an age that would indicate they should be employed; the scarcity of help-wanted advertisements in the classified section of the newspapers; the long lines of men seeking employment, perhaps for one job opening; the bleak news articles that foreshadowed a long recession; and the welfare kitchens in his own neighbourhoods in Harlem and upper Manhattan that overflowed with people seeking meagre sustenance. All this told him that there had to be a flaw in this capitalist society to generate such economic injustice. He saw from his own perspective the difference between the haves and have nots as he was able to enjoy many amenities in the US only because he had an income. Early on he had learned that under Communism there would be no class distinctions and that the means of production would be common to all. The end result would be a society where all would share and prosper. What deficits he was aware of in the new Soviet Union he attributed to the transitory period that had to be faced by an emerging nation. Also, the USSR was about to embark on another five-year plan which would eliminate all problems. Years later, when explaining the Utopian form of government he had envisaged in the Soviet Union, Orlov revealed that, as an ardent Communist, this had been his way of thinking in 1932. He admitted that it had taken only two short months in the US for him to come to the conclusion that Communism was the avenue he would continue to tread as compared to the years it would take before he saw the inherent flaws in the Communist form of government. With this political philosophy, he would depart the United States.

Towards the end of November, Orlov made preparations to leave America. He purchased his passage with the Norddeutscher Line (NDL) and then paid a visit to the AMTORG office for the last time. There he cabled a message to the KGB Centre advising the date of his return. His last official visit was to the INS in New York, where he was obliged to file a federal income-tax return which was required by all departing aliens. However, the income he had received from his Government while in the US was below the statutory limit for paying federal income tax.

Having met all immigration requirements and producing his passage ticket on the NDL for verification of departure, he was able to retrieve his Soviet passport.

Orlov left the US in the evening of 30 November aboard the SS *Bremen* bound for Europe. The GM official who had acted as an interpreter with the INS when he first arrived now saw him off. He arrived in Bremerhaven on the morning of 7 December and took the first train to Berlin. He stayed there, en route to Moscow, for several days and made a point of visiting Eduard Winter.

Winter related that he had received a cable from his company in New York advising that the INS had been unable to verify Orlov's departure and were withholding redemption of the $500 cash bond that GM had posted. The home office could not understand why the INS was unable to verify the departure as one of their officials had personally seen him off. Orlov was astounded at this turn of events and offered to reimburse the $500 in the event that GM was unable to collect the money from the INS. In addition, he furnished Winter with a copy of his federal income-tax return as a supporting document.

The matter dragged on for several months before Orlov learned that it had finally been resolved. Winter explained that he had sent the home office a certified document attesting that he had seen Orlov in the first part of December; he had also obtained a statement from NDL that Orlov had sailed on the *Bremen*'s 30th of November voyage, as well as a statement from the Berlin Police Department that Orlov had registered his arrival in Germany with the police.

Orlov had many fond memories of his visit to the US in 1932, but none was more poignant than when the SS *Bremen* passed by the Statue of Liberty making its way out of the harbour. It was already night time and the statue was fully illuminated. It seemed like everyone aboard had made it to a position where they could experience their own inspiration invoked by the lady who best represented the US spirit of freedom for all. Orlov commented that as he stood on the deck that night watching the

Statue of Liberty fade from view, he had no doubts that he would return someday in the service of his country. What was ironic, and what he had no way of knowing at the time, was that the lady standing on the huge pedestal would in a matter of six years take the Orlov family to her bosom and provide them with a safe haven.

THREE

FIRST DOUBTS

In recognition of Orlov's phenomenal achievements in the field of espionage, the Soviet Politburo in August 1936 decided to send him to Spain as their Advisor to the Spanish Republican Government. This was only a matter of months after the start of the Spanish Civil War. This assignment was of the highest order and of such importance to the Soviet Government that only the most trusted and loyal comrades were considered. The position called for liaison with the Spanish Republicans for counter-intelligence, espionage and guerrilla warfare. The power of the KGB was such that even the Soviet military that came to fight on the side of the Republicans would come under Orlov's purview. He would also be handling the most sensitive of situations with the Republican Government and would be the Kremlin's key man in Spain.

Orlov related that even before he undertook the assignment in Spain he was having doubts about the way in which Stalin was conducting the Government and the effects it was having on the Soviet people. He had only recently returned to Moscow from a long and hazardous assignment in Germany when, on 26 August, he was informed by Genrikh Yagoda, Chairman of the KGB, of his posting to Spain. Orlov was reluctant to accept the assignment as Yagoda had promised that he could remain in Russia for several years before being considered again for another foreign position. Now Yagoda insisted that Orlov had no choice as his name had been nominated by Lazar Kaganovich, a prominent member of the Politburo and trusted friend of Stalin, and the nomination had been seconded by Vyacheslav Molotov, who years later would become known throughout the world as the Soviet's Minister of Foreign Affairs.

In spite of what he felt was a betrayal of a promise on the part of Yagoda, Orlov was not entirely dissatisfied as political conditions in the Soviet Union were depressing and not to his liking. Just a few days before he learned of his appointment, Orlov had attended the show trial of Grigory Evseevich Zinoviev and Lev Kamenev which had begun on 19 August in Moscow. Orlov's previous experience as a Prosecutor in the Collegium of Appeals of the Soviet Supreme Court, and his current status as a high-ranking member of the inner circle of the KGB, made it crystal clear to him that the show trial was the vehicle that Stalin needed as a primary stage to purging the remaining old-line Bolsheviks at future sham trials.

By way of background to the trial, Orlov related that 1934 had been a critical year for Stalin in which he had had to make drastic decisions in order to maintain his prospects for remaining in power. Stalin had plunged the country into a state of financial depression as a result of the gross failure of his policy of forced agricultural collectivisation. Crop failures were the norm and what was produced was barely adequate to feed the populace. Discontent amongst the peasants was at its highest level since the time of the Tsar and the Government under Stalin was at great risk. Orlov later said that this was the time when Stalin felt the ground under his feet tremble, for he was under extreme pressure to pursue a line of action that would keep him in power, no matter what the consequences for those offered up as sacrificial lambs in order to achieve his goal.

Stalin's principal antagonist and closest rival for power was an old Bolshevik by the name of Sergei M. Kirov, who was a prominent member of the Politburo representing the Leningrad faction of the Party. In sharp contrast to Stalin, Kirov was a much younger man and an eloquent speaker, who was able to sway his listeners; above all, he possessed a charismatic personality. Unlike Stalin who was a Georgian, Kirov was also an ethnic Russian, which stood in his favour. Kirov's popularity did not go unnoticed by Stalin at the 17th Party Congress in 1934, when Kirov had stepped up to the podium to be greeted by spontaneous applause that equalled that which was required to be given to Stalin. Perhaps more galling was the fact that the Congress seemed united in its opposition to Stalin while giving Kirov a vote of confidence by electing him to the influential Central Committee Secretariat.

Stalin conjectured that his best ploy would be to recall Kirov to Moscow, where he would have absolute control over him by removing him from his sphere of influence in Leningrad. Stalin greatly miscalculated Kirov's newly acquired independence, which was considerably enhanced by the display of popularity shown at the 17th Party Congress. In the past, an order by Stalin was absolute and could not be ignored. However, Kirov showed no inclination to move on Stalin's order, and it was at this juncture that Stalin knew he was faced with a problem that could culminate in his own downfall and therefore could not be disregarded.

Stalin had no recourse but to eliminate Kirov by assassination. To do so, he required Yagoda's co-operation and total commitment. Yagoda, in turn, assigned the task to Vania Zaporozhets, one of his most trusted lieutenants in Leningrad.

By a fortunate coincidence, the Leningrad KGB office had a report on a young Communist, Leonid Nikolayev, who had recently been expelled from the Party and who had vowed to revenge his expulsion by assassinating a member of the tribunal that had made the decision. Zaporozhets seized on the opportunity and, via the original informant, surreptitiously met Nikolayev. He found Nilolayev to be somewhat slow-witted and a person he felt could be easily manipulated. He concluded that he had the ideal candidate to assassinate Kirov.

The informant was instructed to gain Nikolayev's confidence and convince him that he would gain more notoriety by killing a member of the Politburo than a member of the tribunal. Nikolayev wholeheartedly agreed that this would be his best option and that Kirov would be the logical candidate for assassination. His only problem was that he did not possess the means to carry out the task. Through the auspices of the KGB, Nikolayev was provided with a pistol.

Late in November 1934, Nikolayev entered the Smolny Building in Leningrad with the intention of murdering Kirov. Unfortunately, an alert guard noticed Nikolayev's briefcase and, on examination, found the loaded pistol. Nikolayev was detained, but was soon released on Zaporozhets's orders. The briefcase, pistol and diary that Nikolayev kept were returned to him. Had the diary been examined, the plot would have unravelled.

Nikolayev was unnerved by the incident but soon regained his composure and, at the urging of the informant, decided it was time to make another attempt. This time however he would go in the evening of 1 December, when Kirov was expected to be holding a meeting. Again Nikolayev entered the Smolny Building, where he encountered no difficulty getting past the guard. The building was practically empty at this hour with the exception of the small meeting being held by Kirov. Nikolayev located the conference room, waited in the hallway until Kirov left, and then opened fire. Kirov fell to the floor mortally wounded. Almost at that very moment Nikolayev was arrested by the KGB.

Stalin was immediately notified of the events and, in turn, declared that he was going to Leningrad to assess the situation personally.

Zaporozhets had carried out his part of the plot but realised that he still had to have a confession from Nikolayev implicating Zinoviev and Kamenev as the perpetrators of the conspiracy to assassinate Kirov. Knowing that Stalin would soon be arriving in Leningrad and wanting to be able to take credit for Nikolayev's confession to enhance his own standing in Stalin's eyes, Zaporozhets decided that he could easily coerce the necessary confession out of Nikolayev. However, he also realised that Nikolayev might recognise him as the friend of the informant that he had met previously and then surmise that he had been tricked into killing Kirov. Zaporozhets reasoned that the likelihood of Nikolayev recognising him under the stress he had been subjected to following his arrest was minimal compared to the fruits that would follow by being in Stalin's good graces.

Zaporozhets badly misjudged Nikolayev and the effects of their earlier meeting. Nikolayev immediately recognised Zaporozhets and realised that his friend, the informant, was actually an *agent provocateur* in the service of the KGB and that he had been set up. Nikolayev flew into a rage and refused to co-operate with Zaporozhets.

Stalin soon arrived in Leningrad accompanied by Yagoda. He met Philip Medved, Chief of the Leningrad KGB, as a matter of form as he knew that Medved was not privy to the conspiracy. He dismissed Medved and then summoned Zaporozhets, who brought Stalin up to date on the ensuing events. Next he requested that Nikolayev be brought to him.

Years later, Orlov would admit to me that he had learned of the following sequence of events which had taken place between Stalin and Nikolayev directly from Yagoda, who had been present during the meeting.

As Nikolayev stood before Stalin he was asked by the dictator, in the tone of a father speaking to his son, 'Why did you kill such a nice man?' This conciliatory approach was so out of character that Orlov would not have believed that it had come from Stalin had it not been witnessed first hand by Yagoda.

Nikolayev replied, 'I did not fire at him, I fired at the Party.' Stalin then asked, 'And where did you get the gun?', to which Nikolayev responded, 'Why ask me? Ask Zaporozhets about that!' Nikolayev displayed no remorse for his action or any shred of deference towards Stalin, but rather a firmness in his conviction. Nikolayev's attitude greatly upset Stalin, who had him ushered out of the room.

After Nikolayev's departure, Stalin's rage became apparent when he threw Nilolayev's file at Yagoda and accused him of being a bungler. Stalin then called for Zaporozhets, with whom he had a private conference lasting for about fifteen minutes, after which Zaporozhets was seen hurriedly leaving the room with what could be described as an extremely anguished look on his face.

Zaporozhets's fate was sealed at this very moment. He never achieved the aspirations that he had hoped for as his reward for the part that he had played in the Kirov conspiracy. Instead, he and several other KGB agents from the Leningrad District Office were arrested and sentenced to light terms in the gulags. Zaporozhets was ultimately liquidated on Stalin's orders in 1937.

With the elimination of his chief rival, Kirov, Stalin had achieved success in the first phase of his conspiracy, but laying the blame for Kirov's assassination on Zinoviev and Kamenev was another matter. Nikolayev could not be relied on to give testimony which implicated Zinoviev and Kamenev as the masterminds of the conspiracy. Even if he had agreed to do so, there was the danger that at a public trial he would take revenge and name Stalin and the KGB as the conspirators behind the plot.

This one act on the part of Stalin was responsible for the taking of hundreds of lives. Stalin immediately expressed extreme outrage at the assassination of Kirov and decreed that the perpetrators of the deed would not go unpunished. He pointed his finger at the opposition White Guards as Nikolayev's accomplices and, as a result, over 100 White Guardists were rounded up throughout Russia on charges of terrorist activities and murdered. Nikolayev and over ten of his close associates who might remotely have any knowledge of Stalin's and the KGB's implication in the plot were put on a closed trial towards the end of December 1934. They were all found guilty of Kirov's murder and shot before the year ended. Thus no one was left alive who could testify that Stalin and the KGB were the actual instigators of the plot to assassinate Kirov.

In spite of Stalin's original decision that it would be too risky to tie Zinoviev and Kamenev to the Kirov plot, he could not yet let go of a situation where he felt that he could eliminate more of his enemies. His resolve was stronger than ever to implicate Zinoviev and Kamenev, and therefore, on Stalin's orders, both men were charged with Kirov's murder and placed on trial on 15 January 1935. Again the military trial was closed for fear that revelations would be made that were detrimental to Stalin.

The prosecution was unable to come forward with sufficient evidence to justify an outright conviction of the defendants. However, these men were placed under severe pressure by the KGB and, although denying any complicity in Kirov's murder, conceded that outwardly they must share some of the moral and political responsibility for the act. On this questionable basis the court found them both guilty only to the extent of their confessed culpability. Zinoviev was sentenced to ten years in prison and Kamenev to five years.

In spite of this small victory, Stalin was still not satisfied and wanted the heads of Zinoviev and Kamenev. He had a smouldering and enduring hatred for Lenin and all of Lenin's comrades from the earliest days of the Revolution, because it had been Lenin who had humiliated Stalin by choosing Leon Trotsky as his heir apparent while disavowing Stalin in his last testament. Zinoviev and Kamenev had been old comrades of Lenin and fully understood Lenin's rationale that Stalin was not the person to lead the new Communist Government. Under the unstable conditions in the Soviet Union, these two leaders, as well as other old-line Leninist Bolsheviks, still posed a threat to Stalin's power.

The first step in Stalin's blueprint was to charge Zinoviev and Kamenev with masterminding the Kirov assassination as part of a plot which then called for the assassination of Stalin and other leaders of the Government. By showing that this conspiracy intended to overthrow the Soviet Government, he could then lay the groundwork for future purge trials. Their convictions would be the rope that would tie Zinoviev and Kamenev to the remaining Bolsheviks who stood in his way. Trotsky was the most important of Stalin's living archenemies, but was not an immediate threat as he was in exile abroad.

In order to strengthen his hand in the political arena, Stalin had a new provision enacted into law on 8 April 1935 which would enable him to exert additional leverage over his enemies. The new law decreed that children of the age of twelve and over who were found guilty of crimes would be subjected to the same punishment as adults, up to and including the death penalty. This provision provided the KGB with the means by which they could coerce a confession from a political dissident simply by holding out that false charges would be brought against a family member or loved one.

Stalin's strategy was taking shape and the time for action was at hand. The details of the plan were formulated by Stalin with the assistance of Nikolai Yezhov, his protégé and a member of the Party's all-powerful Central Committee. The execution of the plan would be handled by the KGB under the immediate and close supervision of its Chairman, Yagoda.

Early in 1936, about forty of the KGB's top operatives were summoned to Moscow for a conference. They were advised that a conspiracy against Stalin and the Government had been uncovered and that it would be left to them to secure confessions from Zinoviev, Kamenev and other conspirators.

Part of Stalin's plan called for the bringing of about 300 political prisoners to Moscow, where they would be ruthlessly interrogated and subjected to inordinate pressure. It was expected that a large number of these people would eventually break and thereby provide testimony that could be used in court against the defendants. However, only one prisoner was actually won over after two weeks of intensive KGB interrogation.

Another phase of Stalin's plan called for infiltrating KGB agents into the trial who would act out the parts of defendants to the charges and accomplices of the other conspirators. They were expected to confess their role in the conspiracy and denounce Zinoviev and Kamenev as the leaders of the conspiracy.

The final, yet most important, phase of the plan called for extorting confessions from Zinoviev and Kamenev, or at the least their co-operation during the trial. The KGB's most experienced and qualified agents were put to the task but to no avail. The interrogations intensified when several KGB Chiefs tried their hand, with the added weight of their authority, but again they ended in failure. In the months preceding the trial, the two men were subjected to every conceivable form of interrogation: subtle pressure, then periods of enormous pressure, starvation, open and veiled threats, promises, as well as physical and mental torture. Neither man would succumb to the ordeal they faced.

Stalin was livid that a confession was not forthcoming and continually expressed his hatred towards the men. He made it clear that he expected confessions to be secured and that they should be made fully aware that their lives were at stake.

Towards the end of their ordeal, Zinoviev became sick and exhausted. Yezhov took advantage of the situation in a desperate attempt to get a confession. Yezhov warned that Zinoviev must affirm at a public trial that he had plotted the assassination of Stalin and other members of the Politburo. Zinoviev declined the demand. Yezhov then relayed Stalin's offer: that if he co-operated at an open trial, his life would be spared; if he did not, he would be tried in a closed military court and executed, along with all of the opposition. Zinoviev vehemently rejected Stalin's offer.

Yezhov then tried the same tactics on Kamenev and again was rebuffed. Yezhov finally took advantage of the new law of 8 April 1935 and implied that the KGB possessed evidence on Kamenev's son, which would subject him to harsh penalties under the new law. Kamenev responded in disbelief and then angrily shouted his condemnation of this stratagem with the positive assertion that he still had no intention of co-operating. Yezhov retreated from the room knowing full well that his efforts were a failure.

Zinoviev and Kamenev were both kept under constant surveillance for the slightest indication that they could be vacillating from their stance. The break came in July 1936, following a long and intensive interrogation when Zinoviev asked to talk to Kamenev in private. The request was granted. Zinoviev and Kamenev conversed for about an hour, during which time Zinoviev expressed his view that it might be best for them to go to trial if the promise given to him by Yezhov that Stalin would personally spare their lives if they co-operated at the trial were confirmed by Stalin. Kamenev was reluctant to agree but stated that if Stalin would repeat his promise to spare their lives before the Politburo, he would then co-operate.

When Stalin received the news of their apparent capitulation, he could hardly restrain his pleasure. While listening to the particulars and seemingly staring into space, he stroked his moustache and then uncharacteristically announced that the job had been well done.

Orlov was not present at the meeting of Kamenev and Zinoviev before Stalin but learned the details from Lev Mironov, an old friend who was the Chief of the KGB's Economic Directorate. Mironov was personally known and trusted by Stalin and was a key player in the escapade.

When the two men were brought before Stalin, he asked them what they had to say. They replied that it was their understanding that their circumstances would be presented to the next meeting of the Politburo for consideration. Stalin haughtily retorted that they were now standing before the commission of the Politburo that was authorised to hear their appeal. This startled both men as they now realised their predicament.

Zinoviev started by saying that in the past he and Kamenev had been given many promises, none of which had been kept. When they had agreed to be morally responsible for the murder of Kirov at their last trial, they were given to understand that this would be their last sacrifice. Now it was apparent that Stalin was organising the new trial as a means of besmirching the old-line Bolsheviks to his own benefit. When Zinoviev broke down and started to cry, Stalin looked at him without remorse and stated, 'It is too late for tears. The Central Committee repeatedly warned you that your factional struggle would end lamentably. You didn't listen and it has indeed ended lamentably. You are being told even now to submit to the will of the Party and your life and the lives of those whom you led into the swamp will be spared.'

Kamenev then asked Stalin what guarantee did they have, after so many broken promises, that they would not eventually be shot? Somewhat taken aback by the question, Stalin retorted, 'Guarantee? What guarantees can there be? Maybe you want an official treaty, certified by the League of Nations? You two apparently forget that you are not at a market place haggling over a stolen horse, but at the Politburo of the Bolshevist Communist

Party. If assurances given by the Politburo are not enough for you, then I don't know whether there is any point in talking further with you. As if we could not shoot you without any trial if we considered it necessary.'

Zinoviev and Kamenev listened intently to Stalin's litany and then Kamenev responded that they would agree to go on trial on condition that none of the old-line Bolsheviks who were considered the opposition and charged at the new trial would be executed, that their families would not be persecuted, and that in the future none of the former members of the opposition would be subjected to the death penalty. Stalin looked at the two men sternly and quickly replied, 'That goes without saying!'

Preparations for the trial now went forward at a great pace. The legal aspects for the trial first called for about fifty defendants, but this figure was progressively whittled down to sixteen who would face the dock. Stalin rightfully reasoned that he was not in a position to have a defendant refute his expected testimony in open court by recanting his confession given to the KGB. Only those whom he felt satisfied would follow the script became defendants. Five of the sixteen defendants were actually KGB plants, whose confessional testimony was expected to solidify the state's case by exposing Zinoviev, Kamenev and the other defendants as their fellow conspirators. These pseudo-defendants were co-operating with the KGB knowing that they were not real defendants but heroes of the state.

Stalin insisted that the tightest of controls had to be maintained throughout the trial. He personally selected a very small room in the Hall of Trade Unions as the courtroom for the trial. The room only held 350 people and Stalin directed that the seats would be occupied by KGB personnel in street clothing. In addition, specially coached KGB officers were planted among what was expected to be a very co-operative audience. In the event that one of the defendants got out of control and started to make accusations against Stalin, these stooges would rise at a signal from the prosecutor and drown out the recalcitrant defendant. This would give the trial judge the pretext to call a recess and hopefully give the KGB an opportunity to remedy the situation. Fearing that one of the defendants might blurt out a denunciation detrimental to Stalin, even the most trusted members of the Party were barred from the trial.

The trial formally opened on 19 August 1936. The presiding judge was Vasily Ulrich, who in the past had been a counterintelligence officer with the Cheka. The prosecutor was the very competent Andrei Vishinsky, who would become well known to the West in years to come.

General Orlov was allowed to be privy to an excellent venue from where he could observe the court proceedings in close proximity throughout the trial. In a hallway leading out of the courtroom were several small conference rooms, one of which was used by the KGB as its observation post. The room was fitted with comfortable chairs and a speaker system that transmitted the court proceedings directly to it. The amenities included a large table which overflowed with food and various liquid refreshments. Yagoda hosted the affair with an obvious display of camaraderie in anticipation of a victory at the trial as well as a personal triumph for himself.

However, forsaking for the most part the comfort and amenities of the KGB observation room, Orlov spent most of his time in the courtroom. Here he could actually observe the drama of the proceedings as they took shape, and he was in a better position to judge the unfolding tragedy.

His pity for the defendants extended most sharply to Zinoviev, who now only remotely resembled the prominent hero and leader of the Revolution. Zinoviev looked pale and sickly, and his eyes reflected deep sorrow. His testimony seemed hollow and at times unconvincing, but to Orlov it was just unbelievable.

Throughout the trial Stalin's script was followed to the line with only minor deviations of no actual consequence. The five pseudo-defendants played an important part in denouncing their fellow defendants and provided the larger landscape for the conspiracy. No doubt they must have felt relieved that their part was over and that in time they would be able to resume their lives. On the third day the trial was all but over. Vishinsky had no problem in making a stunning and forceful summation inasmuch as the defence provided him with all the ammunition he needed. In his concluding speech, he strongly dammed the accused parties and screamed that all the defendants should be shot.

The fourth day of the trial was reserved for the presentation of the defendants' pleas to the court, in which each offered their defence and any mitigating justification for their actions should they be found guilty of the charges. However, in this trial each of the defendant's pleas had already been sanitised by Yezhov. All mention of any connection to Lenin and the October Revolution, or any contributing factors in establishing the Communist Party or founding the Soviet Government, was eliminated. This was to be the saddest part of the trial, watching the defendants degrade themselves simply to appease a tyrant. These were the men who had devoted their entire lives to the cause of the Party and now stood naked before the dock in the sense that they could present no defence that was contrary to Stalin's wishes. Even the slightest deviation from the script could provoke Stalin into renouncing his promise to spare their lives if they co-operated in the trial, or still worse that he would retaliate against a family member.

Even though the verdict was preordained, it was not released until the early hours of 24 August. Ulrich entered the courtroom and began reading the long and dull summation leading up to the verdict. Each of the defendants was named and, after a period of hesitation, Ulrich announced that all sixteen defendants were sentenced to death by shooting. Those in attendance fully expected the customary addendum which was used in political trials that stipulated that the sentence was commuted by reason of a defendant's contribution to the Revolution. These words never came, and it was apparent that the death sentence was final when Ulrich placed the summation on his desk and left the courtroom.

Soviet law is clear on the point that a defendant receiving a death sentence has a period of seventy-two hours in which he can make a written plea for clemency and that a sentence cannot be carried out before the expiration of this period of grace. On the morning of 25 August, the Moscow newspapers carried the announcement that all sixteen defendants had been put to death. Stalin had again imposed his will in an obvious transgression of Soviet law.

Even the five pseudo-defendants had not been spared the death sentence as they had expected, even though it should have been apparent to them that Stalin would not allow any witnesses to the counterfeit charges.

The first of the three great purge trials was now over, ending with the result that Stalin had strived to gain. He was now in an enhanced position to lay the basis for the trials that would follow. The convictions of Zinoviev and Kamenev went directly to the heart of the old Bolshevik movement and touched all of Stalin's enemies, real or perceived. These alleged conspirators could now be brought to trial and eliminated one by one without much effort.

Anyone who stood in the way of Stalin's quest to remain in power could be tied to the Zinoviev-Kamenev conspiracy in one way or another. Likewise, those individuals in the KGB who had had a hand in the trial, and were aware that Stalin was the mastermind behind the secret plot to do away with the two so-called conspirators, would now be marking time to their own deaths. Orlov would come to call this source of power Stalin's instrument for 'judicial murder'.

It didn't take long for Stalin to act on his newly acquired power. Within a week of the defendants' deaths, he ordered Yezhov and Yagoda to prepare a list of 5,000 political dissidents who were serving sentences in the various gulags. He then ordered those on the list to be executed under covert conditions. Orlov cited this as the first case in the history of the Soviet Union when mass executions were carried out against Communists without the formality of the judicial system.

Orlov later declared that the two events which had had a profound impact on his life had taken place in August 1936, both within a matter of days of each other. The first was the trial of Zinoviev and Kamenev.

When he had first attended the trial on the opening day, he had done so with an open mind, half expecting a fair trial in spite of the fact that he knew the trial also carried considerable implications for Stalin. As he had only been back in the Soviet Union for less than two months after his assignment abroad, he was never directly involved with the trial nor was he immediately aware of Stalin's connection. As time progressed, however, he learnt about aspects of the plot because of his working relationship with those involved and because he was considered a member of the trusted inner circle of the KGB.

Orlov always considered himself to be a loyal member of the Communist Party and had no reservations whatsoever that the ideals promulgated by Lenin and his followers were the appropriate and fairest course for the Russian people. He also had no reservations about his work for the KGB as he saw this as one of the means to secure the end. However, as the trial progressed, seeds of doubt came into his mind and for the first time he sensed that he was not completely in accord with the hidden objectives of the trial. He also reasoned that the programmed outcome of the trial would provide Stalin with a powerful tool that would not only keep him in power but would hang heavily over his enemies as well as anyone he perceived as opposing him. Up to this time Orlov was well aware that Stalin was an extremely difficult person but expected that this was required of a man in his position.

One evening when Orlov and I were discussing the Zinoviev-Kamenev trial, he reminisced that he often reflected on the historical significance of the trial, but more importantly he reflected on the personal implications that the trial had had for him. He stated that, as time went by, he was more certain than ever that the events of that fateful time in August 1936 set the stage for his defection, although, as he acknowledged, the doubts that entered his mind at the trial did not lead him to consider defection at the time.

The second event that was to have a profound impact on his life took place on 26 August when he was informed of his assignment to Spain. This was to take him to Spain and lead to his inevitable defection from the KGB and the Soviet Union.

FOUR

ASSIGNMENT SPAIN

The early autumn of 1936 in Moscow was a critical period for Orlov as he anticipated his departure for Spain and a new assignment which marked his approval and enhanced his stature not only with the KGB but with the highest level of the Politburo. The recognition bestowed upon him by these two government entities went a long way to balancing out his desire to settle his family in Moscow as well as his apprehension of the harsh course that Stalin and the Politburo had taken to entrench the Communist system of government into the daily lives of the Soviet people.

Following long and frequent absences from his beloved Russia, Orlov felt that he deserved the promised assignment to the KGB Centre in Moscow. These frequent changes of assignment between various Western capitals had brought with them a disruption of normal family life and had played a disastrous role in the health of the Orlovs' only child, Vera, who had accompanied her parents as they both pursued their careers in the espionage field. Maria Orlov's role was minor in comparison to her husband's, but nevertheless her work as a courier and providing her husband with what appeared to be a legitimate cover was an important part of her employment with the KGB.

As already described, Orlov had been dispatched to Paris in the summer of 1926 to become the chief of the legal *rezidentura* at the Soviet Embassy. For Orlov, the assignment to Paris would become a bittersweet experience because it was in Paris that Vera contracted an illness that would eventually take her life at a very tender age.

The Orlov family tragedy began as a pleasurable celebration of Vera's third birthday. The weekend following her birthday, the Orlovs set out for a picnic at the Parc des Buttes-Chaumont in the north-east section of Paris. They had visited the park on several previous occasions, and it was there that Vera had enjoyed the donkey rides and where her parents also took advantage of a wonderful restaurant overlooking a small lake in the park. On the day of Vera's birthday, her parents asked her if there was anything special she wanted, to which she replied that she wanted to ride the donkeys in the park. Most of Vera's park excursions were to the Luxembourg Gardens close to the Soviet Embassy on the rue de Grenelle, but there were no donkey rides there, so they went to the Parc des Buttes-Chaumont instead.

The morning was spent strolling through the park, followed by lunch at the restaurant. In the early afternoon, Vera enjoyed feeding the swans in the lake and then riding in the cart pulled by the donkey. Towards late afternoon the Orlovs decided as a special treat to rent a rowing boat. Unfortunately, while on the lake a sudden downpour of rain drenched them before they could make it back to the dock and some sort of cover. They then returned to their residence.

Vera's wet clothing, combined with rather cool weather that day, produced an immediate chill and a somewhat high temperature, but nothing that alarmed her parents. However, within several weeks of the outing, Vera became tired and listless and developed a sore throat. Becoming alarmed at these developments, the Orlovs now sought the advice of the Soviet Embassy's physician. A thorough physical examination and throat culture determined the presence of strep bacteria, but the extent of damage, if any, was not apparent nor could a long-term prognosis be made. As time progressed, Vera suffered bouts of illness manifested by loss of appetite, a high fever and a sweaty condition, and it became evident that these spells were recurring more frequently and were becoming more severe in nature. Further medical consultation confirmed the Orlovs' worst fears, that Vera had developed an uncommon form of rheumatic fever whose inflammatory properties were attacking her heart and causing permanent damage to her heart valves. This time the prognosis was confirmed as being life threatening and her prospects for a long lifespan were not good. However, proper medical attention would add years to her life and there was always the hope that she would outlive the odds.

Orlov's desire to be posted to the KGB Centre in Moscow, therefore, was based primarily on his concerns for his daughter's health and welfare. He reasoned that the medical facilities extended to him by virtue of his station in the hierarchy of the Communist Party would be superior and therefore comparable to what was available in the West. Even more important, he felt that Vera's needs could be better nurtured by being in a family environment in which his parents and his wife's parents could provide her with loving care. An additional consideration and one of great importance was that an assignment to the KGB Centre would be less demanding of his time and thereby would afford him more opportunity to tend to the needs of the family at a very critical time.

In the end, when he was fully convinced that he had no alternative but to accept the assignment to Spain, he reconciled himself to the fact that the medical attention his daughter would receive in Spain would be better than that in Moscow. He further reasoned that if Spanish medical facilities did not live up to his expectations, his position would allow him to avail himself of the renowned medical skills centred in Paris, which was not too far from Spain. He acknowledged that the family support for Vera would be a concession, but he also understood that it was his duty to make sacrifices for the welfare of the Soviet people.

Preparations now went forward for the Spanish assignment and last-minute briefings scheduled. The first meeting was with Orlov's superior Genrikh Yagoda, who apprised Orlov that Stalin personally considered his appointment as one of far-reaching importance as there was likely to be a confrontation with the German Government of Adolf Hitler, who was already supporting the Nationalist Government of General Francisco Franco. Yagoda related that Stalin had only two priorities on his mind these days: the purge trials going on in the Soviet Union and the Civil War in Spain. Stalin was considering open defiance of his archenemy Hitler by sending Soviet aircraft and pilots to aid the Republicans in their fight against the Nationalists. Yagoda informed Orlov that his principal task in Spain would be to create an intelligence service for the Republican Government, which would direct its operations against the Nationalists and the German forces in Spain, and to organise guerrilla warfare cadres which would operate behind enemy lines. Yagoda stressed the importance of establishing these guerrilla units and noted that the prime reason for Orlov's appointment was his relevant experience during the Russo-Polish War.

Yagoda instructed Orlov to work out a plan of operation and to start out with a small staff, which would be enlarged when needed to meet future requirements. He also scheduled meetings with Maxim Litvinov, the Commissar of Foreign Affairs, and Kliment Voroshilov, Marshal of the Soviet Army.

The following day Orlov and Yagoda met Voroshilov at the headquarters of the Red Army in Moscow. Also present at this meeting were General Uritsky, head of the GRU, and General Jan Berzin, Uritsky's predecessor at the GRU. Berzin had also just been assigned as the Chief of the Soviet Military Mission in Spain.

The previous day Yagoda had said that Stalin was 'considering' sending military equipment to Spain. Voroshilov, on the other hand, made it quite clear that the Soviets would send troops, tanks, aeroplanes and other military hardware as it was imperative to destroy the Nationalist and German forces. He dwelt on the fact that he did not want any military equipment to fall into the hands of the Germans, and should such a situation develop during battle every effort should be made to repair the piece of equipment and remove it from the battle scene, or else to totally destroy the component. At the time Orlov thought it strange that an experienced military officer could conceivably believe that often complex repairs could be made in the heat of battle. In reality, military history supported the fact that military equipment is lost in battle on both sides and the lost equipment becomes the prize of the victor. Orlov realised that Voroshilov's objective to keep Soviet military design and construction secrets from the enemy was logical, but his reasoning that repairs could be made under battle conditions was misguided. Orlov blamed Voroshilov's faulty logic on a recently made propaganda film produced for the consumption of the masses in the Soviet Union and Spain entitled *If War Comes*, which depicted war between the Soviet Union and Germany. The Soviet troops committed to battle did so under conditions that left the impression that they had suffered no losses, and their spotless appearance after battle looked as if they were coming from a dress parade rather than a battlefield. On the other hand, the German troops were defeated and looked the part, with their dead and mangled bodies strewn all over the battlefield.

One message that clearly came out of the meeting was the fact that the Soviet Union was totally committed to aiding the Spanish Republicans. The main objective for doing so was to destroy the German enemy on Spanish soil with a display of Soviet power, which would give Hitler serious reservations about provoking the Soviet Union in the future.

The next meeting with Litvinov was a routine one for Orlov. They had known each other since the early 1930s on a professional basis, which had later blossomed into a warm friendship. Litvinov was a fellow Jew from the old school of Bolsheviks and had been a close and trusted friend of Lenin. His field of expertise was foreign diplomacy, wherein he gained the respect of President Franklin D. Roosevelt It was Roosevelt's willingness to deal with Litvinov that led to the United States' recognition of the Soviet Union as a sovereign government, which in turn led to the establishment of diplomatic relations between the two countries.

Over the years it was Orlov's responsibility to meet Litvinov on his return from an extended assignment abroad. The purpose of these meetings was to report on conditions in Orlov's country of assignment in order that Litvinov would be in a position to make his own assessment and evaluation of the particular country as it would relate to Soviet foreign policy.

Orlov had met Litvinov several days prior to this occasion when they were preparing his diplomatic documentation for Spain. They had both agreed without any reservations that a new identity had to be generated as Orlov (i.e. Feldbin) had to pass through Germany en route to Spain, which might pose an element of danger given Orlov's past assignments in Germany. Litvinov suggested several suitable cover names, one of which was that of Alexander Orlov, the famous eighteenth-century Russian writer. The man who was to become known as Alexander Orlov immediately seized on this particular name as he had first encountered it at the Lazarevsky Institute in Moscow and greatly admired the author's works.

Orlov would have no reason ever to forget the date of his last meeting with Litvinov as it was on that date, 5 September 1936, that the Commissar signed the diplomatic passports of both Orlov and his wife Maria.

On their last meeting, Litvinov was in a depressed mood. He spoke of the recent trial of Zinoviev and Kamenev and questioned their immediate execution. He felt that the trial was a harbinger of coming events which spelt doom for the old-line Bolsheviks. Turning aside from the trial, they spoke of Orlov's role in Spain and the establishment of Soviet influence and control in the area. Litvinov stressed that the British held the key to future world events, the outcome of which could lead to another world war. In his words he stated that, 'If they [the British] insist on preventing the Loyalists from buying arms abroad, the Nationalists will win and Hitler will have his own way. In that case we will be at war by 1938.'

Litvinov warned Orlov to refrain from having any contact with the Spanish Communist Party, saying that he must deal solely with the Republican Government. In the event that things were not going well for the Republicans, they would accuse their own Communist Party first before putting blame on the Soviets.

They both felt sad when they said their last farewells. They

embraced one another in the traditional Russian manner reserved
for a close friendship. As Orlov turned to leave the office, Litvinov
called his name to catch his attention and then wished him the
best of luck. Orlov never saw Litvinov again, although they did
maintain contact through intelligence and diplomatic channels
between Spain and Moscow.

Orlov's last official act in Moscow was a meeting with Yagoda
on 6 September. Most of the day was devoted to Orlov's plans,
which Yagoda approved, to establish an intelligence service for the
Spanish Republican Government and to train guerrilla units to
operate behind enemy lines. All that remained was fine-tuning the
programmes and setting the guidelines that Orlov would have to
operate under in strict compliance with current Soviet policy.
Yagoda emphasised the need for maintaining frequent communication with the KGB Centre and that it must be consulted if there
was the slightest doubt about a plan of action on the local level
that Orlov could not resolve personally. Yagoda went on to stress
that the Spanish Civil War would be the proving ground for Soviet
hardware as well as a measure of the capability of its troops. The
whole world would be watching events in Spain as they unfolded
and it would be then that the power of the Soviet war machine
would be recognised. France and England would realise the advantage of having the Soviets as an ally, and Hitler would recognise
that it would be a mistake to take on the Russian bear.

As with Litvinov the previous day, Yagoda cautioned Orlov to
keep his distance from the Spanish Communist Party and to deal
only with the Republican Government. He noted that Orlov's
presence would be closely watched by the Republican
Government and, as such, he should forget that he was a
Communist but rather should act with dignity and propriety in
the fashion of a British military attaché.

At the conclusion of the meeting, Yagoda walked Orlov to the
door and put his arm around his shoulder. He then reminded
the General that his observations from Spain would be reported
by the KGB directly to the Politburo, and because of its importance the intelligence he would be furnishing the Centre regarding

developments in Spain had to be extremely accurate, highly comprehensive and received by the Centre in a very timely fashion so as to make the KGB's intelligence-gathering competitors, the Commissariats of Foreign Affairs and Defence, look inferior in the eyes of the Politburo. Yagoda even suggested that each night before retiring, Orlov should ask himself if there was anything else he should have cabled to the Centre that day. Neither of these two individuals had any suspicion that within a period of three weeks Yagoda would be dismissed from his post as Chairman of the KGB.

Orlov had three days in Moscow to conclude his personal affairs and bid his relatives and close friends farewell. He would later relate that although it was difficult to take leave of his relatives and friends, he did so with the understanding that it was on a temporary basis as with previous assignments abroad. He noted that it was an emotional parting for him but more so for his wife and daughter. As he looked back on that date, he felt that perhaps it was for the best that he was unaware that he would never see his relatives, his close friends and associates, or Mother Russia, again.

The Orlovs left Moscow on 10 September 1936 and arrived in Paris several days later. They encountered no difficulties in their transit through Nazi Germany, and their fraudulent diplomatic passports were not scrutinised with any degree of suspicion at the two German border control checkpoints. What Orlov personally carried on that journey was of utmost importance to the new KGB Station in Spain, for, in a large brown leather suitcase that he had acquired years before in Vienna, he had the KGB's secret code books. The suitcase never left his sight or his control as the code books could not be compromised and would be the means of communication between Orlov and the KGB Centre. There was no other way the code books could be transferred with such security. Fortunately Orlov's status as a Soviet diplomat made his personal effects immune from customs examinations by any of the countries he passed through en route to Spain.

In Paris, Orlov provided his wife and daughter with a temporary residence until he could eventually see his way clear to bringing them to Spain. He left Paris on 15 September for Barcelona, from where he would have to negotiate transportation to Madrid.

Orlov related what was to become an amusing incident and the beginning of a close personal friendship. On the connecting flight from Toulouse to Barcelona, he encountered an individual who spoke fluent German and excellent English and volunteered that he was going to Madrid on business. However, there was something in his manner that made Orlov suspect that he was actually a Russian, although he never gave the slightest indication that this was the case and Orlov did not pry further. When asked the nature of his business, the stranger replied that he was a furrier. Orlov thought this rather peculiar as Spain was at war and the climate was rather warm for furs, so he asked the stranger if furs were really needed in Spain. An embarrassed look appeared on the stranger's face but he did not reply to Orlov's question. Orlov thought that the stranger was more than likely a munitions dealer. On arrival in Barcelona, the situation was chaotic and finding transportation to Madrid was a difficult task. However, Orlov learned that the huge airport was under the control of the military, so he made his way to the office of the Spanish airfield commander. Here he was met with enthusiasm by a fellow comrade in arms and a small aeroplane was placed at his disposal for the flight to Madrid. Orlov offered the furrier a ride, but the stranger declined as he alleged that his plans did not call for him to go directly to Madrid.

A few days later after Orlov was safely ensconced in his office at the Soviet Embassy in Madrid, the Soviet Military Attaché, Brigade Commander Vladimir Gorev, came to Orlov's office to introduce a friend, who turned out to be the so-called furrier. Both men immediately recognised one another and then laughed at the situation. Gorev's friend turned out to be the Russian General Lazar Stern, whose identity in Spain was concealed under the operational pseudonym of General Emil Kleber. Kleber was destined for fame as the defender of Madrid during the darkest days of the Civil War when the Nationalists were about to capture Madrid and was widely known as the ablest of the commanders of the International Brigades. Their chance meeting under curious conditions turned into a lasting friendship.

FIVE

GUERRILLA WARFARE

The administration of the guerrilla warfare programme during the Spanish Civil War was under the auspices of the KGB rather than where it logically belonged, under the Red Army. Orlov related that this was a throwback to the Civil War in Russia following the Bolshevik Revolution, when intelligence-gathering fully supported guerrilla operations. The two mandates were so closely intertwined that it was reasonably thought that guerrilla activities should be handled by a separate department within the KGB rather than by the Red Army. The Spanish Civil War presented a unique situation in that the Red Army did not actually fight in Spain per se but nevertheless participated through a cadre of Soviet military advisors, who controlled the International Brigades and influenced the Republican Army to the extent that they could be considered a satellite fighting arm of the Red Army. In the end, the Politburo felt it more advantageous to maintain political control over the guerrilla warfare programme than to leave it in the hands of the military, where it could conceivably be turned against the politicians in power during a crisis. The same reasoning applied to the Border Guard, which was a separate department on the same level as the other Chief Directorates of the KGB. What ensued was a supreme instrument of power administered by the KGB and under the direct control of Stalin and to a lesser extent the Politburo.

The Soviet Embassy was located in the Palace Hotel and it was here that Orlov met for the first time Marcel Rosenberg, the Soviet Ambassador to the Spanish Republican Government. Orlov was not favourably impressed with the Politburo's choice.

Rosenberg was a slight man with a noticeable hunchback and an annoying demeanour. He had difficultly maintaining relations with people and was suspicious of everyone. Perhaps his greatest deficits were that he was not considered a true Soviet, having been raised in Danzig, Poland, and that he had only become a member of the Soviet Communist Party relatively recently.

Rosenberg's previous diplomatic experience was with the League of Nations, and he was given credit for laying the ground-work for the 1935 Military Agreement between France and the Soviet Union. However, his appointment by Litvinov to the prestigious position of Ambassador to the Republicans was purely political. Rosenberg was married to the daughter of Yemelyan Yaroslavsky, the head of the Central Control Committee of the Soviet Communist Party. Rosenberg's wife was a much younger woman, who had previously been married to Roman Carmen, a well-known film producer in the Soviet Union.

What became a matter of much conjecture and gossip at the Embassy occurred when Carmen was assigned to the Embassy as an advisor to assist the Republicans in producing anti-Nationalist propaganda films. Orlov was uncertain how Carmen's assignment came about but felt that Yaroslavsky's wife Kirsanova, who at the time was the Director of the acclaimed Lenin School, was responsible. The astute personnel at the Embassy were quick to notice that at official dinners and Embassy functions, Rosenberg's wife and her attractive ex-husband would exchange furtive glances, which did not go unnoticed by the Ambassador. He had forbidden his wife to talk to Carmen and soon resorted to having her placed under surveillance. Within a month, she had left Madrid and returned to Moscow.

Orlov had not yet officially presented his diplomatic credentials to the Republican Government. Rosenberg made separate appointments for Orlov to meet Manuel Azaña, the President of the Spanish Republican Government, and Prime Minister Francisco Largo Caballero.

As with Rosenberg, Orlov was not impressed with Azaña at their first meeting. Throughout the course of the Spanish Civil

War he had frequent official contacts with the President and his initial assessment of Azaña never wavered. He described him as 'a man with an ugly face. He was an apparent weakling, deeply in love with himself and with the lofty positions he had held in Spanish public life since the abdication of the king. The events of the Spanish Civil War proved him an egotist and veritable coward, who deserted his people when the war reached a critical stage.'

Orlov's assessment of Prime Minister Largo Caballero was quite different. The man was a former plasterer, who had risen in the ranks of the Spanish Socialist Party and become the leader of the Socialist-dominated and powerful workers' union, the Unión General de Trabajadores (UGT). The Prime Minister was already in his early seventies and the deep lines on his face reflected a lifetime of turbulence and suffering. He left the impression of a forceful and uncompromising person without the slightest shred of self-importance. Orlov always knew where he stood with Largo Caballero and the two had a common bond of understanding.

On the day of Orlov's appointment with the Prime Minister, Vladimir Gorev also presented his official diplomatic credentials. At the meeting, Largo Caballero asked Gorev what Spain could expect in the form of military aid from the Soviets. Gorev was placed in a position where he could not give a specific answer as not even Stalin had made up his mind as to what aid would be extended. Gorev advised that military aid would be forthcoming but declined to give any details. Largo Caballero then suggested that young Spaniards be sent to the Soviet Union for training as military pilots. Ambassador Rosenberg voiced his opinion that the Prime Minister's suggestion was an excellent idea.

The Prime Minister then turned his attention to Orlov and pointedly asked, 'And what can you do for Spain?' Orlov countered, 'Military intelligence and guerrilla warfare behind the enemy's lines.' The Prime Minister acknowledged the importance of Orlov's mission and noted that the guerrillas could help win the war. He also noted that Orlov would find the Spaniards to be tough guerrillas as Napoleon had discovered a century earlier. He pointed out that the Republicans had not as yet been able to build an adequate army and that the enemy was advancing. However, he felt that guerrilla attacks could at least slow down their advance. Orlov agreed.

When they parted company, Largo Caballero suggested that Orlov should talk to Angel Galarza, the Minister of the Interior. His last words to Orlov were more than a suggestion: 'Come to me in one month and tell me how things are developing.'

The next day a meeting was arranged with Galarza for the following evening at the Ministry of the Interior in Madrid. Rosenberg would also be at the meeting along with Soviet Counsellor Gaikis, who was a member of a Russian family that had migrated to Argentina shortly after the First World War. He had spent his boyhood in the Argentine and, as a result, spoke fluent Spanish. His presence at the meeting was that of an interpreter for Orlov and the Ambassador.

The Soviet group met the Minister, the Deputy Minister and two individuals from the General Staff of the Ministry. The meeting took place in a comfortable room, which appeared to be more like a spacious living-room than an office. Galarza was a tall, handsome man of about forty-five, whose manners suggested someone from the privileged class. He also turned out to be a gracious host when he served his guests cocktails, coffee and tapas.

The major topic of discussion was how to deal with the large number of Franco's spies who had infiltrated Republican territory and how to turn the situation around by infiltrating Republican spies into Nationalist territory. At times the discussion became very provocative and bordered on measures which years later would become known as 'cloak-and-dagger' spying. Galarza's principal concern was that there were Franco spies or sympathisers on Republican soil who, via shortwave radio, broadcast nightly to the Nationalists secrets regarding everything from troop movements to what had taken place at a Cabinet meeting that day. Unfortunately, no one from the Nationalist side was broadcasting Franco's secrets to the Republicans. The meeting lasted well into the night and Orlov felt that much was accomplished.

Orlov reported back to the Prime Minister at the end of the month but had little in the way of concrete measures to report. However, he did have in hand an outline plan for the establishment of the guerrilla warfare training camps as well as the objectives of the programme. Largo Caballero was satisfied and gave his approval. From that day forward the two men maintained a close liaison.

The guerrilla warfare programme started on a small scale with the establishment of two training schools, the first in Madrid and then one in Benimamet near Valencia. Recruitment at the beginning was mostly from the Republican Army for the obvious reason that knowledge of the Spanish language was vital to guerrilla operations. In the early months of the war, the International Brigades were formed with an infusion of foreign volunteers who had flocked to the side of the Republicans in order to fight Fascism. Both the Republican Army and the International Brigades proved to be fertile grounds for recruitment. Both forces were overseen in one way or another by a line of Soviet military advisors, political commissars, and KGB officers and agents in the ranks of the military, who worked both covertly and overtly. The principal objective of all these administrative lines of support was to spot and assess recruits for the guerrilla warfare programme.

Once a potential recruit was selected for guerrilla training, he was transferred to one of the training bases. Orlov's office issued the orders and there was little chance of contravening an order. The guerrilla's personnel file would be maintained at Benimamet along with his passport, which was held for 'safekeeping'. In the event of a guerrilla's death in combat, these essential documents were transferred to Moscow. Orlov related that there was much speculation that the KGB collected passports from the various nationals for purposes of espionage, which was true to some extent. However, by the mid-1930s the KGB had become proficient in manufacturing fraudulent passports and the need for the genuine article declined. However, there was always a need for comparison purposes as well as for the practice of replacing the original identification page with a new one as dictated by the requirements of the service.

By the summer of 1937, Orlov was able to report the establishment of six guerrilla training camps, which operated within three regional districts located in and around Madrid, Valencia and Barcelona. Over 1,600 regular guerrillas had already been trained, along with approximately 14,000 partisans on Nationalist territory who clandestinely supported the regular guerrilla fighters as well as conducting raids on their own. The partisans actively disrupted communications and supply columns and at times would even harass enemy troop movements.

By the time Orlov defected in 1938, he estimated that well over 3,000 guerrillas had been trained by the KGB and the ranks of the partisans had continued to grow and become more widespread in Franco's territory.

Early on in our discussions on guerrilla warfare, Orlov would use the word 'commandos' to define one of his small military units, which could conduct a swift raid on an objective in enemy territory and then return to its home base. When questioned on this term, Orlov was quick to give credit to Leonid Eitingon, his deputy who operated in Spain under the pseudonym Colonel Kotov, as the most probable person to have coined the word and its usage in modern times. Kotov spoke almost flawless Spanish and early on in the planning stages of guerrilla strategy began to use the word 'commando' from the Spanish word meaning 'authority to command'. Soon the word evolved into the name for the military group that had the authority and responsibility to conduct the raid. Orlov also gave credit to Kotov as the man most responsible for developing the strategy for commando raids in modern times, and that the Spanish Civil War was the testing ground for the tactic long before the Second World War. He illustrated how this all came about.

Most of the planning for establishing guerrilla training camps and the schools' curriculum, as well as recruiting candidates primarily from within the ranks of the International Brigades, and overall guerrilla warfare policy and tactical objectives, were resolved and implemented by the end of 1936. The Spanish Nationalist Government had moved the seat of government to Valencia as had the Soviet Embassy and the KGB. Kotov was the officer responsible for the development of the KGB's guerrilla warfare programme and he had displayed an inordinate amount of diligence and administrative skill in carrying out his assignment. Orlov soon came to rely on his judgement.

Towards the end of 1936, Kotov presented a plan to Orlov which he felt was worthy of his consideration. This called for a highly selective cadre of guerrillas to undertake specialised training in firearms, explosives, demolition and physical endurance. These men would be formed into a cohesive military unit, which would stress the importance of teamwork. Each man would have a particular speciality in which he would excel, yet be in a position to take over another speciality if a team member was killed at a critical time in the operation. In addition to their speciality, each member of the unit would be assigned a particular mission within the raid. The operation would have to proceed like a well-oiled machine in order to be successful as much depended on the team effort.

Orlov related that he was somewhat less than receptive to the idea and reasoned that these elements were already in place in the regular guerrilla training programme. Kotov disagreed and argued that the 'commandos' would only be used in the most sensitive and critical of situations, where extraordinary circumstances dictated a lightning strike to accomplish the mission and an equally swift withdrawal before the enemy knew what had happened. He cited as an example the possibility of a strike against a military headquarters or a munitions dump well inside enemy territory. In both instances, complacency would be on the side of the commandos. Orlov immediately saw the flaw in the tactic – it would be easy to get in but difficult to get out – and felt that the loss of life and risk in making their way back to friendly territory did not warrant a hazardous mission that could go wrong at any moment. Neither of them was convinced that the other's position was the correct one, but they continued to debate the matter over a long period of time. In the meantime, Kotov hand-picked a group of guerrilla trainees from the Benimamet training school to undergo the specialised commando training. It was well in his province and he did so without advising Orlov.

Kotov finally came up with the idea of a trial-run commando raid on an actual military target on the Republican side. There would be no bloodshed as it was a training raid and there would be much to learn from such an operation. Orlov agreed and asked Kotov to work out the details for final approval.

Several days later, Kotov presented his preliminary plan to Orlov. When Orlov saw the details, he wondered if his deputy had gone mad. Kotov's plan called for a strike against the head-quarters of the Republican military garrison located in an old fort on the top of a small mountain called Montjuich (Jewish Mountain) in Barcelona. The fort overlooked Barcelona from the south-west quadrant of the city and immediately below it to the south was the Mediterranean Sea. Kotov purposely chose this particular garrison as the objective because there was no way that an attacking army could take the fort from the sea side or from below the mountain without a long drawn-out campaign. He felt that his commandos could make their way to the fortress's west wall by night and scale it just before dawn. They would make their raid on the Staff Office, simulate the capture of several offi-cers along with vital maps and plans, and then make good their escape. He proposed that had this been an actual mission, a sea landing and subsequent sea-route escape would have been the logical approach. However, this facet of the operation could be simulated without any loss in evaluating the mission.

Orlov did not know what to say for several moments and had to regain his composure before telling Kotov that his plan greatly troubled him because of its inherent ramifications. In the first place, he didn't think it possible to carry out such a mission with-out notifying the Republican Army in advance. On the other hand, there was no safe way to alert the Republican Army directly or through the Ministry of Defence as they could not be relied on to withhold the plan of attack from their own people because of the possible embarrassment of a successful raid. In the event that they went ahead with the plan without any notification and something went awry, the situation could escalate into one where there could be a loss of life on both sides. Notwithstanding all these factors, there could be political repercussions which could thwart their already fragile relations with the Republicans.

Kotov agreed somewhat but stated his position, that a raid on an easy objective was worthless and would prove nothing whereas a raid on an objective that entailed difficulties would determine the overall value of this type of warfare. As a compromise, he proposed that one of their own KGB people should just happen to be present in the Staff Office at the time of the attack. Should it get out of hand, the KGB officer could come forth and explain the situation before any defensive action could take place. This solution sounded plausible during the discussion, but in reality the KGB had had no reason to call on the Staff Office in the past and knew no one on the Staff that they could logically call on. Orlov's choice for this particular role fell on the Soviet Military Attaché, Vladimir Gorev. Orlov finally agreed that this was the sensible way to go and that he would make the necessary arrangements with Gorev. In the meantime, he instructed Kotov to start the programme to train the commandos. At this point, Kotov had to admit that the training was already well underway and that all that remained was to obtain Gorev's co-operation and finalise the plans for the operation.

Orlov summoned Gorev to his office and explained the necessity of his services. Gorev acknowledged that he was already known at the Staff Office at the fort but was a little reluctant to undertake the assignment for the same reasons originally expressed by Orlov. Gorev could have been ordered to take the assignment but Orlov preferred him to volunteer. Orlov played on Gorev's work in the past with Soviet military intelligence and, in the end, the General prevailed.

The commando raid was set for the first week in January 1937, sometime between New Year's Day and the sixth day of the month when the religious holiday, the Feast of the Epiphany, is celebrated. The likelihood was good that the fort would be lightly staffed between the two holidays, which, in a real raid, was a valid consideration. The day before the scheduled raid, Gorev called Colonel Garcia, who was in charge of the garrison, from his office in Valencia. He advised that he would be on an inspection tour in the Barcelona area the next day and would like to call on the Colonel. He added that he had a very busy schedule and would like to meet the Colonel first thing in the morning. The Colonel agreed.

Gorev was in the Staff Office the next morning talking to the Colonel when five armed men in military fatigues suddenly burst into the office. Garcia, a junior officer and a desk sergeant were taken by surprise and all four people in the room were disarmed of their personal weapons, bound with rope and gagged with cloth to prevent their outcries. Gorev, whose identity was known to the intruders, was bound in a way that he could easily extricate himself. The raid took only a matter of minutes and the attackers were gone.

As soon as the raiders departed, Gorev untied himself and made for the Colonel. He couldn't help but suddenly notice the deep lines of consternation on the faces of the three other captives. As soon as he had untied Garcia, the man leapt towards the telephone. Gorev placed his hand on that of the Colonel, as he held the telephone, and sternly shouted in Spanish, '*Un momento por favor*'. The Colonel was clearly startled and didn't know what to make of the command. Gorev later recalled that this was among the tensest moments of his career. He then produced an operations memorandum, whose outline reflected what had actually taken place that morning in the Staff Office. Garcia was furious when he realised that he had been the victim of a bizarre plot, but was satisfied that the raid had been a hoax. Nothing that Gorev said regarding the merits and purpose of the assault seemed to calm the Colonel's temper. Gorev estimated that that one incident set back relations between Garcia and the Russians by a hundred years, but in the end felt that the operation was well worth the effort. Gorev never met the Colonel again and suspected that they mutually avoided one another.

Orlov and Kotov were delighted with the results of the operation, and what they learned that day became the groundwork for commando raids throughout the Spanish Civil War. In the days, weeks and months following the caper, Orlov was ever alert to hear of any repercussions as a result of the operation on his daily contacts with officials of the Republican Government. Not one word was ever spoken of the incident during the entire time he was in Spain, and he suspected that Colonel Garcia was too embarrassed to report the matter officially.

Although Orlov was quite modest in underplaying his role in the development of commando operations during the Spanish Civil War while heaping credit on Kotov, whom he characterised as the father of modern commando warfare techniques, I would have to add that Orlov had to at least have been the godfather.

The guerrilla warfare programme was broken down into two distinct types of operation. In the first, a small band of no more than nine highly trained guerrillas would conduct lightning raids into Franco's territory to cut communications and supply lines, derail military trains, demolish bridges and then retreat to a safe area as quickly as possible. In the second, special forces roughly in the strength of a military platoon of about fifty guerrillas would attack heavily guarded military installations, such as airfields and ammunition dumps, to destroy what they could and fight their way out if necessary. Both types of operation called for gathering military intelligence in conjunction with their principal objective. Towards the end of the summer of 1937, these operations became more sophisticated and penetrated deeper into the enemy's territory.

Gathering military intelligence and conducting guerrilla warfare were never far apart. A favourite tactic developed by the Soviets during the Spanish Civil War was used extensively by the German Army during the Second World War. On the eve of a

Republican offensive, Orlov's guerrillas would masquerade as Nationalist Army military police, complete with proper uniforms and fictitious identities, and set up a checkpoint along a road travelled by the enemy. They would then stop all military traffic on the road and make the occupants identify their units, destination and purpose of their journey. By the time they abandoned the checkpoint, they had acquired the intelligence needed to support the Republicans' offensive. The ruse was highly successful and continued without the enemy becoming suspicious throughout 1937. Only on one occasion in 1938 did something go wrong when an alert Nationalist officer detected something not quite right about the fraudulent military police and a bloody skirmish ensued.

There were times when more comprehensive information was required about the disposition of enemy troops garrisoned near the target as well as information concerning the target itself. On these occasions, guerrillas who had family residing near the objective would be sent to visit their relatives to acquire the necessary information. Even in Nationalist-held territory there were always those who were sympathetic to the Republican cause and willing to supply whatever information was needed. Franco's troop movements could easily be monitored in this fashion.

Soon a cadre recruited from the local inhabitants developed into the fighting force known as the 'partisans'. Unlike the regular guerrillas, the partisans remained on Franco's territory to fight clandestinely by night and carry out their usual chores by day, or else to abandon their connections with their family and friends totally and hide out in the hills to await the next attack. The partisans proved to be a very cohesive and elusive fighting machine that demoralised Franco's troops and sapped their strength.

Their credible achievements in the field led the Nationalist Army Chief of Staff to believe that the partisans were far greater in number than they actually were. Orlov's office trained the partisans in the field by sending them regular guerrilla instructors and supplying them with arms, ammunition, explosives and financial support. Their interest and motivation to continue fighting Franco was kept alive by Soviet propagandists preaching the evils of Fascism and the good life to come.

Some of the greatest successes of the guerrillas came in the spring of 1937 in the region of Rio Tinto and Aroche. Located deep within the heart of Nationalist territory, the region was the site of the world's largest copper and pyrite mines, which became the prime targets of guerrilla saboteurs much to the detriment of the Nationalists. They took reprisals against miners whom they believed to be co-operating with the saboteurs and arrested them. These young men had been exempt from military service because of the critical need for the minerals, but were now being drafted into the military. When they began to be drafted, they ignored the call to duty and fled to the hills. The situation became explosive and certainly signified that the sabotage campaign was working. When the KGB Centre was made aware of the situation, they felt that the matter should be exploited to the fullest and sent to Spain four of their ablest and experienced guerrilla experts, who had served in Poland and China.

These four experts were under the command of Major Strik and his assistant, Captain Stepan Glushko. The other two men were Nikolayevsky and Vladimirov. At the age of forty, Strik was the least impressive of the four but turned out to be the most dedicated to the cause. When he heard of the tenuous situation and the great opportunity for achievement in Rio Tinto, he asked Orlov for the assignment in spite of the fact that he spoke no Spanish.

After a brief orientation period at the Benimamet training camp, Orlov was satisfied that the four men were well qualified for the work and gave Strik the assignment to Rio Tinto. The Major took with him Captain Glushko and nine Spanish guerrillas. Travelling by night and sleeping during the day, they finally reached their destination, where they were well received by the miners. When the miners learned that Strik and Glushko had been sent from Moscow for the express purpose of aiding their cause, they were overjoyed and even more committed to the Soviets. Now an additional number of miners joined the renegades in the hills and the number of partisans continued to grow.

Strik organised his first guerrilla campaign simultaneously on a Nationalist air-force school and an army arsenal. Both attacks were highly successful, and soon word spread about the military genius the Spaniards nicknamed the 'Little Russian Devil' because of his small stature and bold exploits. His daring raids became the curse of the Nationalist Army, and no matter how much effort they put into his capture he was always able to elude the pursuer. His band of guerrillas would emerge out of nowhere to attack their objective swiftly and just as quickly retreat to the hills, where they were nowhere to be found. The 'Little Russian Devil' became legendary and caught the imagination of the populace. As a consequence, more volunteers were drawn into the underground conflict and the original band of eleven men grew to over 3,000 partisans in the region. The 'Little Russian Devil' was a constant threat to the enemy and a strict disciplinarian with his men, but to the common peasants in the region he was their hero and saviour.

However, unknown to Orlov was the fact that everything was not going well in the Rio Tinto campaign, although he had no reason to suspect otherwise. Every report he received indicated one success after another. In the late autumn of 1937, he was in his office at the KGB headquarters in the Hotel Metropole, Valencia, when Colonel Kotov appeared at the door and announced that he had something urgent to report. Orlov knew the Colonel well enough to know that the matter had to be important and signalled Kotov to enter.

That morning two Spanish guerrillas had come to the headquarters with a message from Dr Moro, leader of the partisans in Rio Tinto, to the 'Partisan High Command'. Dr Moro was a physician and a former member of the Spanish Socialist Party, who had been drafted into the partisan movement against his will. Despite his original unwillingness to participate with the partisans, he was soon overcome by their dedication to a cause which he also happened to believe to be correct. In time, he became the leader of the movement. Orlov was already well aware of Dr Moro's devotion to the cause and bravery in action to the extent that he could place his full confidence in the man. The message read that although guerrilla operations under Major Strik were very successful and the partisan movement was growing by the day, Moro felt that Strik had overstepped his authority and his actions were causing strife within the organisation. Moro cited a recent incident in which Strik had had a confrontation with a loyal partisan who had refused to obey his direct order. Strik had resolved the matter by shooting the partisan in the head in front of the man's comrades. As a result, Moro felt that Strik's life was in danger and begged that he be relieved of his command before the partisans turned on him.

Orlov called in the two guerrillas who had brought the message. One of them was part of the original group that had accompanied Strik to Rio Tinto. Both guerrillas confirmed the contents of Moro's message and added that Strik was losing control of his faculties and was feeling so self-important that he was harming the movement. They both cited Strik's tendency to settle a difference of opinion by reaching for his revolver and informed Orlov that the partisans were beginning to grumble about the man's behaviour.

Orlov felt that there was too much at stake in the Rio Tinto operation and that there was no point in jeopardising what they had already accomplished. He therefore radioed Strik and congratulated him on his good work in Rio Tinto, and ordered him and Captain Glushko to return immediately to Valencia for another vital assignment. Orlov recommended that Dr Moro be the acting commandant of the partisans.

Ten days later, four Spanish guerrillas from Rio Tinto arrived at the KGB headquarters in Valencia. They explained that they had accompanied Strik and Glushko on the journey but that along the way they had encountered problems with the 'Little Russian Devil'. Strik had become annoyed and argumentative if anyone contradicted his opinion and had gone into a rage whenever they had suggested a different, safer route through the mountains. Finally after another argument which had occurred about fifty kilometres from the Republican frontier, he had ordered the four Spaniards to carry on to Valencia, saying that he and Glushko would continue the journey on their own.

The next morning Strik arrived at the KGB headquarters. Orlov barely recognised him, and for several moments Strik stood before Orlov and two associates without saying a word. Suddenly he burst out in a very clear tone, 'Stepan Glushko', then paused for a few moments and continued, 'is dead.' He then repeated in a more dramatic fashion, 'He is dead!'

Then Strik began his tale of what had happened. He related that after he and Glushko had parted company with the four guerrillas, they made their way past a small village about thirty-five kilometres from the Republican border. They were extremely tired and thirsty when they spotted a young shepherd boy with his flock. They gave him several Franco pesetas and asked him to fetch them water. The village was close by and he returned with the water and a few oranges, so they assumed that he had told no one.

They drank their fill and decided to rest for a while. About an hour later, they were awoken by voices and were able to see a group of men, some in military garb, walking towards them. They had been betrayed by the shepherd. A firefight ensued, but they were able to hold the attackers at bay. As nightfall approached, they planned their escape, but before this could happen Glushko was hit by a bullet square in the forehead. Strik made good his escape that night under heavy enemy gunfire.

Strik stayed at the headquarters for several weeks but seemed emotionally changed from the man who had first reported there less than six months before. He never smiled and always seemed sullen, with his mind and thoughts elsewhere. What was strange to Orlov was the fact that when he first heard Strik's tale about the siege, he felt that it was a cover-up and that Strik had murdered Glushko. Strik claimed that he had fought his way out of the siege taking with him his rifle, two pistols and several hand grenades, but when he had appeared at headquarters he only had with him his military knapsack. Why in the world, reasoned Orlov, would a man trying to escape with his life take with him the additional weight of the knapsack when he was already burdened down with a rifle, pistols and hand grenades and under fire from the enemy? Orlov considered initiating an investigation at the location where Strik claimed the firefight and siege had taken place, but felt that the results would be inconclusive and might risk the life of an investigator in hostile territory.

Orlov decided that he would give Strik the benefit of the doubt and consulted Kotov, who always displayed good judgement and possessed a rare sense of intuition. His first words were, 'In my opinion Strik murdered Glushko.' He theorised that Strik had underscored the dangerousness of the mission by murdering Glushko and concocted the story to bring attention to himself as the hero who had made good his escape through heavy enemy gunfire. The motive for the murder as well as the elaborate scenario were not difficult to understand because, as Kotov reminded Orlov, when Strik had first reported to headquarters on his arrival from Moscow, he was adamant that he would make every effort to earn the highest medal awarded to both military and civilians for outstanding feats, the 'Gold Star Medal', commonly known as the 'Heroes of the Soviet Union' medal.

Despite Kotov's appraisal of the situation, Orlov could not discredit Strik in the absence of concrete proof. He cabled the KGB Centre an account of Strik's escapade and recommended that he be given the 'Order of Lenin', awarded to individuals for special services rendered to the Soviet Union, for his bold exploits during the Rio Tinto operation. Had Strik returned with Glushko, he would have recommended him for the higher award, the 'Heroes of the Soviet Union' medal. Several days later, a cable signed by KGB Chairman Yezhov informed Orlov that his request for Strik had been granted.

In time, the official announcement of the award was carried in the Soviet newspapers. Alongside Strik's name appeared that of Captain Glushko, who had been awarded the 'Order of the Red Banner' in recognition of conspicuous bravery, a somewhat lesser distinction than that given to Strik. What was not noted in the official announcement was the fact that Glushko's medal was granted posthumously, a common practice in those days when the Soviet Government would not acknowledge that the Soviet military was fighting on Spanish soil. Strik was eventually returned to the Soviet Union to an unknown fate.

Captain Nikolayevsky was the most impressive of the four guerrilla experts sent to Spain in 1937, and the one Orlov believed would leave his mark in the Spanish Civil War. A handsome, blond-haired muscular giant, who towered well over six feet, Nikolayevsky was a born leader, who not only led his men but eagerly sought out personal combat with the enemy. Orlov and members of his staff would refer to Nikolayevsky as the 'blond giant'. His daring raids on Nationalist airfields and courageous acts of personal heroism in the field earned him the respect of his men and the admiration of his superiors.

One of Nikolayevsky's raids on an enemy airfield in the summer of 1937 was cited by Orlov. Nikolayevsky and his men approached the vicinity of the airfield in the uniforms of the Nationalist Army. On the road to the airfield, they commandeered two military trucks and proceeded to the sentry gate of the field. The blond-haired Nikolayevsky was often mistaken for a German and readily took advantage of this misunderstanding. On this particular occasion he wore a Nazi Swastika armband and, as the trucks passed the sentry box, he raised his arm and shouted the Fascist slogan, *'Arriba España'*. The sentry was so startled that he failed to challenge the intruders.

Nikolayevsky proceeded to the administration building, where he introduced himself to the duty officer as a captain on a special mission, a statement that was actually true. He produced spurious identification and requested accommodation for himself and his men. En route to their barracks, they noted the disposition of some of the aircraft and auxiliary equipment, but decided to assess the situation more fully in the morning.

In the early light of dawn, they were able to define the targets of the day: large twin-engined bombers that rained havoc on Madrid as well as the smaller fighter aircraft that protected the bombers. At the signal the raid began and, within an hour, the guerrillas were already making their way back to friendly territory.

Nikolayevsky's legend grew along with a string of successful guerrilla raids to the point where even he felt invincible. Headquarters highly prized the man for his ability to plan and execute the most intricate of raids. This would be his downfall as the most dangerous assignments were routinely given to the 'blond giant'. In the summer of 1937, the critical port of Almeria, on the southern coast of Spain on the Mediterranean Sea, was being harassed by daily bomber raids, not only on the supply port with all its facilities but also on incoming Soviet freighters. Approximately fifty miles to the west of Almeria lay the frontier that separated the Nationalists and the Republicans, and not far into the Nationalist side was the airfield that controlled the skies over Almeria. Unquestionably something had to be done, but there was little doubt that the mission would be extremely dangerous. This would be Nikolayevsky's final assignment. During the heat of battle on the tarmac of the Nationalist military airfield, the 'blond giant' was about to throw a hand grenade at its target when the missile prematurely exploded. Sadly, Nikolayevsky became another casualty of the war and never returned to the home base.

The last of the Soviet guerrilla warfare experts sent to Spain by the KGB was the one blessed with good fortune. Vladimirov never saw action and spent his days at the Benimamet training camp. He was a very personable and amusing man, and, by a stroke of good fortune, Colonel Kotov had taken an immediate liking to him. Perhaps his most enchanting quality was his ability to play the balalaika like a professional. When Vladimirov played the musical instrument during the evening off-duty hours, his fellow officers would become nostalgic, with the help of a few vodkas or brandy, with thoughts of Mother Russia. Kotov decided to keep his new friend at the home base, explaining to the KGB Centre that Vladimirov's real importance was training guerrilla personnel. The Centre bought Kotov's argument, which, in the end, turned out to be valid with the additional benefit of keeping the KGB staff happy most evenings.

Orlov related that his involvement with the four guerrillas was very close and that every time he thought about the group, he would recall a rather jocular communication he had received from Abram Slutsky, Chief of the INO. When Slutsky wrote to confirm the assignment of the four men to Spain, he referred to them as 'the four Soviet Musketeers' and warned that they had 'more in common with banditism than with Communism'.

The successes of the guerrilla campaign at Rio Tinto and Aroche far exceeded the expectations of the KGB, to the personal delight of Stalin. Mining of minerals vital for the war effort practically came to a standstill due largely to the great number of young miners who had abandoned their jobs to join the rebels in the hills. As the ranks of the guerrillas swelled, the attacks on military objectives escalated. Franco countered by releasing two army divisions from the front lines to combat the '*guerilleros Marxistos de Orlov*'. Juan Negrin, the powerful Socialist Minister of Finance in the Republican Cabinet, personally congratulated Orlov, writing, 'Besides the harm which you have caused the enemy in his own territory, you have inactivated two enemy divisions. This in itself is a big achievement.' Orlov was surprised when he was also congratulated by a bitter rival, Soviet General Grigorovich.

Grigorovich operated under the pseudonym General Stern during the Spanish Civil War. Later, this pseudonym was a problem for Western writers when they confused him with General Emil Kleber, the pseudonym used during the Spanish Civil War by Lazar Stern.

Grigorovich felt that guerrilla operations rightfully belonged under the province of the Red Army and was jealous of Orlov's successes. One of Grigorovich's top aides in the 4th Department of the Red Army caused him to believe that at least a part of the guerrilla operations should be under his control.

One day while Orlov was at the Soviet Embassy in Paris, he received an urgent telephone call from Kotov informing him that

a Spanish Army unit had just arrived at the Benimamet guerrilla base armed with an order signed by the Chief of the General
Staff of the Republican Army, General Vincente Rojo, transferring the Benimamet guerrilla base to the 'Guerrilla Department'
of the General Staff. Actually, there was no such military organisation as the 'Guerrilla Department', only a subversive creation
in Grigorovich's mind. The Spanish colonel who presented the
order demanded an immediate transfer. Orlov instructed Kotov
to give the impression that they would comply with the order
but that it would take twenty-four hours to make an orderly
withdrawal.

Orlov took the next flight to Valencia and went directly to the
office of Indalecio Prieto, the Republican Minister of Defence.
Prieto immediately issued an order under his signature stating
that guerrilla warfare was subordinate only to the Minister of
Defence and that the order issued by General Rojo was no longer
valid. When the Spanish colonel arrived the next day with a
detachment of his men to take over the base, he was embarrassed
when Prieto's order was handed to him. He and his men made
a hasty retreat, and there was no doubt that Orlov's rival was not
pleased with the turn of events.

The problem apparently did not stop at the gates of the
Benimamet base. Grigorovich took his case to the Soviet Commissar of Defence, Marshal Kliment Voroshilov, who permitted
Grigorovich to organise small guerrilla units within the army.
When Grigorovich began to organise his guerrilla programme, he
sent one of his Staff officers to Orlov to seek advice. Orlov gave
his advice freely, but stipulated that his office had to be advised
in advance of any guerrilla operations that might cause problems
in the field. Orlov had in mind an attack on the same military
installation, which would only duplicate efforts, or worse a simultaneous attack on an objective without either party being
cognizant of the other, resulting in a disastrous situation. The
Staff officer agreed with the necessity to co-ordinate efforts, but
Grigorovich never complied with the request.

About three months later, Orlov encountered Grigorovich at

a meeting of the General Staff of the Spanish Army. Orlov asked how things were going with Grigorovich's guerrillas, to which he replied that he was already operating about a hundred guerrillas and was satisfied with the progress. He mentioned that one of his guerrilla programmes was the dropping of booby traps in the vicinity of Nationalist military installations. The explosives were concealed in articles such as cameras, binoculars and other goods that would attract the attention of a passing soldier. When the object was picked up, the device exploded, rendering the soldier a casualty.

This had not been the type of warfare that Orlov's guerrillas engaged in and he had great reservations. He asked Grigorovich what would happen if a peasant picked up the booby trap. The reply was that there were few peasants near military bases and, if this did occur, it was only to be expected during wartime. He then confided that such an incident could be seen as another weapon of war, which would certainly shatter the morale of the people. Orlov could not agree and told Grigorovich so.

Orlov told me that the KGB Centre was not pleased with Grigorovich's intrusion into its guerrilla province and his efforts to subvert the programme through Marshal Voroshilov. Grigorovich was recalled to Moscow, and Orlov later learned that he had been executed. Orlov claimed that he knew of no connection between the General's recall and his efforts to take over guerrilla operations. Perhaps Grigorovich's name came up on Stalin's list of Red Army generals to be purged.

What was the overall effect of the KGB's guerrilla programme during the Spanish Civil War? Orlov was of the opinion that the impact of the guerrilla operations was so immense that the war was prolonged by at least a year. The guerrilla operations were not decisive and could not in themselves win the war, but what they were able to accomplish was the wearing down of Franco's army by undermining Nationalist forces in scattered operations throughout Spain, thus preventing them from consolidating their efforts for other critical offensive campaigns. Had the Republicans been given support by France and England as allies rather than as non-interventionists, the Civil War could have been won by the Republicans. France and England were in sympathy with the Republicans but were not yet totally committed to taking a stand against Fascism.

Orlov was aware of the success of his guerrilla operations from intelligence gathered in the field, but none was more heartening than an independent confirmation from the other side at the highest level. During February 1938, the KGB was able to penetrate the office of Count Galeazzo Ciano, the Foreign Minister of Italy, in Rome and procured a copy of a letter from Franco to the Italian dictator Benito Mussolini. The period in question was when the KGB's guerrilla warfare programme was achieving its greatest successes in the northern provinces of Spain, especially in the province of Asturias. The operations in the north far exceeded what they had accomplished in the Rio Tinto campaign and had a considerable impact on the operations of the Nationalist Army. In his letter, Franco pointed to the reason why it had taken so long to muster his forces for the offensive to recapture the city of Teruel and why he had to continue to rely on Mussolini's troops. Franco explained that the strength of his army was being sapped by the invisible guerrillas, operated by the 'Reds', that plagued his territory.

Another confirmation of the importance and penetration of guerrilla warfare in the Spanish Civil War can be drawn from a letter that Franco sent to Eberhard von Stohrer, the German Ambassador to Spain, in March 1938. Franco was outlining the military situation in Spain and in part the letter noted:

Unfortunately the regrouping after the ending of the military campaign in the north took more time than expected. The sole reason was the fact, which remained hidden from the outside world, that there continued to be guerrilla warfare, particularly in Asturias, which had not ended until just recently. After the capture of Gijon there were still 18,000 armed men scattered throughout the country; quite recently probably the last ones – 2,000 men with 18 machine-guns and 1,500 rifles – were captured. Thus the enemy was able to seize the initiative and . . . to obtain initial successes which prevented execution of the December offensive against Madrid. [DGPF Document Number 541 (Series D, Volume III), U.S.D.S.]

Orlov lamented the fact that one of his best KGB guerrilla experts, Kirilov, was lost in the Asturias campaign. There were three KGB operatives assigned to the partisans: Kirilov, Lebedev and Nikolaev, who were amongst the group of 2,000 partisans that Franco mentioned as being captured. Lebedev and Nikolaev managed to escape and made their way to the partisans in the hills and eventually to safety in France. Kirilov was never heard of again and was presumed dead.

SIX

SPANISH GOLD

Orlov had been in Madrid for only a month when, on 12 October 1936, his code clerk appeared at his office. There was nothing unusual about this as his code clerk often brought him transcribed secret messages from the KGB Centre in Moscow, but in this instance the code clerk was carrying the secret code book, indicating that the incoming message was for Orlov's eyes only.

The code clerk announced that the message had just come in from the KGB Centre under the category of 'Absolutely Secret' and 'Decode Immediately', with the further caveat that it should only be decoded by 'Schwed', Orlov's operational code name for his assignment in Spain. Orlov dismissed the code clerk and proceeded to decode the message. He immediately recognised that the message was more than a routine matter and of great importance as it did not emanate from the Chief of the Foreign Department but from KGB Chairman Yezhov. The message itself read:

> Arrange with the head of the Spanish Government, Caballero, for shipment of gold reserves of Spain to the Soviet Union. Use a Soviet steamer. Maintain utmost secrecy. If the Spaniards demand from you a receipt, refuse – I repeat, refuse to sign anything. Say that a formal receipt will be issued in Moscow by the State Bank. I hold you personally responsible for this operation. Rosenberg has been instructed accordingly. /S/ Ivan Vasilievich.

The signature on the message, 'Ivan Vasilievich', was Stalin's rarely used code name, a fact known only to a handful of KGB officials. Stalin had personally chosen this code name, which turned out to be a dark touch of irony as the name Ivan Vasilievich was the paternal ancestral name of Ivan the Terrible.

As soon as Orlov realised the importance of the message, he hastened to the nearby office of Marcel Rosenberg, the Soviet Ambassador. As soon as he entered the Ambassador's office, he knew that Rosenberg had received his counterpart of the message in the Embassy's code. When he finished reading the message, Rosenberg looked up with an expression of perplexity and disbelief etched on his face.

There was little doubt that both men knew exactly what was in the other's mind at that precise moment. They questioned whether Prime Minister Largo Caballero would even consider placing the gold treasures of Spain into the hands of the despot Stalin. These were the treasures that had been piling up in the vaults of the Spanish Treasury since the days of King Ferdinand and Queen Isabella, when they had looted the Aztecs and the Incas and seized ships on the high seas carrying gold from South and Central America. Largo Caballero was an honest and patriotic Spaniard, as were his colleagues, so why would they now want to entrust their country's gold to Stalin, the man whose lack of morality and contempt towards capitalists were well established? Why would they think that Stalin would ever return the gold once he had got his hands on it?

The answer in one respect was simple. The Nationalists under Franco were making their way towards Madrid, the capital of the Republicans, at an alarming rate and it might not be long before the capital fell into the hands of the rebels along with the gold and silver reserves lying in the vaults of the Bank of Spain. The Republican Cabinet foresaw this possibility and deemed it necessary to move the treasures from Madrid to a safe location. President Azaña and Finance Minister Negrin signed the secret decree on 13 September 1936 ordering the removal from Madrid. The decree empowered the Finance Minister to transport the precious metals 'to the place which in his opinion offers the best security' and that in due time the transfer would be formalised to the Cortes, the Spanish Parliament. As one might have suspected, this never happened.

At the beginning of October, Franco's armies were within twenty miles of Madrid and the fall of the capital was imminent. The citizens of the city were staging a mass exodus and the roads out of Madrid were clogged with refugees travelling on foot or by whatever means at their disposal. The situation deteriorated to the point that the Republican Government evacuated Madrid on 6 November and moved the seat of government to Valencia.

The secret decree of 13 September was the legal basis for moving the precious metals out of harm's way, but by no stretch of the imagination did it mean moving the gold out of Spain to another country. As the situation worsened, Negrin stepped beyond the scope of his authority and considered storing the gold with their only ally, the Soviet Union. In concert with President Azaña and Prime Minister Largo Caballero, he decided to approach the Soviet Trade Attaché Winzer to sound out his views. Winzer cabled the Foreign Office in Moscow, and they in turn presented the matter to Stalin. He must have jumped up and down with joy as he relished the idea of acquiring the gold reserves of Spain.

Within two days of receiving the secret coded message from Stalin authorising the KGB to procure and transport the Spanish gold to the USSR, Negrin was sitting in the office of the Soviet Ambassador for a conference with Rosenberg and Orlov on the issue. Negrin would later become the Prime Minister, but his political background was that of a novice. He was an intellectual who, before the Civil War, had been a Professor of Physiology. He was also an idealist who was opposed to Communism in theory but still maintained a keen interest in the Communist experiment in the Soviet Union. Perhaps his political innocence explained his apparent willingness to consign his country's gold to a questionable future. Moreover, he was aware that Franco had the benefit of the assistance of Hitler and Mussolini, while the only great power that had come to the aid of the Republicans in their time of need was the Soviet Union. The Soviets and their International Brigades were in the breach to prevent the Nationalists from taking Madrid and, in the eyes of the people, they were at the zenith of their popularity.

Negrin confirmed that he did indeed want the Spanish gold to be transferred to the Soviet Union for safekeeping. He demanded no guarantees that the gold would be returned in the event that the Republicans eventually prevailed in the Civil War, nor was he given any assurances. He felt that he had no choice between the risk of losing the gold to Franco or of entrusting it to an ally, with the prospect that the Soviets would do the right thing and return the gold eventually. He felt that his options were limited because he could not trust the United States, Great Britain or France, as they could not ensure the secrecy of storing the gold and would probably turn the gold over to Franco should he appear to be winning the war.

During the battle for Madrid, the KGB learned that the Spanish gold reserves had been moved to the main naval base at Cartagena. When Orlov asked Negrin to confirm this, he replied in the affirmative and noted further that the gold was stored in caves north of Cartagena, where munitions for the Republican Navy were also stored. This facilitated Orlov's problems as Cartagena was the principal port where Soviet merchant vessels unloaded arms and supplies for the Republicans. Only a week before, the first Soviet Tank Brigade had disembarked at Cartagena and was being billeted at the small coastal town of Archena, some ninety kilometres away. In Cartagena, therefore, Orlov would have a port near to where the gold was stored as well as a port facility where the Soviet merchantmen could pick up the gold. Hopefully he would also have trustworthy Soviet manpower to physically move the gold.

Orlov asked Negrin the identity of all the participants in the plan. He replied that only Azaña, Largo Caballero and himself were privy to the formulation, but that they had to bring Señor Francisco Mendez-Aspe, the Director of the Treasury, into the framework of the scheme. Orlov replied that this secrecy was good as the fewer who knew the plan the better. However, he had to have one more conspirator, whom he identified as Minister of Defence Prieto. Orlov felt that the Republican Navy had to provide protection, at least in the Mediterranean, for the Soviet merchant ships carrying the gold across to the Black Sea and the Soviet port of Odessa, where the precious cargo would be unloaded.

The plan had to be accelerated at all costs and shrouded in deep secrecy. The slightest rumour could alert the German and Italian Navies and the Soviet ships might then be intercepted in international waters. The Germans and Italians were already intercepting suspect Soviet vessels en route to Loyalist Spain and searching them for contraband useful to the Republicans. Another factor to consider was the will of the people. In the event of even the slightest rumour that the gold was being shipped to the Communists in the Soviet Union, there would be an uprising of such magnitude that it would not only kill the whole plan but the conspirators as well. The coalition government, which consisted mostly of Socialists and a few Communists, was not in full control of the Spanish people, and such a move could ignite a desperate situation. In this eventuality, they planned to claim that the gold was being turned over to England or the United States.

In order to perpetrate the latter scheme of feigning the gold was being shipped to England or the United States in the event of a worst-case scenario, Orlov asked if the Finance Ministry could furnish him with credentials attesting that he was an agent of one of the prominent American or English banks. Negrin relished the idea, and it was apparent that he was caught up in the scheme. As a consequence, Orlov had official credentials from the Ministry of Finance that he held concurrent with his true purpose of moving the gold to the Soviet Union. The very powerful and stately looking document signed by Negrin as the Minister of Finance requested that all military authorities render assistance to 'Mr Blackstone, plenipotentiary representative of the Bank of America'.

From the Soviet Embassy Orlov and Negrin went directly to the Finance Ministry, where Orlov met Mendez-Aspe for the first time. He gave an accounting of the gold and how it was stored. The count was approximately 10,000 boxes, each containing 145 pounds of gold cast ingots. Only a handful of Bank of Spain officials knew that the gold reserves had been moved to Cartagena and there was no indication whatsoever that this information had leaked to the general public. Even the security guards watching over the boxes believed that they contained munitions of some type.

The next day Orlov set out for a trip to Cartagena to assess the overall situation at the site where the gold was being stored. A military aircraft was placed at his disposal for this purpose. Shortly after takeoff from Madrid, two German bombers and several German fighter planes appeared out of nowhere to make a bombing run on the city, or some military objective. Orlov's aeroplane was spotted and one of the fighter planes made a strafing pass over the slower aircraft. The pilot was forced to land at an emergency landing strip. Orlov returned to Madrid by car. He was devastated more by the loss of time than by the close call he had had.

The next day he set out again for Cartagena, this time by car. The long journey which took about eight hours was uneventful and rather dull compared to the trip of the previous day. Orlov was not impressed with the quiet city of some 40,000 inhabitants that sat at the edge of the Mediterranean Sea. For the most part, he found the city nondescript and his only positive recollection was the picturesque promenade around the bay.

The Soviet Naval Attaché, Nikolai Kuznetzov, assigned to the Cartagena naval base was awaiting Orlov's arrival. They were old friends from the days when the Naval Attaché had been assigned to the GRU. Orlov informed Kuznetzov that he was preparing to transport 'highly strategic material' and authorised the Naval Attaché to commandeer all Soviet vessels arriving at the port. He was told that all arriving Soviet vessels must be unloaded with the greatest expediency and remain at alert until further orders.

The Soviet merchant ship *Mologoles* was already unloading in the port and was the first freighter commandeered under Orlov's command.

The following morning Orlov and Kuznetzov met the newly appointed commander of the Cartagena naval base, Antonio Ruiz. Ruiz was more than co-operative and anxious to give his full assistance. He pledged to furnish sixty trustworthy seamen to the special task and would have them remain on an alert status until needed. Orlov estimated that the mission would take no more than five days once put into action. Having completed his mission in Cartagena and having set the first elements of the plan in motion, Orlov returned to Madrid.

The next day Orlov met Largo Caballero, Negrin and Prieto, who was taken into their confidence. The plan to remove the gold from Spain was explained to him, and Prieto agreed whole-heartedly to the operation and pledged his full support.

Orlov had been working out the details for the transport of the gold to the Soviet Union and now presented his plans to his fellow conspirators. He felt it wise to divide the gold among as many Soviet vessels as could be mustered expeditiously rather than to place the entire cargo on one freighter. The risk would be too great for one ship considering the long journey to the Bosporus, via the Mediterranean, which was infested with German and Italian warships. Orlov informed the meeting that he had drafted a secret order which would be placed in a sealed envelope and given to each commander of the various Republican naval warships that would be strategically stationed along the route to the Bosporus. He then handed Prieto a copy of this secret order.

The sealed envelopes were to be opened only when the commanders received a specific coded radio message followed by an SOS distress signal. When any one of the Soviet freighters carrying the gold was in a position where they might be intercepted by a German or Italian warship, they would transmit the coded distress call. The sealed orders instructed the Spanish vessels to come to the aid of the Soviet freighter and escort it to safety.

Prieto assured Orlov that all Spanish warships would be deployed to the best possible advantage along the entire route and that each warship commander would be furnished with a copy of Orlov's sealed orders. Orlov felt that the most dangerous stretch of the journey would be the waters around Italy, but none more hazardous than the strait between the African coast and Sicily. With this in mind he sent a coded message to Stalin by way of Yezhov suggesting that Soviet naval vessels under some sort of pretext be stationed along the dangerous span. He never received a reply, although after the mission was accomplished he did learn that Stalin had followed his recommendation.

With everything falling into place at the Madrid end, Orlov returned to Cartagena to fine tune the mission. The major problem was the transporting of the gold from the caves to the piers in Cartagena. He would require trucks and drivers for this particular phase and he felt that none would be more reliable than his own people. He was aware that a Soviet tank brigade under the capable command of Colonel Krivoshein was stationed some ninety kilometres away in the town of Archena. He therefore summoned Krivoshein to Cartagena, where they discussed the best course of handling the shipment to the piers. It was agreed that twenty trucks and drivers would be placed at Orlov's disposal. The trucks would remain on alert in Archena and would only be dispatched when actually needed. They would then proceed to Cartagena and park near the main railway station to await further orders.

Krivoshein held up his end of the bargain admirably. Orlov instructed Krivoshein to detach two of his KGB security officers, Savchenko and Ninkovich, to temporary duty as his aides. He also had Colonel Feodor Gotzul from his own Madrid staff and, with the addition of Savchenko and Ninkovich, completed the personnel that would be responsible for the last days of the operation in Cartagena.

In the interim, three more Soviet merchantmen had made their way to Cartagena and were commandeered by Orlov. He recalled that two of them were the *Neva* and the *Kuban*, but he could not recall the name of the third freighter. Orlov took charge of super-vising the unloading of the vessels.

When Negrin came to Cartagena to see what progress was being made, Orlov decided to give him a bit of excitement and asked if he would care to see a Soviet tank. Negrin reacted with disbelief as, at that time, no Soviet tanks had been known to have arrived in Spain. Together with KGB Captain Savchenko, they drove to Archena, where Savchenko showed them around the tank encampment. There was no doubt that Negrin felt great pleasure at seeing the arsenal of Soviet tanks as he ran his hands over one of their steel plates. With much elation in his voice he stated that with these tanks the Republicans' foes would be beaten and it would be the Nationalists' turn to run. 'Send our thanks to Stalin,' he exclaimed, 'and tell him this war will soon be over.' Orlov stated that he too wished the war would soon come to an end, but realised that of the two combatants the Republicans were the weakest in most respects and more apt to lose the war. There was still much terror to come.

On the return trip to Cartagena, Orlov asked Negrin if the documents to ship the gold to the Soviet Union had been signed. Orlov didn't know if such documents would actually be issued in the name of the Republican Government but thought he should find out. 'To tell the truth,' Negrin replied, 'the others preferred not to put their names on documents. An eye to history maybe, should anything go wrong. . . . General Orlov, I've taken the whole responsibility on myself.'

Orlov later recounted an incident that happened during the time the Soviet freighters were being unloaded, one that almost ended his life and would have spared the Spaniards the loss of their gold, at least temporarily. Orlov, Ruiz and Kuznetzov decided one evening to inspect the railway station, where a shipment of Soviet-made armaments in huge crates had been loaded on to the platform earlier that day. As they completed the inspection and were leaving, an air-raid alarm sounded at the sight of German bombers overhead. Orlov had been smoking and still had a lit cigarette between his fingers, a violation of night-time blackout regulations. A group of sailors standing nearby witnessed the foreigner with the lighted cigarette and one of the sailors yelled as he pointed to Orlov, 'A spy, a spy signalling to the Germans.' The other sailors took up the chant and added 'Kill him' many times. The group of sailors turned into a vicious mob of frightened and furious beasts as one raised his rifle and the click of the bolt was heard. 'Stop,' yelled Ruiz in Spanish, 'this man is our Russian comrade,' but he could not be heard above the roar of the crowd. Then someone else shouted towards Ruiz, 'You're also a spy.'

Suddenly German bombs began to fall all around the railway station. One landed and exploded less than a thousand feet from the station as everyone fell to the ground. This was followed by several more bombs. The German bombers disappeared as quickly as they had appeared with only the remaining sound of anti-aircraft fire being heard in the night. Then the angry mob of sailors reappeared and shouted that they were looking for the German spies that had got away. They checked everyone lying on the ground and, at this point, a young lad still in his early teens who had apparently witnessed the earlier exchange volunteered that the spies had gone in a particular direction. Orlov and his group did not know why the young lad had come to their rescue but appreciated that he had. The mob finally left and the group of erstwhile inspectors hastened to make their exodus from the area.

By 22 October, all preparations had been made and the final phase of the operation was set in place. The twenty five-ton transport trucks from the Archena tank brigade along with the drivers at the Cartagena railway station were given their final orders, and the Soviet freighters were on standby at the docks in anticipation of long nights of loading extremely valuable cargo.

Towards evening when the sun began to set and the sky darkened, Orlov was on his way out of Cartagena going in the direction of the caves where the precious gold was stored. With him was the very nervous Director of the Spanish Treasury, Mendez-Aspe. The twenty Soviet trucks were following Orlov's car and bringing up the rear was another automobile that contained the three KGB men on his ad hoc staff and two of Mendez-Aspe's Treasury subordinates. Their destination was the Spanish naval munitions dump that lay a mere eight kilometres from Cartagena in the hills north of the city.

Night had fallen by the time they reached their destination. The entrance to the cave was covered by huge wooden doors strengthened by a latticework of metal straps and guarded by sailors armed with carbines. The large bolts that held the two immense swinging doors shut were withdrawn and the doors were opened, exposing the interior of a huge cave. It was at best sparsely lit by electric bulbs suspended from electrical cable running the length of the cave. Inside the cave were the sixty Spanish sailors who were awaiting orders to load the crates containing the gold. The identical wooden crates were stacked along the walls of the cave and numbered in the thousands. Each crate contained ingots of gold and gold coinage, the treasure of a primordial nation that had accumulated its wealth over a span of centuries.

Orlov considered the possibility that the sailors who were to load the crates were aware of the nature of the cargo but were not suspicious as to its final destination. He rationalised that had they the slightest apprehension that the gold was being shipped to the Soviet Union, they could easily overpower the guards and make off with their loot. Fortunately, this uncertainty did not become a problem.

The sailors were all youngsters of slight build who barely managed the lifting of the heavy crates. Each crate contained 145 pounds of gold and it took two sailors to lift the weight on to the trucks. The crates each measured 19" × 12" × 7". Each truck was loaded with fifty crates as an easy measure of the total shipment per truck. As a truck passed out of the cave, the Treasury officials and the KGB men would verify the count and the truck would assemble in the immediate area to form a convoy. When ten trucks were thus loaded, they would proceed in convoy and under security to the docks in Cartagena, where they would be unloaded on to the Soviet freighters. Each convoy run took two hours round trip accounting for 500 crates of gold. While the first convoy was making its delivery, the other ten trucks were being loaded in the cave.

Well after the operation got underway, Orlov had to pose a delicate question to Mendez-Aspe, one that he hesitated to ask but knew to be crucial to the operation. 'How many crates are we supposed to ship?' he asked. 'Oh, more than half, I suppose,' came the reply, indicating that the Treasury Ministry had not prepared well for the operation and had not arrived at a specific number of crates to be shipped to the Soviet Union. At that precise moment Orlov calculated that more than half of the crates would be shipped.

The operation went on for three nights from around 7 p.m. to about 10 a.m the next day. Each convoy of ten trucks was led by Orlov's car, which contained himself, one of the KGB officers and a Treasury official. The rear of the convoy was monitored by yet another security vehicle. The nights were extremely dark during those late October days and it was necessary to maintain blackout conditions, which added to the hazards of the journey. Inasmuch as headlights could not be used, a system of short flashes of the headlights from the lead vehicle would indicate a change in direction.

A major problem emerged on the first night because the drivers of the trucks were all Russians, whose experience was driving tanks and not the lighter trucks. As a consequence, they had a problem in steering and tended to veer off the road. The night-time conditions did not help. That night one of the trucks veered off the road and over an embankment. Fortunately, the mishap occurred well out of Cartagena and attracted no attention.

Perhaps more serious in nature was the difficulty the drivers had in keeping the truck ahead of them in sight during the night-time hours. The leading car in the convoy had to keep stopping to ensure that stragglers caught up with the main body of the convoy. This particular phenomenon caused Orlov to have his biggest fright, one that almost paralysed him at the time.

On one of the runs Orlov made in company with Mendez-Aspe, he discovered on reaching the dockside that only six of the ten trucks had made it to the dock. Somehow four of the trucks had eluded the rear security vehicle and disappeared. These four trucks carried a total of 29,000 pounds of gold and had vanished into thin air. It was still night-time when the discovery was made and Orlov and his group retraced the entire route. At each inter-section and sharp curve in the road, he made his driver blink the headlights in spite of the danger of drawing fire from a military patrol. The real danger however was the Soviet drivers, who spoke no Spanish and could be taken for German spies in the event that they were stopped by a military patrol. If this happened, the patrol would certainly open the crates and find the gold, which would compound the situation. Not only would such a catas-trophe set off a political crisis in the long run, but violence could break out at the scene if foreigners were found to be carrying off the Spanish gold. Justice is not only blind but swift and uncom-promising in wartime conditions and the Russian drivers would probably have been shot on the spot. Orlov recalled this incident as being so stressful that he even considered the possibility that the missing trucks had been hijacked and the Soviet drivers murdered.

As dawn approached, the four missing trucks were finally found parked under some linden trees that lined a broad road. The drivers admitted that they had lost sight of the convoy and were unsure as to which turn-off they should take to catch up with it. Orlov asked how they could have missed his vehicle as he had passed the spot several times during the search and had blinked his lights at the nearby intersection, where they should have made the turn with the rest of the convoy. They admitted that they had indeed seen the blinking headlights, but were not positive that they were from Orlov's vehicle and did not feel that they should take the risk of making their presence known. In the end, they had decided it would be best to remain at the spot where they had become lost until daylight, when they knew they would be found. Orlov felt no reprimand was warranted as the drivers had made the correct decision.

During the operation, Orlov and his staff had no more than

four hours' sleep each day. The crews of the Soviet freighters would sleep during the day and the sailors at the cave would sleep sprawled on top of the crates of precious metals. The crates that contained silver had no covers and merely contained the individual burlap bags of silver tied at the top with twine. Although there was no doubt as to the contents of the crates that held the bags of silver, which were easily accessible, none of the silver was pilfered by the sailors. The sailors were of course locked in the cave during the entire operation, and this fact hindered any possible theft. Naturally, Orlov saw to it that only the crates containing gold were shipped off to the USSR.

The principal risk that confronted the operation at the cave was the possibility of the Germans bombing the munitions site. On each side of the cave where the gold was stored were caves that stored munitions, and should one be hit by a German bomb the cave containing the gold would also be blown to smithereens. On the morning of the final day of the operation, German bombers appeared in the skies over Cartagena at about 3.30 a.m. and began their bombing runs on the docks in the harbour. Fortunately, none of the Soviet freighters in the harbour was hit. However, Mendez-Aspe became exceedingly alarmed at the prospect that the German bombers would make their next run on the munitions depot. He pleaded that the operation be halted until the next day and, when Orlov refused, he muttered something to the effect that with all the dynamite among them they would all go up in smoke. Mendez-Aspe and one of his aides then made a quick retreat from the cave. His other aide, who seemed unperturbed by the turn of events, stayed. The German bombers concluded their attack on Cartagena and departed for their air base. Orlov later learned that a Spanish freighter docked near one of the Soviet freighters took a direct hit, which by a stroke of good fortune missed the part of the ship that carried munitions.

At the end of the third day of the operation, Orlov felt it prudent to wind it up for fear that one of the Soviet freighters could be blown up in the next German raid. He therefore informed Mendez-Aspe that it would be best to dispatch the ships as soon as possible and the Treasury Minister wholeheartedly agreed.

During the entire episode, meticulous care was taken to ensure that an accurate count be made as to the number of crates being shipped to the Soviet Union. Orlov had accounted for 7,900 crates and felt that his figure was accurate. However, the final figure that Mendez-Aspe came up with was 7,800 crates, as he added the comment that the gold being shipped was three-quarters of the gold reserves of his country. Orlov did not attempt to argue the final figure as the error was to the benefit of the Soviets; and further he wished to play it safe, that is safe on his side. In the event that Mendez-Aspe was correct, the Soviets stood to gain an additional 100 crates of gold. However, if Orlov's figure of 7,900 crates was accepted and only 7,800 crates were actually received by the Soviets, there would be hell to pay, and it would be Orlov who would have to pay Stalin his dues. The last crate of gold was placed aboard the last ship at a few minutes past 10 a.m on 25 October 1936. By the stroke of noon, all four of the gold-laden ships were en route to the Soviet Union.

The moment of truth finally arrived – one that Orlov did not relish in the least – when Mendez-Aspe asked for a receipt for the gold that had been shipped. Stalin's unequivocal order was that none should be offered or given, so in an offhand manner Orlov replied, 'A receipt? But *compañero*, I am not authorised to give one. Don't worry, my friend, it will be issued by the State Bank of the Soviet Union when everything is checked and weighed.'

Mendez-Aspe's doleful eyes seemed to glaze over and he had difficulty in uttering his reply. 'Don't you understand that in these times it might mean my life? Should I call Madrid?' was all he could say. Orlov told him not to worry and suggested that he could send a Treasury representative on each of the four ships to act as official guardians of the gold. This seemed to placate the Treasury Director and he grasped at the suggestion like a drowning man grabbing a life jacket, even though Orlov knew that such an accommodation would have no meaning to the ruthless Soviet dictator. Time was running out as the Soviet vessels would be departing in less than two hours and Orlov had no intention of holding the ships back to accommodate Mendez-Aspe. First the Treasury Director ordered his two assistants to board two of the Soviet ships, and then, as there were no other Treasury personnel in the vicinity, he and Orlov scoured the few hotels in Cartagena to appeal to patriotic volunteers to accompany the gold.

When they returned to the docks, only one Soviet freighter remained which was preparing to depart. Two of the vessels, each with a Treasury official aboard, had already put to sea and the remaining vessel, the *Mologoles*, was lying at anchor more than half a mile from shore. Orlov commandeered a motor launch and he, Mendez-Aspe and the last volunteer made their way towards the ship. By the time they were over halfway to their target, the *Mologoles* weighed anchor and put out to the open sea. The motor launch had no radio and the ship did not respond to their frantic waving and yelling as it serenely proceeded on its course to the Soviet Union. Unfortunately for the last two volunteers, they were placed aboard the Soviet freighter that was still at the dockside, while the *Mologoles* steamed ahead without the benefit of a Treasury representative. Orlov stated that he did feel concern for the four unfortunates who were on their way to the Soviet Union, but reasoned that it was all for the good of the Soviet Union.

As the last Soviet freighter sailed out of view with its precious cargo of gold, Orlov's only thought was to notify the KGB Centre immediately that the ships were actually en route to Odessa. When the operation began, he had advised the Centre on two successive days that in future communications he would refer to the 'gold' as 'metal' as an additional measure of security, even though the KGB code by which messages were transmitted was virtually foolproof. In a carefully coded message to Yezhov, Orlov informed him that the four ships with their cargo of 'metal' were en route to their destination. That very evening Orlov received what he thought would be a confirmation, but to his distress the reply asked, 'What metal are you talking about?' Orlov could only think that Yezhov was being stupid and therefore dashed off another message, 'See my previous telegrams. Please report sailings to Ivan Vasilievich.'

Orlov spent many anxious days in his Madrid office awaiting word as to the progress of the ships' movements. He finally received the message that all four ships had safely cleared the dangerous passage between Italy and the coast of Africa. He now felt safe to file his report on the operation to the KGB Centre, but again took the added precaution of filing the report in two parts and sending them out on successive days.

The one matter he would now have to deal with was the actual number of crates shipped. He pointed out that the Spanish Treasury's count was 100 boxes less than his own count and asked that an accurate accounting be taken as soon as the four ships arrived in Odessa. By return cable Yezhov inquired, 'Ivan Vasilievich asks whether you are sure of your figure?' Orlov's reply stated that he was almost certain inasmuch as the receipts he had obtained from each of the four masters of the Soviet freighters corresponded with his figure.

When Orlov learned that all four Soviet freighters had unloaded their cargoes in Odessa, he requested a confirmation as to the total count. The reply from Yezhov was swift and to the point, 'Don't worry about figures. Everything will be counted anew in Moscow.' Before he had a chance to comprehend the meaning of the message, a second one arrived from Yezhov saying, 'Do not mention your figure to anyone.' To Orlov, this was the confirmation he wanted although it came in a devious manner. In comparison to the entire shipment, the additional seven tons of gold seemed insignificant, but there had to be a reason for not wanting the correct count known.

It would be some time before Orlov was able to reconstruct what had happened at the Moscow end of the operation. KGB officers coming from the Centre to Spain would report bits and pieces and the final episode was thus established.

When the four Soviet freighters finally arrived in Odessa, the operation was shrouded in the utmost secrecy. The dock area was cordoned off by KGB security troops and only KGB personnel with special orders were admitted. KGB officers from the Centre in Moscow and the Kiev District Office converged to handle the undertaking. The gold was unloaded from the ships by KGB personnel and loaded on to a special train at the dockside. Hundreds of KGB people accompanied the train on its journey to Moscow in a fashion reminiscent of the guarded Bolshevik trains that made their way through White-held territory during the Russian Civil War. The Deputy Chief of the KGB Ukraine District was in charge and rode alongside the engineer. When the train arrived in Moscow without incident, the Ukrainian KGB Chief immediately reported its arrival to Yezhov.

Stalin was beside himself when Yezhov reported the good news. To celebrate the event, he invited all the top KGB personnel to an extravagant party that very same evening. Stalin was in an exuberant mood all night, a disposition that had rarely been seen before. No wonder, for the Spanish Government to entrust three-quarters of its gold reserves to the dictator without any collateral was certainly an exoneration of the man's character in the eyes of the entire world. Unfortunately, the world was not destined to know the facts for some time as Stalin had something else in mind for the gold.

Some time later in February 1937, the Chief of the KGB Foreign Department Abram Slutsky met Orlov in Paris, where Orlov was convalescing from an injury. One of the topics on the agenda was the Spanish gold. Slutsky informed Orlov that he had it on the best of authority that the gold would never be returned to Spain.

Several months later, Orlov's close friend Mikhail Koltsov, the editor of *Pravda* who had been in Spain from the start of the Civil War, made a trip to Moscow. From time to time Koltsov would go to Moscow to report personally to Stalin on the progress being made in the Civil War. On this particular trip he took with him a handsome, two-year-old Spanish boy as a gift to Yezhov, who had recently lost his only child and whose wife desired another child. Orlov thought this a wonderful gesture on Koltsov's part but later wondered what became of the boy when Yezhov was executed.

Orlov had not told Koltsov of the gold operation, but when Koltsov returned to Spain he informed Orlov that he had learned the details of the affair from Yezhov. He informed Orlov that Spain had lost its treasure to Stalin forever. Yezhov had quoted to Koltsov Stalin's words when he had come into possession of the gold, 'They will never see their gold again, just as they do not see their own ears.'

During the twenty-one months that elapsed between the time of the gold operation and Orlov's defection, he was in continuous contact with the Spanish leaders who were behind the affair. The matter never seemed to surface as it became more like a secret they shared and one they kept in silence. No doubt these Spanish leaders had come to realise that they had made a tragic blunder of gargantuan proportions. The anguish must have been unbearable when they realised that there was no turning back and that they had no avenue to retrieve the gold. There was only one occasion when the matter was brought up by Negrin. He asked Orlov if he remembered the four men that Mendez-Aspe had placed on the Soviet ships as representatives of the Spanish Treasury. Then he went on to say, 'They are still in Russia, and it's now over a year. I wonder why the poor fellows are not allowed to come home.' Orlov surmised the answer to the question, but kept his silence.

What he did recall was how he and Mendez-Aspe had hurriedly recruited the two volunteers that day in Cartagena, and in particular the young Spaniard who had packed his suitcase for that quick trip to Russia thinking he was partaking in a fantastic adventure. Orlov related that years later he learned by accident that the volunteers had been permitted to leave the Soviet Union at the end of the Spanish Civil War and that one of them had wound up in the United States.

Orlov later wondered what Franco's reaction must have been when he finally entered Madrid in 1939 only to find that the

Spanish gold reserves had been moved to the USSR. He kept his silence for eighteen years only because he was not in a position to do otherwise. The Spanish nation was paying its debt for the cost of the Spanish Civil War and its currency on the world market was weak as a consequence. The illusion that the Spanish Government had gold reserves had to be maintained at all costs because the slightest indication that the Government did not have the gold reserves to back up its currency would have resulted not only in the collapse of the currency but of its credit standing around the world. The Soviets were not members of the World Bank or the World Court, so Franco had no judicial recourse through these international bodies.

Orlov related that he had no way of knowing if Madrid ever made any discreet inquiries to the Soviets about the matter. He noted that in 1956 there were several press reports that the Spanish Ambassador to France had discussed the issue with his Soviet counterpart in Paris, but nothing came of the inquiry. The official silence was broken only once on 29 December 1956, when the Spanish Foreign Office in a brief statement announced that an official receipt had been obtained in February 1937 by the Republican Ambassador in Moscow for the gold deposited in the Soviet Union. The receipt had been found among the private possessions of Juan Negrin when he passed away in Paris and turned over to the Spanish authorities by his family.

As a consequence of this disclosure, the Soviet Government finally had to give some recognition to the event. In an article that appeared in the 5 April 1957 issue of *Pravda*, they admitted that the Soviet Government had received the Spanish gold in 1936 and that a receipt had been issued. However, the article went on to say that the gold was only the collateral to guarantee payment for the Soviet arms, aeroplanes and other goods of war that had been delivered to the Republican Government during the Spanish Civil War. The gold had been spent during the course of the Civil War to cover these costs and, moreover, $50 million was still owed by the Spaniards to the Soviet Government. There the matter stands.

Orlov had his own opinion about the Soviet claim that the $600 million (in terms of the 1936 dollar) that had been deposited with them in the form of gold ingots only covered a portion of the Spanish debt to the Soviets. He refuted the Soviet claim and expressed the following rationale in his own words:

> The claim that over $600 million of Soviet goods had been delivered raises certain doubts in my mind. In the early months of the conflict, Soviet material contributions were large, but midway in 1937 they began to taper off sharply until they were reduced to mere trickles. Stalin had changed his strategy. While he no doubt wanted an ultimate Loyalist victory, he preferred to protract the war in order to keep Hitler tied up in Spain as long as possible and thus gain time for Russia to get ready to meet Hitler's expected invasion of the Soviet Union. By withholding armaments from Republican Spain, Stalin was deliberately slowing up the contest.
>
> I watched the whole Spanish drama develop and I know that the Republican Government refrained from entering into close commitments with Stalin and waited in vain for a sign of support from England and France. But that support never came. Blind to the march of Fascism which was soon to engulf their own countries in a bloody war, the great democracies abandoned democratic Spain and thus threw the Republican Government of Spain into the arms of Stalin. Stalin did not miss the chance of assuming in the eyes of the world the role of defender of democracy against Fascism and he cashed in on it handsomely in prestige and gold.

When Orlov first told me the details of what he called Operation Gold, he stressed that only a handful of men were privy to the operation of whom only two were still alive, himself and Mendez-Aspe. Now, the only record of this adventure is in the archives of the KGB, and I am positive that they will not tell what happened to the gold once it reached Stalin's control.

SEVEN

THE *DEUTSCHLAND* AFFAIR, 1937

One of the most tragic incidents of the Spanish Civil War was the bombing of the German pocket battleship *Deutschland* in 1937. The implications were so far-reaching at the time that the strong possibility existed that the incident would be the provocation for the start of the Second World War, a full two years before the actual event. The course of history might have been drastically altered by those events in 1937 with a vastly different outcome to the one that finally ensued. The actual instigator of the attack on the *Deutschland* and the rationale behind it was never absolutely confirmed, although suspicion abounded in many directions. To this day, the circumstances behind the event are still a mystery.

However, sometime during the summer of 1972, I became privy to one of the darkest secrets of the KGB, recounted for the first time by Orlov, the man who had personally carried out the plot at Stalin's behest. Orlov unfolded the plot in his usual manner, giving the complete details leading up to the event and discussing every aspect that contributed to the historical significance of the encounter.

Early in the Spanish Civil War, the Great Powers realised that the war in Spain had to be contained to that area lest it spread to the outside world. In September 1936, the Non-Intervention Committee was formed under the sponsorship of Britain and France with Prime Minister Anthony Eden taking a leading role. The Committee was headquartered in London with the British Foreign Office supplying the administrative support. The delegates to the Committee were the ambassadors from the various countries represented in London which maintained diplomatic relations with Great Britain. The signatories to the agreement restricted war material from entering both the Republican and Nationalist sides and limited the number of volunteers entering Spain. In time, the agreement proved to be more of a diplomatic tool than an enforceable mandate as Germany, Italy and the Soviet Union continued to circumvent the agreement and persisted in pouring men and munitions into war-torn Spain. The French and British were on a course of appeasement as they failed to intervene when the Germans and Italians continued to send large numbers of troops and war material to the Nationalists in spite of the agreement. They felt it wiser to reason with the two nations than have them pull out of the Committee. In the end, the Committee had no real impact on the course of the war other than to debate the issues and keep alive the belief that it was responsible for containing the expansion of Communism and Fascism in Spain, thus preventing the war from spreading.

Stalin had no real problem with the Committee until 20 April 1937, when the Non-Intervention Committee Sea Observation Scheme took effect. A merchantman bound for Spain was obliged to carry an impartial observer, who would check the cargo carried by the vessel and verify the identification papers of passengers on the ship and report any violations. The scheme was further backed up by naval warships that would patrol a particular area with authority to board a merchantman solely to verify that an observer was aboard. The warships had no right to search the vessel and could only report any violations. Vessels participating in the scheme bore distinctive marks of identification, although Spanish vessels and non-participating nations were excluded from the agreement. The British and French Navies were charged with the responsibility of patrolling the coasts of Nationalist Spain while the German and Italian Navies had the responsibility of patrolling the Republican coasts. The Soviet Navy had no role in the naval patrol scheme.

The end result was that vessels going to Franco's Spain were almost ignored by the British and French Navies while the

German and Italian Navies in the Mediterranean energetically enforced their end of the agreement, thus hampering Soviet supplies from reaching Republican Spain. The inequality of the scheme did not go unnoticed by Stalin.

Towards the middle of May 1937, Orlov received a coded cable from Yezhov asking if he could arrange to have a German warship on patrol duty in the Mediterranean torpedoed and sunk by a Spanish submarine without revealing the Soviets' hand. Orlov replied that even if there was a way, it would be impossible to keep the matter secret for long as the Spanish leaders were bound to ascertain the facts. Furthermore, the Spanish leaders would not tolerate such an act inasmuch as any meddling on the part of the Soviets could bring the Germans openly into the war on the side of Franco in a more aggressive role.

A week went by before Orlov received another communication from the KGB Centre. This time the message was more belligerent and to the point: 'Why can't a Republican bomber while raiding an enemy port make it its business to hit a German warship on patrol? Such a thing could happen by mistake. Investigate thoroughly and discuss the technical details with our air-force commander. Mandatory condition: The Spanish leaders must not know that this has been planned by us. Let them think it happened unintentionally.'

Without wasting any more time, Orlov contacted Air Commander Smushkevich of the Red Air Force operating in Spain. Smushkevich offered his full assistance and between the two a preliminary plan was formulated. The Air Commander would send reconnaissance aircraft to overfly the Nationalist-held island of Majorca in the Mediterranean to determine if the German cruiser *Leipzig* was at anchor at the island. For some time it was known that the *Leipzig* was operational in the waters off the coast of Republican Spain and was using Majorca as the rendezvous point for meeting German supply and refuelling ships. In the event the quarry was confirmed present, the next stage would be to send two Soviet bombers to attack the *Leipzig* at sunset. The time of the raid had to be precise as the attacking aircraft would have good visibility to view the target but more so the advantage of having the sun at their backs making it difficult for the warship to ascertain the immediate presence of the attacking aircraft let alone their identity. Smushkevich offered his two best pilots and his best bombardiers for the operation, one of which would be the squadron's recognised pinpoint bombardier ace, Livinsky. The plan was not complicated and offered the best chance of success in conformity with Moscow's orders.

Orlov cabled Yezhov the details of the plan and specifically requested that he have discretionary power over the operation. He reasoned that the German warships were highly mobile and, by the time they were spotted in an enemy port, the fact reported to the KGB Centre and authority given for the plan to proceed, they could be gone. Timing was of vital importance to the operation. Orlov observed that the KGB's reply to his cable was the shortest he had ever received from the Centre, 'Agreed. Good Luck.'

On the afternoon of 29 May, three single-engined reconnaissance aircraft of the Republican Air Force made a routine high-altitude observation flight over the Balearic Isles, which included the islands of Majorca and Ibiza. While over the port of Ibiza, they sighted a German warship lying at anchor just outside of the harbour. From their high-altitude position they presumed that the vessel was the *Leipzig*. Back at the Republican air base, the two Soviet twin-engined SB-2 bombers and their air crews designated for the operation were alerted. At sunset they made their glide-angle attack on the German warship scoring two direct hits, one amidships, which appeared to be the major blow, and another on the side of the deck. As the attackers departed the area to return to their base, they could see a huge volume of black smoke and fire coming from the stricken warship.

Back at his KGB headquarters in Valencia, Orlov filed his coded report on the operation to the KGB Centre within two hours of the actual event. Simultaneous with the sending of his communiqué, a direct-coded radiogram from Yezhov was received congratulating Orlov and asking for the names of the Russian air crews that had participated in the operation. This meant that the news of the attack was already public and had been broadcast on the radio. The incongruity of the situation became apparent when Orlov tuned in his radio only to find that it was not the *Leipzig* that had been hit but the German pocket battleship, the *Deutschland*.

Within weeks of the bombing attack, reports on the reception of the news in Moscow began to trickle in from KGB personnel travelling between Spain and Moscow. Stalin was beside himself when he first heard the news and expressed great delight at the plight of the *Deutschland*. From the beginning of the British and Italian naval patrols, his wrath had been provoked and he had sworn vengeance. As time went by, he had seemed more paranoid than ever and his bad temper was showered on anyone who came into contact with him. After the attack, however, his intimate subordinates were the beneficiaries of the 'new Stalin'.

Orlov never knew first-hand the full consequence of his operation at the time and only discovered what he read in the newspapers. The *New York Times* reported quite extensively on the situation from 30 May to July 1937, and over the years a number of scholarly publications have pondered what really happened on that fateful day in May and the far-reaching ramifications thereof. I am quoting some pertinent excerpts from the *New York Times* as the headlines show how newsworthy the incident was and explain the situation for what it was, a crisis that bordered on a world conflict.

The banner headline of Sunday, 30 May, read, 'REICH BATTLE-SHIP SET AFIRE BY SPANISH LOYALIST BOMBS', and the sub-headings read, 'Ship is hit four times: The *Admiral Scheer* Is Accused of Opening Fire on Aircraft'. The article reflects that:

A warship reported to be the German battleship *Admiral Scheer*, which opened fire on two Spanish government airplanes off the Balearic Island of Ibiza, was bombed at 5 o'clock this afternoon. Smoke from several explosions was seen to climb from the battleship. The two planes were said to be have been making a reconnaissance flight over the

Balearic Islands, although some accounts said they were on their way to raid Palma, Majorca. As they passed over the island of Ibiza, the warship stationed 200 yards from the pier in Ibiza Harbor, fired on them without their having taken any aggressive action against the warship or harbor.

The next day's headlines proclaimed, 'SPANISH ATTACK STIRS REICH. ALL NAVY LEAVE CANCELLED. BOMBS KILL 23 ON WARSHIP.' The article informed that,

The German Cabinet in Berlin held a session to deal with the bombing of the pocket battleship *Deutschland*. (The *Admiral Scheer* was erroneously reported yesterday as the ship bombed.) Afterward an official communiqué was issued that 'the German Government is forced to take measures which will be communicated immediately to the non-intervention committee in London'. It was also disclosed that the *Deutschland* had reached Gibraltar and had reported that the bombing had caused twenty-three deaths and that nineteen members of the crew had been seriously injured and sixty-four slightly wounded.

    The nature of the measures to be taken were not disclosed by Propaganda Minister Joseph Goebbels.

The headline of 1 June read, 'GERMAN WARSHIPS SHELL ALMERIA, KILLING 20, IN REVENGE FOR BOMBING. BERLIN, ROME QUIT NEUTRAL PATROL'. The article datelined 31 May in Valencia reflected that,

The Mediterranean seaport of Almeria was bombarded today at dawn by five German warships in reprisal for the Loyalist air attack on the pocket battleship *Deutschland* last Saturday. The attacking fleet stood in Almeria Bay, seven miles offshore, and rained 300 shells on the city, killing and maiming men, women and children. Some of the finest buildings were destroyed.

The same edition also carried a companion article on the front page datelined 31 May, Berlin, saying that,

> Germany notified the International Non-Intervention Committee in London today of her refusal to participate in further deliberations of that body or in patrol service off Spain until complete protection against further attacks on ships of the international patrol fleet is assured. She did so after having retaliated for the bombing of the pocket battleship *Deutschland* by Loyalist planes off the island of Ibiza last Saturday with an early morning bombardment of the fortified Loyalist naval harbor of Almería. Beyond these two actions no further steps will be undertaken by the German Government until the situation is clarified by the Non-Intervention Committee . . . the attack on the *Deutschland* is declared to have been especially unprovoked in that she was off patrol and entitled to anchor off Ibiza.

The same edition, datelined Washington, published Senator William E. Borah's call for the US Neutrality Law to be invoked against Germany and Italy as 'it would appear an act of war had been committed', while in London Foreign Secretary Anthony Eden was reported to have declared in the House of Commons that he had asked the German Chargé d'Affaires 'to represent to his government the hope of His Majesty's Government that the German Government will take no action which would render the present grave situation graver still'. The same edition also carried an article, datelined Paris, under the subheading, 'A Day of Great Anxiety', which said:

> Berlin's announcement this evening that with the bombardment of Almería reprisals for the bombing of the *Deutschland* had been 'terminated' ended a day of great anxiety and much consultation in Paris. It was however, notable that the news of the German action produced no public manifestation or any marked alarm and that in official quarters emotion over

the affair never, for a single moment, prevented clear thinking. Every effort was bent all day in the closest accord with London in seeking to bring the German Government off the emotional plane of action down to reason, and what is considered the most important feature of today's events is that with the reprisals period closed by Germany, Italy cannot do otherwise than follow along.

The most interesting article in the same edition was datelined Moscow under the subheading 'Russia Awaits Details of Bombing of Almeria'. The article reflected that, 'The Russian Government, sympathetic to the Spanish Madrid-Valencia republic, awaited detailed information tonight on the German bombardment of Almeria. There was no official word of Russia's probable action, but unofficial sources said the Soviet regime would align itself with France and Britain.'

The Soviet Government had therefore achieved one tangible result from its illicit adventure: the German and Italian Governments had withdrawn from the Non-Intervention Committee as a consequence of the *Deutschland* escapade and would no longer harass shipping destined for Republican ports. However, the withdrawal would not last, much to the Soviets' chagrin. But the interesting aspect was their denial of knowing the facts surrounding the German bombardment of Almeria. Within hours of the German assault on Almeria, Orlov had notified the KGB Centre about the attack, as had the Soviet Military Attaché's office in Valencia, as there was no doubt that the attack was a direct result of the Soviet bombing of the *Deutschland*.

In the 2nd of June edition, in a lead article datelined 1 June at Rome, it was noted that,

The situation created by the withdrawal of Italy and Germany from the Non-Intervention Committee assumed a totally new aspect today with an announcement that Italian warships would not only remain in Spanish waters, but also would continue to repress traffic in contraband arms and munitions. They would do so not in the name of the London committee but in the name of the Italian Government. In view of the large number of ships, especially Russian, crossing the Mediterranean presumably laden with war supplies, this decision is likely to have a most important effect on future developments, as it may prove a fruitful source of international incidents. It is to be presumed, in fact, that Italian warships would use force if any Russian ships should refuse to halt at their command.

The other lead article datelined 1 June, Washington, announced that US Secretary of State Cordell Hull had appealed to the German and Spanish Governments through their Ambassadors 'for a peaceful adjustment of the situation'.

Mr Hull's action, while not unprecedented, was nevertheless a step infrequently taken. It reflected grave concern over the developing international aspect of the Spanish Civil War and the hope of the US that the conflict might be kept isolated from the rest of Europe. . . . Mr Hull . . . explained to the Ambassadors that the US Government at all times urged peace and he emphasised that in doing so it reserved its own independent course of action in any emergency. The Secretary's representation was followed by a controversy in Congressional circles over US neutrality policy, but there was no indication that this would influence the Government's course.

The same edition carried on its front page an article datelined 1 June, London, with the subheading, 'London Fears Seizure of Russian Vessels by Italian Warships off Spain Might Start an International War':

The Italian Government's announcement that its warships in the Mediterranean had been ordered to prevent Russian war material from reaching Spain caused a slight flurry in London official circles tonight.

Forcible seizure of a Russian vessel or even an attack on one on the high seas when Italy is not at war with Russia might prove to be the spark in the supercharged atmosphere of European politics that fortunately neither the bombs dropped on the German pocket battleship *Deutschland* nor the German bombardment of Almeria, Spain, in reprisal has turned out to be.

Russia, unlike Spain, is not incapable of retaliating for Italian truculence, and a real *casus belli* between the two powers could have far-reaching consequences.

The disposition here is to regard the Italian order as merely another of Premier Benito Mussolini's theatrical gestures and to hope for the best, although it is well realised that the efforts to keep the Spanish conflict restricted to Spanish territory are not yet out of the danger zone.

An article from Moscow which appeared in the same edition noted that the international situation was being weighed there 'with gravity but no outward sign of alarm. The new peril in the Spanish situation has severely shaken the confidence that had recently been visibly waxing here that the danger of a general war had become negligible. The new actions of Germany and Italy are seen as a prelude to increased military activity in Spain, with those two countries doing openly and on a greater scale the things they have been doing half surreptitiously, seriously menacing European peace.' The official press, which was the voice of the Kremlin, reflected 'concern in high quarters' and stated that Russia would continue to act in close contact with France and Great Britain. The great fear was that Britain and France would again 'yield before an aggressor, as they have done so many times, especially in the past two years'. As *Pravda*, the organ of the Communist Party, wrote: 'A policy of toleration and encouragement to an aggressor would have direct results. . . . Fearless, determined resistance must be shown to the provocation of German and Italian interventionists.' Such strong words of denunciation coming from the actual instigator of the tense international situation seemed perfidious at best in light of the dangerous developments spawned by the KGB.

A few days later, on 6 June, Hitler, addressing a meeting of 120,000 Nazi Brown Shirts, assured them that Germany had no intention of 'relinquishing her armed security' and warned that, 'If one thinks, because the German people is peace loving, that bombs can be thrown on ships fulfilling international obligations, then we will show him we know how to defend ourselves.'

How close the world came to the brink of an international war can best be judged by an article that appeared in the 18th of June edition of the *New York Times* under the caption, 'Britain Turns Toward Pact with Germany and Italy'. The article relates that:

In an agreement reached last Saturday in London . . . Germany and Italy have returned to the Non-Intervention Committee despite the desperate resistance of Russian diplomacy. In summing up the steps taken before reaching this point the following was noted in particular:

Things shaped differently when the *Deutschland* was hit and her forecastle ran blood. Hitler met his ministers in council, and immediately afterward German warships appearing out of the mist bombarded the port of Almeria, causing numerous deaths and inflicting material damage.

Europe was shocked by the news of the bombardment. Yet the public is unaware that the attack on Almeria was a pale shadow of the punishment Hitler wanted to inflict on Republican Spain.

Now the British Government has received an account it credits that . . . Hitler began by ordering that war be declared against Republican Spain which he described as a crowd of ruffians in the pay of Moscow. Simultaneously the German Navy was to bombard mercilessly the capital city of Valencia and an expeditionary force was to follow, debarking on the Spanish coast to complete the destruction of the 'Communist nest'.

For six hours Field Marshal Werner von Blomberg, the War Minister, and Baron von Neurath patiently withstood the storm of Hitler's indignation by preaching moderation and explaining the danger of an adventure in the Mediterranean. At times the discussion reached a high level of violence. Hitler was arrogant, his Ministers were respectful but obstinate.

Finally moderation won the day, and Europe does not yet know that it was on the verge of a catastrophe because it is certain France, and Britain with her, could not have tolerated open German invasion of Spain. . . .

Another aspect of the article indicated that the prestige of the Soviet Union was greatly diminished as a consequence of the *Deutschland* affair but more so because of the purge trials that were going on in Moscow concurrent with developments that followed the bombing of the *Deutschland*. Eight Soviet generals, including former Marshal Mikhail N. Tukhachevsky, were placed on trial on 11 June 1937 on charges of treason for having conspired with Germany (see chapter 24). All were executed. The article brings forth the correlation between the two events in that particular time frame:

One may lift now another corner of the veil of mystery enveloping the European situation. London does not profess to know the true nature of the events in Russia, yet the wholesale murders of politicians and military men has created here such an impression of rottenness in Josef Stalin's regime that at the present time Russia is being left outside of political consideration when British diplomacy considers the consolidation of peace on the Continent.

The execution of eight generals has done more harm to the prestige of Russia than all the other political trials together because recently the only remaining card in the hand of Russian diplomacy has been the solidity and excellence of the Russian army organisation. Now that is feared to be equally illusory; so for practical purposes Russia is out of the council of the great powers of Europe. Today Russia by her own act is reduced to the rank of a second-rate power.

This is a feather in Hitler's cap because by force of circumstances the British Government is obligated to consider the possibility of international action through agreement of Britain, France, Germany and Italy.

Orlov related that in time the furore over the *Deutschland* affair disappeared from the front pages of history and was soon forgotten. It was business as usual for the Non-Intervention Committee and, as before, it was reduced to the role of an ineffective diplomatic tool rather than a force that would confine the conflict in Spain to a true civil war between its people. Germany, Italy and the Soviet Union each continued to support their side unabatedly and with impunity. The matter of who fired the first shot in the attack on the *Deutschland* was never resolved in the public arena as each side accused the other. There was never any doubt that it was the aircraft of the Republican Air Force that had carried out the attack, mistakenly or otherwise, on the German battleship, but it was little understood that the air force was Republican in name only as its aircraft, maintenance crews, armaments and pilots were all Russians connected with the Soviet Red Air Force. It was not until the end of 1937 that several hundred Soviet-trained Spanish pilots trickled into the Spanish Republican Air Force.

What was conclusive to Orlov was the fact that Stalin had his revenge on the Germans and the Italians and was instantly gratified, but in the long run the attack on the *Deutschland* was a mistake as it only strengthened Hitler's resolve against the Soviets. As to the role of the KGB in the operation, there was never any indication that its identity or participation in the incident had been compromised, with one possible exception. Months after the event, Orlov's office received intelligence reports that the German naval high command, the Oberkommando der Kriegsmarine, in Berlin suspected that the KGB had been behind the plot to bomb the *Deutschland* but was never able to confirm the fact.

Orlov passed on one small piece of amusing information. Several days after the assault on the *Deutschland*, he was at a private meeting with Indalecio Prieto, the Republican Minister of Defence. The Republicans were unaware that the KGB had been behind the attack on the battleship and had insisted to the world that the bombing had not been premeditated. The topic of the meeting with Prieto was an overview of Orlov's guerrilla operations and, well into the conversation, Prieto interjected, 'By the way, wasn't that German battleship affair one of your guerrilla operations?' Orlov had always considered Prieto to be the most discerning and astute of the Spanish officials he had encountered and noted that other politicians never connected him with the plot. He did not respond to Prieto's question, feigning not to have heard it, but then Prieto looked directly at him, with a questioning expression on his face, as he cocked one eye as if to state that he already knew the answer.

EIGHT

THE GENERAL MOLA AFFAIR

According to Orlov, the Spanish Civil War could have been over by late 1937 had the Republican Government acted and capitalised on an isolated incident that transpired a few days before the first anniversary of the start of the war. When he related this episode, Orlov cautioned that the details were only known at the time to a few leaders in the Republican Government, Stalin and the KGB.

On 3 June 1937, the Nationalist radio announced the tragic death of General Emilio Mola in an aeroplane accident. Mola was one of the conspirators, along with General Franco, who had planned the takeover of the Spanish Government which had led to the outbreak of the Civil War. Generals Mola and Franco were arch rivals vying for power on the Nationalist side.

By the beginning of June 1937, the battle in the north had intensified and the Nationalist Army was tightening the noose around the Republican stronghold that surrounded the city of Bilbao. Mola was flying to the city of Burgos en route to the battle when his aircraft crashed into a mountain and all aboard were killed.

That day, shortly after midnight, Orlov received a telephone call from his next door neighbour, Indalecio Prieto. The two men lived in the small town of Batera just north of Valencia. Prieto said that he had an urgent matter to discuss with Orlov and would he come over to his house as soon as possible. Prieto made one stipulation, that Orlov not bring an interpreter. This was rather a strange request because he had always had one of his Spanish interpreters present at all their previous meetings. Prieto only spoke in his native tongue but this presented no problem to Orlov as he had become fairly proficient in Spanish.

Within minutes Orlov arrived at the Prieto mansion, where he was warmly greeted by the Defence Minister. Prieto was wearing a silk dressing-gown and slippers as though he had already gone to bed when the matter came up which he wished to discuss with Orlov. On the coffee table sat a pot of freshly brewed coffee and a bottle of fine French brandy.

Prieto directed his guest to a chair by the coffee table and, as soon as they both sat down, asked if Orlov had heard the news of General Mola's death. Orlov acknowledged that he had, after which Prieto immediately asked if Orlov could find out through his agents in Nationalist Spain where Mola was going to be buried. Orlov replied that he felt he could readily ascertain this information. What followed took Orlov by surprise somewhat as he and Prieto were the only people in the room. Prieto leaned over towards Orlov and whispered softly in his ear, 'All of them, including Franco, will attend the funeral. We can use this opportunity to destroy all of them, if your Russian pilots pepper them generously with bombs and machine-gun fire.' Orlov could see the excitement on the Minister's face and he recalled that, as he looked at the man, he reminded him of the British film star, Charles Laughton.

'Is this something you could organise?' Prieto asked. Orlov replied that he felt he could but would have to have the approval of his Government. Then Prieto asked with a quizzical look on his face, 'But will you do it?' Orlov thought the question over for a few moments and then replied that war was war and whatever it took to end the war was worth the means. Orlov observed that all of Hitler's and Mussolini's highest-ranking field commanders, as well as those from the Nationalist Army, would attend the funeral. He added that the leadership of the enemy would be demolished with one clean sweep and the havoc that would ensue could bring the war to a swift conclusion. Even if this one major act did not terminate the war, it would be translated into many victorious battles in the field.

It was obvious to Orlov that Prieto felt relieved that he had understood his plan and was delighted that Orlov had concurred with him that the plan had merit. Then he addressed Orlov as 'my friend' and warned that absolutely no one in the Republican Government must know about this. He stated that this would be 'our secret' and explained the reason for such secrecy: 'Some in our government are weaklings, and some are devout Catholics. One cannot talk to them about such things.'

Concluding their business the two men enjoyed a few brandies, after which Prieto relaxed a little and reminisced about his boyhood in Bilbao, telling Orlov of his struggles as an orphan and how he had had to make a meagre living as a newspaper boy. Overcoming these early adversities, he had finally risen to the top as the owner of the widely circulated Spanish newspaper, *El Liberal*, from where he had entered politics. By the time Orlov left Prieto's residence, he saw the man in an entirely different light and, despite his earlier negative appraisal, found some redeeming characteristics in the Minister.

After a few hours' sleep, Orlov went to his office in Valencia and drafted a message to a KGB agent in Nationalist-held territory. He then had the message encoded in time for a regularly scheduled radio contact with the agent. He also cabled the KGB Centre informing them of the substance of his contact with Prieto and recommending approval of the plan; he also requested authorisation to have the Soviet Supreme Air Commander in Spain, General Smushkevich, carry out the air raid.

By that afternoon an answer had been received from the KGB Centre authorising the plan to be put into effect. Smushkevich would be receiving special orders from Defence Commissar Voroshilov and told to place his services under Orlov's control. From the resolute and terse tone of the Centre's message, there was no doubt that it emanated from Stalin personally.

Almost simultaneously, a message was received from the KGB agent that Mola's funeral would be held in Burgos and that details of the time and route of the funeral procession would be forthcoming. Soon after, the Nationalist radio broadcast a story on the arrangements for the funeral including the missing information. Now all of the necessary details from the Nationalist side were in place and the plan could be formalised.

Orlov then flew to the Soviet air-force base, where he met Smushkevich to work out the final details of the plan. The Air Commander was already in receipt of his orders from Voroshilov and was working out the preliminaries for the raid. The attack would be on the funeral procession as it approached the cemetery and in an area of the road where it would be difficult for the vehicles to escape. The first wave would be the Soviet SB twin-engined bombers, which would attack the procession, followed by Soviet fighter planes, which would strafe the area to ensure that anyone missed by the bombers would not survive. In addition, a squadron of Soviet fighters would be in the vicinity in the event that Nationalist fighters were providing air cover for the funeral.

Orlov returned to Valencia and went directly to Prieto's office in the War Ministry building. He outlined the entire plan on a sketchpad, step by step, for the Defence Minister, who gave his wholehearted approval. Prieto then asked if Orlov had revealed his part in the plot to anyone, including Smushkevich, and was assured that no one knew. Prieto was relieved and, when Orlov was leaving, gave him an especially warm embrace, which Orlov had not expected. Everything was now in place for the final attack on Mola's funeral procession.

Orlov returned to his office to catch up on some work he had put aside and later that afternoon he went to the guerrilla training camp at Benimamet, just a few miles north of Valencia. On his arrival, he was told that there was an urgent request for him to call his office as soon as he arrived. When he did so, he learned that Prieto desperately wanted to speak to him. He immediately telephoned Prieto, who was relieved to have found Orlov and who said that he had to see Orlov in person at once.

The very moment Orlov entered the Defence Minister's office, he was told that the operation had to be cancelled. Prieto then explained that he had made a horrible blunder when he had confided the plan to his fellow Basque and lifelong friend Julián Zugazagoitia, the Minister of the Interior for the Republican Government. Zugazagoitia was shocked when he heard about the plan and violently protested the bombing of Mola's funeral procession. Prieto described how the man had gone into a rage and had literally thrown the Bible at him for even thinking of such an outrageous deed. Prieto stated that he should have locked the fool in the office cupboard, but Zugazagoitia ran out of the office declaring that, as a Catholic, he could not let the plan go forward. Zugazagoitia then went directly to President Manuel Azaña, who immediately phoned Prieto at the War Ministry and issued an official order cancelling the attack. He then brusquely hung up. Prieto had no opportunity to object and the order was final. Within minutes President Azaña called again and demanded that Prieto bring Orlov to his office as he wanted assurance that the Soviets would not carry out the attack on their own.

Orlov and Prieto proceeded directly to the Presidential Office, where they were solemnly greeted by Azaña. Without any expression of friendliness on his face, Azaña began talking to Orlov about 'his' plan to bomb General Mola's funeral. He agreed that the plan had some merit from a military standpoint but not in a deeply religious country such as Spain, where it would be considered immoral. He stated that for this reason he wanted Orlov's assurance that there would be no attack on Mola's funeral procession.

Orlov immediately realised that Prieto had misled the President into thinking that the plan had been conceived by him. Although he was dismayed that Prieto had not accepted responsibility for the plan, he was aware that this was an act of desperation on Prieto's part and he therefore did not expose the Minister of Defence to the President. Orlov announced that the plan had already been cancelled, when in truth it had not. He assured the President that the Soviets were only in Spain to act as advisors and that they would not carry out such a plan, or any other plan, without the approval of the Spanish Republican Government. However, he added that the Soviet Government did not consider the plan to bomb Mola's funeral as immoral but one that would shorten the war and thereby save thousands of Spanish lives.

Azaña conceded that Orlov's assessment was probably accurate and that he knew the Russians had the interests of Spain at heart; he added that Spain appreciated the help of their Russian friends.

On the way back to his office, Prieto apologised profusely for having handled the General Mola affair so ineptly. Orlov never mentioned the fact that Prieto had lacked the courage to admit to the President his true role in the matter.

When Orlov returned to his office, he immediately contacted Smushkevich to call off the attack. Smushkevich was appalled at the turn of events after so much preparation on his part, but understood the circumstances. He then cabled the KGB Centre informing them that the attack had been cancelled because of President Azaña's demand. Orlov expected this to be the end of the matter when he received a cable from the KGB Centre. The harshly worded message demanded to know whose orders Orlov was carrying out, those of the Soviet Government or the Spanish Government. Again the terse and decisive tone of the communiqué left little doubt that it had originated with Stalin. The return reply fully explained how Prieto had mishandled the affair and that, under the circumstances, Orlov was not in a position to defy the President. Orlov never heard another word from the KGB Centre regarding the Mola affair but felt that Stalin must have smouldered over it to his dying day.

The affair did take a strange turn for the man who was responsible for putting an end to the plot, Minister of the Interior Julián Zugazagoitia. He had been a lifelong Socialist and was never considered a friend of the Soviets as he openly opposed the Communists in the Republican Government and their Soviet friends. In spite of the fact he had been a protégé of his fellow Basque Indalecio Prieto, and had even worked as an editor for Prieto's Socialist newspaper, he had rejected the plan to bomb General Mola's funeral not out of any opposition to Prieto, or because the plan was contrary to his Catholic beliefs, but because of his intense animosity towards the Soviets. After the fall of Republican Spain in the early part of 1939, he fled to southern France. By the middle of 1940, France was conquered by the German Army and, in the same year, Zugazagoitia was arrested by the Gestapo. He was turned over to the Spanish Government and Franco had him executed in Madrid without the benefit of a trial.

The irony of the situation did not go unnoticed by Orlov. Had Zugazagoitia not opposed Prieto's plan, Franco and all the Nationalist leaders would probably have perished and the Civil War would most likely have been won by the Republican Government. In that scenario, Zugazagoitia would not have been executed and would probably have lived to a ripe old age.

Had the bombing of General Mola's funeral procession taken place, Orlov believed that the outcome of the Spanish Civil War would have been entirely different. With the loss of its top leadership, the Nationalist Government would have been thrown into disarray and, without unity, there was no way they could have won the war. Orlov strongly contended that the Civil War would have been over by at least a year and a half sooner and, as a consequence, the huge loss of life sustained during that period would not have taken place.

NINE

HEMINGWAY – A TRUE BELIEVER

During a discussion on guerrilla warfare during the Spanish Civil War, Orlov wanted to illustrate a point and asked if I had ever read Ernest Hemingway's *For Whom the Bell Tolls*. I told him that I had read the book in High School and had later seen the movie based on the novel. In my view, it was one of his best works.

Citing Hemingway's book, Orlov began to explain a critical guerrilla tactical stratagem that was employed with frequent success during the war. He commented that the protagonist in the book, Robert Jordan, was an accurate portrayal of men engaged in guerrilla warfare although he was in fact a fictional character. The central theme of the book, which concerned the dynamiting of a vital bridge held by the Nationalists, was typical of many guerrilla operations behind enemy lines, although the specific incident that formed the core of the plot was taken from actual events that occurred during the May 1937 Republican offensive at Segovia. Orlov considered *For Whom the Bell Tolls* to be an accurate, although exaggerated in some respects, portrayal of conditions in Spain during the Civil War and overall considered the book excellent. He noted that from a historical point of view, the book was an important contribution as an insight into the Spanish Civil War.

Orlov took up his post at the Soviet Embassy in Madrid in September 1936, the same time as Franco's Nationalist forces captured the Republican-held city of Toledo. Encouraged by this success, they continued on the offensive to take Madrid. Towards the end of October, the Nationalist Army was at the gates of Madrid and on 4 November Madrid's Gatafe Airport was captured and the suburbs of Alcoron and Leganes seized. The final assault on Madrid was to take place on 7 November.

On 6 November, one day before the final assault, the Spanish Republican Government secretly abandoned Madrid and moved the seat of government to Valencia. On the same day, the Soviet Embassy and all its personnel, with the exception of Orlov and Mikhail Koltsov, *Pravda*'s man on the scene, also moved its operations to Valencia.

What turned into a windfall for Orlov was the capture on 4 November of a Nationalist Army intelligence officer along with his secret codes. On the night of 5 November and the two succeeding nights, Orlov managed to send coded disinformation messages to the headquarters of the captured Nationalist intelligence officer under his code name. The first message indicated that a whole division of Russian infantry, about 16,000 men, had infiltrated Madrid during the night; another message implied that 100 Russian tanks had infiltrated the city the next night; and the final message reported that Russian fighter planes had destroyed a group of German Junker bombers. No doubt these false messages were relayed by Nationalist Army intelligence to General Mola as the boasted attack on Madrid, scheduled for 7 November, did not take place on that date.

General Emil Kleber commanding the 11th International Brigade arrived in Madrid on the morning of the 8th and took up positions at Madrid's Casa de Campo, a huge park, and on the campus of the University of Madrid, both locations on the western extremities of the city. These sites would see some of the bloodiest battles of the war. Had the attack on Madrid taken place as originally scheduled, both sites would have been overrun by the Nationalist Army and Madrid easily taken as the Republicans did not have the means to stop the attack at that point. After Kleber's arrival, the Nationalist Army mounted one attack after another to take the bridges over the Manzanares River and enter Madrid, but in the face of Kleber's resistance was unable to do so. Kleber was hailed as the hero and saviour of Madrid.

The 12th International Brigade commanded by General Paul

Lukacz arrived in Madrid on 12 November and took up its position at Carabanchel, a few kilometres from the city. Thus Madrid was saved on the one hand but, on the other, was placed under siege for the next two and a half years until the end of the war in March 1939.

The stage for Ernest Hemingway's entry into the Spanish Civil War was now set, not by default but rather by design, as explained by Orlov. Early in the conflict, it was recognised that world opinion had to be swayed to the side of the Spanish Republicans to win international support. The Soviets had long before learned the art of propaganda and found that there was no better media to spread the word than propaganda films. They had excelled in this direction and over the years had developed skills that were surpassed only by the Nazis. The Spanish Republicans possessed no such experience and were reluctant to import the new methods; however, over a short period of time the Soviets convinced them that this was their only viable option in winning world opinion to their side.

The vehicle would be a documentary film entitled *Spain in Flames*, which depicted the Nationalists as the ugly Fascist aggressor against the rightful government of the poor and proud people of Spain. To the world in general, the film was a product of the Spanish Republican Government as a plea for support, both in terms of finance as well as of men and equipment, as a means to combat the spread of Fascism throughout the world. In reality, it was the behind-the-scenes hand of the Information Section of the Soviet Embassy and the KGB, through their chain of 'advisors', that dictated the true message of the film, although the Soviet role could not be revealed.

It was not a coincidence that the Spanish Republican Government first suggested that Hemingway write the script for the documentary. Since the mid-1920s, Hemingway had been a frequent visitor to Spain and over the years had become a bull fight aficionado who would devote several of his books to the sport. The Spanish people had come to love the author, a feeling he reciprocated.

Hemingway was no stranger to the KGB and the Information Section as they were already aware of his background. A couple of years previously, Hemingway had written an article for the ultra-left periodical *New Masses* chastising the US Government for its handling of relief efforts during the Florida hurricane of 1935. The article focused on what the poor and downtrodden people of the state had had to endure not as a consequence of the hurricane but at the hands of the Government. The article did not go unnoticed by the KGB because, as part of its systematic intelligence-gathering of the media which reflected the thoughts of the people in each targeted government, the most fertile sources were the left-wing periodicals and newspapers. What the KGB analysed in the Hemingway article was a political statement that would be accepted at face value by the American public because of his recognition as a well-known and respected author. The KGB had to conclude that Hemingway was the right man for the job.

Through the efforts of the Republican Government, which was secretly motivated to do so by the Soviets, the North American Newspaper Alliance in New York signed a contract with Hemingway in late 1936 to do the commentary for *Spain in Flames* and to cover the war in Spain. Hemingway arrived in Spain around March 1937.

By the time Hemingway arrived in Madrid, the city was under siege and conditions were in a chaotic state. Nothing was normal. The Nationalists held the high ground on the western perimeter of the city and would constantly bombard the city. As a consequence, it was not unusual to see dead bodies littering the streets and passers-by casually viewing the dead. The inhabitants had been ordered to vacate the city but there were some who had refused to comply with the command. Everything was in short supply, especially food and water. Horse meat became the standard and even that was scarce. By the end of the conflict, there was a noticeable absence of small household animals and pigeons. Gloom, doom and tenseness hung continuously in the shadows as the next attack on the city was always imminent.

For both the foreign correspondents and the Soviet officials, their areas of daily life revolved around three specific locations in Madrid. The official diplomatic establishments of the Soviets were broken down to two entities: the elegant Palace Hotel, which was designated as the official seat of the Soviet Embassy, and the Gaylord Hotel, which housed the Soviet Military and Civilian Missions. The foreign correspondents were housed at the old Hotel Florida.

Although the Republican Government had moved to Valencia, some lesser and more expendable officials remained in Madrid. The Soviet Embassy had also moved to Valencia at the beginning of the onslaught, but when the siege was stabilised the diplomatic staff floated between the two cities. In time, Orlov established his office in Valencia and then moved it to Barcelona.

The hub of most socialising in wartime Madrid was the Gaylord Hotel. In those grey and desolate days of the siege, the Gaylord stood out as an oasis in a desert. Here the Soviets provided food as well as those much sought-after luxury commodities known as the epitome of Russian hospitality, vodka and caviar. This was in sharp contrast to the scarcity of food and liquid refreshments at the few bistros and wine bodegas that remained opened. There was a meagre supply of these goods on the black market, but the Soviet military had no problem supplying the Gaylord. The Soviets felt it a good public relations ploy, and the foreign correspondents flocked to the Gaylord when invited for free food and vodka. Hemingway was no exception.

It was at the Gaylord that Orlov first took notice of Hemingway. Orlov was of course aware of the author's presence in Spain and had read several of his books, yet did not seek him out. For the most part, Hemingway would sit at the table of General Paul Lukacz.

Lukacz was Hungarian and had been an officer in the Austro-Hungarian Army during the First World War. He had been captured by the Russian Army early in the war and was converted to Communism at the time of the outbreak of the Russian Revolution. He fought with the Red Army and became a member of the Soviet Communist Party. After service, he returned for a short period to Hungary, where he became a writer of some repute under his true name, Mata Zalka; however, he eventually went back to the Soviet Union. Orlov had known Lukacz since the early days in the Red Army and, although their paths had led them apart, they had become reacquainted in September 1936 when the Soviets began to pour into Spain. This time Zalka was introduced to Orlov as Lukacz, the pseudonym he would use throughout the war. Orlov facetiously accused Lukacz of purposely taking this particular pseudonym because Lukacz thought that he resembled the well-known Hollywood character actor of the 1930s, Paul Lucas. It saddened Orlov when he learned months later that Lukacz had been killed during the great summer offensive.

On one particular occasion at the Gaylord, the Political Commissar of the 12th International Brigade, Gustav Regler, approached the table where Orlov and his staff usually sat. Regler announced that his General would like Orlov to join his table as he wanted Orlov to meet someone. Orlov replied that he would be happy to do so.

Orlov only knew Regler by name and never had any direct dealings with the man, although some of his KGB staff who worked directly with the 12th International Brigade reported that Regler was co-operative with the KGB. The International Brigades in Spain operated under the same organisational political controls as the Red Army. The senior military officers were all members of the Soviet Communist Party and, therefore, subject to the control of the Party. Independent of the military was the Political Administration of the Communist Party, which operated within the military. These high-ranking officers, although not members of the military, carried the title of Political Commissar and were charged with the political indoctrination of the troops and the enforcing of Party loyalty. Their identities were not concealed. Independent of both the military and the Political Administration were the Special Branches of the KGB, which operated within the military both overtly and covertly. In Spain, these KGB Special

Branch officers acted as 'spotters' to study and select members of the various International Brigades for recruitment into one of Orlov's guerrilla training camps. Once selected, the army commander could not countermand the KGB's order.

Orlov proceeded to Lukacz's table, where he was introduced to Hemingway. Orlov was introduced merely as a political advisor, but he had no doubt that either Lukacz or Regler had informed Hemingway that he was Chief of the KGB in Spain. Orlov found Hemingway to be a robust individual, who did not shy away from making his presence known in a somewhat boisterous manner. He could certainly be best described as a 'man's man'. He was very articulate although prone to using profanities, perhaps to bolster his masculine image. What Orlov could not help noticing that evening was that Hemingway consumed more than his fair share of the vodka. More so, Orlov had difficulty reconciling the fine author whose books he had so enjoyed with the man he had just met. Orlov's first reaction to the author was rather cool and he directed most of his attention to Lukacz. However, Orlov was aware that Hemingway had the reputation of being a 'Big Game Hunter' and, as the evening progressed, the conversation turned to this sport. At last they had found the common denominator on which to base a friendship of sorts. Orlov, who was well versed in firearms, conceded that Hemingway was very knowledgeable regarding firearms and was not a phoney in this regard. The balance of the evening was spent discussing their mutual interest. They parted company with a glass of Spanish brandy and wished one another well. As Orlov reflected on their first meeting, he noted that politics had never entered their conversation.

From time to time Orlov would encounter Hemingway at the Gaylord, but these occasions were infrequent as he now spent most of his time in Valencia and making the rounds of the guerrilla training camps. Likewise, Hemingway was working as a war correspondent, going off to war with the International Brigades and reporting on their successes as well as their failures. Spain was a small country and the battlefields, for the most part, were in close proximity to Madrid. Consequently, Hemingway could be at a dangerous battlefield during the day and that evening enjoying himself at the Gaylord, or one of the bistros, before retiring to the Hotel Florida, where he could sleep in the comfort of clean bedding. Unfortunately, this did not hold true for his friends and companions at the front with the various Brigades.

The very first time Orlov met Hemingway at the Gaylord, there were a number of war correspondents at Lukacz's large table. He couldn't help but notice that an attractive fair-haired young lady was sitting next to the author. Orlov spoke briefly with her and discovered that she was an accredited correspondent from Austria. They discussed their mutual love of Austrian music and food and shared the many delights they had both experienced in Vienna. Orlov found the young lady to be witty as well as exceedingly charming, in fact 'an absolute delight'. On later occasions when he saw Hemingway at the Gaylord, he was always in the company of this lady. He suspected that theirs was more than a casual relationship and soon confirmed through other sources that their relationship was of the intimate type that breaks up marriages. He could not recall the lady's name, but from her family name and some remarks she had made he surmised that she was Jewish. In time, Orlov learned that her name was Martha Gellhorn.

The film *Spain in Flames* was a huge success from the standpoint of the Republicans as well as the KGB. Orlov observed that the propaganda in the film, as well as the control of its release, was subjectivity in its worst form, designed to agitate the world into believing that there was only one side or issue in the conflict. The constant message was the downtrodden against Fascism and the Fascist dictators, Hitler, Mussolini and Franco, and their huge combined war machines. In the propaganda films, posters and media, the Republicans were portrayed as a small group of infantrymen plunging forward against the mechanised might of the enemy. Curiously, the Soviet dictator Stalin and his huge war machine supporting the side of the Republicans were, for the most part, completely ignored and Communism was rarely mentioned. The success of the first propaganda film brought forth a group of left-wing writers who would produce yet another film called

The Spanish Earth. Notable amongst this group was the renowned American author John Dos Passos, whom the KGB already recognised as a leading proponent of Communism in literary circles around the world. The KGB learned that Dos Passos, an old friend of Hemingway's from the days of the First World War when they had served together in the American Red Cross Ambulance Service in Italy, had persuaded Hemingway to do the narration for the film. The KGB and the Republicans gave their blessing to the project.

By the end of May 1937, filming of *The Spanish Earth* was completed with the exception of Hemingway's narration. He returned to America to record the narration and to address the Writers' Congress convention held in New York on 4 June. The KGB was delighted when its sources reported that Hemingway's speech was the high point of the convention and that he had mesmerised the audience when he had torn into the Fascists and shredded them into small bits of unrecognisable bone meal. The vigorous acceptance of Hemingway's speech by the left-wing writers in the audience was to be expected, but the fact that Hemingway had taken such a positive and firm political stance for the first time in public took the KGB by surprise. Orlov revealed that from that moment on, the KGB extended Hemingway *carte blanche* on any wish or endeavour he might hope to pursue on his return to Spain.

Hemingway's wish reached Orlov in the form of a request from Political Commissar Gustav Regler. Hemingway had returned to Spain in the early part of September 1937 and, as usual, spent his off-duty hours at the Gaylord. Regler had been wounded in the spring offensive and was convalescing in Madrid when he met Hemingway at the Gaylord. During his previous visit, Hemingway had learned of the achievements of the guerrillas and the major role that guerrilla warfare was playing in the war, and he told Regler that he wanted to gather more material on the subject. It would therefore be helpful if he could see for himself how the guerrillas were trained. Regler advised him that he could make no promises but would see what he could do. Regler personally made the request to Orlov at the KGB headquarters then located in the Hotel Metropole in Valencia. Without hesitation Orlov said that he saw no problem with the request and that arrangements would be made. Orlov then summoned Colonel Kotov, his top aide who oversaw the guerrilla training camps, and requested that he make the necessary arrangements with Regler. Orlov suggested that Hemingway visit the guerrilla camp at Benimamet as it was only a short distance from Valencia; in this way, he could host a lunch at the Officers' Mess for Hemingway, business permitting. After Regler departed, Orlov instructed that Hemingway be given VIP treatment and that there was no reason why anything of a routine nature should be held back. Kotov agreed.

Orlov stressed that under normal conditions a war correspondent would not have been extended the courtesy of a visit to one of the secret guerrilla training camps, but Hemingway was an exception. Permission to visit one of the camps was a small token of recognition for the extensive efforts Hemingway had expended for the Republican cause.

On the prearranged day, Kotov met Hemingway at the Benimamet camp and the author was shown every phase of the training. Kotov had already orchestrated a programme that was sure to fascinate the author as well as a lunch that would tantalise even a gourmet chef. He also brought along several bottles of fine French wine that Orlov had procured on one of his visits to France for just such a special occasion. Orlov was able to make it to the camp in time for lunch. The private luncheon, which was also attended by the camp commandant and his chief assistant, lasted the better part of three hours. Hemingway was beside himself and expressed his gratitude for the visit and the flawless hospitality that had been afforded. He not only liked the French wine but raved about the vodka, which Orlov had come across on one of his early assignments in Vienna and which was distilled from potatoes rather than grain, unusual even by Russian standards. It was made by a very old distillery in Vienna by the name of Baczewski, and Orlov, who was not a typical Russian vodka drinker, had acquired a taste for it. He was a personal friend of the KGB legal *rezident* in Vienna and had a standing order for this particular treasure. For this occasion he had brought two bottles of the vodka with him and the five luncheon partners had consumed one of them. Orlov gave Hemingway the remaining bottle.

Hemingway had inspected most of what was to be seen in the camp before lunch. Afterwards, they walked around and saw a few attractions that had been missed, and then drove to the rifle range. After watching the trainees on the firing line, Hemingway expressed an interest in shooting a Russian-made rifle that he had never handled before. Orlov was a little reluctant to accede to the request as Hemingway had consumed at least half of the bottle of vodka, although he gave no indication that it had greatly affected him. Orlov agreed, but suggested that he would also shoot, not so much to maintain his proficiency but to keep a close eye on the author should a problem develop. As it turned out, Hemingway was able to hold his own with the KGB sharp-shooter General, and Orlov could only wonder what the results would have been had the author not been under the influence of so much alcohol.

Orlov later remarked that when he finished reading *For Whom the Bell Tolls*, soon after it was first published in 1940, he knew that much of what Hemingway had written in the book regarding guerrilla warfare was based on that visit to the Benimamet guerrilla training camp. This knowledge was then correlated with an incident that took place during the May 1937 offensive in Segovia just before the author returned to America.

One of the people Hemingway befriended, or perhaps the other way around, on his first excursion into Spain in 1936 was Colonel Gustavo Duran, a division commander under the able Spanish Republican General José Miaja. Duran became a highly decorated war hero and commanded troops in some of the fiercest battles of the war. Orlov had seen the Colonel on various occasions at the Gaylord and knew who he was, but had never had the opportunity of meeting him. On several of these occasions he saw the Colonel sitting at the customary table with Hemingway and Lukacz. From time to time he would receive reports that Duran and the author had become close friends and that Hemingway liked Duran and trusted his judgement. What Orlov did not know from those brief episodes at the Gaylord was the fact that Duran was destined to head one of his major projects in the Spanish Civil War and that in time he would get to know the man quite well.

One of Orlov's principal tasks when he was assigned to Spain was to establish a Spanish Republican intelligence service. However, the intention was never to make it a Soviet-style KGB intelligence organisation but rather one directed towards military intelligence. What did come out of his efforts was the Servicio Información Militar (better known by the acronym SIM), a scaled-down version of the KGB devoted entirely towards intelligence-gathering for the military but without the apparatus in place for civilian intelligence matters. Orlov would thus become the father and guiding light of Spain's first intelligence service.

Orlov had presented his outline plan for a military intelligence organisation to Defence Minister Prieto on several occasions but had always met with strong resistance to the idea. He could not understand Prieto's position as intelligence was so vital to winning the war. Prieto finally admitted that it was because of his feeling that by placing the intelligence service in the hands of the Soviets, he and other members of the Nationalist Government might be arrested one day and that the Soviets would then place government power in the hands of the Communists. Orlov assured him that this was not the case and, as proof, suggested that he appoint someone of his own choosing as chief of the new military intelligence service. This satisfied Prieto and thus SIM was born.

The first Chief of SIM was a croney of Prieto's by the name of Angel Baza, whose time in power would be short-lived. Orlov did not like the man and felt that he was unsuited to intelligence work. When Orlov detected that Baza was engaged in a scheme of corruption, he went to Prieto and insisted that Baza had to go. Prieto was embarrassed by the situation and agreed to a replacement. Orlov then recalled his two KGB advisors who were guiding SIM so as to force Prieto's hand into action.

Several weeks later, the Soviet Ambassador arranged a farewell party for the Soviet Military Attaché General Gorev, who had been ordered back to Moscow. Gorev had spent the past year of the siege of Madrid as advisor to General Miaja. Both Miaja and Prieto were guests at the reception at the Soviet Embassy in Valencia. During the evening, Orlov told Miaja of his problem of replacing Baza as Chief of SIM and wisely asked Miaja for his recommendation. Orlov was aware that the General recognised the necessity and importance of military intelligence and, after some reflection, Miaja announced that he had in mind a person who could handle the position ably; however, there was no way that he could spare the man. Gorev, who was sitting in on the conversation, immediately exclaimed, 'Duran!' 'Correct,' retorted Miaja. Colonel Gustavo Duran was the commander of the 69th Division under Miaja and, according to Miaja, was a born leader and spoke several foreign languages. Gorev, who spoke both English and French, spontaneously related that Duran spoke both English and French like a native, and added that Duran was by profession an accomplished pianist and composer. A positive glance from Gorev to Orlov indicated Gorev's approval of the new nominee.

Orlov had to overcome Miaja's resistance as the General wanted to keep his best field commander. He was able to present numerous arguments why Duran would be more valuable in intelligence rather than in the field, and Miaja finally capitulated and told Prieto that he would be willing to sacrifice his own needs for the overall good of the military. Prieto agreed to comply with the wishes of Miaja and Orlov, and promised that Duran would be relieved of his current duties and transferred to SIM as the new Chief.

Within a matter of a few days, Duran reported to Orlov's headquarters in Valencia. He was a man in his early thirties, with light brown hair and light coloured eyes, and looked more like a German than a Spaniard. Orlov purposely spoke to him in English and then in French to evaluate his language abilities. The man's adeptness in these languages was almost faultless, an important attribute in the field of intelligence. What did become apparent was Duran's reluctance to accept the new assignment as he felt that his place was at the front with his troops, but, as a good soldier, he accepted the position without any argument. Orlov liked what he saw in Duran and felt that a wise choice had been made. Moreover, he felt that he could trust the man.

Orlov was not wrong in the confidence he placed in Duran, which was soon reflected in the man's achievements. SIM, under Duran's direction, soon uncovered an enemy spy ring operating within the Republican General Staff of the Army and the Foreign Ministry. Prieto even acknowledged the success and rewarded Duran with a gift of a new car. However, Orlov soon realised that Prieto was still undermining the new organisation with the ultimate purpose of sabotaging SIM into oblivion.

One day Orlov received an urgent telephone call from an agitated Duran, who asked if he could see Orlov immediately. Orlov agreed, and when Duran presented himself it was apparent that he was distraught. On entering Orlov's office, Duran informed him that he had been fired by Prieto and that Prieto had already signed orders for Duran's return to the front. Orlov had already conceded to a request by Prieto to install Angel Pedrero, another of his cronies, in the post of Deputy Chief of SIM, and Duran now explained that Pedrero, who had long coveted the post of Chief of SIM, had finally succeeded. Prieto had even taken back the gift of the car he had so lavishly bestowed on Duran.

Orlov was amazed and outraged at what he heard. He immediately telephoned Prieto, who confessed that he knew what Orlov was calling about but that he had no time to discuss the matter. Orlov told Prieto that he was dropping everything and would be at his office in a few minutes. Prieto took the Duran matter lightly, but Orlov continued to press for an answer as to why he had made such a rash decision. Finally Prieto, who was a Socialist, claimed that Duran had put too many Communists into SIM.

Early on, Orlov had cautioned Duran to maintain a balance of SIM personnel and to give the Socialists the benefit in numbers, so Orlov was prepared for this line of attack as he had anticipated that Prieto would use this issue as a reason for the dismissal. Orlov had therefore brought with him the roster of SIM personnel, and it was evident that the Socialists far outnumbered the Communists. Prieto lost this round but countered that he needed Duran at the front and was going to promote him to a corps commander. Anyway, he had already promised Pedrero the position and could not rescind his word. Orlov did not accept these excuses and warned Prieto that if Duran was not reinstated, he would break off relations with Prieto.

This was the last time Orlov ever spoke to Prieto. Pedrero was made Chief of SIM and Duran reported to the front. Orlov withdrew his advisors and discontinued counter-intelligence in the Republican regions of Spain. The KGB then concentrated its efforts on obtaining intelligence information within Franco's Spain and passing it along to the Republican Minister of the Interior and, in some instances, directly to the then Prime Minister Juan Negrin.

Orlov never lost touch with Duran. He had become fond of the man through their frequent meetings and their respect for each other was mutual. He genuinely felt that the Republicans were the losers because of Prieto's political agenda and his vanity. One thing he did learn about Duran which had no bearing on his military background or his brief work with SIM was the fact that he was a gifted pianist. Duran was invited several times to Orlov's residence in Betera and more often than not their conversation turned to matters other than the war.

Orlov had developed a particular fondness for the music of Spain, both classical and contemporary, which captured the soul of its people. The song 'Granada' had caught his fancy and Duran would oblige him by playing it on the baby grand piano that Orlov had in his house, much to Orlov's delight. Ironically, Orlov never set foot in the town of Granada as the city was held by the Nationalists from the onset of the war.

Duran seemed to be Orlov's link with Hemingway as Duran continued his friendship with the author and Martha Gellhorn. Hemingway had returned to Spain from America during mid-September 1937, and as the focus of the war changed from Madrid to other parts of the country so did Hemingway's base of operation.

The great Republican offensive of December 1937 had as its objective the town of Teruel and the surrounding countryside. Teruel was about 200 miles south-west of Barcelona and less than 100 miles north-west of Valencia. The offensive was launched in mid-December using only divisions of the Republican Army for political reasons. By Christmas, the town of Teruel was taken. Now the Nationalists began their counter-offensive to recapture Teruel, but for the moment the Republicans tenaciously held the besieged city. Winter conditions were horrendous as a severe blizzard enveloped the area and cut off supplies desperately needed by both sides. By early January 1938, the Republicans no longer held out for a purely Republican victory over Teruel and, to save the situation from becoming a complete rout, finally called on the International Brigades for help. The famous General Walter, a pseudonym for Karol Swierczewski, Commander of the 14th International Brigade, came to the rescue and was able to prevent the better equipped Nationalists from marching to the Mediterranean, thus cutting the republic into two parts. In the end, the Republicans lost much of the territory they had held before the battle and the political intrigues instigated by Defence Minister Prieto in the battle led to his downfall and eventually that of the Republican Government.

Orlov's base of operation also changed towards the end of 1937. Although the Soviet Embassy had moved to Valencia in November 1936, Orlov had remained in Madrid during the darkest days of the siege but eventually moved his headquarters and staff to Valencia after the siege became stabilised. Unfortunately, Orlov's residence in Betera was next door to Prieto's house and following their falling out over SIM Orlov could no longer tolerate the man. Also, the Nationalists in the area of Teruel were no more than fifty miles from the Mediterranean, which presented the distinct possibility that the Republican territory could be cut in half. The seat of government in Valencia would then have no land route out of Spain and the only possible escape route would be by air or sea to southern France or North Africa. Under these conditions, Orlov knew that the Soviets would evacuate him should the situation arise, but, as he was already contemplating the possibility of defection, he did not want to be under their control. His preferable alternative was to establish his headquarters in Barcelona, some seventy miles south of the French border, which was far enough north of Teruel that, even if the Nationalists were able to cut to the sea, there would still be a land route into France. It was within Orlov's discretionary power to make such a move and he did so, presenting the same analysis to the KGB Centre in Moscow. The KGB Centre readily agreed with Orlov that his headquarters should be moved to Barcelona. What Orlov did not know at the time was the fact that the Soviet Consul-General in Barcelona was being recalled to Moscow and that the Consulate-General building in Barcelona would come under Orlov's control as the new KGB headquarters in Spain. While he was establishing the Barcelona KGB headquarters and seeking a new family residence, Maria and Vera remained in Betera.

Sometime in early November 1937, Orlov encountered his old friend Colonel Duran in Madrid while on official business. Duran was still chafing over his dismissal by Prieto but was nonetheless content to be back with his troops. The next day, 7 November, was the official anniversary of the Bolshevik Revolution, and Duran told Orlov that he would be celebrating the occasion over lunch with friends at the Gaylord Hotel. Duran noted that Orlov would know most of the guests and one in particular, Hemingway, had recently asked about him. As Orlov was staying at the Gaylord and his family was in Betera, what better way to enjoy the occasion than with friends?

The next day Orlov appeared for lunch and fully expected to meet Hemingway again, but was more than surprised and pleased to find his old friend General Walter at the table. Walter was already famous for his role in the battle of Segovia and the July 1937 battle of Brunete, but was to become best known for his key role in the coming battle of Teruel. As the lunch wore on and more vodka was consumed, Hemingway turned his attention to Orlov. He fondly recalled the day the two of them had spent on the rifle range at the guerrilla training camp at Benimamet, but perhaps what had most impressed him was the bottle of Baczewski vodka that Orlov had given him that day. Hemingway related that he really 'babied' that bottle of vodka and would use it only on special occasions. This time Hemingway directed his attention to politics, perhaps because of his Soviet luncheon companions, or more so because of the anniversary celebration of the Bolshevik Revolution. Hemingway vehemently denounced Franco and the Nationalists while at the same time having nothing but praise for the International Brigades' commanders and the Republicans. There was no doubt in Orlov's mind that the author, and people like him, were the prime motivators of the war in the sense that they swayed world opinion to the side of the Republicans and thereby reaped the harvest of financial support, which needlessly prolonged the war.

Orlov decided to cut short his participation in the festivities as he wished to be with his family in Betera by that evening. He also knew that once the Russians began toasting the Bolshevik holiday with the ever-abundant vodka, they would not know when to quit and would probably retreat to one of the private apartments in the Gaylord to continue their revelries into the early hours of the following day.

Orlov never had the opportunity again to meet Hemingway in a situation where they could sit down and talk. However, in the spring of 1938 he had two occasions to see the author, once when the two happened to meet in the vicinity of Placa Catalunya in Barcelona and they briefly chatted, and on another occasion when Orlov saw Hemingway entering the elegant Hotel Majestic on the fashionable Passeig de Gracia in Barcelona but was on his way to a meeting and was unable to gain the author's attention.

This was the last time he ever saw Hemingway, although through the years Orlov kept up with Hemingway's activities through the media until the author's death.

Orlov had early on informed me that, in his opinion, Hemingway had injected his own character into the role of Robert Jordan, the main character in *For Whom the Bell Tolls*, for whatever reasons but perhaps for vanity. The principal female character Maria, the daughter of a mayor in a small Spanish town, was fictional but based on an atrocity that had actually taken place in the early days of the war. The partisans that assisted Jordan in blowing up the vital bridge preceding the Republican offensive were generic of the townspeople that worked hand in hand with the guerrillas and continually placed themselves in harm's way to assist the guerrilla troops. The core incident described in the book closely resembles one that transpired during the Segovia offensive, but this was only one of many similar incidents that happened during the relevant period as Orlov's guerrillas' principal targets were bridges and rail transportation supplying the Nationalist Army.

What was amazing was the fact that, with few exceptions, the names mentioned in the book – the political and army figures on both sides of the war – were real people whom Hemingway had woven into the plot. Two of the most eminent of these characters were General Golz and war correspondent Karkov.

According to Orlov, the character of General Golz was based on his close friend General Walter. Whenever Walter was in the vicinity of Orlov's headquarters in Valencia and later in Barcelona, he never failed to visit the KGB General. Likewise, Orlov never failed to visit Walter when at the front. On these occasions Orlov would learn more of Walter's connection with Hemingway. It is well worth noting that it was Orlov who rose to Walter's defence when the KGB marked him for liquidation during the Spanish Civil War (see pages 145–9).

Orlov felt that the character of Karkov was based on the real-life background of Mikhail Koltsov, another of his long-time friends from *Pravda* who was actually the eyes and ears of Stalin in Spain as the dictator valued Koltsov's independent judgement on the way the war was going. From time to time Koltsov would leave Spain and report directly to Stalin. However, his personal association with the dictator did not save him from liquidation. Almost everything in the book relating to the Koltsov-based character was true, even down to the physical description, but what did not escape Orlov's attention were the numerous times that Hemingway described Karkov as having bad teeth, a most prominent feature of his friend Koltsov. Orlov was aware of Koltsov's friendship with Hemingway and always attributed the relationship to the fact that they were both war correspondents.

One other character in the book always intrigued Orlov, that of Varloff. The name was only mentioned twice in the same paragraph but in a fashion to indicate a Soviet of high rank and in a context that could possibly indicate that Varloff was connected with intelligence matters. Orlov always felt that Varloff was a character based on himself, pointing out the fact that Varloff rhymed with Orlov.

When *For Whom the Bell Tolls* was first published in 1940, Orlov could hardly wait to get his hands on the book. He related that he had been mesmerised on the first reading as it was like reliving a part of history with old friends and associates in the Spanish Civil War. However, there was one thing that delighted him, a piece of publicity which appeared in a newspaper in connection with the release of the book. A photograph that accompanied the article merely identified the two people as 'Ernest Hemingway and wife', but the wife was Martha Gellhorn, whom he had only met once in war-torn Madrid but never forgotten. He was happy that Hemingway had married her, but felt that the author had got the best of the bargain.

In the mid-1950s, when the Orlovs were in hiding in New York, he became acquainted with the author Max Eastman, who in his early years had been a staunch supporter of left-wing causes but had become disillusioned and eventually supported the far right. During one of their discussions about the Spanish Civil War, the topic turned to Hemingway's participation in it. Eastman told

Orlov about his first meeting with Hemingway in 1922 in Italy and noted that over the years they had remained friends. However, their friendship had come to an abrupt end after Hemingway's book, *Death in the Afternoon,* was published in 1932. Eastman wrote an essay in the June 1933 issue of the magazine *New Republic,* under the title of 'Bull in the Afternoon', which was somewhat critical of Hemingway's book and the sport of bull fighting in general. A reference made in the essay appeared to question Hemingway's masculinity and the matter was soon blown out of all proportion by Hemingway's supporters and then the author himself. Eastman wrote to one of his more vocal critics, Archibald MacLeish, the twice winner of the Pulitzer Prize for poetry and verse drama, assuring him that his essay in no way questioned Hemingway's masculinity and that he was sorry his comment had been misread. MacLeish replied that he accepted Eastman's assurance.

Four years later, Eastman was of the opinion that the matter had long been forgotten by all parties involved. Unfortunately, he was wrong. In August 1937, Eastman was sitting in the office of Maxwell Perkins, editor and Vice President of Charles Scribner's Sons, discussing a recent publication of Eastman's, when in strode Hemingway, who also happened to be at Scribner's that day. They addressed one another in not too complimentary a fashion and it became more than apparent that Hemingway was still smouldering over the previous incident. He then bared his chest and exposed an abundant amount of hair as if to prove his masculinity. The verbal abuse escalated on both sides until Hemingway pushed a book he was holding into Eastman's face; Eastman then wrestled with Hemingway and pinned him to the floor. The mêlée was broken up and Hemingway left the room in a rage. The journalists and literary giants of the day had a field day over the incident and their observations soon became the talk of the town for some time to come. Naturally, their friendship suffered and their paths did not cross again for another nine years. The two met for the last time in Havana in 1946 at the Bar Florida. Eastman was there with his wife Eliena when Hemingway entered. He was friendly and they spoke about their mutual friends, but not a word was said about that infamous day in 1937 when they had scuffled.

For some reason Orlov had never heard of the celebrated incident, probably because his attention was on the Civil War in Spain, and was amused when told about it. He knew Hemingway fairly well and could understand how such an altercation could occur, considering the circumstances. He suggested that Eastman should incorporate the hilarious incident into one of his books, to which Eastman replied that he had written about the episode in a few periodicals in a cursory manner but would keep the suggestion in mind. In March 1960, the Orlovs were visiting the Eastmans when Max presented them with a copy of his latest book, *Great Companions*. As he handed the gift to Orlov, he remarked that he hadn't forgotten Orlov's suggestion of a few years earlier and perhaps Orlov would like to read the full story of Hemingway, his friend from Spain, in his latest book.

From time to time Orlov would read articles on Hemingway in the newspapers and periodicals and he even read his novel, *The Dangerous Summer*, as it dealt with bull fighting in Spain, a sport that had never thrilled Orlov. He was very saddened in 1961 when the news broke that Hemingway had taken his life with a shotgun shell to his head. This event brought back many memories of his brief association with Hemingway in Spain, but none more vivid than that afternoon spent on the rifle range at the guerrilla training camp at Benimamet. It seemed ironic that he should die by a firearm after having dedicated so much of his life to sports revolving around firearms. Orlov concluded that the author's death was a terrible waste of talent as he felt he had more to give to the world of literature.

TEN

BITS AND PIECES

There are a couple of odds and ends that make up Orlov's story during his time in Spain but which don't seem to fit elsewhere, so this short chapter is devoted to them.

Orlov told me of an incident that had happened during the battle of Guadalajara in mid-March 1937 that had resulted in one of the few occasions when Stalin was known to have burst out laughing, something utterly uncharacteristic for the dictator.

During the battle, the Republicans were greatly outnumbered in both men and materiel by the superior Nationalist forces. The mainstay of the Nationalist forces were four Italian divisions under the command of General Mario Roatta. Within the first few days of the Nationalist offensive, the Italian divisions had advanced twenty miles and captured the strategic town of Brihuega, about fifteen miles north-east of the Republican provincial capital of Guadalajara. The Republicans' 11th International Brigade moved into position and was soon followed by the 12th International Brigade and the Garibaldi Battalion. The Republicans were on the verge of losing the battle when a severe change in the weather took place and the advance of the Nationalist Army was bogged down by freezing rain and sleet. The Republicans had the advantage of the nearby Barajas airfield, where the Soviet air force was headquartered and from where missions could readily be flown against the enemy who had no such permanent airstrips to support their troops. By the end of the battle, the Republicans had unexpectedly routed the superior forces of the Nationalists.

In the early stages of the battle, one of the Nationalist Italian divisions captured and held Ibara Castle just a few miles outside of Brihuega. As the tide of the battle turned, the Garibaldi Brigade regained the territory around the castle but was unable to dislodge the Italian division from its fortified position in the castle. After days of fierce fighting, the Italian division finally surrendered to the Garibaldi Brigade.

What was different about this particular skirmish was that it pitted Italian against Italian, brother against brother. Mussolini's Italian division engaged at Ibara Castle was fighting Socialism and Communism whereas the Republican Garibaldi Brigade was composed of Italian volunteers fighting Fascism.

During the battle, Orlov and two of his aides were in Guadalajara directing guerrilla operations behind enemy lines. There the 12th International Brigade reported to Orlov the complete rout of the four Italian divisions. Orlov in turn contacted his headquarters in Valencia and instructed one of his deputies, Colonel Belyaev, to transmit a coded message to Moscow informing the KGB Centre of the successful conclusion of the battle. Orlov provided an outline of what he wanted in the communication and expected Belyaev to execute the message to Moscow in general terms. He briefly wanted Moscow to know that the Italian divisions had been completely routed; that the Chief of Staff of the Italian Corps, General Luizzi, had been killed; that captured Italian soldiers were not volunteers but regulars in Mussolini's army; and that the facts would substantiate a violation of the Covenant of the League of Nations. In his excitement, Orlov made the impromptu comment, relative to the way the battle had gone with special emphasis on the Garibaldi Brigade, 'Mussolini's bastards are fleeing before the sons of Garibaldi.'

With the Nationalists now on the defensive, Orlov was able to return to his Valencia headquarters. While going over the communications that had accumulated in his absence, he ran across the one he had dictated to Belyaev from Guadalajara. He was somewhat astounded when he learned that his message had been relayed almost word for word to Moscow and included his impromptu comment.

Towards the end of March 1937, Abram Slutsky informed Orlov that the Politburo was pleased with his recent objective and timely reports from Guadalajara and that Stalin had personally instructed that henceforth KGB Chairman Yezhov was to prepare a daily summary of Orlov's reports from Spain for distribution to the Politburo and himself. The summaries would bear the title, the 'Schwed Reports', after Orlov's code name.

Several days later, a new member of Orlov's staff reported for duty. KGB Colonel Tolin had been at the KGB Centre in Moscow when he learned that the decision to initiate the 'Schwed Reports' had been taken after Stalin had burst out laughing after reading the phrase 'Mussolini's bastards are fleeing before the sons of Garibaldi' in Orlov's dispatch from Guadalajara. Stalin had allegedly remarked that he could only trust the reports from Schwed and, if he were to believe the reports from the Soviet air commanders regarding the number of Nazi aircraft they destroyed each day, he would have to conclude that the German air force had no more aircraft.

Orlov said that he never realised what the consequence of his dispatch from Guadalajara would be, but at least it did provoke an unusual response from the dictator who was not known for his sense of humour. Orlov's only regret was that he had not been present at the time.

Another incident Orlov told me about was how he and his staff had intervened to save the life of General Walter. What undoubtedly helped to save him was a large silver cigarette box that had served as a bribe.

Orlov related that the Polish Karol Swierczewski was one of the most outstanding commanders of the International Brigades. He had been a colonel in the Red Army and at the start of the Spanish Civil War had been dispatched to France to recruit Poles working in French coal mines for the Spanish Civil War effort. Having successfully completed his mission in France, he was sent to Spain under the pseudonym of Walter. The name General Walter became synonymous with victory on the battlefields of Spain and the General easily won the hearts and respect of all Spaniards through his deeds.

Walter was a shrewd and practical field commander, who was feared by his men yet greatly respected. He commanded the 14th International Brigade and later the 35th Division, where his skills as a commander brought victories and recognition. Orlov had met Walter on the battlefield several times and recalled how Walter would review his haggard troops after a battle and praise each unit as it passed by with comments that it was the best fighting unit he had. To him, they were all the best.

Walter would always visit Orlov's headquarters in Valencia and later in Barcelona. His exchanges with the staff were brief and to the point, and he never allowed himself to be pessimistic regarding conditions at the front. Orlov could only see one fatal flaw in Walter's character: he was not a politician and his pride never allowed him to ingratiate himself with those in high political office. When visiting the capital, Walter would confer with officials of the Republican Ministry of Defence and the General Staff but never with General Jan Berzin, the Soviet Military Advisor to the Republican Government. Orlov would ask if he had met Berzin, only to be given a negative reply and sometimes asked the question why should he meet Berzin when he couldn't tell him anything that he didn't already know. Orlov realised that Walter felt contempt for the armchair General, who had never had a military command, and just considered him another politician. This was a grave mistake in Orlov's eyes as Berzin had high connections in the Soviet Government and the fact that he hadn't received a courtesy call from Walter had not gone unnoticed.

In the early spring of 1938, Orlov received a communication from the KGB Centre asking what he thought Walter would do if he were recalled to Moscow. The communication indicated that the 4th Department of the General Staff of the Red Army had received information to indicate that Walter's attitude displayed great indifference to the war effort, which might lead to his defection. There was no doubt whatsoever in Orlov's mind that the complaint originated with Berzin.

When Orlov received the communication, he was outraged that a shadow of suspicion was being cast on a man who had sacrificed his life many times in battle since he had arrived in Spain. Furthermore, Walter had a twenty-year-old daughter living in Russia and there was no way he would abandon her by defecting. Orlov decided that he would intercede on Walter's behalf and called a meeting of his staff. He read the KGB communication to them and they likewise were shocked about what they considered a miscarriage of justice. They all knew the General personally and quickly came to his defence. Orlov decided that he would send a personal letter of intercession on Walter's behalf to Yezhov with the added observations of his staff.

That day Orlov telephoned Walter, who happened to be on military leave and in residence with his mistress at an abandoned villa about fifteen miles from Barcelona. In the past, Walter had often asked Orlov to come over for dinner but business circumstances had always made it impossible. This time, Orlov offered to come to Walter's residence with his staff. That evening Orlov and his staff were lavishly treated to a wonderful meal and fine wines as well as entertainment presented by two professional Spanish dancers, who were sisters. One of the sisters was Walter's mistress. That night Orlov met the other General Walter. Instead of a man with few words to offer, he met a gregarious person who waxed eloquently about his daughter in Russia and even read her last letter to him. Instead of the determined and hardened field commander on the battlefield, he displayed tenderness and even shed a few tears when he spoke of his fondness for his daughter.

During the evening, Walter was very talkative and in a blissful mood. He spoke of some of the battles he had been engaged in and showed photographs and artefacts from the various fronts as well as a gold inlaid sword that had been presented to him by the town fathers of a Spanish city he had liberated. However, the object that captured Orlov's attention was a large sterling silver cigarette case. The cover of the case was executed with an ornately engraved map of Spain with a ruby set at every battlefield where Walter had engaged the enemy. On the inside of the lid was engraved an inscription from the Socialist-Communist Youth of Spain thanking General Walter for his heroic defence of Republican Spain from its domestic enemies, the Nationalists, and the Fascist invaders. The moment Orlov saw the sterling silver cigarette case, he knew this would be the amulet that would save Walter's life.

The next day Orlov wrote a personal letter to Yezhov pleading Walter's case and specifically challenging the denunciation as being without merit. He cited the General's war record and opined that the General would never defect as he loved his daughter too much to abandon her. He added that his staff concurred with his views.

In spite of Orlov's intercession, Walter was recalled to Moscow a month later. He paid his last respects to Orlov just before departing and asked how he could safeguard his war diary and maps from being confiscated by the Nazis as he had to pass through Germany en route to Moscow. Orlov obliged by granting him permission to send the material via the diplomatic pouch to the Chief of the KGB's Foreign Department, where he could later retrieve the material. It was then that Orlov asked for the sterling silver cigarette case, which he proposed to send along with the other items in the diplomatic pouch as a means of impressing the KGB hierarchy on whom Walter's life depended. Orlov related that he knew the mentality of the men at the top of the KGB and the Kremlin, whose personal integrity would be outweighed by greed, and he had every reason to believe that someone in a position of authority would end up with the cigarette case. He chuckled slightly when he said that I was correct in thinking that the cigarette case was intended as a bribe.

Orlov facilitated Walter's departure from Spain by providing him with the use of his personal diplomatic car, which would enable him to bypass customs formalities at the border. Within a month's time, Orlov received a letter from him in which he expressed his gratitude for the assistance Orlov had given him and mentioned that he had retrieved his material at the KGB Centre. He said that he had felt honoured when he was invited to meet Yezhov and the first thing he noticed on entering Yezhov's office was his silver cigarette case lying on the desk. He related that the piece made a wonderful introduction to their meeting and was happy to hear Yezhov say that he really appreciated the 'gift'. Orlov commented that the 'bribe' had apparently paid off as Walter's life was spared.

Walter, who became Karol Swierczewski again when he returned to Russia, fought and survived the Second World War. As a reward for his wartime services, Stalin made him Minister of Defence for Poland, when the Polish Communist Government and Soviet satellite was created after the war. In 1947, Orlov read a newspaper account which reflected that Swierczewski had been ambushed and killed in Poland by anti-Communist partisans. He was sceptical of the incident as the old General was too wily and experienced to be led into a trap. However, he did suspect that Swierczewski's old enemies from Spain had finally aroused Stalin's enmity again, which had led to his death. Orlov had one final thought on the matter. He related that every time he thought of General Walter, he thought of the sterling silver cigarette case and vice versa.

There is one thing I believe that needs clarification regarding the military intelligence-gathering organisation Orlov created in Spain that went by the acronym SIM. Long after Orlov died, I started to study the Spanish Civil War and noted that historians referred to SIM as the Servicio de Investigación Militar whereas in his memoirs as well as in our discussions Orlov referred to it as the Servicio Información Militar. I would have to assume that as the founder of the organisation, he knew its correct name. Moreover, the aim of the organisation was to gather information related to intelligence matters and not to investigate violations of a military nature. When Orlov first approached the Republican Government, he had wanted to organise a military intelligence service, but Minister of Defence Prieto had strongly objected to a KGB-structured intelligence service that could one day arrest him and other members of the Cabinet and take over the Government. It would seem logical that in order to placate Prieto, the new organisation was called an information service rather than an intelligence service.

While on the subject of the SIM, I should relate another matter that rankled Orlov every time he thought of Prieto and the SIM. As already related in the previous chapter, Orlov broke relations with Prieto over the latter's dismissal of Colonel Duran as Chief of SIM. Up to that time, the two men had been fairly close friends and associates and even lived side by side in the town of Betera. Orlov intervened on Duran's behalf but Prieto would not reinstate Duran. This was the last time Orlov ever spoke to Prieto.

Sometime around 1940, Orlov ran across an account of the Congress of the Spanish Socialist Party which had taken place in Barcelona a month after Orlov defected in July 1938. The account was published in Paris in 1939 under the title *How and Why I Left the Ministry of National Defence* by Indalecio Prieto. In April 1938, Prieto was asked to resign as Minister of Defence and his office was taken over by Prime Minister Juan Negrin, who then handled both Ministries. At the Congress, the still popular Prieto played on the ears of the sympathetic Socialists in a speech he gave noting in particular that he had never been a lackey of the Soviets and that he had steadfastly held his ground against the demands of the Soviets. As an illustration of how he had been victimised by the Soviets and forced to leave office, he cited his dismissal of Colonel Duran as Chief of SIM as a case in point. He related that he had not acceded to the Soviet General Orlov's demands that Duran be reinstated and quoted the General's warning that, 'If you do not reinstate Duran, I will sever my relations with you.' Prieto stated that he had not yielded to Orlov and, therefore, his relations with the Russians had been completely severed. He added that he never saw Orlov again after that episode in Valencia.

Orlov said that in effect Prieto was placing the blame for his failure as Minister of Defence, and the fact that he had been asked to resign his position, on Orlov's shoulders by inferring that Orlov had used his influence to have him ousted. To bolster his claim of why he had dismissed Duran, which had led to his showdown with Orlov and his dismissal as Minister of Defence, Prieto related that Duran had been a member of the Communist Party. This was the part that always annoyed Orlov because Duran was never a member of the Communist Party.

'What if?' was the question that was always at the back of my mind and one which I had to ask Orlov. What if the Republicans had won the Spanish Civil War? How would this have changed conditions in Spain as we know them today? In 1972, Orlov had to admit that he often pondered the question but felt reasonably positive he knew the answer: 'Had the Soviet-backed Republican Government won the Civil War,' he said, 'Spain would be a Soviet satellite today.'

When he was dispatched to Spain in 1936, he was under orders not to undermine or interfere with the political activities of the Socialist Government of the Republicans and, if necessary, to yield to its demands. Although the Republican Government was by far dominated by members of the Socialist Party, there was a small vociferous contingent of Communist Party members in it. Orlov's orders were clear that he should show no partiality towards the Communist Party members. The first priority was to win the war in Spain with everything focused towards this end, the rationale being that the remaining issues would fall into place following the war. Hitler and Mussolini contrived to have a united Europe of Fascist governments and colonies while Stalin, the most megalomaniac of them all, conceived his plan on a more grandiose scale, to spread Communism throughout the world. By the time Stalin died in 1953, he was well on his way to achieving his goal and his masterplan was perpetuated by his successors in the Kremlin. The Soviets already had a foothold in Spain during the Spanish Civil War and a Republican victory would have assured their continued presence by a government that would have owed much gratitude to the Soviets for their aid during the war. Orlov was given to believe that, following hostilities, he would no longer have to placate the Spanish Socialist Party and all efforts would be directed towards gradually placing the Spanish Communist Party in power with an eventual takeover of the Spanish Government by the Communists. During the Spanish Civil War, the Soviets were already grooming Spanish nationals in the Comintern (the Soviet's international apparatus for Communist Parties around the world) for the task. Orlov admitted that when he first went to Spain in 1936, he wholeheartedly supported the plan but in time realised that the Republicans could not win the war.

With this background in mind, Orlov conjectured that Spain would have gone the way of Hungary, Poland, Czechoslovakia, East Germany and the other Soviet satellites behind the Iron Curtain, only at a much earlier time. As with the Central European Soviet satellites, it would have been only a matter of a short time before the Communists had taken over the Spanish Government. The logical candidate to run the new Soviet satellite would have been Jesús Hernandez, the Minister of Education in the Republican Cabinet during the war. Hernandez was a member of the Spanish Communist Party as well as a leading member of the Comintern and would therefore be expected to do the bidding of the Soviets as their puppet in power. He was also an antagonist of Orlov's.

Orlov also projected that had the Soviets taken over Spain, history may have taken an entirely different route. Spain's strategic location ensured control of the Mediterranean Sea from where Communism would have easily spread along the Mediterranean basin. Hitler would have had to rethink his aggressions in Europe with the Soviets on both of his flanks, and undoubtedly there would have been countless possible scenarios and alliances between the Great Powers that would provoke the imagination. The potential to change the course of history was so complex that Orlov was unwilling to speculate further.

Orlov ventured that the people of Spain were far better off under Generalissimo Franco than they would have been under the Soviets. He understood that Franco ran a totalitarian government but, from what he had studied, the Spaniards were far better off than the people of the European satellites that were under Soviet dominance. He observed that there was much discontent amongst the people of Spain under Franco but if they placed themselves in the shoes of the Cuban people under Fidel Castro, with his Soviet-style Communism, they would feel differently. Orlov never lived to see the day in 1975 when Franco passed away and the reins of power were turned over to his selected heir, Prince Juan Carlos de Bourbon, who became King Juan Carlos I of Spain. The new King was the first monarch in Spain in over forty-four years. Orlov was very fond of the Spanish people and I am sure he would have been happy to see a democratic Spain under the rule of a monarch. Today, more than sixty years after the end of the Spanish Civil War in 1939, we find a content and prosperous people in Spain, a situation that would not have been possible under Communism.

ELEVEN

THE DECISION

At the same time as the Civil War was raging in Spain, the power play in the Soviet Union instigated by a paranoid Stalin to solidify and perpetuate his absolute dictatorship was well underway. The great purges that would eventually eliminate all possible and perceived enemies of Stalin through mock trials, questionable executions, unlawful searches and seizures, and unexplained disappearances would bring havoc to the Soviet people. Not even the most highly placed and loyal members of the Party were exempt, and especially targeted were the Chiefs of the NKVD and Jews in particular. Word of the terror sweeping the country would reach Orlov from time to time, and the implications for his own particular situation did not go unnoticed.

At the point when Orlov was selected for the assignment to Spain, he was at the pinnacle of his professional career. His prospects for the Chairmanship of the KGB were enhanced by the prominence of the position he was about to undertake. Orlov realised that a good performance in Spain would certainly not escape Stalin's attention or go unrewarded. However, despite one success after another in Spain, Orlov came to the unmistakable conclusion that Stalin had marked him for execution and that he had no alternative but to break from the Soviet Government and the KGB. To understand what motivated Orlov to take this drastic decision, we must examine the crucial events that transpired from the time he arrived in Spain up to his actual defection which had a bearing on the process.

Orlov was hardly naïve as to what was going on in the Soviet Union on his arrival in Spain but this was of no immediate concern to him. He felt somewhat stifled by the lack of freedom in the Motherland, realised that Stalin's power and brutality were excessive, and that the recent trial of Zinoviev and Kamenev was a mockery of justice, but reasoned that they were all necessary for the good of the nation.

The first harbinger of change that came to his attention occurred within three weeks of his arrival in Spain, when, in the first week of October 1936, he was officially advised by the KGB Centre in Moscow that Genrikh Yagoda had been dismissed from his position as Chairman on 29 September and replaced by Nikolai Yezhov. Orlov was not surprised at this turn of events given the fact that Yezhov was Stalin's protégé, but questioned the tactic as Yagoda was fully aware of Stalin's role in the assassination of Sergei Kirov. Yagoda had not been arrested or charged with any crime but removed to the obscure position of Commissar of Communications. He had been denounced for his failure to tie Zinoviev and Kamenev directly to the Trotsky conspiracy and this was given as the official reason for his dismissal.

Orlov felt that Stalin was walking a tightrope in his manoeuvre to charge Yagoda with the Kirov assassination and thereby divert attention from himself as the true instigator of the plot. Yagoda had faithfully served Stalin since 1934, when he had become Chairman of the KGB, and had since been known as Stalin's eyes and ears. Even on the occasion of their last meeting several weeks before, Yagoda had been basking in the glory of his recent successes and gave no indication that his star was about to descend. Stalin's risk was high but the reward was well worth the effort: in the end, he would be able to claim that the KGB was rotten to the core with plotters against the leadership, and he would have yet another tool to legitimise the liquidation of those members of the KGB whom he perceived as standing in his way.

Yagoda's freedom was not long lasting as he was arrested and charged in April 1937, well in advance of the start of the last great purge show trial. The trial began on 2 March 1938, when Yagoda and the other principal defendants were generally charged with being a part of a conspiracy that had sided with the Western

Powers to the detriment of the Soviet Government. In addition, Yagoda was singled out as the mastermind of the plot to assassinate Kirov and further that he had secretly worked for the German intelligence service. As if these charges were not substantial enough on their own, he was alleged to have signed a confession that he was behind a KGB plot to poison Stalin and members of the Politburo. Yagoda and the other conspirators were found guilty as charged and executed shortly after the conclusion of the trial.

Yezhov, the new Chairman of the KGB, was known to Orlov mainly by reputation, although they had met several times at various social events with mutual friends. Their relationship was superficial at best, yet Orlov had a definite disliking for the man, feeling that he displayed attitudes of petty jealousy and resentment towards his peers for the obvious reason that he was not intelligent and was conscious of this deficiency. Furthermore, his way of dealing with others displayed a vindictive characteristic that Orlov could not tolerate.

Yezhov's rise in the Party apparatus was due solely to his ability to ingratiate himself into Stalin's confidence rather than to the merits of his abilities. For a time he had been the Chief of the Personnel Department of the Central Committee of the Communist Party and, prior to his appointment to the KGB, had been appointed by Stalin to the post of Chairman of the Control Committee of the Communist Party, an all-powerful position that would well serve Stalin's stewardship. It would not be long before it was known that Yezhov was the person responsible for compiling Stalin's list of those marked for elimination under the purges. Suddenly, those who had scorned Yezhov and openly referred to him as 'The Dwarf', and looked upon him as Stalin's lackey, now spoke of him in terms of reverence and were careful not to provoke him in any manner. Even those in the highest echelons of the Politburo were aware that their lives depended on the whims of the very same man they had once overlooked. At the height of the purges it became evident that not even the most loyal and trusted colleagues of Stalin were exempt from 'Yezhov's List'.

In late February 1937, Orlov heard some very disturbing news that would ultimately have a devastating impact on his own future, although at the time he did not fully recognise its significance. At the time he was in a Paris hospital recuperating from a car accident that had occurred while he was inspecting the front. While in the hospital, he had a visit from one of his old KGB colleagues and trusted friend, Abram Slutsky, the Chief of the INO. After the usual greetings, their conversation quickly turned to Yezhov. Slutsky related that, in early December 1936, Yezhov had brought into the fold of the KGB about 300 of his own trusted men from the Central Committee of the Party for the express purpose of establishing a new section of the KGB named the Administration of Special Tasks (AST), which would be under his personal direction and staffed by officials from the Central Committee. Yezhov's intention was complete control of the new apparatus, using men whose loyalty he had already tested at the Central Committee and who could be expected to carry out sensitive assignments without any reservations. The new AST operatives would have no allegiance to any members of the old KGB cadre and would, therefore, have no reason not to carry out an assignment against any one of them.

Within the administration of the AST, a clandestine unit called the Mobile Groups had been created to deal with the ever increasing problem of possible KGB defectors, as INO officers serving abroad were beginning to see that the purges were directed at them as well as at the personal enemies of Stalin. By the summer of 1937, an alarming number of KGB intelligence agents serving abroad had been summoned back to the Soviet Union, and in the event that any one of them refused to return a contingency plan called for their assassination, a task that could not be entrusted to the old-timers. The Mobile Groups would be dispatched abroad under false identities for this purpose.

Now that Yezhov had his mechanisms in place for bypassing the KGB, it did not take him long to put them to the test. In the late spring of 1937, word filtered down to Orlov that all of Yagoda's former deputies and the department chiefs of the KGB, with only a few exceptions, had been liquidated in a plot conceived by Yezhov. During March of that year, he had summoned all the prospective candidates to the plot to his office for a conference. There he informed the group that the Central Committee had commissioned each of them to proceed to the far reaches of the country to evaluate the reliability of local Party leaders. In order to allay any possible suspicion, Yezhov gave elaborate instructions and provided each with a letter of authority from the Central Committee to accomplish their mission.

The following day they all left Moscow for their designated area of assignment. Within a few days, Yezhov repeated the tactic with the deputies of the department chiefs who had already been dispatched. Several weeks went by before KGB officers back at the Centre became wary and questioned the long absence of their leaders. In the meantime, Yezhov had changed the commanders of the KGB troops stationed in Moscow and the KGB guards with those who were expected to remain loyal to him. He also transferred to his own jurisdiction the section within the Foreign Department that issued passports for travel abroad and replaced the commanders of the KGB air squadrons as an added measure to prevent KGB officers from fleeing abroad. Thus the door of possible escape from the Soviet Union was closed. Eventually word leaked back to the KGB Centre that each member of the departed entourage had boarded their respective trains but had been taken off at the first scheduled stop beyond Moscow. They were then taken to prison in Moscow and executed.

What would hit Orlov very hard was the fact that, sometime during July 1937, he received word that his first cousin, Zinovy Borisovich Katsnelson, had been shot that spring as a consequence of the round-up of high-ranking KGB officers. Zinovy was more than just a close relative; he had been a friend and companion from early childhood and their fondness for one another had grown as the years went by. When Orlov had entered Moscow University, Zinovy was in his final year there. While at the university he had shared a room with Zinovy in the small Moscow apartment of Zinovy's mother. Later, they would serve together at the front with the 12th Red Army during the Civil War. Both would achieve high positions with the new Communist Government, Zinovy becoming an assistant and protégé to KGB Chairman Felix Dzerzhinsky in the 1920s. On weekends he would be invited to Dzerzhinsky's country dacha, where he would encounter Stalin, who had not yet become dictator of the Soviet Union. In 1937, Zinovy was a member of the Central Committee of the Communist Party of the Ukraine and held the position of Acting Chief of the KGB in the Ukraine.

In February, while Orlov was convalescing in the Paris hospital, Zinovy had paid him a visit and had informed him of a plan, which was still in its early stages, to overthrow Stalin and for Red Army generals to take over the Government (for fuller details, see chapter 24). The plot was a failure and the Red Army conspirators were arrested on charges of treason, tried and executed the next day.

When word of Yezhov's transgressions reached Orlov, he knew that his own liquidation was only a matter of time. One factor stood in his favour, as it did with all of the KGB officers stationed abroad. Liquidating KGB officers within the Soviet Union was an easy matter, but to expunge officers serving abroad, it was necessary to lure them back to the USSR by whatever means. The task was not simple by any stretch of the imagination and would demand a strategy that would not arouse any suspicion. These KGB officers were the elite professionals in their craft, whose training and experience in the field was such that they would be perceptive of any questionable ploy. Yezhov understood that he had to allay the suspicions of those serving abroad for fear of an exodus of officers who were aware of the KGB's secrets in the countries of their operation and who could possibly expose their spy networks. For over a year the INO remained untouched and its chief, Slutsky, escaped the original purge of KGB department heads. The inescapable conclusion that Yezhov managed to foster was that INO officers were not at risk. However, one by one they were recalled to Moscow on the pretext of being reassigned, or to attend a conference, never to return to their country of assignment.

The summer of 1937 would be a disaster for KGB officers serving abroad. Forty officers were recalled to Moscow using various pretences. The least difficult to lure back were those with families still residing in the Soviet Union. All KGB personnel were well aware of Stalin's promulgated law of 8 June 1934, which held the families of military deserters accountable for their deeds and made them subject to banishment to one of the Siberian gulags. The KGB took the decree one step further by adding KGB officers who fled the country or failed to return to the homeland from a foreign assignment. The officer's closest relative would be subject to ten years' imprisonment or, in the case where the officer divulged state secrets, the death penalty. Those KGB officers with families at stake in the homeland therefore obeyed the order when it came. All knew that they had a difficult decision to make, even those with no strong family ties at home, for the KGB had the benefit of highly placed nationals on its payroll in each of the countries where a defector might wish to hide; these nationals could then ferret out the defector's location for the Mobile Groups to finish the job. Those returning voluntarily did so with the expectation that the mere act of returning would give the impression of loyalty and fortify their innocence of any transgressions against Stalin's regime. Of the forty KGB officers who were recalled that summer, only five decided not to return.

Of those KGB officers who chose to return, the most memorable and pathetic to Orlov was Theodore Mally, whose operational code name was Mann. Mally was one of the best illegals who worked in the capitals of Europe during the early and mid-1930s. His reputation with the KGB was one of capability, and he was well liked and respected not only by his peers but by his superiors. Mally was actually Hungarian by birth and education and had no blood ties to Mother Russia. Prior to the First World War, he had studied for the priesthood and when war broke out he had joined the Austro-Hungarian Army as a chaplain. His military unit was captured by the Russian Army and he spent the remainder of the war in Russia as a prisoner of war. He was in

Russia during the Revolution and, as a consequence of his exposure to Communism, had become an agnostic and a member of
the Communist Party. Following the great Russian upheaval, the
Party assigned Mally to the OGPU, where he became affiliated
with the Counter-Intelligence Department. Subsequently Mally
was assigned to the Foreign Department, where his personal assets
came to the surface. His manner and appearance were that of a
'Continental' European rather than an inhabitant of any one
particular country. He could easily pass as a national of any of
the Central European countries and spoke fluent German,
Hungarian and Russian. His ability to make and keep friendships
in his target countries was amazing and to a large degree made
for his success as an illegal. However, in spite of a long list of
achievements in the field, he could never quite escape an inferiority complex brought on by his earlier endeavour to become a
priest. Mally never felt accepted by his co-associates and believed
that they held him to be inferior because of his failure as a priest.

Mally was ordered back to Moscow from an assignment abroad
in July 1937. En route to Moscow, he met Orlov in Paris, where
they discussed his plight and the turn of events that affected other
KGB officers in the same predicament. Orlov later acknowledged
that he had known Mally personally since the late 1920s and that
they had worked together as illegals in countries that he did not
specify. Orlov made it crystal clear that he considered Mally to
be a close and trusted friend, and further described Mally's services to the KGB as of the highest order.

Years later, I would learn that Mally was responsible for running
the Cambridge Group of spies in England in the mid-1930s.
Today there is no doubt in my mind that Mally was returning
from a covert operation in England en route to Moscow when
he stopped over in Paris to meet Orlov.

At their meeting Mally was totally depressed and his mood
sombre. He spoke of three other Hungarians who, like himself,
had been captured by the Tsarist Russian Army during the First
World War and were later converted to Communism. They had
also joined the Russian intelligence apparatus and had been

arrested in the recent purges and executed. Mally surmised that his fate would be the same as he did not see an alternative reason for his recall. It was at this juncture that Orlov stated that he could not understand why Mally would even consider returning to Moscow and cautioned him against doing so. Unlike the others, Mally had no relatives or close personal ties in the USSR, and he was not even a Russian. In Orlov's eyes, his return to Moscow was not justified by any means.

Unfortunately, Mally did return to Moscow, where he took up an assignment in the KGB's Foreign Department. For the next few months, he plodded along in his unobtrusive manner without attracting any special notice to himself. Perhaps his past achievements and loyalty to the KGB, as well as the fact that he was not a Russian, let him escape the executioner. Even his co-workers at the KGB Centre came to believe in Mally's good fortune, but to no avail as that November he suddenly disappeared from his work area and was never heard of again. Orlov admitted that he grieved on learning of Mally's disappearance but that he had never fully understood Mally's reason for returning. He understood Mally's sense of inferiority and his desire to prove his loyalty to the cause, but these were minor considerations when it came to giving up his life.

Back in Spain, Orlov met his old friend Mikhail Koltsov, who had just returned from a meeting with Stalin in Moscow. On his recent visit, he had found Stalin to be very depressed, a mood which was reflected in his remarks: 'It's awful! We discover traitors every day. My only consolation is the behaviour and performance of our Soviet men in Spain.' He then asked Koltsov to give his personal thanks to the Soviet men fighting in Spain and to commend the Secretary of the Spanish Communist Party, José Díaz, on his behalf.

Based on Koltsov's observations, Orlov reasoned that Stalin was now deluding himself into believing that he was not responsible for the atrocities taking place on a daily basis, in spite of the fact that he was the author and manipulator of the plot. Stalin was now showing another side of his character by acting out a part in which he displayed remorse for having to carry out the executions in order to protect the country from 'traitors'. As to the Soviet Spanish Civil War heroes who were Stalin's only 'consolation', these field commanders were returned to the Soviet Union one by one, given a hero's welcome and decorations, and then executed. Even Koltsov was eventually recalled and murdered on Stalin's orders.

Of the five KGB officers who refused to return to Moscow, the most memorable cases that stuck in Orlov's mind were those of Ignaz Reiss and Walter Krivitsky. Reiss and Krivitsky were both Polish Jews, who had become close friends and members of the Soviet Communist Party, and who were friends and work associates of Orlov's.

The case of Ignaz Reiss, whose real name was Poretsky, was the first to come to Orlov's attention towards the end of July 1937. Reiss was the KGB illegal *rezident* in Belgium when he was summoned back to Moscow. Reiss had the advantage of having his wife and daughter with him when he decided to defect. In July of that year, he sent a letter to the Soviet Embassy in Paris explaining his decision to break with the Soviet Government because he no longer supported the views of Stalin's counter-revolution and wanted to return to the freedom and teachings of Lenin. Orlov learned the details of Reiss's letter and decision to defect through his close contacts at the Soviet Embassy in Paris. He would later learn the conclusion of the matter through the same source.

On learning that Reiss had disobeyed the order to return and intended to defect, an enraged Stalin ordered that an example be made of his case so as to warn other KGB officers against taking steps in the same direction. Stalin reasoned that any betrayal by KGB officers would not only expose the entire operation, but would succeed in placing the most dangerous secrets of the KGB's spy networks in the hands of the enemy's intelligence services. Stalin ordered Yezhov to dispatch a Mobile Group to find and assassinate Reiss and his family in a manner that would be sure to send an unmistakable message to any KGB officer considering Reiss's route.

The task was of such a high priority that Yezhov placed his Deputy Chief of the INO, Mikhail Shpiegelglass, in charge of the Mobile Group that was to locate and liquidate Reiss and his family. Shpiegelglass was able to discover that Reiss had fled Belgium and was hiding in a village near Lausanne, Switzerland. Shpiegelglass enlisted the aid of a trusted Reiss family friend by the name of Gertrude Schildback, who was in the employ of the KGB, to lure Reiss to a rendezvous, where the Mobile Group riddled Reiss's body with machine-gun fire on the evening of 4 September 1937. His body was found by Swiss authorities on a road outside Lausanne.

Reiss's wife and daughter were spared, although it became clear that they had been intended to be victims of a box of chocolates that had been laced with strychnine poison. In her great haste to retreat from the scene of the crime, Schildbach had left behind her luggage at the small hotel where she was temporarily staying. During the course of their investigation, the Swiss police found the box of chocolates. Orlov speculated that Schildbach had neither the time nor the opportunity to give the chocolates to the intended victims, or, more probably, that she did not want to carry forth the murder plot. As a family friend, she had often played with the Reiss child and the bond that had developed with the child was more than likely the factor which caused her to renege on this part of the plot.

The other defector of note was Walter Krivitsky, who at the time of Reiss's demise had been the KGB illegal *rezident* in Holland. His defection would reach the highest levels of the French and Soviet Governments and almost became an international incident. Krivitsky had only been with the KGB since 1935, having previously worked for the Intelligence Administration of the Red Army. He was aware of Reiss's plan to defect and attempted to warn Reiss at his hideout in Switzerland when he learned that Shpiegelglass's Mobile Group had located him. Krivitsky was to learn of Reiss's fate on the morning of 5 September, when he read in a Paris newspaper the details of a macabre murder that had been discovered near Lausanne. The given name of the murder victim was Reiss's pseudonym. Krivitsky soon learned that he had been recalled to Moscow and, being well aware of what had happened to his friend, made the decision to defect. Stalling for more time, he acted as if he were complying with the order while actually planning his escape. On the day of his scheduled departure for Moscow, Krivitsky telephoned his secretary at the Embassy to relay the message to his superiors that he was breaking with the Soviet Government. Krivitsky, his wife and son went to the southern reaches of France, where they had a temporary sanctuary.

On learning what had transpired, Yezhov immediately dispatched a Mobile Group to France with orders to kill Krivitsky and his family. French intelligence soon learned of the plan and placed Krivitsky and his family under the protective custody of the French police. What saved Krivitsky's life for the time being and placed him under the protection of the French Government was an incident of international proportions that had occurred less than a month before in Paris.

General Yevgeny Miller, head of the anti-Soviet émigré organisation in France known as the Military Union of Former Tsarist Officers, was kidnapped off the streets of Paris in broad daylight on 23 September by agents of the Soviet Government (for further details, see chapter 25). The affair provoked an uproar and scandal in France as to how such a prominent person could be snatched in such a manner. The French police mounted one of the most intensive manhunts in their history but never succeeded in finding the perpetrators or the victim. Not wanting another debacle such as the Miller affair, the French Government summoned the Soviet Chargé d'Affaires to the French Foreign Office, where he was told to convey the message to Moscow that another kidnapping on French soil would force the French Government to break diplomatic relations with the Soviet Government.

Stalin was furious at the actions of the French Government but was not in a position to provoke it with yet another incident. He would bide his time for the right opportunity. In the meantime, Krivitsky had a breathing space from the hot pursuit of the

KGB and, during December 1938, would make good his escape to the United States, where he felt that he would be safe. While in the US, he provided the US Government with some intelligence. The end did come for Krivitsky for on 10 February 1941 his body was found lying in a pool of blood on the floor of his room at the Bellevue Hotel in Washington DC. He had been shot through the right temple with a .38 calibre weapon, which was found next to the body; however, no fingerprints were found as the gun had been wiped clean. There were three suicide notes, the nature of which seemed questionable. To some the death was a suicide, but to those who knew him and the ways of the Soviet secret police, the facts were evident and the murder was placed at the feet of the KGB. Orlov would read of the murder in the newspapers, and there was never any doubt in his mind as to the identity and motive of the perpetrators.

Orlov also knew that time was on the side of the KGB, as was evident in the Krivitsky case, but more so as reflected in the case of Georgi Agabekov. Agabekov had been the KGB *rezident* in Turkey when he broke with the Soviet Government in 1929. The KGB kept up its pursuit of him for nine long years until he was tracked down in Belgium and murdered in early 1938. This was one lesson Orlov never forgot and was certainly on his mind when he defected.

By the beginning of 1938, most of the KGB officers serving abroad who had been targeted for elimination had already returned to Moscow. Stalin and Yezhov no longer had to play out the charade that the Foreign Department was not subject to the purges in order to placate the fears of those serving abroad. Therefore, they no longer needed to keep Abram Slutsky as Chief of the Foreign Department in order to maintain this deception.

During the morning of 17 February 1938, Slutsky was summoned to the office of Mikhail Frinovsky, an old friend of Stalin's and now one of Yezhov's deputies. Within an hour of Slutsky's arrival at Frinovsky's office, the latter contacted Slutsky's deputy Shpiegelglass and asked him to come immediately to his office. On entering, Shpiegelglass was alarmed to see his boss slumped over in the chair he was sitting in and his instantaneous reaction was that Slutsky had been murdered. Not wanting to convey the impression that he was alarmed, Shpiegelglass offered to call a doctor, but Frinovsky pronounced that this had already been done and that the doctor had attributed the cause of death to a heart attack. What Shpiegelglass did notice was that on the table in front of Slutsky was a cup of tea and some cakes which had only been partially consumed.

Shpiegelglass was installed as the Acting Chief of the Foreign Department and one of his first acts was to notify all the KGB *rezidents* serving abroad that their comrade and chief had died. At Frinovsky's insistence, Slutsky was described in glowing terms and his death was noted as a definite loss to the KGB. The phrasing of the death notice was designed to calm the fears of the few remaining old-guard KGB officers still serving abroad. The death notice was sent to the KGB *rezidents* by way of the routine diplomatic mail rather than by the more expeditious cable route. Orlov did not receive his notice until twelve days after Slutsky's death, although in the interim he had received cables from the KGB Centre under Slutsky's signature. The issue of *Pravda* which arrived at the same time as the death notice from the KGB contained a brief obituary, which was signed only as a tribute from 'Fellow Workers'. Orlov thought this strange as Russian custom dictated that the leading hierarchy of the KGB subscribe to the obituary.

What was not taken into consideration when Yezhov deemed he no longer had any use for Slutsky's services, and then covered up the cause of his death as a heart attack, was the fact that he was dealing with experienced KGB officers who were well aware of the political intrigue that was decimating their ranks. As Slutsky's body lay in state in the main hall of the KGB Centre, these officers could hardly fail to notice the telltale blotches on his face that led them to the inescapable conclusion that he had been poisoned by hydrocyanic acid.

The elimination of the old guard was not limited to the KGB

but also to the generals of the Red Army, the admirals of the Red Navy, the leaders of the Politburo and commissars of all of the departments of government. The foreign diplomats in Moscow were able to see what was happening and would begin to refer to Stalin as the 'sick man in the Kremlin'. They began to believe that Stalin was insane and that his sinister actions were a reflection of his paranoia. Orlov, on the other hand, felt that Stalin knew exactly what he was doing.

Of the Red Army generals who were caught up in the purges, Orlov's most personal loss was that of General Emil Kleber, who commanded the 11th International Brigade and whom he had met on his arrival in Spain. As already related, Kleber and his 11th International Brigade were responsible for keeping Madrid out of the hands of the Nationalists during the dark days of the Civil War, and when he later commanded the 45th Division he was able to outmanoeuvre the enemy in the battle of Brunete in July 1937 and in the August-September period during the Aragon offensive. He became a hero and foreign correspondents from around the world sought him out for interviews, which he gladly gave. He was a handsome man, who spoke fluent English and possessed the debonair manner of a European aristocrat. Soon articles about the General began to appear in the *New York Times* and the London *Times* as well as other leading newspapers around the world. This publicity and the ensuing notoriety would be Kleber's downfall. He became the envy of other Soviet generals, who felt that he was only seeking personal recognition whereas his deeds should be directed towards the aggrandisement of the Communist Parties of the world.

The personal attacks on Kleber took their toll as Orlov began to discover that the Spanish High Command was not including the General in any new operations. One day in the autumn of 1937, Kleber appeared at Orlov's headquarters to announce that he had been recalled to Moscow and wanted to bid Orlov farewell. Kleber was not happy with the recall although he took it in his stride. Orlov asked if he would prefer to remain in Spain. He agreed that he would because he had become infatuated with a young Spanish farm girl. Orlov cabled the KGB Centre with the request that Kleber be reassigned to his staff as his military background would be invaluable in building up the guerrilla warfare forces. The Centre complied with Orlov's wishes and instructed that Kleber disregard the recall orders and await further instructions while the Centre arranged for his transfer from the Red Army to the KGB. About two months later, the Centre informed Orlov that War Commissar Voroshilov had denied the request for the transfer and ordered Kleber's immediate return to Moscow. Orlov surmised that someone badly wanted Kleber's return. Before departing, Kleber made a request on behalf of his younger brother, who resided in Moscow and who could fall prey to the purges. As a last gesture to a close friend, Orlov cabled the Centre the same day noting the need of a German translator and requesting the services of Kleber's brother, who, as a native of Austria, naturally spoke fluent German. Less than two weeks later, Kleber's brother reported for duty.

General Kleber returned to Moscow. Orlov received only one letter from him in which he related that he was writing a history of the Spanish Civil War. This would be the last contact Orlov would ever have with him and he rightly assumed that Kleber had been liquidated along with the others. Many years later, after Stalin's death in 1953, Orlov would have a confirmation of this when the Soviet newspapers reported that General Emil Kleber (Lazar Stern), the hero of the Spanish Civil War, had been 're-habilitated posthumously'.

Now that we have some understanding of the political climate of the 1936–8 era, we must focus our attention on its effect on Orlov.

In the early part of January 1937, Orlov had received word from Slutsky that Yezhov had dispatched to Spain a former member of the Communist Party Central Committee by the name of Bolodin to head one of the Mobile Groups, which would ostensibly operate throughout Europe. While in Spain, Bolodin would masquerade under the guise of a chief commissar of a Soviet tank brigade. Slutsky wanted Orlov to know that Bolodin was a close friend of Yezhov's and he expected that Bolodin would be in contact with Orlov.

Standard regulations of the day obliged each KGB officer who had any business in Spain, was passing through, or just visiting, to make his presence known to Orlov's office. Bolodin never made any attempt to comply with the regulation. A short time later, Orlov attended a conference of the General Staff of the Republican Army in Madrid, where he noticed that Bolodin was also in attendance. Bolodin's identity had already come to his attention but Orlov did not give the slightest indication that he was already aware of Bolodin's identity and took no overt notice of him during the meeting. However, Orlov did see that Bolodin was making furtive glances in his direction and that, when their eyes happened to meet, Bolodin would turn his head. Orlov realised that Bolodin was studying his physical characteristics for possible future use and came to the plausible conclusion that the Mobile Group under Bolodin's direction was in Spain to liquidate him.

Orlov understood that if his reasoning was correct and that Bolodin's mission in Spain was to murder him, it had to be accomplished in a manner that would not instil fear in members of his own staff that could lead to their defection or alert the Spanish authorities that the KGB had had a hand in a murder on Spanish soil. The mission had to be efficiently planned and executed as an unsuccessful attempt would not only expose the clandestine work of the KGB but, more importantly, would lead to Orlov's divulging the most damaging secrets about Stalin and the KGB to the world.

The task of eliminating Orlov would be difficult at best considering the fact that the building that housed his organisation contained not only the offices but the living quarters of the entire group, including himself. The building was guarded day and night by the Spanish Civil Guard and no one was allowed entry without an authorised pass. When out of the confines and security of his office, Orlov took extra precautions while moving about the country by car. An armed agent of the Spanish Secret Service sat in the front with the chauffeur while Orlov had a .45 calibre automatic weapon strapped to his waist for added protection.

As already noted, Orlov had developed firearms skills during the early days of his career in the 12th Red Army. He had found that he had a natural talent with both the pistol and rifle and went on to become a recognised marksman at Red Army shooting competitions. These skills never left him, but he did take the opportunity to practise firearms while visiting his guerrilla warfare training camps.

The next step in Yezhov's plot to eliminate Orlov came by way of a cable from Slutsky in August 1937 informing Orlov that it had been learned that both the Spanish and German intelligence services had jointly conceived a plan to kidnap him on the Republican side as a means of extracting valuable intelligence information from him. Slutsky went on to say that because of his importance and knowledge of all facets of the Soviets' plans in Spain, he must be protected at all times. Accordingly, the KGB would be sending twelve bodyguards for Orlov's personal protection. Orlov immediately saw through this ploy and had no doubt that someone in the group would be under orders to kill him. He cabled back to Slutsky that there was no need to send the bodyguards as he was already under the personal protection of the Spanish secret police and, further, that his office and living complex were guarded around the clock by the Spanish Civil Guard. It was apparent that Yezhov's plan had failed as the KGB bodyguards never arrived in Spain.

Now realising more than ever that his life had been placed in jeopardy by his own people, Orlov immediately dispatched an aide to the front lines to recruit ten members of the German International Brigade. This Brigade was composed of hardened German Communists and Socialists, who were vehemently opposed to Fascism in their own country and had come to fight on the side of the Spanish Republicans. He specified that they had to be dedicated Communists who had seen action at the front and that their assignment should be viewed by them as a reward for their past services. These were the men who became

Orlov's constant companions in the capacity of heavily armed bodyguards.

For several months no new problems appeared on the horizon and Orlov devoted his attention to building his guerrilla warfare forces. Then, when everything seemed to be going smoothly, Yezhov's top lieutenant and envoy of death, Shpiegelglass, arrived in Spain without any prior warning. There was no apparent reason for Shpiegelglass's presence in Spain and the only assumption Orlov could logically make was that Shpiegelglass was after another victory at his expense. More than ever, Orlov could feel the danger of Shpiegelglass's presence and was aware that he was now in a life-or-death struggle for survival. Being somewhat of a fatalist, he made a solemn commitment to himself that should one of them have to die, it would be Shpiegelglass.

When Shpiegelglass arrived at the KGB headquarters in Barcelona, Orlov knew the cat-and-mouse game had begun. That evening Orlov and Shpiegelglass had supper at the luxurious mansion that had been the Soviet Consulate-General on Boulevard Tibidabo but now served as the KGB headquarters. Consul-General Vladimir Antonov-Ovseyenko had been recalled to Moscow in August 1937 and had never returned. After supper, Orlov took his nemesis on a brief tour of the city along with his chauffeur and ever-present Spanish secret service agent. After the tour they returned to the mansion, where they spent the remainder of the evening sipping wine and discussing events in the homeland. Shpiegelglass was quite open in discussing the shocking events that were taking place in the purges, some of which were very sensitive as well as damaging to Stalin. No doubt Shpiegelglass was doing so as he felt confident that in a short time Orlov would not be around to repeat the stories. Orlov was saddened to learn how his good friend Yuri Pyatokov had been tricked into confessing to crimes against the state and to hear the grizzly details of his murder in the cellar of the KGB building after the second great purge trial. The most startling news was that of Sergo Ordzhonikidze, who was a close friend of Stalin's from the early days of the Bolshevik Party. The Soviet press had reported that Ordzhonikidze had died of a heart attack, but now Shpiegelglass hinted that he had actually died of a gunshot wound under Stalin's direction. Orlov had heard rumours to this effect but, when he pressed for more details, Shpiegelglass turned to another matter. However, the following day he had a change of heart and provided the full background on the Ordzhonikidze affair.

They conversed until the early hours of the morning, when they both decided it was time to retire. When Orlov entered his bedroom with the intention of returning to show Shpiegelglass where he was to sleep, he noticed that Shpiegelglass had followed him. On seeing twin beds in the very large, comfortable room, as well as the balcony facing a park, Shpiegelglass exclaimed that it was such a wonderful room that they could continue their conversation until they fell asleep. Orlov knew that he could not give Shpiegelglass this opportunity and told him that he had a problem sleeping when anyone else was in the same room as him. He already had a room prepared for Shpiegelglass, complete with a regulation army cot, in the chapel of the Consulate. The chapel was very ornate with gold-leaf ceilings, religious works of art and a large crucifix.

Shpiegelglass was impressed by the magnificence and religious spirit of the chapel. As Orlov turned to depart, he recalled bidding Shpiegelglass goodnight with the final words, 'And if the spirits descend upon you, don't be scared.' Orlov returned to his bedroom, locked the door securely and, with his pistol at his side, went to sleep.

The next day he and Shpiegelglass drove to Valencia, where they had lunch with Soviet Ambassador Marchenko. After lunch, they proceeded to one of Orlov's guerrilla warfare training bases at Benimamet. Throughout the journey Orlov's German body-guards followed in another car, and it was obvious that Shpiegelglass was aware of their presence as he occasionally looked back furtively at the car that followed them in such close proximity. No attempt had been made to conceal the fact that the guards kept a tight surveillance on Orlov's car, but an unexpected incident occurred on the road to Benimamet that played into Orlov's hand. The road leading into the guerrilla camp was rather rough and Orlov's car suffered a flat tyre. The car pulled over to the side of the road and, within moments, the guard car pulled alongside and the four guards jumped out and rushed to Orlov's side with pistols and machine-guns drawn. Shpiegelglass appeared to be impressed by the quick response of the guards, but later remarked to Orlov that their actions had seemed excessive. Orlov responded that Nationalist guerrillas had heavily infiltrated the Republican side and, in consideration of Slutsky's warning that the guerrillas' principal objective was to capture him, he had no alternative. Shpiegelglass acted as though this was the first time he had heard of the matter, but Orlov knew better.

On that particular day at the Benimamet guerrilla camp, some 400 trainees were engaged in intensive guerrilla warfare, the likes of which Shpiegelglass had never encountered. He had never served in the military nor did he seem to be knowledgeable about military weapons. Groups of trainees were throwing hand grenades and Molotov cocktails, others were blowing up railway tracks and simulated arsenals, while still others were practising their skills on the rifle range. At the end of the day, when the exercises were completed, Shpiegelglass walked to one of the areas to pick up shards of shrapnel to take back to Moscow as mementos, or perhaps to boast about his ordeal, when several shots rang out in his direction. Shpiegelglass immediately ran, but stumbled and fell to the ground. He covered his head with his hands for protection and only half regained his composure when he heard no further shooting. Orlov had not witnessed the incident, having been in conference with the base commander, but learned that a gunsmith while testing a rifle had fired the shots using harmless blank cartridges. Those who did witness the incident claimed that Shpiegelglass had trembled for some time. Orlov strongly suspected that his assistant Colonel Kotov had had the gunsmith fire the shots, but Kotov strongly denied any part in the episode. Kotov, who was responsible for the day-to-day operations of all the guerrilla bases, just happened to be at the Benimamet camp that day. He was by nature a rascal, who enjoyed playing practical jokes, and it was no secret that he loathed Shpiegelglass.

On the road back to Barcelona, Shpiegelglass asked if he could visit Madrid. Orlov had no objection as he felt that Shpiegelglass wanted to brag back at the KGB Centre about making a dangerous visit to Madrid, which was under siege by the Nationalists. A car and an aide were made available and Shpiegelglass made the journey the following day. A few days later, the aide reported to Orlov that Shpiegelglass had had a private meeting with Bolodin and that he had been made to wait in another room for almost two hours. Following the meeting, Shpiegelglass had cautioned the aide not to tell anyone about it. The aide thought it strange that Shpiegelglass wanted to keep an innocuous meeting secret. What was curious to Orlov was the fact that Shpiegelglass had not mentioned to him that he would be contacting Bolodin while in Madrid. Orlov surmised that the purpose of their meeting was how best to go about eliminating him. No doubt Shpiegelglass had already determined that there was no easy way physically to penetrate his security guards in order to get to him and that they would have to devise another, more subtle means as they could not risk a political scandal in Spain. Orlov knew that it would only be a matter of time before the next stage in their game plan came to light.

The top floor of Orlov's headquarters, directly above his office, was the location of the Communications Section, where the powerful radio transmitter was maintained for contact with the KGB Centre. The alternative means of communicating with the Centre was by coded messages transmitted through the regular telegraph offices. The coding and decoding by this means was handled by two highly trained code clerks, one of whom was Grisha Stepanov, a very intelligent and practical young man. Code clerks were a very special breed of men, who were selected on the basis of their political background, usually membership of the Communist Party or the Communist youth organisation, Comsomol. They had to prove their dedication to the cause and their ability to be trusted with state secrets. After an intensive training by the highly secret Special Department of the KGB, they were assigned to serve with the Red Army or the Red Navy, the Ministry of Foreign Affairs, at Soviet Embassies around the world, or with the Soviet intelligence services at home and abroad. These code clerks not only had a window on the world but a window inside the inner-most workings of the Kremlin, which not even those at the highest level in the Politburo were privy to. According to Orlov, this was the one link in the chain that Stalin had failed to perceive or calculate into his deadly schemes and, accordingly, he neglected to gather the code clerks into his net of destruction. Orlov did not know why Stalin had failed to recognise this weak link, but thought it was perhaps the reticent and obscure nature of their work.

Orlov rated Stepanov as the best and most loyal code clerk he had ever had and one that kept up to date with what was happening in Moscow. Stepanov had followed the murderous path that Yezhov had taken to eliminate all KGB department chiefs and their deputies and was also aware that this path would event-ually lead to his superior. Shortly after Shpiegelglass departed for Moscow, Stepanov informed Orlov that Shpiegelglass had once come into the Communications Section wanting to send a coded message to the Centre. He had asked for the secret code book as he wished to encode the message himself. Stepanov advised him that, because of regulations, he could not give him the code book without Orlov's permission. Shpiegelglass acknowledged the requirement and said that he would obtain Orlov's authorisation. Shpiegelglass never returned to the Communications Section and, therefore, Stepanov felt that Orlov should be made aware of Shpiegelglass's request.

One evening, a short time later, Stepanov appeared at Orlov's living quarters and asked to speak with him. He looked worried and, in the absence of any cables from Moscow in his hands, Orlov knew that there was a problem. Stepanov asked if Orlov knew Commissar of the Tank Brigade Bolodin, to which Orlov advised in the affirmative and asked why he wanted to know.

Stepanov then proceeded to tell him that a former classmate from the KGB Code School, by the name of Sorokin, had recently arrived in Spain to take up his duties as a code clerk to Bolodin. When they had met recently, Sorokin had confided that Bolodin was a personal friend of KGB Chairman Yezhov and that he had been sent to Spain on a special terrorist mission. Stepanov thought that Orlov was probably already aware of this information but wanted to make sure.

They said goodnight and Stepanov started to leave, but stopped in the doorway, hesitated and turned around towards Orlov. In a rather awkward manner, he stated that there was something else. Sorokin had asked him about Orlov's wife and daughter. Sorokin already knew that they were living in the nearby town of La Garrica and that Vera was fourteen years old, but wondered if Orlov had any fears for his family. Stepanov said that he had informed Sorokin that the villa where Orlov's wife and daughter lived was heavily guarded. Without looking Orlov in the eye, Stepanov made one last comment before departing, something to the effect that he thought it best to tell him of Sorokin's interest in his wife and daughter.

The information from Stepanov came as a severe shock to Orlov. It was now apparent that Shpiegelglass was taking a different approach in his assignment to have Orlov returned to the Soviet Union. Undoubtedly he had come to the conclusion that it was next to impossible to get to Orlov on Spanish soil, and the only remaining avenue was to find Orlov's Achilles' heel. Little doubt remained that the meeting between Shpiegelglass and Bolodin in Madrid was a conspiracy to kidnap Orlov's wife or daughter, but more probably his daughter, as the bait to forcing him to return home.

What then crept into Orlov's mind was a matter that had haunted him ever since he had sat in on Zinoviev's and Kamenev's trial in Moscow in August 1936. He had been present from the opening statements through to the announcements of the death sentences for the defendants, and had felt that the trial was a fraud and a travesty of justice, but he had washed his thoughts aside for the moment as it was not of his doing. However, one incident that occurred during the trial had had a lasting effect on him and he had been unable to shake it from his mind. During the trial, Zinoviev had seemed to be a broken man, looking emaciated and fatigued, and at times staring objectively around the courtroom. Orlov was sitting in the front row dressed in the uniform of a KGB general. While another defendant was testifying, Orlov had noticed that Zinoviev was looking directly at him as if asking Orlov to tell him something, or wanting Orlov to do something for him. Zinoviev did not know Orlov personally but the moment their eyes met Orlov felt embarrassed and helpless. Only then did he realise why he had attracted Zinoviev's attention: his eyes were wet and tears were rolling down his face. Orlov had discreetly wiped the tears from his face and hoped that no one else in the courtroom had noticed. He then moved to a less prominent location at the back of the courtroom. That scene never left his mind, and on every occasion when he heard of another liquidation his mind would go back to the moment when his eyes met Zinoviev's. This was the small payment that had been extracted from him to ensure that he would never forget the hopelessness of a man when faced with transgressions beyond his control. Now it was Orlov's time to face these same transgressions.

This was the point that Orlov would later refer to as the defining moment, the moment in which he could no longer vacillate but one in which he had to arrive at a concrete decision. He had long toyed with the idea of defecting since his world in the KGB had begun to crumble around him, and he knew that sooner or later he would have to face squarely the prospect of making the awesome decision, knowing full well that he could no longer postpone the inevitable. His main stumbling block was the effect that Stalin's 8 June 1934 law would have on his mother and Maria's mother, who were both still alive and living in the Soviet Union. He knew that he would have to devise a plan to keep them both out of Stalin's reaches and the consequences of his despicable law.

The decision was made and there was no turning back; only the opportunity was lacking, but that would come once an escape plan had been formulated and perfected. The first consideration now was the safety of his wife and daughter; they needed to be placed in a position where their kidnapping would be near impossible. After thinking over the situation thoroughly, Orlov reached for the telephone and called his wife. Without wanting to alert her suspicion or cause her any alarm, he said that some urgent and unexpected business had come up and that he had to be in France by the next morning. He suggested that they make a holiday of the situation and that she pack enough clothes for at least a two-week stay. Maria was delighted at the prospect of a holiday and looked forward to visiting Paris and seeing old friends at the Soviet Embassy there. It was not unusual for them to make frequent trips to Paris as it was in Paris that Maria did her serious shopping due to the lack of material goods in wartime Spain.

Despite the fact that it was already early evening, Orlov felt that he had no time to waste. Accompanied by his German guards, he arrived at their villa in La Garrica within an hour of the telephone call. There he picked up Maria and Vera and drove straight through to the southern French town of Perpignan, where they stopped at the Grand Hotel. Orlov's office maintained a suite there and he knew the owner of the hotel quite well. The hotelier also owned the Grand Hotel in Toulouse, and Orlov made arrangements for a permanent suite to be secured there. During the journey, Maria was told the true nature of the trip and the need for expedience. She understood the situation perfectly. Maria and Vera were taken to Toulouse and Orlov returned to Barcelona to make future plans for their escape and to await a viable opportunity.

In Barcelona, Orlov felt satisfied that he had made the right move. He knew that Moscow would never consider a kidnapping of foreign nationals on French soil because the French response would be of such tremendous proportions that diplomatic relations between France and the USSR would be severed. After all, the kidnapping of General Miller had taken place only two months before, and a second similar incident would no doubt accomplish what the first incident had not. What Orlov did achieve besides the temporary safety of his family was the very valuable commodity called time.

Maria and Vera were safely ensconced at the Grand Hotel in Toulouse for almost the next three months. The trips to visit his family in Toulouse were long and tedious, so Orlov arranged for another secret hideout closer to the Spanish border. The small French spa resort of Amélie les Bains, which was only a few miles from the border near the road between Barcelona and Perpignan, was known for its hot mineral baths and accustomed to welcoming strangers. Here Orlov rented the Villa Al Soul and left his wife and daughter in the care of a trusted Spanish secret police officer who spoke fluent French.

The sands in the hourglass were about to peter out. On 22 June 1938, Orlov received a coded cable from the KGB Centre wanting to know if he would be able to proceed to an unspecified country adjacent to France during the first part of July for a meeting. He was immediately suspicious that this was yet another trap laid by Yezhov, but cabled back that he would be available. Orlov knew that he had been placed in a 'now or never' predicament. Time had run out and there was no turning back.

TWELVE

THE BREAK

The early months of 1938 were hectic at best with Maria and Vera safely hidden in France and Orlov slowly making plans for the day of defection that most assuredly would come. The top echelon of Orlov's staff were people he had known and worked with in the past and whose loyalty he did not have reason to question. However, what he could not chance was the revelation that he was planning to defect, notwithstanding the remote risk of betrayal by one of his own. He could not conceal the fact that his family was no longer residing in Spain and wisely let it be known that he feared their kidnapping, not on the part of the KGB but by the intelligence services of the opposing countries. However, inwardly he believed that his most trusted friends saw beyond the façade.

The Orlov residence in La Garrica was no longer being used as such but was rather a temporary repository for the family's household and personal belongings until their final disposition could be decided. On each trip to visit the family in France, Orlov sorted out those necessities needed to start a new life and took them with him. Maria would make the final decision as they would be highly restricted as to what they could carry on their journey to freedom and safety. Most of their household goods and excess clothing were inconspicuously given to Orlov's trusted chauffeur and members of the Spanish Civil Guard and secret service whose services he had come to rely on. He would casually mention that he was only getting rid of surplus that was no longer needed.

What Orlov did require was the financial means to make good

his escape. Throughout his long service with the Soviet Government, he had earned a salary well above the norm and had prudently saved and invested a portion for the rainy day that was about to come. He had first conceived a plan to save and invest during his posting to Paris in 1926 and would later open savings accounts in each of the capitals where he was later assigned. Each of these savings accounts had remained untouched through the years, growing with accumulated interest, as Orlov did not feel it prudent to invest money in a shaky Communist Government.

Sometime during early 1938, Maria went to their bank in Paris and had all of their foreign savings accounts consolidated into the one they held there. The Orlovs were more than amazed when they learned that their savings and investments had accumulated to slightly over $13,000 in US currency.

Orlov's financial situation was also helped by his hobby of antique collecting, long before it became fashionable. His collection and field of expertise was rare solid gold European wristwatches in the category of the Duchene Peyrot, Patek Philippe and Rolex, as well as unique American watches. While in Spain, he had also acquired a small collection of valuable Moorish daggers from the era of the 800-year occupation of the southern regions of Spain by the Mohammedan peoples of North Africa. His collections would not be left behind in Spain.

In addition to his watch and dagger collection, over the years Orlov had built up his art collection piece by piece. From their families, Orlov and Maria had inherited a number of fine antiques, including several large ornate Russian icons that were no longer fashionable in the world of Communism, as well as numerous pieces of fine furniture from the time of the Tsars. The watch and dagger collection posed no problem and could easily be transported to their next destination; however, their art collection, antique furniture and the larger inherited items were too bulky to be transported at short notice. They therefore had no choice but to sell the items that could not be taken with them as they had no idea when the time would come to flee, or the place of their final destination, or the means by which they would get there.

Maria made numerous trips to the grand auction houses of Paris which specialised in antiques, taking with her on the train those items she could handle and placing them on consignment. On her next trip to Paris, she would deposit the proceeds from the previous auction in their Paris bank account and so on. In the meantime, Orlov had established contacts in both Toulouse and Perpignan where he could dispose of the larger items, and on each of his trips from Barcelona he would go directly to the dealer with his load of the day.

When they had sold all of their tangible property and put these monies into their Paris bank account, they were surprised to learn that their liquid financial assets were in excess of $22,000. In order to comprehend the purchasing power of $22,000 in today's market, we have to stop and think of the 1938 US dollar. In 1938, the world was still in the midst of a worldwide depression and a US dollar still had a significant meaning. I can only equate the value of a dollar in 1938 to a personal experience that brings some perspective to the situation. In the summer of 1938, my father purchased a brand new top-of-the-line Chevrolet Master DeLuxe Sedan for well under $800. Today the equivalent would be well over $17,000. On the basis of this price comparison, Orlov's $22,000 would translate to $467,500 in today's market. Needless to say, there were relatively few people who had $22,000 in 1938.

When they totalled the grand sum of $22,000, they believed that they had all the money they would ever need to start a new life. They were wrong, it was a good start, but the problem arose when Orlov could not engage in any employment from the time he entered the United States in 1938 until he was able to surface in 1953. For fifteen years the Orlovs were in hiding from the KGB and were forced to live a spartan lifestyle as the cost of living spiralled ever upwards as a result of the Second World War.

Years later, Orlov recounted that it had been a difficult decision to part with his antiques, especially the art collection. He admitted that the sale of these possessions had brought in excess of $14,000, but he shuddered at the thought of what the current value would now be had he been able to bring all of the items to the United States. He noted that his collection had focused on French art, having developed an interest during his first tour in France in 1926. He had been able to acquire two paintings by Claude Monet, which he especially liked, and one painting and three sketches by Toulouse-Lautrec, which he prized the most because they represented the bygone era of Paris that he loved so much. In addition, he had collected prints by some of the famous French printmakers, some of which, because of their small size, he was able to keep, as well as a string of art by lesser known artists whom he liked. He also admitted that in the collection he had had a fairly large oil painting which he disliked but which had been given to him personally by the artist in Spain. He identi-fied the artist as Pablo Picasso, who had come to his attention as a consequence of the German Luftwaffe bombing of the Republican Basque town of Guernica on 26 April 1937. The raid had resulted in the deaths of over 1,600 people and the destruc-tion of the town and the bombing had become an international scandal.

It was in the summer of 1937 at a small social gathering at Defence Minister Prieto's villa next door to the Orlov residence that Orlov had met Picasso. The man was in his late fifties and, to Orlov, he possessed a dour disposition. However, on learning that Orlov was a high-ranking Soviet official and a member of the Soviet Communist Party, Picasso had displayed a more concil-iatory approach and it became apparent that he wanted Orlov's recognition and friendship. Picasso was then engaged in a commission for the Republican Government in Madrid and Valencia, and he and Orlov would meet socially from time to time to discuss art and Communism. One day shortly before Orlov moved his office and residence to Barcelona, he saw Picasso for the last time. At this meeting Picasso presented him with a Cubist painting, noting that the gesture was not only in the name of their friendship but also for Orlov's contribution to the cause of

Communism in Spain. Orlov realised that Picasso was an artist of some recognition and that his paintings were of value, but this was not the style of art he liked. He did appreciate the generosity but the Picasso painting was among the first to be sold.

The spring and early summer of 1938 had been unusually hot and dry in Spain and the fighting had intensified in the Civil War on all fronts with the Nationalists maintaining the upper hand. Orlov's guerrilla units were doing well behind the enemy's lines but support was inadequate to achieve the results that he craved. All this became minor in comparison to the importance of planning for his defection, which he now knew was inevitable. There was no one besides his wife whom he could safely rely on, and no one he could share his plans with or seek their advice; the awesome burden fell squarely on his shoulders alone.

Shpiegelglass's appointment as Acting Chief of the INO following Slutsky's murder was short-lived. His expertise as the butcher in charge of the Mobile Groups far outweighed his usefulness in the administrative position. By late April, communications from the INO were being signed by yet another Acting Chief by the name of Passov. Although the ranks of the Foreign Department had been decimated, there still remained a cadre of older, experienced officers that would be the logical choices to administer the department. However, Yezhov selected a young, inexperienced officer from one of the minor KGB departments for the position. Passov lacked the qualifications to direct the highly important functions of Soviet intelligence on a worldwide basis but did enjoy Yezhov's trust and confidence. He in turn had been an old friend of the Yezhov family and could be counted on for his loyalty. His main task was to lure back to the USSR the few officers still remaining abroad and to recruit new officers into the INO who would be more reliable for the needs of the service and not privy to the treacheries of Stalin. Passov maintained close liaison with Orlov's office in order to meet Stalin's ever-increasing demands for information concerning the conduct of the war in Spain. These frequent communications revealed to Orlov the intellectual deficits that Passov possessed as well as his ignorance of foreign intelligence operations in other countries.

The coded cable Orlov received on 22 June 1938 was under Passov's signature but it was evident to Orlov that it had been sent under Yezhov's direction. The cable inquired whether Orlov could leave his duties in Spain during the first half of July for a meeting in an unnamed country adjacent to France. He reasoned that the unnamed country could be Italy, Germany, Belgium or Switzerland, but he could not guess the specific intention of the meeting other than as a means to secure his return to Moscow for the purpose of his execution. Orlov answered in the affirmative as to his availablity.

Orlov now knew that his defection was imminent and he so advised Maria on his next trip to Amélie les Bains. They were aware that they would be unable to ship all the extra luggage they had packed with the essentials needed for their escape at the last moment. They had long ago decided that the United States would be the only country in the world where they had some hope of escaping the KGB and, therefore, this would be their intended destination. In 1938, there were no transatlantic flights as we know them today but there were very frequent transatlantic sailings of ocean liners from the French ports of Cherbourg and Le Havre, and trains for both ports left Paris from the Gare St Lazare. When the time came to act, Orlov would call Maria from Barcelona and, with the prearranged coded phrase, say, 'Did you hear from your mother?' On hearing this, Maria was to take the baggage immediately to the railway station in Perpignan and have it shipped to the 'Left Luggage' room in the Gare St Lazare. From there, they would be able to pick up the baggage and proceed either to Cherbourg or Le Havre, depending on which ocean liner they were able to book passage. They anticipated that they would have time between the date when he learned of his meeting in the country adjacent to France and the time when he would actually have to leave Barcelona en route to that destination.

The plan was for Maria to make preparations to vacate the

villa at Amélie les Bains. On receipt of his instructions from the KGB Centre, Orlov would telephone Maria on the day he was scheduled to leave Barcelona with the prearranged code phrase, 'How is my darling Vera today?', by which Maria and Vera would be alerted that Orlov was on his way to Amélie les Bains to pick them up. Then together they would proceed to the Grand Hotel in Perpignan, from where they would travel by train to Paris. If there was ample time, as he anticipated, there would be no necessity to conceal the fact that he was going on a business trip and no reason to withhold the date of his departure. However, the elaborate code was an added safety measure in the event that there was a last-minute change of plan beyond Orlov's control; it would also ensure that Maria understood that the plan was to proceed or be aborted.

The message from the KGB Centre arrived on Saturday, 9 July 1938, as Orlov sat in his office preparing a long communication for the Centre which was to go to Moscow by way of the noon diplomatic pouch. Two diplomatic couriers were standing by to take all of the morning's correspondence from Orlov's headquarters to the Soviet Embassy for transmittal to Moscow. Orlov sensed someone entering the office and looked up to see his faithful code clerk Stepanov standing in the doorway. He had in his hand a decoded cable from the KGB Centre and his face bore an expression of despair. In that instant, Orlov knew that it was the communication he was expecting but which he was also dreading to receive. He took the cable in his hand and read the first few sentences, which confirmed his fears. Nonchalantly, he put the cable aside and resumed working on his letter to the Centre. He asked Stepanov to return later after the diplomatic mail had gone out to retrieve the cable for the usual filing procedure.

As soon as Stepanov retreated from the office, Orlov grabbed the cable and quickly read through it a couple of times so as to absorb its contents thoroughly. Yezhov directed Orlov to meet the Soviet vessel S/S *Svir* on 13 or 14 July in Antwerp. On board the vessel, he would meet an unnamed high-ranking official, whose identity would be known to Orlov. The meeting was vital as matters of grave concern would be addressed. Orlov was first to proceed to the Soviet Embassy in Paris, from where he would be taken by an official Embassy car to Antwerp. Soviet Consul-General Biriukov in Paris would accompany Orlov to Antwerp to act as the Embassy's liaison at the critical meeting.

The cable went on to instruct that in the event that Orlov was not comfortable with meeting the emissary aboard the S/S *Svir*, he could use an alternative plan. He should proceed to the American Express Office in the area of the Antwerp docks, where he was to stand across the street from the AmEx Office three times a day on 14 and 15 July for five-minute periods at precisely 2 p.m., 4 p.m. and 6 p.m. He would then be contacted.

Orlov could only conclude that the trap was so transparent that Yezhov had had to add the alternative plan to allay Orlov's suspicions. In the first place, there was no reason why Yezhov could not have identified the official he was to meet in Antwerp by using the individual's code name, which would have been known to Orlov. In the unlikely event that the cable had been intercepted, the emissary's name would not therefore be compromised. Further, Consul-General Biriukov was known to Orlov as a covert KGB officer, who had in the past handled delicate assignments for the Special Department on the staff level of the KGB Centre.

In the event that Orlov opted for the alternative plan, he would be met by KGB operatives who would take him to a hotel room, where he would be sedated and taken to the S/S *Svir* for transporting back to the Soviet Union. Should there be a complication taking him to the ship and the Belgian police tried to intervene, Biriukov would be on hand to attest officially on behalf of the Soviet Government that Orlov was a shell-shocked commander from Spain being taken to the Soviet Union for psychiatric evaluation.

Now it was Orlov's turn to allay Yezhov's suspicions that he would see through the trap and escape. If Yezhov felt this a possibility, he would then dispatch the Mobile Group under Bolodin's command to eliminate Orlov in Spain, no matter what the consequences.

Orlov then replied to Yezhov's cable indicating that he would proceed to Antwerp and come aboard the S/S *Svir* on the 13th. He added that he had many pressing matters to attend to in Spain and was obliged to return as soon as possible. He also added several paragraphs to the long communication he was preparing when Yezhov's cable arrived. He posed several extra questions and requested guidance on other related matters that had not been previously answered by the Centre but which he had to act on when he returned from Antwerp. The last piece of correspondence to the Centre was a reminder that he had to have an answer to Prime Minister Negrin's request for additional aircraft engines and artillery spare parts by the time of his meeting with Negrin, which was to be scheduled as soon as possible following his return from Belgium.

All of this last-minute correspondence was calculated to induce Yezhov into believing that Orlov was not suspicious of Yezhov's true intentions. After all, why would Orlov be concerned with matters that could only be resolved on his return from Belgium if he had any inkling that perhaps he would not be returning?

As soon as the diplomatic couriers had departed with the morning mail, Orlov telephoned his wife. He told her that he would be departing in the morning, 10 July, and would spend that Sunday with the family. He then asked, 'Did you hear from your mother?' Time was now a very precious commodity, and the time it would take Orlov to reach Amélie les Bains was sufficient for Maria to take their luggage to the Perpignan railway station and return by the time her husband arrived the next day. Orlov knew that he would have a passenger from his staff on the trip to Paris and any excess baggage would look suspicious. He had already made it known that he was taking his wife and daughter to Paris for a short holiday while he continued on to Antwerp.

Orlov recalled that he detected something different about Maria's voice after he asked about her mother. He could only describe the strangeness in her voice as a 'quiver' and attributed this to her realisation that the day they had long expected was now a matter of hours away and that there was no more time to reflect on the past.

The few remaining hours the Orlovs had together that Sunday were spent finalising their plans and considering any contingencies that might arise. On Monday the 11th, Maria was to pay off any outstanding bills with the local merchants. On the morning of the 12th, she was to notify the landlord of their villa that they would be moving and pay the rent to the end of the month. The luggage that would travel with them was to be packed and ready. Orlov would arrive at Amélie les Bains by mid-afternoon to pick up the family and proceed immediately to Perpignan to catch the train to Paris.

The one crucial element that fell in their favour was the fact that Vera was not experiencing one of her frequent bouts of rheumatic fever, which would have confined her to bed. She had recently been in good health and this had continued over the vital period. Had this not been the case, the Orlovs' escape plans would have had to be postponed.

Orlov returned to his headquarters in Barcelona the following day, Monday the 11th, to complete any unfinished official business that he felt he should handle personally. He then began the necessary task of destroying all of his personal correspondence with friends and associates which might incriminate them, or reflect an association that might cause them unnecessary pain in the aftermath of his defection.

That evening he called his top assistant, Colonel Kotov, into his office and showed him the cable from Yezhov. Kotov displayed no outward emotion other than to shake his head in disbelief. After some hesitation, during which he seemed to be digesting the contents, he remarked that he felt much concern for Orlov's safety and that he should consider the consequences of complying with the cable. He then added that it did not make any sense for Orlov to travel to Antwerp when the individual whom he was to meet could have come more easily to Barcelona for the proposed meeting. Orlov did not divulge his true intentions, but somehow felt that in the back of Kotov's mind, the spectre of Orlov's defection was present. They had been friends for a long time and he valued Kotov's loyalty to him. As a farewell gesture, knowing that perhaps this would be the last time he would ever see his friend, Orlov suggested a brandy before they parted that evening. Their brandy glasses came together and Kotov made a toast with the epithet, 'To the future, may it all be good', after which Orlov toasted with the phrase, 'To our continued friendship'. The following day would be the last time Orlov would ever see his friend.

As the years took their toll, Orlov often thought about his friend and wondered what had become of him. He had long ago thought that Kotov had gone the way of the other KGB officers of that era, and it was not until August 1971 that he heard the fate of his top lieutenant when he was finally tracked down by KGB officer Mikhail Feoktistov in Cleveland, Ohio (see chapter 21).

Orlov noted that on that evening he showed Yezhov's cable to yet another of his aides. The aide scanned the cable and commented, 'They think they are so clever!'

Before retiring for the evening, Orlov sat in his chair in his private room and reflected on the good and bad times in his life. He then went over every element of his escape plan down to the minutest detail. He slept very little that night. The following day he kept to his usual routine so as not to give any indication that conditions were other than normal. Before retiring, he called his wife to let her know that the plan was definitely proceeding with the coded phrase, 'And how is my darling Vera today?', and that he would pick her and Vera up the next day.

The day of his departure from Spain, Tuesday the 12th, was a sad day for the General, although he did his best to conceal the fact. He would have liked to thank each member of his staff personally for their support during the two-year period that he had headed the delegation, but knew that this was not wise under the circumstances. Normally, when he was going on a business trip, he would delegate his authority and leave without any fanfare. He was surprised on this occasion to find five or six of his most trusted and loyal staff at the car waiting to say farewell. No doubt word of Yezhov's cable had got out. It was an awkward situation as Orlov could not reveal his real intentions even though he felt that with this group his confidence would not be breached. He felt a certain emotional tenseness among them as though they were trying to warn him not to go. As he shook hands with each of them, he felt a warmth in their grasps which he had never experienced before and which seemed to indicate a fondness for an individual they never expected to see again.

Orlov's Spanish translator Soledad Sancha accompanied him on the trip inasmuch as he was going to Paris on business and to have precluded Sancha would have caused suspicion. At the Spanish border town of La Junquera, Orlov's usual entourage of German bodyguards and his Spanish Civil Guard were relieved of their duties as was customary when crossing into France. As Orlov crossed the border, the sadness that he had experienced when saying his farewells to his staff in Barcelona returned. He knew that he would probably never return to Spain, a country and a people he had grown to love and admire.

Orlov picked up his family at Amélie les Bains as scheduled and they arrived in Perpignan in the late afternoon. He had the chauffeur take them to the Grand Hotel and then instructed him to go to the French town of Narbonne, a few miles north of Perpignan, and to wait there for his return in about five days. If he had not returned by the sixth day, the chauffeur was instructed to drive back to Barcelona. Orlov was well aware that the KGB bloodhounds who would be looking for him when he failed to arrive for the meeting aboard the S/S *Svir* would focus their attention on the chauffeur for immediate leads as to his whereabouts. Also, the less the chauffeur knew, the better it would be for him.

At the Grand Hotel the family had a leisurely dinner. Afterwards, Orlov had the opportunity to make reservations at the Crillon Hotel in Paris under a false name. As a safety measure, the reservations were made from a public telephone at a nearby hotel.

They left Perpignan on the evening train, which arrived the

next morning, 13 July, at about 8 o'clock at Paris's Gare d'Austerlitz on the Left Bank. Orlov purposely walked the Spanish translator out of the station to a taxi to make sure that he did not witness his own route out of the station. He suggested several small hotels to the translator and had already mentioned during the journey to Paris that he would be going on to Antwerp. Orlov had purposely chosen to stay at the Crillon Hotel as it was conveniently located on the Place de la Concorde directly across the avenue from the United States Embassy. The Soviet Embassy was located across the River Seine on the rue de Grenelle, and it was therefore very unlikely that anyone from the Embassy would be in the area of the Place de la Concorde and still less likely that anyone would encounter him at this particular hotel. The Orlovs took a taxi to the Crillon, where they registered under their alias.

The Orlovs never unpacked. There was no time to be lost as the 13th was the day he was expected in Antwerp. As soon as the KGB was satisfied that he was not going to appear, all hell would break loose. The KGB had powerful connections within the French Government and it would only be a short time before it picked up his trail. It was essential that the Orlovs leave France as quickly as possible.

Orlov called up the United States Embassy from the hotel and asked for Ambassador William C. Bullitt, only to find that he was out of town because of the Bastille Day holiday the next day. Orlov's elaborate plan had already gone awry and it was only the first day of his long journey to freedom. It was then that Maria suggested they try the Canadian Embassy as the next best alternative. The Orlovs presented themselves at the Canadian Embassy in some despair as the Soviet Union and Canada had no diplomatic relations at the time. They presented their Soviet diplomatic passports at the reception desk, at which point they were accorded diplomatic courtesies. They were taken into the office of the head of the Legation, where Orlov explained that they were seeking visas to enter Canada for a five- to six-week vacation in Quebec. As it turned out, this official had formerly been the Canadian Commissioner of Immigration. His courtesy even extended to a

personal letter for the Orlovs to present to the immigration officials in Quebec requesting that they be extended all possible assistance.

Another stroke of good fortune occurred in the form of a
Canadian priest, who happened to be at the Embassy at the same
time. On learning that the Orlovs intended to vacation in Canada,
the priest volunteered that the Canadian ship S/S *Montclare* was
sailing that evening from Cherbourg bound for Montreal. The
priest had some sort of connection with the steamship line and
was aware that there was space available.

In order to save precious time, Orlov instructed Maria to
proceed to their bank and withdraw their funds. She was then to
return to the Crillon Hotel to pick up Vera and check out. She
was then to proceed to the Gare St Lazare to make the necessary arrangements for their held luggage to be forwarded on the
mid-afternoon train to the dockside at Cherbourg. Orlov would
meet up with the family at the Gare St Lazare in time to catch
the same train.

In the meantime, Orlov went to a travel agency on the Avenue
de l'Opéra which he remembered from past shopping trips. Space
was still available on the S/S *Montclare* and he was able to purchase
cabin class tickets to Montreal. He also purchased round-trip
tickets back to France in another attempt to throw the KGB off
the trail. However, he had not counted on the unusually heavy
traffic due to the next day's Bastille holiday. The taxi went at a
snail's pace, making Orlov wonder why he hadn't walked the short
distance to the Gare St Lazare. With only minutes to spare, he
met up with the rest of the family and they were able to catch
the train to Cherbourg. Within two hours they were at the dockside and had verified that their held luggage would be placed
aboard the ship. Safely ensconced in their stateroom aboard the
S/S *Montclare*, they were only an hour away from sailing time and
an eternity away from the life they had always known.

The S/S *Montclare* left Cherbourg at dusk and, as Orlov and
the family stood by the ship's rail, they could see the lights of
the city slowly fading from view. After Maria and Vera retired to

their cabin, he remained glued on deck while the ship made its passage through the English Channel westwards to the new world. He later recalled that his thoughts were on his unknown future and the anticipation of things to come. Like a drowning man, his life seemed to roll by in his mind and time was of no immediate importance; before he knew it, the land on both sides of the Channel had disappeared and the ship was out to sea. He did not retire until the very early morning of the next day.

The ocean journey was rather uneventful but relaxing and enjoyable. At least aboard ship they had no reason to fear the KGB and thus they experienced freedom at first hand for the first time. Yet despite the temporary tranquillity, there remained one piece of unfinished business that Orlov had to attend to before they reached Canada and one that he dreaded undertaking: he had to tell Vera what was happening. Vera believed that the family was on a holiday and was thoroughly enjoying the adventure with the anticipation of a girl of her age. What she did not realise was that she would never again see her beloved grandmothers, her friends or the land of her birth. Because the Orlovs had spent most of their time abroad since 1926, Vera's love of her native Russia and the Russian people ran very deep in her, probably more so because of these frequent absences. She had led a very sheltered life because of her fragile health and was blissfully unaware of the true suffering of her people or of Stalin's tyranny. These facts had always been hidden from her because of her frailness, not so much to deceive her but to spare her from the truth.

A few days before they were scheduled to arrive in Canada, the Orlovs took their daughter into a secluded section of the ship's main salon. There, with much difficulty, they told her the truth about conditions in the Soviet Union and why Orlov was having to break with his Government. She seemed to understand the gravity of their plight as tears began to roll down her cheeks. It was apparent that the world she knew and understood – all of her dreams, hopes and desires – had at that moment vanished forever. Unselfishly, her hurt was not for herself but for her parents, who had long struggled and suffered in the name of the Communist Revolution. When Orlov told me of this day, he remarked that it was then that Vera left her childhood and became an adult.

Shortly before the S/S *Montclare* arrived in Canada, Orlov made arrangements to disembark in Quebec rather than Montreal, the destination called for when he had purchased the tickets. He felt it reasonable that by now the KGB in Paris could have located the travel agency where he had bought the tickets and would have had ample time to dispatch a KGB Mobile Group from Mexico to meet the ship when it docked in Montreal. On arrival in Quebec in the early morning of 21 July, the Orlovs immediately went to the Hotel Château Frontenac to rest for a few hours and decide on their next step. By that afternoon they had boarded a train bound for Montreal.

The train journey to Montreal was both tranquil and full of anticipation of the unknown. The Orlovs were enthralled by the vast beauty of the countryside that rolled by and were utterly impressed by the passing panorama of small villages and farmsteads. In some respects, the nature of the land was similar to parts of their native Russia. As Orlov sat looking around the coach, he could not help but wonder about his fellow passengers, who appeared to be farmers, businessmen and families. He knew that each one of them had roots in the country and knew exactly where their destination would be, a luxury that he did not have. In his own way he envied them and wished that someday his family's circumstances would be the same.

On their arrival in Montreal they checked into the Windsor Hotel, but within a few days moved to a private apartment where they felt more secure. They had no idea how long they would be in Canada but their ultimate goal was the United States. In the meantime, their financial funds were placed in a Montreal bank under Maria's name, as a prudent contingency for her and Vera's financial support in the event that the General was tracked down by the KGB.

It was in Montreal that Orlov finalised a plan that he had

previously conceived to blackmail Stalin in a brazen attempt to keep him from murdering his mother and mother-in-law, both of whom resided in Moscow. He knew that he could not reason with Stalin to save their heads in the name of humanity as this route had been to no avail previously in similar circumstances. The only force Stalin understood was retribution, not on his terms but on Orlov's. Orlov did possess the instrument of retribution in the form of his knowledge of the dark side of Stalin in his terrorist manipulation of the Soviet Government. Should Stalin take revenge on Orlov by murdering their mothers, Orlov would expose Stalin's secret crimes to the world.

Orlov decided to write two letters outlining his knowledge and intentions. One letter would be for Stalin and the other, a copy of the same letter, for KGB Chairman Yezhov. In this manner, he rationalised, both of these very powerful men would be aware of his position and would not undertake any unilateral action without consulting the other. The letter would be in two parts. The basic letter would forewarn Stalin not to take any revenge against his mother and mother-in-law as he would then carry out his threat. He warned that a copy of Stalin's crimes were lodged with his attorney and should he, or any member of his immediate family, be kidnapped or murdered by the KGB, his attorney was under instruction to have the record of Stalin's crimes published immediately. Orlov knew Stalin well enough to be confident that he would abide by his rules. In order to impress on Stalin that he did possess damaging information about his crimes, he attached a separate addendum to the letter detailing these crimes. For Yezhov's consideration, the addendum also contained references to KGB espionage operations that Orlov had been privy to while engaged in illegal activities on behalf of the KGB in Europe. Orlov made it clear that if Stalin took no action against him or his family, he would not breach his end of the bargain and, accordingly, would not reveal what he knew.

Orlov was well aware that he was playing a dangerous game, but also knew that the stakes were high when it came to his family's safety. He felt secure that Stalin would not take revenge until he could kidnap Orlov and force him to reveal his attorney's whereabouts, thus preventing publication of the letter and its addendum.

Orlov wrote the two lengthy letters on stationery that he had purchased for this purpose in Paris as an additional measure to delude the KGB into thinking that he must be hiding there. He knew that he could not mail the letters directly to Stalin and Yezhov as the stamps would reveal that he was in Canada. He further rationalised that on seeing the letters addressed to two such important people, the postal authorities would turn the letters over to their intelligence service, who would in turn probably reveal the startling revelations to the press, thereby destroying Orlov's only leverage over Stalin. The only way he could safely accomplish this mission was to have a personal messenger take the letters to Europe. He pondered the delivery problem from every aspect and came up with a plan which he believed to be foolproof.

Back in the autumn of 1932, on Orlov's reconnaissance visit to the United States, he had come into contact with several cousins in New York whom he felt he could count on for support. He therefore telephoned his cousin Isak Rabinowich and explained that he was in trouble and that he needed his assistance in taking a letter to France. Rabinowich was unable to attend to the request personally but suggested another cousin, Nathan Koornick, who was a bachelor living in Philadelphia. Rabinowich agreed to contact Koornick and, if Koornick would comply, he was to check in at the Windsor Hotel in Montreal, where he would be contacted by Orlov. Within a few days Koornick was in Montreal, where he checked into the Windsor Hotel and made contact with Orlov, who related that he was in deep trouble with the Soviet Government and needed Koornick to deliver two letters personally to the Soviet Embassy in Paris. Koornick had hardly known Orlov in Russia, but being considerably older had been close to Orlov's father. He therefore agreed to carry out the task because of this strong family tie. However, he needed to return to

Philadelphia in order to obtain a US passport and make further arrangements for the trip.

Koornick returned to Montreal in the first week of August, whereupon Orlov gave him very explicit instructions as to how he was to deliver the two letters. The timing was perfect as the Canadian Pacific Steamship Line vessel that Koornick would take from Montreal was scheduled to arrive in France in ample time for him to be at the Soviet Embassy in Paris on a religious holiday, the Feast of the Assumption, on Monday, 15 August. Although the Soviets did not recognise religious holidays, their diplomatic staff did acknowledge the holidays with a reduced staff.

Koornick was instructed to take a taxi to the Embassy, have the driver wait while he entered the Embassy and lay two bulky manila envelopes on the reception desk, then immediately leave the Embassy and have the taxi depart the area. The letter addressed to Yezhov was contained in one of the manila envelopes addressed to Kislov, the KGB legal *rezident* at the Embassy, with instructions from 'Schwed' (Orlov's code name in Spain) that Kislov not open the letter marked for Yezhov's personal attention but have it forwarded immediately. The letter addressed to Stalin was contained in the other manila envelope, which was addressed to the Embassy's Chargé d'Affaires Hirschfeld. A note contained therein instructed Hirschfeld to forward the inner letter to Stalin immediately and cautioned him not to tell Kislov that he had received the communication for Stalin's personal attention. Orlov feared that if Kislov was aware of the letter to Stalin, he might communicate with Yezhov and the letter might be suppressed. Orlov and Hirschfeld were old personal friends, and he could rely on Hirschfeld to carry out his instructions explicitly. The two letters bore Orlov's thumbprint as a means of positive identification.

Following his departure from the Embassy, Koornick was instructed to go to the main post office in Paris, where he was to mail a letter that had been pre-written by Orlov and addressed to Soviet Ambassador Surits in Paris advising him that the two letters had been dropped off at the reception desk at the Soviet

Embassy. The letter instructed the Ambassador to cable both Stalin and Yezhov to alert each of them that they would be receiving letters from 'Schwed'. As a last precaution to ensure that the two letters came to Stalin's and Yezhov's attention, Koornick was instructed to go to the telegraph office in Paris and send a wire, which had been prepared in advance by Orlov, to the KGB Centre in Moscow, advising that the two letters intended for Stalin and Yezhov had been deposited at the Soviet Embassy in Paris with instructions that they be forwarded to the two leaders. Orlov knew that he had covered all contingencies and felt assured that Stalin and Yezhov would receive the letters.

What Orlov also hoped to accomplish by this elaborate scheme was for the KGB to believe that he was hiding in France, or, perhaps better, to suppose that it had been Orlov who had entered the Embassy. He would hardly have been known to a clerk at the Embassy, and the delivery would be executed in such a speedy manner that it would confuse anyone guessing the identity of the caller. Even if the KGB had traced him to Canada, the roundtrip steamship ticket and the delivery of the letters would indicate Orlov's return to Paris.

Koornick complied with all of Orlov's instructions, but on his return to Montreal found that Orlov had already departed for an unknown destination. He then got in contact with his cousin Isak Rabinowich, who in turn informed him that he should contact Orlov at the King George Hotel in New York. There, Koornick was able to report to Orlov personally that the mission had been successfully accomplished. For the time being at least, Orlov had outwitted his adversary.

About a week after Koornick departed for France with the two letters, Orlov went to the US Embassy in Ottawa to request visas for the family to visit the United States. The secretary of the Embassy whom he dealt with had in the past been assigned to the diplomatic service in Spain for a number of years and was anxious to speak in Spanish with a fellow diplomat. He disappeared with the Soviet diplomatic passports and, on his return, related that the American Ambassador wished to know if Orlov cared to speak with him and senior members of his staff. Orlov was delighted at the prospect and affirmed that he would be honoured to do so. He was then taken into a large conference room, where he met the Ambassador and his aides. There the focal point of the diplomat's interest was the Civil War in Spain on a broad spectrum. The questions asked of Orlov were perceptive, and he tried to answer them as best he could with the exception of those questions which could possibly reveal Republican military secrets. Orlov enjoyed the exchange and was pleased when their passports were returned to him to find that the Ambassador had placed a liberal time limit on their proposed visit to the United States, as each passport was stamped to indicate that the visa was valid for a period of one year.

Orlov stated that when he walked out of the Embassy, he felt so ebullient that he didn't even think his feet were touching the pavement. He had taken a major step on his journey and had done so without the slightest hitch. He had anticipated that he might have a problem in obtaining the visas for entering the US, but wishfully deferred making an alternative plan as he had banked all his hopes on going to the United States.

Orlov's trip to and from Ottawa was by bus. On the return journey, he could hardly contain himself and wished that he could fly bodily to Montreal and break the good news to Maria and Vera. When he did arrive at their apartment and was finally able to break the news, it was apparent that they also shared his excitement. Within two days, the Orlovs had left Montreal for the United States.

The Orlovs entered the United States on 13 August 1938 at Rouses Point in the State of New York, exactly a month to the day after the General had broken with the Soviet Union and the KGB.

When the Orlovs made that first step into the United States, they did so with great joy, anticipation of events to come, and the knowledge that they were in a safe sanctuary for at least the time being. They were all aware that the dark clouds of the KGB still hung heavily over their heads, but were satisfied that the avenue they had taken to freedom was not only the right one but the only one they could logically have taken at the time. Orlov had no way of knowing that he would successfully elude the KGB for over thirty-one years and that he would reside in the United States for almost thirty-five years before he died, without ever again seeing his native land or hearing what had happened to his or his wife's mother. In time, the United States gave much to the General and he in turn reciprocated to the best of his ability without compromising his principles.

PART 2

A SPECIAL AGENT IN THE FBI

THIRTEEN

MY FBI JOURNEY BEGINS

My association with General Orlov began as a result of a rather unique situation which could best be described as an association by default, but in the long run seemed to have been predestined. As with many aspects of life, this path began with the roots that were planted when I was appointed a Special Agent of the Federal Bureau of Investigation back in January 1951.

This was still the era of J. Edgar Hoover, the Director of the FBI, whose leadership and administrative skills built the FBI into a world-renowned investigative organisation. Today I recognise that he is a much-maligned person, but I have no problem countering the misconceptions and falsehoods about him that have been generated since his death. However, here I merely wish to make the affirmation that I was proud the day I entered service with the FBI and, to this date, continue to value my association with Hoover and the FBI.

That winter's day in January 1951 was as bad as it gets for that time of the year in Washington DC and the inclement weather continued throughout the period of my training. At the time, the FBI headquarters were located within the Justice Building on Pennsylvania Avenue, being a function of the US Department of Justice. Training was split between classes at the Justice Building and classes and firearms instruction at the FBI Academy at Quantico, Virginia. I was very excited on the day I first reported to the Justice Building to be sworn in as a special agent and to receive my FBI badge, a .38 calibre Smith and Wesson revolver, a huge number of training manuals and an extra large leather briefcase with a very sturdy lock. I wondered if I would ever need such a large briefcase, but in my first office of assignment learned that it had a direct correlation to something called 'case load'. My official FBI credentials would be received at a later date.

The qualifications to even be considered for an appointment were unusually high and included a law degree, an accounting degree with certification as a CPA, or on a highly selective and very limited basis an experienced federal law enforcement agent. After graduation from the University of Michigan in Ann Arbor, I became a US Treasury agent assigned to the Bureau of Alcohol, Tobacco and Firearms (ATF) investigating criminal violations, thus meeting the preliminary requirements in the process of becoming a special agent with the FBI. Later I would pursue a law degree while with the FBI taking night classes at the University of Miami at Coral Gables, Florida, and at the John Marshall School of Law, which would later become affiliated with Cleveland State University. Having met the basic requirements, the applicant was subjected to personal interviews by FBI officials and a written examination; these were followed by a physical examination. Having met these additional requirements, the next step was a microscopic background investigation, which scrutinised the applicant's life from the date of his birth. The investigation looked into the applicant's character, reputation, honesty and loyalty to the concepts of our democratic form of government in the United States. The applicant had to measure up to the FBI's motto: 'Fidelity, Bravery and Integrity'.

The remaining hurdle was the needs of the Service. As to the process in its entirety, many are called but few survive all of the stages. I was one of the fortunate ones.

Training to become an FBI agent would make the rigorous wartime training that I received to become a commissioned officer in the US Navy seem like child's play. This was my first introduction to long hours under very severe and demanding conditions. The rules and regulations that govern the day-to-day operation of the FBI are well defined and contained in a very large manual; there are no conceivable circumstances of conduct or policy that are not in the manual. I always knew what was expected of me, where I stood and what the penalty would be if I breached any of the rules or even tried to circumvent them. The FBI Academy is located at the US Marine Base at Quantico, and I always suspected that this was because both are highly motivated and disciplined organisations which are totally dedicated to their mission.

Firearms training at the Academy was arduous at any time of the year but more so during the bleak winter months of January and February 1951, when the temperatures hovered at or below freezing point almost every day. No quarter was given, as I recall trying to fire a weapon with seemingly frozen fingers and knowing that I would have to qualify without any dispensation for the weather. The only redeeming factor was that the food and table service at the Academy were excellent.

I would have to rate the calibre of the teaching staff at the Academy superior to that which I had previously experienced in the Navy or at my university; however, as I reflect back on those days, it was perhaps my intense desire to learn and be a part of the FBI that made me reach this conclusion. The FBI has jurisdiction over more than 100 statutes in the Federal Code and the administration for investigating violations of these statutes is delegated to various Divisions headed by an Assistant Director. The Domestic Intelligence Division principally handled internal security, espionage and foreign intelligence matters, while the General Investigative Division and Special Investigative Division handled criminal investigations. Each Division was broken down into Sections or Branches headed by a Section or Branch Chief. These three Divisions were supported by the Laboratory Division. There are other Divisions in the FBI that perform important organisational functions, but the ones I was most concerned with were those related to criminal and security matters. On the field office level, these Divisions are broken down to the security or criminal squads.

Our lecturers were usually Section or Branch Chiefs, or one of their respective supervisors, who would review a particular statute from its legal aspect and then illustrate it with some major cases being handled in the field. I was always fascinated by the cases dramatised by each lecturer and, by the time they had completed their presentations, knew that I couldn't wait to handle their statute in the field. However, the most mesmerising lecturers to me were those from the Domestic Intelligence Division, and in particular Emory M. Gregg and Robert J. Lamphere. Both were the definitive experts on espionage matters in the United States intelligence community and I was spellbound every time I heard one of their lectures.

At the time, Lamphere was handling the most prominent spy case of the century, that of Julius and Ethel Rosenberg, who were part of the KGB spy network that had handed over US atomic secrets to the Soviets. Both Rosenbergs were judged guilty and executed. Lamphere's impressive role only came to light years later when his early work in the VENONA project was made public. VENONA was the breaking of the Soviets' code, which, through intercepts from the KGB and the GRU to their spy network in the United States, was able to identify the Rosenbergs and other members of the espionage ring. Lamphere left the Bureau in 1955 and in 1986 his book *The FBI-KGB War* was first published.

Following graduation from the FBI Academy, I was assigned to the FBI field office at Boston, Massachusetts, much to my dismay. Several weeks before graduation, each candidate is interviewed about his preferred first office assignment. I should have been prepared for my unfortunate destiny as I was certainly not naïve, having served in the US Navy where personal preferences are subordinate to the needs of the Service. This also held true in the FBI, but I thought I held a few aces in this particular game of chance which would get me to one of the more desirable FBI field offices. Long before I ever seriously thought about the FBI as a career, my wife Ruth joined the FBI in 1947 as a stenographer; she would later become the secretary of the supervisor handling the major jewel theft squad at the Florida field office in Miami. One of the special agents on this squad was transferred to the FBI Academy, and it was this particular individual who interviewed me. He fondly recalled his own assignment at the

Miami office and spoke with kindness regarding Ruth, whom he knew quite well. I was lulled into feeling that I had his confidence and stressed that in no way would I feel comfortable with an East Coast assignment and, in particular, Boston. Instead, I suggested that one of the field offices in Texas would broaden my career experiences. To this day I can't recall why I opted for Texas as I had never even set foot in the state, but perhaps I had seen one western film too many in my youth.

Another graduation initiation was the ritual meeting with J. Edgar Hoover. The week before graduation my class, as was the case for all the classes that preceded mine, was primed for the event that took place in the Director's office. In retrospect, this was perhaps the most important and critical milestone of the entire training, and it was aptly known to the trainees as the make-or-break phase. Mr Hoover already had each of our personnel files so as to become acquainted with our individual backgrounds, our performance records during training and, most importantly, the written observations and evaluations that our instructors were obliged to make on each candidate. As we individually met and chatted with Mr Hoover, several Bureau officials and our class counsellor, an agent from the field who was assigned to chaperon the class through training and who perhaps knew us best of all, stood nearby. Mr Hoover took the opportunity to assess our overall appearance, our ability to carry on a conversation and convey our thoughts, as well as the manner in which a candidate responded to a particularly adroit question posed by the Director to elicit a response requiring a degree of concentration. Each candidate had to meet Mr Hoover's personal criteria of what an FBI agent should be; in those instances when someone did not come up to expectations, a slight unseen nod from Mr Hoover to one of the Bureau officials standing nearby for this purpose would end the agent's career, notwithstanding the fact that it was only a week to graduation. Even a 'wishy-washy' handshake, which was not considered masculine, was a cause for Mr Hoover's concern. In all fairness and to give an objective view of this point of the process of becoming an FBI agent, I should note that most of the candidates that did not fit the criteria had already dropped by the wayside. No one in my class was left behind as a result of our meeting with Mr Hoover.

The issue of homosexuality was of prime concern to Mr Hoover and the slightest indication that an agent or employee of the FBI was bent in this direction was the cause of immediate termination. FBI special agents were not covered under the provisions of the Federal Civil Service Act and had no recourse to another authority. This was recognised as a necessity in the operation of an organisation that handled the most sensitive matters of a national interest. I and my fellow agents were comfortable with this arrangement as we understood the necessity for it. Some twenty-five years after Mr Hoover's death, innuendos surfaced that he was himself a transvestite and homosexual. There has never been an established basis for these allegations when investigated to the source, and in my long tenure with the FBI I never heard a word disparaging Mr Hoover's character; had this been the case, the substance of the breach would have spread like wildfire throughout the field.

The day I first reported to the Justice Building to be sworn in as a new agent there were about fifty-five fellow neophyte agents in my class; the next day there were two less. On that first day, I noticed two fellows sitting in front of me who seemed to know one another. The class later learned that they had committed a cardinal sin by leaving their newly issued revolvers and training manuals in their extra large leather briefcases in a locked car but in plain sight of passers-by. The car had been broken into and the government property stolen. These had to be the shortest Bureau careers on record. Although I was compassionate to their plight, I did learn a valuable lesson and henceforth would guard the government property entrusted to my care with the zeal of a mother hen guarding her young.

I will never forget the day I reported to the Boston office as it was on Easter Sunday, 25 March 1951. The office was located in the heart of the city in a commercial building at 100 Milk Street. This was my first encounter with the cow path streets of the city; no one seemed to be able to direct me to Milk Street, so we drove around the downtown area of the city for at least an hour before locating the office.

The closest I ever got to 'spy' work at the Boston office was in the early part of the summer of 1951. Unfortunately, it was not real spy work but rather the type that films are made of. I had been assigned to the criminal squad and had an exceptionally good feeling about this assignment. One day, my partner Russell L. Dagley and I were walking down the hallway in the building that housed the Boston office when we walked past the ASAC (Assistant Special Agent in Charge), Ed McCabe, walking in the opposite direction with an unknown gentleman. Before we could get too far, McCabe caught up with us and informed us that the individual with him was Louis de Rochemont, a producer who was making a film about the FBI using Boston as the location of the story. He told us that when de Rochemont had seen Russ and I, he felt that we fitted the public's conception of FBI agents and wanted us in the film. I could have thought of several thousand SAs who could have fitted this conception as well, but both Russ and I accepted the offer. The feature film was named *Walk East on Beacon* and starred George Murphy, with Finlay Currie and Virginia Gilmore in supporting roles.

Throughout my assignment at the Boston office I couldn't help but notice that all of the first office agents were being transferred to the Bureau's office in New York City for the most part and to a lesser extent to the larger FBI field offices on the East Coast such as Philadelphia, Newark and Baltimore as well as Chicago in the Midwest. It was the Bureau's policy to round out a new agent's career experience by only keeping him in his first office for less than a year and then to move him on to a more permanent assignment. The New York office was the largest Bureau field office and was also the most difficult to staff because of the large turnover of agents who didn't feel comfortable in New York. It didn't take me long to see the handwriting on the wall and I dreaded the prospect of probably ending up in the New York office.

However, I had a stroke of good luck which brought me to the personal attention of the SAC (Special Agent in Charge) of the Boston office, Joseph E. Thornton. As the Boston office was one of the largest in the Bureau, and at the time perhaps an additional 60–100 agents were at the office on 'special assignment' to help solve the then most notorious case of the decade, the robbery of the Brinks Armoured Car Company, the SAC had little time to afford to a new agent other than the customary 'handshake and introduction' on the agent's arrival at the office.

To my good fortune, I was reassigned to a case that fell under the purview of the relatively new Anti-Racketeering Statute. The older and much more experienced agent who had originally been assigned the case was up to his neck in work and could not possibly give the case the full attention that it required. In brief, members of the truckers union were harassing non-union long-distance truck drivers by direct intimidation and, in some instances, were shooting at truckers as they drove along the federal highway in the vicinity of Worcester, Massachusetts. This impeded inter-state commerce and violated the new statute. Somehow I was able to extract five written confessions and on the day the case came to trial, each defendant pleaded guilty; each was then sentenced to various terms to be served in federal penitentiaries. For a number of years, this case became the classic example under the statute and the subject of lectures given at the FBI Academy to new agents and agents returning for criminal in-service training.

The case brought me to the personal attention of the SAC and, as I had a background in Spanish, he recommended me for an assignment to the San Juan (Puerto Rico) field office. Such a recommendation by a SAC for a first office agent was an unusual departure from Bureau policy. I received the letter of transfer to San Juan in early December 1951 and was extremely grateful that it was not to the New York field office or one of the other large East Coast offices.

My wife and I left Boston a few days before Christmas 1951 en route to San Juan, by way of a brief holiday with Ruth's parents, who lived in Miami. It was a typical bitterly cold, snowy day when we arrived at Boston's Logan International Airport. As I entered the terminal, I had visions of future balmy days in San Juan, stopped to take off my protective rubber overshoes and dropped them to the floor. I never looked back.

On New Year's Day 1952 I travelled to San Juan, while Ruth remained in Miami with her parents. In those days it was an adventure to even get to San Juan as Eastern Airlines only had one flight there from Miami which arrived at around 2 a.m. at Isle Grande Airport, an old abandoned Second World War naval air station near downtown San Juan. As I had nowhere to go, I took a taxi to the FBI office, which was located in the Banco Popular Building in the so-called 'old city'. The first thing I observed in gaining entrance to the office was the unusually stringent security measures, which were a result of the attempted assassination of President Harry S. Truman by fervent members of the Nationalist Party of Puerto Rico (NPPR) some ten months before and which had led to upheaval on the island. All FBI offices maintain personnel on a twenty-four hour basis; however, it was unusual to find an agent working on a report that early in the morning. The agent was Charles Peck, a big fellow from near Batavia, New York, who handled the NPPR. This did not bode well as I immediately recognised that I had again landed in an office where much overtime would be expected of me.

I took a room in a vintage residence on Calle McKinley in the suburb of Santurce, which had once been the Honduran Embassy when Puerto Rico was still in the possession of Spain. The house had been leased by Helen Tooker, a reporter for the San Juan daily newspaper *El Mundo*, and as she had more space than she required she rented at least three spare bedrooms, mainly to FBI agents in transit. My bedroom was huge and must have been either a reception-room or the Ambassador's office. It was furnished with extra large pieces made from Honduran mahogany from before the turn of the century.

Ruth joined me at the end of February and we shared the beautiful yet outrageous bedroom for another month. One thing we learned early on was that the house and all the mahogany furniture were infested with termites. We were then able to secure an apartment in the Gallardo Apartments, which were being built on Calle Luis Muñoz in the suburb of Rio Piedras, and we were the first tenants to move into the three-storey building.

The San Juan office was normally one of the smallest in the Bureau but had expanded its agent personnel as a consequence of the NPPR. The vast majority of agents were assigned to the NPPR case and other collateral matters, so I considered myself lucky to be assigned to the criminal squad, which only had five members. Most of my work was mundane handling of criminal violations and, for the most part, tracking down Selective Service Act (SSA) violators. Unlike chasing draft dodgers in the US, the opposite held true in Puerto Rico at the time because of the poor economic conditions on the island. It was not unusual to find a violator who would register at two or more draft boards in a manoeuvre that he felt would enhance his chances of being drafted. He would be drafted by one of the boards and subsequently reported delinquent by the others. There were also those violators who migrated to the Puerto Rican colony in New York on $100 flights aboard war-surplus C-47 twin-engined cargo planes and without malice neglected to notify the draft board of their change of address. I never handled any high-profile criminal cases in Puerto Rico but I did find some challenges and enjoyed the work.

On only one occasion did my work in Puerto Rico have any impact on the national interest. Sometime during the summer of 1953, I received a lead to locate an SSA violator who was believed to be hiding in San Juan. The fugitive, Rafael Cancel Miranda, was not the run-of-the-mill SSA violator but a dedicated and hardened member of the NPPR, who openly avowed independence for Puerto Rico at whatever cost. He was last known to be a resident of Mayagüez on the western coast of the island. I was able to locate him in San Juan, and he was arrested by fellow members of the Criminal Squad and brought before a federal magistrate for arraignment. The arrest went off smoothly although not without resistance on his part. Shortly afterwards, I had to report to Washington for my first criminal in-service training and on my return found that I had been transferred to the Resident Agency at Rio Piedras. Under these circumstances, I lost track of Cancel Miranda.

I reported to the Miami office in the last week of February 1954. A few days later, on 1 March, I was shocked by the news that four members of the NPPR, led by Lolita Lebron, one of its firebrand leaders, had sprayed the floor of the House of Representatives with gunfire. They had situated themselves in the Visitors' Gallery with hidden weapons and, when they commenced their shooting spree, shouted epithets of freedom for Puerto Rico. Five members of Congress were shot and injured, with Representative Alvin M. Bentley (R-Michigan) the most seriously wounded; his life hung in the balance for days. I could identify with this terrorist attack which put our country in harm's way because only a few short months before I had arrested one of the participants, Cancel Miranda.

I can only speculate as to how Cancel Miranda was free at the time of the shooting. When he was arraigned in Puerto Rico, he had been freed on bond awaiting trial and his movements were restricted to the island. It is probable that he jumped bond as the group of terrorists were reported to have come from New York, where they were members of the New York City faction of the NPPR. All were convicted and received long prison sentences. I followed the matter for a number of years and noted that, as the years passed and their cases were brought before parole boards from time to time, they never expressed the slightest degree of remorse for their deeds for fear that this would be an indication that they accepted the laws of the United States. By the mid-1970s, all had been released.

One of the landmarks of our personal life occurred on 6 April 1953, the day following Easter Sunday, when our daughter Kathryn Anne was born at the Presbyterian Hospital in the Condado suburb of San Juan. By a rare coincidence, this was the very same day that the first of four sensational articles appeared in *Life* magazine concerning the heretofore secret crimes of Josef Stalin. The articles were written by a former KGB general by the name of Alexander Orlov, who had defected and now surfaced for the first time to expose Stalin. I was spellbound by the first instalment and could hardly contain myself until the subsequent instalments appeared. Never in the world could I have believed that this man would someday become a close personal friend of mine and a member of my family.

Our joy over the birth of our daughter did not last long. The following Friday I stopped by the hospital to visit Ruth and the baby for my usual daily visit. The second I walked into the room and looked at Ruth I knew that something was drastically wrong. She had no colour in her face as well as an expression that I had never seen before. She seemed unable to get her words out and tears began to roll down her face. After I was able to calm her, she told me the devastating news that a nurse had discovered that Kathy's right leg was shorter than her left leg and had immediately brought this to the attention of our obstetrician, Dr Kodish. He in turn consulted a paediatrician, and they both examined Kathy to learn that she had been born with a bilateral subluxated right hip. They had then gently broken the news to Ruth.

I immediately got hold of Dr Kodish for a consultation. He informed me that one of the leading orthopaedic surgeons in the United States, Dr Karl Horn, happened to be in Puerto Rico and suggested that his services would be indispensable in such a situation. Without any further hesitation, I contacted Dr Horn and he agreed to come to the hospital the same day. He examined Kathy and took a number of X-rays, which confirmed the original diagnosis. He explained our options and recommended the Frejka Splint, which he had helped to pioneer the use of in the US. Kathy was placed in the splint when she was eighteen days old and from that date forward her mother had to tend to her day and night. In August 1953, we took Kathy to the mainland for consultation with a leading orthopaedic specialist in Miami, who recommended that we continue with the splint. She was in it for almost a year and for the next two years the condition was carefully monitored. Today she is as normal as anyone else, and my wife and I are eternally grateful to Dr Horn and the Czechoslovakian doctor who invented the splint.

The San Juan office was considered a hardship office and agents were assigned there for a period of two years under a rotation system. Towards November 1953, I decided to write a personal letter to Mr Hoover explaining Kathy's health problem inasmuch as I was due for rotation in a few months. I wrote to Mr Hoover on 9 November and asked him to consider transferring me to the Miami office, where we could avail ourselves of the expertise of orthopaedic specialist Dr Forrest H. Foreman. I added that in Miami my wife's parents were in a position to give her relief from the burden that had been placed on her. By return letter dated 24 November, Mr Hoover replied that under the circumstances he would gladly bear in mind my request, and on 12 January 1954 he advised me that I was being transferred to the Bureau's office in Miami.

The FBI was a very strong family-oriented organisation because of Mr Hoover's firm belief in family values. The results of his uncompromising parameters is best exemplified by the fact that, during my entire Bureau career, I never knew a married agent who was divorced and only knew four agents that were not married. Mr Hoover looked kindly on the family unit and any deviations from a normal married lifestyle which encroached on the moral relationship of the union was a cause for immediate dismissal. Every agent in the FBI knew Mr Hoover's position.

I reported to the Miami office at the end of February 1954 and was assigned to one of several criminal squads. My squad was rather unusual in that it was a hybrid combination of both criminal and security work. Security work in Florida was minimal at best in the absence of any substantial Communist Party activity, and there were only about five agents who handled this type of work. The fact that this situation did exist would later become a key factor that would take me along the path to General Orlov.

Within a month of my arrival in Miami, I was assigned to assist Melvin M. Jett, one of the old-timers at the office, in a rather complicated sabotage case. Aerodex Inc. was a prime contractor to the US Air Force for overhauling and refurbishing air-force cargo planes. A series of incidents of a similar nature were occurring just after Aerodex had completed work on an aircraft and before the actual test flight. During the final inspection in preparation for the test flight, a key component vital to flight would be found damaged to the extent that it would permit take-off but would fail during flight and cause the aircraft to crash, with perhaps the loss of life. The prime methods that the saboteur used were the severing of most of the strands of one of the steel control cables, which would then fail under stress, or scoring a fuel line to the point that normal flight vibration would sever the critical line. Fortunately, all of the sabotaged components were located by a chief inspector prior to each test flight. What brought him to the attention of the company and made him a hero were also the circumstances that we would come to question. It seemed more than coincidence that the same person found all of the problems. We then explored his past employment records and found a similar pattern at more than one firm. Based on our findings, we confronted the man, who confessed that he had sabotaged the aircraft to bring recognition to himself and praise from the company. He had never intended that the aircraft in question should leave the ground. I felt that he was a sick man, but I also felt that because of the seriousness of the possible consequences of his actions, he deserved the long sentence meted out to him. Aerodex Inc. was kind enough to contact Mr Hoover directly and advise him of their gratitude for the FBI's efforts in solving the matter and requested that a commendation be placed in our respective personnel files.

My career in the FBI as well as my life almost came to an abrupt end that summer of 1954. There are many situations when you have to work with a fellow agent in a 'buddy' relationship, in which you have to share complete reliance and trust as partners. No one is designated as your official partner but it seems you gravitate to one agent that you are comfortable with on the squad. In Boston, my partner was Russ Dagley; in San Juan, there were so few agents assigned to criminal work that they were all partners; and in Miami my partner was Graham C. Hurst. Graham was one of those easy-going Southern boys from Savannah, who could talk an Eskimo out of his parka in midwinter. After I got to know him, I concluded that he must have been the one to set the standard for honesty and integrity. Best of all, I could rely on his judgement and knew he would be the type of person I could depend on in a difficult or dangerous situation. I was not wrong.

Graham had a case assigned to him to locate a dangerous fugitive believed to be in the Miami area. We were able to establish that the fugitive was residing at the downtown Miami YMCA, but were unable to determine his whereabouts during the day. The only recourse was to apprehend him at the YMCA, and we decided that the best way to do so was to surprise him while he was asleep. Graham obtained the key to his room as well as a plan of its layout: the head of the bed was along the wall directly opposite the door and there was a window next to the bed. The hall lights were turned off so as not to give him the advantage of light penetrating the dark room, although we were also well aware that he would have the advantage of the light from the window.

We entered the room and crept towards the bed. As I approached from the right side of the bed, the fugitive reached for a weapon that was hidden under his pillow and, before I could get to him, took direct aim at me. He was moments away from pulling the trigger when Graham was able to grasp the breech of the weapon in a manoeuvre we had been taught at the FBI Academy to prevent the weapon from being fired. The weapon was a .45 calibre automatic, which was capable of putting a rather large hole in a person, and as he was aiming at my head there was no way that I would be alive today had it not been for the quick thinking and action of my partner. Graham and I seldom spoke about this incident while I was assigned to the Miami office, but my respect and gratitude towards him never ceased.

One of the great pleasures I had at the Miami office was meeting and getting to know John S. Knight, the newspaper publisher and founder of the Knight-Ridder newspaper chain. I got this opportunity because of the Atomic Energy Act of 1946, which went into effect on 1 January 1947. The Act authorised the FBI to investigate and report to the Atomic Energy Commission (AEC) on any criminal violations of the law as well as to determine one's loyalty to the US when applying for a position related to the Act. Everyone had to be investigated for a security clearance, from the top executive of a corporation handling work for the AEC down to its janitor. However, by 1951, with the expansion in the atomic energy field due to the Cold War, the FBI asked to be relieved of the burden of investigating all applicants. The 82nd Congress then enacted Public Law 298, which transferred the mass of these investigations to the Civil Service Commission effective from 2 October 1952. The FBI remained charged with investigating only sensitive and high-level positions connected with the AEC.

I was assigned to handle the investigation of Harvey S. Firestone Jr, who was the Chairman of the Firestone Tire and Rubber Company in Akron, Ohio. The company was handling a confidential contract in connection with the Atomic Energy Programme and it was necessary for Firestone to have a security clearance. It was only natural that he would list his good friend John S. Knight as a reference. I was awed as well as impressed by that first interview with Knight, not only by the man but also by his personal office at the *Miami Herald*, which was more like an ornate executive office at one of those high-profile law firms in New York City. I felt a little apprehensive at the prospect of the interview with Knight, knowing that he was a very powerful man in the publishing field and had the reputation of being a taskmaster with his staff. I needn't have been, as he quickly put me at ease with his affable and outgoing style that overcame any fears I might have had. I felt that this would be a one-off situation, but I was wrong as every top executive at Firestone listed Knight as a personal reference. I could only surmise that the company had recently landed a contract in the atomic energy field. The first time I met him he offered me a cup of coffee, which I declined in keeping with professional decorum; after I got to know him better, I would accept his hospitality. What I discovered was that he had a genuine interest in the work of the FBI and held the Bureau and Director Hoover in high regard.

Towards the autumn of 1954, the Bureau allotted the Miami office one slot for the next security in-service class. As I have previously explained, my criminal squad was a hybrid with a small minor staff which handled the security end. The security staff had either recently attended this training course or were embroiled in matters that could not be readily dropped. I therefore became the designated 'pinch hitter', although my work was entirely in the criminal field. I did attend the security in-service session but came away with the resolve that my spirit was in the criminal field. What I did not know at the time was that this random event would leave an indelible mark on my later career.

Everything was going smoothly for me at the Miami office, perhaps too smoothly. I really enjoyed the work, my associates and most of all Miami. Ruth had the company and comfort of her parents, and my parents who resided in Cleveland, Ohio, had decided to make the break and move to the Miami area. I knew that I would be in my third office of assignment for a respectable amount of time so decided to build our first home. We purchased a lot in a very desirable location and, after a few planning hiccoughs, were all set to go, or so we thought.

On 15 April 1955, a letter from Bureau headquarters informed me that I was under transfer to Cleveland, Ohio. The Miami office was being downsized in personnel and, as our daughter's health problem was approaching normalcy, I had become a candidate for transfer. Thus I took another step on the road to my meeting with General Orlov.

FOURTEEN

BY DEFAULT

I reported to the Cleveland field office on Monday, 30 May. My intention was to make a favourable first impression, but this was not to be. I had developed the habit of reporting at least an hour before the start of the working day and my first day would be no exception. The Standard Building, where the Cleveland office was located, was one of the larger commercial buildings that supported a bank of eight elevators. On this particular morning, there was a short summer electrical storm. The FBI office was located on the ninth floor and, as my elevator approached my intended destination, it stopped and remained between floors for over an hour. For some reason unknown to me, none of the other elevators was affected and no one else from the FBI was in the elevator who could support my claim. On a regular day this would not have presented a problem; however, on this particular day another agent, Ernie Kirstein, was also reporting to the office for the first time and the SAC was awaiting my arrival in order to afford us the customary introduction to the office at the same time. I attempted casually to explain my tardiness, but in the absence of anyone else being late that day I had the feeling that at best the SAC was very sceptical of my excuse. It was a great start at my new office.

When I entered the SAC's office, there was no doubt whatsoever that I would be assigned to one of the criminal squads. My previous experience in the criminal field would dictate such an assignment. Ernie and I had briefly spoken to each other before being ushered into the SAC's office, and I learned that we had both served the same length of time with the FBI. However,

Ernie's work experience was all related to security matters and he desired an assignment to the security squad. It all seemed to be working out well for both of us, and there would be no conflict in the event that we were asked our preference. The SAC was an impressive Texan by the name of Oscar Hawkins, who would have looked in place as the hero of a western film. I would soon come to learn that his physical appearance far outweighed his administrative abilities. Ernie and I had no opportunity to express a preference as the SAC bluntly told Ernie that he was to report to a criminal squad and that I was assigned to the security squad. We were both highly disappointed. Logic would have reversed the assignments, and the only explanation I could arrive at was that the SAC had based his decision on the fact that, by a fluke, I had attended a security in-service training class in Washington DC.

What I did not comprehend that fateful day was that had I been assigned to a criminal squad, I would never have met General Orlov. As time went by and the longer I was assigned to the security squad, the more I wondered why I felt that my little world revolved around criminal work. Criminal work was exciting and satisfying but it could never rival the seriousness and purposefulness where the national interest was at stake.

Cleveland supported a large number of Central European immigrants, who, at the turn of the century, had been drawn to its steel mills and factories. Germans, Hungarians, Austrians, Irish and Italians had flocked to Cleveland in the thousands, and Cleveland became the centre of the Hungarian population in the United States. One statistic I have never forgotten is that there are more people of Hungarian extraction living in Cleveland than in any other city of the world with the sole exception of Budapest.

I am a first-generation American, whose paternal side of the family traces itself back to the first of the tribes which existed centuries ago on the banks of the River Danube somewhere between what is now Regensburg and Passau in Germany. My father had emigrated from Austro-Hungary at the turn of the century. The one thing I learned that I had in common with Orlov was that both our families had been engaged in the timber industry. Through the centuries, my family had moved from one site to the next as forests became depleted of their trees to the point where it was no longer convenient or economically feasible to timber the land. Thus, the family continued to trek east seeking precious timber, and its last site was about fifty miles north of Budapest and a hundred miles east of Vienna, near the small German/Austrian settlement of Pranzdorf. The only town of any significance in the vicinity is the market centre of Levice.

My mother was a farm girl, who came from the area north of Vienna that later became part of Czechoslovakia following the First World War. Her father was a travelling master glazier from Vienna, who was working on the great opera houses and art nouveau buildings that were being built in the Austro-Hungarian Empire when he met my grandmother. My mother emigrated to the United States in 1923 and had married my Dad two years later.

With an ethnic background such as this, coupled with the fact that I had spent the summer of 1937 travelling and visiting relatives in Germany, Austria and Czechoslovakia and had been exposed to their languages from childhood, I was a likely candidate for assignment to the counter-intelligence and foreign intelligence section of the security squad.

The vast majority of the agents on the security squad at the Cleveland office handled matters relating to the US Communist Party, the Socialist Workers' Party and other splinter organisations dedicated to the overthrow of the Government. Only a few handled the counter-intelligence, espionage and foreign intelligence side of the work. In the larger field offices, where the foreign embassies, consulates or missions existed, these areas were handled by a separate squad. All of my future formal education in the area would be in Washington at specialised in-service training classes dealing with espionage and counter-intelligence.

In general, the intelligence services of the European countries operate in the same manner, some better than others, but all dependent on funding and the willingness of their respective countries to actively support their efforts. Their missions abroad are balanced between legal and illegal networks, which may have the same objectives but operate under totally different and separate parameters. The legal operation enjoys the cover of the diplomatic establishment and, in most cases, diplomatic immunity, secure communications with the Centre and a readily available administrative control. The downside to the legal operation is the centralisation that enables counter-intelligence to identify its officers and the disruption of the operation in time of war. The illegal network is not a dormant organisation in peacetime as it collects intelligence concurrently with the legal network, but its role becomes critical and indispensable in time of war, or in the event of an emergency when a diplomatic establishment is withdrawn and the legal operation can no longer function. The illegal operation is more susceptible to detection by counter-intelligence in its early stages, when it is in the process of establishing the network; however, once established with its defined sources in place, its own independent line of communication and financial stability, the probability of detection by the FBI is reduced.

Each agent in my section was given the responsibility of handling particular countries that targeted the resources of their intelligence services against the United States. My particular areas of interest were the East German and Hungarian intelligence services. In Cleveland, the AVO (Hungarian intelligence service) was particularly active as the high concentration of Hungarian immigrants and descendants of earlier immigrants provided a relatively easy opportunity for the AVO to assimilate illegals into the fabric of the community with less likelihood of suspicion. The AVO was an exceptionally active and high-grade intelligence organisation, and in the realm of the Iron Curtain countries was second only to the Soviet intelligence service.

The problem escalated severely in 1956, when on 23 October the people of Hungary revolted against their Communist Government. The uprising caught like a brush fire and within a matter of days the Communist Government was overthrown and a democratic government installed. However, the new Government was short-lived when the Soviets sent their army and weapons into Hungary to massacre the rebels and re-establish the Communist dictatorship. On 1 December, the United States initially opened its doors to 21,500 Hungarian refugees. In all, over 200,000 Hungarian refugees escaped to the West as a consequence of the uprising and the vast majority eventually made their way to the United States. On 12 December, the United Nations condemned the Soviet intervention and called for the Soviets to withdraw their troops from Hungary.

The AVO Centre must have had a difficult time containing their delight as an opportunity now presented itself to introduce illegals into the stream of refugees with less likelihood of detection. The FBI did not sit idly by, and every Hungarian refugee that came to the United States was screened and those that were suspicious were actively investigated. Naturally, a large percentage of these refugees came to Cleveland, and I had my hands full for a number of years.

Another significant matter took me in yet another direction when Fidel Castro overthrew the dictatorship of President Fulgencio Batista on 1 January 1959. My Bureau service in the San Juan office, where I had learned the customs and language of the Spanish people as well as having had some exposure to the political intrigues of the Latin Americans, made me the logical choice to handle the Cuban field. The first waves of Cubans to desert their homeland were wealthy landowners and business people, whose land and businesses were confiscated by the new Communist Government. The first groups were followed almost immediately by highly educated professionals, who could no longer tolerate conditions under the Communists. None of these groups posed a problem in terms of espionage, although the possibility could not be ignored. In the beginning, the Castro Government had no intelligence service as such and had to build one from scratch. Originally, this service was crude and ineffective at best, although this eventually changed after the KGB started to train and educate it to its level. I suspect that in the Miami area, it had well-qualified sources who kept its Government abreast of the activities of anti-Castro organisations in that particular area.

Surprisingly, a number of these Cuban refugees found their way to the Cleveland area, where they settled and prospered. My personal relationship with these Cubans was rewarding and I established friendships that have continued to this day.

There were also a number of matters that I handled outside the scope of the field of my expertise during my FBI career that I should briefly mention.

Like my fellow Americans, I was deeply shocked on 22 November 1963 when I heard the news that President John F. Kennedy had been assassinated in Dallas. I was out of the office on that particular day and the announcement was made over the Bureau car radio within minutes of the assassination, instructing all agents to drop whatever they were handling and immediately return to the office. When I reached the office, it was apparent that it was in a state of 'controlled panic' due to the gravity of the situation and the fact that the assassin had not yet been identified. What did come out of that very first meeting was that it was imperative to establish the whereabouts of any individuals known to the office who had been trained in, or were capable of, terrorist activities.

In the early days of the Communist regime in Cuba, the Communist Party established the Venceremos Brigade to attract the young and gullible to Cuba, where they would work on farms during the day and be given every opportunity to indoctrinate themselves into the Communist movement. In the early 1960s, ideological youths from around the world flocked to Cuba to join the Venceremos Brigade (which in Spanish means 'We will conquer/or overcome Brigade'), although the vast majority were recruited in the United States through left-wing organisations. It therefore provided the newly emerged Cuban intelligence service, now trained by and patterned after the KGB, with a source of highly selected recruits that would be trained as terrorists and spies. As with the KGB, the Cuban intelligence service's primary target was, and always will be, the United States.

My squad handled the Venceremos Brigade investigations from the general standpoint that these young recruits would be the future members and leaders of the Communist Party and Socialist Workers' Party in the United States. I had no interest in this facet of the organisation but rather with those members that came to my attention as having been selected by the Cuban intelligence service for special training to become terrorists and spies.

Under the above criteria, I had in the past investigated one such young man who fitted the profile of an individual capable of assassinating President Kennedy. By the night of the assassination, I was able to track and account for this individual's movements that entire day, thus eliminating him as a suspect. I can assure the reader that this was no lone incident as the FBI's programme stressed the importance of intelligence prior to an assassination rather than after the fact.

For some reason that I don't clearly remember now, I was assigned the task of heading the President Kennedy assassination investigation in northern Ohio. Perhaps it was my early entry into the case, but more likely the assassin's (Lee Harvey Oswald) Cuban connection. I was responsible for handling all leads and reporting the results of my investigation, as well as leads handled by other agents within the Cleveland Division (northern Ohio), to Washington in the most expeditious manner possible. The Kennedy case was the most thorough and exhaustive case I ever handled. As they say, no stone was left unturned. I worked the case for months, hardly having the time to take care of urgent matters in my own field. Every thread that intermingled with the life of Lee Harvey Oswald was minutely examined under the strong microscope of the FBI and the Warren Commission. Anyone in military or civilian life whose path had in the slightest manner crossed that of Oswald was located and interviewed. Even the most remotely possible situations were explored in depth.

I specifically recall one situation which I handled for the Warren Commission. In his early youth, when Oswald was perhaps in the eight- to ten-year-old age bracket, he was placed in an orphanage in another state. Every child that had been in that orphanage during the relevant time frame, as well as all of its staff members, had to be found and interviewed. I had to locate one of these former orphans whose testimony really added nothing new or pertinent to the overall picture and at the time I believed that this was an overkill situation. There were many other pieces of that investigation that I felt were superfluous, but of course I had no control over these matters.

In early 1968, I had another case that spy novels are made of. There were two facilities in Cleveland engaged in top-secret work which held the highest priority for the KGB and Iron Curtain intelligence services to penetrate. One was the TRW Corporation, which at the time was headquartered in Cleveland and whose Torpedo Division was manufacturing the most advanced state-of-the-art submarine torpedo in the world for the US Navy. The other was the National Aeronautics and Space Administration's (NASA) Lewis Propulsion Laboratory (LPL), which was situated on a portion of the Cleveland Hopkins International Airport. The LPL was engaged in the most confidential work taking place in the United States relative to our space efforts. Because of the sensitive nature of the work at the LPL, I had been assigned the collateral duty of being the FBI's liaison official at the facility to represent the FBI and to correlate with NASA's Office of Security in matters of interest relating to national security.

One evening in late 1967, I was already home from work when, at about 7 p.m., I received a telephone call from the office. I was instructed to proceed immediately to the LPL and contact the top officials at NASA as an incident had taken place an hour or so earlier which appeared to be a breach of national security. I quickly learned that a mid-level LPL official called Hammonds had returned home from work that day between 5 and 6 p.m. On his arrival at home, he had found a package addressed to him lying on the front porch. He took the package into the house and, when he opened it, the ensuing explosion was of such magnitude that it killed him instantly and tore apart the front of the house.

What I did establish that evening was that Hammonds, by virtue of his position, had access to some of the most vital and sensitive space secrets at the LPL. At the time, the US and the

USSR were engaged in an unrelenting space race, the outcome of which depended to a large extent on the scientific space technology being developed at the LPL. No doubt the KGB or any other Iron Curtain intelligence service would have given their eyeteeth to penetrate the LPL. My attention was now focused on the possibility that Hammonds was a spy in place, or at least an agent of the KGB or one of its satellite intelligence services.

By the following day, the FBI's Bomb Squad from Washington was already at the crime scene collecting evidence. Every particle from around the point of explosion, including shreds of the actual bomb and the package, as well as pieces that had embedded themselves in the structure or had been blown away from the area, were collected. The evidence was taken back to the FBI's laboratory in Washington, where the pieces of the bomb and package were reconstructed and subjected to several areas of analysis.

Several agents from my squad were assigned to assist me and the case was given the highest priority. On the surface, Hammonds turned out to be a respected family man and his moral character appeared to be beyond reproach. There had to be a strong motive for someone to take his life in such a drastic manner but that motive was beyond our reach for the time being. A thorough search of his residence and office at the LPL did not turn up any incriminating evidence or motive for the crime. Nothing was found to tie him to a foreign intelligence service, although this would not be unusual given that this case would have fallen into the category of a deep-cover operation. The investigation began to get bogged down, and I became frustrated knowing that somewhere and at some point in time I would have to discover the key that would solve the case. As with all FBI cases, time was always on our side as an investigation was never closed until brought to its logical conclusion.

One day I decided to search Hammonds's office again, although I felt that my original search had overlooked nothing. This time I would go over every inch of the office and even take apart anything that looked suspicious. My patience paid off as I located a cleverly crafted cavity in a wall partition behind a metal bookshelf. A cursory inspection of the area would not have revealed the hidden location, but I had noticed that the metal bookshelf had left marks on the floor to indicate that it had been moved away from the partition numerous times. When I reached into the cavity, which had been revealed after investigation, and worked down to the floor level, my hand hit on a small bundle of paper. I felt excited as I knew immediately that I had found what I was looking for. No one would take such extraordinary measures to conceal something had it not been of immense importance. I took the papers over to Hammonds's desk and began to examine my find. The papers turned out to be a series of letters contained in their respective envelopes. As I read the letters, it became clear that my major espionage case had fizzled out and become merely a gruesome murder. My find of course was love letters, which revealed a love triangle and provided the clues that finally led to the identity of the murderer. However, the culprit vanished before he could be arrested, and it was not until sometime later that his car containing his body was found submerged in a small lake not too far from Petaluma, California, where he had been employed. It was clear that he had committed suicide rather than face the consequences of his murderous act when he realised, as they say in novels, that the 'game was up'. I personally did not get to play out a role in a major espionage case as I had hoped, but at least had the satisfaction that the secrets of our space programme had not been compromised.

As the 1970s approached, I had handled a number of unusual and interesting espionage cases in the Hungarian and East German fields that were personally satisfying in terms of being resolved in one way or another to the detriment of the concerned intelligence service. However, none would surpass in scope and historical importance the one case that I have always held as my most important service to the FBI and my country: that of KGB General Alexander Orlov.

Somehow I must have been destined to handle the Orlov case, but it was definitely not because I was an expert in the field of Soviet intelligence. I did have an overview of Soviet intelligence as the principal target of the FBI is the KGB, and in all of my specialised training in the field of espionage in Washington the work of the KGB would be stressed and the current major KGB cases in the United States in particular would be discussed and analysed. However, what I did lack was the in-depth knowledge of the key players in the KGB, the background and specific targets of the KGB networks, and most importantly their inter-relationships. In time I would pick up this information, but at a cost. The Cleveland office already had in place one man who possessed the qualified expertise, honed over a long period of time looking after important KGB cases, to handle the Orlov matter. Unfortunately for Special Agent Milton P. Mandt, he was recovering from open-heart surgery when the Orlov case broke. As I have always contended, I got the case by default.

Milt had had a brush with General Orlov long before I arrived at the Cleveland Office. Orlov's four-part series of articles that appeared in *Life* magazine in April 1953, and exposed Soviet dictator Josef Stalin, had hit the world like a bombshell. Who was this General Alexander Orlov, who professed to be a high-ranking KGB official and associate of the dictator? How could this KGB General have defected in 1938 and hidden in the United States until he surfaced with the advent of the *Life* articles without anyone knowing? In particular, the entire US intelligence commu-nity was stunned to learn that such a high-ranking Soviet intelli-gence agent had eluded their detection for all those years. No doubt even the KGB would have liked to have known the answer to this question for their own purposes. As a consequence, the intelligence community had to have answers and the full force of the FBI was immediately summoned and brought to bear upon the task. Agents all over the field scurried to detect and investi-gate every aspect of Orlov's hidden life in the United States and to account for each and every day.

As Orlov had hidden in Cleveland for well over ten years during the period 1942–53, Milt undertook a meticulous investigation to ferret out the smallest evidence of his existence there and did not overlook the most insignificant details. It would be sixteen years before the Orlovs would return to Cleveland, but then Milt would no longer be in a position to lend his expertise to the case.

Milt was no stranger to the work of the KGB and was especially knowledgeable concerning the recruitment and operation of the Cambridge spy ring in England during the mid-1930s. It was through Milt's efforts and extreme patience that one of the most daring and prolific of these early spies was turned and became an asset to Western Intelligence. I always considered Milt's work on the John Cairncross case as his finest inasmuch as the implications were so far-reaching.

Cairncross was the acknowledged Fifth Man in the notorious group of spies that were recruited by the KGB in the 1930s at Trinity College, Cambridge, in England. Their identities and exploits on behalf of the KGB would eventually become known around the world. The names of Kim Philby, Donald Maclean, Guy Burgess, Anthony Blunt and Cairncross would be forever etched into the fabric of history as traitors to their native country and the Western world.

Cairncross was born into a family of modest means in 1913 in a market town near Glasgow, Scotland. He was a scholar and intellectually gifted student, who took notice of the effects of the Depression on the people of the area. These early years greatly influenced him into believing that social change was the answer to the needs of the masses. He spent two years at Glasgow University, where he studied languages, and then went to Paris to attend the Sorbonne for the 1933–4 academic year to enhance his language skills. While at the Sorbonne he won a scholarship to Trinity College. One of Cairncross's tutors at Cambridge was Anthony Blunt, who was a talent-spotter for Guy Burgess. During his weekly sessions with Cairncross, Blunt could hardly escape the conclusion that Cairncross was an intellectually fervent Communist whose abilities could place him in a high-level government position. Blunt passed on his observations to Burgess, and it was James Klugmann who recruited Cairncross into the Comintern as an agent in the secret war against the spread of world Fascism. By the time Cairncross graduated with honours from Cambridge in the summer of 1936, he had severed his connections with the Communist Party in order to facilitate the appearance that he was no longer associated with or supported the idealisms of his youth. The next step was the Foreign Office entrance examination, which Cairncross took and where he achieved a grade 100 points higher than the next highest participant. Thus Cairncross's access to British government secrets was assured.

Cairncross remained with the Foreign Office until October 1938, when, with the guidance of the KGB, he moved to the Treasury. Shortly thereafter he transferred to the top-secret Government Code & Cipher School at Bletchley, where he enjoyed access to the intercepts from the enemy's complex Enigma cipher machines, many of whose keys had by now been broken. By 1944 Cairncross was with MI6. Throughout this period there would be a constant flow of secret information from Cairncross to the KGB.

Possibly Cairncross's most important contribution while in the service of the KGB occurred in September 1940, when he was appointed private secretary to Lord Hankey, who held very high-ranking positions with the British Government at the Cabinet level. Originally Hankey was Minister without Portfolio in Neville Chamberlain's War Cabinet; however, he lost this post when Winston Churchill became Prime Minister in May 1940. Nevertheless, Hankey retained his ministerial rank as Chancellor of the Duchy of Lancaster, thus continuing to receive all Cabinet documents, to have administrative oversight of the intelligence services as well as to chair various secret committees.

As sensitive government documents passed through Cairncross's office with Lord Hankey, the most important would be forwarded to the KGB. Most of the information passed on to the Soviets was extremely vital to the Soviets but none more so than the knowledge regarding the Allies' decision to develop an atomic bomb as early as 1940. In October 1940, Lord Hankey chaired the important British Scientific Advisory Committee, which studied the feasibility of the atomic weapon. Concurrent with their study was the MAUD Committee's secret findings that a powerful atomic bomb could be produced with Uranium 235 by the end of 1943. Hankey's committee met again in the summer of 1941, when it acknowledged the secret MAUD Committee report and endorsed the decision to develop a British atomic weapon. The British recognised that they would require the vast resources of the United States to put the atomic weapon into production. Through Anglo-American co-operation, their joint efforts in this direction were placed in motion. In the autumn of 1941, the British formed the Tube Alloys Consultative Committee to formulate policy for the atomic weapons programme and Lord Hankey became a member of the Committee. The top-secret British atomic bomb project would become known by the code name 'Tube Alloys Project' while its American counterpart utilised the code name 'Manhattan Project'.

There is little doubt that the KGB first learned of the possible development of an atomic weapon as early as 1940 from one of its spies in the Cambridge network. Cairncross had access to this information and so did Donald Maclean. There is some dispute as to which of these two spies was the first to furnish this important information to the KGB; however, this aspect is relatively unimportant when considered together with the fact that the same information came from two independent sources, thereby corroborating the veracity of this vital information.

Now back to Milt's involvement with John Cairncross. Sometime in 1964, word was received from MI5 that it had determined that Cairncross had left Italy, where he had lived since he fled England, and was teaching at Western Reserve University (WRU) in Cleveland, Ohio. MI5 was unable to interview him while he was in Italy and desperately wanted to talk to him regarding unfinished business connected with the Cambridge spy network. It solicited the FBI's co-operation to locate Cairncross and determine if he would speak with a representative of MI5 in Cleveland. Milt located Cairncross, who was residing at the Commodore Hotel on Euclid Avenue in the close proximity of WRU. The Commodore was a residential-type hotel used primarily by professors and staff from WRU. Milt introduced himself and Cairncross graciously invited him into his quarters for a 'spot of tea'. Milt persuasively explained in detail the few options that were open to Cairncross at this juncture, but stressed that talking to MI5 would be his best recourse. After considerable reflection, Cairncross finally looked up at Milt and stated that it was time they had their 'spot of tea' as he had made his decision. He then said that he had no objection to being interviewed by MI5. This information was relayed to MI5 and within a matter of days arrangements were made to have Arthur Martin of MI5 come to Cleveland.

Martin was one of the most knowledgeable experts in British counter-intelligence, whose personal dedication to exposing the Cambridge spy network had become an obsession. He had been on the trail of Cairncross for a number of years without ever having had the opportunity to pin him down in an interview as to his own participation as well as the others in the Cambridge spy ring. Cairncross was interviewed by Martin at the Auditorium Hotel in downtown Cleveland. After Milt introduced Martin to Cairncross, he departed and was not present during the actual interview. Martin later informed Milt that Cairncross was forthright but that there were a number of matters he was unable to pursue and would appreciate it if Milt would continue contact with Cairncross to maintain his co-operation.

Over the next few months, Milt contacted Cairncross at least six to eight times at the Commodore Hotel. On each successive contact Cairncross became more open, and it was apparent that he had placed his confidence in Milt's guidance. Milt assessed Cairncross as an extremely intelligent person, who was fluent in numerous foreign languages. At the time he was translating an ancient book of Chinese poetry into English but was doing so by first translating it into French as the euphonious relationship between Chinese and French provided a better base for the translation into English. Cairncross was also a poet in his own right and presented Milt with a book of his own works. Milt told me that his association with Cairncross was satisfying and from an intelligence point of view a great experience. His overall personal appraisal of Cairncross was good.

An interesting aspect of what prompted him to flee England was recounted by Cairncross. When the news finally hit the newspapers in England that suspected Soviet spies Donald Maclean and Guy Burgess had fled England to Moscow in May 1951, Cairncross became aware that his own circumstances could be in jeopardy. In the past, he had been instructed by his KGB handler that, in the event that his identity and association with the KGB were at risk of being compromised, he would be so alerted through a dead drop. With great haste and without any hesitation Cairncross went to a particular London underground station, where a pre-designated chalk mark would be placed at a specified location within the underground station should the need arise. The chalk mark in the dead drop would indicate that he was indeed compromised and, in Cairncross's own words, meant for him to 'get the hell out of England as soon as possible'. The prearranged chalk mark that Cairncross dreaded and would rather have not seen was present and he knew that he had no alternative but to flee. Cairncross fled to Italy, which proved to be a safe haven from MI5, although he felt it was aware he was hiding there.

A spin-off of these contacts with Cairncross would be the bonanza that every counter-intelligence agent dreams of, the one golden opportunity that seems to be just around the corner, or just slightly out of reach. In this case Milt had it in his hands. Over the course of their interviews, Milt displayed hundreds of photographs of Soviets who were currently or had in the past been assigned to the Soviet Embassy in Washington, or the United Nations in New York, as well as lesser missions. Among the many photographs were those Soviet diplomats and employees who were known by the FBI to be actually with the KGB. Cairncross positively identified at least eight photographs as KGB officers whom he had in the past had contact with in England. As it turned out, all of these KGB officers had previously been identified by the FBI as such, thereby authenticating Cairncross's claim. A number of these KGB people were currently in the United States. Cairncross volunteered to go to Washington or New York on behalf of the FBI and, through a skilfully set-up 'chance' encounter, be placed in contact with one of the known KGB agents from his past. Cairncross had not been in contact with the KGB for a number of years and the KGB was unaware of his present whereabouts or circumstances. Without any doubt, the 'chance' encounter would be reported immediately to the KGB Centre in Moscow. Perhaps with time the fictitious scenario could develop into a redoubled agent situation, wherein the FBI would be able to take advantage of Cairncross to penetrate the KGB in the United States.

The circumstances were presented to Bureau headquarters and they readily acknowledged the motherlode of opportunity. Unfortunately one obstacle in the form of the INS stood in the way of putting the plan in motion. Cairncross was an alien temporarily residing in the Unites States on a work-related visa that in time would expire. During interviews Cairncross did not attempt to conceal, but rather readily admitted, that at one time he had been a card-carrying member of the Communist Party of Great Britain. This information was in the FBI report on Cairncross and because of his alien status the FBI was obliged to furnish the INS with a copy of the report.

The INS and the FBI are both integral arms of the US Department of Justice, each with its own area of jurisdiction. The federal law is clear on the point of membership of the Communist Party and the INS is mandated to deport an alien with a proven affiliation. In this case Cairncross's own admission would suffice. The INS would not agree, compromise or bend the law or its policy to delay the matter, and Cairncross was deported to Italy from whence he had come. My own feeling in my dealings with the INS was that it was rather short-sighted and had no understanding whatsoever of intelligence work. It was somewhat like the horse with blinkers who could only see in one direction. Cairncross was legally in the United States, was under the constant control of the FBI, and his past affiliation with the

Communist Party could in no way harm the national interest of the United States. On the contrary, his contribution could have rendered an immense advantage to the national interest of the US. Today millions of illegal aliens are roaming the United States without the slightest fear of the INS, while at the same time draining American resources. What a contrast in times and policy.

Fortunately, all was not lost. Sometime after the INS deported Cairncross, Milt received a personal letter from him in which he requested Milt's assistance in getting in touch with Arthur Martin. Milt relayed the request to the Bureau, who in turn contacted MI5. MI5 did contact Cairncross in Italy, the results of which were not made available to Milt.

I have maintained periodic contact with Milt over the years and although he doesn't spend too much time these days thinking about his Bureau career, he does reminisce about what could have been had he been able to proceed with his plan to penetrate the KGB through Cairncross.

Monday, 16 August 1971, was the date that my FBI career took a sharp turn along the path to my final destination with the KGB General Alexander Orlov. I was starting the week in anticipation of completing some unfinished business and looking forward to an interview with a recent East German immigrant who had aroused some suspicion. Early that morning I had no sooner sat down at my desk than I noticed the SAC, Charles G. Cusick, enter the office of the security squad supervisor, Thomas A. Corbett. This was highly unusual for this particular SAC as his interest in the work of the security squad was minimal. I didn't have long to wait to find out the purpose of the SAC's visit because Tom soon stepped out of his office and beckoned for me to come in.

No sooner had I entered the office than the SAC started to inform me that an extremely sensitive and urgent matter had developed and it had been decided that I was to handle it. He explained that a few minutes before he had received a telephone call from the Bureau relating that a high-ranking KGB defector in hiding had been located and contacted in Cleveland by a known

KGB officer. He stressed that the matter had the attention of high-level officials in Washington and for this reason it was to be handled with the utmost urgency and the Bureau advised of the results immediately. As I was about to leave the office, Tom interjected that he was aware I was handling the East German matter but that he had no alternative but to assign the case to me in view of Mandt's absence from duty.

I gathered and studied what information we had at the office on General Orlov and then telephoned him to make the necessary arrangements. I was to meet him the next day, 17 August 1971.

PART 3

A NEW LIFE IN AMERICA

FIFTEEN

UNFINISHED BUSINESS

The train ride from Montreal to New York City on Saturday, 13 August 1938, was uneventful for the most part but the anticipation of arriving at a new destination that was to be their safe haven was on the minds of each of the Orlovs. The suspense of what was in store for them on their immediate arrival in New York was difficult, but somewhat allayed by the fact that Orlov had spent several months in New York in 1932 and was familiar with the city.

Orlov did have one major concern that he felt was not insurmountable but could arouse a degree of suspicion on entering the United States on vacation: the inordinate amount of luggage that they were bringing with them, which might alert the immigration and customs inspectors at the border. The Orlovs had in their possession two extra large leather suitcases, a huge steamer trunk and numerous smaller pieces of luggage. This amounted to all of the basic worldly possessions they would require to start their new life. As a precaution, the three larger pieces were shipped in the baggage car of the train so as not to make a direct physical link with the Orlovs. The General recalled the stringent immigration requirements he had had to meet on his 1932 entry into the United States and had no reason to suspect that the requirements would be any less severe this time.

The train stopped at the border checkpoint at Rouses Point, in the State of New York, a month to the day that Orlov had defected. Contrary to what Orlov expected, the border formalities went very smoothly and without any hitches. The 'magic wand' in this case was their Soviet diplomatic passports, which had already been stamped at the US Embassy at Ottawa with their one-year visas. Now their passports would contain the additional stamp indicating that they had been admitted into the US for an 'indefinite' period under the immigration laws of the US.

On their arrival in New York, the Orlovs checked into the Wellington Hotel on Broadway and East 55th Street under the assumed name of Leon Koornick, naturally borrowed in part from his cousin Nathan Koornick, who had been so helpful in delivering his letters to the Soviet Embassy in Paris. Orlov recalled the Wellington from his 1932 visit as a place where he could blend inconspicuously into the crowd as the hotel was in a commercial area in the proximity of Carnegie Hall and Central Park. The Orlovs would stay at the Wellington for about three weeks before moving on.

Orlov had two immediate concerns on his mind when he established residence at the Wellington Hotel. He had to know that his letters to Stalin and Yezhov had actually been delivered to the Soviet Embassy in Paris and he had to make his presence in the country known to the US authorities. As his cousin Nathan was not expected to return from France until about the 21st of August, he focused his attention on alerting the US authorities.

While still in Montreal, Orlov had had ample time to research current world events at the public library. One of the matters he came across was the existence of a committee headed by a Professor John Dewey of Columbia University that was looking into the great purge trials in the Soviet Union, which had been instigated by Stalin, and their implications on Stalin's archenemy Leon Trotsky, who was then in exile in Mexico. He learned that an attorney by the name of John F. Finerty of New York City was the counsel for Dewey's committee, and the information relating to Finerty's work on behalf of the committee strongly suggested to Orlov that Finerty had to be vehemently opposed to Communism.

Not being satisfied with his own preliminary assessment of Finerty, Orlov telephoned his cousin Isak Rabinowich on his arrival in New York for an independent appraisal. Rabinowich was an astute, well-connected businessman, who knew of Finerty through associates who considered him a reputable attorney. His background and expressed views clearly indicated that his ideology ran contrary to Communism. Orlov gave no hint that he was actually in New York, but rather indicated that he would be leaving Montreal soon and wanted to get together with Koornick on his return from Paris. Orlov concluded the call by saying that he would contact Rabinowich again later in the month with instructions as to where Koornick was to meet him.

Within a matter of a few days, Orlov had secured an appointment with Finerty at his New York office. At the onset of the meeting, Orlov initially couched his predicament in vague terms to determine Finerty's reaction as well as to assess the avenues that he would put forth. Finerty's professional demeanour and comprehension of the gravity of the situation were sufficient for Orlov to conclude that his judgement regarding the attorney was correct and that he had placed the matter in well-qualified hands. Orlov was now able to be more straightforward and presented a clearer view of the problem. Finerty did put forward a few immediate possibilities but recognised the sensitive nature of the task and advised Orlov that, because of the uniqueness of the situation, he would have to ponder what their best course of action should be.

At their next meeting the following week, Finerty presented Orlov with what he felt was the best recourse under the circumstances. Recognising the necessity of maintaining Orlov's presence in the United States a secret and yet complying with US immigration laws, the matter had to be presented to the highest level of government concerned with immigration. He suggested that they should take Orlov's case directly to the Commissioner of Immigration in Washington DC. Finerty acknowledged that he did not know the Commissioner personally, but knew influential people who could make the connection. Orlov agreed that this was the best alternative and expressed his view that the plan be put in motion without any further delay. Finerty advised that he would make the necessary arrangements.

A few days later, Orlov met his cousin Nathan Koornick at the King George Hotel in New York. Koornick provided in detail all the facts pertaining to his trip to Paris, thus satisfying Orlov's concern that his instructions had been carried out. Orlov did not furnish any details as to his future plans and only conveyed the fact that he feared for his life and had to go into hiding. Years later, Orlov would relate to me that he was forever grateful to his cousin Nathan for undertaking such an important task without the slightest reservation. They bade each other farewell, not knowing that it would be another fifteen years before they would meet again.

Orlov always stressed that he kept his distance from all of his relatives in the United States from that day forth, and it was only in his twilight years that he felt secure enough to re-establish limited contact. He always reflected that it was not that he did not wish to continue relations with his family but that they could inadvertently lead the KGB to him. He never had any concern that his relatives would betray him to the KGB, but knowing the great lengths that the KGB would be going to in order to achieve this end, he felt it prudent not to take the risk. He would always end with the admonition, 'If they [his relatives] don't know where I am, they can't tell the KGB.'

Now that Orlov had accomplished his two main objectives, he found himself in a position where he had ample time to spare for those matters that he had had to relegate to a lesser priority and had therefore neglected. None had a higher urgency than the welfare and health of his daughter Vera. Ever since her parents had revealed that they had broken with the Soviet Union and that she would probably never see her grandmothers or her home-land again, she had withdrawn into a shell of despondency. She was basically a frail person, but her physical health at the moment was not the problem.

Early in his journey of escape, Orlov had decided that it would not be wise to settle in either New York or Washington DC. The latter of course was the location of the Soviet Embassy, which was teeming with KGB officers working out of both the legal and illegal *rezidenturas*; New York City was the other hub of the KGB's

penetration plan and would likewise have its share of KGB officers. Orlov, by virtue of his stature within the KGB organisational
structure, was a well-known figure, not only by reputation but also
by the sheer number of KGB officers he had personally come in
contact with throughout his long career. To those who did not
know him on sight, it would only be a matter of time before the
entire KGB organisation was alerted to his defection and bombarded with his photograph. It was for this reason that he was
aware that his prospects of spending any time in New York were
minimal. However, in the meantime, he wanted to spend some
time satisfying the emotional needs of his daughter. He therefore
decided to relax and show Vera what her new country was all about,
and there was no better place than New York for this purpose.

The Wellington Hotel was right next to the south entrance of
Central Park, and each morning the Orlovs would take a short
stroll through the southern end of the park. On one occasion,
they walked to a small lake in the park known as 'The Lake', and
the sight of a boathouse there reminded Orlov of the tragic day
in Paris when Vera had caught the infection which had led to her
rheumatic fever. Several days later, Orlov engaged a horse-drawn
carriage to take them on an excursion through the Park but took
the precaution to instruct the driver to take the route around the
lake on the far side of the boathouse as he did not want any bad
memories to recur.

During his 1932 scouting trip to the United States, Orlov had
resided in three rooming houses in the vicinity of Columbia
University and the north end of Central Park. Almost six years
had elapsed, but Orlov had a strong desire to locate these residences and revisit the old neighbourhoods with his wife and
daughter. Afterwards, they had lunch at Orlov's favourite Jewish
delicatessen, which featured the largest pastrami on rye bread
sandwiches that he had ever seen, so much so that both Maria
and Vera could not finish their meal. After showing Maria and
Vera around his old haunts, he decided that the time would be
more wisely spent walking around the north end of Central Park.

What I had always found curious was Orlov's interest in Central

Park. From the very first time we discussed his 1932 trip to the US, ostensibly to look into the purchase of General Motors cars for the Soviet Government, he openly admitted that it was more than a business trip. At the time, it was his belief that his next assignment would probably be the United States inasmuch as the prime target of the KGB was about to shift its focus from England and France to the US. His keen curiosity about Central Park, he would later relate, stemmed from his vested interest in securing dead-drop sites and he had found the park to be quite fertile in this respect.

The Bronx Zoo was another site he had surveyed in 1932 for possible dead-drop sites. He had found the Zoo not only out-standing from the point of view of his original purpose but also fascinating as a zoo. The Orlovs spent an entire day visiting the Bronx Zoo and enjoying its grounds.

According to Orlov, a visit to Manhattan without going up the Empire State Building would be a gross dereliction. On his 1932 trip, he had had neither the time nor the inclination for a visit but had later regretted it. Now he looked forward to what he had previously missed. When he announced that they would visit the Empire State Building, he was impressed when Vera informed him that she already knew of the tower and brought to his attention that this was where King Kong had fought off the aeroplanes in the 1933 film of the same name. The Orlovs were truly exhilarated by the view from the Observation Deck of the Empire State Building and felt the brief visit worthwhile.

However, the high point of the day was yet to come, at least for Vera. When they stopped for lunch at an automat restaurant, Maria and Vera were totally mesmerised by the concept. Where in the world would you see coffee, tea and milk coming forth from spigots projecting from a marble wall and prepared sandwiches and desserts sitting in their little compartments waiting to be purchased by a hungry customer? Vera couldn't stop talking about it for the rest of the day, and it became apparent to Orlov that they would soon have to pay another visit to an automat restaurant.

On the last Sunday of August 1938, Orlov decided to take the family to Coney Island for the day. They took the subway to the end of the line in Brooklyn, from where they walked the short distance to that magic land known as Coney Island. They arrived at an early hour and watched the crowds grow. By the afternoon, the beach had become a sea of people as far as the eye could see. Nothing escaped Vera's attention on the Boardwalk, along Surf Avenue or at the midway, and it seemed to her father that she had not missed any ride, side-show or game of skill. Lunch was 'hot dogs' at one of the many food stands that filled the area. By the time they returned to the Wellington Hotel that evening, they were so exhausted that they all retired early.

The day had been a wonderful adventure and would long be remembered. What really impressed Orlov, and what he brought to my attention, was that the cost of that memorable day, including transportation, rides, entry fees and refreshments, had come to less than $3.00 for the three of them.

I have a memento of the day the Orlovs spent at Coney Island. When they came to the shooting gallery, Vera was quite taken by a small plaster of Paris kitten that was among the prizes. Needless to say, as the General was a skilled marksman, Vera got the kitten. It was to become one of her most cherished possessions until the day she died. She named the kitten 'Schatzi', a German expression for a treasure or someone beloved, because one of her father's German bodyguards had started to use the term when referring to her. Years later, Orlov, who had not yet met my daughter Kathy, insisted that he wanted me to have the prize and instructed me to give it to Kathy some day.

Vera's depressed mood, which had started when she learned that her parents had broken from the Soviet Government, began to lift during the two weeks that the family spent together sight-seeing in New York. The change in Vera was so dramatic that Orlov now felt secure in believing that she would assimilate herself into the new society without any further emotional problems and that he had made the right choice in coming to America.

Orlov recalled it was the first Monday or Tuesday towards the end of September 1938 that he and Finerty travelled to Washington

DC to meet James L. Houghteling, the Commissioner of Immigration and Naturalisation. The appointment had been arranged through an intermediary who was a business associate of Finerty and a friend of the Commissioner. They met the Commissioner at his office at the Department of Labor. There they had a cordial reception and explained the circumstances of Orlov's defection and the danger that had been placed on his life as a consequence. The Commissioner understood the gravity of the situation and summoned an assistant by the name of Shoemaker to handle the details. He instructed Shoemaker to 'take care of Mr Orlov' and bade them farewell. Shoemaker was afforded the same facts they had provided the Commissioner, and it was apparent that he also recognised the magnitude of Orlov's predicament. At the conclusion of this meeting, Shoemaker agreed that the best course of action would be for Orlov to keep his presence in the United States a secret as it was apparent that his life, as well as that of his family, was at stake. During the encounter Shoemaker took copious notes, thereby reducing the proceedings to a government record of the meeting.

Orlov felt that a burden had lifted as he had fulfilled the second task that he had planned to take care of on his arrival in New York. They left Washington immediately, taking the next train back to New York, because Orlov did not want to risk the slightest possibility of an encounter with someone from the Soviet Embassy. Neither Finerty nor Orlov realised at the time that, in a little over two years, they would both be back in Washington to cover the same area under provisions imposed by the newly enacted Alien Registration Act as the United States was about to enter the Second World War.

Orlov had planned to leave New York as soon as he had accomplished his two most urgent goals. As his cousin Nathan Koornick lived in Philadelphia and spoke of the city in glowing terms, Orlov felt that it offered a large metropolitan population that supported a high percentage of diversified ethnic groups as well as a superior library system, where he would be able to research material for the articles he planned to write. He also had to be within a

short commute of his attorney in New York. Philadelphia therefore met all of his requirements and so, by the middle of October,
they were on the move again.

The Orlovs settled in at the Benjamin Franklin Hotel on
Chestnut Street under the name of Leon Koornick. Although the
hotel was situated in a good neighbourhood, they did not feel
comfortable with the constant transient aspects of the hotel. They
therefore moved to the Bellevue Stratford Hotel on Walnut Street,
where they stayed for several weeks until they could find a more
permanent residence.

During the initial phase in Philadelphia, Orlov was undertaking
some research at a library connected with a military museum on
Pine Street. Taking a break from his research, he walked down
the street and passed an antique shop in what appeared to be a
converted residence. As he peered into the shop window, he
noticed that the dealer specialised in Middle European antiques,
which was somewhat strange for a city that he felt would be more
interested in Colonial and English antiques. He decided to enter
and browse around the shop, where he encountered the propri-
etor. The owner turned out to be an Austrian Jew from around
Graz by the name of Jakob. Orlov continued to visit the shop
when in the area and his contacts with the owner developed into
a guarded friendship. Both men had many traits in common based
on their love of antiques, as well as being recent immigrants to
the new world and similar in age and education. Orlov looked
forward to his talks with Jakob and found that they had many
mutual interests and the same political leanings. Of course, the
shop owner never knew the truth about Orlov's background and
was satisfied that he was just an average recent immigrant.

The reason Orlov told me of this chance encounter was the
fact that, when Jakob learned that the Orlovs were seeking a
permanent residence, he offered them the use of a furnished flat
above the shop. Orlov thought long and hard on this generous
offer – there were many advantages to living in this particular
area of Pine Street, the most logical of which was the proximity
of several excellent research sources – but in the end he had to

decline the offer as he thought the relationship would become too close and personal, a situation he felt best to distance himself from. As Orlov moved to other sources for his research material and the family moved away from the inner city, his contacts with Jakob became more infrequent. Orlov related that he had only one regret in respect to Jakob: despite the number of times he had browsed in his shop, he had never purchased one item.

For security reasons, Orlov thought it best for the family to move from the downtown area of the city. He concentrated his efforts on obtaining another residence by reading the classified newspaper advertisements and, after a while, he found the Park Plaza Hotel on Walnut Street, which met his requirements and had an attractive monthly rate. Orlov's original intention was to make Philadelphia their permanent home and for their residency at the Park Plaza to be only temporary, but as it turned out the Park Plaza was home to the Orlovs until they made their next move to California.

One piece of business remained unfinished which Orlov felt was of paramount importance, yet was so sensitive that its disclosure could lead to his being identified by the KGB and thereby compromise his personal security. This concerned a KGB plot that would eventually culminate in the assassination of Leon Trotsky. Trotsky was no hero to Orlov, but at least was not the despot that Stalin had become. Preventing the assassination would in part atone for the numerous friends of his in the KGB that had been murdered by Stalin and at the same time would deprive Stalin of his death-wish victory over Trotsky. In this way, Trotsky would remain a viable thorn in Stalin's side. The problem was how to warn Trotsky in a manner that would not betray his own identity.

Of all of Stalin's enemies, both actual or perceived, none stood higher on his list of persons to be eliminated than Leon Trotsky. Trotsky, whose real name was Lev Davidovich Bronstein, was one of the chief founders of the Communist Party in Russia and second in power only to Lenin in the Communist Government that had followed the collapse of the Tsar in 1917. Although

Lenin's and Trotsky's views often clashed, Lenin nevertheless considered Trotsky the ablest of his followers and heir apparent to lead the new Government in the event of his death. When Lenin died on 18 January 1924, the power play for control of the Government began in earnest. Stalin gradually outmanoeuvred Trotsky and grasped control of the Government. In January 1928, Trotsky and his family were ordered into exile at the desolate outpost town of Alma-Ata in Turkestan near the Chinese border. Distance as well as the ever-present KGB surveillance did not silence Trotsky as he continued to press his opposition to Stalin within the Soviet Union and abroad. Even Stalin's threat to imprison Trotsky did not deter his efforts to dethrone the tyrant. Most of all, Stalin feared that Trotsky's constant agitation and popularity could foment a counter-revolution; however, he refrained from imprisoning or murdering Trotsky because, being so popular with the people, this might have a devastating effect on Stalin's own position.

In January 1929, Stalin banished Trotsky from the Soviet Union by an official decree. Trotsky's first stop was Turkey, where he remained until 1933, when rumours started to float that Stalin had ordered his abduction and return to the Soviet Union in order to stand trial and be executed. The Turkish Government feared an incident on its soil and requested Trotsky to leave. Trotsky spent the next two years in France until Norway granted him political asylum in June 1935. True to form, Stalin had Trotsky tried *in absentia* at the great purge trial of 1936 together with the other 'conspirators' and, as expected, Trotsky was sentenced to death. With an 'official judgement' now in hand, Stalin pressured Norway to extradite Trotsky to the Soviet Union. However, Norway refused to yield to the demand but rather asked Trotsky to leave Norway for the good of relations between the two countries. Trotsky asked for and received political asylum in Mexico, finally arriving there in January 1937. Trotsky, his wife and a small entourage settled in the small town of Coyoacán not far from Mexico City in a house that was constantly guarded by the Mexican police.

Stalin made a great error in judgement when he banished Trotsky from the Soviet Union. Trotsky was now free to collect his thoughts and offer them to the world in a manner that he could not have done as a 'prisoner' in Alma-Ata. Because of Trotsky's constant attacks on Stalin's credibility in light of the purges, Stalin's stature had become greatly diminished throughout the world while that of Trotsky had been enhanced. Stalin became increasingly paranoid and took his immediate revenge on Trotsky's relatives and former colleagues still residing in the Soviet Union, who one by one disappeared from the face of the earth. By 1937, Stalin felt that he had no alternative but to silence Trotsky's denunciations and the only way this could be accomplished was to eliminate the source. Stalin ordered the KGB to plan Trotsky's assassination no matter what the cost or repercussions.

With the background in place, Orlov's narration filled in the blank spaces. As we have seen, Orlov was able to sit in on the first of the great purge trials held in Moscow in August 1936. During this period, he came into contact with many KGB officers and learned that the KGB already had in place a secret agent in the entourage of Trotsky's son Lev (Lyova) Sedov in Paris. The agent was so highly placed that his actual identity was known to Stalin. Sedov ran the Trotskyite organisation in Paris after his father left France in June 1935 and continued the worldwide work of agitation against Stalin from this base.

Orlov could only assume that the planted agent would first ingratiate himself with Trotsky's son and then with Trotsky. This piece of information was so sensitive and so highly guarded that he could not risk asking any questions. What little information he possessed had been volunteered to him by friends and he knew better than to ask for details. In the event of the plant being compromised, each KGB officer who had even the slightest knowledge of him would be scrutinised for the minutest detail that could lead to the source of the leak. Notwithstanding the inherent danger of exposing the plant to Trotsky, Orlov resolved that he would do so at the first practical opportunity. He felt reasonably confident that with the knowledge that the plant was already in place, he was now in a position to recognise other isolated pieces of information that came to his attention from various independent sources, which could result in his identifying the secret agent whose agenda was the elimination of Trotsky.

The next piece of the puzzle, and one that could more readily pinpoint the secret agent, did not come about until over a year later when Orlov was assigned to Spain. Orlov's position in Spain called for frequent business contacts with the Soviet Embassy in Paris and, in particular, with legal *rezident* Nikolai Smirnov, who was an old personal friend of Orlov's in the KGB. On one of these occasions in late August or early September 1937, Orlov stopped for a chat at the office of Valeri Kislov, a KGB officer assigned to the legal *rezidentura*. Kislov was a case supervisor and was in the process of reviewing a file when Orlov sat down at his desk. Kislov handed the file to Orlov and asked him what he thought of it. Orlov's interest was aroused when he noted on the file's cover the code name 'Mark', the customary practice to conceal a source's identity. Orlov gave the appearance of casually leafing through the file, when in reality he was surfing for salient information to pinpoint Mark's identity. While reading the file, Mark's case officer Alexeev came into the room and witnessed Orlov with the file.

Orlov had first met Alexeev in Vienna in 1933. As with any organisation, there are always those who attempt to ingratiate themselves with a superior and Alexeev was no exception. This worked to Orlov's advantage because Alexeev was asked to assist Orlov with some chores and then to take him to the station for the return journey to Spain.

Along the way, Alexeev bragged that the Mark case was a 'hot potato', which could either make or break him, and that Mark was the plant within the Trotsky organisation in Paris. He noted that he had to handle Mark with the utmost care and diligence as any negligence on his part that might expose Mark would mean his head would be in danger. Orlov casually fed the ego of his young friend with a few flattering remarks designed to elicit more information. Alexeev also revealed that Mark worked as a journalist for the Institute of Boris Nikolayevsky, the propaganda arm of the Trotskyite Party in Paris. Now Orlov had a few more key pieces to the puzzle.

The best was yet to come. Alexeev was to have a meeting that day with Mark near the Gare d'Austerlitz and suggested that perhaps Orlov would like to come with him. An offer like this would hardly have been made to the average KGB officer in the same situation, but it was a reasonable offer to a KGB general and anyway Kislov had already shown him the file. Orlov declined to meet Mark but offered to go along to view Alexeev's *modus operandi* in handling a contact with a spy. Without a doubt Alexeev was flattered by Orlov's interest. The meeting was to take place in the Jardin des Plantes, a large park on the left bank of the Seine that was directly across the road from the Gare d'Austerlitz.

Alexeev proceeded to the site of the meeting while Orlov strolled behind him. He saw the two men meet, clearly observed and mentally recorded Mark's physical appearance, and then casually moved to a bench where he could discreetly observe the meeting. It lasted no more than five minutes during which papers were exchanged between the two, no doubt payment for information. The men parted company, walking from the park in opposite directions.

Orlov caught up with Alexeev at the other end of the park and managed to discover a few more pieces of the puzzle. The reason the meeting had been held at the Jardin des Plantes was the fact that Mark's residence was located on one of the streets nearby, where he lived with his wife and baby. Mark's primary position with the Trotsky organisation was as a feature writer on Trotsky's *Bulletin of the Opposition* under the name Etienne. Alexeev failed to offer, and Orlov refrained from asking for, Mark's family name.

Piecing together what he had learned from Mark's file and what Alexeev had volunteered, it became apparent that Mark was the person responsible for the KGB's burglary of the International Institute for Social History, which was also known as the Institute of Boris Nikolayevsky, at 7 rue Michelet, Paris, on 7 November 1936. Trotsky's personal papers and writings against Stalin had been divided into three parts, each in a separate archive, as a secure means to prevent a mass loss. That part of the Trotsky archives which was stored in Paris had been stolen by the KGB on the anniversary of the October Russian Revolution, which had been celebrated on 7 November. The layout of the Institute and the exact location of the hidden Trotsky documents had been obtained and passed on to the KGB by Mark. In order to avoid any suspicion falling on him, Mark had given himself a perfect alibi: he had been the drinking companion of Trotsky's son, Lev Sedov, and fellow Trotskyites, who had been celebrating the anniversary of the Revolution at the very moment the Trotsky documents were being stolen.

Now Orlov was confident that he possessed enough fundamental pieces of the puzzle to enable Trotsky to identify correctly the plant in his son's entourage. What he still lacked, however, was a safe method and secure opportunity to pass the information on to Trotsky. However, Orlov's first attempt to do so was a failure and a foolish error on his part. Because of the inherent danger to himself, he vowed that he would never make the same mistake again.

On his return to Spain, Orlov began to compose a short letter to Trotsky warning him of the infiltration of his organisation in Paris. He printed each letter in ink and forged a style not his own, and was careful not to furnish any incriminating evidence as to the author. He knew only that Trotsky was living in or near Mexico City, so merely addressed the letter to 'Leon Trotsky, Mexico City, Mexico'. The letter was mailed from Paris to divert any attention should it be traced back to its origin. On his subsequent trips to the Soviet Embassy, he kept alert to any information regarding Mark, but everything appeared normal. Mark was still sending his information to the KGB as if nothing had happened. Had such a valuable source been compromised, all hell would have broken loose at the Embassy. Orlov surmised that his letter had never reached Trotsky because of the incomplete address; most probably, a Mexican postal worker had relegated it to the waste-paper basket. Nevertheless, Orlov had some consolation that the letter did not fall into the hands of the KGB.

The strange death of Trotsky's son Lev Sedov on 16 February 1938 was also of concern to Orlov and perplexed him considerably. From what he knew of the son, there was no valid reason why a person barely past the age of thirty and in robust health should pass away. Sedov had a history of abdominal problems and had recently complained of stomach pains. After a severe attack, he had been taken by ambulance to a hospital and, following an emergency operation for appendicitis, had appeared to be out of danger and on his way to a normal recovery. Less than a week after the operation, the patient had had a dubious relapse manifested by hallucinations and verbal obscenities towards the staff and other patients. His condition deteriorated rapidly and he died on the 16th. A cursory autopsy revealed no unnatural causes for the death. Sedov's wife was convinced that he had been poisoned by the KGB.

What concerned Orlov greatly was the fact that the hospital Sedov had been taken to, and where he expired, was the small clinic of Professor Bergère in Paris. Exactly a year earlier, Orlov had been in the same clinic because of his car accident while at the front. He had been cared for at the Bergère Clinic because it was a hospital that was trusted by the KGB to take care of high-ranking Soviet officials. Professor Bergère and his staff were sympathetic towards the Communist cause and under the influence of the KGB. Orlov was in Spain at the time of Sedov's death and was unable to ascertain the complete facts, but speculated that at the moment the KGB Centre had been apprised of the circumstances by Mark, the decision had been made to take advantage of the situation and eliminate Sedov. The autopsy performed by the KGB hirelings had to have been bogus to conceal the true cause of death.

Within five months of Sedov's mysterious death, Orlov was to learn that yet another of Trotsky's leaders had been eliminated. Rudolf Klement was a former German Communist, who had turned against Stalin and strongly supported the Trotskyites in both words and deeds. He had become a trusted member of

Trotsky's proletariat and at the time was organising the founding conference of the Fourth International, the vehicle that Trotsky expected would propel his views to the world. Klement had disappeared from his Paris residence in the middle of July 1938. Within a week of his disappearance, Trotsky had received a letter from Klement addressed to him in Mexico and bearing a New York City postmark. The letter chastised Trotsky for allegedly aligning himself with the Fascists. A copy of the same letter was also received by other Trotsky luminaries. By the end of the month, a headless body was found floating in the River Seine. Because of peculiar scars and marks on the body, it was identified as that of Klement. According to Orlov, the Klement letter to Trotsky was a KGB forgery designed to make it appear that, after the denunciation, Klement had disappeared for his own reasons. Years later, Orlov would learn that when Trotsky received Klement's denunciation letter, he had been positive that the letter was a KGB forgery and that the KGB was responsible for kidnapping and then assassinating Klement.

The KGB hadn't taken into account the possibility that Klement's corpse would emerge from its watery grave, nor that the headless body would be identified. Orlov never made a direct link between the Klement assassination and Mark, but strongly felt that Mark had to have been a key player. Now Mark was the head man in Trotsky's Paris organisation and in a position to report on all its activities to Moscow.

From the moment Orlov first recognised that he must warn Trotsky until he actually decided to defect, he had not yet devised a plan to do so. The KGB's Mobile Groups had already been dispatched to Spain to assassinate him and, as a consequence, all of his time was now devoted to preserving his and his family's lives and planning their eventual escape. Less than three weeks before he crossed the border into France, providence stepped in in the form of what Americans call an 'all points bulletin' from the KGB Centre. KGB General Lushkov, Chief of the KGB Border Guard for the far eastern maritime provinces of the Soviet Union, had defected from his post in the middle of June and all legal *rezidents* abroad were being alerted. Lushkov had been recalled to Moscow under the same set of circumstances that his doomed comrades in the KGB had previously faced. He finally surfaced in Japan and worldwide coverage was given to his plight.

With Lushkov's defection, Orlov could now concoct a legend around his escape and use it as a basis for his warning letter to Trotsky. Fortunately Orlov and Lushkov had been contemporaries in the KGB and had become friends during their careers. As a consequence, Orlov was somewhat familiar with Lushkov's family background. He then had to gather information regarding Lushkov's defection through research first in Montreal and then in Philadelphia as the details had to hold up to scrutiny. Orlov also had to seek out Trotsky's exact address in Mexico. With all the necessary details committed to memory, Orlov then wrote and rewrote the letter, which had to conceal all traces of his identity while being forceful and convincing enough to gain Trotsky's attention. In the final version, Orlov purports to be an un-named close relative of General Lushkov, from whom he obtained the damaging information regarding Mark.

The original letter was written in Russian on an English-language character typewriter rather than on the customary Russian-language Cyrillic character typewriter, which was unavailable to Orlov at the time. Pertinent excerpts from the letter are reproduced verbatim so that the reader can understand the complex nature of the scheme. Lev Davidovich is the polite salutation in Russian for Trotsky. Cheka is one of the KGB's previous names.

27 December 1938

Dear Lev Davidovich,

I am a Jew who came from Russia. In my youth I was close to the revolutionary movement. Later I emigrated to America, where I have been living for many years.

I have close relatives in Russia. Among them there was one by the name of Lushkov, a prominent Bolshevik and chief of the Cheka. It is the same Lushkov, who, being afraid for his life, fled eight months ago from Khabarovsk [Russia] to Japan. That story was printed in all newspapers. From there he wrote to me in America, asking me to come to Japan and help him. I went there and helped him as much as I could. I found him a lawyer to make sure that he is not extradited to the Soviets and gave him a little money.

[The letter goes on to give Lushkov's prominence with the KGB and why he defected. Then it notes that the author read several books on Trotsky when he returned to the US. These books had opened the author's eyes to the Trotsky movement in a positive manner.]

. . . Under the influence of these books I decided (a little late to my regret) to write to you about the most important thing which I learned from Lushkov: about an important and dangerous *agent provocateur*, who has been a long-time assistant to your son, Sedov, in Paris. . . .

Lushkov gave me detailed information about this *agent provocateur* with the understanding that no one, even yourself, should know this information came from him. In spite of the fact that Lushkov forgot the last name of the *agent provocateur*, he supplied enough details to enable you to establish without any error who that man is. . . .

Lushkov is almost sure that the *agent provocateur*'s name is 'Mark'. . . . He wormed himself into the complete confidence of your son and knew as much about the activities of your organisation as Sedov himself. Thanks to this *agent provocateur*, several officers of the Cheka have received decorations.

This *agent provocateur* worked till 1938 at the archive or institute of the well-known Menshevik, Nikolayevsky, in Paris and, maybe, still works there. It was this Mark who stole a part of your archive from Nikolayevsky's establishment (he did it twice if I am not mistaken). These documents were delivered to Lushkov in Moscow and he read them.

[Here the author of the letter gives extensive background

on Mark and suggestions on how to ferret out the *agent provocateur.*]

When I asked Lushkov whether this *agent provocateur* was in any way responsible for the death of your son L. Sedov, he answered that this was not known to him, but that the archive was definitely stolen by Mark.

Lushkov expressed apprehension that the assassination of Trotsky was now on the agenda and that Moscow would try to plant assassins with the help of this *agent provocateur* or through *agents provocateurs* from Spain under the guise of Spanish Trotskyites. . . .

I ask you not to tell anybody about my letter and especially that this letter came from the United States. The Russian Cheka, no doubt, knows that I made the trip to Lushkov, and if they learn about this letter they will understand that Lushkov supplied the information through me. And I have close relatives in Russia to whom I send food parcels and they might be arrested as a reprisal for this letter.

. . . Don't tell anybody about this letter. Ask your trusted comrades in Paris to find out whether Mark belonged to the Union of Repatriation to the Homeland, to check on his past and see whom he meets. There is no doubt that before long your comrades will see him meet officers from the Soviet Embassy.

You have all the right in the world to check on members of your organisation, even when you have information that they are traitors. And besides, you are not obliged to believe me.

The main thing: be on your guard. Do not trust any person, man or woman, who may come to you with recommendations from this *agent provocateur.*

I am not signing this letter and I am not giving you my address; the Stalinists might intercept and read this letter at the post office in Mexico. They might even confiscate this letter.

In order that I may know that you have received this letter,

I should like you to publish a notice in the newspaper *Socialist Appeal* in New York that the editorial office has received the letter from Stein; please, have the notice appear in the newspaper for January or February.

To make it safer, I am sending two identical letters: one addressed to you and the other to your wife, N. Sedov. I have learned your address from the book *The Case of L. T.*

Respectfully, your friend [not signed]

Orlov sent the letter registered from Philadelphia to Trotsky's residence in Coyoacán, Mexico, and mailed an exact copy to Trotsky's wife, Natalia Sedov. He sent two letters for fear that they could be intercepted by Mexican postal workers in the employ of the KGB, and with two letters the prospect that Trotsky would receive the information was greatly enhanced.

Thereafter, Orlov carefully scanned each issue of the *Socialist Appeal* for the confirmation that he hoped to receive. At the end of January his appeal was answered with a classified notice in the newspaper which read, 'I insist, Mr Stein, I insist that you go to the editorial offices of the Socialist Appeal and talk to Comrade Martin.'

This was not the confirmation that Orlov expected. He felt that Trotsky would take his warning at face value without the necessity of any further dialogue. Surely the warning contained sufficient information to identify Mark without the danger of exposing himself any further. He consulted Maria and they both agreed that a meeting with Comrade Martin would be too risky.

They had already planned to leave Philadelphia and were only awaiting the confirmation. Orlov had scheduled a final meeting with his attorney in New York as he had to keep in touch with Finerty in the event of any developments on his immigration status. Maria was unable to make the trip to New York as Vera was having a bout of her illness, but she warned him not to even consider contacting Martin while in New York. After his business with Finerty was concluded, Orlov decided to go to the editorial offices of the *Socialist Appeal* to size up the situation and, perhaps with luck or subterfuge, find out something about Martin. The Comrade was pointed out to Orlov, and he had the opportunity to observe the man casually without being noticed. What Orlov saw was not a Russian but perhaps a Hungarian. However, his intuition told him that something was not right. If the KGB could penetrate Trotsky's organisation in Paris, it was highly possible that they had also penetrated Trotsky's *Socialist Appeal* and that Comrade Martin was an agent in the employ of the KGB. On his return to Philadelphia, Orlov never mentioned the fact that he had visited Trotsky's newspaper. Like the best laid plans of mice and men, Maria only learned of the incident during hearings of the Senate Committee on Internal Security in September 1955.

Orlov was still not satisfied that he had done enough to alert Trotsky to a possible KGB plot to assassinate him. Shortly afterwards, the Orlovs moved to Los Angeles, where Orlov conceived another plan. The family went to San Francisco on holiday and while there he placed a telephone call to Trotsky in Mexico. In the event that the call was traced, at least it would not be from Los Angeles. Orlov identified himself as 'Mr Stein' to Trotsky's secretary, who took the call, and said that he had an urgent message for Trotsky. After several minutes the secretary replied with a feeble excuse why Trotsky could not come to the phone and said that she had been instructed to take Stein's message. Orlov left no message for Trotsky and this was the last attempt he would ever make.

Testimony in the 1955 Senate Subcommittee hearings revealed that Trotsky had considered Orlov's warning letter to be a hoax perpetrated by the KGB and aimed at the destruction of Trotsky's organisation. By the time of the letter and Orlov's telephone call, the KGB had already penetrated the Trotsky household. Orlov never believed that Trotsky considered his letter a hoax as Trotsky's urgent appeal for him to contact Comrade Martin would indicate otherwise. He felt that Trotsky could have pretended that he did not believe the letter so as to allay any fears on the part of his staff. My own feeling is that the secretary who intercepted Orlov's phone call was in the service of the KGB and never relayed

Orlov's message to Trotsky. There was no valid reason why Trotsky would not want to speak with the author of the warning letter as he had nothing to lose and everything to gain, in this instance his very life. What she probably hoped to accomplish by this *modus operandi* was to elicit more information from the caller with which to identify 'Mr Stein'. The only good that transpired as a consequence of Orlov's efforts to warn Trotsky was the huge amount of funds and manpower the KGB expended in Japan and the United States in their pursuit of the elusive 'Mr Stein'.

Leon Trotsky was felled by a blow to his head with a piolet, an ice axe used in mountain climbing, on 20 August 1940, in his study at his residence. He succumbed the next day. The assassin was an agent in the service of the KGB, who had inveigled himself into the confidence of the Trotsky household. Had Trotsky acted more rationally on Orlov's warning letter, he may not have been assassinated and history may have taken another direction.

As to Mark, there was no direct link to the Trotsky assassination, although he was in a position to pave the way. It was not until seventeen years later that Orlov learned of his true identity.

Following publication of his book *The Secret History of Stalin's Crimes*, and the death of Stalin on 2 March 1953, Orlov became more open although he was still reluctant to give up the personal safety precautions that he had developed over his years in hiding. One of the people he came in contact with was a prominent Russian Social Democrat by the name of Abramovich, who had lived in exile in Paris and was familiar with Trotsky's organisation there. Orlov informed Abramovich of the salient facts concerning Mark. In reply, in an oblique manner, Abramovich asked Orlov if he knew of a man by the name of Zborowsky. The question was not directly related to their conversation about Mark and only appeared to Orlov to be a suggestion that Zborowsky might be Mark. Abramovich never directly implied that the two names were one and the same person; however, he suggested that perhaps Orlov should report his suspicions to the federal authorities. Orlov felt that the incident did not present enough evidence for reporting an individual to the authorities and, furthermore,

Mark would only be of interest to the intelligence service of the country where he resided in the event that he was still alive in the mid-1950s. However, what had come out of the meeting with Abramovich was that for the first time an actual family name had tentatively been associated with the KGB cryptonym.

At the beginning of July 1954, Orlov received a letter from David J. Dallin, an author who claimed to be writing a review of Orlov's recently published book and who was also writing his own book, for which he wanted Orlov's advice. Dallin was no stranger to Orlov, and his wife Lidya was known to Orlov as a Trotskyite who had had a close association with Lev Sedov and the Paris organisation. There was no doubt that she would have known Mark. Orlov agreed to a meeting with Dallin at the Wellington Hotel in New York on 6 July, which excluded Lidya. Orlov and Maria met Dallin as planned and chatted with him briefly in the lobby of the hotel. Maria, as cautious as ever, noticed an individual who seemed to be taking more than a casual interest in the three of them, so the meeting was terminated. Maria arranged for a taxi and the group resumed their meeting at a nearby restaurant.

Orlov recalled the meeting as very strange. Both he and Dallin were very reticent and cautious, until Orlov finally broke the ice and asked Dallin if he knew 'Mark, the *agent provocateur*' in Sedov's Paris organisation. Dallin replied in the affirmative and asked if Orlov knew Mark's last name. Orlov replied that he did not, to which Dallin asked if the name Zborowsky was known to him. After Orlov's negative reply, Dallin asked if he had ever seen Mark. Again Orlov feigned ignorance. Dallin then suggested that there had been two Etiennes – one of whom wrote his column under that name – who had worked on Trotsky's *Bulletin of the Opposition* in Paris and that Orlov might be confused about his facts. Orlov now felt that it was Dallin who was confusing the issue. Orlov asked if he knew the present whereabouts of Mark, but Dallin stated that he did not. Orlov suggested that, in recognition of Mark's dedicated service to the KGB and because of his Polish background, he was probably holding down a high-level position with the KGB in Poland. Maria ventured that Mark had probably been stranded in France during the German occupation of Paris. Dallin replied that Mark had been able to get out of France, thus revealing that he knew far more than he was saying. More than ever Orlov was convinced that Zborowsky was Mark.

What transpired next came as a shock to Orlov. Dallin suggested another meeting as he needed advice from Orlov on his own book. He also added that he would see to it that his wife would not be present; however, Orlov retorted that he had no objection to her presence. They agreed to meet at Dallin's Central Park West apartment on Christmas Day.

At the start of the meeting, Lidya Dallin again offered the scenario that there had been two Etiennes and that this must have confused Orlov. However, Orlov insisted that he knew of only one Etienne, that being Mark. Dallin sensed that they had got off to a bad start and signalled to Lidya to get off the subject of Etienne; he also verbally admonished her that the matter was irrelevant. Orlov knew that he had to demonstrate that he was totally aware of Mark's spying activities in Paris. He related several incidents that would have been known only to Mark and the KGB as well as those in very close contact with Mark. One incident he related completely crushed Lidya as it would have been known to her and Mark alone. During Sedov's last illness, he had been confined in the clinic in Paris where the Chief of Staff was a female doctor by the name of Ginsburg, whose husband was Lidya's brother. During his illness, Sedov had had an urge for an orange, and it was Lidya who had provided Lev with one, a fact that was known only to Mark. Mark had related the incident in his KGB report, specifically mentioning that it had been Lidya who had provided the orange for Lev. Lidya looked horrified at the reference to the orange and immediately responded that she now knew that Orlov was telling the truth and was fully aware of Mark's KGB role.

Lidya retreated to the kitchen to make some tea while Maria followed to make sure that no poison was added to their cups. Still in shock, Lidya blurted out that she and her husband had got themselves into a grave situation as they had been responsible for bringing Mark to the United States, where he still resided. Lidya also acknowledged that she had been in Trotsky's household in Mexico as one of his secretaries at the time Orlov had made his attempt to speak to Trotsky from San Francisco. Maria rushed back to the living-room to inform her husband of these facts.

Orlov couldn't wait for the following Monday, 27 December, for the federal offices in Foley Square to open in order to report the presence of a known KGB spy in the United States. He presented his information to United States Attorney Boudinot Atterbury, who immediately summoned the FBI.

What the Dallins revealed on that eventful Christmas Day in 1954 was confirmed later during US Senate Subcommittee on Internal Security hearings held in September 1955. Placed on the record was a statement previously made by Dallin, which asserted that his wife had known Zborowsky since 1935 and he had become acquainted with him a few years later. They had continued the relationship through to 1953. Zborowsky had been born in Uman, Russia, but during the Russian Revolution his family had escaped to Lodz, Poland, where he had grown up. Zborowsky had become a Communist and was arrested in 1930 for his Communist activities. He was placed on bond but escaped to France. Dallin believed that it was then that Zborowsky was recruited into service for the KGB and that he had entered France on forged documents provided by the KGB. Around 1933 to 1934, he was given the task of infiltrating Trotskyite organisations in Paris and continued in this capacity until the outbreak of the Second World War. He was successful in his efforts and became Lev Sedov's trusted confidant. When Sedov fell ill in February 1938, the identity of the hospital to which he was taken was reported to the KGB by Zborowsky. A few days later Sedov died but, according to Dallin, there was no proof that the death was other than natural.

Dallin also claimed that Zborowsky had played a role in the preliminary planning of the KGB assassination of Ignaz Reiss in Switzerland on 4 September 1937, although he had no proof of Zborowsky's direct involvement in the actual murder. When Walter

Krivitsky defected from the KGB in the autumn of 1937, it was Sedov who placed Zborowsky in contact with him, and from that day forward it was Zborowsky who reported Krivitsky's activities to the KGB. The KGB had attempted to assassinate Krivitsky at the railway station in Marseilles, presumably located via Zborowsky, but failed. There were few indications that Zborowsky was connected with the KGB in the United States, although Dallin went on record to state that Zborowsky had admitted that, some time after his arrival, he had been contacted by KGB agents in the US. Dallin said that he doubted Zborowsky's admission as being the whole truth. He continued that in 1943 or 1944, it seems that Zborowsky was assigned to report on Russian émigré groups in New York and to this end approached various émigré leaders.

It was Orlov's firm belief that the Dallins had only come forth with this information about Zborowsky, and testified before the Senate Subcommittee, as a consequence of the confrontation with the Orlovs on that Christmas Day of 1954. They knew that Orlov would report the matter to the FBI and their gesture had been self-serving. Orlov also believed that Lidya had always known about Zborowsky's KGB connection and that she was herself a KGB agent.

Zborowsky and his family had lived under the German occupation of France until 1941, when they were able to escape, and emigrated to the United States with the help of the Dallins. In June 1947, he became a naturalised US citizen.

As to Zborowsky, Orlov never wavered from his contention that Mark's activities in the United States were on behalf of the KGB and he never ceased to reiterate this allegation to the FBI. What did trouble him immensely was the fact that Zborowsky seemed to be able to roam at will in the United States without any fear of reprisal for his past deeds. Early on the FBI made it clear that Zborowsky could not be prosecuted in the United States on the Espionage Statutes because Zborowsky's spying activities in France for the KGB were beyond the jurisdiction of the US. However, Orlov never gave up hope that Zborowsky would some day face the consequences of his past acts.

That day did eventually come about in a very circuitous manner. In the early 1940s, the KGB had in place a spy network that had among its tasks the penetration of Russian émigré organisations in the United States. Zborowsky had become a member of the network, which was headed by two brothers, Jack Soble and Robert Soblen, who had emigrated to the US from Russia under their true family name of Sobelivius. Each brother had Americanised the family name differently. Another member of the spy network was the famous Hollywood producer Boris Morris, who was best known for his series of Laurel and Hardy films. Morris had first been identified as a suspect and later as a member of the Soble spy network when, in 1943, the FBI had witnessed a clandestine contact Morris made with Vasili Zublin, who had previously been identified by the FBI as the legal *rezident* at the Soviet Embassy. At the point when exhaustive investigation had conclusively established that Morris was a KGB spy, and was perhaps the one link in the network that could be broken and turned, Morris was approached in July 1947. After a period of persuasive interviewing by the FBI agents involved, in which he realised that he was in a totally untenable position, Morris agreed to co-operate. What proved to be a bonanza for the FBI was the fact that Morris's business operation, The Boris Morris Music Company, was also the cover for the spy network. As the company had offices both in New York and Los Angeles, the FBI was able to double the scope of its penetration.

For more than a decade the FBI built its espionage case on the Soble spy network and finally decided to bring down the curtain in 1957. The network's members were brought to trial and each was convicted of espionage.

Unfortunately from Orlov's point of view, not all the members of the spy network were convicted. Zborowsky had escaped trial as he had severed his activities with the Soble network around 1945. However, the matter of Zborowsky was not dropped by the FBI but was rather diligently pursued. Zborowsky was brought before a Federal Grand Jury investigating the Soble spy network during February 1957 and vehemently denied under oath that he knew any of its members. However, what he did not know was that Jack Soble had identified him as a member of the ring who had been paid for his services. In November 1958, Zborowsky was charged with perjury. Much to Orlov's satisfaction, he was convicted, but that was short-lived as on appeal the conviction was overturned on a technicality. Zborowsky was retried in November 1962 and this time the jury convicted him of perjury. Orlov testified against him, but the defence was able to bar his testimony as being in the realm of hearsay and therefore not admissible. Zborowsky was sentenced to a term of four years in a federal penitentiary.

Some twenty-four years had elapsed since Orlov had first come into possession of the information about Mark. His persistence and desire to expose the KGB spy first to Leon Trotsky and then to the US authorities strongly attested to his loyalty to the United States.

When the Orlovs had first arrived in Philadelphia in the early part of September 1938, there were apparently no new health problems for Vera and she was in high spirits. She seemed to take delight in every new experience and adventure. Unfortunately, her physical health soon began to decline. By early December, as the colder weather began to set in, she again started to have bouts of rheumatic fever. The attacks seemed to persist for longer durations and the interval between attacks became shorter as the seasonal changes became harsher. The Orlovs immediately took her to a doctor, who recognised that Vera's condition was serious. By early January 1939, her heart palpitations had become more severe and her general practitioner arranged for her to be examined by a specialist in children's heart diseases at the General Hospital in Philadelphia. Vera's condition was diagnosed as critical but not life-threatening, but the long-term prognosis was not good as there was evidence that her heart had become strained and there were signs of heart damage. As Vera's attacks seemed to be less severe during the summer months, the doctor strongly suggested that climatic conditions in southern Florida or California could prolong Vera's life. Before they had even departed from the hospital, they had made the decision to move to Florida.

Orlov had sent his letter of warning to Trotsky at the end of December and as the middle of January was fast approaching expected to receive the coded confirmation of Trotsky's receipt of the letter at any moment. Although time was of the essence, another week or so would not make that much difference. The problem was that a small circulation political newspaper might not be available in a Florida library and he could not chance this possibility. Having researched all the material available on Florida, he decided that Miami would best fit their requirements.

Now having made the decision where to move to and with spare time on his hands, he decided to pay a farewell visit to Jakob, the antique dealer on Pine Street. When Orlov mentioned that he would be moving to Miami, Jakob expressed immediate concern. He related that several years earlier he had visited Miami and was aghast to find that all of the hotels on Miami Beach had signs posted with the caveat, 'Gentiles Only'. Orlov related that although he didn't look Jewish and no one would have to know that he was Jewish, he had seen so much racial intolerance and injustice towards the Jews under both the Tsar and Stalin that he would not feel comfortable under such circumstances. There and then he reversed his original plan and opted to move to Los Angeles. One of his major considerations in choosing Florida over California in the first place was the fact that he would be closer to his attorney in New York. However, his new decision was more than compensated for when he learned that the film industry in Los Angeles was heavily dominated by Jews and there appeared to be little racial discrimination.

By the end of January 1939, the Orlovs were on their way to their new home on the West Coast of the United States. What they did not know was that in less than a year and a half the elder Orlovs would be returning to the East Coast of the United States, this time without their precious daughter Vera.

SIXTEEN

SORROW IN LA

Before leaving for the West Coast, the Orlovs spent a few days in New York, where Orlov had some unfinished business with his attorney John Finerty. At their meeting, Orlov presented Finerty with a sealed blank envelope with instructions that the envelope be sent by registered mail to him in Los Angeles when he had established an address. Orlov stressed the importance of the contents and made Finerty aware that the envelope contained photocopies of his and Maria's Soviet diplomatic passports. The Orlovs would be carrying the original passports, but this identification was so vital that they needed supplementary assurance in the event that something happened to the originals. Finerty agreed that this was a precaution well taken and bade his eminent political client a fond farewell.

After two days enjoying themselves in New York, the Orlovs boarded a train to Chicago. From there, they took the Santa Fe Railroad's crack train, the Super Chief, directly to Los Angeles. The accommodation and food were outstanding, and Vera's fascination with the changing scenery never diminished.

Shortly after departing from Chicago, the Orlovs took note of a young couple sitting across the aisle from them. After they had settled in, Orlov introduced himself to the couple, who told him that they were residents of Los Angeles and had been visiting relatives in Toledo, Ohio. The couple were very congenial and expressed a great attachment to Los Angeles; needless to say, Orlov realised that he had found a fountain of information that would pave his entry into his new destination. His immediate concern centred on where they should live in LA which would meet their needs as well as be near any necessary medical facilities. The couple suggested the neighbourhoods around Wilshire Boulevard and Douglas MacArthur Park, which were good sections of the city and were near the City Library and downtown LA. They also suggested the classified section of the *Los Angeles Times* as a good source for available apartments in the area. On their last night, Orlov invited the couple to supper in the dining car as a sort of payment for their generosity in supplying such helpful information. It was apparent that the couple were on a budget and he wanted to express his appreciation for their help.

The Orlovs got off the Super Chief at the end of the line at Los Angeles's Union Station. When they stepped out of the station's front entrance on to the street, they immediately sensed that they were in a new world. Not since their last vacation on the Côte d'Azur in the South of France had they seen palm trees. The buildings were all low and light coloured in the style of architecture they had been accustomed to in Spain. The most imposing building they could see from Union Station they would later learn was LA's City Hall. Everything looked clean and appealing, but most evident and exhilarating was the weather, which was warm and somewhat balmy, in sharp contrast to the extreme cold they had left behind in New York. The difference in the two cities was so overwhelming that Orlov immediately knew he had made the right choice in moving the family to LA.

Acting on a suggestion made by the young couple on the train, the Orlovs took a taxi to the Park Plaza Hotel overlooking Douglas MacArthur Park. The hotel was more expensive than they expected and looked as if it was part of a film set, with its intricately carved façade and spectacular lobby with a massive staircase, but Orlov knew that their stay there would only be temporary.

The next morning a casual inquiry at the hotel's news-stand led to their next residence. The clerk on duty happened to be from the area and recalled seeing a vacancy sign on a nearby residential hotel. Following the clerk's directions, Orlov located the

Hershey Hotel in the 2600 block of Wilshire Boulevard. The exterior of the hotel and the neighbourhood satisfied his requirements, so he selected a furnished apartment which would meet their needs. The Hershey Hotel would be home to the Orlovs for the next few months. Here they registered under the name of Alexander O. Berg of New York City, the name they would use during their entire stay in Los Angeles.

The month following their arrival in Los Angeles, March 1939, would be a devastating one for Orlov. In mid-March, the German Army occupied the greater part of Czechoslovakia after having annexed the Sudetenland in October of the previous year. Towards the end of the month, the Spanish Civil War came to an abrupt end when General Franco and the Nationalists finally succeeded in capturing Madrid and the Spanish Republican Government crumbled. The German Army had proved its capabilities in Spain and had bullied its way through Czechoslovakia. With the release of its military manpower from Spain and a series of successes brought about by poor statesmanship on the part of the West, there would be no way of stopping Hitler unless the might of the Soviets be brought to bear against the tide. Orlov's worst fear was that some unknown factor would prevent Stalin from committing the Soviet Army to stand up against Hitler.

The unknown factor that would open the gate for Hitler's future aggression first surfaced in May 1939 in what at the time did not appear significant to most of the world. Maxim Litvinov, the Soviet's Commissar for Foreign Affairs, was relieved from his position and replaced by Vyacheslav M. Molotov. Orlov had been a personal friend of Litvinov's from the early years and found him to be not only an outstanding diplomat but a decent and honourable human being. Litvinov was pro-British and French and his diplomatic design was for an amalgamation with these powers to prevent Hitler from undertaking any future adventures. Although subservient to Stalin, he was nevertheless respected by the leaders of the Politburo and his political shrewdness was esteemed in political circles. On the other hand, Molotov was identified with the faction that favoured alignment with the

German dictator and could be better manipulated by Stalin, who wanted conciliation with Hitler. When Orlov heard the news that his old friend had been replaced by Molotov, he knew that the tide had turned away from Hitler. In August, the Soviets and Germans signed a non-aggression pact in Moscow which astounded both the Communist and non-Communist spheres and confirmed what Orlov had suspected all along, that the team of Stalin and Molotov had swayed the Politburo into the belief that this was the best course of action for the Soviet Union. Whatever Stalin wished to achieve by the pact, the world had now become partitioned into two parts with opposing goals and ideology, with the result that a world conflict was inevitable and perhaps just around the corner.

Litvinov was not entirely discarded even though he was later officially dismissed from the Party's Central Committee and more or less driven into obscurity. However, Stalin did spare his life despite the fact that he was a Jew, an old Bolshevik and an important member of Lenin's entourage. Why Stalin went against his own general policy during the great purges and spared Litvinov would always remain a mystery to Orlov. Orlov would later say that whenever he heard Litvinov's name, or let his memory creep into his mind, his thoughts would go back to their last meeting in 1936 and, without exception, a peculiar sadness would overcome him. Litvinov died in 1951 and, on learning the news, Orlov lamented that he had indeed lost a good friend.

Closer to home and more personal to Orlov as a consequence of the defeat of the Spanish Republican Government was the fact that the thousands of men he had caused to be trained in guerrilla warfare in Spain would now become prisoners of war and subjected to the capricious nature of the Generalissimo. He also wondered what would now become of the Red Army generals and political commissars who commanded the various International Brigades. Most of them he knew personally and with some he had developed more than a business relationship. He would in time learn that a few did made it back to the Soviet Union as newspapers during the Second World War gave glowing accounts of the exploits of some of these Red Army generals, who had served their battle apprenticeship with the International Brigades. His heart went out to the common soldiers of the various Brigades who had volunteered to go to Spain from their homelands far away to fight for a cause they believed in.

His thoughts were most focused on the members of his own staff with whom he had had daily contact during his two years in Spain. Most were close personal friends from the early days of the KGB with whom he had shared the most confidential secrets. As he reflected on the situation of his former comrades, he could not help but wish them the best in an extremely critical situation.

The Orlovs were totally satisfied with the area in the vicinity of the Hershey Hotel but soon found that they could not cope with the congestion in the area and especially the heavy vehicular traffic on Wilshire Boulevard. The only apartments available at the time were on the street side of the hotel, which for the most part interfered with Vera's ability to get a good night's sleep.

The Orlovs had long ago developed a habit of walking as a form of exercise and on one of these occasions spotted an apartment that would fill their needs better in a tranquil neighbourhood not too far south of Wilshire and somewhat west of Hoover Boulevard. No apartments were available for an immediate move, but one would become vacant on 1 June 1939. Then and there, the Orlovs agreed to sign a one-year lease for their next residence at the Mayan Apartments, 3049 West 8th Street. The Orlovs actually moved into the sparsely furnished apartment on 1 June and would remain there for the year.

The Orlovs grew fond of the area around Wilshire Boulevard because of its convenience for many shopping sites, ornate cinemas built in the 1920s and fine restaurants. The nearby parks afforded a serene venue to pass the time and the nearness to downtown Los Angeles proved to be a strong attraction.

The Orlovs would often shop at the huge Bullocks Department Store because it was a place to view America on display with all of the latest fashions and state-of-the-art goods. About the middle of August 1939, the family was browsing in the radio department when Vera spotted a small wooden radio, which was a Philco model and which also supported a police radio band. It was apparent that Vera was impressed with the radio and Orlov decided that she should have it for her birthday, which was just a few weeks off. Several days later, Orlov returned to Bullocks, purchased the radio and brought it back to the apartment, where it was hidden until the big day.

Vera's sixteenth birthday was on 1 September 1939, which turned out to be a rather eventful day not only for Vera but for the entire world. There was nothing very unusual for the Orlovs at the start of the day. They had lunch in the apartment, followed by the ritual of a Russian birthday party with all the expressive salutations and wishes for the celebrant, in this case mostly for Vera's good health. Maria then produced the gift-wrapped radio and presented it to Vera. As she opened the box, the smile of delight on her face more than made up for the cost of the radio. Vera couldn't wait to plug it into the wall socket. The results were tragic: the news at that moment and for most of the rest of the day was of the German Army's invasion of Poland in the early hours of the morning. Orlov knew that this was the beginning of the end; the Second World War had begun.

No personal calamities appeared on the horizon for the remainder of 1939 for the Orlovs. Vera's frequent bouts of rheumatic fever seemed to be in remission although she remained weak and easily tired. She continued to read at an accelerated pace and listened to her radio at every opportunity. The radio proved to be the vehicle the Orlovs depended on to keep up with world and local events, but best of all it seemed to help them improve their proficiency in English. Because of their quasi-legal status in the United States and because they were in hiding, Orlov could not engage in any employment; as it turned out, he would never hold any recognised daily employment. In one way this was a financial disadvantage, but in another it further brought the family together in what would be a critical time.

From time to time during our discussions, Orlov would tell

me of minor incidents of a personal nature that occurred during the time the family was in hiding. Most of these events were of no particular significance to the world of intelligence but to the reader they do hold some importance in exploring the character of the man and his family and perhaps provide the basis for some of his decisions. The reader is entitled to know the man as I did and therefore I have included a couple of these minor brush-strokes in painting the overall picture.

The Orlovs were not the typical US movie-oriented family. In fact, films were considered decadent by the standards of the Communist Party of the USSR and most of the inhabitants of the homeland were bound to this convention through censorship. Orlov had occasionally broken out of this restrictive mould during his KGB assignments in Europe, seeing a film if it attracted his attention; however, these visits to the cinema were few and far between. Likewise, Vera preferred to read and was not inclined towards the movies, although she was more conversant with Hollywood and some of its stars than her parents. This changed once they settled in Los Angeles as there was no way of escaping the glamour of Hollywood. The Orlovs saw only a handful of special films as a family but did allow Vera to attend the Saturday matinees at the famous cinemas that were in their Wilshire neighbourhood. As a European family and because their situation called for tight security precautions, they would escort Vera to the Saturday matinees and return to the cinema just before the conclusion of the programme.

Towards the end of 1939, Orlov read rave reviews of a film that was a parody on Communism. This was the famous *Ninotchka* starring Greta Garbo and Melvyn Douglas. Garbo plays the part of a dedicated Communist commissar who has been sent to the US on a trade mission with several other commissars. Douglas plays the part of the decadent bourgeois playboy, whose capitalist views sharply clash with the Communist views of Commissar Ninotchka. Slowly the views of her fellow commissars are won over to the capitalist side while she remains adamant about the virtues of Communism. Naturally Douglas wins her over by the end of the film. Orlov related that he and his family found the film to be hilarious and they had burst out laughing at scenes at which others in the audience remained silent as they did not understand the nature of the portrayal from the Communist standpoint. Orlov had often gone abroad on KGB assignments under the cover of a trade mission and could easily picture himself in the film. He also felt that Garbo handled her role as Ninotchka in a true light. He was aware that the film would never be shown in the USSR, but wondered what its reception would be had it been allowed to be played.

One thing that always stuck in my mind was Orlov's statement that the radio and the cinema resulted in the 'Americanisation of Vera'.

I was always curious as to Vera's education in the US while the Orlovs were in hiding. The answer was a simple one: Vera had no formal education in the US for several reasons. Firstly, Orlov explained that Vera was an exceedingly intelligent child whose educational development was far above the level of her contemporaries. Secondly, there was a security risk as school enrolment would be an area the KGB would look into as a means of locating the family. In the early stages of their concealment, they were aware that home study was not a major problem, although in time they knew that they would have to confront the issue. There was no doubt that Vera would in time pursue a professional career and would therefore have to enrol in a university.

In the meantime, Vera's education was not neglected. A minimum of four hours was set aside each day, five days a week, for this purpose. Both of the Orlovs were university educated and worldly wise. Maria usually handled the chore of tutoring Vera in the English language and history, and setting aside part of the time for a specific area of self-study. Vera's progress was self-evident. The only phase of her education that was lacking was in the field of mathematics as neither parent had a proficiency in this discipline. Vera despised the subject and recognised this as one of her hapless failures. Her talents lay more in the field of literature and creativity, and her reading skills were superior. By an early age she was reading and understanding the works of Lev Tolstoy, Fyodor Dostoevski, Alphonse Daudet and Alexandre Dumas, as well as other great authors and ancient philosophers. Her favourite novel was *La Dame aux camélias* by Dumas, which she read and re-read several times. This slightly bothered Orlov as he suspected that Vera saw herself in the heroine, who was dying from tuberculosis; however, he realised that a young girl would also be attracted to the romantic mood of the novel.

Vera was able to speak and read in French and German as a result of Orlov's assignments in France and Germany. There the family had had access to radios and local newspapers. In this regard, Orlov would say that a child's brain was like a sponge and easily absorbed everything that came to its attention. In France and Germany, he had been the chief of the legal *rezidentura* and had been able to avail himself of the educational support provided for the children of the diplomats. Within their own confines, Russian was always spoken and was Vera's mother tongue.

Religion was a subject we never touched on to any great extent. I was acutely aware that Orlov was a man of high moral standards and principles to the extent that he lived by the golden rules. It was not until years later, when I attended Maria's funeral, that I noticed both a rabbi and a minister officiating. Orlov explained that his parents had been Orthodox Jews and Maria's parents had been Christians with some Jewish ancestry, and accordingly he supported both religious views. His formative years under the Communist system, which had espoused atheism, had had little hold on him and there was never a time when he did not believe in God. He acknowledged that the family celebrated both Jewish and Christian religious holidays. What had occurred as a result of Communism was his retreat from the formal weekly religious services at the synagogue, although he did attend services on the most important religious holidays after his arrival in the US as a walk-in so as to go unnoticed.

Towards the end of 1939, Vera's medical condition still seemed to be in remission although she was physically frail. She had suffered no acute attacks for some time and her health was closely monitored. The year would end with Vera in good spirits and optimistic about the future. The turn of events that seemed to project a longer lifespan for Vera was attributed by her parents to the warmer climate in California.

The new year of 1940 brought several events that would have an impact on Orlov's status as a refugee in hiding in the US. On 28 June, Congress passed the Alien Registration Act (ARA) and on the following day President Roosevelt signed it into law. This made it unlawful for an alien to belong to any organisation that advocated the overthrow of the US Government and further required that all aliens residing in the US be registered and finger-printed. Orlov's membership of the Communist Party of the USSR clearly brought him under the purview of the new law although technically his defection had ended the relationship. Orlov was greatly concerned as to how the new law would affect his particular situation. He immediately consulted Finerty, who advised him that there was ample time to comply with the law and that he would research the new law as to its effect on Orlov's particular situation.

Another event was the Selective Service Act of 1940 (SSA), which was passed by Congress on 16 September and signed into law by President Roosevelt. The SSA called for the first peace-time draft of men into the military. Men between the ages of twenty to thirty-six were required to register for the draft. Orlov escaped the first round of the draft and would not have to register due to the fact that he was over age. However, as war conditions prevailed and the draft consumed a greater number of men, Orlov would come within the purview of the law. At the moment it was of no immediate concern to him, although in a matter of less than two years he would have to face the consequences of regis-tering for the draft.

The hopes that the new year would continue with Vera's seem-ingly good health disappeared in mid-February when she caught a cold. She was immediately taken to her neighbourhood doctor, Dr Russell W. Lyster, at his office on West 3rd Street. Dr Lyster was not pleased with this development but hoped that the cold would have little effect on Vera's already strained heart muscles. The cold did disappear as expected, but by early May another cold took hold and lingered for longer than usual. Then her heart palpitations returned. By this time, there was no doubt that Dr Lyster was deeply concerned for her health and felt that the only alternative was to commit her to the Good Samaritan Hospital, where he could closely monitor her condition.

Vera remained in the Good Samaritan Hospital from 22 May until she was discharged on 7 June. The Orlovs spent every hour of each day at her bedside. Her condition did not seem to deteriorate nor did it seem to get better. Dr Lyster confided to Orlov that there was nothing more that could be done at the hospital and Vera's prospects for recovery were not good. The best that could be hoped for was a few additional years of life, although in this case Vera's physical activity would be severely restricted. The Orlovs held out in the hope that God would intervene to save their daughter.

Less than a week after Vera was admitted to the hospital, world events took a turn for the worse when Holland and Belgium surrendered to the German Army on 28 May. Within a week of Vera's discharge from the hospital, the German Army had taken Paris. Orlov's attention was not squarely focused on the world events taking place because of his own problems, but at the back of his mind he knew that the situation was not good. For days after the fall of Paris the family would reminisce about the times they had lived in or visited the City of Lights.

Another problem then came to the fore that could not be avoided. The Orlovs' lease on their residence at the Mayan Apartments expired on the last day of May and the landlord had already leased the apartment to another party. Fortunately, the Orlovs had anticipated the problem and found another apartment on the next street. By 1 June, they had moved what few belongings they possessed to The Westbury, an apartment house located at 3360 West 9th Street, where Vera was taken on her discharge from hospital on 7 June.

The next five weeks would be the longest and saddest period of time the Orlovs would ever have to endure. They were reconciled to the fact that there was little hope for Vera, yet prayed for that elusive miracle that would sustain their daughter's life. Vera's emotional output was generally optimistic and outwardly she held out hopes for the future, in spite of the fact that the look in her eyes betrayed her. She never uttered one word to indicate that she knew she was dying, although the ever-present extrasensory communication between the family members indicated that she knew.

During that time Vera was confined to her bed. During the day both parents were usually at her bedside and at night they would take turns to sit in a chair near the bed and attend to any of her needs as well as to monitor her condition. More often than not, her nights were restless and as time progressed so did her frailties. Towards the end, the palpitations returned with unremitting frequency as though a harbinger of bad news to come.

On the night of 14 July, Orlov had taken his turn at Vera's bedside. She had been especially restless that night and perspiration appeared on her forehead somewhat after midnight. He recognised the signs from previous occasions as the bad omen that signalled an attack of rheumatic fever. The following day she had a more serious and sustained attack. Just before dawn on the 15th, signs of another attack started and Orlov immediately summoned Maria with the bad news. A few minutes after 8 a.m. the palpitations increased in intensity and frequency. The Orlovs had no telephone so he went to the manager's office to telephone Dr Lyster. The doctor had been called to another emergency but would be given Orlov's message as soon he called in. The manager knew of another doctor in the neighbourhood and proceeded to make the call for help. In a matter of minutes, the doctor was at The Westbury, had taken note of the gravity of the situation and given Vera an injection of adrenaline, but to no avail. Vera had already expired. Dr Lyster appeared on the scene in a matter of minutes but nothing further could be done.

Vera's body was immediately moved to the Glasband &

Company Mortuary for embalming. Here Orlov made arrangements to have a rabbi and a minister officiate at the brief funeral rites. That afternoon her body was taken to the Los Angeles Crematorium and was cremated that same day, in accordance with Jewish custom that called for burial or cremation by sunup of the day following death. One of the last matters the Orlovs had to accomplish before Vera was cremated was to obtain a lock of her hair. Following Orlov's death, I opened by court order his two safe-deposit boxes in Cleveland. Among the contents was the lock of Vera's hair, a highly valued remembrance of his daughter which had been kept under such secure conditions for all those years.

Maria could not stand the thought of spending another night at the apartment where their precious daughter had died. That same evening they moved to Apartment 204, 669 South Union Avenue. Orlov later confessed that there was no way that he could have remembered this specific address as they had only stayed there until the end of the month. However, he had retained the final funeral statement from Glasband & Company, dated 27 July 1940 and addressed to the South Union Avenue apartment.

On 1 August, the Orlovs moved to the Ansonia Apartments, 2205 West 6th Street, with the intention of deciding whether to stay in LA or to move on. As with all their previous residences in LA, the Ansonia was in the Wilshire Boulevard neighbourhood where they felt most comfortable. They liked everything about LA, especially the weather, with the sole exception that this was the place of Vera's death. They also felt reasonably secure from the KGB in California. However, Maria was so distressed that she cried every day and became upset at the mere mention or thought of Vera. Soon it became apparent that they could not remain in LA and would have to move on. The only questions that remained were where to move to and when. In the end, the Orlovs decided to move to Boston, for reasons I will explain in the next chapter.

Just ten days before they left LA, Orlov was subjected to yet another shock. He happened to be walking past a news-stand when the headline of a newspaper caught his attention: Trostsky had been assassinated. The fatal blow had been delivered on 20 August 1940 and Trotsky had succumbed the following day. The assassin had been caught but not identified; however, there was not the least shred of doubt in Orlov's mind that the murder had been carried out by the KGB. Orlov's initial response was anger that Trotsky had not heeded his warnings when he had gone out of his way to forewarn him at risk to himself. Anger then turned to logic when he rationalised that nothing could have prevented the determination of the KGB to consummate its highest priority. Logic then turned to sorrow when he realised that a great Russian leader, who had placed his priorities solely for the good of the Russian masses, to his own detriment, was now gone.

The full impact of Vera's death on her parents can best be summed up in an eloquent passage written by Orlov:

> Care for our daughter was the supreme goal of our life. She was only 15 [when Orlov defected], too young to fathom the nightmare which we had left behind and the crisis we were entering upon.
>
> She picked up the English language quickly and came to love and admire this beautiful country. Because of her knowledge of several languages, she dreamed of becoming a foreign journalist and taking care of us. This thought kept her very happy. But the periodic recurrence of rheumatic fever wore her heart out until one fateful morning, in July 1940, after several days of uncontrollable violent palpitations, it stopped beating. This was the biggest blow to my wife and me. The light had gone out of our eyes. . . . In our misfortune there was one consolation – that she died in our arms, surrounded by love.

The Orlovs left Los Angeles on Sunday, 1 September 1940, en route to Boston, the very day on which Vera would have been seventeen years old. Unknown to them at the start of their long journey, there would be an unexpected happenstance along the way that would come to shape their lives for a period of almost eleven years. It was also this one incident that would eventually make it possible for me to meet the Orlovs.

SEVENTEEN

BOSTON

The Orlovs arrived early at Union Station in downtown Los Angeles for a last look at the city they would have reason to remember for the rest of their lives. They had grown to like California and had apparently been able to elude the KGB for yet another year. The prospects seemed to indicate that they had found a safe sanctuary. Within that year all their dreams for the future had been shattered.

When they boarded the Santa Fe Railroad's Super Chief bound for Chicago, they carried with them Vera's ashes in an urn contained in a cardboard box. The ashes had been put into a small box inside the urn, and the urn had then been placed in a larger box which was covered with wrapping paper and sealed. The final product was addressed to Attorney Finerty in New York and the parcel contained the correct postage. In the unthinkable event that the parcel was somehow lost during the journey, the rear side of the parcel contained a notice that clearly stated that the contents were the ashes of a family member and of no value to anyone but the family, and that the finder should forward the parcel. In addition, the finder was asked to write separately to Finerty as the family was offering a reward for the parcel's return. Orlov related that he took these extraordinary precautions to ensure the safety of his daughter's ashes despite the fact that they fully expected to transport the box with paramount diligence. He remarked that it was his KGB training which had come to the fore in the current situation.

The journey to Chicago was uneventful with the exception that sadness prevailed throughout the trip. There was little spoken communication between the Orlovs and most of the time was spent aimlessly staring out of the window. The box never left Maria's person and for the most part it sat on her lap with her hands continuously and gently fondling the precious cargo. At night the box remained close to her in her Pullman berth. The General recognised early on that the situation was not good for Maria's emotional stability as the box unremittingly reminded her of her daughter and only prolonged her agony and sorrow. By the time they reached Chicago, it was evident that Maria was emotionally and physically exhausted.

In Chicago, they made their connection on the eastbound train for Boston. As the train approached Toledo, Ohio, it was apparent that Maria was ill and unable to cope with the journey. Normally Maria was an extremely strong person, both in mind and body, but the events since Vera's death were now taking their toll. Orlov felt it wise to break up the journey and afford Maria a good night's sleep in a hotel. He contacted the train conductor and found that their journey could be interrupted but that it would be impossible to make the necessary arrangements for their luggage travelling in the baggage car in the time remaining before their arrival in Toledo. The conductor informed Orlov that the next stop after Toledo was Cleveland, where there would be ample time to make arrangements to have their excess baggage continue on to Boston and placed in storage. He also informed Orlov that the train would be arriving in Cleveland late in the evening and suggested that he might want to stay at the Hotel Cleveland, which was part of the Terminal Tower complex that also housed the Cleveland Union Station, where they would disembark from the train. That evening the Orlovs checked into the Hotel Cleveland under the identity of Mr and Mrs Alexander Berg.

For the first time since leaving LA, Maria slept and felt much better in the morning. Orlov noticed the difference and felt it wise to remain in Cleveland for another night to continue the fine progress. That morning they walked around the downtown area and were impressed with the wide thoroughfares, the number of large imposing department stores and the huge public library, situated near their hotel just off Public Square. They spent the remainder of the day at the world-renowned Cleveland Museum of Art.

The next day the Orlovs continued their journey to Boston. The short and unexpected stay in Cleveland had rejuvenated Maria, but perhaps the most innocuous aspect of the stopover was that it would set the stage for their eventual move from Boston. They liked what they saw in the friendly city, but there was no doubt that the Cleveland Public Library would be the magnet that would draw the Orlovs to Cleveland in a matter of two years.

They arrived in Boston in the late evening of 5 September 1940 and registered at the Essex Hotel under yet another fictitious name, Mr and Mrs Leon A. Berg of Los Angeles, California. This would be the name they would use during their stay in Boston, with one exception which called for yet another cryptonym. The name Leon is the Westernised version of Orlov's true Russian name Leiba, and he purposely used the middle initial 'A' for Alexander in case he had a lapse in memory. During his hiding in the US, Orlov out of necessity resorted to many fictitious identities that were usually variations of names of some significance and therefore more readily remembered. However, he related that he also kept a diary, where he listed these names in a code known only to him and Maria.

He had chosen Boston because during his visit there in 1932, when he had been researching dead-drop sites, he had discovered a cemetery adjacent to Harvard University. The cemetery turned out to be the Mount Auburn Cemetery on Mount Auburn Street, and Orlov was impressed with the sheer beauty of its landscaping and the tranquillity that prevailed throughout; it was indeed a natural site for a dead drop, although he was unaware if it had ever actually been used as such.

After the Orlovs were settled in at a permanent residence at 36 Highland Avenue, Cambridge, the time had come to consider a final resting place for Vera's remains. Orlov wanted it to be Mount Auburn, and this was the prime reason why they had taken up residency in Cambridge. However, Maria also had to be satisfied before a final decision could be made. They soon visited the cemetery, but Maria could not make up her mind conclusively. They then visited several other cemeteries in the environs of Boston but found none they liked better than Mount Auburn.

On 24 October 1940, Alexander Berg paid the sum of $150 to the Mount Auburn Cemetery for Niche No. B-10, Columbarium No. 3, in the Bigelow Chapel for the right to deposit in perpetuity the cremated human remains of Vera Orlova Berg. Orlov was able to procure another document dated on the same day to the effect that he reserved the right to extract Vera's remains if he so chose at any time, and further Mount Auburn agreed to refund the $150 paid in that eventuality. Orlov felt that he had to cover every contingency. Orlov also reserved the right to purchase additional space in Niche No. 10 for his and Maria's burial.

By the time the Orlovs decided to leave Boston in the summer of 1942, they were satisfied that there was no foreseeable reason why they would have to remove Vera's remains from Mount Auburn. They further decided that this would also be their final resting place as it would give them comfort knowing that in death their remains would be together. The additional space in Niche No. 10 was purchased on 14 July 1942 and granted in perpetuity for the right to deposit the remains of Maria O. Berg and Alexander O. Berg. The sum of $150 for the additional space also covered perpetual care for and repair of the niche.

The Orlovs' new home on Highland Avenue was only about three miles east of the cemetery and they had chosen it for this reason so that they could walk the short distance to visit their daughter's niche.

As soon as the Orlovs obtained a permanent address, they contacted their attorney, John Finerty, as the first step in complying with the newly enacted Alien Registration Act. By the early part of December 1940, Finerty had finalised arrangements for the Orlovs to register under the provisions of the ARA in a manner that would not compromise their specific whereabouts in the United States. Finerty was a long-time friend of the then Attorney General of the United States Francis Biddle. Biddle recognised the gravity of the situation and turned the matter over to Earl G. Harrison, Director of Alien Registration, for personal handling.

The Orlovs met Finerty in New York and they proceeded jointly to Washington. On 19 December 1940, they met Harrison at his office. The circumstances regarding Orlov's defection from the KGB and the obvious need to conceal Orlov's whereabouts in the US were made clear to the government official. He agreed to suspend the requirement of a specific address for the registrant as long as the Orlovs could be reached through Finerty. No doubt Biddle's personal interest in the matter significantly influenced the making of arrangements for the Orlovs that were unusual to say the least. Harrison's assistant personally took the Orlovs to the office of Richard E. Eggleston, Postal Inspector-in-Charge, in the US Post Office, Washington DC, where the actual registration took place. The Orlovs furnished their address as care of John F. Finerty, 120 Broadway, New York City. Orlov was greatly relieved with the manner in which his registration was facilitated and now had yet another obstacle behind him.

News at the beginning of 1941 did not bode well for Orlov. On the morning of 10 February, he had read in the newspapers that the body of Walter Krivitsky had been found in a pool of blood in his room at the Bellevue Hotel in Washington DC. There were many unresolved questions and theories concerning Krivitsky's death, yet the path of least resistance was suicide. In the days before the US knew much about the operations of the KGB, this theory was acceptable. To a KGB professional like Orlov, it was obvious that Krivitsky's death was at the hands of the KGB.

Orlov was deeply shaken when he heard the news of Krivitsky's death but nevertheless learned something of immense value in the form of a lesson that would keep him steps ahead of the KGB. Krivitsky had made the fatal mistake of openly testifying before the Dies Committee in Washington DC, which was investigating Communist infiltration in the US, and had co-operated with British intelligence, a fact that would certainly have come to the attention of the KGB through its sources. Krivitsky had shown his hand and the KGB had taken advantage of his mistake. Orlov would not make the same mistake. When Orlov broke the news of Krivitsky's murder to Maria, she was more adamant than ever that they remain in deep cover and not do anything pointless that could possibly reveal their whereabouts.

They kept to themselves more than ever and made no friendships of a personal or casual nature. They were ever vigilant as to their own security by keeping their apartment dimly lit throughout the night so as to be able to see a possible intruder, as well as placing loose obstacles at the door and windows in a manner that would alert them to any unwanted presence. They also used an old anti-surveillance tactic even when walking the streets in their own neighbourhood. One of them would walk ahead on one side of the street while the other walked on the opposite side at least a block behind in order to observe if the first person was being followed.

They made only one lasting friendship during the entire time they were in Boston. This was with Mrs Katz, who managed their apartment house. Mrs Katz and Maria had a genuine affection for one another and it was good therapy for Maria to have at least one person she could express her thoughts with and while away some time. For a number of years after the Orlovs left Boston, they exchanged greetings cards with their former landlady on some of the holidays.

A few days after their arrival in Boston, on 7 September 1940, the Orlovs opened a safe-deposit box (number 7165) at the Pilgrim Trust Bank, which was located at 31 Milk Street, under the name Alexander L. Berg. The bank was located a few steps from the FBI office and I must have passed it several times each day.

A year later, on 16 August 1941, the Orlovs appeared at the Pilgrim Trust Bank only to be told that they could not retrieve certain contents from their safe-deposit box because of an Executive Order by President Roosevelt, which had been issued after they had rented the box. The Executive Order foresaw the shadow of the war that would eventually engulf the entire world and in part placed restrictions on the banking activities of aliens. As the Orlovs were unable to produce naturalisation papers to prove that they were US citizens, they fell under the purview of the new regulation. However, under these same regulations they were able to reclaim their two passports and a Canadian bank book under the scrutiny of an observant bank official. This official's curiosity was aroused by the fact that the Orlovs were also anxious to repossess a quantity of 'roll and flat pack' film from the box. No doubt his suspicions were kindled when he saw that the object of their obsession was ordinary film of apparently little monetary value rather than items of more tangible value. The Orlovs were not allowed to take the film and it remained in custody in the safe-deposit box until long after the Second World War had ceased, along with the termination of the Executive Order.

The Pilgrim Trust Bank did not report the matter to the FBI office at 100 Milk Street until 24 January 1942. Orlov never returned to the bank to claim the film after his initial attempt, although he did pay the annual rent on the box throughout the years that he maintained the account. The one mishap that probably encouraged the bank to report the incident was the fact that their September 1941 rental bill for the box addressed to the Orlovs care of the Essex Hotel in Boston was returned with the stamped notation 'Not Found'. This, together with the Orlovs' strange behaviour when trying to retrieve the film from the safe-deposit box, probably motivated the bank to report the matter.

The FBI initiated an investigation into the Orlovs under the only name reported to them, Alexander L. and Marie Berg, under the administrative category 'Internal Security – G'. The 'G' was the category which stood for the wartime enemy, the Germans, as the bank official who reported the matter related that, although the Orlovs represented themselves as Russians, he found them to be 'people of some breeding' and was left with a 'very definite impression that they were Germans'.

The Boston office conducted an exhaustive investigation throughout the United States based on the limited amount of information available but were never able to identify the Bergs. There was never sufficient evidence on which a subpoena could be obtained with which they could legally open the Orlovs' safe-deposit box for examination. Each cheque sent to the Pilgrim Trust Bank for the rental payments on the box was the basis for additional investigation, but to no avail. The FBI reasoned that they should continue to investigate the Orlovs because not only were they still eluding the Bureau but they were continuing to pay the rent on the box in order to protect its contents. When the Second World War ended, so did the FBI's legal interest in the Bergs and the case was closed. It was not until 9 May 1950 that Orlov reappeared in person at the Pilgrim Trust Bank to claim the film.

By the summer of 1941, the general character of the Second World War changed again. In June, Germany broke its non-aggression treaty with the USSR and invaded Russia. Before the end of the year, the Germans were at the outskirts of Leningrad as well as at the gates into Moscow before the tide of war shifted again. On Sunday, 7 December, the Orlovs were listening to Vera's radio when a broadcast was interrupted to announce that the US naval base at Pearl Harbor had been bombed by the Japanese. The next day President Roosevelt announced that a state of war existed between the United States and Japan. Before long the whole world was engulfed in the Second World War.

All of these new complexities would leave their mark on Orlov. He had escaped the peacetime draft because he was over age, but with the war being accelerated at an unprecedented pace the need for manpower was unabated and the age limits for registration were adjusted accordingly to take the old as well as the young. Orlov had every intention of complying with the draft registration, but a salient problem existed. For the past year and a half he had been living at the same Boston residence under the name of Leon O. Berg. The procedure called for the registrant to register with a particular draft board and then a draft card would be issued and sent by mail to the registrant's home address. Orlov was aware that he had to register under the name that he had used when he entered the US as his immigration status was in the name of Alexander Orlov. However, if a draft card arrived at his residence in a name other than Berg, he would no doubt come under suspicion and be reported under the prevailing war-time conditions. This was a problem he neither wanted nor needed, so a plan was therefore devised.

The Orlovs registered at the Eliot Hotel, 370 Commonwealth Avenue, Boston, on 25 April 1942, under the name of Mr and Mrs Alexander O. Berg. They did not vacate their residence at 36 Highland Avenue but simply advised the management that they would be away on vacation.

The following day Orlov registered with Selective Service Local Board #18 on Boylston Street under the name of Alexander Orlov Berg at the Commonwealth Avenue address. He was careful to record that he was also known by the name of Alexander Orlov as well as his true name Leon Feldbin. Towards the middle of the following week he received his draft card, which had been mailed to the Eliot Hotel. The Orlovs then ended their 'in-town' vacation and returned to their home in Cambridge, no one being the wiser. Orlov never let go of the draft card and it was among his possessions when he died.

Their daughter's death was never forgotten, and the Orlovs made the pilgrimage to the cemetery almost every day during the two years they resided in Boston. The anniversaries of Vera's birthday and death were especially hard on the Orlovs, but more so on Maria. On these dates, they would bring cut flowers to the niche and spend the day in mourning. As time wore on, Orlov noticed a definite change in Maria, which progressed to the point where he became concerned for her emotional health. She became more depressed after each successive visit to the cemetery and on those special anniversaries would cry unremittingly, to the point where Orlov would have to insist that she leave the cemetery for her own good. He finally conceded that they must move from Boston before Maria's condition resulted in a nervous breakdown.

The question was where should they go. Orlov was aware that nothing would keep them from visiting Vera's niche from time to time, so it had to be in the somewhat close proximity of Boston yet far enough away that Maria would not insist on more frequent visits. The West Coast was too distant and the East Coast too near to the centres of the KGB's operations. Then Orlov remembered the few days they had spent in Cleveland. The city offered them many possibilities but best of all there was every indication that it would be a safe place to hide with its large ethnic population. While in Boston, Orlov's thoughts had turned to writing a book that would expose Stalin's crimes, and what he would require towards this end was a research base that he could avail himself of. He could think of none better than the Cleveland Public Library. Based on all these considerations, they finally decided that Cleveland would be their next destination.

EIGHTEEN

CLEVELAND

The Orlovs arrived in Cleveland on the first day of December 1942 and from that date forward until their departure some ten years later would be known as Mr and Mrs Alexander Berg. They took up temporary residence at the Hotel Cleveland. Within a few days, they were able to find an apartment at the Bertland Apartments, 2384 Euclid Heights Boulevard, located on the east side of Cleveland in the suburb of Cleveland Heights.

They chose this particular location because it was immediately available and, under wartime conditions, they had only a few other options for housing. The apartment was close to the cultural centre of Cleveland, which included the Cleveland Museum of Art and Severance Hall, home of the Cleveland Orchestra. Public transportation into the heart of Cleveland was convenient as well as inexpensive.

By the time the Orlovs arrived in Cleveland, Orlov was convinced that he would have to pursue a more formal education to hone his skills in the English language and as a means for possible employment in the future. On his arrival in Cleveland, therefore, he immediately researched the colleges and educational institutions in the area and focused his attention on a small business college, Dyke and Spencerian College, which specialised in the commercial field. Dyke College, the more recognisable name by which the institution was referred to by its students and faculty as well as the general public, enjoyed an excellent reputation and was well perceived by the local commercial and industrial community. The College was located in the Standard Building in downtown Cleveland. Orlov paid several visits to the College and spoke to its counsellors, who suggested that his background and goals were appropriate for the Business Administration course, which was well structured to enhance his English-language proficiency. Orlov recalled that after having made his final decision, he enrolled in the course on the Monday preceding the Christmas 1942 holiday. He felt fortunate in not losing any time as he was able to enrol in the spring semester, which started shortly after the holidays.

For the next two and a half years Orlov's principal endeavour was his studies at Dyke College. Shortly after enrolling, Orlov also applied for a part-time position as a translator at the Berlitz School of Languages in downtown Cleveland. He was told that his English-language skills did not meet the demands of the school but that his application would be kept on file in light of his studies at Dyke College and he would be given consideration in the future.

An interesting coincidence was the fact that Dyke College and the Cleveland Office of the FBI were both housed in the Standard Building during these years. Dyke College was located on the third floor of the building and the FBI on the ninth floor. Undoubtedly during those two and a half years, Orlov rode the elevators with hundreds of FBI agents. When I asked him if he was aware of the situation, he replied in the negative with the added explanation that he assumed the FBI was located in the Federal Courthouse building.

Orlov accelerated his studies and graduated on 15 June 1945 with a degree in Business Administration. He was favourably disposed towards Dyke College and especially appreciative of the extra efforts the teaching staff had made during a critical transitional period. He considered his greatest achievement during the two and a half years was the development of his proficiency in English to the point of fluency. I can attest to this fluency and articulation in English and was always amazed at the extent of Orlov's vocabulary and his ability to formulate sentences in a clear and concise manner. I was trained to be alert to traces of a foreign accent and speech patterns of a questionable nature, but as to

Orlov I was only able to detect the presence of a minimal foreign accent and a speech pattern that was almost flawless.

Shortly before graduation, Orlov again applied for a position with the Berlitz School of Languages. He felt that he had greatly enhanced his English-language skills and with his knowledge of Russian, German, French and Spanish, he would have an appropriate background for a position with the firm. What was more pressing was the fact that his financial means were dwindling and at some point in the not-too-distant future he would have to secure employment. The Berlitz officials were now very receptive to him, having re-evaluated his English proficiency, and indicated that a position would be available for him on graduation from Dyke College. However, by the time he graduated, Orlov had come to the decision that he must write a book dealing with Stalin's crimes notwithstanding the fact that this would mean continued financial hardship. He withdrew his name from any further consideration and was assured by the Berlitz officials that, should he ever change his mind, a position would be available.

The Orlovs came to enjoy their circumstances in Cleveland Heights and had no intention of living elsewhere for the time being. They felt comfortable in the neighbourhood, probably because it was predominantly Jewish. They took advantage of the close proximity of the Cleveland Art Museum and often attended concerts by the Cleveland Orchestra at the Severance Hall. They became particularly fond of the Cleveland Orchestra under the baton of Polish conductor Artur Rodzinski and were somewhat dismayed when he left the orchestra following the 1942–3 orchestral year. However, their dismay was short-lived when the orchestra came under the baton of Erich Leinsdorf and then, at the end of the 1946 season, of Austrian conductor George Szell. It was soon apparent that Szell came out of a quite different mould than his predecessors. He had the reputation of being a difficult disciplinarian who demanded nothing less than perfection.

The Orlovs' lifelong love and appreciation of classical music was their one indulgence on their now meagre budget. In this connection Orlov observed that, during the ten years they were in Cleveland, there was never an orchestral year in which they did not attend at least two concerts of the Cleveland Orchestra, and if their financial resources had been such they would have attended all of them.

After becoming somewhat complacent in their Cleveland Heights apartment, their tranquillity was soon shattered. Towards the beginning of the autumn of 1943, their Jewish landlord informed them that they would have to vacate the apartment as he intended to move his own family into it. There was no animosity on either side and the landlord graciously afforded them ample time to find another residence. The landlord's reason as to why he wanted the apartment was vague but the Orlovs suspected that it was because of the wartime rent controls, which froze rents at the level they were at when the law came into effect. By occupying the apartment himself for a short period of time, a landlord in effect could terminate the previously set rent level, then move out and establish a new higher rent level with the next tenant.

What had at first been perceived as an inconvenience soon turned into a distressing situation for the Orlovs. In a period of less than a year since their arrival in Cleveland, the nation had gone into high gear in its war effort. Production of the hard goods of war centred on industrial cities like Cleveland. Every day there was a huge influx of new factory and steel-mill workers into the greater Cleveland area. Consequently, a severe shortage of housing existed. Each morning the Orlovs would scan the local newspapers for prospective housing that would fill their needs. While Orlov attended his classes, Maria would check out the day's possibilities. For well over a month she had nothing but bad news to report to her husband on his return home from school. Finally, she located an apartment in the suburb of Lakewood, Ohio. When Orlov returned from school that day, they immediately went to the apartment and rented it. The Lake Apartments, 12040 Lake Avenue, would be home to the Orlovs for the next nine years.

Not long after the Orlovs settled in Cleveland, Maria started to feel that something was not right with her physical condition. At times she felt an extreme tension in her body and blamed it on the stress that had been brought about by the defection and Vera's death. She had kept her condition to herself for some time so as not to alarm her husband, but he had already sensed that something was wrong. The powerful bond that had grown between them throughout their long marriage and tribulations communicated the inner message long before the spoken word.

Orlov made numerous inquiries followed by intensive research to find the right doctor for Maria. He finally focused on a young cardiologist, who was viewed by his peers as an outstanding performer in the field. Dr Henry A. Zimmerman, whose offices were in the Hanna Building in downtown Cleveland, would not only become their personal physician but a lifelong friend and the doctor who would eventually sign both their death certificates.

Maria's first examination by Dr Zimmerman brought news that was neither good nor bad. She had a very mild case of rheumatic heart fever that could easily be contained by proper medical attention. There was no need to worry was the last statement made by Dr Zimmerman as she left his office. But she did worry, not for herself but with feelings of guilt that she had been responsible for the death of her own daughter by passing on the condition to her. Although through the ensuing years Dr Zimmerman assured her that there was no correlation between her own illness and Vera's, the mere possibility haunted her for the rest of her life.

The end of the Second World War in 1945 set in motion a new direction in Orlov's life. He was greatly troubled by the Yalta Conference and the subsequent conference at Potsdam between the leaders of the three Great Powers as he could see Stalin gaining the upper hand in each instance through intimidation and forcefulness coupled with the weakness and willingness to placate Stalin on the part of US President Roosevelt, then US President Truman and British Prime Minister Churchill. He felt that the Western Powers were acceding to Stalin's demands to a

KGB General Alexander Orlov: early 1930s photo for a fraudulent passport.

Maria Orlov, Berlin 1930.

Vera Orlov, aged 3, enjoying her favourite donkey rides in Paris during Orlov's assignment there.

Orlov on holiday in the French Alps, 1931.

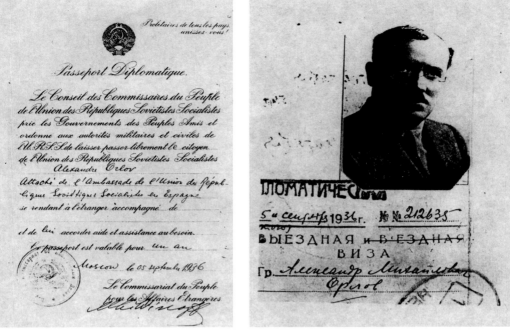

Orlov's 'insurance' – his 1936 diplomatic passport, signed by Foreign Minister Maxim Litvinov. This was found in Orlov's safe-deposit box after his death.

Ardent Communist Vera Orlov giving the International Brigade salute during the Spanish Civil War.

Vera and Maria Orlov by their residence in La Garrica, Spain, late 1937.

KGB guerrilla warfare training camp at Benimamet, near Valencia, where Ernest Hemingway was introduced to Soviet-style guerrilla warfare, which became the basis for his book *For Whom the Bell Tolls*.

Vera Orlov accompanied her father on a visit to the Benimamet training camp in 1937. Photo taken by General Orlov.

Spanish Civil Guard member who was Orlov's personal guard and chauffeur during the Spanish Civil War. He drove Orlov to France when the latter made his break with the Soviets.

Orlov's office and bedroom off the balcony at his KGB headquarters in Barcelona. The radio and code room was immediately above in the Mansard roof.

Vera Orlov, with a dagger for personal protection, at their residence in Batera, when rumours first surfaced of the Mobile Groups' plot to kidnap Orlov in about July/August 1937.

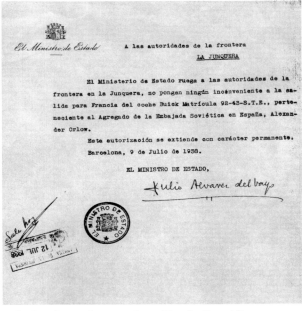

Orlov's safe conduct pass issued by the Republican Government on 9 July 1938, the day that he received his cable from the KGB Centre. Orlov passed into France at La Junquera, Spain, on 12 July as noted by the date stamp and handwritten notation, 'departed today'.

FBI Academy class of 1951. The author is third row from the bottom, third from right, with arms folded. Russ Dagley, his partner at the Boston field office, is in the same row, fifth from right.

The author's first intelligence assignment, as courier taking the secret revised code book from Washington DC to San Juan, September 1953. Pictured with his wife Ruth and daughter Kathryn Anne (in Frejka Splint) in Miami.

The author about to depart on a naval reserve training cruise, pictured with Ruth, Kathryn Anne and son James.

Photo of Vera Orlov taken on her sixteenth birthday, 1 September 1939. The sad news that day was the invasion of Poland by Germany and the start of the Second World War.

The Westbury Apartments, 3360 West 9th Street, Los Angeles, where Vera Orlov died on 15 July 1940 under the fictitious name of Vera Berg.

The house in Cleveland, Ohio, where Orlov gave the FBI the full details of his background.

Clifton Park Apartments, Orlov's last place of residence.

The last photo of General Orlov taken in late summer 1972 by the author's son James.

point that in time would jeopardise the stability of the world. He was certainly in a position to know, having himself been in the inner court of the dictator and witness to the monstrous ploys that Stalin had engaged in to destroy his enemies, both actual as well as those wrongly perceived.

His decision to write a book denouncing Stalin came at an awful price, but he was resolved to go ahead no matter what the sacrifices or consequences might be. He owed this much to his adopted country, which had taken him in when he needed refuge. He also wanted to expose Stalin's tyranny to the people of the free world. More so, he later admitted that he wanted personal revenge against Stalin, not only for his own case and for that of his beloved cousin Zinovy Katsnelson, but for his numerous friends who had perished during the Stalin purges. In the end, he also realised that he had to enlighten the common people in Russia, who were totally unaware of what was happening in their country.

However, he was now facing a financial crisis, which would have been solved by employment at the Berlitz School of Languages but which he had turned down. One evening I questioned him as to why he had reached such desperate financial straits considering that, when he had defected in 1938, he had accumulated the sum of $22,000. He answered in two words: mismanagement and unemployment. In addition, the escalating cost of living as a consequence of the war was a factor that could hardly have been taken into account when he defected. He explained that when he had entered the hierarchy of the KGB, he was expected to lead a bourgeois lifestyle rather than that of the popular conception of a Communist, especially while serving abroad. This lifestyle dictated the best hotels, the best restaurants and even tipping for services, which would have been prohibitive in the Soviet Union. He noted that one became accustomed to these amenities and he was no exception. From the beginning of his stay in Canada he tolerated nothing but the best, and it was not until he left California that he finally realised he was on the wrong financial course. The medical expenses for his daughter had also proved to be a greater than expected drain on his finances. By the time the Orlovs arrived in Cleveland, they had to take a severe look at their finances and recognised that a new lifestyle was necessary. However, the one item that could not be dropped from the budget was their annual visit to their daughter's niche in Cambridge.

One other concession they would not make was their place of residence. From the first apartment they rented in California to the last in Cleveland, they were always in a good neighbourhood, which supported professionals and people of above average means. Orlov reasoned that a secure neighbourhood would also be safer for his own situation. Likewise, he always attempted to rent an apartment on the upper floors and at the end of a hallway, where he felt more secure. A security entry system at the main door and locked secondary doors were not only of prime importance but mandatory features that were normally found only in better apartment houses. He concluded that a higher rent was an inexpensive sacrifice for his personal safety.

Frugality became the key word in their new lifestyle. Breakfast cereals were the main staple of their diet for breakfast and lunch; eating at restaurants was a thing of the past; and the only entertainment they indulged in was a couple of concerts a year at Severance Hall. Orlov related that when he made the decision in 1945 to write his book rather than seek employment, he and Maria came up with an uncompromising budget that would carry them through the next five years barring an unexpected catastrophe.

The one factor in their favour was the practice they had developed early on in their KGB careers of placing their funds in a bank where they would earn interest. After the war started, they began to buy US war bonds, which brought a better yield than the banks. They steadfastly adhered to their stringent budget, which in later years would raise the eyebrows of sceptical federal investigators. When they surfaced in 1953, both the FBI and the INS made a critical assessment of their finances and concluded that the Orlovs had truly subsisted on what in terms of today would be the poverty level.

Oddly enough, the book *Deadly Illusions* makes an assertion that Orlov stole about $60,000 from the KGB Barcelona office. The book bases its conclusion on information from Orlov's KGB personnel file:

> Secreted in their hand baggage, the Orlovs carried a small fortune in US currency. The Soviets would later claim that their cash hoard was NKVD operational funds stolen from the Barcelona *rezidentura* office safe. Supporting evidence is found on page 170 of volume one of the Orlov file which contains a certificate of examination of the safe made out after his disappearance. This records that about $60,000 was missing, presumably taken by Orlov. This was far in excess of the money that Orlov later testified he carried with him when he arrived in North America. Significantly he never accounted for the discrepancy, nor is it clear from the NKVD file whether there was any other explanation for the disappearance of such a substantial sum.

Firstly, I would question that KGB operational funds would be in US dollars as specifically stated. Logically, in Spain, the currency needed for operational purposes would have been Republican or Nationalist Spanish pesetas, or perhaps even French francs, but not the US dollar. As to why Orlov never accounted for the discrepancy, how could he have done so if he had not taken the funds? However, the door was left open to a small extent because the NKVD file was not clear as to an explanation for the theft. We have to assume that at least one other person had access to the safe because of Orlov's frequent absences from his office. Perhaps it was his trusted deputy, Colonel Kotov? It is therefore reasonable to suspect someone of having absconded with the funds after realising the golden opportunity that could easily be covered by Orlov's sudden defection.

Orlov's finances were twice audited by the INS and the FBI, and his frugal lifestyle was compatible with the $22,000 he had when he defected and entered the US in 1938. By the end of

1952, the Orlovs were almost financially destitute and had to virtually beg a cousin in New York for a loan of $1,000 to keep the wolf from their door. Had they had that extra $60,000 the KGB alludes to, there would have been no reason for them to humble themselves. Also, when I opened Orlov's two safe-deposit boxes after his death, I found his financial records which indicated that his funds were not excessive in relation to his income and commensurate with his lifestyle. There was no evidence of that elusive $60,000.

Orlov finally began to put his thoughts to paper in the summer of 1945 and for the next six years worked continuously and arduously on his manuscript. Most of his days were spent in the White Memorial Room of the Cleveland Public Library, where he would research the relevant world history and reduce the findings to notes. The rest of the afternoons and evenings were spent at home drafting the narrative of those crucial events with Maria's assistance. The manuscript was originally written in longhand in Russian as Orlov felt that he did not have enough mastery of the English language. By the time he completed the Russian draft, he was sufficiently confident of his ability to begin translating the entire manuscript into English, again in longhand.

Towards the end of 1951, the English version of the manuscript was completed with the exception of a few minor details. During the entire period Orlov had handwritten each page twice realising that he still did not have the final product. Maria would assist by proofreading each page. At some point he would have to submit the final manuscript to a publisher in an acceptable typewritten form.

Orlov again turned to his old friend Dyke College. By this time he was aware that he had to learn to type, so he enrolled in the school's typing course in early December 1951 and completed the course four months later. He then acquired a used Royal office model typewriter and began the laborious task of transforming his handwritten English draft into the finalised typewritten version; he completed this by the end of the summer of 1952.

The only minor problem that remained was a name for the book. The Orlovs considered numerous titles and finally settled on *The Secret History of Stalin's Crimes*. What never came into question was the dedication, 'To the memory of our daughter Vera'.

Concurrent with the completion of the book was the depletion of almost all of their financial resources. The budget which they had strictly adhered to since 1945 would cover their normal living expenses for at least another nine months, even though this went far beyond the five years they had originally calculated. Unexpected medical and living expenses had had to be covered by selling personal possessions and selected items from Orlov's watch and dagger collection. Now there would be additional expenses connected with promoting the book with the national publishing houses, most of which were in New York.

Orlov had no one to turn to but a relative, and the one that he felt would be most sympathetic to his plight was his cousin Florence Kellerman, who was now living in the Bronx. Florence was the daughter of Orlov's father's sister, Itka Koornick. They had been close in childhood and shared a special fondness for one another. Florence graciously lent Orlov $1,000 without any questions asked or a deadline for repayment; however, within a year of the book's publication, the loan was repaid.

The hard part was yet to come: to find a publisher who would be interested in the manuscript. Orlov cites and gives credit to two individuals – George E. Sokolsky and Max Eastman – who were able to open the doors that led to the eventual publication of his book. Both had ties to Russia and were also prominent in the United States.

Sokolsky was a boyhood friend of Orlov's in the Byelorussian town of Bobruysk, where they had both grown up. The Orlov family had moved from Bobruysk at the beginning of the First World War and it was not until twenty-four years later that the two friends encountered one another by chance. By August 1938, Orlov and his family were in New York and, just prior to leaving the city in mid-October, they attended the service of Yom Kippur, the holiest of the Jewish holidays, at the synagogue. There Orlov spotted his old friend Sokolsky. They got together after the service and reminisced about their boyhood. Sokolsky told Orlov that he was now a journalist and was doing quite well. Orlov informed him that he had only recently immigrated to the United States and that he would be leaving New York at any moment, perhaps for Pittsburgh. On recognition, Sokolsky had addressed Orlov by his boyhood nickname 'Lyova' and his real name 'Feldbin'. Orlov had made no attempt to correct him, or to tell him that he was a high-ranking official in the Soviet Government who had recently defected. They parted on friendly terms and both expressed the hope that they would meet again in the not-too-distant future. That date would not come about for some fifteen years.

Over the years Orlov watched with great pleasure the rise of his old friend in the field of journalism. Much more to his delight was the fact that Sokolsky was now a conservative syndicated columnist for the Hearst newspaper chain and a journalist for the *Washington Times Herald*. By the time he had completed his book, Orlov was again in contact with Sokolsky. This time he no longer concealed his true background and openly solicited his friend's help. Sokolsky readily took the matter under advisement and offered what assistance he could. He suggested that Orlov should consider contacting Max Eastman, the author and founding editor of the magazine *The Masses*, as they had 'both been over the same road'. Orlov was cognizant of Eastman's early adventures into Socialism, his break from Socialism and finally his strong stance against Communism. Eastman was a friend of Leon Trotsky and had become his literary agent; he was also responsible for translating several of Trotsky's important works into English. Based on these factors, Orlov willingly agreed to Sokolsky's offer to make the introduction.

Within a month, Orlov met Eastman in his Greenwich Village apartment. They would become lifelong friends and maintained close contact with one another until Eastman's death in 1969. The introductory contact was spread over several days because of the secure manner in which Orlov maintained physical control over the manuscript, which he never let out of his sight. Orlov first verbally apprised Eastman of his background with the KGB and then let Eastman speed-read the manuscript while he watched. Eastman was impressed with Orlov's background and agreed that the revelations in the manuscript were indeed sensational. Eastman initially suggested that he would be in a position to act as Orlov's literary agent and would represent him for the customary fee. Orlov was reluctant about this arrangement as it would mean letting the manuscript out of his sight, and further Eastman did not yet have his full confidence. Orlov made no commitment one way or another.

Then a fortuitous circumstance took place towards the end of the third day. When they had first met, Eastman had made Orlov aware that he had married a Russian native when he had visited the USSR in the 1920s; however, his wife was nowhere to be seen. When Orlov was about to leave on the third day, Eastman's wife entered the study. They spoke in Russian about their mutual backgrounds and it surfaced that Eastman's wife Eliena was the sister of Nikolai Vasilievich Krylenko, an old and admired friend of Orlov's.

Krylenko was a lawyer by profession and had actively participated in the Russian Revolution. He had become a charter member of the new Communist Party and gained the reputation of being a hard-nosed Bolshevik. When Orlov became an Assistant Prosecutor in the Collegium of Appeals of the Soviet Supreme Court in 1921, he had worked under Krylenko. During the almost four years that Orlov held this post, a more than casual relationship developed between them. Orlov later learned that Krylenko had given him a highly flattering recommendation when he was brought into the KGB.

Krylenko incurred the wrath of Stalin a short time after Lenin's death in January 1924, after which the leadership of the new nation was up for grabs. As a leader of the Party, Krylenko gave an impassioned speech at the May 1924 13th Congress of the Central Committee of the Communist Party in which he implored the delegates to publish Lenin's Testament. Stalin strongly opposed publication as the organisational structure and procedures proposed by Lenin would not be in his favour. Stalin never forgave Krylenko for his actions that day. The last Orlov heard of Krylenko was in 1937, when he learned that his former superior had been relieved of his post as the People's Commissar of Justice. He always felt certain that Krylenko had perished in the great purges, but it was not until Eliena confirmed that Stalin had ordered her brother's execution in 1938 that he knew for certain.

Orlov stayed longer than he had anticipated as the conversation then turned to friends and conditions in Russia. When he finally departed, he and Eliena said farewell with a typical Russian bear-hug embrace.

When Orlov returned the following day, he could not help but notice an entirely different atmosphere. Eastman seemed less business-like, more conciliatory and extremely friendly. Orlov could only surmise that it was Eliena's persuasiveness that had brought about the change. Eastman now told Orlov that perhaps he did not really need a literary agent as the merits of the manuscript stood on their own; all that Orlov needed were the right introductions. He added that he would be glad to supply this end. He also mentioned that he was under contract to *Reader's Digest* as a freelance editor and reporter and that the conservative publication might have an interest.

Orlov declined to furnish Sokolsky or Eastman with his home address or his newly acquired telephone number, which he reasoned he would now need in conjunction with his efforts to publish the manuscript. He advised Sokolsky and Eastman that he would contact them periodically to determine if their efforts on his behalf had proved fruitful. Both men understood the necessity of Orlov's tight security measures.

Towards the end of February 1953, Sokolsky made arrangements for Orlov to meet William L. White, a professional friend of his who was an author and editor with connections to *Life* magazine. White was perhaps best known for his 1941 book *Journey for Margaret* and the wartime book *They Were Expendable*. Sokolsky related that he had provided White with the background to the matter and that White was sufficiently impressed to want to meet Orlov. White was no stranger to Orlov as he had written numerous articles highly critical of Stalin. Orlov agreed to meet White and advised that he would be in New York on Monday, 2 March, for the meeting. Orlov then contacted Eastman, who informed him that the people at the *Saturday Evening Post* in Philadelphia were interested in reviewing the manuscript. He advised Eastman to go ahead and make the necessary arrangements with the *Post* staff for a Monday, 9 March, meeting. Eastman also said that he had mentioned Orlov's manuscript to Eugene Lyons, a fellow editor at *Reader's Digest*, and that Lyons also wanted to meet Orlov. Eastman felt that it wouldn't hurt to get together with Lyons as he could open some doors, but thought that *Reader's Digest* was not looking for book-length material and therefore would not be receptive to the manuscript.

The Orlovs checked into the Wellington Hotel in New York on Sunday, 1 March, under the name of Mr and Mrs Leon Koornick. The following morning Orlov met White at his office and the remainder of the day was spent going over the manuscript under the watchful eye of the author. By the end of the day, White told Orlov that he was satisfied that the people at *Life* would be interested, but that they would require several days to read the manuscript and his presence might be somewhat annoying. He impressed on Orlov that he should have no qualms regarding their integrity or trustworthiness and that he could place the manuscript in their care with the utmost confidence. Orlov decided to take the risk. White placed a telephone call to *Life* and a meeting was set for the next morning.

Orlov met Edward Thompson, Managing Editor, and John S. Billings, Editor, of *Life* at their offices in the Time and Life Building at the Rockefeller Center. Also present at a meeting that subsequently followed were several members of the *Life* editorial staff, who were apparently specialists in the field of foreign affairs with emphasis on the USSR. The manuscript was not touched on that day as the entire time was spent going over Orlov's background from his birth to his defection from the KGB. Towards the end of the meeting, he briefly presented a summary of the contents of the manuscript and stressed that above all else he expected the trust and confidentiality of all those present at the meeting. He was assured that this was the case. Prior to his leaving, Billings gave each member of his staff specific chapter assignments, with instructions that they review each chapter looking for information suitable to *Life*'s requirements and make a final recommendation by that Friday morning.

Billings requested that Orlov return to his office at 3 p.m. on Friday. He made no commitments but his demeanour did indicate to Orlov that he had more than a passing interest in the manuscript.

At this Friday meeting, Billings was optimistic to the extent that his staff had reported earlier that day that the manuscript did present certain possibilities for publication. However, some of them considered the material to be outdated and did not meet the specific needs of *Life*, which normally covered current events and issues. There was no doubt whatsoever as to the material's historical importance, Billings said, but perhaps it was more suitable for publication as a book. He advised that he personally liked the manuscript but was not prepared to go ahead with publication in light of his staff's recommendation. However, he told Orlov that his decision was not final and that the matter would be held in abeyance. Orlov picked up his manuscript and furnished the name of his attorney, John F. Finerty, should *Life* want to reach him in the future.

Orlov admitted that he was deeply disappointed with the results of the meeting with *Life* but felt that the meeting with the *Post* would be more promising as the publication was not devoted entirely to current issues.

During the time the Orlovs were in New York, they also managed to meet Eugene Lyons at his *Reader's Digest* office. They learned that Lyons had been born in Russia and had come to the United States at an early age. In his early career, he had been a foreign correspondent with UPI and covered the Soviet Union from Moscow. His political view of the Soviets was on the conservative side and coincided with that of Orlov. The Orlovs also met De Witt Wallace, Editor of *Reader's Digest*, and Paul Palmer, the Executive Editor, who were both eager to hear about Orlov and his work with the KGB. Orlov's expectations were not great, as Eastman had already warned him that *Reader's Digest* was not looking for book-length material, but he felt that he made a good impression and they showed more than a casual interest. Perhaps some good would come out of the meeting. He was correct in this assumption because he would write several articles for *Reader's Digest* in the near future. As to Lyons, they became good friends.

By the time Orlov had picked up his manuscript at *Life*, it was late in the day so he and Maria decided to stay overnight in New York and travel to Philadelphia the following morning. On Saturday, 7 March, Orlov received the shock of his life. The morning newspapers all carried the banner headline that Stalin had died. Orlov bought the various New York newspapers and carried them up to his room, where he and Maria read each one. Stalin had died on 5 March but the news had not been relayed immediately to the world. At last his old enemy was gone, but the wise old General knew that this would not stop the KGB from trying to track him down and take revenge.

The Orlovs arrived in Philadelphia that afternoon and registered at the Benjamin Franklin Hotel as Mr and Mrs Leon Koornick.

On Monday, the 9th, Orlov took his manuscript to the editorial department of the *Saturday Evening Post*, where he met its Editor Ben Hibbs and two of his staff members. For the better part of the day, Orlov explained his credentials for writing the book and highlighted the material in it. Hibbs told him that they would turn their full attention to reading the manuscript without any undue delay and would contact him at his hotel. Around noon on 12 March, the Orlovs received the harbinger of bad news in the form of a *Post* messenger, who personally delivered a letter to Orlov at the door of room 665. Orlov recalled closing the door in haste after tipping the messenger and ripping open the envelope. He quickly scanned the communication but it was not difficult to realise that his manuscript had once again been rejected because, as Hibbs wrote,

> the material is far too outdated. If this book had been offered to the *Saturday Evening Post* in, say, 1937 or 1938, it doubtless would have been accepted, and it would have created a sensation. . . . I do agree your book contains some interesting revelations about the purges and other matters, and that it is a contribution to the history of the period about which you write, but we can't feel that these worthwhile qualities are sufficient to overcome the defects mentioned above. Please believe that I am very sorry about this.

Orlov was devastated by the rejection. Now he had no more immediate avenues to turn to but also realised that he had no alternative but to continue his quest.

The Orlovs returned to Cleveland on Saturday and no sooner had they stepped into their apartment than the telephone rang. It was John Finerty in New York, who informed them that he had been desperately trying to get hold of them for the past week. The news was good: *Life* had decided to publish parts of the manuscript. Orlov authorised his attorney to proceed with the negotiations and told him that he would be in New York in the first part of the following week.

The Orlovs appeared at Finerty's office on the morning of the 18th. Negotiations were going well and *Life* had committed itself to paying the sum of $40,000 for sufficient material from the manuscript for a series of four instalments to appear as soon as possible. Only one obstacle stood in the way of a binding contract: Orlov's bona fides had to be established before *Life* would go ahead. They had to be certain that he was the man he purported to be.

This was not an easy task considering that Orlov could not call on the KGB for verification. He had to have someone who knew him in Russia or Spain, but there were no KGB defectors alive that he knew of in a position to corroborate his background.

Then his thoughts turned to Ernest Hemingway, who was certainly in a position to make the verification and one that *Life* would accept positively. Orlov contacted Hemingway's publisher, Scribner's, but was told that he was in Cuba. They refused to divulge the author's address but said that they would forward a letter to him if Orlov cared to write one. Unfortunately, this uncertain route would take too long and time was now of paramount importance.

Then Orlov recalled an American journalist he had met years before in Spain. When he had first arrived in Madrid in September 1936, he had maintained his office in the Palace Hotel, which also housed the Soviet Embassy. The same month of his arrival, the Soviet Ambassador to the Spanish Republican Government, Marcel Rosenberg, had come to his office with the express purpose of introducing him to Louis Fischer, an American journalist who was heavily in favour of the Republican side of the war. Any reservations Orlov had had about Fischer were dispelled when Rosenberg later returned alone to see him and clearly indicated that Fischer could be trusted to be on their side. There was no doubt that Fischer had been informed by Rosenberg that Orlov was head of the KGB in Spain. Orlov related that, during the course of the war, he saw Fischer on numerous occasions and even encountered the journalist on a business trip to Paris. Being a trained intelligence officer, I strongly suspected that at the least Fischer was a KGB source in the field of journalism.

Orlov once again solicited the help of Max Eastman, who was deeply entrenched in the literary and journalistic worlds. Fortunately, Eastman knew Fischer personally and gave Orlov Fischer's address and private telephone number. At the time, Fischer was a journalist for the *New York Times*. Orlov telephoned Fischer on 19 March, relating only that he was a friend from Spain and wished to meet him that day if at all possible regarding an urgent matter. Orlov did not reveal his identity but sensed that Fischer probably guessed who the caller was because, when they did meet later that day, Fischer did not seemed surprised. When Fischer opened the door and recognised Orlov, he reached for his hand and called him 'my old friend Orlov'. Orlov briefly explained the circumstances of his predicament and Fischer readily agreed to make the verification. Orlov then telephoned Finerty from Fischer's apartment to finalise the arrangements and waited for an answer. Within minutes Finerty returned the call, advising him that a meeting with the people from *Life* had been arranged for the next day at his office.

Representatives of the editorial and legal staff of *Life* magazine met the Orlov group as scheduled at Finerty's office. Fischer's prominence as a journalist met *Life*'s criteria for verification of Orlov's bona fides and the contract was subsequently signed. During the negotiations, Orlov learned that Stalin's death was the turning point that had prompted *Life* to reconsider its decision to publish the manuscript. *Life* felt that the world would now want to know about Stalin's hidden secrets more than ever and that Orlov's sensational revelations would only whet their appetite for more facts. It was ironic that in life one of Stalin's principal objectives was the elimination of his archenemy Orlov but that as a consequence of his death Orlov was flourishing. The gods of fate had strangely intervened on Orlov's side and no doubt Stalin would forever turn in his grave at this shift of events.

Time was of the essence as *Life* was determined to publish the revelations while Stalin's death was still fresh in the memory of the world. It was decided that there was enough material available to stretch the instalments over a longer period of time in order to capture a larger audience. The script would contain the key elements of Orlov's book but was more of a condensed version of some of the major incidents that had taken place. *Life* entitled the series of articles, 'The Ghastly Secrets of Stalin's Power', with the first instalment coming out on 6 April 1953 followed by three additional weekly instalments. The articles proved to be sensational and the talk of the nation. With each successive instalment, the circulation of *Life* reached new heights.

In several ways, the Orlovs that had gone to New York were not the same as the ones that returned to Cleveland. Orlov had in his pocket an advance on the *Life* articles and their financial situation would be secure to the end of their days. However, there was the inevitable trade-off for this success: their lives would now and forever be in harm's way. The Orlovs had surfaced to the world and no one would be more interested in this fact than the KGB.

Publication of the *Life* articles brought many changes in the Orlovs' lives. Both *Life* and Finerty were bombarded with requests for interviews with Orlov, although in all probability the KGB using a third party might also have made innocuous inquiries as to his whereabouts. By the middle of April, the Orlovs realised that their future lay in New York, the heart of the publishing world, and not in Cleveland. The decision to leave Cleveland was a difficult one as they loved the city and had grown accustomed to their Cleveland lifestyle. Their main concern was the fact that they would no longer be under the care of Dr Zimmerman, but recognised that he must have a counterpart in New York.

The Orlovs made it known to their neighbours that they were moving to California because of Maria's health. They left Cleveland in the first part of May 1953 believing that they would never return. They had what they assumed was their last look at downtown Cleveland when they boarded the train bound for New York. Orlov lamented the fact that they were leaving the city and compared it to leaving behind a dear old friend whom he would never see again. However, almost seventeen years later they would return.

New trials, tribulations and successes would meet the Orlovs in their next destination. New York City would be their home for the next nine years.

NINETEEN

MANHATTAN

Regarding the period he spent in New York, Orlov would compare it to being swept up by a cyclone, deposited on a roller-coaster for an exhilarating yet horrifying ride of ups and downs, and then ending the journey on a note of tranquillity; an awe-inspiring adventure at the time but nothing he had any desire to repeat.

No sooner had the Orlovs settled in Manhattan than the cyclone part of the adventure began. The fall-out from the publication of the *Life* articles began soon after the final instalment appeared. Several publishing houses approached *Life* regarding publication of Orlov's book and they were referred to his attorney. Orlov finally settled on Random House because of its publication of Whittaker Chambers's 1952 book *Witness*, in which he denounced Alger Hiss, a high-ranking US government official, as a Soviet spy. By the autumn of 1953 Orlov's book, *The Secret History of Stalin's Crimes*, was published.

No sooner had this matter been settled than *Life* asked Orlov to write an article on the notorious KGB Chief and personal henchman of Stalin, Lavrenti Beria. Orlov had known Beria since 1925, when he was the brigade commander of the OGPU Border Guard in Tiflis. Beria had then been a promising officer and Deputy Chief of the OGPU in Georgia. The article, 'The Beria I Knew', appeared in the 20th of July 1953 issue of *Life* magazine.

The Voice of America (VOA), an integral arm of the United States Information Agency (USIA), in Washington DC, also expressed an interest in the *Life* articles and the book as a propaganda vehicle in the war against Communism and the Kremlin.

The *Life* articles and a condensed version of the book penetrated the Iron Curtain when the VOA beamed the material into various Communist countries over a period of time in thirteen languages. From May to December 1953, the VOA transmitted a series of ten broadcasts. Radio Free Europe, another entity dedicated to halting the spread of Communism in Europe, also recognised the propaganda value of Orlov's intelligence and undertook to broadcast to its area of endeavour.

Orlov freely consented to the use of his material by the USIA, VOA and Radio Free Europe and modestly told me that he had never allowed himself to accept any monetary remuneration in return. What he did gain was the knowledge that his efforts would strike a decisive blow against Communism and the KGB at the height of the Cold War and alert the people of the free world as well as those behind the Iron Curtain to the evil perpetrated by Stalin and his regime.

In the same vein, the USIA on 30 July 1954 asked for Orlov's consent to publish his book in Hong Kong in the various Chinese dialects and to have it serialised in Chinese newspapers. Orlov signed a contract with USIA for the printing of 7,500 copies of the book and gave permission for the serialisation of the book in Chinese-language newspapers. The USIA also arranged for the serialisation of the book in the Malayan language in a trade-union journal in India. In 1954, the book was also published by Jarrolds in Great Britain and, in 1955, a Spanish edition appeared with worldwide distribution rights in all Spanish-speaking countries. Subsequently, the book was published in Germany, Austria and Switzerland.

The Orlovs had resided incognito in the United States from the time they had entered the country on 13 August 1938 until the April 1953 *Life* articles exposed their presence in the US to the world. They had met all legal requirements regarding their immigrant status and, because of Orlov's leading position in the hierarchy of the Soviet Communist Party and especially the KGB, their actual whereabouts had always remained a secret. They had been accorded a special dispensation on reporting their specific whereabouts in the US because, if they had handled it in a routine manner, their lives might have been placed in grave danger. They could always be reached by the INS or any federal government agency through Orlov's attorney, who was on record for this purpose.

In 1938, when the Orlovs entered the United States, there had been no specific federal agency designated to gather foreign intelligence. What little foreign intelligence was gathered was handled by the US State Department through its diplomatic establishments and the US military through its military attachés (Army and Navy) stationed at strategic US Embassies throughout the world. Naturally, their gathering of intelligence was limited to their own particular scope of interest. This *modus operandi* would change drastically on the advent of the Second World War, although the roots were actually planted in 1936 when President Roosevelt became alarmed at the rise and spread of Communism and Fascism in the United States, which he construed as a threat to the country. He quietly called FBI Director Hoover to a private meeting at the White House to discuss the matter in August 1936. The FBI had no legal jurisdiction to gather intelligence or to investigate subversion at the time. Hoover suggested that under the provisions of the Appropriations Act, which financed the operations of the FBI, the FBI could undertake an investigation on behalf of the US State Department should they be requested to do so by the Secretary of State. Roosevelt felt it rather strange that the US President could not directly request the FBI to undertake an investigation but that the Secretary of State could. Following consultation and agreement with Secretary of State Cordell Hull, the final details were worked out by 1 September. The FBI would co-ordinate domestic intelligence-gathering with the Military Intelligence Division of the War Department, the Office of Naval Intelligence and the State Department. Thus the embryo of an intelligence-gathering mechanism came into being. Hoover's position was clear: information should be gathered from all possible sources concerning subversive activities being conducted in the US by Communists, Fascists or other groups or individuals advocating the overthrow of the US Government by illegal means; however, no investigation could be initiated without specific authorisation from FBI headquarters. This limited authority pertained only to investigations in the United States.

By a confidential directive dated 26 June 1939 to his Cabinet, President Roosevelt made it clear that the investigation of all espionage, counter-espionage and sabotage matters was solely under the control of the FBI and the Intelligence Divisions of the War Department and Navy, thus for the first time clearly defining the roll of the FBI in domestic intelligence.

By early 1940, when Europe was already at war, the Administration realised that the German Government had established bases in Mexico City and throughout South America from which it could direct espionage activities against the US. In May–June 1940, the problem was approached by Hoover, the State Department and the Chiefs of Army and Naval Intelligence. What evolved was a proposal for a Special Intelligence Service (SIS) to operate in the foreign field. Assistant Secretary of State Adolf A. Berle Jr agreed to present the plan to the State Department and the President for approval. Thereafter, President Roosevelt issued a directive on 24 June 1940 that the FBI would have responsibility for non-military intelligence in the Western Hemisphere. Within thirty days, experienced FBI Special Agents, who were already fluent in Spanish and Portuguese, were being dispatched to all countries south of the border in overt capacities with US Embassies and covertly as undercover agents. The FBI soon established an SIS training school to prepare its agents for foreign assignments. Espionage and sabotage techniques of the enemy were taught along with code and cipher training. Special emphasis was placed on teaching Spanish and Portuguese language skills. Vital intelligence information soon began to flow to FBI headquarters in Washington, and during its existence the SIS was able to penetrate and destroy a number of enemy spy rings. For the first time in its history, the United States Government had a viable and very capable civilian foreign intelligence-gathering organisation.

During the Second World War, a noticeable degree of friction occurred between the FBI and the Office of Strategic Services (OSS). At the end of the war, the need for intelligence was never greater but the OSS and Joint Chiefs of Staff felt that a new super agency with worldwide intelligence-gathering capabilities should be created to this end. The FBI proposed expanding its SIS into a worldwide intelligence organisation, but by this time the FBI had lost its champion, the late President Roosevelt, and it was no secret that the new President by default, Harry S. Truman, had an intense dislike for Hoover. In January 1946, President Truman directed the formation of the National Intelligence Authority under which operated the Central Intelligence Group (CIG). The CIG was originally meant to be a co-ordinating agency to plan and develop intelligence operations abroad. In June 1946, the CIG operation was taken over by Army General Hoyt Vandenberg, who wanted to establish an independent worldwide intelligence agency. The National Intelligence Authority by directive finally gave Vandenberg authority to take over the basic intelligence field as well as to handle foreign espionage and counter-espionage matters. These events led to the demise of the FBI's Special Intelligence Service and the creation of the Central Intelligence Agency (CIA) in 1947.

Thus, with this climate regarding intelligence-gathering in 1938, there was no apparatus in place, let alone any form of repository, where the vital information that Orlov possessed could be recorded. US authorities were well aware of his connections to the Soviet Government and had to assume that he possessed vital information; however, in the placid era before the war, they were not conditioned to the importance of foreign intelligence and had no interest in taking advantage of the situation. Orlov was able to remain anonymous for almost fifteen years without any agency of the US Government attempting to contact him. This all changed when the *Life* articles appeared in print during April 1953.

What must have been a shock to the FBI and the CIA was the fact that the highest-ranking official of the KGB ever to defect had been residing in the US for fifteen years without their apparent knowledge. Just who was he and what crucial information regarding the KGB did he bring to the West was their first reaction. From that moment on, the FBI focused its attention on the General and was able to develop extraordinary and crucial intelligence information regarding the innermost operations of the KGB. Much of the operational information was outdated but did provide an insight into the KGB that had never been known before, although it had been suspected in some cases.

Years later when I became involved with the General, I was privy to some of the information he had afforded the FBI in the early years and it became quite clear that he had played an important role in the struggle against the Soviets during the height of the Cold War. This information is still secret and thus cannot be revealed, although I am able to report on matters of historical significance that were revealed to me during my close relationship with General Orlov but which have no particular intelligence value today.

During 1953, Orlov made many friends connected with *Life* magazine, the *Reader's Digest* and Random House Publishers, who strongly believed that Orlov's revelations merited favourable consideration on the part of the United States Government and that US citizen status should be conferred on the Orlovs. They sought the advice of Democrat Congressman Francis E. Walter of Pennsylvania, who was the Chairman of the all-powerful House Committee of the Judiciary. Walter was a conservative whose influence on the Judiciary Committee was well known. The Congressman was impressed by Orlov's credentials and revelations but more so by the fact that so many prominent people were willing to stand together to vouch for the defector. He agreed that the US Government should give something back to the Orlovs in return for their many years of sacrifice before they had been able to bring forth their information.

On 20 January 1954, Walter introduced a private bill, H.R.7427, in the 83rd Congress that would grant the Orlovs the status of permanent residents in the United States. This legalised status would then allow them to apply for US citizenship.

A necessary part of the procedure was a full background investigation of the Orlovs by the INS. In this connection, the Orlovs were summoned to the office of the INS, at 70 Columbus Avenue, New York, for an immigration hearing on 29 April 1954. They testified under oath during the proceedings. Orlov related that he had testified freely and truthfully but that the hearing entered a problem area for him. When he had entered the US in 1938, he had made every effort to make his presence known to US government officials and in doing so had made it clear that up to the date of his defection he had been a member of the Communist Party of the Soviet Union. He had never attempted to conceal this fact and, at the point where he severed relations with the Soviet Government and the KGB, he had in effect broken with the Communist Party. However, at the hearing, the INS produced records relating to his entry into the US on 23 September 1932 and his departure on 30 November. These records reflected that Orlov had testified before a Special Board of Inquiry of the INS on 26 September at the immigration facility on Ellis Island as a part of the procedure to gain admittance into the United States as a visitor.

In answer to the questions whether he had ever been a member of any Communist Party or had advocated the overthrow of the US Government, he had responded in the negative. At the current INS hearing he was asked if he recalled denying Party membership at the 1932 hearing. Orlov related to me that he actually had no recollection of the questions posed to him in 1932, but that there was no doubt in his mind that he would have strongly denied both of them, although at the time the truthful answer would have been the opposite. What has to be understood is that in 1932 he was on a KGB assignment under the fictitious name of Lev Leonedovich Nikolev. His KGB position therefore dictated the correct KGB responses.

H.R.7472 was never acted on and, when the 83rd Congress adjourned later in the year, it became a dead issue. Orlov was somewhat bitter towards the INS as he later learned from his attorney that the required INS report never reached Congress, although he felt that the INS had had ample time to complete the investigation and report its findings to the Judiciary Committee.

The unwanted attention drawn to Orlov as a consequence of his surfacing in April 1953 did not go unnoticed by the Federal Grand Jury investigating the influence and spread of Communism in the US. To this end, Orlov was subpoenaed to testify before the Federal Grand Jury convened for this purpose in the southern district of New York on 17 August 1954. Orlov, as a very cooperative witness, was able to provide a new insight into the KGB from his personal perspective as well as his intimate observations on Marxism.

The low point of 1954 was when the bill for his permanent status in the US failed. Nevertheless, Orlov never gave up hope that he would be able to remain in the US.

In the spring of 1955, Orlov was surprised to learn through his new attorney, Hugo Pollock, that a second private bill had been introduced in the US Senate by the Republican Senator from Ohio George H. Bender. Several of his friends from Ohio, spearheaded by Dr Zimmerman, had approached the Senator for his support when the first bill did not make it through the House. On 10 March 1955, Bender introduced Senate Bill 1627, which was referred to the Senate Committee of the Judiciary for consideration.

Everything seemed to be going well for the Orlovs until the day they received a notice to appear at the office of the INS for another immigration hearing on the morning of 22 June 1955. There was no doubt in their minds that it was another required hearing in connection with Senator Bender's pending bill. They arrived at the INS office as scheduled without the benefit of their attorney in the belief that it was nothing more than a routine matter. The unexpected turn of events shocked them when they were informed that the INS considered their status in the US as illegal and that deportation proceedings would be initiated. Orlov would be charged under the provisions of the Immigration Act of 1924 as being an official of the Soviet Government and a member of the Communist Party at the time he had entered the United States. Likewise, Maria would be charged with being the spouse of an official of the Soviet Government. They were apprised that arrest warrants had already been prepared and would now be served. After the initial shock and surprise, the instincts of Orlov's legal background came into play. He requested that prior to service of the warrants of arrest, he be afforded the opportunity to consult his attorney. The INS had no recourse at this juncture but to comply with the request as the Orlovs were without benefit of legal representation. The Orlovs agreed to return to the INS office later that day.

The Orlovs immediately contacted Hugo Pollock, who had taken over from Finerty in 1953 when he had left the law firm of Olwine, Connolly and Chase. Pollock was of the opinion that the INS stood on firm ground based on a strict interpretation of the law but in Orlov's case there were mitigating circumstances that should prevail, his service to the country notwithstanding. Pollock felt that the Bender bill had more than a fair chance of succeeding but that they would have to buy more time before the wheels of Congress would legalise their immigration status. Even if the issue of buying time failed, the worst-case scenario would be their deportation, the bill would pass and they would then be allowed back into the country as legal immigrants. Pollock promised that he would do all in his power to see to it that no time would be lost in complying with any issues brought about by the Bender bill.

A letter to the INS was carefully drafted that in effect laid down a logical course of action in requesting a delay of ninety days that should be acceptable to the INS. Pollock felt that ninety days would be ample time for the Senate Judiciary Committee to make its recommendation. Unfortunately, Pollock badly miscalculated the time it would take for the Judiciary Committee to come to a decision, which did not happen until the spring of 1956. On the other hand, it was the long drawn-out INS investigation for the benefit of the Judiciary Committee that prevailed in the end.

By mid-afternoon, the Orlovs returned to the INS office with the letter in hand. They were both served with arrest warrants, after which they formally presented the letter to the officiating INS officers. The letter dated 22 June 1955 read as follows:

Having learned now from Immigration Officers Messrs Caudino and Mason that there is a decision to serve my wife and myself with warrants of arrest and to start deportation proceedings against us, we wish to inform the Immigration and Naturalisation Service that we have decided to leave this country voluntarily. We are taking immediate steps to find political asylum in another country and we ask you to grant sufficient time for this purpose.

We have decided to leave voluntarily to spare my wife the bitter experience of deportation proceedings. We hope to be able to obtain an immigration visa to another country within ninety days. However, if during this period, while we are seeking political asylum in another country, we shall be lucky to see the bill introduced on our behalf by US Senator George H. Bender, pass through, we shall be most happy to remain in this country.

The INS officials informed the Orlovs that the INS was not pressing for criminal charges against them because of their unique circumstances as well as the fact that they had co-operated with the Government. However, they were now in a conditional parole status and must report to the Parole Section of the INS. The following day the Orlovs did report to the Parole Section, at which time they were advised that they had to report their presence to a parole officer in person once a month. In addition, the special dispensation not to furnish their actual address, rather than their attorney's address, was rescinded and it was now mandatory for them to provide a current address. The Orlovs were more than outraged and disturbed at this news because their very lives depended on secrecy, but no amount of pleading could persuade the INS parole officer from enforcing the mandate.

The Orlovs mistrusted the INS's ability to keep their address confidential and, as it turned out, they were fully justified. Within weeks they were to receive an INS notice directed to the address they had given to the INS on 23 June 1955 and addressed to 'Alexander Orlov' rather than the alias of Alexander Berg, which they had so carefully explained to the parole officer. They considered this a major blunder on the part of the INS which could easily lead to their detection and possible assassination at the hands of the KGB. As a consequence of the torment they suffered on receiving the INS notice addressed to Alexander Orlov, they decided to move from that address and, in so doing, would impress upon the INS the necessity of confidentiality regarding their new address.

From the time the Orlovs entered the US, they had taken great pains to conceal their identity and their whereabouts. Only their attorney knew their place of residence. The only exceptions were the FBI and now the INS. Orlov had complete confidence in the FBI to keep his whereabouts secret and his trust was never breached. I never knew where he lived in New York and, after I got to know him quite well, I asked him out of sheer curiosity. He told me that he had lived on the seventh floor of a large apartment house located at 711 West End Avenue in Manhattan. The apartment house, which was in a predominantly Jewish neighbourhood, met all his security requirements but was also located within an easy walk of Central Park and near transportation to his good friend Max Eastman. He told me that he and Maria had developed a close relationship with the Eastmans and it was because of this friendship that they had moved to easy commuting distance to their apartment.

Several factors that could compromise, or perhaps even fatally jeopardise, Orlov's prospects under Senator Bender's bill first came to light during the 22 June 1955 meeting with the INS and a subsequent meeting on 27 June. The first area of INS suspicion was the fact that the INS questioned his account of events that had led up to his defection, principally the date he had furnished the INS when he alleged that he was to meet the Soviet ship *Svir* on 14 July 1938 in the port of Antwerp. The INS investigators made him repeat the date and then told him point-blank that the *Svir* had never been in the port of Antwerp during the month of July 1938. They contended that another unnamed US government agency had checked the shipping records in Antwerp and there was no record in July for the *Svir*, although the vessel did make it to the port later in the year. This was a serious flaw in Orlov's legend if it proved to be correct, but as Orlov did not meet the ship as scheduled, he had no way of definitely knowing whether the vessel had reached Antwerp as scheduled. However, he did have one confirmation that the *Svir* was actually in Antwerp during the summer of 1938 rather than the autumn of that year. He recalled some information that another of his close boyhood friends had earlier passed on to him. He identified this friend as Boris Rosowsky, who then resided at 527 West 110th, in New York. Fortunately for Orlov, he had made the effort to renew their friendship when he returned to New York. Orlov had told his friend about his defection and Rosowsky recalled that when he had lived in Belgium before immigrating to the US, a fellow Russian émigré had mentioned meeting a mutual friend from Bobruysk who was an engineering officer on the Soviet vessel *Svir* when it had made port in Antwerp during the summer of 1938. Rosowsky was certain that the year was 1938 as it fitted the time frame when he resided in Belgium and also when he was in contact with the Russian émigré. He felt almost certain that it was either July or August of that year.

Orlov related that had he been in the shoes of the INS investigators, he would also have been sceptical of the sighting of the *Svir* in Antwerp as told by the Russian émigré, as on the surface the corroboration seemed flimsy at best. However, he believed that Rosowsky's facts were correct as he had no information to the contrary. But the overriding factor was his keen knowledge of how the KGB operated: if they said the vessel would be in Antwerp on or about 14 July, it would be there as planned. The problem was how to go about verifying the facts and thereby establishing his veracity. If there were shipping records available to the unspecified US government agency, he should be able to find their source and make his own inquiry.

As the following letter shows, Orlov was able to find and present to the INS the dates that the *Svir* was in Belgium:

> I wish to correct the erroneous assertion made by investigators of the Immigration and Naturalisation Service by presenting here a photostat of a certificate issued by the official agency Scaldis appointed by the Belgian Government to signal vessels to the port of Antwerp. The certificate, dated September 20, 1955, states that 'The Soviet steamer *Svir* from Leningrad, had been in Antwerp once during the month of July 1938 and that it entered the port on July 16 at 2.25 a.m. and left on July 22 at 8.20 p.m.' Thus the Soviet ship which was sent to Antwerp to kidnap me waited for me 6 $^{1}/_{2}$ days. [The certificate was placed in evidence as exhibit #1. The letter was quoted in the report of the US Senate Committee of the Judiciary dated 31 May 1956 regarding Committee findings relative to Senate Bill 1627.]

Orlov admitted that he had felt certain that it had been the FBI which had made the erroneous search. However, years later he learned that the government agency that had conducted the search was in fact the CIA.

Orlov had won the first battle, but the war was far from over. Now a new challenge of a more serious nature was brought forth by the INS investigators. During the interrogation by the INS on 22 June 1955, he was asked if he had been implicated in the kidnapping and murder of Andrés Nin, the head of the Trotsky/Marxist POUM (Partido Obrero de Unificación Marxista/United Marxist Workers' Party) during the Spanish Civil War. Orlov vehemently denied any connection with the Nin affair but realised that the matter would not be dropped. He suspected that the source of the allegation was a book by Jesús Hernandez, the former member of the Comintern who had been the Minister of Education for the Republican Government during the Spanish Civil War. The book, which was titled *Yo Fui Un Ministro de Stalin* (*I Was Stalin's Minister*) and which placed the blame for Nin's murder on Orlov, had been published in 1953, well after Orlov's revelations appeared in April 1953, but had not been available until 1954.

There was not enough time during the INS inquiry to substantiate fully his position relative to the allegation, other than to deny it, and Orlov felt that a formal presentation of the facts was in his best interests. In a letter dated 25 June 1955 to the INS, Orlov charged that the spurious allegation which had appeared in Hernandez's book was a total fabrication.

In the book, Hernandez alleges that he met Orlov several times during the Civil War and that at one of their meetings Orlov insisted that Hernandez make arrangements for Nin to be arrested; it also says that Nin was eventually murdered on Orlov's orders. Orlov contended that he had never met Hernandez personally and was only aware of him by reputation because of his official position in the Republican Government. Hernandez also gives a literal account of a meeting with Abram Slutsky, Chief of the Foreign Department of the KGB, in the autumn of 1936, when Slutsky talked to him about the planned murder of Nin. Orlov pointed out that there was a fatal flaw in the book, which clearly indicated that Hernandez had never met either Orlov or Slutsky personally and which therefore rendered his allegations pure fabrication.

For example, in the book Hernandez describes Orlov as being 6 feet 6 3/4 inches tall, whereas Orlov was barely 5 feet 8 inches tall. He did no better with Slutsky, describing him as a very tall, thin man with stooped shoulders, sunken chest and a sharp-featured face. In reality, Slutsky was short and very stout, weighing about 200 pounds; he had a barrel chest rather than a sunken chest, and a fat, round face rather than a sharp-featured face. It was obvious that Hernandez had never seen Slutsky or Orlov.

Orlov provided the INS with photostats of the pertinent sections of Hernandez's book along with translations from the

Spanish. The INS could then make its own judgement from visual contact with Orlov. As to Slutsky, this would be a problem as he had already been liquidated on Stalin's orders. There were also no other KGB defectors available to confirm the description as they too had been liquidated. However, there was one man in the US who had known Slutsky personally, and to this end Orlov directed the US authorities to Alexander Barmine, who was head of the Russian Desk of the Voice of America and who could certainly confirm the description of Slutsky from an unbiased position.

Orlov felt certain that the INS would also interview Hernandez in Mexico, through its sources at the American Embassy in Mexico City, and confront him with Orlov's rebuttal. Information regarding Orlov's alleged implication in the Nin affair was presented to the Judiciary Committee investigating the merits of the proposed law giving the Orlovs legal residency in the US.

When I later asked Orlov about the Nin affair, he replied that it had to be seen in context with events that were taking place during the Civil War and not as an isolated incident. Orlov stressed the fact that the Republican Government had been composed of many factions, the most powerful of which were the Socialist and Spanish Communist Parties, who had distrusted each other. There was no cohesion in the Republican Government as each party, including several splinter groups, was pulling the Government in diverse directions rather than calling for a unified front first in order to win the war. Franco's Government, on the other hand, was united in its determination to win the war. To Orlov, it was inevitable that the Republican side would eventually lose the war.

From the very beginning of the Spanish Civil War, the Soviet Government had backed Prime Minister Francisco Largo Caballero, the ever popular Socialist head of the largest workers' union, the UGT. They felt that under his leadership he could unite all parties into a solidarity that would win the war. Therefore, all Soviet efforts were designed to make concessions to the Prime Minister and never usurp his authority. Soviet policy in Spain dictated that the Republican Government had direct command of its troops and that the Soviet advisors never went beyond advising.

However, this did not go as planned. At the very beginning of the Civil War, the Nationalists under Franco had made their way to the very heart of Spain, the city of Madrid. Fortunately, the International Brigades and the Republican Fifth Regiment had stemmed the advance at the very gates of the city. Largo Caballero seemed unperturbed at this turn of events and, when it was suggested that fortifications be erected around the remaining vital Republican cities, he took no action. Franco's armies continued their advances into Republican territory, although they were never able to take the besieged city of Madrid until the waning days of the war. The major problem was the fact that Largo Caballero held two positions within the Government, those of Prime Minister and War Minister, whose duties detracted from each other. In doing so, he completely lost sight of the reality that Madrid had to be saved at all costs.

As described earlier, the Republican Government was moved from Madrid to Valencia on 6 November 1936, during the darkest days of the Civil War. Madrid was temporarily saved by foreigners in the International Brigades but this was at the expense of the popularity of Largo Caballero. Soon the men in the trenches knew that it was the Soviets, and only the Soviets, who had come to their rescue with men and armaments at a time when they were desperately needed. During those days, the popularity of the Soviets rose to new peaks as civilians and the military flocked to join the Spanish Communist Party. Socialists in the Government soon began to support the Communists in the Government and both parties found it possible to co-operate with one another, at least for a while.

Slowly Largo Caballero's popularity diminished to such an extent that his influence was evaporating. He therefore had to do something drastic to curtail the haemorrhaging of his power and popularity in the eyes of his people. As the War Minister, he devised a plan for an offensive attack in the region of Estremadura, which he calculated would cut off the province of Burgos, and

Franco's headquarters in the city of Burgos, from Andalusia. None of his top field commanders or Soviet military advisors concurred with the plan, knowing that it would draw troops from Madrid, weaken their position and thereby give Franco an opportunity to take Madrid. When the matter came before the War Cabinet, it was strongly rejected, even by Indalecio Prieto who would come to play a major role in future events.

Stalin and the Politburo were kept advised of these critical developments and of Largo Caballero's leadership. The office of the Soviet Ambassador, the Comintern (on matters related to the Spanish Communist Party), the Soviet military attachés (on matters related to the war effort) and the KGB (on political as well as military aspects of the war) were each charged with furnishing a weekly report to Stalin and the Politburo. Orlov's reports were in the form of an overview of the week's events, both military and political, which also included information from official as well as unofficial sources. He would receive the reports of the other entities without making his report available to them. In one of his weekly summations to the Kremlin during March 1937, he stressed the fact that the Civil War was going well but that a critical situation in the future could preclude a final victory. He went on to build his case against Largo Caballero in his capacity as War Minister, but suggested that Largo Caballero be kept on solely as Prime Minister, which was at most a position of limited power.

Orlov felt that nothing would come of this weekly communiqué and he was much surprised when he received a reply in early April from KGB Chairman Yezhov, admitting that the Kremlin was worried about the situation and agreeing that Largo Caballero's handling of the war effort was detrimental to the cause. Could the matter be discussed in confidence with Juan Negrin, a Socialist member of the cabinet, and his views obtained? Orlov had in the past informed the KGB Centre of Negrin's co-operation with his office and that he could be trusted. Orlov replied by cable that he would only discuss the matter with Negrin if the latter consented beforehand to keep it confidential. In return, Yezhov gave his blessing to the task.

Negrin did agree to confidentiality and confessed that he too, as well as other members of the cabinet, was concerned about the manner in which Largo Caballero was handling the reins of government, especially in his capacity as War Minister. However, he cautioned that it might be very dangerous to shift the balance of power at that time because there was a great amount of tension and dissension between cabinet members. He felt that this could lead to a loss of determination to win the war on the part of some of the key members of the cabinet, who would then prefer a negotiated peace with Franco. He identified these key players as President of the Republic Manuel Azaña and Indalecio Prieto. He said that he knew Prieto was already alarmed at the course of the war as a few days earlier he had remarked, 'I already see myself in Mexico City delivering a lecture on "Why has Republican Spain lost the war? Admission 2 pesos".' Both men laughed at Prieto's remark, but Orlov knew it to be a correct quotation as he had heard the same remark from Prieto himself a few days before.

Orlov suggested that Negrin would be the man for the post. Negrin discounted this proposal and added that he had enough problems administering his Finance Ministry, which was far less complicated and demanding than the War Ministry. He then remarked that the man for the post would not only have to have the ability to run the Ministry but would have to be acceptable to the other members of the cabinet. He knew of only one cabinet member that would meet both criteria, Prieto. Orlov was taken aback by this observation in view of Negrin's previous comment, but Negrin explained that Prieto was an outstanding administrator and that, if he knew he had the full backing of the Soviet Government, he would regain the confidence in himself to strive aggressively for victory. Negrin agreed to sound out Prieto's willingness to make the attempt to become Minister of War without revealing that Orlov had intervened.

In less than a week, Orlov had his answer. Negrin reported that Prieto would accept the position if it were offered to him.

Prieto had expressed the opinion that if the United States could be swayed from its position of non-intervention, a victory over Franco was certain. He was buoyed by the fact that he had it on good authority that information coming from US Ambassador Claude Bowers indicated that President Roosevelt, and more so his wife Eleanor, were sympathetic to the Republican cause.

Unrest was the key element of the strife that would come about in the very near future. From the onset of the Civil War, members of the FAI (Federación Anarquista Ibérica) Party, commonly known as the Anarchist Party in the Catalonia region of Spain, had taken over the administration of the customs houses along the Spanish-French frontier. Their arbitrarily established checkpoints were soon overrun with corruption as the border guards unlawfully confiscated commodities coming into Spain. On 26 March 1937, the FAI members of the Catalan Generalitat (Catalan Regional Government) resigned in protest at a proclamation issued by the Chief of State Security Auguade demanding that these checkpoints be abolished and all firearms turned over to the police. In turn, the Anarchists demanded Auguade's dismissal and the rescinding of his order. The Central Government then ordered the Carabineros to take over the customs posts. When the Carabineros attempted to take over the customs post in Puigcerda, they were met with gunfire from the resisters. The pot was beginning to boil.

Another point of contention also revolved around the Anarchist Party and only worsened the situation. In the earliest days of the Civil War, they had taken over the Telefónica Building in Barcelona, which housed the vital telephone communication system in Republican Spain. There was no doubt that the Anarchists were listening in on conversations of government officials and when a conversation in progress did not agree with their agenda, the line would go dead. The Central Government decided that this practice had to stop and, on 3 May 1937, sent its crack assault guards, under orders from the Councillor for Public Order Rodriguez Sallas, to take the Telefónica Building. The assault guards were met with gunfire and only succeeded in taking the ground floor.

By the time the Catalan Generalitat met the following day, the situation was smouldering and ready to ignite. The Anarchists protested against Sallas's action of the previous day and demanded his immediate dismissal. Their demands were rejected, after which the Anarchists called for a general strike and agitated for the workers of Barcelona to erect street barricades and stand up for their rights. Elements of the extremist faction of the Anarchists were joined by members of POUM, whose membership mandated the overthrow of the Republican Government in favour of a Leninist Socialist Government. They then took to the streets, where they fortified strategic points of ingress and egress to the city and kept their members posted there with a wide array of weapons. In all, almost 6,000 men took part in the uprising, most of whom were from the Anarchist Party with smaller numbers from the FAI and POUM.

The rebellion lasted only a few days but it came at a difficult time for the Central Government when its troops were in a life-and-death struggle against odds that were strongly in favour of the Nationalists. On the third day of the rebellion, the Anarchist leader José García Oliver, having realised the impact of the rebellion on the war effort, went on radio to beseech the revolutionaries to lay down their arms for the good of the country. Thanks to his efforts, the revolt quickly petered out. The final official toll was around 950 men killed and over 2,600 wounded.

The Central Government, fearing that the still smouldering embers of the revolt could easily re-ignite, transferred 5,000 troops to the Catalonia region under the able command of General Sebastian Pozas-Perea. Soon Pozas-Perea had the situation under control, but this was at the expense of diverting troops from Madrid.

The tense situation now presented the Spanish Communist Party with a golden opportunity to avenge itself against POUM and its leader, Andrés Nin. Nin had come to power under the cloak of the Comintern when he was one of the founding fathers of the Spanish Communist Party. He had become the First Secretary of the Party and was a man of great influence. However, in 1931 he had broken with the Comintern, thereby severing his ties with the Kremlin. Nin felt that the Communists had lost sight of the ideals of Marxism and thus formed a splinter Communist Party called POUM. The Spanish Communist Party never forgave Nin for his sin and cautiously waited for the day when they could take revenge against him and his party. That day finally came.

The Central Government also had its own agenda concerning the revolt. The cabinet met on 15 May 1937 and two of the Communist ministers, Vincente Uribe and Jesús Hernandez, demanded that POUM be outlawed for its part in the revolt. However, Prime Minister Largo Caballero, a strong Socialist and enemy of the Communists, would not go along with their demands. As the Communists continued to press their demands, Largo Caballero only became more agitated and uncompromising. As the matter came to an impasse, both Uribe and Hernandez walked out of the meeting. The Prime Minister then moved to the next item on the agenda, but he had hardly begun when the majority of cabinet members, including those from his own Socialist Party, walked out of the room. Among them were Ministers Negrin and Prieto, who had no love for POUM and felt that the party should be outlawed, but made their move knowing that it would probably be the end for Largo Caballero. Prieto had the most at stake as he felt that this would be his opportunity to take over the post of War Minister. In the end, he had made the correct assumption.

The Government was now in crisis and the matter could only be resolved by Manuel Azaña, the President of the Republic. He wholeheartedly endorsed a plan presented to him by Largo Caballero that a new cabinet be formed which would be composed of members of his own party, the UGT, the CNT and the Anarchists but which would exclude the Spanish Communist Party. Several members of the cabinet, including Prieto, Negrin and Alvarez del Vayo, saw the flaw in this composition and informed Largo Caballero that the Communists had to be retained in the new government. They reasoned that, without the Communists, the Soviets would no longer support the Republicans and would withdraw their military aid. They also advised that they could not sustain the Civil War without the benefits derived from the Soviets. They then played their best hand with the warning that they would not take part in the new cabinet if it did not contain any Communists. As insolent as ever, Largo Caballero stayed his course.

The Communist Party then took their turn at Largo Caballero. They agreed to support him as Prime Minister if he relinquished the post of War Minister and declared that matters relating to the war could best be handled by a Supreme War Council. No friend of the Communists, Largo Caballero rejected the offer. The next day he resigned his positions of Prime Minister and War Minister.

Juan Negrin became the next Prime Minister and formed a new cabinet with Prieto as Minister of Defence. The Anarchists refused to join the cabinet. In the end, Negrin and Prieto became the most formidable forces in the Republican Government.

Orlov always considered his relations with Negrin to be very good and he always knew that he was dealing with a man of great integrity. Orlov soon called on Negrin to congratulate him on his new position. Negrin immediately asked Orlov if any outside forces had propelled him into the post of Prime Minister. Although unsaid, it was apparent that Negrin thought the Soviets had had a part in the selection. Orlov assured the new Prime Minister that there had been no outside influences at play and that he should accept the fact that it had been political strategy which had manoeuvred him into the position. However, he did admit that when Largo Caballero resigned, the Kremlin had instructed the Spanish Communist Party to give their full support to Negrin.

Orlov always felt that Negrin handled the position of Prime Minister with self-confidence and dignity. During his tenure in office, Negrin was often criticised by his enemies as being under the thumb of the Soviets and acceding to their demands. Orlov related that this was never the case and, as with any high political office, there was the matter of juggling the issues which could be interpreted in many ways.

Soon after the formation of the new cabinet, the Communist Party press began to circulate news releases and editorials demanding the arrest of POUM leaders for their collaboration with the enemy. The most formidable voice in this direction was that of Jesús Hernandez, the Minister of Education. He demanded retribution, claiming that the POUM leaders were Franco's spies who were agitating and destroying the Republican Army from the rear.

The demands of the Communists aroused the Government into action. Julián Zugazagoitia, the Socialist Minister of the Interior, signed warrants of arrest on 16 June 1937 for Andrés Nin and other leaders of POUM. Within weeks of their arrest, the prison where they were being held was raided by a band of armed men, who overpowered the guards and took Nin with them. There was an outcry that this could happen and soon the finger of accusation was pointed towards the Communists as the perpetrators. The Communists retaliated by putting the blame on Franco, who, they insisted, came to Nin's rescue because he was a spy for the Nationalists. Soon graffiti appeared on the walls of buildings in Barcelona asking the question, 'Where is Nin?' This was soon covered over with the Communists' answer, 'In Salamanca [Franco's stronghold] or Berlin.'

The other leaders of POUM were charged with leading an armed rebellion in May 1937 in Barcelona against the Republican Government in time of war and spying for the Nationalists. The investigation turned up documents that allegedly linked members of POUM with Franco's intelligence service. A few Fascist members of POUM confessed and implicated other POUM members in the spying charge. In October 1938, they were brought to trial for their rebellious acts, although the charge of spying was dropped because of insufficient evidence. Of the seven defendants brought to trial, five were convicted and two were acquitted. The victory for the Government was indeed a hollow one as a few months later the war was over and the Republican Government no longer existed. As to the documents presented at the trial purporting that POUM members were Franco's spies, Orlov always felt that they were forgeries.

However, despite this Orlov did believe that there was some merit in this claim. He cited a released report on German foreign policy in which is reflected a report dated 11 May 1937 from the German Ambassador to Spain, Wilhelm Faupel, to the German Foreign Ministry. Faupel states that Generalissimo Franco had apprised him that his intelligence service had precipitated the street fighting in Barcelona with the active help of his secret agents. Orlov felt that Franco's claim was exaggerated, although he had no doubts that it was one of many factors that had contributed to the uprising.

The disappearance of Andrés Nin has never been fully explained nor were the kidnappers ever identified. Without doubt, this was a matter of political vengeance. The blame has been laid at many doorsteps, with the finger pointing to a different person or group depending on the political expediencies at the time. At various times the POUMists have laid the blame for the crime on Spanish Communist Party members; on Erno Gerö, the Communist Prime Minister of Hungary during the 1956 Hungarian revolt; on the Italian Communist Vittorio Vidali; on the French Communist leader André Marty; on the Comintern agent Stepanov; on the Soviet Consul-General in Barcelona Vladimir Antonov-Ovseyenko; and, last but not least, on Alexander Orlov.

In the book in which Jesús Hernandez accuses Orlov of being behind the plot to kidnap Andrés Nin, he also cites an event that has been proved to be a fabrication, thereby casting doubt on his credibility. He relates a story of a secret meeting of the Spanish Communist Party held in Valencia in March 1937, in which the only topic of discussion was how to remove Prime Minister Largo Caballero from office. In addition to himself, he lists the following as being in attendance: Palmiro Togliatti, Stepanov, Codovila, Erno Gerö and André Marty. He also notes that Soviet Chargé d'Affaires Gaikis and Alexander Orlov were present.

Orlov related that he had never attended such a meeting, was never aware that this meeting had taken place and, moreover, did not believe that such a meeting had ever occurred. He strongly believed it to be a fabrication on the part of the KGB for the benefit of Hernandez's book. The Soviet policy of manipulating foreign Communist Parties was always through the Comintern and was very specific that Soviet representatives not attend meetings of foreign Communist Parties.

What Orlov was not aware of when he was challenged by the INS regarding the Hernandez accusation in 1955 was the fact that a biography of Palmiro Togliatti had already been written in 1953, which proved the secret meeting to be pure fiction. Years afterwards, he read the biography, *Conversations with Togliatti* by the authors Marcella and Maurice Ferrara, which says that Togliatti reported to Spain as a representative of the Comintern in June 1937, four months after the fictitious meeting he was supposed to have attended. Orlov acknowledged that he had known Togliatti personally but, to the best of his recollection, he had only met him towards the end of 1937. He further noted that the KGB in Spain tracked all of the Comintern members as part of their intelligence duties and it was not until around the time he first met Togliatti that this individual appeared on the KGB screen. Had he been aware of this information when he originally stood accused by the INS, he would naturally have directed its attention, as well as that of the Senate Judiciary Committee, to the Togliatti biography.

Orlov was highly disturbed at Hernandez's accusation, but more so by the fact that it perpetuated the claim, as an accepted fact, that he had ordered the Nin murder. He always felt that the more times a lie is repeated, the more it is accepted as the truth. He cited as cases in point two books on the Spanish Civil War which repeat Hernandez's accusation. The authors both claimed to have done extensive research in the Spanish archives and had reviewed Spanish newspapers of the time. How could both authors have failed to contact him, the highest-ranking Soviet official in Spain during the Spanish Civil War with discretionary authority over the Soviet Ambassador and the Soviet military, despite their claims that they had meticulously researched the facts. He was the man in the field whose reports to the KGB Centre, the Kremlin and even Stalin provided the most valued information upon which decisions as to the direction of the Civil War were made. He had direct and personal access to the highest echelon of political leaders in the Spanish Republican Government as well as his own people, who were responsible for the International Brigades and advisors to the Republican military. He was the man that organised and trained the troops of the XIV Corps, which carried out the guerrilla warfare that kept Franco's armies at bay, destroyed communications and supply lines, and more often than not diverted the Nationalists' attention away from the true area of a Republican offensive. Both books had been published after Orlov had surfaced and become known around the world. The authors could easily have contacted *Life* magazine, Random House Publishers or *Reader's Digest* and their inquiries would have been forwarded to him. If they had been seeking the truth, he would have been more than happy to help them. Orlov's only explanation as to why these authors never contacted him was his belief that they must have been guided in their work by biased advisors from among the various Spanish splinter groups, whose views had influenced their research.

One of the authors greatly upset Orlov when he doubted that Orlov had actually written the book, *The Secret History of Stalin's Crimes*, noting in a footnote that 'I have been unable to establish whether this book is a forgery or the work of a ghost.' When I asked Orlov the identity of this particular author, he casually shrugged off the matter, noting that it was unimportant. Later, my curiosity aroused, I did some research and finally came up with the footnote in question on page 503 of Hugh Thomas's book, *The Spanish Civil War*, which was published by Harper & Brothers, New York, in 1961. I later casually confessed to Orlov that I had run across the aforementioned footnote while reading Thomas's book. He seemed impressed at my interest in the Spanish Civil War and thought that I should read the other book, which he identified as *Communism and the Spanish Civil War* by David Cattell (Berkeley Press, 1955). He stated that Cattell did make a shrewd observation in his book that he thought worth mentioning as it summed up the myriad of allegations on all sides that came out after the Civil War ended. Cattell stated that after the defeat of the Loyalists by Franco in 1939, the various Republican groups threw the blame of defeat on someone else. The Communist Party was unanimously chosen as the scapegoat by all non-Communist Spanish émigrés. In their rush to place the stigma on Communism, attempts to analyse the truth were often forgotten. Old hatreds that had been set aside during the war were now focused on the Communists. This fanatical recrimination therefore makes most of the Spanish reports written after the war almost worthless to the conscientious investigator.

I discussed the Nin affair on numerous occasions with Orlov and there was never any doubt that he truthfully portrayed his position. The more I delved into the matter, the more I realised that it was a very complex situation with few concrete answers. However, Orlov did make a few observations that made sense to me. As Hernandez was the Minister of Education in the Republican Government, why in the world would Orlov seek his help to liquidate Nin when it would be more logical to go through the Ministry of Police or the Ministry of the Interior? When I suggested that perhaps one of the KGB Mobile Groups had been dispatched for this purpose, Orlov thought not, as up to that time they had only ever targeted their own people. The KGB would not have resorted to the Mobile Groups as the matter could have been handled with ease by a Spanish agent of the Comintern, the proclaimed enemy of the POUMists and their leader Nin.

One thing Orlov questioned was the strange coincidence that Hernandez's denunciation of him had followed on the heels of the publication of his own book. He strongly believed that the Hernandez book had been used by the KGB to retaliate against his own revelations about Stalin, the KGB and the men in the Kremlin. He knew for certain that Hernandez had been an agent of the Comintern at the time of Nin's death and later learned that he had been sent to Mexico in 1943 to direct Communist activities in South America. Hernandez had dedicated his book to his mother and sister, whom, he noted, resided in the Soviet Union, which could amount to the traditional KGB hostage situation to ensure his obedience. The fatal blunders that Hernandez had made in his book could be attributed to the long line of communication between the KGB Centre in Moscow and Hernandez in Mexico, but more so to the rush to get the book out as quickly as possible.

I have often thought of the Nin affair and speculated as to the perpetrator of Nin's murder. I long ago dismissed Orlov from my list of suspects as I was in the unique position of being able to confront him face to face. I was not a novice in interrogating nor could I have been easily led or deceived. I further had the benefit of confidential information that would not have been available outside the confines of the US intelligence community. If I had been able to take my investigation one step further, I would have had a closer look at the logical suspect who had a political motive for the vengeance murder of Andrés Nin. My focus would have been on the accuser, Jesús Hernandez, and his ties to the Comintern and the KGB.

Orlov never distanced himself from the fact that the guerrilla operations he was sent to Spain to organise were responsible for the deaths of thousands of people; nor did he deny the fact that he had masterminded the bombing of the *Deutschland*, which resulted in the bombing of the city of Almeria with the combined loss of nearly 100 lives; nor the fact that he was about to execute a bombing attack on the funeral procession of Nationalist General Emilio Mola which would have resulted in the deaths of hundreds. All of these deaths are well documented in Orlov's personal memoirs, so it makes no sense for him to deny responsibility for one more, that of Nin.

Long after I completed this chapter, I read Max Eastman's book *Great Companions*, which was published in 1960. In one of the chapters revolving around a 1937 incident, my attention was drawn to the fact that Eastman and Nin had been personal friends, a fact that I had not previously known. In discussing Nin, Eastman noted that his POUMist friend had recently been taken from jail and murdered by the Stalinists. He added that Nin had been one of the finest men in the revolutionary movement.

From the time Orlov and Eastman first met in 1953 until Eastman's death in 1969, they were close friends, a relationship based on mutual respect and trust. Had Eastman had the slightest suspicion that Orlov was implicated in Nin's murder in any manner, there would have been no friendship or any kind of relationship between them. This information convinced me more than ever of Orlov's innocence.

The Orlovs were now under the microscope of the INS in connection with their deportation proceedings. They dutifully reported to the INS parole office every month until they finally received permanent resident status. In the meantime, Orlov considered the possibility that the Bender bill might not make it through Congress. As with any good general, he had a contingency plan. He contacted the Canadian Government and explored the possibility of obtaining a visa to enter Canada as a permanent resident alien. The Canadian Government's reply was not encouraging, but it did offer to study his request further. It later asked Orlov if he would require security guard protection in Canada, noting that such protection being afforded GRU defector Igor Gouzenko had become a financial burden. Gouzenko had been a cipher clerk in the office of the military attaché at the Soviet Embassy in Ottawa, operating under the diplomatic cloak. In September 1945, he defected bringing with him secret details of Soviet espionage directed against the Canadian Government. The information was of immense value to the West. Gouzenko and his family were given new identities and protection by the Royal Canadian Mounted Police. The Canadian authorities also asked why Orlov had not become a US citizen after residing in the States for seventeen years.

He then explained his situation at length with respect to protection requirements and also that he was making efforts to remain in the US, but suggested that the INS be contacted as it was in a better position to give an official answer regarding his immigration status in the US. In the end, the Canadian Government turned down Orlov's request as it stated that he did not meet its requirements for immigration. Orlov had no doubt that his immigration appeal was turned down because of the financial commitment the Canadian Government would have to have undertaken to provide him and his wife with protection.

The Senate Committee of the Judiciary continued its investigation of the Orlovs in connection with Senate Bill 1627 through 1955 and into 1956. In April 1956, two separate letters were directed to the Honourable James O. Eastland from Eugene Lyons and Max Eastman, both of the *Reader's Digest*, and one to Senator George Bender from William L. White, now connected with *The Emporia Gazette* of Emporia, Kansas. All three letters on behalf of the Orlovs cited the Orlovs' contribution to understanding Communism and recommended favourable action. These letters were printed verbatim in the final report of the Committee.

The final recommendation of the Senate Committee of the Judiciary, 2nd Session of the 84th Congress, on the legislative date of 24 May 1956, after consideration of all the facts in the case, was of the opinion that Senate Bill 1627 should be enacted. An Act identified as Private Law 810 was enacted by the US Senate and the House of Representatives to the effect that Alexander Orlov and his wife Maria should be considered to have been lawfully admitted to the US for permanent residence as of the enactment of this Act. The bill in its last legislative stage was passed by the House on 17 July 1956 and then sent to the President of the US, Dwight D. Eisenhower. The legislative process had dragged on for so long that Orlov had hardly managed to keep abreast of developments. He was therefore taken by surprise on 25 July 1956 when he received a telephone call from his attorney, Hugo Pollock, informing him that the President had signed his bill. Pollock forwarded the telegram that had brought the good news:

PLEASED TO ADVISE PRESIDENT EISENHOWER SIGNED YOUR BILL THIS AFTERNOON. CONGRATULATIONS. YOU WILL HEAR FROM IMMIGRATION SERVICE SOON REGARDING PAPERS TO BE PROCESSED. WARMEST REGARDS
                    SENATOR GEORGE H BENDER OHIO

From the day he received the telegram at his residence in New York to the day he died in Cleveland, Orlov kept the telegram in a frame on his desk. He told me that every day when he looked at the telegram, he realised his good fortune at being able to make the United States his home and thanked God for the privilege.

Towards the end of March 1956, *Life* magazine learned that Orlov was writing an essay on Stalin and made him an offer he could not turn down. On 2 April, he signed a contract giving publication rights to *Life*. The article, entitled 'The Sensational Secret behind the Damnation of Stalin', appeared in the 23rd of April issue of the magazine. As noted in the title, the word 'sensational' became synonymous with the article itself and led to other requests for the author's works. The article ended with the warning that although the successors to Stalin – Khrushchev *et al* – had distanced themselves from Stalin the person, they had not truly broken with the Stalin legacy. I am sure that the article was not well received by the Kremlin.

Orlov testified before the Senate Subcommittee of the Committee of the Judiciary to investigate the administration of the Internal Security Act and other internal security laws in Washington DC in September 1955 and again during February 1957. He furnished valuable information of an intelligence nature not previously known, some of which is reflected elsewhere in this book. Needless to say, these episodes added another dimension to an already hectic schedule.

In about 1971 or possibly 1972, I discovered another dimension to the General that I would never have suspected: he was an aspiring playwright. I was visiting him one afternoon when I spotted a manuscript in his office bound in an embossed manila folder bearing a label which read, 'LOVE IN MOSCOW (The Americanochka)'. When I asked him about the manuscript, he smiled as usual and said that it went back to the days when he was living in New York. He explained that towards the end of the 1950s, when his articles no longer seemed to be in demand, he took to writing plays. He wrote three in all, but only kept the most promising one. He admitted that he had never had the courage to promote the play as the theatre was a field outside of the scope of his expertise as well as his contacts in the publishing profession.

As my wife Ruth noted when she read the play, it gave

the feeling that [Orlov] used this to give a detailed and no doubt very honest picture of some of the methods used by the MVD (KGB) to recruit foreigners (in this case a twenty-year-old American girl employed by the State Department in the US Embassy in Moscow) into their spy network. The play shows very clearly how the MVD used their own Soviet citizens to entrap young and naïve US government employees who had access to top-secret information. Who would suspect a famous singer with the Moscow Bolshoi Theatre of being an agent of the MVD assigned to captivate a young and easily impressed young woman from America for the purpose of using her to provide the Soviets with first-hand information that came across her desk?

There is no doubt in my mind that the characters . . . were very real to Mr Orlov and could have even been taken from some of his actual experiences during his career prior to his defection. The constantly changing plans . . . as well as the 'bending' of the laws by the MVD to suit their needs to achieve their ends is a reaffirmation of the depth of deception to which the MVD would go to bring their plan to a successful end for them with no regard for what kind of turmoil it was bringing to not only their own agent but also to the young woman.

Towards the end of November 1958, Orlov suffered a severe heart attack. He felt chest pains early one morning and was rushed to the New York Hospital at 528 East 68th Street, where he convalesced for almost two weeks. By disposition he was physically strong for his age with a good mental outlook to match; however, the years in hiding had taken their toll. This was nature's way of telling him that he had to slow down and he took the advice.

From the moment the Orlovs defected and went into hiding, they were constantly plagued with anxiety and stress. They could not lead normal lives as the fear of detection by the KGB was ever present. Their every move was calculated on the basis that the KGB was closing in on them. The situation only intensified in New York after they had been exposed to the world. Every time the Orlovs left their apartment, they would use counter-surveillance techniques to detect any interest in their movement. In the parlance of the intelligence trade, these measures are known as 'dry cleaning'. They would walk several blocks in a direction opposite to their actual destination, stopping at various shop fronts to assess the pedestrians and vehicles behind them. Often they would dart down a side street and into a recessed doorway or alley to see if anyone questionable passed by. They would then retrace the same route back towards their apartment while observing the pedestrian and vehicular traffic coming towards them. They would then pass their apartment and walk several blocks in the opposite direction from their first excursion using the same detection methods. Finally, they would hail a cab when they had to go some distance. Even a visit to a neighbourhood grocery store or butcher shop around the corner, or down the street, was a time-consuming chore, but without doubt a necessity considering that they had to abide by this daily ritual if they valued their lives, which they did. Not even their closest friends knew their actual address, with the exception of the Max Eastmans in time, and they could only be contacted through their attorney Hugo Pollock. Any socialising would take place away from their home and preferably at a predesignated restaurant. It was a difficult way to socialise because the slightest unintentional remark could betray their whereabouts. In New York, their privacy from their neighbours was not a problem as this was the way it was in the Big Apple, but in other cities they kept to themselves, made a few select friends in the apartments and were probably classified as aloof, anti-social or just plain unfriendly. This was not the way the Orlovs wanted it to be but the way it had to be.

In 1957, with his immigration problems now behind him, Orlov felt that it was time to move on. His thoughts turned to Cleveland, where he had many fond memories. Another consideration was his wife's health, which had certainly deteriorated since their arrival in New York, and he thought it would be best to place her under the care of their friend and medical advisor, Dr Zimmerman. Orlov also felt that he wanted to teach at a university and recalled the conservative Jesuit college in Cleveland, John Carroll University. In July 1957, he contacted the university and was advised that there were no suitable openings that would match his experience. He speculated that he had received little consideration because of the notoriety brought about by the Andrés Nin affair. He therefore dropped the idea of moving for the foreseeable future.

By the early 1960s, the Orlovs definitely decided that they had had enough stress and that it would be best to make a change. The demand for Orlov's writing had diminished and the prospects in this regard did not look good. He knew that he would have to occupy his time in some manner and still wanted to teach or do research at a university, preferably in a small town. He and Maria felt that a small town would be less susceptible to their detection and, conversely, they would be more able to detect any surveillance on them. The unresolved questions were what would he do and where would he do it.

A friend suggested the University of Michigan in Ann Arbor as a place that could satisfy his requirements. Orlov contacted the university and was advised that they would consider an appointment. Would he contact Roger W. Heyns, the Vice President of Academic Affairs, the next time he was in Ann Arbor? In the early part of June 1962, the Orlovs travelled to Ann Arbor to look around the town and to meet Heyns. Orlov discussed at length his background in law and with the KGB and how his official positions with the USSR related to the history of his country of birth. Heyns seemed impressed and advised that he would get back to him. Orlov thought that the interview had gone well and, from what Heyns had told him, felt that there was a good possibility there would be an opening. Based on this assumption he and Maria spent another day looking around Ann Arbor. They liked what they saw and concluded that should an offer be made, it would be accepted.

Almost a month went by and nothing was heard from the university. Orlov now felt that another possibility had slipped through his fingers but still was not discouraged. Then the letter that he hoped for finally came and met all his expectations. On 3 July 1962, Heyns wrote offering an appointment, which would enable Orlov to continue his research and writing. He felt that the university's first interest would be the preparation and publication of Orlov's personal memoirs as the university believed them to have enormous historical value. Also other projects dealing with Soviet law and the history of the Spanish Civil War would be within the range of the university's interests. The appointment, should one materialise, would be in the Law School, and if any works were produced the University of Michigan Press would have first publication rights. The letter concluded that if such an appointment were of interest, the university would bear the expenses for Orlov to come to Ann Arbor to work out the details. By return letter dated 7 July, Orlov affirmed his interest in the appointment and said that he would be available to discuss the details at the convenience of the university.

As arranged, Orlov met the Dean of the Law School, Allan F. Smith, on Thursday, 26 July, in Ann Arbor. The following day Smith confirmed by letter their conversation of the previous day in which Orlov had indicated that he would accept an appointment as a Senior Research Fellow at the Law School beginning 1 September 1962. The letter noted that it should be regarded as a formal offer of an appointment on the terms that the University of Michigan Press would have publication rights to any works produced. If the terms were satisfactory, a written acceptance would be appreciated.

Orlov accepted the appointment by return letter dated 30 July with a sense of deep satisfaction and responsibility. He wrote that he was ready to put all of his past experience and knowledge to the service of the great university and was confident that he would make a valuable contribution to the study of the Soviet Union. He then extended his sincere thanks to Dean Smith and Vice President Heyns for making it possible for him to continue writing.

The Orlovs would be in Ann Arbor by the end of August 1962. Thus the stage was set for their next adventure, one they would hardly ever forget, an encounter with the KGB.

PART 4

KGB STRIKES AND DISINFORMATION

TWENTY

THE KGB STRIKES IN ANN ARBOR

Of all the cities in the United States where the Orlovs hid from the KGB, Orlov considered Ann Arbor, Michigan, to be special. It was in Ann Arbor that they finally threw off the shackles of fear and began to believe that the KGB no longer had an interest in them. For the first time they lived a more normal life in most respects and began to disregard the harsh security measures that had governed their daily routine ever since they stepped into their safe haven back in 1938. Orlov realised that it was Ann Arbor, where they were lulled into a sense of complacency, that brought about their downfall.

On numerous occasions Orlov compared his plight in Ann Arbor with Charles Dickens's historical novel *A Tale of Two Cities*. He had read the book in the late 1920s, when he was assigned to the Soviet Embassy in Paris, and admitted that he was first attracted to it because of its tale of the political intrigues that surrounded the French Revolution, much as with his own country's revolution. He noted that he had been favourably impressed with the opening lines of the book and had even memorised the potent message of the opening paragraph. Those lines never left his memory and after the KGB finally tracked him down in Ann Arbor, he often heard them in his head as if they were being played on an invisible phonograph that repeated the message over and over. In his own version of those lines, he said, 'Ann Arbor was our best of times and hope for the future that became our worst of times and despair for the future.' What they had achieved and enjoyed came to an abrupt end one cold November day in 1969, when an officer of the KGB knocked on their apartment door.

The Orlovs were settled in Ann Arbor just before the new school year. They took up residence in the modern Maynard House Apartments at the corner of E. William and Maynard Streets, just a block from the main campus of the University of Michigan and its famous 'Diagonal', the focal point of the university since its foundation. They were able to acquire an apartment on an upper floor of the building, which met their security requirements.

Orlov's office was no more than a brisk fifteen-minute walk down S. State Street, past the Michigan Union Building, to the Law School complex at S. University Avenue and Tappan Street. The main building of the complex, the Law Quadrangle, was an imposing and beautiful stone structure that would not have looked out of place at Cambridge University in England. Orlov's office was situated on the seventh floor of another building in the complex, the Legal Research Building, where he would take up his duties as a Senior Research Fellow.

Up to this point and for the next seven years that the Orlovs resided in Ann Arbor nothing seemed out of the ordinary and almost none of Orlov's colleagues at the Law School knew what had really brought him to the University of Michigan. Although Orlov's work was bound in secrecy, Alfred Slote, a freelance writer for the monthly magazine *Ann Arbor Observer*, was able to provide another reason for Orlov's tenure at the Law School of the University of Michigan.

When *Deadly Illusions* was published in 1993, the answer to part of the riddle of Orlov's time in Ann Arbor was made public for the first time. Because of Orlov's connection with the university, Slote took the matter one step further when he established that Orlov had been brought to the campus by the CIA and that his salary and expenses while at the Law School had been underwritten by the CIA. The results of Slote's investigative journalism appeared in the December 1993 edition of the *Ann Arbor Observer* under the caption, 'The Spy in the Law Quad'. The salient portions of the article that explain Orlov's presence in Ann Arbor are reproduced as follows:

Professor Emeritus Whit Gray, who taught a course on Soviet law, says that it wasn't unusual then for the CIA to fund research at universities. 'You have to remember that it was a different time. There might have been a hundred members of the U-M [University of Michigan] faculty receiving CIA funds for research. Back then it was the patriotic thing to do. I can assure you no eyebrows were raised about a former NKVD general being here. No one thought it was unusual.'

But at least one person did think it was unusual enough to worry about. That was the man who appointed Orlov a research associate, set up the special account through which to pay him, and gave him his Law School office. That man was Allan Smith, then Dean of the U-M Law School and later the acting president of the university.

Smith says with a wry smile, 'It was my one affair with intrigue, and I worried about it a good deal. I remember worrying whether we really should get involved with this sort of thing.'

Smith was approached by the CIA in 1961. As Smith recalls, 'I was told that the CIA had an important Russian defector they wanted to place so they could continue to try to find out what he could tell them about Russian espionage. The CIA would pay his salary and overheads.

'I thought hard about this and decided my justification for having Orlov here would be that he might be able to tell us something about the Russian criminal justice system at the time of the revolution, and also he'd be willing to do a little writing. He didn't do any teaching.

'The man himself was very cool, a mild sort of fellow, calm, reserved, slight – a little guy. I remember thinking he'd be a perfect spy.' Smith smiles, 'According to the CIA they didn't get much out of him. He was, I guess, acting as a sort of consultant to them.'

What writing or research did Orlov do in his Law School office in the years from 1962 to 1969? No one seems to know. He did write one more book, *A Handbook of Intelligence and*

Guerrilla Warfare in 1963, the year after the Orlovs' arrival in Ann Arbor.

Did the CIA also provide funds to the university to publish Orlov's *Handbook*? A CIA representative [named in the article] says he wouldn't be a bit surprised. A handbook on guerrilla warfare is certainly an unusual subject for a university press, and $6,000 was an enormous chunk of money for the U-M Press to advance. But the real smoking gun is a letter in the press's files. Dated November 29, 1960, it was written by the late Fred Wieck, then director of the press. Wieck states that 'Mr Alexander Orlov has just agreed to write for us a Soviet intelligence handbook. . . . We have agreed to make him an advance against royalties in the amount of six thousand dollars. Mr Orlov will deliver his manuscript in approximately thirteen months.' The letter was addressed to the CIA in Washington DC.

I would have liked to have put Smith at ease over his concern whether the university should have got involved 'with this sort of thing' because Orlov did indeed provide a valuable service to the United States while he was at the Law School. Unfortunately, Smith had died before I could convey this message to him.

In no time at all, the Orlovs assimilated themselves into the academic and social world of his new Law School colleagues. For the first time since the defection, they were able to take on a social life and make many friends at the Law School, as well as a few select friends in the community. Life was definitely getting better. One of their closest social relationships was with Law Professor Marcus L. Plant and his wife Geraldine, whom Orlov affectionately called Mark and Gerry. They had four children who were favourites of the Orlovs and I in turn learned that the Plant children were equally fond of the Orlovs. There was no doubt that a strong bond existed between the Plants and the Orlovs and, as the General once advised me, Mark was 'the kind of man you can trust'. His remarks came to have more meaning to me years later.

Other than socialising, their primary interest was in the cultural field that they had cultivated over the years. They hardly ever missed a classical concert or individual performance of a classical artist at the U-M Hill Auditorium and always looked forward to the next concert. The changing exhibitions at the U-M Museum were also a prime source of pleasure for the Orlovs. They never participated in the U-M spectator sports, but during the summer months they would travel the short distance to Detroit to visit its museums and shops. What the Orlovs found of particular interest was the Henry Ford Museum and Greenfield Village in Dearborn, which they made a habit of visiting at least once a year.

At the Law School Orlov completed the final draft of his book, *Handbook of Intelligence and Guerrilla Warfare*, which was published by the University of Michigan Press in 1963. In conjunction with the release of the book, an article appeared in the *Ann Arbor News* on 2 May under the caption, '"U" Press Issues Book by Former Soviet Spy Trainer'. The article relates that 'Alexander Orlov, a former Red Army commander and NKVD General, knows more about Soviet intelligence operations than any other man living outside of Russia', and goes on to describe the contents of his book. The interesting part of the article is the care given not to reveal any clues that might lead to Orlov's whereabouts, in particular the closing paragraph of the article which states that, 'University officials have declined to make public the whereabouts of Orlov and there was no comment from the author.' Orlov's telephone number was always unlisted.

Less than ten months after the release of the Orlov *Handbook*, the magazine *Newsweek* in its 24 February 1964 issue carried an article under the caption, 'The De-Briefing Process for the USSR Defectors', which dealt principally with the then recent defection of KGB officer Yuri I. Nosenko to the United States. An interesting historical appendage to the main thrust of the article related in brief what had happened to three previous KGB defectors and mentioned in particular 'General Alexander Orlov, perhaps the highest ranking Soviet secret police officer to defect to the West'.

It added that, 'Today, twenty-six years after his defection, Orlov is still convinced that the KGB will get him one day. He lives on a farm "somewhere" in the US. Only a few CIA and FBI agents know exactly where he is.' There is no doubt that this article went a long way to convincing the KGB that it would be a difficult task to locate Orlov and, at the least, diverted its attention away from the place where Orlov's *Handbook* had been published. Had it focused its investigative attention on Ann Arbor in 1963, it would have been a simple matter to locate the General.

By the summer of 1969, the Orlovs decided to leave Ann Arbor and the Law School was advised. The past seven years had been the happiest and most tranquil period since the defection and they hated to leave Ann Arbor and the environment of the university. What became the deciding factor was Maria's health. She was becoming more nervous about her heart problem as time progressed and was never able to settle on a physician that she felt comfortable with. In spite of the top medical facilities at the University of Michigan, which were practically around the corner from their residence, Maria would settle for nothing less than her true and time-tested Cleveland cardiologist, Dr Zimmerman. Her husband concurred, feeling that much of her problem was her constant fear that any day they would be discovered by the KGB. Over the years he had detected that Dr Zimmerman's counselling had managed to calm her fears.

They made several house-hunting trips to Cleveland during the early autumn and were able to lease an apartment not too far from where they had lived in the 1950s. The apartment would be vacated by the end of November and they expected to move into it on Monday, 2 December 1969.

On their return to Ann Arbor, the Orlovs made arrangements with Bekins Movers to have their furniture picked up during the week of 23 November and delivered to Cleveland around 2 December. What they had no way of knowing was that these dates would be changed because of an unwelcome development.

Nothing could have forewarned the Orlovs of the unexpected and catastrophic event that came to pass on Friday, 14 November.

They had spent the morning packing some of their smaller items and planning the details of the move. After lunch, they were expecting a young Japanese friend to drop by. Kyoko Sato and her husband Hiroshi had been close friends since the Orlovs came to Ann Arbor and they were particularly fond of the Satos' children. Hiroshi was employed as a physicist at a nearby Ford Motor Company plant and Kyoko was a housewife who was also taking classes at the university. On this particular day, Kyoko had volunteered to help the Orlovs pack and expected to be at their apartment around 2 p.m. following a scheduled class.

Sometime around 1.30 p.m., the Orlovs heard a knock on the door and assumed that it was Kyoko as they had not released the mechanism to open the front entry door. In the past, Kyoko had often bypassed the electronic front door release device by entering when someone else had opened the door to enter or leave the building. Orlov opened the door cautiously expecting to see Kyoko. Instead, he was confronted by a man in his late thirties wearing a dark-coloured trench coat. The man had an envelope in his hand and announced in English that he had a letter for Alexander Mikhailovich Orlov that he wished to deliver to him. He commented that the letter was from one of Orlov's former officers. Orlov then asked for the man's name, to which the caller simply replied, 'Feoktistov', and then in Russian expressed a desire to speak to 'Orlov' for a few minutes. At this moment Orlov realised that the caller did not recognise him and therefore took the letter from the caller's hand and told him that he would give the letter to 'Orlov'. Orlov closed the door on the caller, suspecting that he now had a major problem on his hands, and couldn't wait to examine the contents of the envelope.

The unsealed envelope was typewritten and addressed to Alexander Orlov, 400 Maynard, Ann Arbor, Michigan. Orlov quickly perused the letter and confirmed his worst suspicions. The letter, which was written in Russian, mentioned by name several of his KGB subordinates from the Spanish Civil War as well as the code name 'Schwed', which he had used in traffic communications between Spain and the KGB Centre in Moscow.

Whoever wrote the letter must certainly have been connected with the KGB to have known these intimate details. After reading the letter, Orlov was naturally alarmed and secured a small Spanish dagger just in case he required protection. At this point he was unaware as to what the caller's intentions were as, when he accepted the letter, he had not promised to return and the caller had given no indication that he would wait for a reply. Orlov cautiously opened the door a fraction of an inch and observed that the caller had not departed. As he was doing so, Maria, who was aware of what was going on and had heard the unseen caller speak in Russian, brushed her husband aside and advised him to remain in the apartment while she confronted the caller. It would be another twenty-one months before Orlov lay eyes on Mikhail Feoktistov again in Cleveland.

Maria's description and appraisal of the confrontation was graphic and enlightening as well as highly interesting. She had immediately perceived an element of danger when she first realised that the caller was not Kyoko, coupled with the fact that whoever it was spoke in Russian. When she saw her husband reading the letter, he had appeared visibly shaken, and when he took out the Spanish dagger she knew that there was a problem. She decided that there would only be a slight risk for her to confront the caller and that the nature of the intrusion had to be resolved. She therefore stepped into the hallway and asked the caller his identity, to which he replied with a slight Russian accent, 'I am Mikhail Aleksandrovich Feoktistov.' On hearing the name Feoktistov, she recalled having recently heard of a Russian classical musician by the somewhat common Russian name and so asked him if he were a musician. He replied that he was no musician but was with the Russian delegation to the United Nations. Then he produced some sort of official-looking identity card, which Maria at first believed was a passport. The document was dated 1966 and contained the complete name of the caller as he had stated and indicated an official connection with the Soviet Government. She asked whether he worked in Washington or New York and he replied New York. She was convinced that the document was genuine and returned it to Feoktistov.

Not long into the encounter with Feoktistov in the hallway, Kyoko Sato appeared on the scene. With a few spoken words and then a gesture, Maria motioned for Kyoko to enter the apartment.

Feoktistov then said that he wanted to speak with Alexander Mikhailovich and would only take a few minutes of his time. At this moment the far-fetched thought entered her mind that he might possibly be considering defecting and wanted to consult her husband. On this remote possibility, she asked if he wanted to live in the US, to which he strongly protested that he had no intention of living in America and would only live in his own country. He repeated that he wanted to speak with Orlov and asked why she would not permit him to do so. Maria replied that Orlov issued the orders and she was only obeying. He asked again and this time Maria said that she would have to search him. He replied that if this allowed him to see Orlov, she was free to do so. He then opened his overcoat in a manner to indicate that she should proceed. Maria conducted a painstakingly careful search of his entire body and was convinced that he carried no weapons of a harmful nature. When she had completed the search, Feoktistov chided her and asked how she could ever think any evil of him. I have never forgotten her reply to Feoktistov: 'If not today, then tomorrow.' She was well aware of the nature of the KGB and conceded that if it didn't carry out an assassination on a particular day, it always had tomorrow to accomplish its mission. Feoktistov didn't let the matter go away and admonished Maria for thinking badly of him.

He then asked if Maria had read the letter he had given to the man that had answered the door. Feoktistov gave no indication that he knew the man was Orlov although she sensed that, by the time the encounter in the hallway ended, he had reached the conclusion that the man was indeed Orlov. She replied that she had not read the letter, at which Feoktistov addressed her as Maria Vladislavovna, the polite Russian form of addressing a female with reference to her parentage to indicate that he was aware of her identity. He then stated that the letter brought greetings from her two sisters, who still resided in Russia. He informed her that he had made the trip to Ann Arbor to tell her and her husband about her two sisters. Maria replied that she had no interest in hearing about her sisters, not because she did not love them but out of fear that any contact with a family member in the free world might end to their detriment at the hands of the Soviet secret police. She added that even the receipt of a completely harmless letter from a relative abroad would be sufficient for the KGB to construe an association with the enemy of the Russian people and place an innocent person in prison. Feoktistov objected to Maria's observation and stated that she and her husband were not enemies of the Soviets; he further noted that Alexander was well respected in the Soviet Union. He repeated that his only purpose in coming to Ann Arbor was to deliver the letter and inquire about their health. In an apparent attempt to placate her, he added that he had only wanted to find out how the Orlovs were getting along and how they liked living in the United States.

Maria informed Feoktistov that she and her husband loved the democratic form of government in the United States and that she could only find fault with Communism. She had compared the two systems of government and her study and observations had led her to conclude that the Marxist system had failed to provide agricultural produce and goods for the people. Feoktistov interjected that the people of Russia were now living in better conditions than ever, to which Maria replied that this was not good enough as she wanted the Russian people to be able to eat and enjoy life as in a democracy and that there should be a choice as to how their children should be educated. She added that the Soviet Communist Party had been holding the Russian people by the neck for the past fifty years and she didn't believe this could go on forever. She blamed the leadership for lacking education and effective managerial skills and proclaimed the trial-and-error philosophy of the Soviet Union a failure. Before concluding, she admonished Feoktistov for coming to Ann Arbor for the purpose of establishing communication between his Government and her husband as it served no useful purpose. She re-emphasised that they had cut off their relations with the Soviet Government forever and for all intents and purposes they did not recognise the legitimacy or the existence of the Soviet Government. She added that even if she were made President of the Soviet Union, she would not go there nor would she ever 'break bread with the Communists'.

After I got to know Maria, I knew that she meant every word of what she said to Feoktistov. She was vehemently opposed to Communism and her expressions were not merely window-dressing for my benefit. Orlov was not as outspoken and tended to keep his views to himself, but I knew that he shared the same opinions as his wife.

Maria also prophesied to Feoktistov that in about twenty years the Soviet Communist Party would be dissolved and the people of Russia would be free. The adventurers in the Kremlin would be swept away by change and the country would not be governed by members of the Communist Party but by educated people such as professors, economists and scientists. She told Feoktistov that he was young and would come to see the day when the power structure in the Soviet Union would collapse; however, because of her advanced age she would not be alive to witness the change.

Towards the end of her discussion on the merits of democracy as opposed to Communism, Maria told Feoktistov that she had something to show him that would fortify her argument. Leaving him in the hallway, she entered the apartment and soon returned with a handful of published books and articles that her husband had written. She declared that she was proud of her husband's published works and stated that every word in the books and articles were true. She suggested that Feoktistov should read these writings to discover the truth for himself. He agreed to read the material and asked for a copy of Orlov's book, *The Secret History of Stalin's Crimes*, claiming that he had found it impossible to buy a copy. Maria replied that she would like to give him one but this was the only copy they had.

Feoktistov then repeated his request to speak to her husband. Maria re-entered the apartment and discussed the matter with Orlov, who was adamant that he would not speak personally with the KGB officer because of the inherent danger, but agreed to speak to him by telephone as in this manner he had more to gain than to lose. Maria returned to the hallway and apprised Feoktistov of the terms if he still wished to contact her husband. He reluctantly agreed to telephone but only if the Japanese lady were not present. Maria informed him that she would ask Kyoko to leave. As he departed, Feoktistov wished both of the Orlovs good health.

Orlov estimated that his wife was engaged in conversation with the KGB officer for slightly over two hours as she returned to the apartment at about 3.30 p.m. with the announcement that the KGB man had departed. Kyoko was not asked to leave and she was present when Feoktistov telephoned about a quarter of an hour later.

In the meantime, Orlov had carefully studied the letter and found several unresolved and questionable issues that he wished to challenge. He concluded that the letter had to have been drafted by the KGB because it contained intimate details regarding his staff in Spain as well as the identities and present circumstances of Maria's two sisters. The writer of the letter simply identified himself as 'Nikolai from Almeria' and referred Orlov to an incident in which 'Schwed' had admonished him for participating in a birthday party that had turned into a drunken escapade. Orlov could recall no such incident and further the mention of 'Nikolai from Almeria' meant nothing to him in identifying the writer of the letter.

What was perhaps the real purpose of the letter was the conveyance of a message to Orlov from the KGB in an oblique manner. The writer offhandedly refers to 'Schwed', not as being Orlov but as someone mutually known to both of them. The writer expresses that 'Schwed's' fateful decision had come as a shock to him and that he could neither condone nor condemn him for his action. However, the writer indicates that his own views have changed over the years having learned that 'Schwed' had carried out the promises he had made in his farewell letters to Stalin and Yezhov and, for this reason, the writer feels 'Schwed' to be a man of personal honour. The letter concludes with a statement that there is more to be told about Orlov's relatives and, if this contact proves favourable, more details can be provided.

When Feoktistov telephoned, he spoke in Russian and gave his salutation to 'Alexander Mikhailovich'. He said that he was sorry that he had been unable to speak to Orlov in person and asked if Orlov had read the letter. Orlov replied that he had and asked for the identity of the man who signed the letter as 'Nikolai from Almeria'. There followed a slight hesitation and a period of silence as though Feoktistov had to think about the answer. He finally replied, 'Prokopyuk . . . Nikolai Prokopyuk'. Orlov then stated that he had never had a member on his staff by the name of Prokopyuk and, as he knew every member of his staff personally, there was no such person. Feoktistov then said that he understood that Prokopyuk had been Orlov's staff member assigned to the port of Almeria. Orlov retorted that this was not the case and, even after thirty years, he could still identify his man in Almeria as Colonel Kremnev, who had formerly been an officer with the KGB Frontier Guards.

Feoktistov appeared to be a little disconcerted that Orlov had not accepted his explanation as to the identity of the letter writer and changed the subject to Orlov's book on Stalin. He again claimed that he had been unable to secure a copy of the book and would Orlov kindly give him one. Orlov replied that he had no spare copies to give, but even if he had an extra one he would not give it to him as he would probably brag about receiving the book from 'Orlov the defector' at the KGB Centre and claim that he had won over Orlov's co-operation. Feoktistov then attempted to ease the situation by noting that everyone knew Orlov's book to be a truthful account of Stalin's crimes and that he would like to know more about the assassination of Kirov. Orlov replied that all of this was known to the Kremlin and the KGB and that it was up to them to publish the facts.

Then Orlov asked the question that was uppermost in his mind: was his assumption correct that Feoktistov had travelled all the way to Ann Arbor just as a favour to this 'Nikolai from Almeria' while taking a great risk to deliver the letter to an enemy of the people. 'It took great courage to take this risk,' he said, 'yet you were afraid to call me by telephone. Were you afraid your conversation would be recorded?' Feoktistov answered that Orlov must be under some misapprehension as he had taken no risk in coming to Ann Arbor and had been asked to deliver the letter by his KGB superiors. As he was going to Michigan, his superiors had asked him to deliver the letter and inquire about Orlov's health. He added that Orlov was not considered an enemy of the people and was highly respected by everyone who knew him. Feoktistov then asked to see Orlov in person, but the request was denied on the grounds that such a meeting was impossible. Feoktistov ended the conversation with the wish that Orlov have many more years of good health.

Orlov commented that throughout the ordeal Feoktistov maintained a polite attitude and never made any threats to him or his wife. He realised that somehow the KGB had learned of his whereabouts in Ann Arbor and used the letter as a means of introducing the KGB officer with the intention of establishing a line of communication with the KGB through him. Orlov was not clear as to the long-term motive, but in the absence of any physical harm felt that the KGB was assessing the situation with the possible motive of paving the way for a future attempt to lure him back to the Soviet Union. By this time, Orlov had little fear of being assassinated on American soil as over the past thirty years he knew of only one such instance, the death of Walter Krivitsky in 1941. Orlov was not saying that the KGB had changed its ways as the KGB had continued its revenge assassinations primarily in Europe, most recently with the assassination of a Bulgarian defector in the heart of London by means of a lethal injection delivered by a concealed device. Orlov strongly felt that the KGB had met its match in the FBI and would not risk an assassination attempt in the US. The Orlovs had one consolation, that the authorities were alerted to the contact and, although they could not provide twenty-four hour protection, they were in a position to go all out should circumstances reach that point.

Having described Orlov's account of this incident, I would now like to challenge a few points mentioned in *Deadly Illusions*, which gives a different version of events. Firstly, the KGB account of the interview places Feoktistov inside the Orlov apartment, where at one point Maria charges him with a pistol shouting, 'I'm going to shoot you! You came to kill us.' While in the apartment, he is able to observe an ink-stained copy of the Soviet magazine *Communist*, which he later claims was the basis for finding the Orlovs in Cleveland after they had disappeared from Ann Arbor (see pages 391–3). However, the fact of the matter is that Feoktistov never entered the Orlov apartment nor was there any pistol. What the KGB did not build into its equation was a witness to the contrary, which the KGB Centre was probably unaware of.

Deadly Illusions goes as far as to say that Feoktistov did not mention the gun incident to the KGB Centre when he filed his report on his contact with the Orlovs in 1969, noting, 'Surprisingly, his report contains no mention that Mrs Orlov had threatened him with a gun. This, Feoktistov explained, was because he withheld this fact so as not to jeopardise the possibility of a second meeting with the Orlovs.' Buried in a footnote relating to the incident is mention of the fact that the co-author of *Deadly Illusions*, the former KGB officer Oleg Tsarev, did not note the episode with the gun in an article he wrote on Orlov in the Soviet trades union newspaper, *Trud*, on 20 December 1990. Tsarev wrote the article based on a review of Orlov's KGB archive files, which did not mention the gun incident, and he only learned the full story when he interviewed Feoktistov in 1992. The footnote goes on to clarify that Feoktistov had realised that his concealment of the gun episode in his official report was a breach of discipline but he was confident in his professional intuition and was prepared to take calculated risks which would, and in fact did, bring him success.

Indeed, the KGB file could be changed to reflect an incident that had never taken place but there was no way of changing the *Trud* article to add the gun episode. The damage was already done and there was no way of knowing in 1990 that the KGB files would be opened within a few years. The KGB had to do some fancy footwork to circumvent the truth and come up with a new explanation tailored to a new set of circumstances.

For years Orlov had asked the FBI for a 'gun permit' in order to carry a gun and was always dissuaded. After Maria died, he again brought up the subject and I conceded only to the extent of a rifle, which I felt was the safest weapon for him to possess and which would give him a degree of mental security in the absence of his ever-protective wife. After his death, I meticulously searched his apartment and found no pistol.

Kyoko Sato had arrived at the Orlovs' apartment shortly after the start of the contact. She observed Feoktistov and Maria conversing in the hallway and joined Orlov in the apartment. She related that Orlov was alarmed by the caller, whom he identified as a Russian, and briefly told her of the contents of the letter which the caller had brought from Russia. Orlov expressed fear for his life and did not want to talk to the Russian as he felt that the caller might have a gun and could assassinate him. Sato saw a dagger lying on a table next to Orlov but made no mention of seeing a gun. She observed Maria enter and leave the apartment twice, once to converse with Orlov in Russian and then to pick up a handful of books. At no time did the Russian caller ever enter the apartment. Maria again entered the apartment and announced that the caller had left but would telephone Orlov. Within about ten minutes a telephone call was received and Orlov spoke to the caller in Russian. Sato then departed. I recalled that another neighbour had also witnessed Maria speaking with a stranger in the hallway that day.

There is one other factor worth discussing which reflects on who is telling the truth. When Orlov was recounting the story to me of how he was contacted in Ann Arbor, he told how he disclaimed knowing 'Nikolai from Almeria', who had been identified by Feoktistov as Nikolai Prokopyuk, and how he remembered that his subordinate in Almeria was Colonel Kremnev. I recalled that when Orlov surfaced in 1953, he had furnished a list of his entire staff in Spain during the Spanish Civil War, and like any FBI agent I checked this out. His staff list contained the name of Colonel Kremnev but not that of Nikolai Prokopyuk, or anything similar. I can only conclude that Orlov was telling the truth as the list had been compiled by him sixteen years before the KGB contacted him in Ann Arbor.

Deadly Illusions relates that the obvious candidate for this delicate mission had been Nikolai Arkhipovich Prokopyuk, but the risk of being apprehended by the FBI was too great as he had been involved in many sensitive missions since the war. The alternative who had been considered for the task was Fyodor Zimovievich Kimochko, a Soviet pilot who had saved Orlov's life when a White Guardist shot at him from close range. In the end, KGB officer Mikhail Feoktistov was chosen for the mission.

When I read this, Orlov was no longer alive to tell me about Kimochko, but I did not recall him describing such a dramatic episode in his life nor did I remember such an event in his memoirs. He had written extensively about that stage of his life in the Red Army fighting the White Guardists, so I retreated to his memoirs and combed each page devoted to this period without finding any reference to Kimochko. It was odd that a man who paid so much attention to comparatively inconsequential events in his memoirs and in his conversations with me would fail to mention a man who had saved his life. It was not like Orlov to neglect to give credit where it belonged.

After Kyoko left that fateful day, the Orlovs discussed their plight. Their worst fears that they had harboured for over thirty years had come to pass and they now had to face the future knowing that the KGB had finally found them. They both agreed that their decision to move to Cleveland had come at an opportune time and perhaps the move would distract the hound from the scent. However, their immediate problem was what to do in the interim as they had no idea what the KGB's next move would be. They felt reasonably secure for that evening as it was unlikely that Feoktistov would return that day. Orlov recalled that that night was one of the longest he and his wife had ever spent as they didn't know what to expect but dreaded what might be in store for them the next day. As it turned out, nothing happened.

By the next day Orlov realised that his wife was so stressed and nervous about the events of the previous day that the best course of action would be to move out of the apartment. Unfortunately, because of a sporting event they were unable to find a hotel or motel room in the city that Saturday. They then decided to stay at the apartment as they had to finish packing but, after the movers had picked up their household goods, they would move into temporary quarters until they finally left for Cleveland. In the meantime, they would take all the necessary security precautions and admit no one into the apartment.

Orlov and I often discussed and analysed how the KGB had come to find him on the campus of the University of Michigan but never came to a definite conclusion. He maintained that it was complacency which had led him to drop his guard. In the past, he had always covered his tracks, but in Ann Arbor he had carelessly listed his name in the directories at his apartment and for his office at the Law School and made no real attempt to conceal his true identity, although he never went out of his way to make any pronouncements. Thirty-one uneventful years in the United States had managed to cloud his good judgement and optimistically he had wanted to believe that the KGB no longer had an interest in finding him. The publication of his *Handbook* in 1963 had only fortified this view as it was reasonable to assume that the KGB could have focused its attention on the University of Michigan, from where it could have easily located him. This didn't happen until six years after publication. Also, following the publication of the *Handbook*, there was every reason to assume that his colleagues at the Law School were aware of his true identity but there was no motive for any of them to betray him to the KGB, nor would they necessarily know how to do so.

Another supposition that there was a KGB spy on the university campus is also unreasonable, at best from a practical standpoint. *Deadly Illusions* does supply an answer to this but not one that stands up to logic. The book reflects that 'The Orlovs' KGB dossier shows that it was not until 1969 that information reached the Centre from a "reliable source" (who is named in the file but who Russian intelligence prefers not to identify) giving his address and telephone number in Ann Arbor where he resided openly using his own name.'

It then took the KGB twenty-one months to locate the Orlovs again in Cleveland, as described in the next chapter. However, if the KGB had a 'reliable source' available, why did it take so long to find the Orlovs again? The term 'reliable source' in intelligence parlance refers to a source that has been utilised over a significant period of time in which the reliability of information furnished is deemed accurate beyond any doubt. I suggest that there was no 'reliable source' and that the KGB located Orlov by other means. I hold to the more probable conclusion that it had come across a piece of information which had led it to look on the University of Michigan campus for its quarry.

Whilst researching this book, I came across two likely possibilities that could perhaps solve the riddle. Orlov had mentioned to me a young U-M graduate student by the name of John Howard Wilhelm, whom he had befriended in Ann Arbor, and after Orlov died I took it upon myself to inform Wilhelm. I recently re-established contact with him and what he had to tell me about his association with Orlov was certainly interesting as well as informative.

Sometime in the mid-1960s, Wilhelm was shopping at an Ann Arbor drug store when he noticed an older gentleman apparently trying to find an item without any success. Wilhelm offered to help the man find a particular brand of toothpaste and they struck up a conversation. Wilhelm was doing graduate work in Russian Studies as well as work towards a Master's Degree in Economics, and with this background was able to detect that Orlov was a

Russian. The chance encounter soon developed into a personal relationship.

Wilhelm would look towards Orlov for his views on the Soviet economic system and would meet Orlov at his office in the Legal Research Building. Often these meetings were at the end of Orlov's working day and, after they had concluded their discussion, Orlov would always telephone his wife to announce that he was on his way home. Orlov explained that this was a security measure. He would also call his wife when he arrived at his office in the morning. He would always take a precise route along S. State Street, past the Michigan Union, and if he did not arrive at his apartment or report his arrival at the office by telephone within twenty to thirty minutes of departure, Maria would look for him along the prescribed route. The plan called for her to alert the authorities if she could not locate him. Invariably, if he happened to saunter or stop along the route to chat with someone, he would find Maria dashing towards him.

I asked Wilhelm his view of how he thought the KGB had located Orlov on the U-M campus, although I realised that I was grasping for straws. I was surprised when he recalled that in the late 1960s, a student in the Slavic Language Department was jokingly called 'Mischa the Spy' because he seemed to lean towards the Soviet economic system. At the time, there were people in the Department who were aware of the former KGB General's presence on campus. The possibility that someone connected with the Slavic Language Department may have inadvertently mentioned Orlov being on campus or posed an innocent question about Orlov to a Soviet official, seems quite remote but nevertheless within the realms of possibility.

The second strongly viable possibility came to my attention when I tried to re-establish contact with Professor Marcus Plant, whom I discovered from his wife had died unexpectedly in 1984. In May 1997, Plant's daughter Nancy forwarded to me a copy of a letter, the original of which was on the letterhead of the University of Michigan Law School, that the family had found among the pages of one of Orlov's books shortly after her father's death. She believed that her father had sent the letter on Orlov's behalf in 1967 and I had to concur with her view, knowing some of the background.

By 1967, Orlov had completed the bulk of his work on his memoirs and was researching the field of jurisprudence in the Soviet Union from the time of the Russian Revolution through to 1923. As we have seen, at the time of his tenure as an Assistant Prosecutor in the Collegium of Appeals of the Soviet Supreme Court, he had been responsible for drafting the original Soviet criminal code in 1922 and 1923.

The letter was dated 4 April 1967 and addressed to Professor M. S. Strogovich, Member of the Academy of Sciences of the USSR, Moscow. It was ostensibly from and signed by Professor Plant but in reality had been written at Orlov's request to further his research efforts in the field of Soviet law. He had been unable to make the request openly under his own name as this could have brought his whereabouts to the attention of the KGB. The letter stated that during his research into the first period of the Soviet Criminal Law and Procedure (1917–23), he had come across a footnote reference to a publication titled *Piat' Let Verkovnogo Suda* (M. Iurizdat, 1923) commemorating the fifth anniversary of the Soviet Supreme Court. As this publication was unavailable in the Library of Congress or at major US universities, could Strogovich obtain a copy for the writer? The salient paragraph in the letter, set forth verbatim, is as follows:

A knowledgeable colleague of mine, an expert in Soviet legal bibliography, advised me that among the legal scientists of Russia you are probably the only one whose work in the field of Soviet law goes far back to the very beginnings of the Soviet legal system and that in the early 20s you had already occupied an official post in the Soviet Supreme Court and that you, no doubt, would remember the edition, which had apparently been published by the Supreme Court in the form of a jubilee journal, commemorating the fifth anniversary of the Soviet courts.

Whatever prompted Orlov to add the above paragraph to the letter is not known as it provided little in the way of enhancing the request and was only marginal to it. However, as it turned out the paragraph was perhaps a monumental mistake, which led to Orlov's discovery by the KGB. Orlov and Strogovich had both been officials with the Soviet Supreme Court during the same period and the jubilee journal had carried a tribute to Orlov for his work on the original Soviet criminal code.

The Soviet Government has always maintained a highly structured society and assiduously monitors its citizens, but never more so than during the height of the Cold War when mail from the US was very closely scrutinised by the KGB. At face value, the letter would have been of negligible interest to the KGB and a copy thereof would likely have been indexed and relegated to its file system and the original forwarded to Strogovich. On the other hand, Strogovich would have taken a more personal interest in the letter and wondered about the identity of the expert in the Soviet legal field who knew he had been an official with the Soviet Supreme Court in the early 1920s. This was information that would not have been known outside of the Soviet legal community and most certainly would not have been known in the US legal community. The somewhat strange request for the commemorative material might seem innocuous on the surface but could have looked suspicious to a trained legal mind like Strogovich's.

Something relevant to the above jogged my memory when I read the following paragraph in *Deadly Illusions* regarding Feoktistov's interview with Orlov in Cleveland during August 1971:

One request which Orlov made of Feoktistov was that he promise to try to find and send over a copy of a picture which appeared on the cover of the journal of the Law Institute of the Academy of Sciences that marked the five-year anniversary of the Supreme Court of the USSR. Orlov explained that he had been in the group photograph and would like it as a memento of old times.

According to Orlov, Feoktistov had already known about the commemorative journal and the photograph, which is a coincidence that will be explored in the next chapter.

The Orlov-inspired letter was written well over two years before the KGB contacted Orlov, a long time between the two events but not an unusual length of time considering the many pieces of the puzzle that had to come together before the contact could take place. It might have taken Strogovich some time to realise that Orlov was the letter writer, and even then he might have set aside the matter or even procrastinated and agonised for a while before reporting the letter to the KGB. In turn, the KGB could not be certain as to what it had and had to make a decision to determine whether active investigation was warranted. At this juncture it might have correlated the information in the letter with the fact that Orlov's *Handbook* was published by the University of Michigan Press, which should have raised eyebrows and been sufficient justification to warrant a full investigation. However, before it could begin any course of action, it had to verify Orlov's presence in Ann Arbor. Having done this, it then had to conceive a plan of action. All of this took time.

The foregoing is only a supposition drawn from an established set of facts, which indicates a strong probability but is not conclusive. Of all the scenarios that have been considered in the Orlov matter as to how the KGB came to find him on the campus of the University of Michigan, for me this is the most plausible one to date.

In less than a week after the KGB contact, the Orlovs moved from Ann Arbor to the Howard Johnson's Motor Lodge in the heart of downtown Detroit. On Sunday, 23 November 1969, their good friend Marcus Plant picked them up at the motel and drove them to their new home in Cleveland. Orlov never forgot this act of kindness and often spoke with affection about the Plant family.

As the Orlovs drove away from their home in Ann Arbor for the last time, they prayed that the KGB would not find them in their new home. They were totally unaware that in less than two years they would again be contacted by the KGB and that in two years, almost to the day, of their first contact with the KGB, Maria would be dead.

TWENTY-ONE

THE KGB STRIKES IN CLEVELAND

The day that I was finally to meet General Orlov had arrived. He had been contacted by the KGB in Cleveland the previous week and I was assigned to gather the details. The day before our meeting, we finalised arrangements for him to come to the FBI office in downtown Cleveland on Tuesday, 17 August 1971, at 10 a.m. Security Supervisor Tom Corbett and I would handle the interview. It was highly unusual for a supervisor to accompany the case agent, but in this situation the arrangement was dictated from the highest level at Bureau headquarters in Washington.

I was going over old reports on the General in preparation for the interview when I received a telephone call from him around 9.30 a.m. He requested that we meet him at 10 a.m. at the main entrance to the Cleveland Public Library on Superior Avenue, a few blocks from the FBI office. From what I had read about Orlov, he could be difficult to deal with at times so I posed no objection. I assumed that he might feel more secure being escorted to the office but also thought it strange that he would have any reason not to come directly to the office. We exchanged descriptions of our physical appearances and of what we were wearing. What came next really surprised me; he stated that as a means of positive identification he would resort to a physical parole by carrying in view a *Reader's Digest* magazine in his left hand and a folded newspaper under his right arm. This is the classic method for an intelligence officer and an agent to meet for the first time when unknown to each other. Under the circumstances, I thought it a little more than unusual but again did not object.

Tom and I approached the main entrance to the Library and

immediately recognised Orlov standing at the top of the steps. What I had not expected was the presence of his wife, who was standing next to him. Both were very well dressed and he possessed the proper parole. They in turn recognised us and came down the steps to meet us. I had been warned that it would be best to interview the General without the presence of his wife as she would dominate the situation, but, as I soon learned, it was impossible to meet him alone. When we had made the arrangements for the meeting, he had given no indication that his wife would accompany him. Also, it was my understanding that she was a semi-invalid because of her heart condition. This turn of events foreshadowed a very difficult interview and, in the end, I was right.

After a brief introduction, we walked to a secluded area nearby, where Orlov asked to see our FBI credentials. He scrutinised them carefully as if he was memorising every word. After he was fully satisfied as to our identities, he announced that he did not want to be interviewed at the FBI office. Instead, I suggested that we could handle the interview in a Bureau vehicle in a safe location. He declined this suggestion and indicated that he had made other arrangements. In fact, he had rented a day room at the nearby Sheraton-Cleveland Hotel. Not only was this another surprise, but by now I felt that I was being put through a series of difficult gymnastics in order to conduct this interview.

Our little group finally settled into the day room on what I recall was the top floor of the hotel. As anticipated, the interview was a difficult one because Maria Orlov tended to monopolise the conversation without any objection from her husband.

By way of background, the Orlovs related the circumstances of the KGB contact in Ann Arbor in November 1969 and their subsequent move to Cleveland, where they had taken up residence in Apartment 507, Clifton Park Apartments. 11406 Clifton Boulevard, under the name of Alexander Orlov. The apartment house met their security requirements with entrance through the front door controlled by an electronic door-release device activated from the individual apartments.

At about 10.30 a.m. on 10 August 1971, the Orlovs had heard a slight knock on the only entry door to their apartment. They waited a few moments and the knock was repeated. As was customary in these situations, Maria would open the door and Orlov would retreat to a position where he could not be seen by the caller. Before opening the door she asked for the caller's identity, to which she heard the response, 'Your friend.' As the front door buzzer had not been activated, she concluded that it was the apartment house janitor. She opened the door slightly to make visual contact but realised that it was not the janitor or anyone else she recognised. Although she did have some difficulty seeing the caller as she was suffering from cataracts, she advised him that she did not know him. Before she could close the door, the caller announced in English, 'You are Russian like me. You know me.' From what she could see of the caller, she concluded that he was either a hippie or intoxicated and closed the door. The man was wearing walking shorts that appeared rumpled, a beige-coloured sports shirt hanging loosely at his waist and sandals.

About 11 a.m. they heard the buzzer that signalled that someone was at the front entrance wishing to be admitted. Maria answered but no one responded at the other end. Within a few minutes, they again heard a soft knock on their apartment door. Maria opened the door slightly with the security chain in place and observed that it was the same unkempt caller she had turned away half an hour before. This time the caller advised her in Russian that he was 'Feoktistov' and addressed her as Maria Vladislavovna. He then insisted in English that she open the door. Under the circumstances she opened the door a little further to scrutinise the caller, at which point she recognised him as the KGB officer who had located them in Ann Arbor almost two years earlier. The caller reminded her of their past encounter and produced his diplomatic passport. He stated that he only wanted to speak with the General and that he would take no more than ten minutes of his time. Maria then asked to examine the passport, but he retorted that it was the same one she had previously seen in Ann Arbor and that it was not necessary for her to examine it again. She disagreed and started to close the door when Feoktistov pushed it, repeated that he only wanted ten minutes of Orlov's time and reluctantly surrendered the passport. Maria closely examined it and recognised it to be genuine, based on her own diplomatic passport. She noted that the passport had been issued to Mikhail Feoktistov in August 1966. She returned the passport to him and, as she closed the door, told him that she would be back to him.

Now the question was what to do. During the encounter, Orlov had been standing out of sight next to the door and was able to hear the entire conversation. He felt that there was nothing to gain and more to lose by admitting the caller. Maria felt differently. She judged by the non-professional appearance of his attire and his agitated manner that this was perhaps not an officially sanctioned contact by the Soviet Government but that there was another motive. She speculated that Feoktistov had defected, or was considering defecting, and was therefore seeking Orlov's counsel. Orlov concurred with this possibility but was also curious as to the reasoning behind a second attempt by the KGB to contact him in person. They decided that they would admit the caller only under the strictest security measures to protect their well-being. Orlov placed a butcher's knife under the cushion of the sofa where he would sit. Maria placed a large pair of scissors in her handbag, which she would hold on her lap. Feoktistov would be seated in a chair on the other side of the living-room from the sofa. Before allowing him entry, he would be physically searched for any concealed weapons. In this manner, they reasoned that they would have ample time to produce their weapons should he make a threatening advance towards them.

Maria related that she had subjected Feoktistov to a head-to-foot search in the hall, where she felt she would be safe and where she could scream for help if he made any unwarranted advance. She meticulously examined his person as well as each item of clothing and even had him extend behind him one foot at a time while she took off each sandal to look for any hidden device or

weapon. She also took off his wristwatch for a closer examination. In this situation, she was aware that the KGB was the master
of the art of inventing innocuous and mundane-looking items,
such as a wristwatch, that in reality were concealed weapons for
assassination.

I should add that when Maria told us that she gave Feoktistov
a comprehensive body search, she meant just that. After I got to
know her better, I realised that she was a very determined and
resourceful woman, who was unabashedly devoted to the safety
and welfare of her husband. She was the type of woman who
would have no qualms about extending her search to areas of a
private nature.

After Maria was satisfied that her search was conclusive, she
admitted Feoktistov into the apartment. The first thing she asked
was when he had broken with the Soviet Government. He looked
extremely astonished and somewhat embarrassed, and then
replied that he had not and that he was making an official call
on behalf of his Government. As prearranged by the Orlovs, he
was seated at the far side of the room.

'Why have you come?' Orlov immediately asked. Feoktistov
explained that as his first attempt to contact the General in Ann
Arbor in 1969 had been a failure, he thought that the matter had
been dropped. However, after his return to the Soviet Union, he
was told that he should make another attempt to contact the
Orlovs. He added that Orlov was held in the highest regard in
the Soviet Union and that the hierarchy held no animosity towards
him; in fact, he was a hero in the Soviet Union and so popular
with the people that the very mention of his name invoked the
gratitude of the masses for his contribution to the Bolshevik
Revolution and his service to the Soviet Government during the
Spanish Civil War.

Feoktistov stated that he had returned to Ann Arbor on 23
September 1970, only to learn that the Orlovs had moved and
their whereabouts were unknown. Maria asked how he had now
found them in Cleveland, to which he replied that he could not
disclose his source. He then went on to say that the Orlovs needn't

move again just because he had found them because the KGB meant them no harm and only wanted to help them. His trip to Ann Arbor had been to secure Orlov's permission to use his name, along with all the others from the Soviet Union who had contributed so heavily towards the Soviet intelligence service and guerrilla warfare during the Spanish Civil War.

Feoktistov then reverted to small talk that Orlov felt was designed to gain their compassion and make them understand that his first priority was their welfare and not that of his Government. He spoke of his birth in a small town outside Moscow and of the death of both of his parents from heart problems. He noted that his own family had been caught up in the purges and that an uncle, who had held a high position with the Government, had been sent to Siberia. He ended by saying that, like Orlov, he had also graduated from the Law School at Moscow University before becoming a KGB officer.

The Orlovs both believed that Feoktistov's legend had been tailored to highlight similarities in their backgrounds with the intended purpose of allaying any suspicion and making himself appear to be a 'regular fellow' in their eyes. However, they both doubted the validity of his presentation and questioned whether he had ever attended law school as his general level of intelligence did not appear to reach the standards dictated by a law school education. Also, Feoktistov displayed no degree of sophistication that such an education would have provided.

Feoktistov informed them that he had news of two of Orlov's old colleagues whom Orlov had asked about during their telephone conversation in Ann Arbor in November 1969. Orlov had asked what had become of two of his friends, Lev Mironov and Leonid Eitingon, who had been Orlov's subordinate in Spain. Feoktistov related that Mironov had survived the purges and had gone on to become a chief in the Central Committee of the Communist Party. He continued that in 1959 Mironov had been chosen to become Chief of the State Administration for State Security but had been killed in an air crash in Yugoslavia. As to Eitingon, Feoktistov said that he was now retired on a pension and living near Moscow, where he continued to contribute his past knowledge and experience to the good of the Communist Party. Feoktistov also mentioned in passing several other friends of Orlov's but offered little information.

Orlov said that he detected several falsehoods and inconsistencies in Feoktistov's narrative regarding his old friends but did not bring these factors into play as he did not want to let the KGB officer know that he knew better. For one thing, he already knew Mironov's fate. During the third Moscow purge trial in January 1938, KGB Chief Yagoda had introduced evidence against Mironov that had led to his execution. Orlov was still in Spain when the news of Mironov's death came to his attention. As to his old assistant Leonid Eitingon (alias Colonel Kotov), he never doubted that the man was scheduled for execution during the purges and hadn't lived to lead the serene life that Feoktistov portrayed, but more recently he had learned that Eitingon had actually escaped the purges and did not die until 1953.

What also crossed Orlov's mind was the previous contact with the KGB in Ann Arbor in 1969 when Feokistov had brought a letter of introduction from 'Nikolai of Almeria', someone he didn't even know. Wouldn't it have been more logical to bring a letter from Colonel Kotov, his trusted friend and deputy in Spain? If Kotov was alive and well and living in Moscow on a KGB pension, it should have presented no problem to have him write the letter. This only endorsed Orlov's belief that Kotov was dead and that Feoktistov was lying.

Feoktistov then volunteered to inquire about other friends of Orlov's and determine what had become of them. He asked Orlov to compile a list of his friends, but Orlov vehemently declined to do so.

Then followed a litany of flattery, which only nauseated Orlov. How could he believe that he was still revered as a Soviet hero, let alone that his name was even known to the people? According to Orlov, this was a highly dubious statement considering the fact that he was a sworn enemy of the Soviets.

Eventually, the true purpose of Feoktistov's visit came to light.

Would Orlov return to the Soviet Union, where he would be welcomed as a hero by the Soviet Government and where he could also claim the medals he had been awarded for his services to the country? If he desired, he could then return to the United States at any time he wished. However, if he decided to remain in the Soviet Union, he would receive a liberal pension and a commodious apartment in Moscow commensurate with his rank of a KGB general. Orlov had no hesitation in answering this question with an unqualified negative reply. Then Feoktistov turned to Maria and asked if she would visit the Soviet Union, where she would be welcomed as the wife of a hero and would be able to visit her two sisters. The Soviet Government was willing to bear the cost of the trip. Again, the offer was rejected.

Orlov informed me that he didn't have to be a rocket scientist to understand the underlying nature of the KGB's generous solicitation. If he and Maria jointly returned to the Soviet Union, they would never be allowed to go back to the United States, and he would probably be disposed of in an unobtrusive manner that would never come to the attention of the world. In the event that Maria returned alone, she would be held hostage and he would have no alternative but to return to suffer the same consequence.

Feoktistov then turned his attention to Orlov's book, *The Secret History of Stalin's Crimes*. He claimed that he had not yet read it because he was still unable to find a copy. Did Orlov have one which he could have or borrow? Orlov replied that he had one but could not spare it, nor would he let him borrow it. Maria interjected that she saw no harm in giving Feoktistov a copy as he would learn the grim reality of the old Bolshevik Government under Stalin and the part the KGB had played in the purges. She looked over at her husband as he nodded his approval. She then found Feoktistov a copy, but when he asked if Orlov would inscribe the book to him, or at least autograph it, Orlov declined.

Feoktistov's visit was fast approaching the noon hour and he hinted that he had not eaten since early morning. The Orlovs had no intention of inviting him to lunch as they did not wish to prolong his stay. In the absence of the invitation he hoped to receive, he then mentioned that his pregnant wife and five-year-old daughter were sitting in his car, which was parked outside the apartment. Perhaps the Orlovs would like to meet them? They again declined. What seemed strange to them in retrospect was that when he hinted that he had not eaten since early morning, he was obviously ignoring the fact that his family were sitting in his car nearby in the intense August heat. Had they extended an invitation to him, his pregnant wife and child would have paid the penalty. But on reflection, it would have to be considered in light of the KGB's interests.

Before he left, Feoktistov again declared that the KGB meant no harm and that the Orlovs should not consider moving again as it was too expensive for them to do so. At this juncture Maria felt it the opportune moment to ask how he had found them again, to which he replied that he could not tell them. He then reiterated that they should not fear the KGB as it only wanted to help the Orlovs. Maria retorted that they didn't expect help from the people who wanted to murder her husband. Feoktistov was taken aback by her statement and said that he was hurt that the Orlovs felt this way about his motives. He then looked squarely at them and asked how they could think such a thing of him. Maria quickly replied that she didn't trust him as she knew he would do whatever he was instructed to do by the KGB.

As he was about to leave, Feoktistov urged Maria to write to her sisters in the Soviet Union as they would no doubt like to hear from her. He reminded her that he had previously provided their addresses with the letter from 'Nikolai from Almeria'. In case she no longer had their current addresses, he would be more than happy to have her letter forwarded to the Soviet Union and he would personally ensure that her sisters received the mail. Maria shrugged off the suggestion with the comment that she had not corresponded with her sisters since 1938 and had no intention of doing so at the present time.

Throughout their conversation, Feoktistov remained in his seat, with the exception of a couple of times when he had looked out of the window, apparently checking his car as he made some comment to this effect. Orlov did not dare to move from his position on the sofa, where his weapon was handy in case he had to protect himself. When it was apparent that Feoktistov was actually leaving and they got up to escort him to the door, Orlov furtively took the butcher's knife from under the sofa's cushion and concealed it in his sweater, which was lying on the arm of the sofa. This opportunity took place while Maria was speaking to Feoktistov and diverting his attention.

Maria first walked to the door with extreme caution, unlocked it and then beckoned Feoktistov to leave. Orlov kept his distance should there be a last-minute confrontation of some sort. As Feoktistov walked into the hall, Maria sternly told him never to return to their residence as he would not be admitted under any circumstances. Feoktistov just shrugged his shoulders, made no comment and then retreated to the elevator.

Both of the Orlovs rushed to a window to see their unexpected caller leave the apartment house and walk towards his car. When Orlov was satisfied that they had seen the last of Feoktistov, he rushed to the telephone to call his CIA friend in Washington to report the KGB contact, which had lasted from 10.30 a.m. until 12.15 p.m., when he was able to make the call. Although the time element was not a matter of great concern to us, I questioned why the contact had not been reported to FBI headquarters until Monday the 16th. The CIA agent who had handled Orlov later related that Orlov's call was logged in on the 10th at the time specified by Orlov. However, the agent who normally handled Orlov was out of touch and Orlov did not want to speak to anyone else. He was not in contact with Orlov until Friday the 13th.

The book *Deadly Illusions* contains portions of my interview with the Orlovs that had been obtained from the FBI through the Freedom of Information Act. But perhaps more revealing to me was the report that Mikhail Feoktistov had purportedly made to the KGB right after his interview with the Orlovs. The FBI report of the interview is attacked paragraph by paragraph to justify the KGB's official position, and the book states that 'Feoktistov's account in both the report he filed at the time and his recollections during an interview twenty years later paints a very different picture.' Now it is my turn to analyse the book's version of the Orlov interview and let the reader come to his own conclusion.

According to *Deadly Illusions*, in 1969 the KGB learned through a reliable unnamed source that Orlov was living at a specific address in Ann Arbor under his own name. Mikhail Feoktistov, a KGB officer already assigned to the Soviet Mission at the United Nations in New York, and operating under the code name Georg, was given the assignment to contact Orlov. Feoktistov located and interviewed the Orlovs for the first time in Ann Arbor on 14 November 1969.

Feoktistov never physically interviewed Orlov in the 1969 contact but was able to conclude from a brief telephone conversation with Orlov that he had never betrayed the KGB and was not a traitor. Based on this conclusion, the KGB Centre authorised Georg to recontact Orlov to find out what information he had actually furnished the US Government. Feoktistov returned to Ann Arbor in early 1970, only to learn that the Orlovs had been spirited away to a new hiding place.

However, there is no way that Feoktistov could have concluded from his brief telephone call with Orlov that he had never betrayed the KGB and that he was not a traitor to the KGB. Here the KGB is laying the ground for its new version of the interview, which is as follows.

Feoktistov returned to Ann Arbor in the summer of 1971 in an attempt to discover where the Orlovs had moved to. He verified that Orlov was no longer on campus by checking the list of lecturers on the board in the Physics Department and began a systematic search of every library on campus and in the vicinity. His diligence paid off with a lucky break. He stated that in one of the libraries he actually discovered the Soviet magazine *Communist*, number 11 of 1969, which 'was the very same one I saw in Orlov's apartment because it had the same ink blot on the cover'. When he asked the librarian to check the records, she discovered that the elderly Russian couple had left town more than a year before, but told him that she did not believe they had moved too far because she recalled them telling her that they did not want to leave their beloved daughter's grave site. The librarian did not know their new address, but helpfully suggested that Feoktistov, who identified himself as an old family friend, could probably find them in either Detroit, Toledo or Cleveland.

What the KGB apparently did not know when it came up with the story of the magazine with the blot on the cover is that periodicals are not placed in general circulation and are intended only for use at the library.

The reference to a search of the directory of the Physics Department for Orlov's listing is nothing more than a clumsy attempt to divert attention away from the KGB source at the university. Why search at the Physics Department when it already knew that Orlov was connected with the Law School? It is highly probable that the source who first reported Orlov's presence in Ann Arbor in 1969 was connected with the Law School in some way. When Feoktistov returned to Ann Arbor in 1970 to contact Orlov again, perhaps this source was unavailable for some reason, or more probably was not contacted. When the Orlovs left Ann Arbor in November 1969, they kept their departure a secret and purposely told only a handful of people their true destination. It took the KGB almost two years to locate the Orlovs in Cleveland, which strongly suggests that the few people whom the Orlovs trusted with this crucial piece of information did not breach their confidence, but more so indicates that none of these close friends was the KGB's source for their original information. What probably happened was a mere slip of the tongue some years later when the information no longer seemed that relevant. This innocuous violation, in conjunction with a little prodding by the source, then led the KGB to what it wanted. This is not to infer that the source was a KGB spy in the true sense but rather a person who may have unwittingly been seduced in some fashion by the KGB.

The part about Feoktistov finding the specific library and the actual magazine with the ink blot that he claimed he saw almost two years earlier in Orlov's apartment is unbelievable. More so is the fantasy that a librarian could produce such detailed personal information about a couple who had left Ann Arbor two years earlier. The librarian refers to the Orlovs as the 'elderly Russian couple', as though she knew them both, when in reality Orlov had no occasion to undertake research at any library accompanied by his wife. Orlov had little need to go beyond the extensive library at the Law School and any references he needed for his work were purchased for him by the Law School. As to the librarian advising Feoktistov that the Orlovs had not wanted to move far from Ann Arbor because they did not want to leave their beloved daughter's grave site, the fact remains that Vera's grave was in Cambridge, Massachusetts, a detail that was perhaps unknown to the KGB when they restructured history.

The librarian then suggests that the Orlovs could probably be found in either Detroit, Toledo or Cleveland. As a result, 'Feoktistov, a methodical investigator and one of the KGB's most accomplished "manhunters", decided to drive the 160 miles to Cleveland as it was the most distant of the three from Ann Arbor.'

Given all factors being equal, as the KGB scenario would indicate, I or any FBI agent assigned to seek a fugitive starting from Ann Arbor, Michigan, and progressing to the New York City area, where Feoktistov worked and lived, would logically look for the fugitive first in Detroit, then in Toledo and finally in Cleveland, as the rational progression to New York. Common sense does not dictate otherwise. Perhaps it was because of the methodology used by the KGB in the Orlov case that it took so long to find the Orlovs in the first place. In my view, the lengthy description of the KGB's search for the Orlovs in Cleveland, as noted in *Deadly Illusions*, was a subterfuge provided by the KGB to conceal its source and embellish Feoktistov's story.

In his report to the KGB, Feoktistov described Orlov as smiling conspiratorially when they went into the kitchen to be a safe distance from what he had called, with a gesture towards the radio and telephone, the 'modern listening apparatus'. According to Feoktistov, their long, detailed conversation lasted almost five hours.

However, none of this was true at all. The only telephone that the Orlovs had was one hanging on the kitchen wall. I know because while visiting the Orlovs I often used that telephone to call my office for any messages. It would be strange to retreat to the kitchen to avoid the telephone when it was already in the kitchen. As to some sort of listening device in the radio, Orlov had none as by this time he possessed a television. I never saw a radio during my first visit to the Orlov apartment a few days after the KGB contact or on any of my subsequent visits. When in 1972 Orlov gave my son Jim the Philco radio that had belonged to Vera, he had to dig it out of a cupboard to give it to me for Jim. The radio was still in the original box it had come in back in 1939. I don't see how Orlov could have pointed out a radio to Feoktistov when there was none.

As for an interview lasting almost five hours, Feoktistov didn't enter the Orlov apartment until at least ten minutes past 11 a.m. after Maria's examination of his diplomatic passport, followed by a consultation with Orlov on the merits of admitting him and finally a body search. Feoktistov departed at 12.15 p.m. as told by the Orlovs and verified by records. This leaves at most only sixty-five minutes for the interview.

Much of that time was taken up with Feoktistov's attempt to ingratiate himself: talking about his background, relating fictitious tales about Orlov's old KGB friends, flattering Orlov about what a hero he was in the Soviet Union, asking the Orlovs to return to the Soviet Union, suggesting that Maria write to her sisters, requesting a copy of Orlov's book and then wanting it inscribed, warning the Orlovs that they need not move again, etc.

Feoktistov reported to the KGB that, 'Once the residual ice of Orlov's trust had melted', he had begun to learn the details about everything the Centre wanted to know. Orlov had told him about the principal cases he had been involved with in Europe, naming Kim Philby and four other Cambridge agents who had been recruited into the network before his posting to Spain in 1936 (for more details see chapter 28). He said that Orlov had spent hours relating, in the smallest detail, everything that had happened to him and his family after he had received the ill-fated telegram from Moscow in July 1938. Then Orlov proceeded to dictate to the KGB agent a long list of names and positions of American officials, who, he said, could be of interest to the Soviet intelligence service. All this in less than sixty-five minutes!

If the Centre had any remaining doubts, Orlov apparently told Feoktistov that the acid test of his loyalty was that he had never given any hint of, or revealed anything about, his role in establishing the 'illegal' NKVD networks in Europe and Britain before the Second World War. 'On the back of his official report to the Centre, Feoktistov made a handwritten note that Orlov named to him five British agents of the Cambridge group, which indicated that he had kept abreast of the development of the network after he left London in 1935.'

Apart from the fact that this was all supposed to have been revealed within the critical sixty-five-minute time frame, it seems implausible that the most crucial piece of information to be revealed by Feoktistov, that Orlov named five British KGB spies, is reduced to a handwritten notation on the back of the report of his interview to the KGB Centre. Wouldn't this major development be a matter for the body of the report? I contend that the notation was added to the original Feoktistov report some twenty years later, when the KGB was revising the original version of the report. There was hardly any possibility that the original report would ever be held up to public scrutiny, but with the transition from Communism to a more traditional form of government in Russia, a possibility, however remote, did exist. A handwritten notation on the back of the original report, therefore, was better than nothing.

Feoktistov was interviewed some twenty years later by the authors of *Deadly Illusions*, at which time he made the following observations. After the librarian in Ann Arbor suggested that Orlov could probably be located in either Detroit, Toledo or Cleveland, Feoktistov decided to drive to Cleveland as it was the most distant of the three from Ann Arbor. In Cleveland, he checked the telephone directory and failed to find a listing for Orlov. He then proceeded to the main library, where he was directed to the second floor where the street directories were kept. 'It was my good fortune to find the door of this section was not locked,' Feoktistov recalled, and there was no one to be seen. 'But from behind a curtained cubicle at the end of the room full of book stacks, he heard noises which left him in no doubt that a couple was busily engaged in love-making. The curtain didn't quite reach the floor and he could see a pair of black legs belonging to a man and a pair of white legs just as obviously a woman's. He slipped into the room and silently closed the door with a practised hand.' As it was already late on 'Friday' afternoon, 'he wasted no time locating the stack containing the directories he was after. Following a hunch that the Orlovs were now living under their own name, he pulled out the "O" volume first and had no difficulty in finding their address. The clerk had evidently been too preoccupied with his amorous activity to notice that he was leaving.'

However, as anyone who has ever been in the main Cleveland Public Library knows, and having spent a considerable time there myself, the reference section is on the main floor in a huge Reading Room, not in a locked room as Feoktistov reports. The assignation that Feoktistov speaks of would certainly have been a source of great amusement to the more than fifty people who would have been carrying out research on any particular day. Also, the Cleveland City Directory, as with all city directories, is an alphabetical listing of names and there is not a separate 'O' volume.

Another salient point to consider in this respect is Feoktistov's reply to Orlov's query as to how he had found them in Cleveland. He replied that he could not tell them. If it were true that he had resorted to a city directory and found their listing, there would have been no logical reason to withhold this information. This only reinforces the supposition that there was a source or investigative technique in 1971 that had to be protected and that the city directory scenario was conceived in a later time frame. To me, there is no doubt that when Feoktistov left New York in 1971 to seek out his quarry, he knew exactly where to locate Orlov in Cleveland.

As Feoktistov relates, he drove to a motel about eleven miles from the city. 'It had been his experience that on "Fridays" [author's emphasis] motel managers left early for a weekend off, leaving their establishments in the hands of service personnel.' When Feoktistov was asked to fill in the registration form, he played a standard KGB trick of handing over a $10 bill to cover the accommodation charge, saying that, as he would be leaving early the next day, he would leave the completed slip in the cabin. '"Needless to say, I didn't fill in the form, but I did leave at 5 a.m. the following morning before anyone was around,"' Feoktistov said. '"The motel receptionist pocketed the $10, which was what he had been counting on, and I did not leave behind any clues of my stay in the Cleveland area, which was what I was counting on."' Shortly after 6 a.m. on 10 August, Feoktistov was 'at the wheel of his Plymouth Valiant driving past the Orlovs' apartment house on Clifton Road on the outskirts of Cleveland'.

Unbelievably, the KGB seems to have failed to check the dates when it revised the original interview. According to Feoktistov's account, he arrived in Cleveland on a Friday to contact Orlov. He specifies that it was a Friday not once but twice, noting this particular fact quite clearly in two places, describing events at the library and then at the motel. He also notes this all happened at the 'weekend'. The next day, which for the first time in his narration he actually mentions by date as 'the morning of 10 August 1971', he contacts the Orlovs and interviews them. There is no disagreement by either the KGB or the FBI as to the date of the interview being the 10th of August 1971, but the 10th of August 1971 fell on a Tuesday, so the Friday preceding the contact with Orlov was actually the 6th. However, Feoktistov's narration clearly indicates that he went directly from the motel to Orlov's apartment.

I find it inconceivable that the KGB failed to check the 1971 calendar to verify the dates it claims as the core to its narration of events leading up to the interview with Orlov. Such a blunder completely shatters its claims and casts a long shadow of suspicion on any information provided by it.

Another matter worthy of consideration is Feoktistov's declaration that Orlov was still considered a great Soviet hero, which gives the impression that Orlov's loyalty to the Soviet Union and the KGB had never wavered and, accordingly, he was not a traitor but a hero. In reality, the KGB honours and takes care of its own. The KGB, like its US counterparts the CIA and the FBI, sports a huge new complex in the Yasenevo district on the outskirts of Moscow. The centrepiece is a tall skyscraper, which houses the headquarters of the First Chief Directorate, the apparatus that directs foreign intelligence matters. Within the building is a revered shrine that I have heard referred to by many names, including the Hall of Honour, the Memory Room and the Hall of Heroes. Here the portraits of the great illegals who served the KGB so well are displayed. Many of Orlov's contemporaries and personal friends, such as Arnold Deutsch, Jan Berzin and Theodore Mally, are so honoured because, despite being caught up in Stalin's purges, they never turned their backs on the KGB. However, Orlov's portrait is not amongst those selected because he did turn his back on the KGB and placed his loyalty with the US Government.

In recent years, there has been an era of openness in the former Soviet Union in which members of the US intelligence community have been allowed to visit the KGB Yasenevo complex. As recently as 1996, several of my acquaintances have toured the KGB shrine and the portrait of former KGB General Alexander Orlov is conspicuous by its absence. Surely, if the account of Feoktistov's report in *Deadly Illusions* is a true reflection of the KGB's position, then Orlov's portrait should be on display?

Finally, sometime during the summer of 1972 when Orlov and I were going over Feoktistov's contact of the previous year, we were speculating on the possibility of another contact. By this time Orlov felt more secure that the KGB had given up any hope of luring him back to the Soviet Union as he had been extremely vehement that he would never return under the current regime. He continued by noting the time lapse since the last contact and Feoktistov's parting admonition that the KGB meant no harm and that the Orlovs should not consider moving again as it was too expensive. He had given Feoktistov no indication of his future plans, whether they would stay or move, but one item had come up in the interview which puzzled him. Feoktistov had mentioned that he had seen Orlov's photograph in the fifth anniversary commemorative publication of the Soviet Supreme Court and asked if Orlov would like a copy. Orlov replied that naturally he would like a copy but sending one was up to Feoktistov. Orlov felt that this was Feoktistov's devious way of ascertaining his intentions of moving again. At the time, Orlov wondered how Feoktistov knew about the commemorative article as this had been published long before Orlov had joined the KGB and it would therefore not be part of his KGB personnel file. Orlov mentioned that Feoktistov had never sent him a copy of the publication nor did I find such a publication in Orlov's possessions after his death. My feeling at the time was that the matter was inconsequential. However, in light of what I now know, I think it was more than coincidence that Feoktistov brought up the matter of the publication – and not Orlov, as Feoktistov asserts in *Deadly Illusions* – as he must have been aware of Orlov's letter to Strogovich. What appears certain to me years later, with the benefit of knowing about the Orlov/Plant letter and Feoktistov's own words in *Deadly Illusions*, is that there was a connection between what Orlov thought was an innocuous request for the fifth anniversary commemorative publication and how the KGB came to find him.

Tom Corbett and I concluded our interview with the Orlovs with the admonition that they contact the Cleveland office immediately, day or night, should they be contacted again by the KGB. We made it clear that the FBI could not provide them with day-to-day protection but would be at their disposal at any time the KGB ventured in their direction by whatever means. They both acknowledged that they understood the FBI's position in these matters and noted that it would be to their benefit to comply with our request to report any future incident. We left on a very cordial note.

As with all interviews, I had to make a preliminary judgement as to the veracity of the information and the degree of co-operation that had been afforded during the interview. With the Orlovs, there were never any areas of suspicion and their responses were straightforward, sincere and without the slightest hesitation. There was no reason to doubt any of their statements and their co-operation was without any reservation. What I did see were two very frightened and concerned people, who outwardly feigned composure.

Naturally, I had my own personal observations on that first meeting with the Orlovs. Orlov came across in the true meaning of what one thinks a military general should be. He had a military bearing and a 'presence', a quality of confidence and self-assurance. He also struck me as an extremely intelligent person. Maria came across as an intelligent and very strong-willed person, who was also uncommonly compassionate and loyal to her husband. I detected in her a degree of sophistication that I had not expected and a manner that was more official than friendly.

When Tom and I returned to the office, we immediately telephoned Bureau headquarters in Washington to report the results of the interview. I was instructed to prepare a written report of the interview by no later than the next day.

I continued to contact the Orlovs at least once and more often twice a week during the first month after our initial contact to determine if there had been any new developments, as well as to ensure their continued co-operation and to let them know that we were closely monitoring the situation. As time went by, the frequency of my contacts diminished to one visit every other week. The Orlovs once actually admonished me for neglecting them and told me that they looked forward to my visits. I recall visiting them only once during November 1971 and that was at the beginning of the month. My other work had been neglected to the point that I had some catching up to do.

As I continued my contacts with the Orlovs, I detected a certain degree of fondness on my part for them, which appeared to be mutual. I found that Maria was actually a very warm person and it was only the barrier that she placed between herself and others for the sake of her husband that made the first impression difficult to escape. When I visited, they always adhered to the European custom of offering the visitor a drink and some cakes. At first I would decline, in keeping with my professional code, but after the ice was broken I never failed to accept their hospitality. Unlike her husband, Maria spoke with a definite foreign accent although she was fluent in the English language.

On my first visit to the Orlovs' apartment, they showed me a hard rubber wedge they had just purchased at the local hardware store. Should anyone come to the apartment unannounced, they intended to position the wedge under the door and with one foot pressing on the wedge against the door they would have more leverage to keep an intruder out. At night they placed pots and pans on a chair immediately in front of the door in order to warn them should anyone try to force an entry. I thought these devices were unnecessary but knew that they gave them some peace of mind. On my next visit, Orlov asked my thoughts about purchasing a revolver for protection. I knew that he had been an expert in firearms in his day but cautioned him against this move. I explained that the KGB was well aware of the US's interest in their safety because of our protest lodged with the State Department. Should they encounter any foul play, the FBI would logically suspect the KGB. Orlov took my advice for the time being.

Soon the Orlovs came up with another innovative idea that they put in place without bothering to consult me and one with which I found no objection. They lived on Clifton Boulevard, a major artery in and out of the city, and only two blocks from a major intersection where they did most of their shopping. The neighbourhood was mostly apartment houses and commercial buildings. As a consequence of the KGB's intrusion in their lives, they now restricted their travel to the immediate neighbourhood and kept to places where there were a lot of people about. The Orlovs purchased two whistles, like the ones used by military drill instructors and football referees, which produced an extremely high-pitched sound that was bound to draw attention. They each secured their whistle to a shoe-string and pinned them on the inside of a garment, out of sight yet readily available when needed. In the event that one of them was accosted by Feoktistov in the future, or anyone they believed to be connected with the KGB, the other would blow their whistle to attract attention. This sounded a little childish when they first told me about it, but after I thought about it for a while I could not come up with a better idea. What really convinced me was when Maria unexpectedly demonstrated the effectiveness of the whistle: she was rather close to my ear and I continued to hear the sound for several days.

I only knew Maria for a period of three months but what I could not help but notice during this short period was the deterioration of her health. At our first meeting, she had appeared vibrant and fierce in her agitation over the KGB contact. Her health, at least on the outside, seemed robust and her mental outlook showed no abnormalities. However, my frequent contacts with her were sufficient enough to notice a slow yet incessant progression to a state where she seemed at times sullen and her attention seemed to drift. There was no doubt that a matter of great concern was on her mind and, as I look back, I suspect that she knew her time span was closing. It seemed that Vera was always on her mind as she incessantly brought her daughter into the conversation in one way or another. I was shown every family photograph of Vera, as well as the cherished pieces of teenage jewellery, trinkets and toys that had brought so much joy during her short life. What could not escape my attention was the array of medicine bottles on the kitchen table. On one occasion, the General caught me glancing at the medicine bottles and, in his manner, lowered his head and nodded dejectedly while pointing with his hand to his heart. At another time, when Maria was preparing refreshments in the kitchen, he leaned towards me and softly said that, although Maria put up a good front, she was constantly in fear of another visit by the KGB and that the situation was visibly wearing her down. There was no need for him to tell me that he was worried but he did. I hoped that my visits would lift her spirits and that her health problems would go away.

Maria Orlov passed away on 16 November 1971 from a massive heart attack, exactly three months and one week from the day the Orlovs had been contacted by Feoktistov. I lay the immediate blame for her untimely death directly on the doorstep of the KGB. What it could not accomplish in her lifetime by direct means, it insidiously accomplished by an orchestrated scheme of harassment. The KGB had achieved in a matter of months what it had been unable to accomplish over a thirty-three-year span when the Orlovs were in hiding from its henchmen.

TWENTY-TWO

LONG-STEMMED RED ROSES

I received a telephone call at the FBI office from Orlov on the morning of 17 November 1971. This was rather unusual as I was always the one who called him when I wanted to set up a meeting with him. He informed me that Maria had passed away the previous evening and could I recommend a funeral home that could handle the arrangements. I recommended the Corrigan Funeral Home, which was personally known to me for their dignified services in burying both of my parents.

I met Orlov as soon as I could and arrangements were made to have Maria's body taken to the funeral home. I learned that it had only been a matter of an hour from the first sign of a massive heart attack until she had been pronounced dead. Her long history of rheumatic heart fever had caused the mitral valve to her heart to become scarred and, along with congestive heart failure, her fate had been sealed. Orlov knew that the KGB's recent contact with them, and her fear of another entanglement with the KGB officer in the future, had only hastened the path towards her death. At least he now knew that she would have peace of mind and would never again have to fear the KGB.

We went to the funeral home, where the final arrangements were made: the service would be held the next afternoon followed by cremation. Afterwards, Orlov asked if I could take him home as he had been up most of the time since Maria had died and now needed some rest. I thought that he was handling the situation quite well and for all appearances behaved in the manner expected of an old general. However, I also suspected that he was putting on a façade, perhaps for my benefit. Sometime later, when our personal relationship was closer, he admitted that when I left him that day, he had sat alone in his apartment and suddenly realised what a terrible loss Maria's death was for him. Earlier that year they had celebrated fifty years of marriage and since his defection in 1938 not a day had passed by that they had not been in each other's company. He revealed that at that moment he had been unable to control his emotions and broke down. He also admitted that he had very rarely let his inner emotions get the better of him, but this occasion was the hardest he had ever had to endure.

When I left his apartment, he casually mentioned that he would be contacting an old friend with the CIA to break the news. Earlier that day I had notified Bureau headquarters in Washington about Maria's death. Shortly before leaving the office that evening, I received a telephone call from the Bureau advising me that a CIA official would be attending Maria's funeral the next day. Would I meet him on his arrival in Cleveland and take him to the service? The CIA official was identified as Raymond G. Rocca, a long-time CIA operative who was deputy to James Angleton, Chief of the CIA's counter-intelligence division. That evening I telephoned Orlov to determine how he was holding up and learned of no problems. He did relate that 'Rock' (Rocca's nickname) was coming to Cleveland for the funeral and he was surprised when I told him that I was already aware of this fact. He was happy to learn that I would be meeting his CIA friend.

The following day I picked up Rocca and had no problem recognising him at our rendezvous. The day was rather brisk with a chill wind blowing in from Lake Erie, and he was wearing the proverbial light-coloured CIA trench coat with a felt hat while I wore the typical dark-coloured FBI trench coat with the customary felt hat. There was immediate recognition on both sides. Ray, the name I would call him when I got to know him better, was a tall, big-boned man who was neither muscular nor overweight. He had the commanding presence of a self-assured individual, expressed himself in an articulate and intelligent manner, but on our first meeting I felt him to be a little aloof and somewhat officious. This first impression was not unusual as I, as well as my FBI colleagues, always found CIA personnel to be different from us FBI types. No doubt this characterisation held true for the CIA people who felt that FBI officers were different. With time my appraisal of Rocca changed and I found the warmer man. We became friends on a professional level.

The religious service for Maria was impressive but the attendance at the funeral was very sparse as their lifestyle had precluded socialising and they had made few friends during the short time they had been in Cleveland. The one thing that I could not help but notice about the funeral was that the religious service was officiated by both a rabbi and a Protestant minister. This was the first time I had witnessed such an arrangement but it would not be the last time. When the time came for the General to be buried, I handled the funeral arrangements and never deviated from the pattern that had been previously set at both Maria's and Vera's funeral services. Maria Orlov's remains were cremated on 19 November at the Sunset Memorial Park Cemetery in the Cleveland suburb of North Olmsted, Ohio. In time, her ashes were interred at the Mount Auburn Cemetery in Cambridge, Massachusetts.

Early in the following week, I received a telephone call from Orlov in which he expressed a desire to take me to lunch. I agreed and picked him up at his apartment. We went to the rather exclusive Pier W Restaurant in the Winton Tower Complex in the suburb of Lakewood. We discussed trivialities over lunch although I felt that he had something on his mind but he didn't feel the place was appropriate. As I was taking him home, he asked me to pull over to a parking place on a side street. I knew that the time had come for him to discuss whatever was on his mind. As we sat there, he started the conversation by saying that Maria had become very fond of me and had looked forward to my visits. She had told him that my visits afforded her an opportunity to appraise me and she had liked what she saw. She had confided that she placed a considerable amount of trust and confidence in me and felt that I was the person who would take her place as Orlov's 'protector' and 'confidant'. She had then made him promise that he would at least approach me when the time came to express her feelings towards me and felt that I would recognise the sincerity of her final wishes. Orlov seemed relieved that he had complied with Maria's last request and looked towards me for an answer. I hardly knew what to say, but I was extremely flattered that Maria had felt that way about me. Before I could reply, he said something to the effect that he too felt comfortable with me and knew I could be trusted. He added that he wanted to be my friend. I detected a sincereness and a modicum of loneliness in his demeanour. I had to admit to him that I had also grown fond of Maria and him and that I expected to continue our friendship. As we parted company, I had a strange feeling about our relationship and in my heart felt a deep satisfaction at the turn of events.

Sometime later he told me something I shall never forget, an analogy that related to that day. He said that on that particular day he had been overcome by a feeling that he had only experienced once before. The previous occasion had been when he had defected and had tried to get hold of the US Ambassador in Paris as everything depended on getting a visa to the United States. On that day the Ambassador was absent and he had nowhere to turn. He said that he had felt like a man who had just abandoned ship and climbed into a lifeboat only to find that he had no valid plan for survival and little hope. When Maria died, it was a similar situation, only this time Maria was the ocean liner and he had fallen overboard. While the ocean liner faded in the distance, symbolising her death, he was floundering in the water unable to attract anyone's attention. It was now more apparent than ever that Orlov was a very lonely man who had no place to turn to and was reaching out to me as his last hope.

In the coming weeks, we would have lunch together at least once a week and in between I would telephone frequently to see how things were going. We went to a number of fine restaurants and, as time wore on, settled on two excellent German restaurants, Hertzog's on Lorain Avenue at West 131st Street and

Kieffer's on Detroit Avenue near West 25th Street. It turned out that we both loved European food and German cuisine in particular.

In the first week of January 1972, my wife Ruth and I decided to invite Orlov to our house for supper. When I extended the invitation, he seemed more depressed than usual and explained that earlier that day he had read that Maurice Chevalier, one of his and Maria's favourite singers, had passed away a few days before of a heart attack in a hospital in Paris. He recalled that he and Maria had first encountered Chevalier in Paris in late 1927 or early 1928, when they had seen him several times in a musical revue at the Casino de Paris. They had never met him personally, but had continued to follow his career as they both enjoyed his singing and dancing. After reminiscing about his early days in Paris, Orlov accepted my invitation.

Ruth prepared one of my favourite Austrian dishes, Steak Esterhazy, for the occasion. That evening I picked Orlov up at his apartment on my way home from work. It was on my usual route and presented no problem. When I asked if he cared to have wine with the meal, I learned that this was his custom. He loved drinking wine with his meal and a small brandy afterwards. This would set the pattern for the many memorable occasions that we would have together from then on. Our son Jim was in high school so he also had the pleasure of meeting Orlov. During the meal there was never a lull in the conversation as we discovered that Orlov was a natural storyteller. What he had to say was always of interest, touching on subjects that were rare and worldly, yet entertaining. That evening was one of the shortest I had ever experienced and we were still sitting at the table at about 10.30 p.m. Orlov bade Ruth and Jim farewell, and I then took him home. When I returned home, Ruth and I discussed the evening and she was thoroughly impressed with Orlov's graciousness and European charm, which had put her at ease. She said that she had a good feeling about him and suggested that we invite him over again. I agreed.

The next afternoon the front doorbell rang and Ruth noticed

a florist's truck parked in front of the house. When she opened the door, she saw a uniformed man holding a long, white cardboard box. She thought that the driver had made a mistake, but when she verified her name on the little card that accompanied the box her mouth dropped open. I only gave flowers to Ruth on very rare occasions as my Depression-era upbringing called for more tangible gifts that could be useful in the long run. She could hardly wait to open the envelope and when she did the enclosed card read, 'Thanks for a wonderful evening, Alexander Orlov.' The box contained a dozen beautiful long-stemmed red roses. She was 'flabbergasted' and, after regaining her composure, she immediately telephoned Orlov and thanked him profusely for the flowers. She also tried to impress on him that as much as she appreciated the gesture, it was not at all necessary.

Ruth and I thought that this was a wonderful act of gratitude, but soon learned that this was not an isolated instance but rather one that reflected Orlov's generosity.

The following week we again invited Orlov to supper and the next day another box of long-stemmed red roses arrived for Ruth. At our next luncheon, I told him that Ruth really appreciated the gift but that it was totally unnecessary. He replied that he enjoyed the visits to our house and that it gave him great pleasure to send the roses to Ruth. I dropped the matter with the admonition that I would prefer him not to send flowers in the future. However, after his next visit to our house, he still sent a dozen long-stemmed red roses the following day. When we met again, I was more than upset. I threatened that I would not invite him to our house again if he insisted on sending roses as his way of thanking us. He appeared a little shaken at my threat, but from that day on Ruth received no more long-stemmed red roses.

Ruth and I continued to invite Orlov to dinner and he continued to come. In time, it became more like a family reunion and the more he came, the more we wanted to have him. He was at the house at least once a week and more often than not twice a week. To this day, Ruth recalls Orlov sitting at the dining-room table relating humorous stories about people he had known and events he had experienced over the years. Although Orlov and I discussed more serious matters in our private conversations, at the dinner table with Ruth and one or both of our children present he spoke only of the happy times in his life. In spite of the fact that he had suffered years of hardship while in hiding from the KGB, as well as the tragic loss of his young daughter Vera and his ever-protective wife, he never dwelt on these matters.

Orlov and I also continued our luncheon engagements at least once a week. In time, both Ruth and I found that we were getting very fond of him and sensed that the feeling was mutual. I began to look upon him as a father figure, in part because I had lost my father at a very young age and more so because both my father and Orlov had been born in the same year, 1895.

Towards the middle of February, a more serious side to our dinner encounters began to emerge. After dinner, Orlov and I would retreat to my Bavarian Room in the basement, where he would tell me fascinating stories about his career in the KGB along with the exploits of his fellow KGB officers. He seemed to have an endless supply of anecdotes from a long and colourful career. During the winter of 1972–3, we would have a fire blazing in the fireplace and one of the things Orlov liked to do was to add a log to the fire when needed.

One evening Orlov mentioned that he had already written his memoirs and suggested that I might wish to read them. I was more than delighted at the suggestion and told him so. The next week when he came to the house, he brought the memoirs with him. They were in two volumes, typewritten and bound in coloured pressboard binders. I perused the contents and found that the two volumes contained nearly thirty chapters that spanned a lifetime of history for Orlov. He had titled his memoirs, *March of Time (Reminiscences)*, and noted in his handwriting that they were his copyright. He left the two volumes in my possession saying that they were an exact copy of the original, which he would keep in his possession.

He suggested that I should read one chapter at a time and at our next meeting we would discuss that particular chapter. He would amplify on its contents and explain anything that was not clear to me, and he would not object if I wished to make notes during the review of each chapter. This became the set procedure until we finished discussing the memoirs towards the end of the summer of 1972.

During these discussions, I learned that Orlov had submitted the memoirs to several publishers, including the University of Michigan Press. He felt that as he had written part of his memoirs while at the Law School of the University of Michigan, and as the Michigan Press had published his *Handbook*, he was obliged to give them the first opportunity to publish. However, the manuscript had been rejected by the Michigan Press, as it was later rejected by the publishers who had produced his earlier works. He had also submitted the memoirs to other publishing houses to no avail. The heyday of the mid-1950s when his work had been published around the world was over and the name Alexander Orlov was no longer a household word.

The lack of interest in his memoirs greatly disturbed Orlov, not so much from the monetary side but from his wish to expose the evils of Communism and the KGB. What he had to say about the deeds of his former masters was of historical significance and should not go unforgotten in an unpublished manuscript.

We pondered the situation quite extensively and came up with the idea of placing his memoirs under the control of a legal document known as a Revocable Agreement of Trust because of his advanced age and the constant fear of reprisals by the KGB. He felt that the revelations recorded in his memoirs were highly detrimental to the Soviet Union and that the KGB would therefore take extraordinary measures to procure them illegally and thereby stop their publication. He was certain that the Soviets would take every means of preventing the unfavourable and heretofore unknown clandestine activities of the USSR and the KGB from becoming known to the free world. At his suggestion and final approval, his memoirs were placed under the control of the Revocable Agreement of Trust.

When he first voiced great concern that his manuscript and other records could be burgled by the KGB, I thought that his fears were somewhat exaggerated and told him so. He then became more adamant and pointed to the case of Leon Trotsky, whose personal papers and writings had been stolen by the KGB in Paris in 1936; he also mentioned several other cases in which the KGB had resorted to burglary as a means of achieving its goal. I finally agreed with the need to protect his secrets, but even more so years later when I came to suspect that the KGB had in fact burgled his papers (see chapter 28).

I was appointed custodian of the memoirs with discretionary powers as to their final disposition in the event of Orlov's death, but acting in this capacity without remuneration.

In the event that the memoirs were published for profit, or that any of his previous publications were reprinted, the royalties thereof would be for the benefit of the American Heart Association and/or the College of Law at the University of Michigan. As to the American Heart Association, any monies generated and designated to this institution would be specifically for research in the field of rheumatic heart fever in order to try to develop preventative medicines and a cure for this illness. Orlov declared that he was doing this in memory of his beloved daughter Vera, with the hope that a programme would be established and named after her.

As to the College of Law at the University of Michigan, any monies generated and designated to this institution were specifically for a programme to enhance the prestige of the Law School in the field of International Law as a means of expressing Orlov's appreciation and gratitude to his fellow associates at the Law School. In the event of his death and in the absence of the publication of his memoirs, Orlov directed that the memoirs be placed in the hands of a repository dedicated to exposing the evils of Communism and the KGB and/or a repository where they would be made available for their historical value in the study of Communism and the KGB. For this purpose, Orlov requested that consideration be given to the US National Archives or the

Hoover Institution on War, Revolution and Peace at Stanford, California, as the final repository.

Early on in our relationship, Orlov gave us quite a scare. He would always inform us well in advance when he would be away for any length of time, but on one occasion he failed to tell us. I don't recall the specific date but it was probably in late April 1972. I telephoned Orlov several times one Monday and never received a response. It was not unusual for him to be out of the apartment as he was not the type to sit at home and brood. For the most part, he would take long walks in the neighbourhood or take the bus to downtown Cleveland, where he would spend time reading at the Cleveland Public Library. His absence did not alarm me at first, but on the following day when I tried to reach him again, I again got no response. I walked over to the Library to look for him but to no avail. I then drove to his apartment, but again received no response. I drove all around the neighbourhood, but there was still no sign of him. That evening, I called his telephone number continuously and, in the absence of any response, made a point of stopping at his apartment very early the following morning en route to work. Orlov was not there. I now feared the worst – that the KGB had struck again – and so I advised Washington of Orlov's disappearance. The Section Chief at the Bureau told me to hold on for the moment and they would do some checking. Later that day I had the answer, much to my relief. Orlov had been sighted in the Washington DC area, where he had paid a visit to his CIA friend, Ray Rocca, and had then gone on to Boston.

Orlov returned to Cleveland by that Friday and I was able to get hold of him. I didn't mention what had happened and only asked him over to the house for dinner. After dinner, I finally did tell him of the consternation he had caused. He looked rather sheepish and apologised profusely. He said that it would never happen again and it never did.

There were two deaths in 1972 that caused Orlov substantial distress, one was human and the other literary: J. Edgar Hoover,

Director of the FBI, passed away on 2 May and *Life* magazine ceased publication.

Orlov had nothing but praise and admiration for Hoover and considered him and his organisation an early bulwark against Communism and the KGB. He felt that Hoover's 1958 book, *Masters of Deceit*, which exposed Communism for the threat it was and outlined his strategy for fighting espionage and the spread of Communism, was truly the standard by which Americans would know and understand the enemy. As to *Life* magazine, he considered its demise a loss to the American public. As he commiserated the event, he vividly recalled that it had been *Life* that had given him his opportunity to pursue his personal battle against Stalin and Communism at a time when other publishers had not been interested.

There was more to Orlov than his serious side, although I would have to say that this side of him prevailed. Often when he came over for the evening, I would suggest seeing a particular film after dinner to break our usual routine. His negative reply became the standard response and he would note that we could spend the time more profitably at home. However, to my surprise on one occasion he suggested that we go to see *Cabaret*, starring Liza Minnelli and Joel Grey, as a review of it had intrigued him. He explained that the story took place in Berlin about the time he was there and he wanted to see whether the depiction of that era measured up to his own observations of those times. Afterwards, his only comment was that he had enjoyed the film but found it to be a closer replication of the Berlin he had known in the late 1920s than the pre-Hitler early 1930s' version reflected in the film. He also mentioned that he had seen many similarities between *Cabaret* and the classic German film, *The Blue Angel*, starring Marlene Dietrich, which had been the rage in Berlin about the time he left Germany in the early part of 1931. I never knew him to see another film after this.

Ruth and I would often pick up Orlov at his apartment on Saturdays so that we could spend the day together, as well as take him away from his usual monotonous routine. We were seriously interested in antique hunting and there was normally a Saturday auction somewhere in northern Ohio selling early Americana and primitive antiques. We all enjoyed these outings and soon learned of Orlov's own interest in antiques, although he never bought anything at auction as his preference was for European antiques. We would always return to Cleveland via an alternative route, usually along the more scenic country routes and side roads. Orlov never seemed to tire of our Saturday excursions.

One Saturday afternoon, Orlov said that he had always wanted to visit the boyhood home of Thomas A. Edison. This came as a surprise considering the Soviets' claim to have invented every-thing from the wheel to the aeroplane. When I jokingly brought this to his attention, he retorted with his usual sly grin that perhaps the Soviet claims were slightly exaggerated. He told us that he was aware that Edison was America's greatest inventor and had admired the man and his achievements long before he had ever come to the US. As Ruth and I had never been to Edison's birthplace, the decision was an easy one. Edison was from the village of Milan, Ohio, about fifty miles west of Cleveland, and we visited the small wood-framed house where he had been born and the Edison Museum. The turn-of-the-century architecture proved interesting and we all enjoyed the day, thanks to Orlov's suggestion.

Orlov loved animals, especially the wild kind, and one of our Saturday trips was to the Cleveland Zoo, one of the oldest in the nation. Orlov was enthralled by the animals and stood at each cage as though he were seeing that particular animal for the first time and making a study of its habits. What attracted him most were the bears, in particular the darker brown and black-shaded ones. He led us back to the bear pits for a last viewing when we had already decided to call it a day. On the way home, I found out why he had been so riveted by the bear pits, although I should have known if I had thought about it for a moment. Firstly, the bear was the symbol of both old Russia and the Soviet Union, and secondly these bears reminded him of his boyhood in

Bobruysk. Each summer a man with a trained black bear would perform at the small village, to everyone's delight. His routine became an annual ritual, which everyone expected. The huge bear would be dressed like a girl, complete with hat, ruffled shoulder piece and skirt. It would assume an upright position by standing on its hind legs and would then balance a large ball on its nose while attempting to mount a colourful platform. The trainer and the bear would toss the ball back and forth and the act would usually end with the bear dancing about. Sometimes an accordionist playing Russian folk songs would accompany the trainer and the bear would then dance to the music. Orlov recalled that the bears brought him and everyone in the village immense joy, but he felt that the small pittance the trainer received when he passed his hat at the end of the act was far less than he deserved. Orlov reminisced that Vera must have taken after him as she had always looked forward to seeing the bears when they had gone on a family outing to the circus.

Orlov had a rapacious appetite for reading and he would spend most days at the Cleveland Public Library; in the evenings, he would read the books he had borrowed from the Library. He shunned television and only watched it to see the national news broadcasts. The last book I know that he read was Alexander Solzhenitsyn's novel *August 1914* and we discussed it in late 1972. Normally he did not read novels as he found non-fiction more interesting, but he had made an exception because of the author and the subject matter, which was the tip of the iceberg of events that had brought down the Tsar. As implied by its title, in August 1914 the Russian Tsarist Army engaged the German Army at Tannenberg and was soundly defeated. The Tsarist Army did not lose because the German Army was superior but because of the ineptness of the Russian generals. From that battle onwards, the Russian Army never seemed to gain the high ground and as time progressed the army in the field became demoralised as a viable fighting machine. Russia sued for peace in 1917 and the formalities of war ceased with the signing of an armistice between the Russians and Germans at Brest-Litovsk. This culminated in the

Russian Revolution at the end of the year, which led to a Communist government and the birth of the Soviet Union. Orlov had been drafted into the Tsarist Army in 1916 and had missed being in the battle of Tannenberg by two years, but its historical significance had caught his attention.

Orlov did not know Solzhenitsyn personally as the author was a much younger man and his works were not known when Orlov defected. Sometime in the early 1960s, Max Eastman had referred him to the recently published book *One Day in the Life of Ivan Denisovich*, which Orlov was impressed by, but he was more interested in the background of the author. In 1945, Solzhenitsyn had openly denounced Stalin in a letter to the Soviet people in which he pointed out that Stalin was not the man on the pedestal that he had them believe. The KGB arrested him and he was sentenced to eight years in a labour camp in Siberia. After his release, Solzhenitsyn continued to be a thorn in the side of the Soviets and, as a consequence, was expelled from the Soviet Writers Union (SWU), a sentence that was harsher than it would appear. Without the sanction of the SWU, he was not able to access Soviet libraries and research material or to be published. However, by the 1970s he was an internationally recognised author, who was the recipient of the 1970 Nobel Prize for Literature. Orlov considered him to be an important writer of our times and one that loved Mother Russia.

To describe Orlov is not a simple task as he was an extremely complex man. In fact, there were two distinct Alexander Orlovs, the KGB general on the one hand and, on the other, the defector whom I came to know intimately. As I never knew Orlov the KGB general, I can only base what I know of him from my firsthand association and what I learned from government documents. Orlov the KGB general was a very forceful, resourceful and uncompromising leader. Without doubt, he was a planner and doer with the ability to deal with world leaders and high-level issues and have his ideas prevail. He was certainly a mysterious and cunning figure, who had had to play many deceptive roles during his lifetime in espionage. Some of the attributes of Orlov the KGB general no doubt carried over to Orlov the defector, but by the time I knew him he had mellowed somewhat like a vintage wine.

My personal observations of Orlov were all positive. Although he was lean and short in stature, probably no more than 5 feet 7 inches tall, he had cast an enormously large historical shadow. Like a general, he carried himself in an erect military manner, which commanded attention and exuded that elusive condition known as presence. He had the flair for saying the right thing at the right time and what he had to say was organised and concise. His suave manner and dapper appearance reminded one of a European aristocrat and suggested that he was a man of the world, which he was. He was an immaculate dresser and I never saw him without a formal shirt and tie. When he again became financially solvent, his lifestyle dictated the very best; all his purchases, such as clothing and personal items, were from the very best stores, which I suspect was a result of his days in the top echelons of the KGB. Despite his sophistication, he was self-effacing and humble, a combination that few people possess. He never spoke down to anyone and had the ability to listen patiently to the other side. He was an extremely intelligent man of immense character and integrity. I never knew him to lie to me and I had plenty of opportunity to discover if he had. Perhaps he didn't tell me everything about himself during his life as Orlov the KGB general, but then again I never asked.

At the end of January 1972, Orlov took the ashes of his beloved wife Maria to the Mount Auburn Cemetery for interment. He anticipated that he would have a problem as the niche had been purchased in the name of Alexander O. Berg and his daughter had been interred under the name Vera O. Berg. However, when he returned to Cleveland, he was much relieved as he had had no problem in changing the name of ownership for the niche to Orlov.

Orlov last visited the family niche at Mount Auburn towards the end of September 1972. Just before his final illness and death, he was planning another visit during the first week of April 1973.

He did make it to Mount Auburn in April 1973 but not as planned: he passed away on 7 April 1973 and his ashes were sent to Mount Auburn for their final resting-place during the month he had anticipated making his visit.

TWENTY-THREE

KGB DISINFORMATION

Sometime during December 1971, I received a telephone call from Orlov that clearly indicated he was distressed. His voice teemed with urgency so I dropped everything and agreed to meet him.

On contact, I learned that Orlov was concerned about two major newspaper articles that had appeared separately on Sunday, 21 November 1971, in the *Chicago Tribune* and the *New York Times*. Both articles reported on the funeral of KGB spy Rudolf Abel in Moscow, and the thrust of the articles was that several old-time KGB officers associated with Abel were conspicuous by their absence at the funeral. One of those identified was Leonid Eitingon. The articles also related that Alexander Orlov, a top-ranking official in the secret police who had headed the Soviet intelligence network in Spain during the Spanish Civil War, had testified before the United States Senate Committee on Internal Security that Eitingon, Orlov's chief deputy during the Spanish Civil War operating under the pseudonym Colonel Kotov, had engineered the assassination of Leon Trotsky on 20 August 1940 outside Mexico City.

Orlov informed me that the assertion he had testified that Eitingon was the man behind the plot to assassinate Trotsky was totally incorrect, and what he had actually said at the hearing had been indisputably recorded by the Senate Committee on 28 September 1955 and was readily available to the public as well as the press. Orlov had testified that he had written Trotsky a warning letter in 1938, when he arrived in the US soon after his defection (see pages 260–3). Unfortunately, Trotsky had taken

Orlov's warnings as a hoax perpetrated by the KGB.

The *New York Times* reported the article under the heading, 'Abel, the Soviet Spy, Is Reported to Have Protested the Jailing of 2 Associates, One Linked to Trotsky Slaying'; the article was datelined 20 November, Moscow, as a Special to the *New York Times*. The *Chicago Tribune* reported the article under the heading, 'Brutality, Terror Emerge in Soviet Spy Apparatus', also datelined 20 November and by James Yuenger, Chief of the Moscow Bureau. Both articles attributed their revelations to the death of Rudolf Abel, the KGB spy who had been apprehended by the FBI and spent nearly five years in an American penitentiary after his conviction on espionage charges. In 1962, Abel had been released from his incarceration in exchange for the U-2 pilot Francis Gary Powers, who was being held in the Soviet Union after his aircraft was shot out of the sky over the Soviet Union while on a spy reconnaissance mission.

The *New York Times* reported that 'an unusual glimpse into the murky past of Soviet foreign intelligence operations of Stalin was provided this week in connection with the death of Colonel Rudolf I. Abel, the Soviet master spy who operated in the United States for eight years until he was seized in 1957'. The article continued that,

> usually reliable sources said that Colonel Abel, on his return to the Soviet Union in 1962, joined in a protest to Soviet authorities over the imprisonment of two close associates who had been arrested after Stalin's death in 1953.
>
> The sources identified the two men as Leonid Eitingon, the mastermind behind the assassination of Leon Trotsky in Mexico City in 1940, and Pavel Sudoplatov, head of foreign intelligence under Stalin. These men were jailed, the sources said, because they had been too closely involved with the internal security activities of Lavrenti P. Beria, head of Soviet intelligence and the secret police, who was executed on charges of treason after Stalin's death.
>
> Mr Eitingon, who served a twelve-year term in the

penitentiary of Vladimir, north-east of Moscow, was reported working for a Soviet book-exporting organisation. Mr Sudoplatov was said by the source to have gone blind during the fifteen-year term he served in Vladimir. . . .

Little is known about the past of Mr Sudoplatov. Mr Eitingon's career was described in 1957 by a Soviet defector, Alexander Orlov, in testimony before a United States subcommittee on internal security.

Mr Orlov, who headed a Soviet intelligence network in Spain during the Spanish Civil War, said that Mr Eitingon had been assigned by Beria or by Stalin to engineer the assassination of Trotsky, Stalin's old rival, who was in Mexico City.

Trotsky was slain on August 20, 1940, by a man who got into his heavily guarded villa in Coyoacán, a Mexico City suburb. The assassin was arrested and sentenced to a twenty-year term and only then was identified as Ramón Mercader, a Spanish Communist. His mother, Caridad, was reputed to be a close friend of Beria's, according to the Orlov account.

Some of this information was used by Issac Don Levine in the book, *The Mind of an Assassin*, published in 1959.

The assassin, also known in Mexico as Jacques Mornard, was released after completing his sentence and is now believed to be in the Soviet Union.

Orlov responded to the *New York Times* article by a registered letter dated 30 November, with his return address care of his attorney, Hugo Pollock. In his letter, he took umbrage with the falsehoods attributed to him in the article and referred the newspaper to the true facts, which were readily obtainable in the published text of his testimony before the Internal Security Subcommittee of the Senate (85th Congress, First Session) of 14 and 15 February 1957.

Orlov's letter also came to the defence of the mother of Trotsky's assassin, Caridad Mercader, and what he had to say could be of some significance to historians by giving them another insight into the assassination of Trotsky. In response to the assertion that Orlov had testified that Caridad Mercader was reputed to be a close friend of Beria, Orlov emphatically denied that he had ever made such a statement and noted that this could easily be verified in the minutes of his testimony published by the Government Printing Office. What he did add to the letter from his personal knowledge was his statement:

> Mrs Mercader had been depicted in this country as a woman of easy virtue who enjoyed dancing in the nude to entertain the members of the Politburo of the French Communist Party, which is nothing but deliberate slander. In reality Mrs Mercader was a high-grade idealist, who was respected in the socialist circles in France and Spain. She is a victimised mother, whose son was skilfully brainwashed by Stalin's agents into killing Trotsky, the man she greatly admired and whose views on the Russian Revolution she shared. Bewildered, Mrs Mercader waited twenty years for the release of her cheated son.

Orlov related to me that he had known Caridad Mercader personally during his time in Spain but was never privy to what her relationship was with Eitingon or her connection with the assassination of Trotsky. He did not know if there had been a romance between Eitingon and Mercader, although he was aware that they knew one another. His close working relationship with Eitingon, as well as their personal friendship wherein they shared confidences, would have brought to the surface any dalliance between the two. When he defected in 1938, Orlov was positive that Eitingon would be next in line to be purged by Stalin unless he also defected. He was therefore surprised when he learned that Eitingon had survived the purges. However, he was even more surprised to learn many years later that Eitingon was the mastermind behind Trotsky's assassination and that Caridad Mercader was Eitingon's mistress. Orlov was never aware of a specific KGB plot to assassinate Trotsky, or that an assassin had been designated at the time he defected, so he concluded that all these elements had come into place after his defection.

To the credit of the *New York Times*, they did respond to Orlov's letter with an acknowledgement. They advised him that the Moscow correspondent who was responsible for the article was on another assignment and, consequently, they were not in a position to reply directly to his letter. I kept track of the matter but Orlov never received another communication from the *New York Times* in his lifetime. Nor did his attorney Hugo Pollock, even after Orlov's death.

The two separate articles appearing in the *New York Times* and the *Chicago Tribune* were unmistakably similar in context. The *Chicago Tribune* article added that,

The death this week of Rudolf Abel, the Soviet master spy, has prompted reliable Russian sources to give a rare glimpse of the brutality and terror which existed at the top levels of the Soviet Union's espionage apparatus.

Ironically, considering the callous nature of that shadowy world, it is a story of honest human resentment at the shabby treatment of men who, on orders, successfully organised two of Josef Stalin's most ambitious schemes, the murder of Leon Trotsky and the theft of America's atom bomb secrets.

The story emerged because three top ex-spies were not permitted to attend the funeral or cremation of their good friend Abel.

It seems, the sources said bitterly, that the current Kremlin leadership wants to leave elements of the Stalinist past – even, in Communist eyes, the most honourable deeds – to the dust of history.

[When Abel returned to the USSR in 1962, he] reportedly was amazed to find two of his old comrades in arms were being held in a maximum security prison at the ancient city of Vladimir, 110 miles east of Moscow.

He quickly organised twenty-three other top agents, all of whom had been designated 'Hero of the Soviet Union', the nation's highest honour. Together, the sources said, they signed a letter of protest to the Communist Party Central Committee.

The letter pleaded that the two men had risked their lives to ensure a Russian victory in World War II and that they did not deserve to be in prison. But the effort was in vain. The two served out their full prison terms. The appeal never received an official answer.

One of the men involved, who was not invited to Abel's funeral (attendance was by special pass only) is a mysterious figure named Leonid Eitingon.

Now an old man, Eitingon was thought before now to have been shot by Stalin's heirs in 1953 along with Lavrenti Beria, Stalin's hated secret police chief. Sources said, however, that after twelve years in prison, Eitingon is alive and working at the International Book Publishing House in Moscow.

Eitingon's name is not known to have turned up in public since 1957, when a Soviet agent named Alexander Orlov, who had defected and been a top-ranking official in the secret police, testified before a United States Senate Subcommittee.

Orlov said that Eitingon, using the name of Kotov, was a secret police general who had directed Soviet counter-intelligence during the Spanish Civil War. In the late 1930s, Orlov added, Eitingon selected Ramón Mercader del Rio, the son of his mistress in Barcelona, Spain, to carry out the task of assassinating Stalin's archenemy, Leon Trotsky. . . .

Eitingon was close not only to Beria but to Stalin himself. Stalin is said to have once told him: 'Eitingon, if a hair of your head should fall, Stalin is no longer alive.' He was arrested shortly after Stalin died in 1953.

The other man named in the appeal organised by Abel was one named Pavel Sudoplatov, who was chief of espionage under Beria. While serving a fifteen-year prison term he went blind, but he also could not attend Abel's funeral.

The third man noticeably absent was one known today as Kheifetz – probably not his real name. He knew Eitingon and Abel well, sources said.

An intelligence agent since 1922, Kheifetz served as Soviet vice consul in New York and returned to the USSR in 1946. That was four years before he was identified and indicted *in absentia* as 'Anatoli Yakovlev' – the man who masterminded the atom bomb spy ring which consisted of Julius and Ethel Rosenberg, David Greenglass, Harry Gold and Morton Sobel.

The same year the Rosenbergs went on trial, 1950, Kheifetz – Yakovlev – was arrested. The reason is not known. It is known, however, that he was beaten so severely in prison that his spine was broken.

Other than his record, little information is available. There is only a hint from Greville Wynne, the British businessman spy who was imprisoned at Vladimir. After his release in 1964, Wynne wrote that he had seen two of Beria's assistants there.

The *New York Times* went a little further in defining the relationship between Wynne and the two prisoners in Vladimir prison. The article notes that,

There appeared to be corroboration of the imprisonment of the two Beria associates in an account written by Greville Wynne, the British agent, after his release. After an espionage trial in May 1963, Mr Wynne served nearly a year at Vladimir until he was freed in another spy exchange. That one involved the late Gordon Lonsdale, a Soviet agent then held in Britain. Mr Wynne wrote in the *Sunday Telegraph* of London in October 1964 that he had learned that two close associates of Beria were in Vladimir prison.

I was curious to find out exactly what Wynne had said in his article that could identify Beria's two associates as Eitingon and

Sudoplatov. I found Wynne's essay was a five-part series that had appeared in the *Telegraph* from 6 September to 4 October 1964. The Sunday, 27th of September, instalment under the heading, 'My Life in a Soviet Prison', described how Wynne had shared a prison cell at Vladimir during 1963–4 with an American student by the name of Marvin Makinen. The relevant part of the article reflects that, 'I found I was sharing with Makinen the cell in which Gary Powers, the American U-2 pilot, had been kept. On our right side were two elderly Russians, the secretaries of Beria, Stalin's secret police chief. One of them, I was told, had been a lieutenant-general and an ambassador.' None of the instalments carried any reference to Eitingon or Sudoplatov by name, and the description furnished by Wynne of Beria's two associates in the next cell could have fitted an untold number of individuals. It was therefore a long step between what Wynne had actually said in his article and the inference reported by the two US newspapers that the two men were Eitingon and Sudoplatov.

Orlov responded to the *Chicago Tribune* article as he had done to the *New York Times* and expected a retraction of the story, or perhaps an apology for attributing false information about him, or in the least that his letter would be printed. Unlike the *New York Times*, the *Chicago Tribune* did reply to Orlov's letter two months later, on 31 January 1972. In his letter, the Editor, Clayton Kirkpatrick, wrote:

We have examined your letter criticising a news story which appeared in the *Tribune* November 21. We have discussed your letter with individuals involved in writing and editing the story. We have read the transcript of your testimony before the Senate Internal Security Subcommittee.

As a result, we have concluded that this sentence was incorrectly attributed to you: 'In the late 1930s, Orlov added, Eitingon selected Ramón Mercader del Rio, the son of his mistress in Barcelona, Spain, to carry out the task of assassinating Stalin's archenemy, Leon Trotsky.'

Other sources have said that Eitingon, in fact, did make the selection. You have testified that you learned an assassin was selected and that you wrote Trotsky warning him of this. History shows the warning to have been appropriate.

It seems to me that the error in the story is minor and very technical in nature. The space that would be required to set the record straight is out of proportion to the error, in my opinion.

Orlov was outraged by this reply, but he also realised that there was nothing more he could do to remedy the situation. The error printed in the *Tribune* was not 'minor and very technical in nature' but rather one of historical significance. The murder of Leon Trotsky has spawned a vast amount of literature as well as numerous unresolved issues, and to this day there still exists a forum that debates the mysteries of the assassination. Another dark cloud only perpetuates the matter. Orlov was a major player in the Trotsky case and is widely recognised as such, so what he had to say was important. Therefore, it is outrageous that the space required to correct the falsehood in the *Tribune* was considered 'out of proportion to the error'.

Orlov didn't lose his sense of humour over the matter. He smiled when he said that for the small sum of 25 cents, the newspapers in question could have bought the entire transcript of the proceedings before the Senate Internal Security Committee from the Government Printing Office.

What Orlov did not tell either newspaper was the fact that he was certain, or at least as certain as he could be, that the stories concerning the funeral of Colonel Rudolf Abel had been planted by the KGB so as to send an innocuous message to him. The KGB had a long history of resorting to disinformation as a means of securing their objective and the Abel story was no exception.

Orlov related that back in November 1969, when Feoktistov had contacted him in Ann Arbor, he had asked the KGB officer what had happened to his old comrades Lev Mironov and Leonid Eitingon. As already discussed Feoktistov informed Orlov, when he tracked him down in Cleveland, that Mironov had perished in an aeroplane crash at the end of 1959 and that Eitingon was retired on a pension and living comfortably near Moscow. In passing, Feoktistov also mentioned several of the old guard from the KGB Centre, including Pavel Sudoplatov, whom Orlov had only known briefly as a junior KGB officer in the mid-1930s. At the time, Sudoplatov worked in another department at the Centre and Orlov had never had the occasion to work with him.

When Feoktistov had told Orlov that Mironov had not died until 1959, he knew that this was not true as he was still in Spain when Mironov had been put on trial in January 1938, found guilty and executed. As to Eitingon, he had learned in 1955 that his former subordinate had indeed survived the purges but had been executed in late 1953. The wily old General had purposely asked Feoktistov these questions in order to test his veracity, and the KGB officer had fallen headlong into the trap. When Orlov was explaining all this to me, he mentioned an old Russian adage, which seemed applicable to this situation: 'If one tries to hide one's tracks from the truth, one will eventually fall into a pit of lies from where one will never be able to extricate oneself.'

The first solid indication that Eitingon had not met a bad end in the 1930s came to Orlov in the spring of 1955. Up to that point, Orlov was certain that Eitingon, who also happened to be a Jew, was next in line to be summoned to Moscow and executed after his defection in 1938. However, in April 1954, Vladimir Petrov, the KGB legal *rezident* at the Soviet Embassy in Canberra, Australia, defected along with his wife Evdokia. Petrov and his wife remained in Australia under government protection. In the same year, Petrov learned of Orlov through his book, *The Secret History of Stalin's Crimes*, and contacted him through his publisher. The two began to correspond. Petrov was writing a manuscript about his involvement with the KGB and solicited Orlov's help. While going over Petrov's manuscript, Orlov came across some material on Trotsky's assassination which had inadvertently come to Petrov's attention in 1948 during the course of his official duties with the KGB. The information indicated that Eitingon had been the mastermind behind the KGB's plot to assassinate Trotsky in 1940. Petrov had not had a close relationship with Eitingon, although he recalled seeing him occasionally at the KGB Centre in the 1940s, nor did he have any knowledge of what had become of him. Petrov's book was published in 1956 under the title *Empire of Fear*.

The second indication that Eitingon had not perished during the purges came to Orlov's attention later that same year during the September 1955 US Senate Subcommittee Hearings on Internal Security. One of the individuals to testify was Nikolai Khokhlov, a KGB officer who had defected in early 1954. Khokhlov had engaged in guerrilla warfare behind enemy lines during the Second World War and before his defection was the leader of one of the KGB's assassination teams. He had come to know Eitingon quite well during the war when they had served together in partisan warfare. The name of Khokhlov was brought up again during the subsequent Senate Hearings in February 1957, as well as in considerable newspaper publicity, because in 1957 the KGB had attempted to murder him by radioactive poisoning but had failed. According to Khokhlov, his friend Eitingon, who at the time was deputy to Pavel Sudoplatov in the Spetsburo (the KGB assassination department), had been imprisoned by the KGB in early 1950 but through Beria's intervention had been released in April 1953. Beria's KGB Chairmanship was short-lived as he was arrested on 26 June 1953 at a meeting convened by the Praesidium as a result of a power struggle with Khrushchev, then the First Secretary of the Central Committee of the Soviet Communist Party. Beria was tried in December 1953 and executed. Having lost the protective cover of their mentor Beria, Sudoplatov and Eitingon were both arrested in the autumn of 1953 and then disappeared, believed to have been executed according to reliable KGB defectors of that era.

What surprised me was Orlov's statement that the articles in the *New York Times* and the *Chicago Tribune* had been a direct result of Feoktistov's contact with him on 10 August 1971. The articles had been 'planted' by the KGB in order to allay his suspicions regarding Eitingon's death by clearly indicating that Eitingon was very much alive. In his view, the KGB's motive for planting the articles was its hope that he could still be enticed back to the Soviet Union. Orlov maintained that the KGB's duplicity only strengthened his resolve never to return to the Soviet Union under any circumstances.

I saw no apparent connection between the two events – Feoktistov's contact and the newspaper articles – and only acquiesced with a slight degree of amazement on my face, which Orlov readily took note of. I knew him well enough to know that he would not have made such a damaging assessment without being able to prove his position. I also knew that I had only to wait for him to explain. Knowing that he had captured my attention, he began to take me step by step through the somewhat complicated process from the standpoint of his experience with the KGB.

During Feoktistov's contact on 10 August, he had furnished information about Mironov and Eitingon which Orlov believed to be untrue. The motive for this deception was to have one or both of the Orlovs return to the Soviet Union, where they would undoubtedly have been put under the control of the KGB. If Orlov thought that his close friend was well, he would have no fear of returning to the Soviet Union. Whether Feoktistov had made the statement on his own initiative, or whether it had been dictated by the KGB Centre in Moscow, Orlov had no way of knowing, but what was clear to the KGB was that the tactic did not work. As their plan had backfired, the KGB now had to convince Orlov that Eitingon was still alive; otherwise, its cause was dead. It did not have long to wait to put forth its next stratagem. A little over two months later, the KGB's golden opportunity appeared on the horizon in the form of Colonel Abel's death.

On 15 November 1971, Moscow announced Abel's death. In a strange twist that had nothing to do with Orlov's scenario, Maria Orlov died exactly one day after the Moscow announcement was made.

Colonel Abel had been a KGB officer since the mid-1920s and his most important assignment came about in 1948, when he entered the United States under false documentation. The name he adopted was that of an actual person, Andrew Kayotis, who had obtained US citizenship and had later returned to Lithuania, his place of birth, where he had died. Less than two years later, after having travelled extensively around the US to become familiar with its way of life, Abel took on yet another false identity. He now became Emil Robert Goldfus, the name of a deceased individual who had been born in New York City of foreign parentage. The practice of building a legend around the documents of deceased persons was not new to the KGB as it had perfected the technique over many years.

Abel's downfall came about in a rather innocuous manner. In 1952, a KGB officer by the name of Reino Hayhanen was selected by the KGB Centre to go to the United States to assist Abel in his spying work. Since 1948, Hayhanen had been in Finland, where he was building up his legend under the name of Eugene Nicholai Maki. The real Maki had been born in the US but his family had returned to Finland at the end of the 1920s, after which all traces of them were lost. Armed with a photocopy of Maki's US birth certificate, Hayhanen was able to procure a US passport and entered the States on 20 October 1952. Hayhanen was everything that Colonel Abel was not; he was irresponsible, undependable, incompetent and, worst of all, indiscreet. He soon turned to alcohol to the point where he was unable to carry out his KGB responsibilities. These crucial defects did not go unnoticed by Abel and, as a result, Hayhanen was recalled to Moscow under the pretence that he was being promoted to the rank of lieutenant-colonel. Hayhanen might have been an alcoholic but he was not stupid. En route to Moscow he stopped off in Paris, where in April 1957 he defected at the American Embassy. He was returned to the United States and co-operated with the federal authorities.

Abel had breached one of the cardinal rules of being a spy: never let anyone know where you reside or work, not even your fellow KGB agents. Hayhanen had been given $3,000 by the KGB to set up a cover business in New York, but had squandered the money on his own passions; therefore, when the time came for him to set up a photo shop, he did not have the money to pay for the equipment. In March 1955, Hayhanen leased a shop in Newark, New Jersey, and had to turn to Abel for help. Abel had assumed the cover of an artist and maintained a studio at the Ovington Building on Fulton Street in Brooklyn Heights. Abel took Hayhanen to his studio and gave him some of his equipment and supplies.

Although more than two years had elapsed, Hayhanen still remembered the location of Abel's studio. FBI surveillance was placed on Abel, which eventually took them to the Hotel Latham in New York, where Abel was living and where he was arrested on 21 June 1957. He was indicted by a Federal Grand Jury on 7 August and brought to trial on 14 October. He was convicted on 25 October on three interrelated espionage charges and sentenced on 15 November to thirty years' imprisonment on the most serious count.

I never had any direct involvement with the Abel case but even today I can recall two related incidents. About 1955, I attended one of my first espionage in-service training courses in Washington DC. Our class was introduced to a very clever 'concealment device', which was a hollowed-out nickel that contained a microfilm of a coded message. The nickel had been given to a young newspaper carrier in Brooklyn, New York, in 1953 as part payment for the subscriber's weekly newspaper bill. The boy happened to drop the nickel and it split into two, thus revealing the secret message. The young boy handed it in to the police, who in turn gave it to the FBI. I was really amazed at the cleverness of this device and never forgot the circumstances. The hollowed-out nickel remained at the FBI laboratory for years without the FBI managing to break the code. When Hayhanen defected in 1957, he provided the key that decoded the secret message. Coincidentally, it had been through his carelessness that the nickel had been lost in the first place.

The nickel became an important piece of evidence in the chain of Soviet espionage.

The second matter relates to a minor detail that aided in the investigation and eventually the conviction of Abel. A year or so after Abel's conviction, I was again in Washington and had the good fortune to meet a number of FBI agents from the New York office who had worked on the Abel case. During the Bureau's surveillance of Abel, it was of paramount importance that they find his place of residence as there was little doubt that he would have hidden his espionage paraphernalia at home, and the link was needed to convict him on the Espionage Statute. The surveillance always started at Abel's studio in the Ovington Building and it was from there that the hard part would begin. Caution was the keyword in any surveillance and never more so than in an espionage case. Abel was extremely clever and no tenderfoot when it came to surveillance techniques. He always took the routine precautions that would disable a surveillance, even in those instances when he was unaware that he was the target of one. The Bureau's policy was to drop the surveillance rather than to take a chance on compromising it, especially in this particular case when they could always resort to a known starting-point. Also, in this case the FBI had a definite ally on their side in the name of Colonel Rudolf Abel. Abel was a bald-headed man, who consistently wore a dark-coloured straw hat with a sharply contrasting white hatband either to conceal his baldness or his vanity. This straw hat served as a beacon to those agents following him and eventually led them to his residence and the evidence needed to convict him. This was probably the first time in history that a conspicuous straw hat had helped to break a major espionage case.

The Abel story would probably end at this point were it not for a sad episode that occurred during the bleak days of the Cold War. On 1 May 1960, Francis Gary Powers, a pilot employed by the CIA, was flying his U-2 aircraft on a spy mission over the industrial town of Sverdlovsk, deep in the heart of the Soviet Union, when it was hit by a missile. Powers survived the crash but was convicted on espionage charges and sentenced to an eighteen-year term in prison.

The U-2 incident proved to be an international embarrassment to the US and a propaganda coup for the Soviets. Before the dust from Powers's trial had settled, there was talk of a 'spy swap' between him and Abel. In less than two years after Powers's conviction and almost four and a half years after Abel's, negotiations for the exchange had been completed.

The famous Glienicker Brucke of spy novels and fact was chosen as the site for yet another exchange of spies. The bridge, which spans the Wannsee lake, sits on the extreme south-west quadrant of the then divided city of Berlin on the road to Potsdam. On an ordinary day in February 1962, Powers walked to the West and Able to the East; as they both neared the midpoint of the bridge on their respective roads to freedom, neither man bothered to look at the other when their paths met.

The remaining character in this saga was Reino Hayhanen. To some he was a traitor to his cause, to others a hero. Hayhanen disappeared from the public's view under mysterious circumstances during the later part of 1962. Unsubstantiated reports surfaced that he had been killed in a car accident on the Pennsylvania Turnpike. Others believed that his alcoholism had finally taken him, while there were those who thought that he had started a new life under yet another legend. Perhaps the most widely accepted theory was that he had been assassinated by the KGB in retribution for his defection and betrayal of Colonel Abel. In the absence of any concrete evidence to the contrary and although I have no solid proof to substantiate my position, I personally subscribe to the latter conjecture.

When Abel was indicted in August 1957, there was an immense amount of publicity concerning him and Orlov recognised his photograph as a KGB officer he had known briefly at the KGB Centre. He immediately made this information known to the proper federal authorities. However, in *Deadly Illusions*, the authors assert that Orlov took advantage of Abel's arrest by confirming that he was a Soviet agent, thus reinforcing Orlov's bona fides as a true defector. This is simply nonsense as there was never any information to indicate that Orlov was not what he represented himself to be by his deeds or his actions.

Up to this point, Orlov had not resolved to my complete satisfaction the basis for his assessment that the stories appearing in the *New York Times* and the *Chicago Tribune* had been planted by the KGB as a consequence of the KGB contacts with him in Ann Arbor and Cleveland.

Orlov pointed out that it was apparent that both newspapers had relied on the same source for their information as the content and thrust of each article was practically the same. The announcement of Abel's death had only been used as the medium by which to introduce the real intention of the articles: to purport that Eitingon was still alive. Someone at the KGB Centre had seized upon the opportunity to use Abel's death in this fashion but, because they had had to act quickly, they had not been able to think through their plan thoroughly.

The idea that Abel had been so amazed to find two of his old KGB comrades in arms, Leonid Eitingon and Pavel Sudoplatov, being held in Vladimir prison that he had organised twenty-three other top agents, who all happened to be 'Heroes of the Soviet Union', into signing a letter of protest to the Communist Party Central Committee was incredible at best. Orlov related that it was no secret in the KGB that such a foolish gesture would only mean forfeiture of one's pension and continued eligibility for housing, not to mention the fact that a strong protest could even result in a long stint in Siberia under very unfavourable conditions. After all, this was still in the midst of the Cold War and such a penalty was not uncommon. The fact that the appeal never received an official response only indicated to Orlov that the appeal had never existed. He explained that the Central Committee was required to publish its decisions and policies in the official organ of the Communist Party. In the absence of any such publication regarding the alleged appeal, the KGB had nowhere to point to for an affirmation and so had resorted to the spineless answer that the appeal had never received a reply.

Orlov pointed to the case of Alexander Solzhenitsyn, who, when he had dared to criticise Stalin openly in 1945, had been sent to the gulag in Siberia for eight years. Therefore, how could Abel have organised twenty-three former KGB officers to sign a letter of protest when they were aware of the probability of being harshly punished for such an act?

Orlov recalled that although he had specifically asked Feoktistov about Eitingon, Sudoplatov's name had only come up in conjunction with a number of other old KGB comrades who were mentioned in passing by Feoktistov. Orlov never mentioned the name of Anatoli Yakovlev to him. Yakovlev is described in the *Chicago Tribune* article as the third man noticeably absent from Abel's funeral and goes on to describe him as the intelligence agent who served as a Soviet vice consul in New York and was the mastermind behind the atom bomb spy ring. Orlov suspected that Yakovlev was only mentioned in the article as 'window dressing' in an attempt to divert his attention from any possible suspicion that he may have harboured that the KGB was the source behind the articles.

Orlov also informed me of one piece of evidence which, more than anything else, clearly pointed to the KGB's involvement: for the first time ever, his name was mentioned by sources in Moscow. Since his defection, he had closely monitored European and US newspapers, which had correspondents in Moscow, and had never found any reference to himself. He explained that for all intents and purposes the KGB considered all defectors as nonentities and, therefore, among the dead. The last thing they would ever admit to was that someone had defected from their service unless, of course, the admission served their purpose. He was convinced that the real purpose of the articles was to convey to him that Eitingon was still alive and to confirm that Feoktistov was telling the truth.

I never doubted that Eitingon and Sudoplatov had perished after Beria's fall in 1953. However, in 1994 Sudoplatov's memoirs were published under the title *Special Tasks*. By that time Sudoplatov was an old man – he had been born in 1907 – and was in ill health. He claimed that he and Eitingon had been prisoners at Vladimir and that Eitingon had died in 1981. Sudoplatov briefly mentions that they had known 'that Gary Powers and Greville Wynne were in an adjacent cellblock, but we never saw them'.

I now had to give credit to Feoktistov for being shrewder in one respect than I had originally perceived him to be. As noted, Orlov had been very sceptical of Feoktistov's information but had tried hard not to convey this scepticism to the KGB officer. However, it is now apparent that Feoktistov had detected Orlov's suspicion and realised that, before they could make any progress with him, they would have to overcome this suspicion. Nothing in Orlov's reasoning at the time changed with respect to his belief that the newspaper articles were disinformation planted by the KGB, other than Sudoplatov and Eitingon being alive at the time.

There was no doubt whatsoever in Orlov's mind that the KGB was laying the groundwork for another contact to entice him back to the Soviet Union, more so now because he was probably perceived as being more susceptible to such an advance without his protective wife standing in the way. I fully expected the KGB to make another call on him and realised more than ever that I would have to maintain close contact with the General.

PART 5

FURTHER DEBRIEFINGS AND MYSTERIES

TWENTY-FOUR

STALIN'S 'HORRIBLE SECRET'

In the summer of 1972, I became privy to a historical secret that had only been alluded to in Orlov's 1953 book, *The Secret History of Stalin's Crimes*. In his book, Orlov had taken up the matter of the trial of Red Army Marshal Mikhail Tukhachevsky and seven Soviet generals on 11 June 1937 and the official announcement the following day that the eight traitors had been put to death. The punishment for their alleged spying for a foreign government and conspiring to plot a war against the Soviet Union was swift and shocked the civilised world.

What followed made the first two purge trials fade in comparison. The first trials eliminated the old-line leaders of the Bolshevik Revolution and the founding fathers of the Soviet Union, who had adhered to the policies of Lenin that disavowed Stalin. The rationale for these trials was clear: Stalin was eliminating old enemies from the leadership of the Communist Party who could pose a threat to his dictatorship. What no one could understand was the logic behind the next great purge of the Soviet military.

Following the Tukhachevsky trial, the wave of executions of the officer corps of the military was like a wind blowing over a huge field of wheat; no one escaped. Any officer, no matter how remotely connected to Tukhachevsky and the seven deposed generals in the past or present, was rounded up and executed. In turn, the military subordinates of the newly executed commanders became the next group of candidates for elimination and so on, like a never-ending web of destruction. Even the top echelon of Soviet marshals and generals, who had signed the verdict for the actually non-existent trial of Tukhachevsky and the other generals, disappeared one by one, never to be heard of again. By the end of the reign of terror, the officer corps of the Soviet Army had been decimated beyond recognition.

What could not be understood was why Stalin had purged his own military machine of its leadership, the only thing that stood between the Soviet Government and its foreign enemies, especially in light of the fact that the Red Army was devoid of politics and posed no threat to his dictatorship. The ever-growing menace of Adolf Hitler could not be ignored as the prime threat to the Soviet Union and this was not the time to weaken the Red Army. Stalin himself had appointed the most able commanders of the Red Army and was now annihilating them. Rumours began to spread that the man in the Kremlin had gone mad under the strain of the previous purge trials.

Now it was Orlov's turn to tell me that Stalin was not insane and knew exactly what he was doing when he purged the Red Army officer corps. He then referred me to a passage in his book in which he declared that 'when all the facts of the Tukhachevsky affair are disclosed, the world will realise that Stalin knew what he was doing'. It went on to say that the case of Tukhachevsky was of less historical significance than the first two purge trials but was destined to occupy a place in history beyond what it deserved because of Stalin's involvement. In this light Orlov wrote in 1953, 'I am making this assertion because I know from an absolutely unimpeachable and authoritative source that the case of Marshal Tukhachevsky was tied up with one of Stalin's most horrible secrets which, when disclosed, will throw light on many things that seemed so incomprehensible in Stalin's behaviour.'

Nineteen years after he made that assertion in his book, Orlov was about to disclose this 'horrible secret' to me. I could hardly wait.

Orlov's story went back to January 1937, while he was assigned to Spain as the Soviet's Advisor to the Spanish Republican Government. However, to better understand Orlov's relationship with Stalin, a few observations must be made. Over a period of time, it had become apparent to me that Orlov was never a close personal friend or confidant of the Soviet dictator and that in time he had actually come to despise the man. In fact, he had said that 'Stalin was personally offensive and easy to dislike.' Their association was more of a professional relationship in the context of conferences rather than one-on-one encounters.

Orlov first became casually acquainted with Stalin in the early 1920s, when he was an Assistant Prosecutor in the Collegium of Appeals of the Soviet Supreme Court. Stalin was then the General Secretary of the Soviet Communist Party and showed more than a casual interest in Orlov's efforts to draw up the new criminal code of the Soviet Union. In those days, Stalin was referred to as the '*Gensek*', which means the General Secretary. The officers of the KGB usually referred to Stalin as 'The Boss' or 'The Big Boss'. It was not until the early 1930s, when Orlov was a chief in the Foreign Department at the KGB Centre in Moscow, that he came to know the Big Boss on a more intimate basis.

The KGB, or more plainly the secret police, was the apparatus by which Stalin controlled the Government as well as foreign affairs. Orlov's realm was with the KGB's Foreign Department rather than domestic intelligence, but it was one in which the dictator took a particular interest and consequently they would meet frequently. From 1931, when he was first assigned to the KGB's Foreign Department, until he left for Spain in September 1936, Orlov often had conferences with Stalin. By the beginning of 1936, with the world on the brink of another war, it was Orlov's responsibility to brief Stalin personally on a weekly basis on issues regarding foreign espionage and KGB intelligence operations as well as to provide the dictator with an overview of political conditions throughout the world. Assessing world political conditions was really the province of the Foreign Office but, for some reason, Stalin felt that the KGB was better suited to handle the responsibility. Orlov felt reasonably certain that these weekly meetings with the Big Boss led to his appointment in Spain.

On those occasions when Orlov personally had to present a KGB plan for a new high-level operation that required the dictator's approval, or make a progress report on a KGB operation already in place, he would usually be accompanied to the Kremlin by either the KGB Chairman or the Chief of the KGB Foreign Department, but more often than not by both parties. Stalin would always listen intently while smoking his pipe and occasionally nod his approval or disapproval. After Orlov finished his presentation, the dictator would either shake his head in agreement or frequently go into a rage if it did not suit his views. Stalin was always decisive in his views and any rebuttal only incurred his wrath, so Orlov learned to live with the situation and conform to the whims of the dictator. Stalin was neither warm nor friendly during these encounters and Orlov dreaded meeting him.

I asked Orlov for his personal assessment of the dictator, which he readily offered. He started by noting that by birth Stalin was a native of the Russian region of Georgia and that his real name was Josef Djugashvili. During his lifetime he used numerous aliases, including the name Koba, which he adopted while in the underground movement against the Tsar, but eventually settled on the name Stalin, which he apparently favoured because it referred to him as a man of steel. Rather than a man of steel, the dictator was a rather ordinary and insignificant person, who did not stand out in a crowd. He was short, perhaps no taller than 5 feet 5 inches, although in official Soviet state paintings he always appeared to be quite tall and imposing. The world was well acquainted with Stalin's face and his abundant amount of hair, bushy moustache and eyebrows, but not as well known was Stalin's deeply pockmarked face caused by a childhood disease. This abnormality, as well as a shrivelled arm that was slightly shorter than the other, was kept from public view as much as possible. He was not only a dark-complexioned man but possessed a dark and sinister personality not generally known to the Russian people, who idolised the man. Often at their meetings Stalin would use vulgar and profane language and resort to telling sexually oriented jokes, or make sexual references to otherwise well-respected persons. In these instances, it was wise to join in the laughter at his remarks or run the risk of alienating him. Most times during a personal briefing Orlov would sit at a desk directly across from the dictator and at these times it was apparent that Stalin had extremely bad breath. In time, Orlov learned that the cause of his bad breath was decaying teeth, which was apparently why he would normally nod an affirmative or negative reply rather than open his mouth with a vocal response. Orlov admitted that when he first became acquainted with Stalin in the 1920s, he had actually admired the man and felt that he had something good to offer the Russian people. However, as time went by his views changed to the diametrically opposite position and he then described Stalin as a conniver and manipulator to achieve his ends; a falsifier of historical facts to make himself look good in the eyes of the Russian people; a vindictive man against anyone who stood in his path; a born tyrant, who needlessly took the lives of an untold number of his subjects; and, worst of all, a megalomaniac of the highest order.

Orlov clearly remembered the day in Valencia when events occurred which would eventually lead to his learning Stalin's 'horrible secret'. It was shortly after his deputy Colonel Kotov had made his infamous and fraudulent commando raid on the Republican fort on Montjuich (see pages 62–5) that he began to receive reports of a build-up of Nationalist forces along the front just south of Madrid and north of Toledo. The area between the towns of Arganda and Aranjuez was especially critical and all intelligence indicated that the next Nationalist offensive would be in this particular region. Orlov decided that he would make a personal inspection and departed for the front on 11 January 1937.

Orlov recalled that the early January morning was relatively warm and he had thought of how harsh the winter would be in Moscow at this time of the year. Passing through the vast orange groves west of Valencia, he couldn't help but wonder what people in the Soviet Union would think about the warm climate and oranges practically growing in the back yards. Driving through the great plain with views of mountains in the background reminded Orlov that he was indeed fortunate to have received the assignment to Spain. Unfortunately, the tranquillity of the journey did not last as they finally reached the front. Driving along an unpaved country road leading to the sector that would be the front line, Orlov realised that something was wrong when the car suddenly lurched off the road, down a steep incline, and came to a sharp stop. He later learned that his chauffeur had fallen asleep at the wheel.

Suddenly, from out of nowhere Spanish Republican soldiers appeared and within minutes a military ambulance came on the scene. Orlov instructed the chauffeur, who was not injured in the accident, to remain with the damaged car while he was taken to a nearby army field hospital. There it was determined that he had injured his back and that nothing more could be done for him, so he was transported by ambulance to a hospital in Valencia. At the hospital Orlov was diagnosed with two broken vertebrae. As Orlov was suffering excruciating pain and the condition did not seem to improve, the Soviet Embassy in Valencia consulted with the Soviet Embassy in Paris and it was decided that he would receive better treatment at the clinic of the well-known surgeon, Professor Bergère, in Paris.

Orlov was taken by ambulance to Paris on Sunday, 17 January, with an overnight stop at the Grand Hotel in Perpignan. He then spent over a month in the Bergère Clinic lying flat on his back. The treatment was successful and he was released from the clinic on 21 February; he was able to return home to Betera the following day.

Orlov recalled that the month he spent at the Bergère Clinic was one of the most boring in his life, with the exception of the day he learned of Stalin's secret life. The Soviet Embassy in Paris would bring the daily communications from Moscow and Spain and twice a day he would dictate replies to his secretary. He kept in touch with his staff in Valencia by telephone. His wife and daughter resided nearby in a small hotel and spent the days entertaining the sick patient as best they could. His only other regular visitor was Nikolai Smirnov, the chief of the KGB legal *rezidentura* at the Soviet Embassy in Paris. Most of the time, when he was not engaged in conducting official business or enjoying the company of his wife and daughter, he would think of the terrible events that were taking place in the Soviet Union. Much of the information that was being funnelled to him was from two of his old KGB comrades, Lev Mironov and Boris Berman. Both men were KGB Chiefs who had been forced by Stalin to become his accomplices in falsifying evidence used in the purge trials. As a consequence, both men were broken in spirit, a condition Orlov was determined would not happen to him.

As already described on page 157, towards the end of his stay at the Bergère Clinic Orlov received a surprise visit from Abram Slutsky, Chief of the KGB's Foreign Department. Slutsky had been in Czechoslovakia on a high-level mission when he decided to make an inspection trip to Spain. He was already aware of Orlov's confinement in Paris and had stopped off to visit him. It was during this visit that Orlov first learned of the existence of the AST, which had been set up to track down and assassinate Stalin's enemies who had fled the Soviet Union. Slutsky's deputy, Mikhail Shpiegelglass, was handling the new operation and its special Mobile Groups. At the time, Orlov had no reason to believe that within a short period he and his family would be one of the 'special secret assignment' targets of the Mobile Groups.

Orlov telephoned his deputy Kotov in Valencia and informed him that Slutsky was on his way to the KGB office there and should be extended every courtesy. When Slutsky returned to Paris after spending a few days in Spain, he again visited Orlov, who was preparing to leave the clinic. Slutsky was thrilled with the trip to Spain and spoke highly of the guerrilla warfare training camp at Benimamet, which he had inspected, and of the journey with Kotov to visit the front near Madrid. He claimed that he had come within inches of being hit by shrapnel at the front and couldn't wait to tell the fellows back at the KGB Centre about his 'war experiences'.

As they parted company that day in Orlov's room at the Bergère Clinic, Orlov did not know that this would be the last time he would ever see Slutsky. They had become close friends during their many years of professional association to the point that they could safely share confidences. After Orlov returned to Spain, he and Slutsky continued to maintain both official and personal communication. On 17 February 1938, almost exactly a year to the day after they had last met in Paris, Slutsky died at the KGB Centre under mysterious conditions, although it was strongly believed that he had been murdered at the hands of Chairman Yezhov (see page 167).

On the afternoon of 15 or 16 February 1937, Orlov received a telephone call at his bedside from Nikolai Smirnov, who was calling from the Soviet Embassy. Smirnov sounded exceedingly jubilant and announced that he had the surprise of a lifetime for Orlov. Another voice then came over the phone which Orlov immediately recognised as that of his dearly loved cousin Zinovy Borisovich Katsnelson. Zinovy informed Orlov that he was at the Soviet Embassy in Paris on business when he had learned of his convalescence in Paris. He advised Orlov that he was coming right over to the clinic.

When Orlov put down the telephone, his thoughts turned to the happier days of his youth. His cousin Zinovy was not just another relative, but a close childhood friend. Through the years their affection for each other had only grown stronger and they had never lost contact with one another. Zinovy had rapidly moved up the career ladder and by 1937 was a member of the Central Committee of the Communist Party of the Ukraine and Acting Chief of the KGB in the Ukraine. He had enjoyed an early friendship of sorts with Stalin in the 1920s and courted among his friends the most influential figures in the Soviet Union, including Politburo member Stanislav Kossior.

Zinovy and Smirnov arrived at the clinic and what followed was a joyous occasion that dwelt mostly on old times in Russia. Zinovy related that he had just been transferred back to the KGB Centre in Moscow on the orders of the newly installed KGB Chairman, Nikolai Yezhov, and explained that he was in Paris on an assignment for Yezhov to contact two important Soviet agents. One of them was a Ukrainian émigré and former general in the Tsar's army. The Soviet agent had recently been in contact with

Alfred Rosenberg in Berlin, where they had discussed a plan to organise a training school in Germany for young Ukrainian refugees to become officers in the German Army. Rosenberg was Hitler's Foreign Policy Advisor and held a position of power in the Nazi Government. Zinovy felt that Rosenberg was already laying the groundwork for Germany to seize the Ukraine in the eventual war that Germany was planning against the Soviet Union.

The conversation turned to lighter matters and then to a point where they seemed to have run out of topics to discuss. Orlov knew Zinovy well enough to know that he was becoming impatient and annoyed by Smirnov's continued presence. Finally, Smirnov announced that he had work to do at the office and departed.

As soon as Smirnov left, Zinovy dropped the pretence of being light-hearted, which he had displayed in front of Smirnov, and suddenly took on a serious demeanour. He informed Orlov that when he had arrived in Paris, he had been unaware of Orlov's presence in the city and had planned on going to Spain to discuss an important matter with him. Fortunately, he had learned of Orlov's stay in the clinic.

Zinovy's next statement startled Orlov: 'It's unfortunate that Smirnov knows that we have met.' Normally, there would have been no problem about two cousins meeting and certainly no reason to conceal such an inconsequential event. Zinovy then went on to tell a story that made Orlov realise that he was hearing about an event of immense magnitude, which could only have been placed into his confidence by a trust and mutual respect that had developed between two cousins during a lifelong relationship. The story Zinovy told him that day unfolded in the following manner.

During the period when Stalin was making preparations for the first of the purge trials with the then KGB Chairman Genrikh Yagoda, he suggested that it would be to their advantage to show a relationship between the Bolsheviks being put on trial and the Okhrana, the Tsar's secret police before the Revolution. What Stalin had in mind was for the KGB to find a way to prove that those to be liquidated had been agents of the Tsar's secret police. Of course, Stalin's suggestion was regarded as an order by Yagoda.

Yagoda was no fool and understood that what Stalin wanted was fabricated proof. This would be no problem as by this time the KGB had become quite adept at forging documents to the point where it was a routine matter. However, in this particular case the documents would have to be placed into evidence at the trial and, accordingly, would be held to the highest degree of scrutiny. Yagoda felt that this would present a certain amount of risk at a public trial, where the false evidence would be on display to the world and possibly recognised for what it was, an attempt to supplement the truth with a falsehood. In this event, public opinion would backfire against the Soviets.

Yagoda finally settled on a much safer method, which would bring about the same results. He decided to locate a former officer of the Okhrana who had somehow survived the Revolution and have him testify against the defendants by exposing them as *agents provocateurs* of the Tsar. He would then use every means available to extract a confession from the defendants in order that the testimonies of both the witness and the defendants were identical during the course of the trial. This would provide shocking proof that the old Bolsheviks on trial had been spies for the Okhrana, the most despicable of crimes in the minds of the Russian people.

Yagoda's plan to find a living Okhrana officer proved easier on paper than in practice. By the 1930s, most of the Tsarist secret police officers had already been located and murdered during the hectic years of the Revolution, and those that had escaped the dragnet had fled abroad to safety. Some had even resorted to new identities by acquiring false documents and starting new lives in the outreaches of the Soviet empire, where it would be difficult to ferret them out. It was on this latter group that Yagoda focused his attention. He decided that the old Okhrana personnel records should be thoroughly examined and that relatives of Okhrana officers believed to have taken on new identities would be contacted to learn their current identity and whereabouts.

Yagoda knew of one KGB officer capable of handling the assignment with the tenacity required to complete the task. That man was Stein, the Assistant Chief of the Political Department of the KGB, who was responsible for the interrogations and technical aspects of the purge trials. Stein was released from his duties and given the full-time assignment of reviewing the old Okhrana files. This was not an easy task as the Okhrana files were scattered throughout the Soviet Union in the cities where the Okhrana had operated under the Tsar. However, a majority of the files were in the old capital of Russia, St Petersburg, which by now was called Leningrad. Another large mass of files was located in the office formerly occupied by the late KGB Chairman Vyacheslav Menzhinsky. These files were brought stack by stack to Stein's office, where he painstakingly reviewed each one for a clue that would lead to that elusive former Okhrana officer who would be the key in the forthcoming trials of the old Bolsheviks.

Days turned into weeks as Stein continued with his tedious task without finding what he was looking for. Finally, he came upon a file that quickly grasped his attention. The file was not an ordinary personnel file but one that belonged to Vissarionov, the Deputy Director of the Okhrana, in which he kept his personal work-related papers. This was the type of file in which documents were kept that were not intended to be seen by others in his department. Going through the file, Stein came upon a personnel questionnaire with a small photograph of Josef Stalin as a young man attached to the front. His first reaction was that he had discovered an artefact from the past when Stalin had been in the underground of the Bolshevik movement and an enemy of the Tsarist Government. He could hardly contain himself, and his first thought was to take the file immediately to Yagoda and show him how the historical document highlighted Stalin's achievements in the Revolution, which would no doubt put him in good favour with the KGB Chief.

By a stroke of good fortune, Stein decided to give the file his further attention; perhaps before taking it to Yagoda, he would find more evidence of historical value that would benefit Stalin's reputation. As he read through each page of the Stalin document, his felicity soon turned to pure horror. The file did in fact concern Stalin, but not as one of the great leaders of the Revolution; instead, it described Stalin's work as *agent provocateur* for the Tsar's secret police. The file contained reports and notes to Vissarionov in Stalin's handwriting, which was so familiar to Stein. In addition, the file contained documents regarding another high-ranking official of the Bolshevik Party, who, like Stalin, was also an informant of the Tsar's secret police and under the control of Vissarionov.

The problem for Stein was what action should he take with this newly discovered revelation about Stalin. He kept the file for days considering his options without seeing a clear-cut way out of his dilemma. His conscience told him to take the file to Yagoda and forget what he had seen, but he realised that the implications were far-reaching and well out of the scope of his ability to take advantage of the information. He finally decided to share his find with V. Balitsky, a close and trusted friend. Balitsky was Stein's former superior in the KGB and the current Chief of the KGB in the Ukraine. In addition, he was an influential member of the Politburo of the Communist Party of the Ukraine and a member of the Central Committee of the Communist Party of the Soviet Union.

Balitsky was well known and respected in both the Communist Party in Moscow and in the Ukraine and was considered a man moving up the political ladder. He had good connections with the Politburo in Moscow and, when KGB Chairman Menzhinsky died, his friends in the Politburo pushed for his appointment as Menzhinsky's successor. Stalin rejected the nomination, fearing that Balitsky had too many connections in the Politburo and that, if in a very powerful position in the KGB, he might someday turn on him and side with his friends in the Politburo in a power play for the dictatorship. In the end, Stalin chose Yagoda to become the new KGB Chairman based primarily on the fact that Yagoda was intensely disliked in the Politburo and was therefore less likely to join forces with the Politburo to overthrow him.

Stein flew to Kiev, the capital of the Ukraine, and presented the file to Balitsky. His reaction on making a cursory review of the file was total amazement. He immediately summoned his Chief Deputy, Zinovy Katsnelson, to share the information. They both went over every document in the file and came to the same conclusion that Stein had reached days before, that they had a 'hot potato' on their hands. Stein was now out of the picture and was considerably relieved when he boarded the return flight to Moscow.

In the coming days, the Stalin file was scrutinised by Balitsky and Katsnelson not only as to its contents, which without doubt were extremely damaging to Stalin, but more importantly as to the question of its legitimacy. Both KGB men were experienced in the way that documents could be forged, but on the face of it the Stalin documents appeared genuine. However, this was insufficient evidence for making a final judgement on their authenticity. Handwriting analysis was made with readily available samples of Stalin's known handwriting, along with chemical testing to establish the age of the reports' paper and ink. The findings were conclusive: Stalin was the author of the reports found in the Okhrana file and the reports were authenticated as being from the period in question. Stalin had therefore been an informant for the Tsar's secret police from 1912 to early 1913, with references in some of the documents to indicate his relationship with the secret police prior to 1912.

A number of Stalin's reports in 1912 were on the Russian Imperial Parliament, known as the Duma. The Duma had consisted of numerous political factions, one of which was the Bolsheviks with six deputies headed by Roman Malinovsky. Following the first revolution, more commonly known as the February Revolution, the archives of the Okhrana were opened and revealed that Malinovsky had been an Okhrana informant. He had betrayed his Party and his Bolshevik comrades on a colossal scale and he was shot for treason to the Party in 1918.

During the time Lenin was banned from Russia, he had directed the activities of the Bolshevik Party from abroad through

Malinovsky. Lenin highly regarded Malinovsky and trusted him completely, even when the Mensheviks, the minority political faction that often opposed the Bolsheviks, claimed that Malinovsky was a secret agent of the Tsar. Lenin had staunchly defended his protégé and representative in the Motherland. In the Duma, Malinovsky had been considered a gifted orator, who, with intense passion, denounced the Tsar and the regime as well as everything they had accomplished. Often speeches written by Lenin would be smuggled into Russia and given before the Duma by Malinovsky. In Lenin's absence abroad, Malinovksy was the reputed leader of the Party with the power to make appointments to the Central Committee of the Party. In this capacity, he had appointed Stalin to the Central Committee in 1912. At the time, Stalin was living in St Petersburg and often acted as the channel of communication between Lenin and Malinovsky.

Like Lenin, the Tsar's secret police also valued the services of their informant Malinovsky. Through him, they knew every move made by the Bolshevik Party and, in some cases, were able to influence the Party's policies. For his services to the secret police, Malinovsky was paid 700 roubles a month and given a generous expense account, occasionally with a bonus for exceptional work. However, the secret police did fear that some day the Russian people and the Tsar might learn that the man making the scathing attacks on the floor of the Duma against the Tsar and the Government was actually an informant of the secret police and doing so with their approval.

Stalin's reports to Vissarionov in the file clearly indicated that he was aware that Malinovsky was in the employ of the secret police. However, there was nothing in the file to indicate that Malinovsky was aware that Stalin was a fellow traveller.

One of Stalin's critical reports concerned a meeting that had been convened in the first part of January 1913 at Lenin's apartment in the Polish city of Cracow, then a part of the Habsburg Empire. The meeting was so sensitive that extraordinary precautions were taken to mislead the secret police by referring to it in all communications as the 'February Conference'. The incongruity of the situation was the fact that both of the secret police's informants, Stalin and Malinovsky, attended the meeting.

Also in attendance were Lenin's wife Nadezhda Krupskaya; leading Party members Grigory Zinoviev, Lev Kamenev and Troyanovsky, the future Ambassador to the United States; representatives from the various Russian districts and four of the six Bolshevik Duma members, including Malinovsky. Stalin's report on the meeting to the secret police was quite extensive and detailed all those in attendance as to the extent of their participation, conflicts of views between participants and what conclusions were finally reached.

A review of the documents in the file indicated that Stalin had been disturbed and resentful of the power that Malinovsky held in the Bolshevik Party and openly criticised Malinovsky's influence with the secret police. He felt that he should be the principal police informant and pointed out in writing that Malinovsky's dual role could prove an embarrassment to the secret police if he were uncovered. As expected, the secret police did nothing.

Shortly after the Cracow conference, any good judgement that Stalin might have had deserted him. His unrelenting ambition drove him to do the unspeakable, to go over the heads of his immediate police supervisors. The Vissarionov file contained a letter written by Stalin to Assistant Minister of the Interior Zolotarev, the man who supervised the operation of the Police Department of which the Okhrana was an integral part. In his letter, Stalin respectfully reminded Zolotarev that they had met in the past at a restaurant in Moscow. Stalin then went on to attack Malinovsky and pointed out that he had closely observed Malinovsky at the Cracow conference and believed, without reservation, that the accused was a true supporter of Lenin and was more inclined towards the Bolsheviks than the secret police.

In the margin of Stalin's letter there was a handwritten notation made by Zolotarev to the effect that, 'This agent should be deported to Siberia for good. He is asking for it.' It was obvious that Zolotarev was displeased that Stalin had gone over his head;

in fact, he was not in agreement with Stalin's assessment and re-routed the letter to Vissarionov.

Orlov recounted that shortly after Stalin returned from Cracow, sometime in the spring of 1913, Stalin and a few other Bolsheviks were arrested in St Petersburg in a trap set up by Malinovsky.

This was not the first time Stalin had been arrested by the Tsarist Government for anti-Government activity and, in Orlov's opinion, this was how Stalin had originally been recruited to work as an agent for the secret police. Stalin had been banished to remote areas of Russia several times but each time had managed to escape and resume his underground activities. He never revealed how he had managed to escape nor did anyone else. While other revolutionary leaders told of their escapes in their writings, or details were discovered in their police records, no such records or general information existed in Stalin's case. Orlov felt that this lack of information was unusual.

After Stalin's arrest in 1913, he was sentenced to four years' banishment in the far reaches of the Russian Empire, to the Turkhansk region north of the Arctic Circle. Escape from there was almost impossible and he remained in exile until the February Revolution.

This was the crux of the file that was discovered by Stein and found by Balitsky and Zinovy Katsnelson to be indisputably authentic. The perplexing problem of what to do with the file was the next step in the political adventure.

Balitsky and Zinovy next shared the contents of the file with two of their most trusted friends, who were also the most politically powerful men in the Ukraine: General Jonah E. Yakir, the commander of the military forces in the Ukraine, and Stanislav Kossior, a member of the Politburo and Secretary of the Communist Party of the Ukraine. Both men were alarmed at what they saw and Yakir decided to take the matter one step further. He flew to Moscow, where he conferred with his close friend Marshal Tukhachevsky, the Supreme Commander of the Red Army. Tukhachevsky was a rival of Stalin's and their personal dislike for one another was well known. Tukhachevsky in turn took into his confidence the Deputy Commissar for Defence, Yan Gamarnik, who was a man of high moral integrity and who was well liked by the people.

On that day in February 1937, Zinovy identified to Orlov only four of the military leaders of the Red Army connected with the proposed conspiracy to rid the Soviet Union of Stalin's dictatorship: Tukhachevsky, Gamarnik, Yakir and General Vitovt K. Putna. However, when news of the conspiracy broke, it was announced by the media that eight traitors had been involved in it.

Orlov related that the 'conspiracy' led by Tukhachevsky was more like a 'palace revolution'. The claim that the conspirators were spies of the Nazi Government was a complete fabrication on Stalin's part in order to bring charges against them. The proof of the falsehood lay in the fact that three of the eight generals were Jewish. In no way would the Jewish generals Yakir, Eideman and Feldman have acted in concert with the anti-Semite Hitler, thus making the charges ridiculous at best.

The eight executed generals were patriots of the highest order, who were bound by a sense of duty and honour to their country. They had witnessed the terror of Stalin's blood purges, which had enveloped the country and exposed the moral decay of the dictator. Now they had in their hands the evidence that would expose him for what he actually was, a murderer and tyrant who was the creation of the Tsar's secret police and not the revolutionary hero that he had led the Russian people to believe.

In the quiet of Orlov's hospital room, Zinovy told him that at that time the Red Army generals were in the process of 'gathering forces' and had not as yet settled on a firm plan of action for the overthrow of Stalin. However, Tukhachevsky favoured the following plan.

He would contact Commissar for Defence Kliment Voroshilov under a suitable pretext to persuade him to call a top-level conference with Stalin to discuss critical problems of a military nature in the Ukraine. The commanders of the Moscow and Ukraine Military Districts, who were privy to the conspiracy, as well as their trusted aides would be in attendance at the conference. At a prearranged time, two elite regiments of the Red Army would seal the roads into the Kremlin to prevent the entrance of KGB troops. With the Red Army regiments in place. Tukhachevsky would arrest Stalin and proclaim a new government. Tukhachevsky anticipated no problems in the takeover within the walls of the Kremlin and felt that the *coup d'état* would be bloodless.

Zinovy explained that there were two views as to the final disposition of Stalin. The Red Army generals believed that he should be killed on the spot and that a special plenary session of the Central Committee of the Soviet Communist Party should then be called and the Okhrana secret police file on Stalin placed before the session. On the other hand, the non-army members of the conspiracy, Kossior, Balitsky, Zinovy and others not known to Orlov, held the view that Stalin should be arrested and charged with being an *agent provocateur* for the Tsar.

Orlov recounted the facts surrounding the conspiracy, as told to him that afternoon in Paris by his cousin, like an experienced intelligence agent. He said that he was crystal-clear about the facts because, 'It was the kind of history-making information that burns sharply into one's mind, like acid on copper plate.'

Before leaving that day, Zinovy shyly asked Orlov a meaningful favour. If the coup failed, and he and his wife Elena were shot, would the Orlovs take care of their three-year-old daughter? Orlov knew that Zinovy was a devoted father and instantly realised that this was why Zinovy had planned to travel to Spain to reveal the conspiracy plot to him and to ask the favour. Without hesitation, Orlov assured Zinovy that his daughter would be taken care of but also reassured him that he saw no way the plan could fail. In order to allay Zinovy's noticeable apprehension, Orlov said that Tukhachevsky was a respected Red Army leader and had control over the Moscow garrison as well as free access to the Kremlin. He also had frequent contact with Stalin and would not be suspected of any treachery by the dictator. Orlov added that all that remained was for Tukhachevsky to arrange the conference and to alert the two Red Army regiments; everything else would fall into place.

As a last word of encouragement, Orlov noted that there was very little likelihood that any of the plotters would betray the conspiracy to Stalin because the inherent danger of betrayal was absent in this case. Only a fool would have the nerve to tell Stalin that his Okhrana file had been uncovered as the reward would be immediate execution to keep the betrayer's silence.

The two cousins embraced and kissed each other on both cheeks. As Zinovy passed through the doorway, he turned around for a last look at Orlov and gave a slight farewell motion with his hand. This was the last time Orlov would ever see his beloved cousin.

A few days later, Orlov was well enough to be discharged from the clinic and returned to Valencia. In the weeks and months that followed, he was always alert to any news of the expected overthrow of Stalin and in time feared the worst. Finally, on 11 June 1937, he heard the news in a radio broadcast from Toulouse, which interrupted the regular programme with a special bulletin saying that Red Army Marshal Mikhail Tukhachevsky and a number of other Soviet generals had been arrested, charged with treason and would be court-martialled.

The following day, the French radio announced that Tukhachevsky and the seven other Red Army generals had been tried, found guilty of spying for a foreign government and executed. What followed was an ever-mounting avalanche of arrests and executions, which Orlov learned of on almost a daily basis. Towards the middle of July, Orlov received word that his cousin had been executed for treason. Orlov never discovered what had happened to Zinovy's wife and small daughter, but he had to assume that Elena at least went the way of her husband. Even the unfortunate KGB officer Stein, who had found the Okhrana file on Stalin, took his own life at the KGB Centre with his service revolver.

Then came word that Gamarnik, one of the early plotters, had allegedly committed suicide thirteen days before the other conspirators had been executed. The judges that presided over the sham Tukhachevsky trial and signed the fraudulent verdict all suffered the same destiny, one by one. Not even the highly placed member of the Politburo, Stanislav Kossior, was able to escape with his life.

The purge of the Red Army commanders reached epidemic proportions when the long arm of Stalin reached into Spain that August to pluck some of the most able of the commanders assigned to the Spanish Republican Government as advisors. Most of those recalled to Moscow and executed without the benefit of a trial were attached to the General Staff of the Republican Army. Among those were Brigade Commanders Kolev and Simonov (whose true name was Valua), who were instrumental in modernising the Republican Army; Orlov's friend Brigade Commander of the Soviet Tank Forces and Military Attaché Vladimir Gorev; and General Jan Berzin, the Chief Military Advisor to the Republican Government. In spite of his close friendship with Marshal Voroshilov, the Supreme Commander of the Red Army, Berzin had no better luck than the others.

Within a short time, Orlov was able to piece together the remaining details of the conspiracy. Almost to the very last moment, members of the Politburo had no knowledge that Stalin was about to destroy the most prominent leaders of the Red Army. Several days before the executions, Stalin called an extraordinary meeting of the Politburo, in which Voroshilov reported that Tukhachevsky and seven other generals had been caught conspiring against their own Government in concert with Hitler. The members of the Politburo knew better than to challenge or even criticise Voroshilov's report as their reward would be dismissal from the meeting and probable imprisonment.

Soon after the first of the military executions, Orlov learned that the Fourth Department of the Red Army, the vital arm of the Red Army dealing with military intelligence, had been placed under the control of KGB Chairman Yezhov, the very man who was ruthlessly carrying out Stalin's orders to purge the Red Army of its Stalinist enemies.

That October, Shpiegelglass, the KGB officer in charge of the

Mobile Groups, was in Spain on a business matter. He confided to Orlov that there had been no formal trial for Marshal Tukhachevsky and the other seven generals and that they had been summarily executed on Stalin's personal orders. Shpiegelglass exclaimed that the conspiracy must have been gargantuan and of enormous consequence judging by the turmoil that had been caused in the Kremlin. The KGB's special troops had been alerted for immediate action and all passes to the Kremlin were suddenly invalidated. Orlov was already aware that, as a result of the conspiracy, the policy of utilising a system of political commissars at all levels of the Red Army had been reinstated, after a lapse of many years, as a means of spying on the officer corps in order to ensure that another Tukhachevsky affair would not come about.

Stalin never felt it necessary to present the facts of the Tukhachevsky case to the Russian people and the conspirators were only mentioned in a brief official communiqué as convicted traitors and spies. Nevertheless, in the name of public opinion Stalin wanted the Western Governments to believe that Tukhachevsky and his fellow generals had conspired with Hitler against their own country.

What was troubling to Orlov was the fact that to a great extent Stalin had convinced the Western world that he was correct. As years went by, historians and writers came to regard Stalin's version as an accepted fact. This conclusion emanated from unsubstantiated information furnished to the free world by President Edvard Beneš of Czechoslovakia. As the statesman Winston Churchill wrote in his book, *The Gathering Storm*:

> He [Beneš] became aware that communications were passing through the Soviet Embassy in Prague between important personages in Russia and the German Government. This was a part of the so-called military and Old Guard Communist conspiracy to overthrow Stalin and introduce a new regime based on pro-German policy. President Beneš lost no time in communicating all he could find out to Stalin.

Thereafter there followed the merciless, and perhaps not needless, military and political purge in Soviet Russia, and the series of trials in January 1937 in which Vyshinsky, the Public Prosecutor, played so masterful a role.

In our discussion of these events, Orlov posed the following questions to me: how could President Beneš have authenticated a set of circumstances that never existed? And what would Churchill's reaction have been had he known that it was Stalin that had fabricated the charges against Tukhachevsky? I didn't have the answers, but Orlov went on to supply the following explanation, which he felt in today's free world would be corroborated by a number of former Czech officials.

During the era prior to Hitler, the Soviet intelligence service had the initiative in Germany and through various spy networks was able to procure Germany's top secrets. With the advent of Hitler and the Gestapo, the Nazi secret police, there was a drastic change in security and spying by the Soviets became a very dangerous game. The KGB mandated that extreme caution be exercised in all spy operations in Germany.

The assistant KGB *rezident* at the Soviet Embassy in Berlin in 1936 was an officer by the name of Israelovich, who happened to be a good friend of Orlov's. At the time, Israelovich was running two very important German army officers, who were on the General Staff and in a position to acquire extremely sensitive army information of immense value to the Soviets. In accordance with KGB policy in effect at the time, because of the high risk of exposure Israelovich had to travel to Czechoslovakia, where meetings with the two German spies could be made safely.

On one of their clandestine meetings in 1936, Israelovich and the two German spies met at an out-of-the-way *kavarna* (café) just off the Old Town Square in Prague. The Germans left first and then Israelovich departed. As he exited the *kavarna* on to a small alley, the KGB officer was arrested by the Czech police and taken to police headquarters. There he was searched and a roll of undeveloped film, which he had just received from the

German spies, was confiscated. Israelovich was told that he had been under surveillance by the Czech police and had been observed with the two Germans. The Czech police official charged Israelovich with spying for the Nazis.

Orlov recalled Israelovich as an individual who lacked resoluteness and who would often lose his composure under pressure. In this predicament, Israelovich should have refused to talk to the Czech officials and demand that the Soviet Embassy in Prague be notified immediately of his arrest. Instead, the KGB officer began to defend himself, which was a very unwise move under the circumstances.

In a sudden gust of professional vanity, Israelovich proclaimed that it was the Germans who were his agents and not the other way round. As proof, he referred to the confiscated roll of film and noted that the film contained photographs of secret documents of the German General Staff. By this time the shrewd Czech official realised that he had broken through any defence that Israelovich might have had and took the opportunity to press the issue without showing any compassion towards Israelovich. He soon had Israelovich boasting of his intelligence accomplishments and, in the end, Israelovich provided the Czech police with a signed statement of his deeds and was released from police custody.

The matter was referred to the Czech Foreign Office, which in turn supplied the information to President Beneš. During this period, the Czech nation was well aware of the threat from Nazi Germany and was making every effort to enhance its relations with the Soviet Union as a precautionary measure. Beneš personally decided to send the Czech police report and Israelovich's signed statement to the Czech Ambassador in Moscow along with instructions that the matter be reported directly to Stalin, or, if this were not possible, then to Foreign Commissar Maxim Litvinov. The report and signed statement were received by the Soviet Foreign Office, which extended its appreciation to Beneš for a friendly act towards the Soviet Government.

Orlov learned of the Israelovich incident in 1936 while at the

KGB Centre. Israelovich was recalled to Moscow and arrested. His actions were somewhat mitigated because the affair had been resolved without any recrimination from the parties involved. The German Government was totally in the dark as to what had happened that day in Prague as the KGB's role with the two German spies was never revealed. Israelovich was sentenced to five years' hard labour and served his time at the Kem gulag near the White Sea.

A year after the Prague incident, Tukhachevsky and his collaborators were executed for treason. As proof of their involvement, Stalin intimated that Israelovich had been the link between German military intelligence and the Tukhachevsky traitors. The Czechs knew better but needed Stalin's help against the Nazis more than ever and so kept their silence. Worse still was the fact that Beneš propagated the false version of the Israelovich affair to a world that at the time remained naïve to the machinations of Stalin. The Soviet dictator now felt secure in the belief that the true facts surrounding the framing of the conspirators would never come to light.

Stalin's reputation was shattered nineteen years later, in 1956, when one of his own lieutenants, Nikita Khrushchev, denounced him at the 20th Congress of the Soviet Communist Party. Khrushchev's declaration stunned the Russian people as well as the world with the following damning statements:

1. Stalin had fabricated charges of treason against Marshal Tukhachevsky and seven other leaders of the Red Army in 1937, had had them executed without trial and followed up those assassinations with the murder of 5,000 innocent officers.

2. Stalin had slaughtered hundreds of old Bolsheviks, including 70 out of 133 members of the Central Committee of the Party.

3. Stalin had liquidated so many thousands of industrial managers and technicians that the Soviet economy was almost paralysed.

4. Stalin had been a coward, who had deserted Moscow at the approach of Nazi Germany's troops.
5. Stalin had been a sadist, who had tortured men until they stammered out their false confessions.

Khrushchev went on to say that whenever he and other members of the Government had had personal contact with Stalin, they never knew 'whether we would come out alive'. At the end of his vehement denunciation of his former master, Khrushchev broke into tears. What Khrushchev failed to say was why the new leadership of the Soviet Union had finally disowned their former master. Orlov was convinced that the leadership had had to disown the dictator and distance themselves from him when they had learned that Stalin had been an agent of the Tsar's secret police. But the critical question remained unanswered: why did the Soviet leadership remain silent until the 20th Congress?

Orlov told me that he had answered this question in an article he had written for *Life* magazine on 23 April 1956, shortly after the 20th Congress of the Soviet Communist Party, as well as in his personal, unpublished memoirs. By the very nature of his status within the Soviet hierarchy, having personally known Khrushchev and having been privy to knowledge shared by few, the following observations by Orlov become important from an historical viewpoint:

> It has been argued that Khrushchev and his associates wanted personal revenge on Stalin who had so long humiliated them. Whoever believes this does not know the men who spent twenty years as Stalin's apprentices; he taught them always to put political expediency ahead of personal feelings. Stalin personally hated Lenin, who had disowned him in his last testament; he hounded Lenin's widow; he destroyed all of Lenin's personal friends. But Stalin the politician knew what was good for him. Year after year he built Lenin up as a deity and established himself as Lenin's true prophet.

Why didn't Khrushchev and his colleagues do as Stalin did? They had been Stalin's closest aides for many years. As such, they had inherited his power. Why did they not perpetuate Stalin's cult and profit from it?

By means of rewriting and falsifying history Stalin had succeeded in building himself up as the supreme strategist of the October Revolution and the only infallible leader of world Communism. He had transformed the backward country of Russia into a powerful industrial empire. He had won military victories unequalled in the history of Russia. He had outwitted his Western allies at Teheran, Yalta and in China. He had extended the power of the Soviet Union over 900 million people. With such a record Stalin was not good enough for Khrushchev, Bulganin and the others as an ancestor?

Moreover, it is obvious that Khrushchev and the others must have realised that by indicting Stalin they would gravely endanger themselves. They had been closest to him. They had condoned and abetted many of his crimes. Their sudden attack on Stalin was bound to rouse in the minds of the Russian people angry recollections of how Khrushchev, Bulganin, Kaganovich, Miloyan and Malenkov had glorified Stalin and his policies before huge audiences of Communist Party activists, how they had justified Stalin's bloody Moscow trials and how they had hailed the shooting of the Red Army Generals as a 'just punishment of traitors'.

The bosses of the Kremlin no doubt knew that in the minds of the Russian people pertinent questions were bound to arise as to their complicity in Stalin's crimes and their fitness for continuing as leaders of the Soviet Union and world Communism. But in spite of that, Khrushchev and the rest found it necessary to bring into the open the story of Stalin's crimes. Why did they take such a risk? Why did they do it now, at this time?

Something must have happened to the new oligarchs which had left them only one way out: to disown Stalin completely and to do it fast. That 'something', I am convinced, was the discovery of the incontrovertible proof that Stalin had been an *agent provocateur* of the Tsarist secret police.

Orlov recalled that on that fateful day in 1937 in Paris, his cousin Zinovy Katsnelson had told him that several photocopies of the contents of Stalin's secret police file had been made. Over the years, he had asked himself a thousand times what had happened to the file and the photocopies of it, and had speculated that the conspirators had been tortured and possibly revealed the whereabouts of some of the photocopies, but perhaps the original file and some of the photocopies may have survived.

Orlov strongly believed that the original Okhrana file, or one of its copies, had finally been brought to the Kremlin leaders by someone who had kept the file secretly in his possession for all those years. He felt it most likely that the file was in the possession of a military man who had guarded the file with his life, or perhaps a relative or friend of someone in the military. He speculated that it could have been Red Army Marshal Georgi Zhukov, who was given the file sometime in 1937 and who, days before the 20th Congress was convened, had surprised his fellow members in the collective leadership of the Soviet Union with the revelation.

Orlov knew Zhukov from the early days of the Spanish Civil War, when Zhukov was a Red Army general who frequently came to Spain as a military observer. Through their official relationship Orlov became aware that Zhukov was not a lackey or courtier of Stalin's but a military man through and through, exactly the type of person who could be entrusted with such a secret file without the slightest possibility of betraying the trust. There was no doubt that the 1937 moral blemish on the honour of the Red Army must have rankled with Zhukov over the years. Even during the Second World War, the victories that took place were inequitably credited to Stalin while the defeats were attributed to the Red Army generals. This must have taken its toll on Zhukov and, under these circumstances, he was the logical Red Army officer to be given the Stalin secret police file knowing that he could be counted on to act on the matter.

No matter how it happened, the documentary proof that Stalin was an informant for the Tsar's secret police was placed before the collective leadership of the Soviet Communist Party. In the words he recorded in his memoirs, Orlov wrote:

> The Kremlin leaders then had no real alternative but to try to cut the umbilical cord that tied them to a usurper and impostor who had few parallels in all human history. The risk was enormous, but unless they dissociated themselves fast and fully from the Tsarist agent, they might themselves have been doomed. They could not take a chance on keeping the dreadful secret from leaking out ultimately, now that Stalin himself was not there to keep it smothered. And possibly there were those – Marshal Zhukov or others – who warned that the facts would not remain secret unless the Stalin myth was completely deflated.

Orlov related that not even when he defected did he reveal to Stalin that he was aware that he, Stalin, had been an agent for the Tsar because he feared that this information would only infuriate the dictator and make him double his efforts to locate him and take revenge. When Orlov wrote his letters to Stalin and Yezhov following his defection, he outlined what secrets he knew about Stalin and the KGB and felt confident that this was sufficient insurance to keep the hounds away from his door. By 1953, he felt that his mother and mother-in-law must have died so, without fear of reprisal in this direction, he had gone ahead with the publication of *The Secret History of Stalin's Crimes*. In his book, he had only alluded to the fact that the execution of the Tukhachevsky conspirators was connected to Stalin's 'horrible secret'. Even after the death of Stalin in 1953, he did not reveal his information for fear that the new leadership in the Kremlin were loyal to Stalin and would continue to pursue him vigorously. However, what did bother him was his guilty conscience;

he knew Stalin's 'horrible secret' but feared that if he were liquidated by the KGB, or died of natural causes, the world would never discover it. On that premise, Orlov told me, in 1953 he wrote down the narrative of what his cousin had revealed that February day in 1937 in the Bergère Clinic. He sealed the chronicle in an envelope, which he placed in the safekeeping of a bank vault. Then he instructed his attorney to open the envelope only at the time of his death. Fortunately, the revelations at the 20th Congress of the Soviet Communist Party made it possible for him to reveal for the first time the connection between the execution of the Tukhachevsky conspirators and Stalin's secret as there no longer existed a motive for Orlov to remain silent.

Orlov's article in *Life*, which appeared under the heading 'The Sensational Secret Behind the Damnation of Stalin', was the first time the world had any solid knowledge that Stalin had been an informant for the Tsar's secret police. For years a rumour had persisted to this effect in the Russian émigré colonies around the world and even within the Soviet Union, but this was the most damaging tangible evidence to surface so far. The article reflected the salient elements of the affair, but not to the extent of the far-reaching coverage reflected herein.

The same issue of *Life* also carried a companion article by Isaac Don Levine titled, 'A Document on Stalin as a Tsarist Spy'. Levine had written extensively on the Russian Revolution as well as on Lenin and Stalin and was knowledgeable about Russian affairs. In 1947, an original document in the form of a letter had come into Levine's possession from a Russian émigré residing in the United States. The letter dated 12 July 1913 was from the headquarters of the Okhrana in Moscow, under the signature of one 'Yeremin', to the Chief of the Yeniseisk Okhrana Section, A.F. Zhelezniakov. The letter reflected that in 1906 Stalin had been arrested and given the Chief of the Tiflis State Gendarmerie Administration valuable denunciatory information; in 1908, the Chief of the Baku Okhrana Section received a series of intelligence reports from Stalin and afterwards, upon Stalin's arrival in St Petersburg, he had become an agent of the St Petersburg

Okhrana Section; after Stalin's election to the Central Committee of the Party in Prague, he openly opposed the Government and discontinued his connection with the Okhrana completely.

Laboratory tests determined that the paper the letter in question was written on was of European origin and not of recent manufacture. The typed lettering was the same style as that on the Remington Model #6 typewriter, with its Russian Cyrillic keyboard, which was in general use in Russia before the First World War. In addition, an archival letter from the St Petersburg police, typewritten eight months before the document and dated 5 November 1912, bore the same characteristics although not from the identical typewriter. The genuineness of Yeremin's signature was proved beyond much doubt, although by this time both the sender and recipient were deceased. In the end, the letter was deemed genuine, or at least as genuine as possible without the author's testimony, on a preponderance of evidence and the editors of *Life* magazine chose to run the Levine article in the same issue as Orlov's article in order to reinforce Orlov's contention of the existence of an Okhrana file on Stalin.

In 1972, Orlov informed me that he had been quite perturbed when *Life* printed the Levine story alongside his article in 1956; he had strongly objected because he considered the 'Yeremin' letter to be an outright forgery. Over the years he had reflected on the matter and, as time passed, he began to consider that the letter could be genuine. What was important to Orlov was the fact that in the twenty-five years since the 'Yeremin' letter had surfaced in 1947, not one other such letter damaging to Stalin had appeared in public. Had this been a vendetta by a sole émigré or émigré organisation to expose the dictator, he reasoned, more forged documents with similar contents would probably have made their way to other recipients over the years.

A more conclusive piece of evidence appeared in Levine's book, *Stalin's Great Secret*, which was published later the same year. The conjecture of the book, which was based on research and a correlation of known facts surrounding the life of Stalin, was that Stalin was a spy for the Tsarist secret police. However, the subject of

Stalin's Okhrana file was never addressed and it was apparent that its existence was unknown to the author.

The Levine book explores in part the relationship between Stalin and Marshal Tito of Yugoslavia as it relates to the premise of the book. Tito deserted the ranks of Stalin's Communist movement and the men became bitter enemies. Levine writes that caches of documents exposing Stalin's service in the Okhrana may have fallen into the hands of Tito, and there was no doubt that certain information concerning Stalin's treason to the revolutionary movement had been in his possession for a long time. A section of this proposition rests with the Politburo member and Secretary of the Communist Party of the Ukraine, Stanislav Kossior. The interesting revelation notes, 'Recent inquiries in Belgrade have confirmed the suspicion that Tito had known all along of Kossior's possession of documents incriminating Stalin as a Tsarist spy, and met his fate because of this.' This is the same Kossior to whom Orlov's cousin, Zinovy Katsnelson, had given the damaging and secret Okhrana file on Stalin in 1937.

After we had concluded our discussion of the Tukhachevsky affair, Orlov added a colourful vignette that seemed to explain further his early reticence in making known the connection between the Red Army purges in 1937 and Stalin's secret. In the autumn of 1937, while visiting the Soviet Pavilion at the French International Exhibition in Paris, he ran into his old friend Pavel Alliluyev, who happened to be Stalin's brother-in-law. Pavel's sister Nadezhda was Stalin's second wife. Orlov and Alliluyev had first met in early 1929, when the latter was assigned to the Soviet Trade Delegation in Berlin as a subordinate to Orlov. In the following two years they became close friends. By 1936, Alliluyev was the Commissar of the Tank Corps of the Red Army and could count among his friends Red Army Commissar Voroshilov and his deputy Gamarnik as well as Marshal Tukhachevsky. However, Alliluyev fell out of favour with his brother-in-law and, when the two old friends met again in Paris, Alliluyev held a minor position at the Soviet Pavilion. Alliluyev seemed greatly depressed and troubled so Orlov invited his friend to dine with him that evening.

After supper, the two friends walked along the River Seine. They spoke of the horrendous events taking place in the Soviet Union and at one point Orlov asked his companion what was the truth behind the execution of Tukhachevsky and the Red Army generals. Alliluyev stopped walking, grasped Orlov's upper arm and then, in a very slow and deliberate manner, addressed Orlov with the words, 'Alexander, don't ever inquire about the Tukhachevsky affair. Knowing about it is like inhaling poison gas.'

Orlov had to wonder how much 'poison gas' his friend had inhaled when, several years later in 1939, he read in one of the official organs of the USSR, either *Pravda* or *Izvestia*, an obituary saying that Alliluyev, Commissar of the Tank Corps of the Red Army, had died unexpectedly while carrying out his official duties. The announcement was signed by Voroshilov and several other Red Army officers, but to Orlov the absence of Stalin's signature was suspicious. The cause of death was not given.

But, on the other hand, Orlov wondered what Alliluyev would have thought had he known that, while strolling along the Seine, Orlov's lungs were already full of that 'poison gas', the insidious secret of what was behind the purges of the Red Army in 1937.

To this day neither the original nor any of the photocopies of the Okhrana file on Stalin have ever surfaced. There is no doubt that when the Tukhachevsky conspirators were arrested, many of these documents were retrieved by Stalin. Through a systematic reign of torture of the remotest of suspects, more of these documents fell into Stalin's hands. Despite all of Stalin's efforts to erase the existence of his Okhrana file from the face of the earth, I still believe that somewhere out there, perhaps buried beneath the ground in a container, or lying in a dusty attic, one of these documents will yet be discovered.

TWENTY-FIVE

GENERAL MILLER

One of the most fascinating chapters in the history of the KGB was the kidnapping of General Yevgeny Miller off the streets of Paris in September 1937. Orlov had no direct connection with the kidnapping but was able to learn of one facet of the operation which had not gone according to plan and which KGB Chairman Yezhov covered up by lying to Stalin. As Orlov told me, 'When I learned Yezhov lied to Stalin in order to cover his blunder . . . I realised I could have his head.' In Orlov's defection letter to Stalin, with its duplicate copy to Yezhov, he revealed that Yezhov had lied to him. By this time, most of Orlov's close friends and associates in the KGB had been recalled to Moscow and executed on Yezhov's orders and Orlov never had a kind word for him. When I told Orlov that I suspected he had taken revenge on Yezhov for his past misdeeds, I expected his usual wry grin to indicate an answer. This time, without the slightest trace of emotion, he sternly replied that his motive had been both personal revenge for the execution of his KGB colleagues and vengeance for the murder of his cousin Zinovy Katsnelson. He knew Stalin well enough to realise that the dictator would be furious that his subordinate had lied to him and would punish his KGB Chairman. Orlov added that if he had to write the letter again, this was one item he would not exclude.

I had read several accounts of and references to the kidnapping of General Miller and it was apparent that little was actually known about the covert phase of the operation. The information Orlov furnished was contemporary with the incident and complete to the extent that the only entity that could provide more information would be the KGB archives. In February 1937, while recuperating in Paris, Orlov had first heard from Abram Slutsky about the special Mobile Groups under the jurisdiction of Mikhail Shpiegelglass. When Shpiegelglass arrived in Barcelona during the first week of December 1937 for what Orlov believed to be the first phase of Yezhov's plan to eliminate him, he learned the details of the plot from the man that had masterminded General Miller's kidnapping. What information Shpiegelglass failed to provide through his boastful revelations, Orlov was able to obtain from Kislov, the new chief of the KGB's legal *rezidentura* at the Soviet Embassy in Paris, who had replaced Smirnov when the latter was recalled to Moscow. When Orlov began his revelatory account of the General Miller kidnapping, I was mesmerised.

Following the kidnapping of General Alexander Kutyepov in broad daylight in Paris in January 1930 (see pages 531–2), his deputy in the Union of White Russian Veterans (ROVS), General Yevgeny Miller, was named his successor. During the Civil War in Russia, Miller had commanded the Northern White Army in the region of Archangel and, after the defeat of the White Armies, had fled to France, where in time he joined the ROVS. Under Miller's tenure, the ROVS was no longer a force to be reckoned with as most of their efforts were concentrated on keeping the organisation together and helping the indigent Russian émigrés make their way in the new land of their asylum. Besides, one of their top officials was on the payroll of the KGB so there was no problem in keeping track of the organisation.

By 1936, Stalin's purges had begun and, in March 1937, the KGB Chairman who had orchestrated Stalin's purges, Genrikh Yagoda, had in turn been purged and replaced by Yezhov. The new Chairman was determined to make a name for himself with Stalin and remembered how his predecessor, when he had been the Acting KGB Chairman, had successfully abducted General Kutyepov, after which his influence and esteem had grown in the eyes of both Stalin and the Politburo. Yezhov decided that he would also demonstrate his capabilities to Stalin by kidnapping

General Miller, but unlike Yagoda, who had the unfortunate experience of having his quarry die before he could be returned to Moscow, he would not only kidnap Miller but bring him back to Moscow alive.

Yezhov therefore sent for Shpiegelglass, who had just returned from Switzerland after successfully arranging the assassination of KGB defector Ignaz Reiss, and asked if Shpiegelglass's Mobile Groups could handle the assignment. In the past, such assignments were handled by foreign nationals, who were members of the Communist Party of their country and associated with the Comintern; the Soviet Government could then deny any responsibility. Shpiegelglass acknowledged that the task could be done but that it would take at least three months of planning because of the strict personal environment surrounding Miller and because the vigilant French police made such an operation fraught with danger. Shpiegelglass suggested several possible scenarios for the kidnapping, but in the end Yezhov wanted immediate action. He proposed that Miller be lured under a suitable pretext to a house on the outskirts of Paris, where he would be drugged and then taken to a Soviet vessel in one of the French ports for delivery to the Soviet Union.

Shpiegelglass acceded to Yezhov's demand that immediate action be taken and proceeded to Paris, where he contacted General Nikolai Skoblin, the KGB's informant in the ROVS. Skoblin had commanded the famed Kornilov Division during the Civil War and had earned the distinction of being a ruthless but brave leader. His division had won many battles against the Red Army and was dreaded by the enemy because of its reputation for hanging or shooting captured Communists on the spot. In 1921, Skoblin had married the well-known Russian folk singer Nadezhda Plevitskaya. Soon after, they moved to Paris, where the General became one of the directors of the ROVS. It was in Paris in the late 1920s that Skoblin had been recruited by Shpiegelglass, with the help of Nadezhda, into the ranks of KGB informants. With Skoblin now in place, the KGB was able to know every move of the ROVS.

Shpiegelglass met Skoblin and a plan was soon conceived to lure Miller into a trap. Miller was to be told that two officers of the German General Staff attached to the German Embassy in Paris were interested in establishing communication with the ROVS as a means of securing information on the Soviets through the ROVS's intelligence-gathering apparatus. The Germans were prepared to pay for the information, which would appeal to the financially strapped ROVS and at the same time further its cause against the Soviets. Miller would be told that Berlin had authorised the contact with him and that it should be carried out in great secrecy so that the French Government did not learn of the liaison.

With a suitable plan now in hand, Shpiegelglass arranged to rent a villa in the environs of Paris, where Miller's meeting with the two Germans was to take place. Skoblin made his preliminary approach to Miller and found the General receptive to the idea of meeting the Germans. He also gave his word that he would tell no one. Skoblin left with the notion that he would make the final arrangements with the Germans. In the meantime, Shpiegelglass was in contact with Yezhov, who made arrangements for the Soviet merchant marine vessel S/S *Maria Ulyanova*, so named in honour of Lenin's sister, to make for the port of Le Havre, where it would be in position to take on the unsuspecting and unwilling passenger. The date of the operation would coincide with the arrival of the Soviet vessel at Le Havre. All the pieces were now falling into place.

Shpiegelglass had at his disposal all of the KGB personnel at the Soviet Embassy in Paris. He chose for this critical mission Kislov, who was accredited to the Soviet Embassy as the Vice Consul-General; Beletsky, who was accredited as an employee of the Soviet Trade Delegation; and Dolgorukov, the Soviet Embassy's chauffeur. Beletsky was by profession a doctor, who had abandoned his medical training for the excitement of working for the KGB.

There was one other key player that would be indispensable to the operation, Skoblin's wife Nadezhda. She would help her husband establish an alibi to account for the time frame during which the kidnapping would take place. Shpiegelglass worked out all the details for the alibi beforehand.

Before the date of the operation could be set, Kislov and Shpiegelglass met the captain of the S/S *Maria Ulyanova* at the port of Le Havre to give him final instructions. The operation was then arranged for 22 September 1937.

Around noon on the 22nd, General Miller left his ROVS office on the rue du Colisée to keep his 12.30 p.m. appointment with Skoblin at the corner of rue Jasmin and rue Raffez in the heart of Paris. There, Miller entered Skoblin's car and they drove directly to the villa which the KGB had rented. A KGB surveillance car followed at a discreet distance to ensure that the French police were not taking an unwanted role in the operation.

At the villa, Miller and Skoblin were met by the two German officers, who in reality were Kislov and Shpiegelglass. They spoke for a few minutes and Skoblin left the room. As he left, Beletsky and Dolgorukov entered. At that moment the formalities were over; the KGB men grabbed Miller and secured his arms while Beletsky injected him with a sedative.

Skoblin immediately returned to Paris, where he picked up his wife for the purpose of establishing an alibi for the period when he was taking Miller to the villa and returning to the city. The plan was carefully crafted by Shpiegelglass and executed by the Skoblins. That day the Skoblins ate at a Russian restaurant, where they were well known and which they left at 11.50 a.m. with the agreement that, if asked, they would say they left at 12.30 p.m. From there, they went to Madame Skoblin's dressmaker, where she looked through the latest fashions and purposely pointed out to the owner that her husband was waiting for her in the car. She mentioned several times that her husband must be bored waiting for her but continued looking for her dream dress. Suddenly, she told the dressmaker that she remembered she had to see an acquaintance off at the Gare du Nord but would return another day. That day the daughter of the late General Kornilov and her husband were actually leaving for their home in Brussels and a small contingent of Russian friends were seeing them off.

Madame Skoblin was already at the station when her husband arrived and joined the group. His absence had not been noticed as everyone assumed that he had been speaking to someone else while they were speaking to his wife. Skoblin now spoke to all his friends on the platform and, when he saw Miller's wife amongst the group, walked up to her and pointedly asked about her husband. She told him that he was expected at the gathering and wondered what had detained him.

From the Gare du Nord the Skoblins visited a few friends, while keeping track of the time, and even drove into the countryside for a short excursion with a fellow ROVS officer. They then returned to the city, where they spent the remainder of the evening at the Gallipoli Club. Here they were seen by the White Russian clientele who frequented the club. Exhausted, they finally returned to a hotel room they permanently maintained in the city knowing that they had secured their alibi.

Meanwhile, back at the villa the sedated General was placed into a large wooden container, which had been purposely provided with numerous air holes. The container was then placed in the Embassy's van and the reluctant passenger was taken to Le Havre by Shpiegelglass, Kislov, Beletsky and Dolgorukov. They arrived at the pier by late afternoon and Kislov made arrangements to have the container taken carefully aboard the S/S *Maria Ulyanova* and placed in a stateroom. With anticipation the container was opened and, with much relief, Miller was found to be alive but still under sedation. Within the hour, the S/S *Maria Ulyanova* left the harbour with Shpiegelglass, Kislov and Beletsky aboard, while Dolgorukov returned with the van to the Soviet Embassy.

The operation was still not out of danger as it was certain that when General Miller's absence was brought to the attention of the French authorities, there would be a maelstrom in the press and a demand to find the missing General. Any Soviet vessel departing France that day would be suspect and subject to search as it passed through the Kiel Canal. To preclude this possibility, Shpiegelglass ordered the captain to bypass the Kiel Canal and take the route north of Denmark to St Petersburg. There was also the possibility that the S/S *Maria Ulyanova* might be intercepted and searched on the high seas by French naval vessels. If this occurred, Shpiegelglass had arranged for the General to be dropped into the sea.

Miller's wife was not unduly concerned by her husband's absence as that day a contingent of veterans of the Northern White Army was expected to arrive in Paris for a reunion with their old comrade in arms. These reunions were lengthy affairs as the old timers reminisced about the past, caught up with what the ROVS were now doing and finally had dinner together. Indeed, the veterans arrived in Paris about 6 p.m. and went to the ROVS headquarters, where they expected to meet the General. They waited until 9 p.m. but he had still not appeared. By this time they telephoned the General's home and informed Mrs Miller that her husband had not shown up for the reunion. She then called up several of her husband's ROVS friends, only to find that he had not been seen since around noon that day. With much concern and trepidation she now called up her husband's Chief of Staff, General Kussonsky.

Kussonsky was shocked at the news and last recalled having seen her husband when he left the ROVS headquarters around noon that day. Miller had informed Kussonsky that he was on his way to a very important meeting and, as he departed, had handed Kussonsky a sealed envelope. As he did so, he had remarked that if he failed to return, Kussonsky should read the contents. Miller then added that he 'expected to return, but just in case'. Kussonsky had placed the envelope in his desk and had forgotten the incident.

Kussonsky dropped what he was doing and rushed to the ROVS headquarters to retrieve Miller's letter. He hurriedly tore it open and found a message indicating that Miller had a rendezvous with General Skoblin, who had arranged for him to meet two German officers connected with the German Embassy. Miller considered that this could be a trap and was leaving the note, just in case.

In spite of the late hour, which was now almost midnight,

Kussonsky telephoned Miller's deputy, Admiral Mikhail Kedrov, and broke the news to him. Kedrov immediately came to the ROVS headquarters, from where they dispatched a colonel to proceed to the Skoblins' residence in the suburb of Ozoir with the request that General Skoblin come to the ROVS headquarters immediately on an urgent matter. Skoblin was not to be found in Ozoir so the colonel went to the small Parisian hotel where the Skoblins were known to maintain a room. There the colonel found Skoblin and requested him to report to the ROVS headquarters. Skoblin dressed, but as he left the room he made one critical mistake that would come to haunt him. For some reason he could not reconcile later with the KGB, he threw his wallet containing all his money to his wife, a move he would come to regret and the incident that would lead to Yezhov's lie to Stalin.

Skoblin knew that things were not right the moment he entered the ROVS headquarters. Kedrov and Kussonsky immediately demanded to know Miller's whereabouts. Skoblin denied any knowledge and claimed that he had not seen Miller that day. He was directly challenged again and denied knowing anything. This time the accusers asserted that they had proof to the contrary, to which Skoblin swore that he hadn't seen Miller and wondered why he was a suspect. The Admiral then informed Skoblin that he knew he had had an appointment with Miller at 12.30 p.m. that day to see a couple of Germans and that if he again denied knowing Miller's whereabouts he would be turned over to the French police. With a demonstration of indignation, Skoblin replied that he was eager to have the French police settle the matter.

The men stepped into the reception room adjacent to the office where the colonel was waiting, but Kussonsky called Kedrov back into the office to tell him something he did not want Skoblin to hear. In that brief moment, Skoblin quickly opened the door into the hallway and fled down the stairwell. The colonel was aware of Skoblin's departure but made no attempt to stop him as he had not been told that Skoblin was implicated in Miller's disappearance. Skoblin was nowhere to be found at the street level and by his actions it was now apparent that he was involved in Miller's disappearance. The matter was reported to the Commissariat of the French police shortly after midnight and the hunt for Skoblin was underway.

The minute Skoblin emerged from the ROVS headquarters he ran for his life, knowing full well that his former comrades held him responsible for Miller's disappearance. He ran as far as he could until he felt relatively safe for the time being, thinking that he would then be able to formulate a plan to make good his escape. Unfortunately, he knew of no one to turn to, spoke no French despite the fact he had resided in France for a number of years and, worse still, realised that he did not have a single franc to his name as he had left his wallet with his wife.

Skoblin did have a regularly scheduled contact with a KGB courier from the Soviet Embassy, to whom he passed his information about the week's activities of the ROVS, but the man's identity had always remained anonymous and their next scheduled meeting was almost two days away. Shpiegelglass had furnished him with a KGB contact at the Soviet Embassy by the name of Sokolov and a telephone number where he could be reached in case something went wrong, but the telephone number was in the wallet he had left with his wife.

What Skoblin needed most was money to facilitate his escape. He had no money to telephone his wife nor could he go to the hotel as by this time she would be in the hands of the French authorities. He was aware that by morning the news of General Miller's kidnapping would be in every Paris newspaper and his chances of escape would be greatly diminished as his name and perhaps his photograph would be on every front page. Knowing that he had only a few hours before the news broke, he was now desperate to reach someone who could give him financial assistance before they discovered his part in the plot. He therefore walked the short distance to the apartment of a colonel in his old Kornilov Division only to learn that the man and his wife were on vacation. Then he went to an all-night garage where another of his officers worked only to find that the man had the night off. Finally, he made his way to the home of a captain from his former division in Neuilly and was more fortunate this time. The captain was out but his wife recognised the famous General, who claimed that he had lost his wallet and needed the taxi fare to get home. She lent him 200 francs.

His only remaining course of action was to try to contact Sokolov, who might already have been alerted by Shpiegelglass to this possibility. He telephoned the Soviet Embassy and spoke to the switchboard operator in Russian asking for 'Sokolov'. The operator was a French Communist, who only understood a little Russian but who did recognise the name Sokolov. This time Fortune was with the hapless Skoblin as Sokolov was a code clerk who lived at the Embassy and was in residence at the time of the call. Without revealing his identity, Skoblin explained that Shpiegelglass had given him his telephone number and that he had to see him. Sokolov asked the caller his identity and when he learned that it was General Skoblin, he immediately realised that there must be a grave problem. Sokolov had coded the communications between the Embassy and the KGB Centre and knew of Skoblin's participation in the operation. He advised Skoblin that he would pick him up in thirty minutes at the entrance of a nearby Metro station.

Sokolov knew that it was a violation of Soviet espionage policy for him to make contact with an underground KGB spy, but felt that the present circumstances far outweighed the policy. In the event that the French police apprehended Skoblin, or if he surrendered, the Miller plot could be compromised. Sokolov picked up Skoblin and brought him to the Soviet Embassy, but the problem was where to hide the conspirator. Sokolov was not a trained KGB officer and did not have the means to provide a safe-house for the fugitive, but he was shrewd enough to know that Skoblin had to be kept from the French authorities.

Sokolov arranged a small room for Skoblin in the section of the Embassy that was restricted to the KGB and in an isolated area between the third and fourth floors. Only he and the wife of the legal *rezident* Kislov knew of Skoblin's presence in the

Embassy. Sokolov dutifully reported to the KGB Centre that Skoblin had been provided with asylum in the Embassy and, with much apprehension, awaited the furore from the Centre and his possible recall to Moscow. Nothing happened to Sokolov, but someone had to pay for his decision to hide the errant General in the Soviet Embassy.

By that afternoon, all the newspapers in Paris had reported the kidnapping of General Miller and the escape of General Skoblin. Miller's letter clearly pointed to Skoblin as one of the perpetrators of the plot and, unlike the kidnapping of Kutyepov a few years earlier, the conspiracy began to unravel. Witnesses had seen a van registered to the Soviet Embassy deliver a large crate to the S/S *Maria Ulyanova* in the port of Le Havre shortly after the kidnapping. Within an hour of the delivery, the Soviet vessel had pulled anchor and departed the port without clearing with the French port authorities. The French police knew that the instigation of the Miller kidnapping lay with the Soviet Embassy but were never able to track down General Skoblin.

Skoblin's wife Nadezhda was questioned intensively by the French police through an interpreter but was unable to provide any information as to where her husband could be found; she also denied any knowledge of the crime. She became uncontrollably hysterical and the police had no recourse but to leave. When they departed, she also left the hotel room and spent the day trying to locate her husband but to no avail. She spent the night with friends and the following morning her friend's husband took her to the French police headquarters fearing that in her emotional state she might commit suicide. Nadezhda again denied any knowledge of the kidnapping and added that she did not believe her husband had anything to do with the crime. Despite the fact that she had a cast-iron alibi, she was arrested as an accessory to the crime.

In the meantime, Skoblin remained hidden in his sanctuary in the Soviet Embassy, only knowing the facts of what was happening on the outside through White Russian émigré newspapers and French newspaper accounts which he struggled to translate with the aid of a small French-Russian dictionary. Sokolov informed him that the KGB had undertaken to hire an attorney for his wife's defence and genuinely believed that she could not be convicted because of her firm alibi.

The French public's outrage grew by the hour and demands were made by the conservative members of the French Chamber of Deputies for the S/S *Maria Ulyanova* to be intercepted at sea and searched for General Miller. The ROVS and White Russian officers met to agitate the French Government into action and at one point there were rumours that 200 White Russian émigrés were preparing to invade the Soviet Embassy. Both the Soviet Ambassador in Paris and the People's Commissar of Foreign Affairs, Maxim Litvinov, kept Stalin and the Politburo advised about the growing public outcry.

When the rumour that the ROVS were about to storm the Soviet Embassy came to his attention, Stalin had no fear that Skoblin would be found there as Yezhov had personally reported to him that Skoblin was being hidden in a safe-house on the outskirts of Paris. It was now that Yezhov trembled with fear that the true facts would be revealed if the White Russians invaded the Soviet Embassy and found Skoblin hiding there. For the next three weeks, Yezhov was in constant terror that his lie to Stalin would be exposed, but as time went on the clamour to storm the Embassy subsided and the invasion never took place. It was not until a year later that Stalin would learn the truth from a most unlikely source, the KGB defector General Alexander Orlov.

By the time the S/S *Maria Ulyanova* was a day out of the port of Le Havre, General Miller regained consciousness and was surprised to find himself in what appeared to be a hospital room complete with all the paraphernalia of the trade. At his bedside was a physician dressed in a white medical gown and customary stethoscope who answered to the name of Dr Beletsky. Miller questioned the doctor in French and then in German and was told that he was on an Estonian vessel bound for the port of Reval. Miller was informed that he and another individual had been rescued from a sinking rowing boat off the coast of France.

Unfortunately, the other man was already dead. Miller remembered very little at first but soon regained enough memory to recall his own name and identified the dead man as General Skoblin. He only remembered that he and Skoblin had set out to a meeting but had no recollection whatsoever of the villa. When he became too inquisitive, Dr Beletsky reminded his patient that it was best to rest and not be so concerned for the time being.

Soon Miller had another daily visitor who came to observe the condition of the patient. Miller was taken by the concern of the ship's captain but had no way of knowing that man was in fact Shpiegelglass wearing a borrowed captain's uniform. Miller's suspicions should have been aroused because all the people he was in contact with spoke Russian; however, he dismissed any suspicion because most Estonians spoke Russian as their second language. As to Shpiegelglass and Dr Beletsky, Miller had no recollection of having encountered them in Paris.

Within a day or so, Miller recuperated with no side effects. The more he thought of his situation within the limited bounds of what he remembered, the more he placed the blame for his predicament on those 'dirty Bolsheviks'. He asked the bogus captain to send a wireless message to his wife in Paris explaining what had happened to him and telling her that he was aboard a vessel bound for Reval, from where he would write further. The captain gladly agreed to send the message but needless to say that never happened.

By the end of the six-day voyage, Miller had regained his strength and was able to roam the ship freely. When the S/S *Maria Ulyanova* entered the harbour, he was able to see the roof lines of the Isaak Cathedral and immediately realised that he was in Leningrad and not the port of Reval, which he had been led to believe was the port of destination. At this point the charade was over and Miller knew he was in deep trouble.

Miller and the KGB entourage were met at the port by Leonid Zakovsky, Chief of the Leningrad KGB Station, and taken to an estate on the outskirts of the city. The following day, the group took the Red Arrow Express to Moscow. There, Miller was treated like royalty on arrival and was the honoured guest at a banquet celebrating the success of the operation. He fell into the spirit of the festivities and enjoyed the camaraderie of the occasion without the slightest realisation as to his final disposition. However, at one point he did ask about the possibility of talking to his predecessor at the ROVS, General Kutyepov, which appeared to be a feeble attempt to learn his own fate. His request evoked amusement on the part of the KGB officers who were present as they were aware that Kutyepov had not survived his kidnapping and had been dead for over six years.

Three weeks later, Kislov and Beletsky openly returned to Paris after the commotion surrounding the Miller kidnapping had subsided. Stalin felt it was best for them to return as otherwise their absence would be construed as evidence that they had participated in the plot. It was then that Orlov learned from Kislov that General Miller had been executed. This was later confirmed by Shpiegelglass in early December 1937, when he visited Orlov in Spain.

Skoblin fared no better than Miller. In November 1937, when the focus of attention on the Soviet Embassy had shifted, the hapless White General was smuggled out of the Embassy and taken aboard a Soviet vessel bound for Leningrad. Kislov had already left the Soviet Union by the time Skoblin arrived in Russia but speculated that he had met the same fate as Miller inasmuch as he was now out of reach of the French authorities and could therefore not implicate the KGB in Miller's kidnapping; he was also no longer useful to the KGB. Shpiegelglass never commented on the fate of Skoblin and Orlov never asked as he knew that Kislov's explanation was the logical outcome for a man who had outlived his usefulness to the KGB and was now a burden to them.

The KGB took one other precaution to ensure that Skoblin's wife did not turn on the Soviets as she had been part of Shpiegelglass's plot to kidnap General Miller and had been privy to at least her husband's part in the abduction, which could have proved fatal to the Soviets in a court of law. Shortly after the

Miller affair broke, relations between the French and Soviet Governments were so strained that the Soviets had good reason to believe that the bungled kidnapping might lead to the breaking of diplomatic relations with the French if there was tangible evidence to prove Soviet participation. To this end, they made Skoblin write a series of brief, undated letters to his wife while he was still in hiding in the Soviet Embassy with the view to them being useful at a later date. Orlov never knew how these letters came into play, or when they were posted, but assumed that they were sent to her periodically before and during her trial to keep up her morale but also to prevent her from revealing what she knew about the kidnapping.

Nadezhda Plevitskaya, Skoblin's wife, was the only scapegoat in the General Miller affair. She was brought to trial on charges of being an accessory to the crime and throughout the trial defended her husband and proclaimed that their alibi proved that her husband could not have had the time to participate in the kidnapping. She claimed that it was impossible for her husband to have been involved because he could not have met General Miller at 12.30 p.m. as he was sitting in their car outside her dressmaker's shop while she was shopping. Had she remained silent, she might have been acquitted; however, her dressmaker happened to look out of the window several times that day and did not see General Skoblin or his car. Orlov related that this was the proverbial case of the lady who protested too much. At the end of the sensational trial that lasted four days, Nadezhda was found guilty and sentenced to twenty years' hard labour. Years later, Orlov learned that she had died in prison from a heart ailment, but shortly before she had confessed to a Russian priest that her husband had been a participant in the Miller kidnapping and that he had informed her that, soon after he had introduced Miller to the two fictitious German officers, he had left the room but later, as he passed by the partially open door, he had caught a glimpse of Miller lying prostrate on the floor.

There were several areas in the book *Deadly Illusions* dealing with the kidnapping of General Miller that contradicted known facts and were in direct conflict with information provided by Orlov. In fact, the book attempts to link Orlov with the kidnapping, perhaps another example of KGB disinformation.

The book claims that, 'The NKVD records reveal that Orlov's role [in the Miller kidnapping] was not as he described it to the CIA. So far as can be identified there are three separate documents that link Orlov directly to the case of General Miller.' The first link was apparently disclosed to Feoktistov at their meeting in Cleveland in 1971, when Orlov gave as one of the reasons he had fallen out with Yezhov the fact that 'he had declined to approve the plan for the kidnapping operation'. The second link was that, in his defection letter to Yezhov in August 1938, Orlov had stated that he still had in his possession 'FARMER's ring – FARMER was the code name of General Skoblin'. The third link refers to Orlov writing to Schpiegelglass on 10 May 1938 about another operation from Barcelona 'in which he mentioned the possibility of chartering an aircraft: "For $15,000 we could buy an airplane of the type in which you and I whisked away FARMER."'

I will now individually explore Orlov's alleged three links with General Miller.

As to the first alleged link, there would have been no logical connection for Orlov to have been involved in an operation to kidnap anyone in France. At the time of Miller's kidnapping, Orlov was in Spain as a direct representative of Stalin and the Politburo and his total attention was concerned with high-level matters pertaining to the Spanish Civil War. Besides, the KGB's Mobile Groups were designated to handle such matters under Shpiegelglass's supervision and, in this particular case, with the assistance of the KGB legal *rezident* in France, Kislov. There was no need for Orlov's expertise as there was ample brain and manpower at the place where the kidnapping was to occur. It seems rather obvious that Orlov was not consulted as he only met Shpiegelglass for the first time in Barcelona following the kidnapping.

As to the second link, this appears to be a contradiction in terms of what is stated in the book. The inference seems clear that Orlov's possession of Skoblin's ring was being used as a threat to Yezhov not to take any punitive action against Orlov's defection otherwise he would expose the Miller affair. However, in another section of the book it is stated, 'It is also significant that, despite Orlov's assertion that he had supplied information to Stalin which proved that Yezhov disobeyed his express orders during the kidnapping of General Miller, when Skoblin took refuge in the Paris embassy, it does not appear anywhere in the letter [Orlov's defection letter] in the KGB files. This, it appears, was another element in the General's monumental deceptions.'

Based on the above, I would have to submit that the monumental deception was on the part of the KGB and not Orlov. In addition, there is the matter of Skoblin's ring, an item which I had never heard of. If such a ring actually existed, Orlov would have had every reason not to bring it to the attention of the FBI or the CIA as it would have implicated him in the Miller kidnapping. However, I never knew Orlov to wear a ring – and this is evident in the last photographs of him taken shortly before his death – and although I was not specifically looking for a ring after Orlov died, I spent over six weeks searching and conducting an inventory of the contents of his apartment and never found a ring. There is no way that Orlov would have pawned Skoblin's ring if it really did exist, as he did with so many of his treasures during his financial crisis, as the letter would indicate that it was his insurance to stay alive. Also, the attorney for Orlov's estate, a bank official, an Ohio tax official and I searched and made an inventory on paper of the contents of his two safe-deposit boxes and no ring was found, as testified by the official inventory. In my view, if a prudent person depended on such an item, I would expect it to be in a readily accessible and secure place, such as a safe-deposit box. Therefore, with no ring, there is no story.

As to the third link, that Orlov conspired with Shpiegelglass to buy an aeroplane like the one used to whisk away FARMER, this is tantamount to the bank robber writing to a colleague after a recent bank robbery about a gun, 'just like the one we used when we robbed the First National Bank in Miami'. It just isn't done, especially by an intelligence professional like Orlov, who would know better than to link two separate intelligence matters even when coded. The book also makes another reference to the aeroplane incident noting that, 'What Orlov did not tell the CIA in 1965 [the Miller kidnapping debriefing] was that on Shpiegelglass's orders he hired a plane to fly Skoblin out to Spain.' The classic KGB method of exfiltrating someone out of a foreign country, in the era before commercial air travel was so common, was by Soviet vessels, such as in the case of General Miller's kidnapping. If it were true that Skoblin's destination was Spain, why not route him through the underground networks that had infiltrated thousands of International Brigade recruits into Spain during that same period to fight for the Republicans, or else give him a fictitious identity which was the practice of the KGB and the Red Army when bringing their people into Spain during the war. Skoblin was hiding in the Soviet Embassy for well over a month, which was more than ample time to forge a passport; and by that time, the furore over finding him had subsided. It is just not reasonable to believe that the KGB had any need to charter an aircraft at an enormous cost when it had simpler, more expedient and less expensive methods available. The bottom line is that Skoblin had outlived his usefulness as a KGB informant and its only interest was to keep him from talking. The only way that this could be accomplished was for him to be exterminated and the logical place of choice would be the Soviet Union. I am therefore prone to believe Orlov's version that Skoblin was taken to Russia on a Soviet vessel over the KGB's dubious scenario which does not stand up to close scrutiny.

Perhaps the most glaring statement to consider is whether Orlov knew Shpiegelglass prior to the kidnapping. Shpiegelglass was not a professional KGB officer but a crony of Yezhov's. When Yezhov became Chairman of the KGB in 1936, he brought about 300 of his trusted friends and associates from the Central Committee of the Communist Party into the KGB, and chose his personal friend Shpiegelglass to head the Mobile Groups. It was not until early December 1937 that the two antagonists met for the first time. However, had Shpiegelglass been a KGB career officer, it would be reasonable to expect that they might possibly have known one another. This factor alone challenges the credibility of the KGB version.

As already described, Shpiegelglass became Acting Chief of the KGB's Foreign Department in February 1938 following the mysterious death of Abram Slutsky. However, his days in the sun did not last long as he was arrested in the autumn of the same year and was believed to have been executed shortly afterwards. An interesting and revealing glimpse of the repercussions surrounding the whole affair was afforded in *Deadly Illusions*, which stated that there was an item in the KGB files which confirmed how swiftly Yezhov had caved in to Orlov's blackmail letter. In Shpiegelglass's file, amongst the confession he made six months after his own arrest for treachery in November 1938, was a reference to Orlov's letter in which he threatened to expose compromising material if he detected any hint of a KGB surveillance. 'After that Yezhov issued a directive not to touch Nikolsky [Orlov]. The stakes were high in Orlov's "dangerous game" and it would be clear to Yezhov and Stalin that his was no idle bluff.'

There is one other area that cries out for an answer pertaining to Orlov's defection letter, which had been sent separately to Yezhov and Stalin. *Deadly Illusions* implies that Orlov never sent a copy of his letter to Stalin and in a footnote records that, 'there is no evidence to be found in the NKVD files that Orlov addressed a separate copy of his letter to Stalin'. Then the question is asked, 'Why did Orlov go to such great lengths to maintain he also sent a copy of his letter to Stalin along with a note revealing that Yezhov had disobeyed orders not to get the embassy involved in the Miller kidnapping?', and is answered with the statement, 'It is conceivable that he wanted to enhance his importance and make his case more dramatic.'

In the footnote which followed, it was also stated that, 'Corroboration that there was no such missive appears in the discovery of two copies of the note that Orlov sent accompanying his letter to Yezhov. They are addressed to Kislov, the Paris *rezident*: "Today I have handed to a concierge at the Embassy two packets addressed 1) to Kislov 2) to Ambassador Surits. Both are to be forwarded to Nikolay Ivanovich (Yezhov). signed Schwedlov."' Contained in the same footnote is the somewhat contradictory statement, 'Certainly two copies of Orlov's letter addressed only to Yezhov have been found in the files. It is clear that one was seen by Beria. But it is impossible to know from the surviving records whether he showed it to Stalin.'

It would not be difficult to answer the question why Orlov sent a copy of his letter to Stalin denouncing Yezhov. It was certainly not vanity but pure revenge on the man that had liquidated many of Orlov's friends in the KGB, had caused him to defect in order to save his life, and had been responsible for the execution of his cousin Zinovy Katsnelson.

It is absurd to believe that Orlov sent both copies of his letter to his archenemy Yezhov with the expectation that Yezhov would forward one of the copies to Stalin. Orlov was a professional in every respect and was certainly not naïve in any way. On the contrary, he was streetwise in matters of human nature and would have taken every measure to safeguard the transmission of his letter to Stalin. Orlov took elaborate precautions from the very moment he drafted the letters, having them carried by hand by his cousin halfway around the world aboard an ocean liner and shrewdly having them deposited on the reception desk at the Soviet Embassy in Paris on a religious holiday when the Embassy would be lightly staffed. This does not sound like a man who would entrust his life to his worst enemy.

The beginning of the end was fast approaching for Yezhov by the time Orlov's letters were delivered to the Soviet Embassy on 15 August 1938. The previous month, the notorious Lavrenty Beria had been transferred to the KGB Centre as the Deputy Chairman of the KGB, the date almost coinciding with Orlov's defection. In August, Yezhov was relegated to the obscure position of Commissar of Inland Water Transport, although he was ostensibly still in charge of the KGB. He was officially dismissed as the head of the KGB on 8 December 1939 and Beria was appointed in his place. Yezhov mysteriously disappeared from the scene and was believed to have been executed.

The sequence of interrelated events strongly suggests that Stalin did receive Orlov's letter and the corroboration lies with the fact that Yezhov was dismissed from his exalted position with the KGB and executed in this time frame. It appears that Stalin was already disenchanted with Yezhov as early as July 1938, when he had his new protégé Beria in place to take over the reins of the KGB at the point when Yezhov had outlived his usefulness to the dictator. There is no doubt that when Stalin received Orlov's letter, he must have felt betrayed and outraged to learn that Yezhov had been disloyal and lied to him. Orlov's letter could well have been the straw that broke the camel's back.

As for the reference in *Deadly Illusions* questioning whether Beria had shown Orlov's letter to Stalin, I would have to suggest that it was Stalin who turned his copy of the Orlov letter over to Beria with the intention of eliminating Yezhov in the near future. This would explain why both copies of Orlov's letter now lie in the KGB archives in Moscow.

I once asked Orlov if he felt that Beria, as the new Chairman of the KGB and protégé of Stalin, could have intervened and saved his life in 1938 had he chosen to return to Moscow rather than to defect. They had been professional associates since 1926, when Beria had been a subordinate of Orlov's, and Beria owed a few favours to Orlov. His reply was that even if Beria had interceded with the dictator, this would not have made any difference as Stalin was highly unlikely to have changed his mind. Furthermore, Orlov added that he had never looked back and had no regrets about his decision to defect. When we spoke of matters relating to Yezhov and his fall from grace with Stalin, Orlov never displayed the slightest hint of emotion or remorse when we came to the part about Yezhov's mysterious death. In my mind, I visualised that deep down in his heart he was thinking of his cousin Zinovy Katsnelson.

TWENTY-SIX

REILLY, ACE OF SPIES

No book on Alexander Orlov would be complete without a chapter on the British Ace of Spies, Sidney Reilly. Although Orlov never met the British spy in person, it was apparent that he greatly admired the man. Over the years there have been numerous works written about the flamboyant British spy but none from the perspective of the KGB. What Orlov related to me is well worth repeating inasmuch as it provides historical insight that he acquired while a KGB official.

The period in question is shortly before and after the end of the Russian Civil War in 1920, which was a time of turbulence when the fate of the newly formed Soviet Government hung in the balance and only a slight push could bring it down. In April 1920, Poland invaded Russia with such success that it occupied Kiev and most of the Ukraine and precipitated the Russo-Polish War. By the early part of 1920, the Anti-Bolshevik White Armies were on the defensive but the Polish invasion breathed new life into their cause, at least temporarily. The Civil War was finally over but unrest on the part of the White Army generals continued from abroad with the unrealistic hope that the masses within the new Soviet Union would rise against their Communist masters and return the Government to the monarchy. The newly formed KGB under the direction of Felix Dzerzhinsky correctly calculated that its immediate enemy was the leaders and remnants of the defeated White Army who continued to pose a threat to the Soviet Union.

Against this backdrop, the KGB created one of its most enduring and rewarding illusions, which served to convince the

Western Powers that it was dealing with real dissidents and their organisation within the Soviet Union through a legitimate anti-Soviet monarchist organisation. The fictitious creation came to be known as the TRUST, after the Russian word '*Trest*', the so-called 'Monarchist Organisation of Central Russia', and became the vehicle which fed misinformation to the Western Powers. In time, the TRUST was the avenue by which the prime enemies of the state were lured back to Russia and executed. Sidney Reilly and Boris Savinkov, the fanatical White Russian General who ran the anti-Bolshevik organisation People's Union for the Defence of the Homeland and Freedom from abroad, would both be successfully lured back to Russia and their deaths by the TRUST. The third prize target of the TRUST was General Kutyepov, the head of the ROVS, who was kidnapped off the streets of Paris in 1930 by the KGB and eliminated.

Reilly was destined to become Britain's most famous intelligence ace, although there was considerable doubt concerning his true background. He claimed that he was the son of a Russian mother and an Irish father, who was a sea captain, and had been born in Odessa and educated in St Petersburg and the University of Heidelberg in Germany. He was considered to be handsome, intelligent and noble by those who knew him, but to others he was a dreamer, a charlatan and a con-man. His close associate, the British envoy Robert Bruce Lockhart, said of him, 'A man cast in the Napoleonic mould . . . who deserves to be ranked with the bravest men of his time.'

Early in his career, Reilly was successful in business as an agent for the naval armaments company of Mandrochovich and Count Chubersky in St Petersburg; and at the start of the First World War, he was a munitions broker and agent of the Banque Russo-Asiatique. In 1916, he posed as a German naval officer and was able to penetrate the German Naval High Command and steal the secret naval code, bringing him recognition on his very first intelligence escapade. The German code was turned over to British intelligence, thereby opening for Reilly the door into the secret world of intelligence. Reilly was not a professional in the

British Secret Intelligence Service (SIS) but more of a gentleman spy, who did not depend on the Service for a living. In this manner, he was able to choose his projects to some degree and be in a position to criticise his superiors and the foreign policy of the British Government when he saw fit to do so.

At the beginning of 1918, Reilly was dispatched to Russia, which was now under the control of the Bolsheviks. His Russian background and influential friends in the new nation no doubt were the factors that had brought him the assignment. This was still in the period before the peace treaty of Brest-Litovsk of March 1918 between Russia and the Central Powers. The Allies felt that their main concern was to have the Soviets continue their pressure on the Central Powers in order to prevent the Germans from transferring their troops from the Russian front to the Western front. What Reilly proposed after seeing what was going on in Russia was a common front against the Bolshevik Communists, whom he regarded as the true enemy of the people. He did not consider the Germans as the enemy and could not understand why England did not realise that the monstrous cancer against mankind, which was growing in Moscow, had to be crushed immediately. There was no room for doubt that Reilly was highly motivated towards the destruction of the new Soviet regime and, in doing so, propelled himself into the position of the prime enemy of the Bolsheviks.

Reilly feverishly went about re-establishing old contacts among his former Russian associates and, in a short time, was able to form his own network of spies. He was then able to supply SIS with a steady flow of information regarding the Red Army and the Soviet Government as well as giving an accurate portrayal of the political climate in the Soviet Union.

In the early summer of 1918, Lenin was convinced that the French and British Governments were plotting to overthrow the Soviet Government and proposed to Dzerzhinsky that these plotters could be exposed to the world if their spies were caught in the act of espionage. Dzerzhinsky took the matter up with his aides and a pragmatic operation was conceived.

The KGB had on its books a young informant by the name of Smidchen, who was of Lettish origin and who had been a junior officer in the Tsar's Army. This informant had reported several contacts with the British Naval Attaché in St Petersburg, Captain Cromie. In these contacts, Cromie had attempted to prevail on Smidchen to obtain Red Army secrets for him. The KGB seized on this opportunity to expose the SIS and asked Smidchen to contact Cromie with the information that he had a friend in the Lettish artillery, Colonel Berzin, who despised the Bolsheviks and would be willing to work for the British cause. Cromie made no immediate commitment but within a week contacted Smidchen with a request that he bring Berzin to a private apartment on Khlebny Lane in Moscow for a private meeting with Bruce Lockhart. This was the beginning of a celebrated operation in the annals of the KGB that would become known as the 'Conspiracy of the Ambassadors'.

Smidchen and Berzin met Bruce Lockhart on 14 August and the latter was convinced of the Colonel's bona fides, his sincerity and the fact that the Lettish troops had no desire to fight the British; in the event that they were called upon to do so, Berzin said that he would surrender his troops to the British rather than fight. Berzin also mentioned that his troops might be dispatched to Archangel in the north to fight the British troops that had recently landed there under the command of General Poole. In this contingency, he requested a pass in order to send a delegate to make contact with Poole for an orderly surrender.

Berzin stressed that all he desired after the cessation of hostilities was an independent Latvia and the return of the Lettish troops to their homeland. Bruce Lockhart was convinced that Berzin was legitimate and asked both men to come back the following day.

The next day, the two KGB plants met Bruce Lockhart and two other individuals, the French Consul-General Grenard and an important SIS member by the name of Constantine. Bruce Lockhart was impressed with the fact that the Lettish military was disposed towards the interests of the British, and he in turn impressed on the two callers the importance of indoctrinating the Lettish military against the Soviets. He stressed that they could expect unlimited funds in this direction. Grenard went one step further: in return for any assistance in overthrowing the Bolshevik Government, the Letts could be expected to gain their independence. He said that he could not state this position officially but was convinced that this would be their reward for their help. Berzin was offered 4 million roubles to be paid in two instalments with which he was to influence his troops towards the Allies' cause. As the two impostors were about to depart, Bruce Lockhart gave Berzin a handwritten pass that authorised free passage for him through British lines. The pass was the first solid piece of evidence that the KGB had against the British.

On 17 August, Constantine met Berzin at the Café Tramble in Moscow for the purpose of paying Berzin the first instalment of 900,000 roubles. In addition, Constantine outlined a plan that had been proposed by a French general, which called for two Lettish regiments to be assigned to the city of Vologda, where they would surrender to the Anglo-French forces and thus pave the way for the Allies to advance from their landings in Archangel. In the meantime, the remaining Lettish troops in Moscow would seize the Soviet Government and assassinate Lenin and the other top leaders of the Government.

Constantine was none other than Sidney Reilly, the man who would be entrusted with the plan to overthrow the Soviet Government. As they sat there that day, Reilly felt proud that he had been instrumental in moving forward the plan to defeat the Communist menace.

On their next meeting, Reilly requested that Berzin should make a trip to St Petersburg, now called Petrograd, to establish contact with the Lettish community and determine what their role would be in the coming uprising. Reilly would follow by the next train out of Moscow. He then gave Berzin the address of a safe-house in Petrograd where they would meet. Berzin proceeded to the specified address, where he was told by a maid that the lady of the house was not in but that he should wait. In the apartment, he noticed a letter on a table that had apparently just been delivered. The letter was from Reilly and bore the return address of 'Apartment 85, Sheremetiev Lane #3, Moscow'. Berzin made a note of the return address and left.

At about the same time, René Marchand, the Moscow correspondent of the French newspaper *Le Figaro* and a Soviet sympathiser, brought to Dzerzhinsky the news of a highly secret conference held at the American Consulate-General on 25 August. The French Consul-General Grenard had presided over the conference, which had been attended by the diplomatic and military staffs of the Americans, French and British. The topic was the imminent departure of the diplomatic missions from Russia and the need for the embassies to leave behind their intelligence personnel to continue espionage activities on Soviet soil. Reilly, who was an active participant at the conference, was to head the British intelligence mission with the assistance of Captain George Hill of SIS.

The most unexpected news to come out of the conference was the disclosure by Reilly of the plan he had devised with Berzin that the Lettish troops could be counted on to surrender and throw their lot in with the Allies in return for Latvia's independence. He added that he had bribed the Lettish commanders with money and promises of high posts in their new government in the expectation that they would do his bidding. Without hesitating, he announced the most shocking and compelling part of the conspiracy. On 28 August, only a few days away, a series of meetings of the All-Russian Congress of Soviets would take place at the Bolshoi Theatre with all of the Soviet leadership in attendance. Reilly and his fellow conspirators planned to conceal themselves behind the curtains armed with weapons and hand grenades. At a predesignated signal given by Reilly, the soldiers would cover all exits to prevent anyone from escaping. Reilly would jump on to the stage and seize Lenin, Trotsky and the other leaders. They would all be shot on the spot.

Marchand's story seemed unbelievable to Dzerzhinsky, although he was already aware of the part that Berzin had reported to him and, therefore, had to assume that the story was correct. He immediately contacted Lenin, who asked if Marchand was willing to put his report on paper. Marchand replied in the negative, advising that if he furnished this information to the Soviets in writing, his journalistic career would be ruined and he would be criticised by his Government and ostracised by his fellow journalists. However, he did mention that there would be no problem if he were furnishing the information to his own Government. Lenin immediately knew the answer to the problem. He asked Marchand if he would be willing to write this information in a letter to French President Raymond Poincaré and, if he were, the KGB could then find the letter during the course of a surreptitious search of his apartment under a suitable pretext. Marchand agreed and wrote a lengthy letter to Poincaré, under the guidance of Dzerzhinsky, detailing the events of the Allies' secret meeting. Marchand did not have long to wait for the KGB to search his apartment and find the incriminating letter. The contents were eventually published by the Bolsheviks in the Soviet press on 24 September, which cited the facts as a case of treachery against the Soviet Government.

Fate intervened when the conference of the Congress of the Soviets at the Bolshoi Theatre was postponed until 6 September. In the meantime, Reilly decided to use the remaining days to work out minor details of his plan. Then several other events took place that would have drastic consequences on the plan. On 30 August, a man by the name of Kenigisser, who was alleged to be a member of Savinkov's anti-Bolshevik organisation, stalked Moses Uritsky, the Chief of the KGB in Petrograd, and shot him dead as he was leaving his office. Lenin was outraged at this assassination and ordered Dzerzhinsky to raid the French and British Embassies, as well as their other diplomatic establishments, in Moscow and Petrograd in retaliation for the murder.

If this was not enough confusion to add to the situation, there was more to come. Within hours of Uritsky's murder, Lenin himself was shot. The perpetrator was a young Jewish woman by the name of Fanya Kaplan, who also went by the name of Dora

Kaplan and was a known member of the Socialist Revolutionary Party. That day Lenin gave a speech before the workers at the Mikhelson factory in Moscow and was shot by Kaplan as he was leaving the building. Kaplan was immediately arrested. On his specific orders, Lenin was taken to his home rather than to a hospital. He was gravely wounded but survived. Kaplan was not as fortunate; within days of the assassination attempt, she was executed. Kaplan never revealed what brought her to this terrible act nor whether she had any accomplices, but many believed that she had acted on the orders of Boris Savinkov, who denied the allegations.

The next day, 31 August, KGB troops surrounded the British Embassy in Petrograd and their officers entered the Embassy. As the KGB officers charged the stairs to the second floor, they were met by Captain Cromie, who opened fire on the intruders. He killed one KGB officer by the name of Lisen and wounded several others. They in turn killed Cromie. Meanwhile, the KGB carried out a similar raid on the diplomatic establishments in Moscow and arrested Robert Bruce Lockhart at his Moscow apartment.

The KGB also raided the apartment at Sheremetiev Lane #3 in Moscow, the location which Berzin had found on the letter in Petrograd with Reilly's return address. The apartment turned out to be the residence of Elizaveta Otten, an actress with the Moscow Art Theatre. She admitted that she had a deep affection for Reilly and had permitted him to use her apartment as a meeting place for his conspirators; she also said that she had acted as a liaison between Reilly and his spy network. With this information, the KGB placed a surveillance on Otten's apartment and was able to apprehend several members of Reilly's spy network. The first spy arrested was Maria Friede, the sister of Colonel Friede of the General Staff of the Red Army. She walked into the apartment with a large number of secret documents which she had received from her brother. Shortly afterwards, Colonel Friede walked into the trap and was arrested. He admitted that he had been furnishing Reilly with vital military information from the files of the Red Army.

While Captain Cromie was shooting it out with the KGB at the British Embassy in Petrograd, Reilly was sitting at a table in a café waiting for his friend Cromie to arrive. Oblivious to what was happening, he was nevertheless apprehensive as to why his normally punctual friend had not appeared at the scheduled meeting. He decided to go to the British Embassy to determine why Cromie had failed to turn up. As he approached the Embassy, he noticed the military presence and several bodies lying near the entrance. He realised that there was a major problem and walked away from the Embassy without being noticed.

The hunt for the elusive British spy now went into top gear in Moscow and Petrograd. The Soviet newspapers all carried stories about the crackdown on the Western conspirators and the name Sidney Reilly became a household word. Reilly's photograph was published in the newspapers as well as being posted in public places. By now, Reilly realised his predicament and was aware that he would be shot if apprehended. A prudent individual would have made it to the Finnish frontier and crossed to safety, but not Reilly. His first consideration was the members of his spy network who had placed their loyalty in him. If he could help them in any way, this was the time to do so in spite of the ever-present danger. Changing his identity again, he boarded the train to Moscow without incident even though his identity papers were scrutinised by the officials at the Petrograd railway station.

In Moscow, Reilly warned those members of his spy network that had not been detected by the KGB, despite the danger of betrayal. Satisfied that he had done as much as he could under the circumstances, he again changed his identity and returned to Petrograd. There he learned of a Dutch vessel in the port and bribed the captain to take him out of the country. His adventure finally brought him to London and safety. However, his return did not bring him the adulation he expected from the British SIS but suspicion on the part of his fellow spies. Some were envious of his exploits while others questioned how this man could have such courage in the face of the enemy. Soon the pettiness turned to the suspicion that this extraordinarily brave man could possibly be a Soviet spy who had turned against his own people.

In December 1918, the Soviet Supreme Revolutionary Tribunal in Moscow convicted Reilly, Bruce Lockhart and several of the lesser members of the conspiracy to death *in absentia*. Although the event was known in the KGB as the 'Conspiracy of the Ambassadors', to the world at large it was the 'Lockhart Conspiracy'. This is how the matter stood in December 1918.

By the end of 1920, the KGB had in hand the apparatus that would bring Reilly and other enemies of the state to their end. In charge of the operation that would become known as the TRUST was the Chief of KGB Counter-intelligence Artur Artuzov and his chief deputies Pillar, Puzitsky, Kiakovsky and Fedorov. Because of his many successes in the TRUST operation, Artuzov was destined to become the chief of the all-powerful First Directorate by the end of the decade. Although Artuzov is given credit for being the founding father of the TRUST, it was Fedorov who conceived the idea of the TRUST. Another faction of the operation was known under the name of the SINDIKAT and conceived to collect and disseminate military rather than political information. Both operations were under the jurisdiction of the KRO (counter-intelligence) but were so intertwined that the TRUST became the dominant organisation while the other was of minimal usefulness.

Orlov never had an official connection with the TRUST, or for that matter the Reilly affair, but took a keen interest in both interconnected operations. Because of his official position with the KGB, he knew most of the key players personally and was privy to the secrets of both operations. His prime informants for the story related here were Artuzov, Fedorov and, to some extent, a former Red Army officer by the name of Grisha Siroyezhkin.

Orlov was a skilled teacher and to illustrate an important point he would often resort to an interesting metaphor. Such was the case when he first introduced me to the TRUST and it so impressed me that I wrote it down. Orlov related that the TRUST was nothing more than the old 'cat-and-mouse' game. In this case, the cat was the Great Powers: England, France and America, and the mouse was the newly emerging Soviet Government, which possessed limited power assets, no leverage with which to be in a position to broker their demands, and an absence cf international recognition. However, the twist in the case of the TRUST was the fact that it was the mouse which was manipulating the cat.

Orlov's assessment was that the TRUST was well conceived from the start and ably managed throughout its existence. No operation was ever undertaken without complete consultation of the chief planners and, although there were disagreements and dissent, any differences were resolved before any action was taken. The only exception was when Stalin would personally interject his views and wishes. Orlov specifically related that throughout the history of the TRUST, the managers walked a tightrope as to the information they would feed to the West but always came down on the side of expected results that would benefit the Soviets in the long term. In order to build up confidence in the TRUST and to perpetuate its continued existence, it was necessary to disseminate both factual and verifiable information, however, that information was either of an inconsequential nature or was already in the hands of the West from other sources. On the other hand, they also furnished disinformation that for the most part would be impossible to verify.

This is how the TRUST evolved. In order to promote the illusion of a monarchist organisation within the Soviet Union dedicated to the overthrow of the Bolshevik Government, it was necessary to have an organisation with recognised leadership that would appear to be legitimate and acceptable to the anti-Bolshevik émigré organisations abroad. For this purpose, the KGB already had on its payroll two very well-qualified agents. Alexander Yakushev was a well-known monarchist, who had become a KGB agent after being caught in an anti-Bolshevik operation. Lieutenant General Nikolai Potapov had close connections to the late Tsar and was considered the titular head of all White Russian veterans living abroad. He was living in France as a political exile but, unknown to his associates, was a secret agent of the KGB. Both men made frequent trips abroad to meet the White émigré leaders, Generals Vrangel and Kutyepov, and feed them information ostensibly from the non-existent TRUST organisation. Although under severe scrutiny, their information was always favourably received as being authentic. In time, other so-called monarchist members of the TRUST came out of the Soviet Union to do their insidious work.

Yakushev and Potapov were able to win over the complete confidence of Vrangel and Kutyepov and through them were able to establish relations with foreign intelligence agencies to whom they claimed that they were building up a large anti-Bolshevik spy network within the Soviet Union. The doctored information they brought out of Russia was so skilfully prepared by Fedorov that the deceit was never uncovered; it was considered reliable and above suspicion. The Western intelligence organisations were lulled into the belief that the TRUST's intelligence-gathering ability was so efficient that they never bothered to establish their own spy networks in the Soviet Union. The TRUST succeeded in infiltrating the ROVS and recruited a number of former Tsarist generals to its side. One of them was General Monkewich, Kutyepov's expert in terrorist acts, who was bribed by Fedorov, after which he became an ardent supporter of the TRUST. All in all, the KGB reaped a rich harvest through the TRUST.

Before each mission Potapov and Yakushev, as well as other TRUST representatives, were briefed extensively by Artuzov and his staff because of the danger that one wrong word or one miscalculated action could bring down the entire operation. Every detail was measured for accuracy so as to overcome any pitfalls they might encounter. At times Dzerzhinsky would join the briefings to satisfy himself that the operation was going according to plan. In order to safeguard the integrity of the operation, a regular KGB staff member accompanied Potapov and Yakushev on each mission in the guise of a subordinate. In fact, if any unforeseen event occurred and a spontaneous decision had to be taken, it was made by the KGB officer. The man chosen for this position was Fedorov.

Fedorov was around thirty-two years of age when he was chosen for the assignment. He was rather short in stature and somewhat portly. He was by disposition a very modest person, who spoke with sincerity in a slow and deliberate manner. Beneath his personal appearance was a tenacious man of deep imagination and intelligence, who, by nature, was a psychologist. He inspired confidence and had the ability to present a proposition in both a negative and positive light and in such a manner that the person being interrogated would come to the conclusion sought by Fedorov. By the early 1930s, Fedorov had earned two top Soviet decorations and was appointed Chief of the Foreign Department of the Leningrad KGB.

Much has been said about Fedorov's achievements with the TRUST but none would be more acclaimed than his next assignment. In 1924, Fedorov was given the task of luring the KGB's archenemy Sidney Reilly back to the Soviet Union to face the consequences of his conspiratorial acts against the country. The KGB and the Soviet leadership had never forgiven the famous British spy for his intrigues and now had in hand the instrument to bring their foe back into their waiting arms. Unknown to Reilly, his new adversary was the unrelenting KGB officer that other KGB officers dared to call in private 'Bulldog' Fedorov.

What Reilly had on his side was the knowledge that a year before Boris Savinkov had been lured back to the Soviet Union and to his death. Reilly had even cautioned Savinkov not to return to the USSR fearing that he was falling into a trap, but Savinkov did not heed his warning. What prompted Reilly to ignore his own good advice will never be known.

Savinkov had been the thorn in the side of the Bolsheviks that had to be eliminated. He was the fiery Socialist revolutionary whose bands of guerrillas roamed Byelorussia during the 1920–2 period committing acts of sabotage and terrorising the local Soviet officials. During the Russo-Polish War, Savinkov's guerrillas joined forces with the Polish Army and Savinkov recruited the Russian People's Army, which fought side by side with the Poles. However, at the end of the war in March 1921, the Soviets insisted that the Poles dissociate themselves from Savinkov's band. In January 1921, Savinkov formed the Union for the Defence of the Homeland and Freedom for the purpose of operating a spy network in the USSR and to prepare for the uprising that would topple the Bolshevik Government. Savinkov moved his headquarters from Warsaw to Prague and finally to Paris.

The first crack in Savinkov's armour came about in 1920, when his guerrillas played havoc with the Red Army behind their own lines. The Osoby Otdel (a special department within the army roughly equivalent to military intelligence) of the 16th Red Army devised a plan to gather information on Savinkov's guerrillas, who were well supported by the Russian peasants. A small Red Army military unit would appear at a Russian village near the Polish border that had been suspected of giving aid and comfort to Savinkov's guerrillas, ostensibly to collect a levy from the villagers. The commander of the unit would advise the village elders that his heart was not in collecting taxes from the poor and that he and his unit were deserting. The junior officer chosen to lead the supposed Red Army renegades was a young and ardent Communist by the name of Grisha Siroyezhkin.

The plan went better than expected. The villagers informed Savinkov's guerrilla leader in the area, one Ivanov, of the Red Army deserters' presence and the fact that the group planned to surrender to the Polish forces. Under a pretext, Ivanov met Siroyezhkin in order to evaluate the veracity of the group; when he was satisfied to this end, he asked Siroyezhkin and his men to join his guerrillas. Soon Siroyezhkin and his men were participating in a variety of guerrilla operations against their own country, but still under the watchful eye of the Osoby Otdel as Siroyezhkin was reporting the guerrillas' activities through an underground channel. In time, Siroyezhkin won over the confidence of Ivanov and was asked to participate in a secret conference of guerrilla commanders. At the conference, Siroyezhkin met Colonel Sergei Pavlovsky, Savinkov's overall field commander who operated behind the Russian lines. Siroyezhkin later learned that the true reason for his presence at the conference, as well as several other junior field commanders, was that Pavlovsky wanted to select a few reliable couriers to carry messages between himself in the field and Savinkov in Warsaw. Siroyezhkin was one of the selected candidates for the position, which he readily accepted.

The original motive for Siroyezhkin's penetration was to determine the best opportunity for a massive attack on Savinkov's guerrillas as well as to explore the possibility of capturing the guerrilla leaders. When the Osoby Otdel received the word that Siroyezhkin was going to become a courier for Savinkov, they cancelled the original plan and ordered him to concentrate his efforts on his new role.

Siroyezhkin played his part well. On his first crossing into Poland as a courier, he met Savinkov in Warsaw. On his third crossing, he was wounded by a Soviet patrol and convalesced at the Hotel Brul in Warsaw, where Savinkov maintained his headquarters. Had there been any suspicion regarding Siroyezhkin, being a wounded courier only added to his bona fides. Savinkov became fond of his trusted courier and soon appointed him commander of all the other couriers. Siroyezhkin knew that this meant he would have access to all intelligence flowing between Russia and Savinkov.

Savinkov was a brilliant organiser and leader. Within a year, he had created a vast anti-Soviet organisation within the Soviet Union, which operated from an underground centre in Gomel. He succeeded in establishing anti-Soviet cells in the villages and the army as well as in various government departments. The principal objective was to gather a force that would overthrow the Bolshevik Government. He also had the financial resources of the Western Powers. The uprising was planned for the end of the 1921 harvesting season. In July 1921, the Soviet military raided Savinkov's underground establishments in a number of cities and arrested the conspirators. The organisation was badly bent but not broken. The Soviets took great pains not to disrupt Siroyezhkin's work as a spy in Savinkov's camp in order to maintain the flow of vital information from their prime source. Savinkov continued to rebuild his shattered organisation.

Orlov surmised that it was during this period that the KGB gradually took over the operation of Siroyezhkin from the Osoby Otdel. He became a KGB officer and was destined to become one of the key players in the field operations of the TRUST. It was also about the time Orlov first met him and they became friends. Orlov disclosed to me that part of his insight into the TRUST had been provided by his friend Siroyezhkin.

By 1923, the KGB felt that it could allow Savinkov's organisation to exist as it knew all the key members and could arrest them at any time; and further, interest in the organisation had waned to the point it was no longer a real threat. What they did not have in their hands was their real enemy, Savinkov. Artuzov therefore came up with a cunning scheme to instil in Savinkov's mind that the Communist experiment was a total failure and that the masses would soon rise to overthrow the Government. He intended to paint a picture indicating that Savinkov's organisation was growing in strength daily and that the time was ripe to seize power. The mechanics of the scheme was to have Siroyezhkin intercept the handwritten communications between Savinkov and Pavlovsky and substitute letters fabricated by the KGB. This was not as difficult as it would seem as both men had a distinctive style of writing that was easy to imitate. The gist of the forged letters indicated that the Soviet Union was unravelling at the seams due to unemployment, food shortages and rivalry amongst the Communist movement. On the other hand, the Union for the Defence of the Homeland and Freedom was gaining strength continuously and was poised to overthrow the Government. All went well until April 1924, when one of Pavlovsky's real letters was read by Artuzov in which the Colonel advised Savinkov that he would no longer write and that no one should be trusted. Artuzov was apprehensive as to what had brought about this suspicion and had Pavlovsky arrested in order to stop him from possibly giving Savinkov damaging information by means other than the courier service. Meanwhile, Savinkov knew nothing of Pavlovsky's arrest but felt that something was not quite right with Pavlovksy's letters, so he summoned Siroyezhkin to Paris.

Siroyezhkin assured him that there was no problem and said that Pavlovsky insisted that he come to Russia. Savinkov was still not satisfied and decided to send a retired and trusted chief of the Warsaw secret police to Russia to meet Pavlovsky in person in order to evaluate the situation.

Artuzov now had a problem of major proportions. At first he thought they could find a suitable double for Pavlovsky, but common sense prevailed when they considered the fact that Pavlovsky had commanded the anti-guerrillas near the Polish border and might be personally known to the Polish police chief. He then ordered Pavlovsky to be brought to him from prison with the intention of laying all his cards on the table. He showed Pavlovsky photographs of all the intercepted correspondence between him and Savinkov, the fictitious lists of all the members of Savinkov's organisation, the non-existent location of the organisation's secret printing plant and places where they were supposedly storing arms and ammunition for the uprising. Then he made his best play: he informed Pavlovsky that there was no such thing in the Soviet Union as the Union for the Defence of the Homeland and Freedom as ninety-five per cent of its membership had been created fictitiously by the KGB. Looking straight at Pavlovsky, Artuzov sternly interjected that before the KGB had humbled him, he had caused much harm and bloodshed on Russian soil and it was time to pay for these crimes.

Artuzov related that Savinkov was sending an emissary to size up the situation and consult with him in regard to the uprising. Artuzov warned that the emissary should be told that the time for the uprising was imminent and that Savinkov was needed in Russia to lead the rebellion. Artuzov promised that in return for this service, Pavlovsky's life would be spared. Pavlovsky, like the good soldier he was, was visibly unnerved by the news but made no commitment. Finally, under the pressure of continuous interrogation all day and night, he succumbed to Artuzov's demand.

The next part of the operation was planned meticulously by Artuzov to the smallest detail. Stalin himself had taken a personal interest in the operation and had been the one to suggest the wily scheme to bring Pavlovsky to his knees by revealing the fact that Savinkov's organisation was nothing more than a paper tiger. In his usual way, Stalin then denigrated his subordinates in the operation by stating, 'I can already see that it will end in a flop!' Orlov felt that this was Stalin's unorthodox way of goading the best efforts out of his subordinates. With Stalin's personal admonition before him, Artuzov knew he had no room for failure.

The Polish chief of the secret police crossed the border into Russia and was met by a member of the TRUST operation. Puzitsky was one of the chiefs in the operation and a Russianised Pole, who spoke perfect Polish. He passed himself off as a colonel in the Red Army and told the Pole that Pavlovsky was in Tiflis attending a secret meeting of Georgian activists that had several contentious factions; when they received word from Pavlovsky, they would go to Kharkov to meet him. Artuzov reasoned that there was no way he could allow the Pole to meet Pavlovsky face to face for fear that at the last moment Pavlovsky might blurt out the truth, or make some sort of facial expression to indicate that the Pole was being told lies. Artuzov therefore came up with another scheme, which fortunately went according to plan.

The next day, Puzitsky received a telegram instructing him and the Pole to proceed to Tiflis rather than to Kharkov. On the train to the new destination, they heard a knock on their compartment door and a young Georgian entered. Puzitsky was ecstatic at seeing the man and introduced him to the Pole as one of the leading members of the Georgian branch of the Union for the Defence of the Homeland and Freedom. The Georgian related that he bore bad news: a brawl had broken out at the secret meeting between two opposing factions and, when Pavlovsky had intervened, he had been badly wounded. He was now in a hospital in Tiflis, where he would meet Savinkov's emissary.

When they did meet in the hospital room, it was apparent that Pavlovsky had survived the altercation by the narrowest of margins. He was lying in bed with bandages around a supposed wound and some old blood-stained bandages were visible on an adjacent medical tray. The Pole related that the Commander,

Savinkov's pseudonym, had only two questions he wanted answered: did Pavlovsky believe the time had come for the uprising and what was the strength of their forces? Pavlovsky hesitated for several moments as if considering the questions and finally replied that the time had come for action. However, he wanted to give more consideration to a final answer. The Pole then asked Pavlovsky if he thought the Commander's presence in Russia was vital for the success of the uprising. Yes, replied Pavlovsky, while adding that he could only give his final answer when he was out of hospital. At that moment a new patient was wheeled into the room and the conversation was terminated for the time being. The visitors agreed to come back the next day, which they did; however, they were barred from seeing Pavlovsky as it seemed he had developed a high fever and could receive no visitors.

The short meeting of the previous day had accomplished everything Artuzov hoped for. Everyone in the hospital room, with the exception of the Pole, had acted out their part according to the TRUST script in a first-rate fashion. There was never any doubt that when the Pole returned with his report to Savinkov, it would be favourable.

Savinkov was still not satisfied that he would not be risking his life by entering the Soviet Union and he felt time was on his side. In this direction, he consulted three experts. The first was Vladimir Burtsev, who had ferreted out numerous spies from the old revolutionary parties during the time of the Tsar. Burtsev felt that Savinkov's organisation was viable and that it was his destiny in history to serve the Russian people. The second person consulted was the dictator of Italy, Benito Mussolini, who cautioned Savinkov to wait for more facts. The third person consulted was the famous British spy and his personal friend, Sidney Reilly. The British spy was extremely apprehensive and emphatically warned Savinkov that he would fall into a trap and should not enter Russia.

Time was mounting and Stalin accused Artuzov of bungling the operation. Thus Artuzov was forced into another ploy. He sent two *agents provocateurs* to Paris to plead with Savinkov. They painted a dire picture that indicated there was much ideological divergence in the organisation in Russia and said that Pavlovsky no longer had the prestige to correct the situation as only Savinkov could. They even delivered a bogus letter to this effect from Pavlovsky. Notwithstanding these latest efforts, the 'Great Conspirator', as Orlov would often refer to Savinkov, did not spring into action but erred on the side of caution.

By this time, Artuzov was at his wits' end but had one more card to play. Savinkov was infatuated with the wife of his personal secretary Derental. The lady was attractive although much younger than Savinkov. In his younger days, Savinkov had been the proverbial 'ladies' man' and had many conquests to his credit; however, in his waning years this would be his last fling. For whatever reason, the husband closed his eyes to the romance between his wife and the man he idolised as a political figure. Knowing these facts and because of the high priority of the Savinkov matter, the KGB *rezident* in Paris approached Madame Derental and was able to recruit her. However, her services came at a high financial cost as she demanded and received almost three times the pay of an informant in a similar situation.

Madame Derental now had the financial incentive and began her insidious campaign step by step. She played on Savinkov's egotism by putting him on a pedestal and telling him that he had to assume his rightful place in Russian history as the liberator of the Russian people. He had no choice but to go to Russia in person to lead the revolt and meet his destiny. In time, Savinkov was convinced by her that he must go.

While Savinkov was making his arrangements to go to Russia, Madame Derental met her Soviet contact and related that she and her husband would be making the trip with Savinkov. She demanded an excessive amount of money for her services to be paid up front; if the KGB did not meet her demands, Savinkov would not cross the border. The sum of $5,000 in French francs was therefore placed into her Paris bank account. The KGB felt that this was extortion on her part but had no alternative. In the end, the KGB would make her pay for her greed.

Savinkov and the Derentals left Paris on 10 August 1924 for Warsaw. Savinkov travelled under false documentation issued in the name of Stepanov. On a dark and rainy night, they crossed the Polish border into Russia, where they were met by two men dressed in military uniform. Savinkov was delighted when one of the men turned out to be his old friend Siroyezhkin. The Paris group was then taken to a cabin in a nearby forest, where they now met two more actors from the TRUST, Artuzov and Pillar. After calming any fears the group might have harboured, Siroyezhkin directed his attention to the Great Conspirator. 'Boris Viktorovich,' he said, 'you must believe this is the saddest day of my life, but I must place you under arrest. I came to like you very much, but revolutionary duty comes first.'

The cabin was immediately surrounded by troops of the KGB's border guard to prevent any escape. Savinkov and the Derentals were taken by car to Minsk and from there to Moscow by rail. Savinkov was incarcerated in the Lubyanka prison in a comfortable and well-furnished cell, which had been prepared for him. He was served food from Dzerzhinsky's private kitchen and had all the amenities of home at his disposal. There was a purpose to this lavish treatment as Savinkov soon found out. Dzerzhinsky did not threaten Savinkov with death and only told him that he was living in a fantasy world, where he believed that an army of dissidents was awaiting his word to set the uprising in motion. There was no such army and conditions in the Soviet Union were not what he had been led to believe. He said that he admired Savinkov's courage but the time was at hand for him to tell the world the truth about Russia and that he had been mistaken. In exchange for Savinkov's compliance, the KGB Chairman suggested that there would be a light term of imprisonment and perhaps even rehabilitation, wherein he could again work to the benefit of the Russian people. Savinkov did make a plea to save the Derentals, especially Madame Derental, whom he claimed was entirely innocent and had only crossed the border because of her devotion to him. Dzerzhinsky agreed to order the release of Madame Derental and to look into the case of her husband.

Savinkov was taken around Moscow daily to see for himself the great changes that had taken place in Russia since the Revolution. He was delighted that his guide and companion for these excursions was his old friend Siroyezhkin. One day Savinkov informed Siroyezhkin that he had long suspected a spy in his camp, which might result in foul play, but had never thought that he would be sold out by his friend. Siroyezhkin answered that he had never sold him out and briskly explained, 'I was never with you. I was a Red battalion commander and a Communist, when I infiltrated your guerrilla band.'

There was no doubt that Savinkov was shocked when he learned that his entire anti-Soviet organisation, and everything connected with his dream to liberate Russia from the Bolsheviks, was only a fantasy conceived and manipulated by the KGB. He came to realise that the former White Army generals and anti-Bolshevik politicians were but shadows living in the past and could not change history. Now he was given the opportunity to make his own subjective assessment of the Bolshevik experiment. What Savinkov always held paramount was the people of Russia, whom he loved and had always sacrificed and risked his life for; this element would be uppermost in his mind when he made his final judgement.

Orlov related that he had spoken with all the key figures in the TRUST and, without exception, they were convinced that Savinkov's reappraisal of the situation was genuine and that his transformation was legitimate. At his trial on 27 and 28 August 1924 in Moscow, he gave a dramatic speech in which he said that he now unconditionally recognised the sovereignty of the Bolshevik Government and threw himself on the mercy of the court when he noted that he had never asked anything for himself and that he had dedicated his entire life to the cause of the Russian people. The Military Collegium of the Supreme Court sentenced Savinkov to death; however, this was commuted to imprisonment.

When the world learned the news of Savinkov's capture and confession, his friend Sidney Reilly rose to the occasion to protest the affair in a letter to the *Morning Post* of London, which appeared in its edition of 8 September 1924. In his letter, Reilly wrote that he had full confidence in Savinkov and that he had been one of the few who knew of Savinkov's intentions to penetrate into Soviet Russia. He had spent every day with him up to the day of his departure for the Soviet frontier and must now help to vindicate the name and honour of Boris Savinkov. Reilly insisted that Savinkov must have been killed crossing the border and that the man who had appeared at the trial in his guise must have been an actor playing the part.

When verification was received through foreign correspondents for various newspapers that it actually had been Savinkov who had stood in the dock in Moscow and not an impostor, Reilly wrote another scathing letter to the *Morning Post* in which he denounced Savinkov's treachery and betrayal of his organisation, his cause and his friends. He stated that by this act Savinkov had erased forever his name from the scroll of honour of the anti-Communist movement.

Reilly sent a copy of his letter to Winston Churchill, who was an admirer of Savinkov's, to which Churchill replied that Savinkov had been placed in a terrible situation and that he should not be judged too harshly. He added that only those who have successfully sustained such an ordeal have the full right to pronounce censure. He concluded that he would wait to hear the end of the story before changing his view about Savinkov.

Savinkov spent his days in prison writing and would occasionally receive a visit from Madame Derental. Siroyezhkin continued to take him for rides in the country and around Moscow. A year later, he was still not released from prison, contrary to what Dzerzhinsky had promised. Each time he asked, he would receive the same reply: just wait a little longer. He finally suspected that Dzerzhinsky had deceived him and so wrote Dzerzhinsky a letter on 7 May 1925 deploring his status as a prisoner. He explained that he had believed he would either be executed or pardoned to continue to work for the people but had never considered that he would be left to languish in prison. He appealed to Dzerzhinsky to be set free so as to work in some capacity, no matter how menial.

In fact, Dzerzhinsky had recently suggested to the Politburo that Savinkov be released in order to write his memoirs; however, the idea had been rejected. He again asked for Savinkov's release but this time the Politburo could not come to a decision.

Several days after his letter to Dzerzhinsky, the Soviet newspapers announced on 12 May that Savinkov had committed suicide by jumping out of a window on the upper floor of the prison. Several KGB officers were reprimanded for negligence and steps to improve the physical security of prisoners were taken. Whether Savinkov committed suicide or was pushed to his death will never be known; however, Savinkov's constant companion and friend, the KGB officer Grisha Siroyezhkin, implied to Orlov that Savinkov did not take his own life.

There was one last piece of unfinished business for the KGB to attend to: what should they do about Madame Derental? She was free from imprisonment but not in the total sense. She insisted that she be granted an exit visa in order to return to Paris but the KGB could not take the chance as, once she was out of the USSR, she could reveal her own participation in the scheme to lure Savinkov back to Russia and convincingly claim that Savinkov had been framed into his confession. Always the actress, she went before Artuzov, staged a tantrum and demanded her release. She threatened and cajoled and even promised to continue working for the KGB. Finally, Artuzov reminded her how she had blackmailed the KGB *rezident* in Paris for an exorbitant amount of money in exchange for her services and now she must face the consequences of her folly and greed.

After Savinkov returned to the Soviet Union, the full weight of the KGB was brought to bear on its other prime objective, to lure Sidney Reilly back to the Soviet Union and his death. In 1924, Artuzov chose for this extremely difficult task his most able deputy, Fedorov, the man who had conceived the idea of the TRUST. Fedorov was no fool and realised the enormity of the task of luring Reilly into the mouth of the demon. Reilly had already escaped the Soviets by minutes in 1918 through his skills as an adventurer, but now more than ever was alerted to the

KGB's deceit in the Savinkov caper. Fedorov would have to devise a foolproof plan that would convince the ever-wary British spy.

Fedorov had everything at his disposal towards this end, including KGB personnel and financial means. Fortunately, he already had one indispensable resource totally suited to the task within arms' reach. This was a female KGB operative by the name of Maria Zakharchenko, who went by the name of Maria Schultz. Following the defeat of the White Army in 1920, she had settled in Yugoslavia with other Russian émigrés. Her father was a Russianised Pole, who had been an officer in the Tsar's Army and, as the daughter of an officer, she had attended prestigious schools and acquired a degree of sophistication. She had been recruited into the KGB by one of her lovers, who had convinced her that the Russian monarchists stood in the way of Russia's progress and that only the Bolsheviks held the key to Russia's future. The KGB had been interested in her because she was the niece of the White Army General Alexander Kutyepov. However, throughout her relationship with the KGB, she never betrayed her uncle and continuously refused to entice him to return to the Soviet Union. This arrangement did not extend to General Kutyepov's associates and friends, whom she would betray at a moment's notice.

Kutyepov had the greatest love and respect for his niece and trusted her completely. In 1923, he had assumed the operation of the ROVS underground activities inside Russia and Schultz became his confidential courier. She was truly a 'double agent' in all respects; while crossing the border on a mission for her uncle, she would be assisted by the KGB in order to facilitate her passage. Often she would return with a message for her uncle from the anti-Bolshevik TRUST knowing full well that the TRUST was operated by the KGB.

Schultz was an attractive and skilful actress who could play any role, although deception was her forte. She was so adroit that not even the men she had betrayed to the KGB ever suspected her, although the slim thread of treachery could easily have been traced back to her. For whatever reason, even those that did suspect her as their betrayer could not bring themselves to believe she had wilfully done so.

Schultz would play a vital role in the Reilly affair but there was yet another player whose services to the operation were indispensable. A year earlier, Fedorov had recruited a young Englishman who was a British intelligence officer with SIS in the anti-Soviet field. This Englishman had no political convictions and served the KGB solely because of his greed for financial compensation. He was a colleague of Reilly's during the 1918 period in Russia and was now stationed with the SIS in Tallinn, Estonia. In his personal papers and memoirs, Orlov never revealed the identity of the Englishman for reasons unknown. In 1972, while Orlov and I were going over the Reilly affair, I was not concerned with the identity of the British intelligence officer who was compromised by the KGB as it was of no particular intelligence significance in the modern sense and consequently I never thought to ask the name of this individual. To the best of my recollection, Orlov never mentioned or volunteered the man's identity, or if he did it is now long forgotten. However, based on additional facts that Orlov provided at the time combined with independent documentation, I was able to deduce the identity of this key player. Inasmuch as Orlov never directly furnished this identity, I originally felt it prudent to do likewise; however, on further reflection I realised that SIS was already aware of the man's identity and so, as this information was historically relevant, there remained no valid reason to stay silent. The man in question who betrayed Reilly and served as the principal who ultimately sent Reilly to his death was Commander Ernest Boyce.

By 1925, Reilly was on the brink of financial ruin and political bankruptcy. The political motivators no longer believed that the Russian monarchists would or could overthrow the Soviet Government and they no longer felt inclined to support any anti-Bolshevik organisations financially. Savinkov's recent capture had greatly diminished any support that Reilly might have had but Reilly had also spent a considerable amount of his own funds to support the Savinkov conspirators and consequently was himself in desperate financial straits.

Reilly and his wife, the former British actress Pepita Bobadilla, travelled to the United States, where he was engaged in another of his business schemes. While in New York in the early part of 1925, Reilly received a letter from his old friend Boyce informing him that a Russian couple would be contacting him in Paris on his return to Europe. The couple were representing a strong rebel group in the Soviet Union that wanted the support of Great Britain in their fight against the Bolsheviks. Reilly could be of some value in this direction.

Reilly was interested in the new development but business in New York kept him from returning. He received further correspondence from Boyce indicating that the couple were in fact the Schultzes and that the new anti-Bolshevik organisation in Russia was willing to meet him in Finland to discuss his views on obtaining British help in their fight. Reilly was already aware that the Schultzes were close collaborators of General Kutyepov and, therefore, felt the new organisation must be legitimate.

Reilly finally returned to Europe and had two meetings with Kutyepov, Boyce and the well-known industrialist Alexander Guchkov, who had been a pre-revolutionary Russian statesman. These gentlemen all felt that Reilly should meet Maria Schultz in Helsinki, where the leaders of the Russian conspiratorial organisation hoped to confer with Reilly. The British intelligence ace had little to fear in such a meeting outside of Russia considering the fact that all those privy to the meeting were reputable individuals in the anti-Bolshevik movement. Kutyepov was in a position to vouch for his niece and had no reservations; in fact, he had made several trips to Finland on his organisation's business and had never encountered any problems. Also, General Vallenius of the Finnish Army General Staff was a personal friend and would take care of Reilly's safety. Despite what would appear to be on the surface a safe venture, Kutyepov repeatedly warned Reilly that under no circumstances should he agree to cross the border into Russia. He insisted that, 'It has been arranged that they will come to Finland to see you. If they don't, drop the whole thing and come back. Don't go to Russia.'

During the latter part of September 1925, Reilly arrived in Helsinki, where he met Maria Schultz and her supposed husband. The young man who played the part of her husband was a KGB operative by the name of George Radkevich, who was actually Schultz's bodyguard and aide. Reilly was instantly impressed by Schultz's personality and attractiveness but more so by her involvement with the new anti-Bolshevik organisation in Russia. He was taken to the home of a White Russian in Helsinki, where he met Yakushev, the well-known monarchist who had thrown in his lot with the TRUST. Reilly was inspired by what the conspirators told him of the new organisation and agreed to go with Schultz to Vyborg in Finland, which was much nearer to the Russian border, where leading members of the organisation would meet him.

Just before departing for the border, a messenger delivered a sealed envelope to Reilly which contained a handwritten message from Boyce. Reilly was able to authenticate that Boyce was the author of the letter as he was familiar with his handwriting. The letter conveyed the information in veiled terms that an important Soviet diplomat had recently been in London on business and had dropped a hint to a British statesman that a group of leading Kremlin dissidents were planning to go to Finland in an effort to contact the British regarding their efforts. There was no doubt in Reilly's mind that this was a reference to his proposed trip to Vyborg. Had Reilly harboured any reservations about making the trip to Vyborg, they melted like snow in July. The letter from an old friend within SIS was reassuring and eliminated most, if not all, of the danger inherent in Reilly's latest adventure. He felt that after years of chasing the elusive pot of gold at the end of the rainbow, he was closer than ever to the fulfilment of his dream. What Reilly had no way of knowing was that the text of Boyce's letter had actually been composed by the KGB officers, Artuzov and Fedorov, for the purpose of luring him into Russia.

On the long trip to Vyborg, Reilly questioned Schultz about the leaders of the anti-Bolshevik organisation and their connections. She claimed that she was not in a position to reveal their identities, but took from her purse several old clippings from Russian newspapers and displayed one of them to Reilly. The clipping contained a photograph of Lenin standing with a large group of men, mostly well-known figures from the October Revolution. She pointed out a man standing behind Lenin and asked Reilly to take a good look at him, remarking that she hoped this would be the man coming to meet him in Vyborg. Reilly was sufficiently impressed at what he saw.

The man that Schultz pointed out was actualy a KGB operative with the TRUST by the name of Deribass. KGB technicians had skilfully superimposed his photograph over that of the actual person standing behind Lenin and reprinted the newspaper article containing the altered photograph.

Reilly was taken to a residence in Vyborg, where he met two emissaries from Moscow. He immediately recognised one of them as the man in the newspaper clipping. This was certainly reassuring and brought credibility to the meeting. Reilly was told that there would be a new government in Russia within a short time and that the coup was expected to be bloodless, or at least of short duration. What they wanted to know was what help they could expect from Britain and on what terms. They said that they would be willing to meet responsible British officials anywhere in Europe to explore the situation. Deribass asked if Reilly had such contacts in the British Government, to which Reilly optimistically replied that he had all sorts of influential friends in government, banking and industry and, with the right economic concessions, they would come to the aid of the new revolutionary government. Deribass replied that the new government would give them all the concessions they could possibly handle inasmuch as it would need all the foreign capital and technology it could get.

Years later, Deribass related that, at that very moment, 'I knew I had him in the bag. His eyes began to glitter, as if he already saw millions of dollars flow into his pockets for helping the bankers to arrange concession deals.' Acting on this intuition, he told Reilly that he wanted him to go with him to Moscow in order to discuss these possibilities further with his fellow comrades, after which they could meet in conference with the British representative. He shrewdly added that there was no time to waste.

For a moment Reilly hesitated, knowing that he had promised not to enter Russia. He stated that he had no passport to enter Russia legally and was afraid he might be apprehended. 'No problem,' replied Deribass as he turned to his companion and asked what he could do. The companion produced a Soviet passport from his pocket in the name of Nikolai Steinberg and noted that this would do. 'What if I'm caught?' asked Reilly. 'No problem,' replied Deribass in a somewhat contemptuous manner, noting that he was still an official with the Party and had the power to fire the Chief of the KGB in Leningrad without having to explain his actions. This seemed to satisfy Reilly.

Whatever apprehensions Reilly might have possessed quickly faded when he rationalised that this could not be a trap to lure him into the Soviet Union. These were the dissident Kremlin officials that Boyce had told him would make the contact in Finland; besides, Deribass was the man in the photograph with Lenin. A prominent Bolshevik official from Lenin's entourage would certainly not demean himself by allowing the Russian secret police to use him to capture a British agent. All of Reilly's good sense had vanished in the face of the huge financial gains to be made.

Before making the journey, on 25 September Reilly wrote to his wife that he had to go to Russia in spite of the fact that he had promised her he would never set foot there. He advised her not to worry; he would be safe and the rewards would be high. Even if he were caught, his new friends were powerful and would secure his release. He ended by saying that he would be back in a few days and they would be together again.

To the outside world, Reilly seemed to vanish from the face of the earth, except for a brief announcement that appeared in the Soviet newspapers several days later: 'On the night of

September 28th to 29th, four contrabandists tried to cross the Finnish frontier. As a result, two were killed; one, a Finnish soldier, taken prisoner, and the fourth so badly wounded that he died on the way to Petrograd.' This false announcement had been planted by the KGB in order to mislead the British.

Reilly, one of the two Russian emissaries, Schultz, Radkevich and a captain from Finnish military intelligence made their way to the Finnish border on 25 September. The area was found to be clear of Russian border guards. Reilly, Radkevich and the Russian emissary crossed into Russia and made their way to a village railway depot not too far from Leningrad. Radkevich watched as Reilly and the Russian boarded a train for Leningrad.

Reilly was met in Leningrad by Yakushev and a man by the name of Shchukin, who was in reality Orlov's KGB friend Siroyezhkin. Reilly was well acquainted with Leningrad (formerly Petrograd and St Petersburg), the scene of his escapades in 1918, and strongly wanted to look around the city. However, prudence dictated that he stay in the safety of Shchukin's apartment during the day. That evening, Reilly and Yakushev boarded the train for Moscow, where they arrived the next morning. On arrival, they were taken to a dacha outside the city, where they met a group representing the TRUST's political council. Here they discussed the new conspiracy and ways to finance the movements.

The members of the political council fully expected Reilly to be allowed to return to Finland and that the charade was solely to enhance the TRUST. However, a telephone call was received from the KGB Centre ordering Reilly's arrest. They felt that such a foolish move would bring down the TRUST as there was no way the TRUST could survive another blow, such as the capture of Savinkov under the guise of the TRUST. A quick call was made to Artuzov with this argument, but the KGB Chief insisted the order be carried out.

Reilly intended to return to Finland, via Leningrad, following the conclusion of the meeting and was taken by car supposedly to Moscow's railway station. En route, he expressed a wish to send a couple of postcards from Moscow as sort of a trophy of his adventure into the forbidden land. He was obliged as the KGB deemed it worthwhile to know the identity of Reilly's collaborators. They stopped off at the Moscow apartment of one of the group, where Reilly wrote a postcard to his wife and another to the captain in the British SIS who was collaborating with him in the operation.

Again the group re-entered the car, ostensibly resuming the trip to the railway station. As they neared the KGB headquarters in the Lubyanka building, Puzitsky, one of the key players in the TRUST who was sitting next to Reilly, suddenly pulled out a pair of handcuffs and placed them around Reilly's wrist. He then announced that Reilly was under arrest. Everyone in the car was tense with excitement with the exception of Reilly, who remained unmoved. Reilly was taken to Pillar's office in the Lubyanka building, where Pillar and Fedorov were the first to interrogate him. These two KGB officers were among the original instigators and operational planners of the TRUST, and had successfully guided the fictitious organisation since its inception, but at this point they were nervous at the prospect of interviewing Reilly. Reilly however remained calm as though waiting to be seated at a restaurant.

Pillar informed Reilly that he was in a very tenuous position and that it would be best for him to co-operate fully. He reminded Reilly that he was already under a death sentence as a result of his conviction *in absentia* in 1918 and there would be no escape this time. All that was required of him was the identities of all British spies on Russian soil and details of the operations they were involved in. Reilly was undisturbed by these threats and informed his interrogators that a British agent did not co-operate with the enemy. When word of Reilly's attitude and resilience under pressure came to the attention of the KGB Chiefs, they had only admiration and respect for the man.

Despite all the direct pressures and psychological measures taken by Artuzov, Pillar and Styrne, the best interrogators the KGB possessed, the British intelligence agent never confessed. This was corroborated to Orlov by two of his KGB colleagues,

Fedorov and Puzitsky, who also related that Reilly was never subjected to physical abuse during the interrogations. In November 1925, Reilly was executed. As Orlov later said, Reilly had been 'a British gentleman spy in the classic sense, but a fool to walk into the lion's den'.

An interesting aspect surrounding Reilly's execution came to light several years later, rather than at the time of his death, to the effect that in his last days Reilly had written a letter to Dzerzhinsky seeking clemency in exchange for revealing what he knew about the British and American intelligence services.

The book *Deadly Illusions*, which deals with this letter from the viewpoint of the KGB, describes this as 'turncoat Reilly's 'grovelling' letter to Dzerzhinsky. This sounds unlike the man that Orlov admired for his professionalism and bravery. The consensus of the Western intelligence community is that the Reilly letter was a fabrication conceived and floated by the KGB. Had such a letter existed at the time of Reilly's execution, it is certain that Orlov would have known about it. What Orlov did not say, therefore, becomes a matter of great importance because, in his papers and personal memoirs and in the numerous discussions I had with him regarding Reilly, he never mentioned the purported letter to Dzerzhinsky. There is no doubt in my mind that Orlov did not know of the existence of such a letter when he died in 1973 as he would have certainly addressed the matter with me. Also, based on simple logic, it is my view that the letter was a KGB fabrication. When Savinkov was captured through the efforts of the TRUST, he was afforded a public trial that became a forum for worldwide Soviet propaganda. Had Reilly actually confessed, he would have likewise been placed on trial if only for the Soviets to reap an extraordinarily bountiful harvest of propaganda. Savinkov was relatively unknown outside of Russia whereas Reilly was famous internationally because of his exploits and flamboyant style. The propaganda benefits that the Soviets derived through the Savinkov trial would have paled in comparison to what might have been expected had Reilly been placed on trial. Therefore, I must conclude that no such Reilly confessional letter ever existed.

In his memoirs, Orlov wrote extensively about the major players that had participated in the TRUST, or had been victims of it. When his memoirs are finally published in 2002, the world will be enlightened further. In the meantime, I will render a few brief sketches to bring to a close the matter of the TRUST.

Following Reilly's disappearance, his widow strongly suspected Maria Schultz of treachery as all the pieces of the puzzle seemed to lead to her. Pepita had gone to Helsinki to investigate her husband's disappearance and while there Schultz came on the scene. Schultz admitted her part in the tragedy to the extent that she blamed herself for persuading Reilly to undertake the mission. Schultz vowed that she would never rest until she found out what happened to Reilly – even though at that point she knew Reilly was languishing in the Lubyanka prison, although she might not have known he had already been executed – and that she would crawl on her hands and knees to organise his escape. Pepita fell under her charm and by the time she returned to London was convinced of Schultz's innocence.

Schultz was a woman of deep passions and immensely enjoyed the intrigue that her work for the KGB afforded her. Men were romantically attracted to her and she to them, but never to the extent of lasting relationships. It seemed that men quickly lost interest in her. George Radkevich, her KGB bodyguard who posed as her husband on foreign assignments, had fallen in love with her but she had rejected him as being too effeminate. The year following Reilly's death she found the one true man in her life.

In the autumn of 1926, Artuzov summoned Schultz to his office and advised her that one of his valued agents, Edward Opperput, was going through some sort of moral crisis and that he should be watched for his own good. Opperput had been one of the original field operatives in the TRUST and could be relied on to handle dangerous missions abroad. However, he was usually at odds with and jealous of his superiors at the KGB Centre over policy and the manner in which they handled the day-to-day operation of the TRUST. Most recently, he had openly criticised the arrest of Reilly and felt it a blunder that would expose the true nature of the TRUST.

Schultz was asked to spy on Opperput and she readily accepted the assignment. In fact, she was quite pleased and flattered by the request, feeling that she was now considered an insider by the KGB hierarchy.

Opperput was divorced and lived alone in an apartment, within the compound designated for employees of the Commissariat of Foreign Trade, under the name of Staunitz. The KGB made arrangements for Schultz to move into an apartment in the same building and before long they began seeing one another by Schultz's design. The inevitable happened: they both fell in love. Schultz disclosed to Opperput that she had been assigned to spy on him to judge his reliability and henceforth only reported inconsequential pieces of information to the KGB. Opperput was outraged that the KGB had questioned his loyalty after all the personal risk and sacrifice he had undergone on its behalf.

Their love and trust only grew stronger and in time they felt that their only course of action was to break with the KGB and flee the Soviet Union. Opperput had only one thing on his mind, vengeance. He decided that he would expose the TRUST and reveal how the TRUST had successfully penetrated the Western intelligence services and lured Reilly to his death. He also harboured a plan to conduct terrorist acts in Russia with the aid of the ROVS prior to defecting.

Schultz went to Paris in January 1927 to contact her uncle General Kutyepov and pave the way for Opperput's political asylum. She informed Kutyepov that a member of the TRUST had confessed to her that he was a spy for the KGB and wanted to quit and tell all he knew, providing he were granted political asylum in France or Britain. She did not inform her uncle that the TRUST was a fiction created by the KGB and made her uncle promise that for the time being he would not report to the British and French intelligence services that a KGB agent had penetrated the TRUST, knowing that these intelligence services were themselves infiltrated by the KGB and thereby possibly jeopardising Opperput. Having accomplished her mission, she returned to her lover in Russia.

Schultz and Opperput appeared at a Finnish frontier post on 13 April 1927 and asked for political asylum. They asked that General Vallenius, Chief of Staff of the Finnish Army, be notified. Both were taken to Helsinki, where they were interrogated by Finnish army intelligence and then taken to Vallenius. Opperput's revelations were shocking at first and unbelievable, yet he was able to provide specific details regarding secret operations that clearly indicated that the Western Powers had been duped by the Russians for years, and that more often than not the Western intelligence service's reports to their Governments were exact copies of misinformation planted by the KGB. Kutyepov was the first to realise that he bore a large share of the blame and responsibility for the situation by having placed his trust in the aptly named TRUST, thereby sealing the fate of the numerous White officers he had sent on missions inside Russia. Opperput deliberately failed to reveal all of the TRUST's operations in order to insure his own life and the question arose as to what to do with him; after all, he was personally responsible for many of the crimes perpetrated by the TRUST. Kutyepov was of the opinion that Opperput should prove his right to asylum by returning to the Soviet Union and carrying out terrorist raids. Schultz disagreed but Kutyepov would not be swayed. Opperput immediately accepted Kutyepov's challenge and when Schultz announced that she would accompany her man on the mission into Russia, Kutyepov strictly forbade her to go. He even posted guards to enforce her obedience but she was able to outfox them.

Schultz, Opperput and four experts in terrorism crossed the border into Russia on the night of 31 May carrying with them the necessary implements for conducting terrorist raids. After crossing the border, they split into two groups. One team under the command of Captain Larionov headed for Leningrad, where they blew up a meeting of some Bolsheviks and wounded about thirty men, several critically. They were able to return safely to Finland.

The other team, consisting of Schultz, Opperput and an explosives expert by the name of Voznesensky, was not as fortunate. They attempted to blow up the community apartment house known as the Malaya Lubyanka on Lubyanka Square, just a short distance from the KGB headquarters. Opperput knew that numerous KGB officers resided in the Malaya Lubyanka and it was his intention to assassinate as many as he could. On the night of 3 June, the explosives were placed in the hall of the apartment house; however, they were found before the devices could explode and demolish the building along with its sleeping residents. Obviously, Opperput was quite serious about taking revenge on his former lords. On 9 June, the official Soviet organ, *Izvestia*, placed the blame for the attempted sabotage on the British Government and General Kutyepov. A day later, the Soviet Government struck back and announced that twenty prominent British intelligence agents had been executed in Russia, among them a number of personal friends of General Kutyepov, whose connection to the ROVS was known to Schultz.

The KGB was well aware of the identity of the perpetrators who had planted the explosives in the Malaya Lubyanka and put into effect a huge dragnet that extended west from Moscow to the Polish border. Descriptions of the fugitives Schultz, Opperput and Voznesensky were circulated in every town and hamlet in the region. Opperput was the most recognisable of the group so he decided to part company with Schultz and Voznesensky to give them a better chance of escaping the manhunt. Opperput was correct in his assumption as he was spotted at an alcohol distillery near Smolensk on 18 June. He fought off several militiamen and escaped. The next day he was again spotted in the area and this time his luck did not hold; he was mortally wounded.

In the meantime, Schultz and Voznesensky were making their way to the Polish border when, on 23 June, they wandered into the village of Dretun. The village was the location of a Red Army regiment and the wife of an officer happened to spot the two fugitives. The officer's wife screamed out an alarm as she ran off to alert anyone she could. Schultz shot the wife in both legs to stop her, but the harm was already done and the fugitives were soon surrounded by angry soldiers. Instead of surrendering, Schultz shot it out with her pursuers; however, she had enough sense to save the last bullet for herself.

On 5 July 1927, the Soviet press announced the death of Schultz, Opperput and Voznesensky. The following day, the official Soviet newspaper published an interview with Acting KGB Chief Genrikh Yagoda in which he gave the complete details of the manhunt for the three fugitives. However, at no time did he mention that Schultz and Opperput had been connected to the KGB and had broken relations with the Soviets. They were only described as agents of the British who had infiltrated Russia.

The KGB operating through the TRUST had already captured two of its three prize quarries, Savinkov and Reilly. Only General Kutyepov remained untouched. The undoing of Reilly had exposed the true nature of the TRUST and, at the same time, eliminated the means to lure Kutyepov into Russia. Suffice to say that Kutyepov was the most intelligent of the three, or else his strong instincts kept him from going to Russia despite the TRUST's incentives to point him in that direction. In the winter of 1929, an attempt was made on the life of Stalin and the dictator concluded that Kutyepov had had a hand in the assassination plot. Stalin ordered Kutyepov to be kidnapped and brought to Moscow to suffer the consequences. The man chosen for the assignment was Yasha Serebriansky, who was not a member of the KGB or even a member of the Communist Party. He had previously carried out special assignments abroad for Yagoda.

Kutyepov and his wife lived in a modest section of Paris. At approximately 10 a.m. on Sunday, 26 January 1930, he left the residence to attend services at the Russian Orthodox Church and was expected to return by 1 p.m. When he failed to return, the manhunt that followed discovered witnesses to the abduction, which indicated that he had been taken to the north coast of France. Suspicion immediately fell on the Soviet Embassy in Paris and the bold kidnapping off a Paris street in broad daylight spawned a wave of indignation and protests.

A month after the kidnapping, Orlov, who was in Berlin at the time, returned to the KGB Centre for a briefing. The Kutyepov affair was the sensation of the day yet the secrets of the operation were known only to KGB Chairman Menzhinsky, Yagoda, Artuzov and a few select KGB members. While in a private conversation with Artuzov, now Chief of the Foreign Department, Artuzov mentioned that the kidnapping had been carried out by Serebriansky, who had received the Order of the Red Banner for this feat. Later that day, Orlov and Artuzov went to Yagoda's office to brief him on the KGB's work in Germany. During the briefing, the kidnapping was casually mentioned and, although Orlov assumed that Kutyepov had been brought to Moscow, Yagoda stated that the KGB did not have Kutyepov. Orlov knew better than to ask for details. Orlov had to wait another year and a half, when he had been reassigned from Berlin to the KGB Centre, to learn the truth. One day Artuzov informed him that when Kutyepov was kidnapped, he was given an overdose of an anaesthetic and died before he could be taken to Russia.

Later, one of the key players in the TRUST became a subordinate of Orlov's during the Spanish Civil War. Siroyezhkin operated in Spain under the pseudonym of Gregory Shchukin, the same pseudonym he had used in the TRUST operation to lure Reilly back to Russia. During the Spanish Civil War, Siroyezhkin was one of Orlov's principal deputies handling guerrilla warfare.

He was a giant of a man and became known throughout Spain as 'Grisha Grande'. He was also a heavy drinker, possessed an explosive temper but was well liked by his fellow officers. He was well known for his exploits with the TRUST and at times, but only when under the influence of alcohol, he would speak of his connections with Savinkov and Reilly during the last days of their lives. Although terribly incoherent during these episodes, he implied that he had been present when both Savinkov and Reilly were executed and that there was more that he could reveal. When sober, he would brush off the matter, although Orlov felt that he knew more than he was telling regarding his personal involvements with these deaths. Sometime during the summer of 1938, Siroyezhkin was recalled to Moscow and Orlov never heard of him again. He surmised that Siroyezhkin had been executed along with the rest of the KGB personnel that had been recalled under similar circumstances.

TWENTY-SEVEN

FINAL ESCAPE

I had good reason to remember the last time General Orlov was at my home as it was only two days before the events that led to his death. We spent the evening of Friday, 23 March 1973, together in one of our usual weekly encounters. Nothing in the course of our meeting indicated that anything was out of the ordinary and I found him to be in a particularly good mood. He never complained of any health problems and I had no reason to ask. I had had lunch with him earlier in the week and again there was nothing that warned me of the impending disaster. In fact, he told me that he was making a trip in the near future to visit Ray Rocca, his good friend in the CIA, in Washington DC; from there he was going to the Mount Auburn Cemetery to visit the burial niche of his wife and daughter. He asked if I and the family could possibly accompany him on the trip and volunteered to pick up the expenses. This was typical of him as I always had a problem taking care of the lunch bill. However, I told him that the trip was out of the question because Jim was still in school and his mother would never agree to leave him at home alone to go on a vacation. He said that he understood and mentioned the possibility of us all taking a trip together during Jim's summer holiday from school. I told him that I would certainly consider this.

Following supper that evening, Orlov and I retired to the Bavarian Room, where we always had our private discussions. We always sat across from each other at a large German trestle table, on which we would spread out our work papers. Following the conclusion of the evening's work, he would normally sit in a Boston rocking chair to relax and chat. On this particular occasion, he opted to sit in his favourite rocking chair rather than at the trestle table as we had already concluded going through his memoirs and he just wanted to socialise that evening for whatever reason. He suggested that Ruth join us as soon as the kitchen chores were finished, which was a slight departure from the usual as she would normally join us after we had finished our business. I felt that he had something on his mind. He did make one request: he asked if I could build a fire in the fireplace. This was no problem as I had already intended to light a fire that evening; as anyone who has ever been in the Cleveland area in March knows, it can be quite cold and this March was no exception.

It didn't take long to find out what the General had on his mind. When Ruth joined us, he immediately asked if we could take a summer vacation with him. He directed his remarks to Ruth as he probably knew that she was the boss in the family when it came to holidays. He put forward a really strong case and one that we could hardly turn down. He said that as he felt like family with us, he more than anything wanted us to visit his family niche in Cambridge. This would please him enormously as no one else had ever visited the niche nor had he ever extended the invitation to anyone. He added that it was about time Ruth met his wife and Ruth and I his daughter. I was quite flattered by his invitation and this gave me the opportunity to tell him that we also considered him as part of our family. As I looked over at Ruth, I could tell that she was also quite taken by his kind thought and the way he had expressed himself as it was evident that her eyes were moist with tears.

Ruth and I agreed that we would make the trip sometime that summer. Orlov suggested that we stop off in Washington DC and then travel on to New York and Philadelphia, where he wanted to show us around. Our last stop would be the Boston area and the Mount Auburn Cemetery. I added that I would like to show him the terraced house in Boston where Ruth and I had lived when I was assigned to the FBI Boston office and, in particular, the location of the old FBI building on Milk Street, which was just a few steps from the bank where he had kept his safe-deposit box for a number of years. He thought this would be interesting. Again he said that the vacation would be his treat and stressed that it was his way of repaying us for our kindness towards him. Further, he could not think of a better way to spend his money than on his adopted family. However, he did intend to make his spring journey to Mount Auburn as well.

That evening, when the three of us were together, I felt he was a little more nostalgic than usual. He spoke about Maria and Vera in terms of his love for them and said how much he had adored his parents. He spoke of the halcyon days of his youth in Russia and admitted that before he died he would like to revisit Russia and Spain. However, in the same breath, he stated that he would never visit Russia under the Communist regime, no matter what. It was always clear to me that Orlov had a deep-rooted love for Mother Russia although he equally clearly despised Communism and what it stood for. I knew him well enough to know that he was not pulling the wool over my eyes as the KGB would want me to believe. Perhaps his impassioned nostalgia that evening was a premonition of things to come, but if this were the case he never gave me any indication and I believe he did not have any awareness of what was about to happen.

The three of us had our usual nightcap and I drove Orlov back to his apartment. Before I dropped him off, I mentioned that we would get together at the beginning of the week for lunch. He agreed. In retrospect, I am certain that at this point he had no inkling whatsoever of any medical problem. Had he had the slightest apprehension, he would have told me and would not have made long-term plans for the summer.

The following Sunday, 25 March, Ruth and I attended our usual 9 a.m. mass at St Christopher's Church in Rocky River. Ruth is a convert to Catholicism and part of the group that I feel are better Catholics than people like me who were raised in the religion. As usual we arrived at church early as Ruth insisted that we sit as close as possible to the altar, but this particular Sunday it was to our detriment. I had no way of knowing that at the very moment we left the house, Orlov tried to telephone me when he had the first sign of a heart attack.

The next morning I telephoned him to set up a time for our luncheon engagement. There was no response so I assumed that he had already left for the Cleveland Public Library, where he usually spent his time reading. I intended to call him later in the day but got tied up. The following morning, I called earlier and again got no response. It was too early for him to have gone downtown so I became alarmed and drove to his apartment to look for him. I called his apartment from the front lobby without getting a reply and there was also no response from his landlord's apartment. Fortunately, an elderly lady was leaving the building and I asked if she had seen Mr Orlov that day. She did not know Orlov's name but informed me that an elderly man from one of the upper-storey apartments had had a heart attack on Sunday morning and had been taken by ambulance to St John's Hospital nearby. My heart sunk as I knew this had to be Orlov. This was not a good omen for me as my father, mother and stepfather had all died at St John's Hospital.

I don't suppose it took me more than five minutes to reach the hospital and confirm that it was indeed Orlov who had had the heart attack. The lady at the reception desk informed me that he was in intensive care and no visitors were allowed. I insisted as it was now an official government matter. When I got to his room, I could see that he was connected to a multitude of life-sustaining supports and was apparently in a comatose condition. The attending physician, Dr B.P. Konanahalli, was optimistic but pointed out that Orlov was a patient of Dr Henry A. Zimmerman, who would have the last word. Dr Zimmerman in turn informed me that his condition was critical and it was too early to give a concise opinion. I stayed at the hospital for several hours but it was apparent that Orlov's life was now in the hands of God and the good doctors. There was nothing more I could do so I returned to the office and contacted the Bureau in Washington with the sad news. That day or perhaps the next day, the Bureau advised me to drop my other work and place all my attention on the

Orlov matter. I was to telephone my report on his progress to Washington daily and inform them immediately of any new developments.

The following day I spent in Orlov's room at St John's Hospital mostly with the medical staff as he was unaware of my presence. By early evening, he was out of the coma and able to recognise me. I recall that he lifted his right hand slightly and acknowledged my presence with a feeble motion of the hand. I felt reasonably certain that his condition had stabilised and that he was out of the woods. By this time, the administrator at the hospital was aware of the Government's interest and assured me that should there be any adverse change in Orlov's condition, I would be notified immediately day or night. I left the hospital with somewhat less of a burden on my shoulders.

When I walked into Orlov's room the next morning, he greeted me with a grin and I knew that everything would turn out fine. He told me that he felt relatively good although very weak. He mentioned how he had tried to contact me when he first realised that he might have a problem and had turned to a neighbour instead when he couldn't reach me. I didn't let him talk too much as he needed to conserve his energy and he would doze off occasionally. Early in the afternoon, Dr Zimmerman came to the hospital and, after examining his patient, proclaimed that Orlov was out of danger and the prospects for his recovery were good. During this period, Dr Zimmerman or a member of his medical staff were in daily attendance at the hospital but this proved a burden as none of the doctors with Dr Zimmerman's practice were on the staff of St John's Hospital. Instead, they were accredited as staff members of St Vincent's Charity Hospital, which was near downtown Cleveland and in the close proximity of Zimmerman's office. Dr Zimmerman felt that he could serve Orlov better at St Vincent's and expressed the opinion that his patient's condition had improved to the point that there would be no danger in transferring him by ambulance. I had confidence in the doctor's opinion and knew he was dedicated to saving Orlov, so agreed with him. However, I felt that the final decision should be Orlov's. As Orlov also had complete trust in Dr Zimmerman, he decided to make the move. Dr Zimmerman withheld his final decision pending another examination the next day. On Friday, 30 March, with Dr Zimmerman's final approval, Orlov was moved mid-morning by ambulance to St Vincent's.

I followed the ambulance to St Vincent's and, after Orlov was settled in, joined him in his hospital room. He was quite chirpy considering his condition and definitely more like his old self. I was pleased that he was recovering and told him so, but on the other hand felt somewhat melancholy at the turn of events. I did something that day I never expected of myself. Basically I am a very private person and keep my emotions to myself, but on that day I told Orlov that I had grown very fond of him and now looked upon him as a substitute for my own father, who had passed away when I was twelve years of age. I also told him that this had not been the case at the beginning, but over time he had grown on me like the character Jacobowsky in the Franz Werfel play, *Jacobowsky and the Colonel*. He then grabbed my hand and told me that he had also grown to love me and my family. He would not let go of my hand and, at that moment, I noticed tears begin to appear in his eyes. The moment had been very emotional for both of us.

Orlov asked me about the Werfel play and I briefly told him what I remembered. He was aware of Franz Werfel but not the play. As anyone who has spent time in a hospital with a close relative can tell you, time seems to drag as though the hands of the clock are made of stone. I asked him if he would like me to read him the play and he replied with a humble, 'That would be nice.' The smile on his face told me that this deed would be greatly appreciated. I returned to downtown Cleveland, grabbed a quick lunch and borrowed a copy of the play from the Cleveland Public Library. I recall that the Date Due card reflected that the play was seldom checked out.

I immediately returned to the hospital and throughout the afternoon and early evening read the play to Orlov. At times he would doze off and I would stop, or else his mind would wander and he would ask me to fill him in on what he had missed. The play is not that long and we had completed the reading before I left. He told me that he had really enjoyed the play and noticed the similarities between the characters and us. I mentioned his play, *Love in Moscow*, and he just smiled and shrugged his head as if to indicate that his play was of no consequence in comparison to Werfel's play. I in turn commented that his play was not that bad and he seemed pleased at my appraisal. I suspect the playwright in him got the best of him. When I left that evening, I told him that Ruth would accompany me the next day as she really wanted to visit him. His eyes lit up this time and he said that he was looking forward to her visit.

Ruth and I spent the whole of Saturday with Orlov with the exception of lunchtime. He looked exceptionally good and I was more convinced than ever that he would make it. He told Ruth what I had said the previous day about being fond of him and he told her that he wanted her to know that he loved her like a father and that, in some measure, she had filled in for his daughter Vera. He added that had Vera lived, she would have been a few years older than Ruth and he would have been very pleased had she turned out to be such a 'fine lady'. He stated that our relationship was very important to him and he highly valued our friendship and the fact that we had taken him into our family.

I had always sensed that Orlov really liked us but never knew to what extent. We were soon to find out how much he cared when he smiled and said that he would be pleased if we would accept his estate. He told us that he had almost $50,000 in various bank accounts and knew of no one he would rather give it to. When he stated how much money he had in the bank, I was a little flabbergasted and felt that perhaps he was not getting sufficient oxygen through the plastic tube inserted in his nose. He asked if I would draw up his Last Will and Testament naming me as executor and leaving his assets to Ruth and I. He informed us that this was not a sudden decision as he had been thinking about leaving his estate to us for some time, but because of his illness he felt it prudent to take the necessary legal steps. I replied that I greatly appreciated his generosity but more so the fact that we meant so much to him. However, I clearly explained that it would be ethically incorrect for me to accept the inheritance in view of the official position I held with the FBI, which would be in conflict with our relationship. He could not understand what this had to do with his wishes, but I was adamant that this could not happen. He then said that he would leave his estate to our children, Kathy and Jim. Again, I had to explain that leaving his estate to our children was tantamount to leaving the estate to me and was, therefore, totally unacceptable. He seemed puzzled and did not understand my position. I agreed that I had no objection to handling his estate as the executor and suggested that he leave his estate to charity. He had made it clear that he was not close to any of his relatives and those that he might consider were already financially well off. We ended the conversation with my saying that he had plenty of time to rethink who his heirs would be and then I would draw up his will.

We spent much time reminiscing about the previous summer when we had made our antique-hunting trips and our visits to the country. He also reminded us that we would be making the trip to the Mount Auburn Cemetery in the summer but felt that he would have to forego the visit he had planned to take in a few weeks' time.

Before departing, I informed him that I would be back the next day but perhaps after lunch. He agreed that this would be wise as he knew we must have better things to do than spend the entire day in the hospital. I assured him that there was nothing more important to me than spending the day with a close relative. He seemed to like my reply. I asked if there was anything I could bring him, books, magazines, etc., but he replied that he did not feel like reading. Perhaps I might read to him again? I asked if he had any preferences, to which he quietly replied that he wouldn't mind if I read Hemingway's *For Whom the Bell Tolls*. I could understand his request for this particular book as he had never forgotten Spain and her people, from the very ordinary peasants to those in the highest positions with the Spanish Republican Government.

Ruth kissed Orlov goodbye and this would be the last time she would ever see him alive. As I left the room, I looked back at Orlov and was confident that he was well on his way to recovery.

The next morning, Sunday, was spent at St Christopher's Church, where Ruth and I prayed for Orlov's recovery. After lunch, we planned to visit Orlov. Before leaving for the hospital I received a telephone call informing me that Orlov had suffered another heart attack but was alive. There was no point in Ruth accompanying me to the hospital as there was nothing she could do, although, in fact, there was nothing I could do but sit and wait. Again I saw Orlov comatose in the intensive care unit with all the support systems in place. It seemed like a repetition of his previous heart attack. Someone from Dr Zimmerman's office, I believe it was a Dr Demany, informed me that the situation was extremely critical and it was too early to prognosticate. By midnight, there was no apparent change in Orlov's condition so I left.

Monday was another day of sitting and waiting. I made my usual daily telephone call to Washington but had nothing good to report. Every time I looked in on Orlov he was totally unaware of my presence. I left by midnight but my spirits were low as I saw no improvement in his condition. By Tuesday afternoon he had improved to the point where I realised that he was aware of what had happened to him. He was disgusted that he had had another heart attack but was reconciled to the fact. Dr Zimmerman informed me on Wednesday that Orlov had a better than average chance of surviving and that each day his condition seemed to improve. Dr Zimmerman and members of his staff never failed to check on the General as they made their daily rounds at the hospital.

I started to read *For Whom the Bell Tolls* to him but found he didn't have the attention span or the resolve to devote to the book. He would doze off as well as lapse into periods of momentary confusion, but for the most part he remained rational and was able to recognise me. A great part of the time he would just hold my hand.

Sometime during Thursday afternoon he informed me that he hoped that he still had time to become a US citizen and regretted that he had never made the effort when he had had the opportunity. He said that he had always intended to do so but had never got round to it. He felt that when he finally became a permanent resident, he had achieved a goal towards this end and in his heart felt like a citizen. I told him that it was never too late to become a US citizen and urged him to make good on his promise. He agreed that he would and then asked for my help. I told him that he did not need my help but I would assist in any way I could. He thought that his past problems with the INS might hinder his efforts but I told him I didn't think so. He added that because he had been born in Russia, he still had a strong love for his homeland but, as he had resided in the US for the better part of his adulthood and was reconciled to the fact that he would die in the US, he should become a citizen. I felt good that he had made this admission and looked forward to the day when I could see him sworn in as a US citizen.

We again discussed his will and he came to the conclusion that he would leave his estate to the Law School at the University of Michigan and/or the American Heart Association but he could not reach a conclusive decision between the two. I decided to draw up his Last Will and Testament leaving blank spaces for the beneficiary and/or beneficiaries, which we could fill in later. I felt it most important that he not die intestate; if he changed his mind when his condition improved, a codicil to the will could be added or else the will could be completely rewritten at his request.

On Friday afternoon, he made a statement that I had often heard from him in the past but this time I was convinced that he was finally about to tell me something very important related to his work with the KGB. I thought I knew all his secrets but in the past he kept telling me that he had something 'sensational' – he always used the word 'sensational' or 'revelation' to emphasise importance – to tell me and that it would have an impact on history. I was not the first FBI agent to have heard these words as I recalled FBI reports dating as far back as 1953 that contained similar statements. I remember one incident in particular after he had several publications to his credit when he informed an FBI agent that he had more to write and what he had to tell would 'shock the world'.

I never pressed him about this 'sensational' information as I was well aware that he was not the type of man to succumb to pressure and that he would reveal his secret in time. I did not feel that the information was forthcoming that day but I did venture to ask him what he wanted me to do with it. His only reply was to the effect that, 'You'll know what to do, I trust your judgement.' I had long wondered what his secret might be and considered that there could only be two possibilities.

The first and most probable one was that he had a copy of the Okhrana reports proving that Stalin had been a paid informant of the Tsar, or else he knew of the existence of copies of these reports that had survived through the years in a secret hiding place and he would reveal their whereabouts to me so that they could be readily retrieved. This would certainly be 'sensational' and settle once and for all the rumour of Stalin's association with the Tsar's secret police.

The second possibility was more in the realm of imagined romanticism but nevertheless highly plausible. When Orlov removed the Spanish gold reserves during the Spanish Civil War and had the gold transported to the Soviet Union, he was presented with the possibility of retaining one or more crates of gold at his own discretion. This would place the gold into the category of Dashiell Hammett's 1930 thriller, *The Maltese Falcon*. Perhaps I was about to discover the whereabouts of Orlov's Maltese falcon.

As described in chapter 6, when the Spanish gold was moved from the naval ammunition storage caves to the port of Cartagena for shipment to the Soviet Union, one of the trucks transporting it veered off the road and went over an embankment. It became necessary to remove the fifty crates of gold that the truck carried in order to pull it back on to the road. When the truck did not arrive at the port, Orlov went looking for the missing vehicle and found it just before dawn. With his political power, it was possible that several crates never made it to Cartagena and lay hidden in the ground, or in a secret hiding place, even to this day. What enhances this scenario is the fact that the count of the crates was never accurate despite the value, because Orlov's count was 100 crates higher than the Spanish Bank's figure and therefore several crates would not show up in the official tally. In the end, the Spanish Bank's count was accepted by Orlov to the benefit of the Soviet Government. It is also possible that en route to Cartagena one of the trucks could have been off-loaded at a particular rendezvous and the crates taken to one of the guerrilla camps, where they were hidden. Each crate contained 145 pounds of gold, which, at today's value of around $300 per ounce, would amount to $696,000 per crate.

Today I would have to consider a third possibility, which seems the most likely avenue that Orlov would have taken me to had he lived long enough to tell me his sensational secret. Since the recent publication of the book *Deadly Illusions* in co-operation with the KGB, I learned many facts surrounding Orlov that I did not previously know in 1973. This, coupled with some mysterious circumstances that transpired at the time of his death, led me to consider that the KGB wanted to prevent the world from learning one of Orlov's KGB secrets, perhaps the one that he referred to as 'sensational', and that they accomplished this end. This scenario will be considered in the next chapter.

At the time, my thoughts were on formalising Orlov's will and not on his sensational secret, as I believed I could learn about that later when he had recovered. In the early hours of the evening, Orlov finally decided to leave his estate to the Law School of the University of Michigan with the stipulation that if his memoirs were published at a later date, this should be taken into account for the benefit of the American Heart Association. I knew he was very favourably disposed towards the Law School yet wanted to remember the American Heart Association as a memorial to his deceased daughter, Vera. I anticipated no problem in obtaining witnesses to the document, but I was wrong. I decided to fill in the beneficiary to his will in the presence of the witnesses so as to preclude any legal question in the future. The medical resident on duty flatly refused to be a witness and the room and floor nurses on duty were reluctant to witness the document. I suspect that it had something to do with hospital policy. I didn't feel this was a crisis situation but still thought it prudent to execute the will. I therefore decided to telephone an old friend, George Feldman, and ask him to pick up my wife and bring her to the hospital, where they could both witness the will. George had been a former FBI employee and could be depended on for his discretion and trusted to keep the matter confidential. Unfortunately, he was not at home. His wife said that she would ask him to call me at the hospital on his return. I didn't receive his call until a few minutes past 10 p.m. and decided, at that late hour, to postpone the matter until the next day. Had I known Orlov's death was imminent, I would have moved heaven and earth to have the will witnessed that evening as the extra effort would have eliminated much consternation in coming months.

Orlov for the most part slept lightly that evening, although from time to time he would look up and nod, and a few times we engaged in short conversations. I realised that he was exhausted. I told him that I had made arrangements to execute his will the next day and that Ruth would accompany me as soon as we finished a few necessary chores. He expressed his desire to see Ruth and remarked that he was looking forward to her visit. Before he fell asleep again, we said our goodbyes. The nurse had given him a strong sedative and, as there were no new medical problems, I felt it was safe for me to leave. When I finally left around midnight, he was in a deep sleep and I was satisfied he would have a comfortable night. As I left the room, I turned around for a last look at the General not knowing that this would be the last time I would ever see him alive.

The next morning, 7 April 1973, Ruth and I were having breakfast and planning the day when the telephone rang. Ruth took the call and then, turning to me, announced, 'Mr Orlov is dead.' This came as a great shock to me as, although a very sick man,

I never expected him to succumb because he was a strong person whose instincts for survival were paramount. I realised that I had lost a very close friend and a father figure.

However, I also felt a sudden sense of relief when I realised that after thirty-five years of running, living a secret life under deceptive conditions and, most of all, living in constant fear of his life, Orlov had finally made good his final escape from the clutches of the KGB. As he had once said to me when describing his fugitive life, 'There was never a time when I didn't have to look back over my shoulder.' I am sure that this continual fear must have taken a terrible toll on him and no doubt shortened his life in never-ending increments.

I made a hasty telephone call to Washington with the news and then went to St Vincent's Charity Hospital, where I claimed Orlov's body and the possessions he had taken with him when he had had the first heart attack. I spoke to Dr Demany, who had attended Orlov that day. He explained that Orlov had passed away at 9.40 a.m. within minutes of a cardiac arrest, which had been brought about by his recent myocardial infarction. I signed a release for Orlov's body that authorised the Corrigan Funeral Home in Cleveland to pick it up. As Orlov had been satisfied with Corrigan's handling of Maria's funeral arrangements, I felt he would want the same for himself.

I immediately proceeded to Orlov's apartment and contacted the landlord. I notified him that the apartment was now under government seal and no one was authorised to enter it. I also picked up the landlord's set of keys to the apartment to ensure the integrity of the contents. I took a quick look around the apartment to familiarise myself with the scene as it must have existed on the day Orlov was first taken to St John's Hospital. Everything seemed normal.

I then proceeded to Corrigan's Funeral Home, where I made the necessary arrangements with the funeral director, Thomas Corrigan, whom I had known for a number of years. There were to be no obituaries in any of the local newspapers and no response to any media inquiries that might be made. We did not want to release any publicity concerning his death in order to keep the news out of the hands of the KGB, at least momentarily. At the time, there was no indication that it had in place the means to know this information immediately, although recent developments indicate otherwise and strongly suggest that the KGB was aware of Orlov's death concurrent with the event.

The next step on my agenda was to retain an attorney to handle Orlov's estate. This actually presented no problem as I already had one in mind: George Lowy, whom I had known since the early 1960s when I first became aware of him through a mutual friend. His office was in the Standard Building, where the FBI office was, and we had had ample opportunity to see each other frequently. More importantly, Lowy enjoyed an excellent reputation in the legal community and was recognised as one of the leading experts in the field of probate law. I knew that he was not only a person of high moral character and assiduous diligence but, more important, that I could depend on his integrity and discretion. He had also handled Maria's estate on my recommendation and Orlov had been satisfied with him.

There was to be no viewing of Orlov's body at the funeral home on Sunday or Monday with the funeral service set for the morning of Tuesday, 10 April 1973. As expected because of his past association with the KGB, Orlov had been a very private person and had rarely made close personal relationships.

On Monday morning, 9 April, Lowy and I met Probate Judge Francis J. Talty at the Probate Court for Cuyahoga County at Cleveland, where I had to establish my personal relationship with the deceased. Inasmuch as Orlov had died intestate, the Probate Court had the power to appoint an administrator to handle the deceased's estate. That day, Judge Talty granted me Letters of Administration to handle Orlov's estate.

On the day of the funeral, I picked up Orlov's good friend Ray Rocca at the airport. Ruth was already at the funeral home when Ray and I arrived. Ray paid his last respects by Orlov's casket as Ruth and I stood by. Ray had brought with him a rare orchid in a flower box and placed the orchid in Orlov's hands. I learned that Ray's hobby was growing exotic flowers, which was quite a contrast with the work he did for the CIA. Later that evening, Ruth told me that when Ray placed the orchid in Orlov's hands, he was visibly moved with tears in his eyes. I was aware that Orlov had thought a great deal of Ray and this sign of affection showed that Ray thought likewise of the master spy. I also became aware of the deep emotional bond between my wife and Orlov. That day she bent down and kissed Orlov on the cheek. I said farewell to my good friend in my own way.

In keeping with Vera's and Maria's funerals, I had a rabbi and a minister officiate at the memorial service. Both Rabbi Donald Heskins and Reverend Eugene Z. Szabo gave eulogies worthy of the occasion. As it turned out, apart from the clergy and the funeral home staff, Ray, Ruth and myself were the only ones to attend the funeral service. At the time, I thought it very sad that a wonderful man like Orlov did not have more friends to pay their last respects but understood that this was in keeping with how Orlov had lived after his defection, in complete anonymity. In contrast, had he continued in the Soviet Government without being purged – a rare conjecture given the facts at the time of his defection – he would have been given an official state funeral attended by thousands by virtue of his high government rank and his achievements. When I thought more of this scenario, I understood that Orlov's actual funeral service was the way he would have wanted it.

After the service, Orlov's body was taken to the crematorium, where he was cremated the same day. Tommy Corrigan arranged for the ashes to be sent to Mount Auburn Cemetery in Cambridge for interment in the Orlov family niche. At last Orlov joined his wife and daughter in their last common resting place.

Following the funeral service, Ray and I made a cursory examination of Orlov's apartment and found that several items believed to have been in his possession were missing. However, we did find two safe-deposit keys, which we felt were possibly the clues to the missing items.

By Probate Court order I was able to enter both of Orlov's

safe-deposit boxes on 4 May and conduct an inventory of the contents in the presence of three witnesses. Safe-Deposit Box A-109, as maintained by the National City Bank, Cleveland, contained miscellaneous papers and books. Among its contents was a 'flat pack' of developed film that later played a prominent part in the book, *Deadly Illusions*. This was the film that Orlov had kept in his safe-deposit box in Boston in 1940 and which *Deadly Illusions* speculated was the film of Orlov's 'insurance policy', his letter to Stalin and Yezhov. The film was indeed an insurance policy as it contained photographs of Orlov's Soviet diplomatic passport and not Orlov's defection letter. Orlov had last entered this safe-deposit box on 18 January 1972, well over a year before he died.

Safe-Deposit Box D-809, as maintained by the Central National Bank of Cleveland, contained bank passbooks for savings accounts held at three banks to the amount of $43,020.48. Orlov had last entered this safe-deposit box on 8 January 1973, almost three months before his death.

What was not found were the missing items that Ray and I noted when we first examined Orlov's apartment on 10 April and which we expected to find in the two safe-deposit boxes. I meticulously searched the apartment until the end of April and then for the following four weeks thoroughly examined every item from the apartment at the FBI office. Any suspicious film that might have contained hidden microdots, as well as any suspect material, was forwarded to and examined by the CIA in Langley, Virginia.

Orlov's furniture and miscellaneous items were sold and the proceeds placed into his estate. A final accounting determined that the original amount of $43,020.48 found in the safe-deposit boxes had grown to $48,500.85 with the accumulated interest on the bank accounts and the sale of his personal items. I accepted no compensation for the more than two years of personal effort I had expended while handling my friend's estate, although by law I was entitled to a substantial monetary remuneration.

Some of Orlov's personal effects had little or no monetary value and the cost of an estate sale would not make this avenue feasible.

His sizeable collection of books was donated to the Cleveland Public Library, where he had spent so much of his time. The receipt for this donation acknowledged 208 bound books, 87 unbound books and 18 periodicals, and noted that the material was found to be interesting and a valuable addition to the collection. I suspect that he would have gladly approved of this donation. Many of the smaller items were donated to the Salvation Army for the benefit of the poor.

There was one donation that especially pleased me as it not only helped a worthy cause but benefited the Eskimos that lived in Alaska in the area of the Seward Peninsula. Here the Bering Strait separates the United States from the Soviet Union by no more than fifty miles. I found it ironic that Orlov would be able to aid the Eskimo people who lived in the proximity of his homeland and took advantage of the situation in his name. Ruth and I had known a very gregarious lady by the name of Betty Abele, who was chairman of the garage sales in the Cleveland area for the Alaska Catholic Mission of the St Ann Chapter in Anchorage. All Orlov's kitchen utensils, tableware and clothing were turned over to Mrs Abele for resale.

Orlov's personal papers were donated to the National Archives in Washington DC on 23 October 1974 on the authority of the Probate Court for Cuyahoga County. This was in the depth of the Cold War and, because of national security interests at the time, his papers were sealed for a period of twenty-five years. However, these papers were subject to selective review by US government agencies charged with the internal security of the United States and/or agencies concerned with foreign intelligence, or representatives or individuals designated by those agencies. Today, I only have a slight recollection of the specific contents of his personal papers but I do recognise that they will have a strong impact on history.

In coming to a decision on donating Orlov's personal papers to a repository where they would be of historical significance, I solicited the observations of Ray Rocca, who then made the following comments which he had reduced to writing:

Orlov's personal papers and correspondence include yearly appointment books, photographs, and many folders of notes, clippings, and exchanges with people and institutions, many of them academic, during the whole period of Mr Orlov's active public life in the United States from 1953 until the time of his death. All of this paper is essentially unsaleable; however, it is of prime importance as a monument to the man, his work, and his character. It, therefore, should be preserved and kept intact for the historical record.

The probating of Orlov's estate dragged on for almost two and a half years after his death. This was due to the large number of heirs that eventually surfaced, thanks for the most part to the diligence and tenacity of Attorney Lowy. By the time the Final and Distributive Fiduciary Account was filed on 26 August 1975 and approved on 29 September 1975, there were fifty-four heirs to Orlov's estate. If Orlov had been alive in 1975, he wouldn't have believed that he had so many relatives residing in the United States.

There were a few first cousins but, for the most part, they were distant relatives, none of whom could attest to a close personal relationship with Orlov let alone having ever laid eyes on him. His cousins Isak Rabinowich and Nathan Koornick, who had come to his assistance when they were needed, well deserved an inheritance from the estate but both had predeceased Orlov. The division of the estate between the numerous heirs would have left none with a significant amount of money; therefore, it was suggested that the next of kin consider donating their share of the estate to a worthy cause in keeping with Orlov's last request. Sadly, they rejected the proposal. I was highly disturbed at this turn of events and felt remorse that Orlov's last wishes could not be met legally. I was well aware of the legal consequence of dying intestate but did feel a moral justification for adhering to his last request.

However, there was one thing I could do for my friend. I petitioned the Probate Court to set aside $500 to be paid to the

Mount Auburn Cemetery for floral arrangements to be placed in perpetuity at the Orlov niche on specified dates. As none of the heirs appeared at the hearing in Cleveland to protest the petition, the Court approved it. Therefore, every 7 April, 15 July and 16 November, the anniversaries of Orlov's, Vera's and Maria's deaths respectively, as well as on 25 December, flowers are placed at their niche.

One of the positive things that came out of Orlov's death was meeting CIA officer Paul Hartman, which culminated in a life-long friendship. CIA headquarters in Langley sent Hartman to Cleveland to assist me in searching and cataloguing the contents of Orlov's apartment. As usual with this sort of relationship, at the beginning our working association was professional and somewhat restrained. Fortunately, Hartman was the type of person whose warmth could melt the ice of any of the glaciers in Iceland. I soon found that he was in the mould of Orlov, a man I genuinely liked. I saw him officially for a number of years and even after the Orlov case was concluded, he never failed to look me up whenever he was in Cleveland on business or passing through. We met one another almost every year and corresponded until he passed away in 1991. Years ago he encouraged me to write a book about General Orlov but until now I had not heeded his advice.

There was one piece of unfinished business that was left hanging when Orlov passed away. Sometime during the autumn of 1972, Orlov approached me with the idea of writing to Maria's two sisters in the Soviet Union. When he had first been contacted by the KGB in Ann Arbor in 1969, Feoktistov had given him their addresses: Vera Babanova resided in Yaroslavl and Olga Vladislavovna lived in Kharkov. Orlov hadn't seen his two sisters-in-law since the early 1920s and naturally had not written to them since his defection. Orlov mentioned that his daughter Vera had been named after Maria's sister. Feoktistov had told them something of their present-day circumstances but Orlov wondered about other members of their families.

What did weigh heavily on his mind was whether Maria's

mother had a proper tombstone on her grave as he assumed she must have passed away by this time. He realised that there could be some consequences if he wrote but felt that he really did not have much to lose and more to gain if he could help his wife's sisters financially and provide a headstone for his mother-in-law. I let him know that it was up to him to make the decision and concurred that he had little to chance.

That November I knew he was serious about writing to Maria's sisters when he asked me to go shopping for a headstone. I knew of two monument dealers that were located near the West Park Cemetery in Cleveland and agreed to take him one Saturday. He had no idea what was available or suitable for his needs so I suggested he might wish to see my parents' grave site in the West Park Cemetery to get some idea. My mother, father and step-father are all buried in a row next to one another and when Orlov saw the headstones on their graves, which are all identical in size and style, he stated that he wanted a similar headstone for Maria's mother.

We stopped at the first monument dealer and found a head-stone similar to my parents'. The cost with engraving came to around $300. The shop's manager estimated that with crating and shipping to Russia the total cost would be around $500. He claimed that he handled shipping within the United States so I assumed he had some experience, but shipping to the Soviet Union was an entirely different matter. In my mind, I could see the final price escalating by several hundred dollars when he determined an actual shipping cost. We also visited the other monument dealer in the area and found a similar headstone at about the same price, but when Orlov mentioned that it had to be shipped to the Soviet Union the dealer lost interest.

About the first or second week of December 1972, Orlov informed me that he had written to Maria's two sisters and showed me copies of his letters. They were typewritten in the Cyrillic script and meant nothing whatsoever to me. He said that in the letters he had reminded his sisters-in-law of when he had last seen them in the Soviet Union, when they were still teenagers;

he had also informed them that in the United States he had made his living as an author with several published books and articles to his credit, inquired about various family members and offered to buy a headstone for their mother if this would be appropriate. Orlov explained that both letters were practically identical in content and asked each of the sisters to reply care of his attorney, Hugo Pollock.

Orlov never received a reply from either sister during his lifetime. However, whenever he told me that he had not had any reply from them, I could see that he was still concerned about the headstone. Even on his deathbed he mentioned the fact that he had never heard from his sisters-in-law. Although I never said so, I strongly suspected that the KGB had had a mail intercept on both sisters' addresses and felt certain that this possibility had also crossed Orlov's mind.

In early November 1973, I received a letter from Hugo Pollock forwarding a letter for Orlov that had been sent to his office by Maria's sister Vera Babanova. I asked one of our Russian-language experts to give me a translation, which on the surface seemed to indicate an innocuous reply to Orlov's letter. Orlov was brought up to date on the status of his relatives in the USSR and his kind offer of a headstone for their mother was rejected as she had been adequately taken care of in this respect. Vera Babanova asked about Orlov's daughter Vera, making it apparent that she did not know that Vera had passed away as a teenager. One interesting piece of information in the letter was that Maria's mother had not passed away until 1958. When Orlov surfaced in 1953, he had done so in the expectation that both his mother and Maria's mother were no longer alive and that the KGB would not be able to retaliate against them. Had he known that Maria's mother went on to live to a very ripe old age, he would probably have reconsidered surfacing in 1953.

One thing in particular caught my eye in Babanova's letter. She speaks of attending some sort of war veterans' gathering in Yaroslavl, where she happened to meet a man by the name of Nikolai who had known Orlov in Spain. By some strange coincidence this

Nikolai appears to be the 'Nikolai from Almeria', whose letter to Orlov was the means by which Feoktistov tried to initiate contact with Orlov in November 1969 in Ann Arbor. I would have to speculate that this was more than sheer coincidence and more in line with the KGB's probable hand in drafting Babanova's letter with the intention of allaying Orlov's suspicions regarding the bona fides of 'Nikolai from Almeria' as the interlocutor in the initial KGB contact. Maria's other sister Olga never responded to Orlov's letter. It would suffice to say that the KGB got across its message in Babanova's letter.

I must make one final observation on Orlov's correspondence to the USSR. If Babanova had taken up Orlov's kind offer to send a headstone to Russia for her mother's grave site, I would have seen to it that the headstone was sent. Orlov's estate was not closed when Babanova's letter was received and I would have petitioned the Probate Court on the basis that this was a deathbed wish. As the cost was relatively small in comparison to the size of the estate, it is probable that the petition would have been granted. On the other hand, probate law is clear on matters outside the scope of a will and a deathbed wish may not have prevailed. I did have one card up my sleeve that I would have played in the latter event: I would have claimed the legal compensation that I was entitled to as the administrator of the Orlov estate and then purchased the headstone with the proceeds. Orlov's wish would also have been my wish.

When the estate finally received probate, I felt somewhat let down as even this indirect connection had kept me remotely in touch with my good friend Orlov. Twice a day going to and from work I would pass Orlov's apartment house, which prompted me to think about him. I will always value my friendship with the KGB master spy and I do miss him. However, I was also glad that he would no longer have to fear the KGB.

TWENTY-EIGHT

THE MYSTERY

Following Orlov's death, there were a number of circumstances I was aware of that were unusual and somewhat difficult to explain but in no manner did I connect them with the far-reaching arm of the KGB. My conclusions were more mundane at the time. Years later when my attention was drawn to the book *Deadly Illusions*, I saw these events in an entirely different perspective and found that what was then the colour white was now black, and vice versa. By nature and training I am highly critical and sceptical of all the conspiracy theories that pop up after every major national event, such as the assassinations of President Kennedy and Reverend Martin Luther King. Years after the event, the theorisers come out of the woodwork and suddenly become experts on the incident, questioning the findings of those who were actually at the scene and usually putting forward theories that convolute the facts. This is not to say that there have never been instances where the newly emerged conspiracy theories have proved to be legitimate and supported by evidence that clearly finds the original suppositions to be wrong. Unlike many of the theorisers, I was at the scene at the time of this occurrence and, therefore, feel qualified to present my own conspiracy theory.

Sometime during the summer of 1972, Orlov began to mention a family that had recently moved into his apartment building. This in itself was not unusual other than the fact that the family were Hungarian nationals who had not been in the United States for any great length of time and were not US citizens. The head of the household was a man I shall call Janos Nagy – a common Hungarian name that I will use for the purpose of this text – his wife and two small children. Nagy was unemployed during the whole time I was aware of him. As time progressed, Orlov would frequently speak about the Nagys and as usual expressed his fondness for their children. He admitted that he was giving money to Nagy to support the family as he felt sorry for them and knew they were having a hard time financially. As for the Nagy children, he was always buying them gifts, which I could see gave him great pleasure.

I was totally grounded in the ways of the Hungarians as I was the Cleveland FBI office's expert on the Hungarian secret police (the AVO) as a result of the October 1956 uprising in Hungary (see pages 225–6). The FBI was well aware that the steady stream of Hungarian refugees, who were drawn to Cleveland as it had the largest Hungarian ethnic community in the United States before the revolt, was the vehicle the AVO would take advantage of to infiltrate its agents into the United States and was therefore charged with the responsibility of detecting them.

In time, I realised that Orlov was having more than an average relationship with his new Hungarian neighbours but I saw nothing evil or out of the ordinary in this. However, I eventually felt that Nagy was taking advantage of Orlov's generosity but nothing more. I could not understand why a healthy man like Nagy could not obtain employment in Cleveland, where positions of all sorts were readily available to anyone who wanted to work. He may have had a language problem but this was no deterrent for anyone in the largely ethnic community of Cleveland.

One other factor about Nagy bothered me. The Hungarian community lives in one concentrated area on the east side of Cleveland in the Buckeye Road district. Probably ninety-nine per cent of the refugees that came to Cleveland following the 1956 Hungarian uprising settled in the Buckeye Road Hungarian community and I could count on one hand the number who had settled on the west side of Cleveland. Why hadn't Nagy settled in the Buckeye Road community, where housing was more modest and certainly more affordable for an unemployed person of no visible financial means? And, more to the point, why would an unemployed refugee move into the fashionable Clifton Park Apartments on the west side of Cleveland when he could have found a more modest rent somewhere else in the Cleveland area? I didn't know the answer but I did check out Nagy's immigration records and found nothing suspicious to challenge his bona fides, nor any questionable areas to warrant further investigation. However, here I should mention the fact that from the KGB or AVO standpoint, this was how they planned for such eventualities. Had I been aware in 1973 of what I know today, I would have had the basis to request a full field investigation that would have reached into Europe and quite possibly covert sources in Hungary.

When I finally got to search Orlov's apartment, there were obviously a few missing items that I felt had been stolen and attributed the loss to opportunity and greed. I had a good suspect in mind but my primary duty was to retrieve any information or paraphernalia pertinent to the national security and not to investigate a burglary. During the course of my investigation, I was able to determine that several other items of security interest were missing but had no way of knowing if these items had been in the apartment at the time of Orlov's death. Therefore, I could not tie these missing items to the suspected burglary. Today I feel beyond any doubt that they were one and the same crime perpetrated on behalf of the KGB.

The last time Orlov was at my house was Friday, 23 March 1973, just two days before the onset of his last illness. We concluded the evening with our usual nightcap. His nightcap of choice was the liqueur Drambuie but for some reason he opted for a glass of brandy. I would soon learn why he did not have his favourite refreshment that evening. He mentioned the fact that he had recently purchased a bottle of Drambuie and the next time I visited him we would 'break it in'. When I took him home that evening, he insisted that I come up to the apartment to have a Drambuie. I declined his kind invitation but he kept insisting and his persuasiveness won me over. He seemed to be in a particularly good mood so I went along with his wish. I noticed that the bottle of Drambuie had not been opened until he poured out the drinks. He toasted our good friendship and our forthcoming summer trip to Boston. It was getting late so I left immediately after drinking the Drambuie.

Within the very first days of my search of Orlov's apartment following his death, I noticed that the bottle of Drambuie was missing. In addition, I became aware that one other item was also missing: a .22 calibre Mossburg rifle, which I had tacitly given Orlov permission to purchase for his own protection. He had kept the rifle by the entrance to his apartment at all times and I had seen it on the evening of 23 March. It was now obvious that the apartment had been burgled some time between the 25th of March, when he was first taken to hospital, and the 10th of April, the date I started the search in earnest. The burglar obviously took the rifle as it was both easy prey sitting by the entrance door and a tempting souvenir. What the burglar did not know was that there was a heavy canvas gun case that went with the rifle, which Orlov kept apart from the rifle. I was able to locate the gun case in a bedroom closet, which would indicate that the burglar had found most of what he was looking for and that the rifle was a bonus, which he felt no one would miss. I would also have to take the scenario one step further: that the burglar may have made a reconnaissance of the apartment during Orlov's hospital confinement but certainly did not actually burgle it until after Orlov's death.

On Orlov's death, when I picked up his possessions from the hospital, I was given a copy of the inventory of the items on him when he had entered the hospital, which is now part of the Orlov estate's files. The box indicating 'keys' was blank. I immediately retrieved the spare sets of door keys from Orlov's landlord but apparently there was one more set, the set he would have used, that was not accounted for, which at the time I failed to notice. When Orlov could not reach me at the onset of his first heart attack at his apartment, he later informed me that he had got hold of his neighbour, who called the ambulance. I never specifically asked the identity of this neighbour as the manner in which he related the incident clearly indicated it was Nagy. During the events of that day, I would have to assume that Nagy came into possession of Orlov's set of keys – his apartment key and the key to the entrance of the apartment building. Throughout Orlov's last illness, he never once mentioned anything about the key(s) so apparently he either had no concern or never gave them a thought. From the very beginning, my only logical suspect as to the perpetrator of the burglary was Nagy. Although additional factors came into focus that clearly indicated the identity of the burglar to be my original suspect, I never remotely suspected the KGB. I never took the matter beyond the motive of personal greed and opportunity.

As already related, following Orlov's funeral Ray Rocca and I made a preliminary search of Orlov's apartment. We found a number of yearly appointment books that Orlov had meticulously kept but curiously the appointment books from the mid-1930s were missing. These were the years that the KGB purports Orlov was in England recruiting the famous Cambridge University traitors, who became productive spies for the KGB. Another item that Rocca considered to be of immense value, as a tool for propaganda against the Soviets in the midst of the Cold War, was Orlov's Russian-language version of his book, *The Secret History of Stalin's Crimes*. However, the Russian-language version has never been found and I have every reason to believe that it was stolen on behalf of the KGB before Rocca and I entered Orlov's apartment.

Probably in part to keep up my interest in finding the Russian-language version of Orlov's book and stressing the immense value of this particular work, in March 1974 Rocca wrote me the following pertaining to the original Cyrillic transcript version of manuscript:

The original version of *The Secret History of Stalin's Crimes* was written in Russian by Mr Orlov. He himself did the translation and rendering into the final English. The Russian version is eminently publishable and saleable. Again, the financial return would probably not be large, but the impact of the book in Russian would still be considerable if the work appeared abroad or here in its original language. It is known that Mr Orlov himself gave some consideration to this kind of publication, and it would be worthwhile in his memory to give some thought to publication by his heirs or a foundation or an institution.

During the almost two weeks that Orlov was confined to hospital, Nagy never visited his sick friend. Orlov even made some comment to this effect and wondered why Nagy had not been to see him. Visits were restricted to relatives or with my approval, but this was only a formality in order to know the identity of any callers and did not preclude visits by friends. I was with Orlov most of the time and Nagy never made an attempt to visit him. I thought this rather strange even then.

On Monday morning, 9 April, two days after Orlov's death, when I was at the Probate Court making arrangements to administer Orlov's estate, my wife received a telephone call from an attorney by the name of Frank C. Gasper inquiring about my status with regard to the Orlov estate. He said that he had been retained by Mr and Mrs Janos Nagy, who were making a claim on the estate. The Nagys claimed to be 'Orlov's closest friends' and said that 'Orlov was almost like a father' to them. My wife advised Gaspar that, as far as she knew, I was handling Orlov's estate. Like any FBI wife would have responded under similar conditions, she made no mention of the fact that I was with the FBI. Ruth immediately contacted the FBI office and her message was relayed to me at the Probate Court. George Lowy, the attorney for the estate, was with me when I received the message and agreed to contact Gasper after I had formally received my appointment as administrator of the Orlov estate. Lowy knew Gasper to be a reputable attorney and had frequent contact with him as both their offices were in the Standard Building. Lowy apprised Gasper of the facts and this was the last I heard of the matter.

What I did wonder about was how Nagy had got my name and home telephone number. It didn't take long to find out that he had learned from the hospital that Orlov's body had been taken to the Corrigan Funeral Home, but St Vincent's was obliged not to furnish my identity in keeping with the prior arrangements I had made with the hospital administrator. That Sunday, the day following Orlov's death, Nagy contacted Tommy Corrigan claiming to be a 'close relative' and wanting to know who had authorised the release of Orlov's body to the funeral home. Corrigan felt that the inquiry was legitimate and had no alternative but to give him my name and telephone number. What he did not do was identify me as being with the FBI; he had known me for a very long time and knew better than to volunteer this bit of information. What Corrigan did feel was strange under the circumstances was that Nagy never once mentioned that he wanted to view Orlov's body or make an inquiry as to the viewing times. It was obvious to Corrigan that Nagy only wanted to learn my identity and had no real interest in his 'close relative'.

What surprised me at the time was the speed with which Nagy had found out where Orlov's body had been taken and what my identity was. Also, that within an hour of Gasper's law office being open for business on the Monday morning, Nagy was laying a claim on Orlov's estate. He had certainly wasted no time and for a recent immigrant he seemed to be well versed in how to gain information surreptitiously and how the judicial system worked.

Naturally at the time I realised that Nagy was more than a casual bystander but still only suspected he was attempting to cash in on the Orlov estate for the monetary bonanza as I attributed his motivation solely to greed. Today, my thinking is radically different. Had he succeeded in obtaining the administration of the Orlov estate, he and the KGB would have had a field day.

Before the funeral, there was an allotted time for anyone wishing to view Orlov's remains although the parlour in which he was laid out was locked at all times. Corrigan confirmed that Nagy never contacted him again and that, if he had approached someone else on the staff to have a private viewing of Orlov's body, the request would have gone through him as he held the keys to the private parlour. On 10 April, the day of the funeral service, I purposely looked to see if Nagy attended. For one thing I had never met the man and wanted to know what he looked like. However, neither he nor his wife appeared.

At the time, I suspected that the man who claimed Orlov was like a father to him was just an opportunist only interested in Orlov's estate. However, based on what I know now, the reason for the Nagys' absence from Orlov's funeral service was that at that very moment they were burgling his apartment in complete safety, knowing that this would be their last chance before an inventory was made of the estate.

It wasn't until the book *Deadly Illusions* was published in 1993 that I was generously given, undoubtedly unintentionally, the smoking gun that tied the KGB into the burglary. When I first became acquainted with the Orlovs following their encounter with the KGB in Cleveland during August 1971, on my first visit to their apartment they showed me a professional portrait of Orlov with his daughter Vera. This was a typical situation of loving parents wanting a visitor to view a photograph of their pride and joy. Orlov casually mentioned that the photograph had been taken in the early summer of 1938, during the time Maria and Vera were in hiding from the KGB's Mobile Groups in France. I later learned that the picture had been taken in Paris. On one occasion Orlov was on his way to the Soviet Embassy in Paris on official business when he picked up Vera at Amélie les Bains in order to take her to Paris for a short holiday. Maria was busy preparing for their eventual escape from the KGB and was unable to accompany them. Perhaps with some degree of trepidation as well as a premonition of events to come, Orlov and Vera had gone to a professional photographic studio in Paris, where they had the portrait taken. In his Cleveland apartment, Orlov kept the portrait in his bedroom on top of a chest of drawers, which was visible from the living-room. On my frequent visits to the apartment, I could not help but notice the portrait.

Following Orlov's death when I catalogued the contents of his apartment, I failed to notice that the portrait of Orlov and Vera was missing. This inventory took about six weeks of painstaking endeavour going through voluminous amounts of material with my mind set on finding specific items and records, and I now realise that the intensity of my search distracted me from any thoughts of the portrait. In fact, I never thought of the portrait again until I saw it illustrated in *Deadly Illusions* and realised for the first time that the reason why I had not found it in 1973 was because it had already been stolen along with the other items by the time I started my search. The mere fact that the portrait was in this book badly jolted me and I wondered how it had fallen into the hands of the authors; I could only presume that it must have been via the KGB.

The portrait appears in the only photo section of *Deadly Illusions* on the lower right side of the last page of photographs. It is easily identified by the explanatory caption, 'Veronica Orlov with her devoted father shortly before her illusions were shattered when the family fled from Spain to their American exile in July 1938.' Orlov is wearing a light-coloured summer suit and Vera is in a short-sleeved summer dress, which reflects that the portrait was taken in the summer as Orlov told me.

Without being able to ask Orlov himself, I only had the photographs of each page of his Soviet diplomatic passport to help settle the crucial issue of the exact, or approximate, date that the portrait was taken. The passport reflects the stamped entries and departures for his travels between Spain and France. From Barcelona, there were two border crossings into France that Orlov used to travel to the Soviet Embassy in Paris. He most frequently left Spain at Port-Bou and arrived across the border at Cerebre, and vice versa on his return to Spain. This was a somewhat longer route that hugged the Mediterranean Sea but was certainly the most scenic. Perhaps he took this route as a security measure as it was further removed from the front. In the spring of 1938, the passport noticeably reflects Orlov taking the alternative route into France. He would cross the border at La Junquera and declare himself at Le Perthus, and vice versa when returning to Spain.

This route is on the main road to Perpignan and shortly after crossing the border into France there is a secondary road that travels the 10–12 kilometres west to Amélie les Bains. In June 1938, Orlov made a trip to France; when he returned, he departed France at Le Perthus on 14 June as indicated by the border stamp. The corresponding border stamp indicating the exact date of entry into France is illegible. However, it is logical to assume that this was the period when the portrait was taken as it corresponds with information furnished by Orlov. He dropped Vera off at Amélie les Bains on his way back to Barcelona via Le Perthus.

The date becomes critical as the portrait was taken the month before Orlov defected. As Orlov was by then aware that he would have to defect at a moment's notice, he would hardly have taken the portrait to Barcelona where the portrait could have fallen into the hands of the KGB's Mobile Groups. Although Orlov never said, the probability is quite high that he left the portrait with Maria when he dropped Vera off at Amélie les Bains. Even in the most unlikely scenario that he took a copy of the portrait to Barcelona for display at his office, it is extremely improbable that one of Orlov's subordinates would have turned it over to the KGB's Mobile Groups. The explanation that he left the portrait at his office when he defected so as not to arouse any suspicion because its absence would be immediately noticed does not carry much weight either in light of the short length of time that the portrait had to sit on Orlov's desk before he defected. In that brief one-month time span, no one would have become so accustomed to its presence as to notice its disappearance. Orlov and his chief deputy Colonel Kotov were extremely close and it is probable that Kotov would have covered Orlov's trail. At the time, Orlov felt that Kotov was aware that he was defecting and, as Kotov could expect a similar fate at the hands of Stalin, there was little likelihood that he would betray Orlov. Orlov was no fool and understood the value of his recent photograph as an investigative tool to track down a fugitive; accordingly, he would have protected the portrait from falling into the wrong hands.

The bottom line is that the portrait did fall into the wrong hands but not at the time of Orlov's defection. This could only have happened as a consequence of the burglary at Orlov's apartment in 1973. All the events that transpired at or near Orlov's death, as well as the missing items from the apartment, point in the direction of one conclusion, that Janos Nagy was in fact a cleverly placed KGB agent who took advantage of Orlov's trust. Let me explain further.

My field of expertise, the AVO, was patterned after the KGB. There has always been a close working relationship between the two organisations since Hungary became a Soviet satellite after the Second World War. In 1973, the KGB had an influential liaison with the AVO to the point that many factions of the American intelligence community also felt the KGB had a strong measure of control over the AVO. To the best of my recollection, after Nagy escaped from Hungary during the October 1956 uprising, he made his way to Austria, where he remained for a number of years until he migrated to the United States. The FBI was well aware that the AVO had taken full advantage of the 1956 uprising in Hungary by infiltrating the vast stream of refugees leaving Hungary with illegals and AVO agents. Some of these illegals and agents made their way to the United States; others stayed in a third country such as Austria, where they remained on an inactive status until a specific circumstance arose that would require their services. In the meantime, they built up their legend, which would corroborate their alleged background in Hungary. What the residency in the third country did, depending on various factors, was to allay suspicion. This type of illegal or agent is referred to as a 'sleeper'.

The KGB had already made two unsuccessful attempts to subvert Orlov for whatever motive. It therefore had to reason that it could not break Orlov by normal means but was still determined to accomplish its mission. There was something Orlov had in his possession, or something Orlov knew about old KGB operations, that the KGB desperately wanted to obtain and keep out of the reach of the American authorities. What could be more logical than to plant someone in the Clifton Park Apartments with the intention of befriending Orlov and waiting for the opportune moment to burgle his apartment?

Even if burglary was not the original intention of the KGB, it would at least have in place the means to keep track of Orlov. The KGB was well aware that it could not plant anyone with a Russian background as this would immediately arouse Orlov's suspicion. What could be more natural than a family man with a wife and two children who had suffered the hardships of the 1956 Hungarian Revolution, and who, by chance or more probably by design, had moved into the Clifton Park Apartments in 1972, when Orlov was at his most vulnerable after the recent death of his beloved wife? The AVO had in hand a 'sleeper' who was well suited to the needs of the KGB.

The fact that Nagy was unemployed only played Orlov into the hands of the miscreant by taking advantage of his compassion for people. Nagy and his family ingratiated themselves into Orlov's heart and in time won his confidence and trust. At no time did Orlov ever cast the slightest shadow of suspicion on his new-found friends. If the Nagys were genuine friends, where were they during Orlov's last illness and why did they not express any sorrow or pay him any respect after his death? As they were unsuccessful in their attempt to gain control of Orlov's estate, they resorted to burgling his apartment for the KGB.

I was aware that Orlov was lending the Nagys money and this was confirmed at the time of his death, when the landlord informed me that Orlov had given Nagy 'perhaps a thousand dollars'. At the time, I suspected that Orlov was also paying Nagy's rent. If they were such good friends, why hadn't they attempted to repay the loan to the estate?

From time to time I would check the directory of the Clifton Park Apartments for the status of the Nagys following Orlov's death. I wasn't too surprised to find that their name was removed from the directory a short while later and just assumed that they had fallen into arrears on the rent and had to move. Now I suspect that Nagy had accomplished his mission for the KGB and had fled the scene of the crime.

The KGB has a well-documented history for burglary and assassinations and these avenues cannot be ignored as possibilities in the Orlov matter. As to the burglary, I have no doubt that this did transpire under the auspices of the KGB as there is more than sufficient proof. However, what has haunted me since I came to this recent conclusion is that Orlov's death might also have been stimulated by the KGB.

I consulted an eminent cardiologist by the name of Dr Esten S. Kimbel, who stated frankly that a person with a history of heart problems can suffer a heart attack induced by certain drugs. Also, it is more than likely that the root cause of an induced death of a heart patient by drugs can easily be overlooked without the advantage of an autopsy and, even with the benefit of a routine autopsy, the presence of an innovative drug can go undetected. I was with Orlov two days before he had his first heart attack on 25 March 1973 and there was no indication whatsoever that he was having a health problem; he even stated that he felt great and was making long-term plans. This was certainly not what one would expect of a man who would be gone in two weeks. Although these circumstances could be normal for a person with a past history of a heart condition about to have a heart attack, there is still room for suspicion. Orlov's death was attributed to natural causes and he was cremated without the benefit of an autopsy. I had no suspicions at the time so I did not request an autopsy; today I have an entirely different perspective on his death and, if it were at all possible, I would request an autopsy to lay the matter to rest.

The real mystery is not so much that a burglary had been perpetrated by the KGB but why the KGB had taken such an extraordinary measure. The KGB badly wanted to retrieve something that was extremely important to them, and it was certainly not the bottle of Drambuie or the Mossburg rifle, or the Orlov portrait which, although somewhat baffling, can perhaps be explained by a vain burglar wanting a prize or proof of his accomplishments. There is no doubt that other items of value to the estate were taken out of greed. The Russian-language translation of Orlov's book was of some propaganda value but hardly an item that would warrant such extreme action. Perhaps the KGB was looking for the original or copies of the Ohkrana file proving that Stalin was an informer of the Tsar's secret police? However, by 1973, the Cold War leaders of the Soviet Union had distanced themselves from Stalin and the value of the Ohkrana file on Stalin was questionable. Also there was little reason to suspect that these documents were in Orlov's possession.

In 1994, another possibility came to my attention while reading *Deadly Illusions*. In the very last paragraph of the book in the Afterword section, dated February 1993 under the name John Costello, the author drops a bombshell that would have lit up the sky for anyone trained in intelligence and espionage. The matter deals with a KGB spy ring that was recruited in the 1930s at Oxford University in England contemporary to the spy ring at Cambridge University. It appears that Costello may have stumbled on a piece of crucial information that revealed Orlov's connection to an Oxford University spy network in one of the documents that was probably inadvertently given to him from the KGB archives when he was researching his book. Costello writes that,

> One of the most tantalising clues that has dropped out of the KGB Orlov dossier appears in the 1964 'damage assessment report' which finally absolved the runaway General of treachery. It records that agents whose names Orlov 'knew very well' continued to operate from the time he surfaced in 1953 until 1963, 'that is until their exfiltration into the USSR'. Since the only known 'exfiltration' was that of Philby in 1963, it is possible that he was followed by other British comrades, whose names appear in the Oxford Registry for 1938.

However, before he could reveal anything further, the fifty-two-year-old Costello died on 26 August 1995 aboard a transatlantic flight from London to Miami. The *Washington Post* in its 31 August

1995 edition published an obituary of him, but perhaps more revealing and to the point was a companion article in the London *Times* that Costello's death may not have been from natural causes but may have been the result of a conspiracy theory that involved the KGB. In this article, entitled 'Mystery over spy writer's death', by Andrew Pierce, it was observed that an inquiry was under way into the death of Costello, who was threatening to expose an Oxford University spy ring contemporary with the Philby, Burgess, Maclean cell at Cambridge, noting that conspiracy theories were a favourite subject of Costello's. I thought how ironic – considering that Costello championed several conspiracy theories in his various writings – that he would now be at the centre of yet another conspiracy theory.

It is apparent that Costello uncovered more from the KGB archives than he admits to in *Deadly Illusions* for, at the time of his sudden death, he was researching his forthcoming book, *A Feast of Scorpions*, which planned to expose the Oxford spy cell. It is clear that Costello knew the identities of members of the Oxford cell by the following statement that his editor, James Wade, made at the time of Costello's death, relative to the book Costello was working on: 'It will cause a stir. But, for legal reasons, it is unlikely to name KGB contacts who are alive. There are household names, however. It will also indicate that there was a Soviet cell at Oxford, less famous than the one at Cambridge, which was operating at the same time.'

It is highly conceivable that Costello met his untimely death at a point when he was about to expose the 1930s' KGB spy cell at Oxford. The only beneficiary that had a motive and stood to gain from the death of Costello was the KGB and it is possible to assume that, if Costello did not die of natural causes, the only remaining suspect is the KGB. Costello's research indicates that Orlov 'knew very well' the identities of the Oxford spy cell. Perhaps therefore Orlov met the same fate in 1973 that Costello met in 1995, both at the hands of the KGB.

The possibility that Costello was eliminated by the KGB cannot be ignored by the same standards that today I judge that Orlov's death may have been at the hands of the KGB. The motive behind Costello's and Orlov's deaths could have been the same, the KGB's prevention of the exposure of the Oxford spy cell.

For those sceptics who believe that the KGB is untainted in these matters, I refer them to United States Senate Internal Security Subcommittee Hearings of 21 September 1960 and 26 March 1965. This judicial body compiled fifty-one instances during the period 1926–60 where the Russian intelligence services disposed of their enemies through abduction, murder, assassination, kidnapping and imprisonment as well as failed attempts through these methods. In addition, two cases of KGB burglary are recorded. Since 1960, I am aware of additional KGB crimes that would add substantially to the original list.

Corroboration that the KGB used poison as a means to eliminate its enemies came as late as 1994, when the memoirs of KGB General Pavel A. Sudoplatov were published in the book *Special Tasks*. Sudoplatov was recognised in the American intelligence community as the post-war chief of the KGB's Spetsburo, which carried out foreign assassinations, and he admits in his memoirs that he was responsible for assassinations, including that of Leon Trotsky, under the direct order of superiors. Sudoplatov had been a deputy to KGB Chairman Lavrenty Beria and after Beria fell from grace in 1953, Sudoplatov was arrested and held for five years before he was given a formal trial in 1958. Among the charges were that as head of the Administration of Special Tasks under Beria, Sudoplatov had carried out secret assassinations of people hostile to Beria by administering poisons and then covering up the deaths by making them appear to be accidental, and that from 1942 to 1946 he had supervised the work of the toxicological laboratory that tested poisons on people condemned to death. Sudoplatov maintained that the charges were flimsy and not supported by specific cases or examples. He denied any involvement in the 1948 KGB murder of the Jewish leader Solomon Mikhoels, whom he claimed was killed under the direct orders of Stalin, as well as the charge that he had conducted experiments in the toxicological laboratory on people condemned to death. At the trial, Sudoplatov's contention was supported by testimony from Grigori Maironovsky, the former head of the KGB's toxicology research group, that he had never fulfilled orders from Sudoplatov for experiments with poisons or for executions, and that he was not Sudoplatov's subordinate. As with all Soviet trials of this nature where the verdict is known before the trial, Sudoplatov was convicted and sentenced to fifteen years' imprisonment without the right to appeal. He was released from Vladimir prison in 1968 and it was not until the fall of the Soviet Communist regime that he was exonerated and rehabilitated in 1992 after years of appealing his case. After reading his memoirs and comparing his information with what was known to me, I felt this was the most objective piece of KGB history coming from a former KGB officer that had crossed my path.

Sudoplatov traces the programme of toxicological research to the time of Lenin, when it became a special section of Lenin's Secretariat. In 1937, the research group under Maironovsky at the Institute of Biochemistry was transferred to the jurisdiction of the KGB. Maironovsky became chief of the toxicological research group and, in addition to his research, carried out death sentences on the direct orders of ministers and commissars of security Beria, Yezhov and Merkulov. In Sudoplatov's time, the KGB toxicological laboratory was called 'LAB X' in official KGB documents.

Sudoplatov cites the complex case of Issac Oggins, a US citizen, who was a member of the Communist Party of the USA (CPUSA), veteran of the Comintern and an agent of the KGB in the Far East. His wife Nora was a member of the KGB spy network in France during the 1930s. Issac was arrested in the Soviet Union by the KGB in 1938 and sentenced to eight years in a concentration camp for anti-Soviet activities. In 1939, Nora returned to the US and Sudoplatov had reason to suspect that she was co-operating with the FBI and other government agencies. At the time, there was concern that Issac's case could be used against the CPUSA by the US House Un-American Activities Committee and in particular the Russian intelligence services feared that Nora's revelations to the FBI could jeopardise the Soviet spy networks in the US. Stalin and Foreign Minister Molotov decided that Issac had to be eliminated. During the course of a routine medical examination in 1947 at the prison where he was being held, Issac was given a lethal injection by Maironovsky. He was ordered to be buried in the Jewish cemetery in the city of Penza. Sudoplatov stated that, as he looked back at this episode, 'I feel sorry for him; but in the Cold War years we did not concern ourselves with what methods we used to eliminate people who knew too much.'

As I look back, I cannot help but feel that Orlov and Costello 'knew too much' and could have been eliminated at the hands of the KGB's 'LAB X'. There is no reason to believe that 'LAB X' does not exist today because of the end of the Cold War. Whatever name the toxicological laboratory is now called, its mission is the same.

An interesting note worthy of attention is the fact that Costello's demise in August 1995 was long after the end of the Cold War. In 1991, the KGB ceased to exist under this name and by 1992 the organisation became known as the SVRR (Foreign Intelligence Service of Russia). This was in an era of supposedly placid co-operation between the United States and Russia. However, whatever the Russians call their intelligence service, they will always strive to penetrate their chief enemies, the United States and its Western allies. In my opinion, the leopard does not change its spots by changing its name and, whatever the KGB is now called, I and the Western intelligence communities are still afraid of its bite.

The principal thrust of *Deadly Illusions* insinuated that Orlov was never a true defector; that he was always loyal to the KGB and the Soviet Union; that he never betrayed the KGB by exposing its operations and KGB spies to the Western intelligence services; and that he never fully co-operated with the FBI and the CIA as he concealed information from them. The book builds up a strong case to substantiate its claims. It also attempts to destroy Orlov's character by false accusations, especially in the area of his work in Spain during the Spanish Civil War, and attributes such Spanish crimes as the assassination of the anti-Trotskyite Andrés Nin to Orlov in spite of the fact there is no strong evidence to support its conclusions. However, as I have already pointed out throughout this book, based on my personal knowledge, the records and pure logic, these accusations are fallacies.

A more accurate and impartial observation of Orlov's loyalty was made by Sudoplatov in his book *Special Tasks*. Sudoplatov was a contemporary of Orlov's at the KGB Centre in the mid-1930s although they had no close association. After Orlov defected, Sudoplatov was given the task of tracking down the fugitive General. Sudoplatov's crucial assessment noted, 'I don't believe that loyalty to the Soviet system was the reason Orlov did not expose the Cambridge group or the kidnapping of General Miller in Paris. Orlov was simply struggling to survive.'

As the reader is already aware, Orlov was genuinely in fear of his life when he defected and he continued to be afraid of retribution by the KGB throughout his lifetime. Clear evidence of his continued fear of the KGB is the fact that in 1972, less than a year before he died, he placed his personal memoirs exposing the KGB and some of its clandestine operations into a legal Trust Agreement under my care. He specifically states in the Trust Agreement that he was doing so 'because of my advanced age and ill health but more so knowing my life has been in continual danger of reprisal on the part of the Soviet secret police, better known as the KGB'; he further noted that the revelations in his memoirs 'are highly detrimental to the Government of the USSR and would therefore be the subject of extraordinary and inordinate measures on their part to illegally procure and thereby prevent publication of the memoirs'. This extreme measure was not the act of an Orlov that was never a true defector, remained loyal to the KGB and the Soviet Government throughout the years he was in hiding following his defection, and never betrayed the KGB. To believe otherwise would be extremely naïve.

This is not to say that there are not suspicious areas or unanswered questions relating to this man of mystery. The period in the mid-1930s, when *Deadly Illusions* asserts that Orlov directed the recruitment of the Cambridge spy ring in England, is certainly a grey area. Originally I did not want to believe this thesis but in time felt that it was probably correct. Orlov contended that during this period up to the middle of 1935, he was Chief of the Economic Department for Soviet Foreign Trade for the KGB; thereafter, he was Deputy Chief of the KGB's Department of Rail and Sea Transport. He held the latter post until July 1936, when the Politburo appointed him their Advisor to the Spanish Republican Government and Stalin's personal representative in Spain. The mundane jobs that he claimed prior to his posting to Spain never seemed to be compatible with his extremely high-level position in Spain, and I could never reconcile the disparity between the importance of this position and the others that he claimed before he was dispatched to Spain. It was like the middle management official suddenly becoming the Chief Executive Officer of the General Motors Corporation.

Orlov's position with the KGB prior to Spain would have been at least lateral to that of the Chief of the KGB's Foreign Department, and I suspect that had he survived the purges he would have been in line for the chairmanship of the KGB. Throughout our conversations, he would casually mention that he had visited this Soviet Embassy or that one – specifically mentioning at various times Berlin, Prague, Vienna, Rome, Warsaw, Zurich and Paris – in connection with KGB matters during the mid-1930s, but there was one notable exception which, for some reason, went over my head, London. I always suspected that he was like one of the FBI's inspectors handling major investigations of national interest anywhere they may occur, such as the 1993 World Trade Center bombing in New York and the 1996 TWA Flight 800 explosion off the coast of Long Island. In Orlov's case, he must have supervised every one of the KGB's legal *rezidenturas* operating from Soviet diplomatic establishments as well as the illegal *rezidenturas* in Western Europe. He would direct and guide the major spy rings in various Western countries through the chief legal and illegal *rezidents* with the power to make on-the-spot decisions as to matters of spy recruitment and KGB policy. He had to have been chosen to handle the most important Soviet position in Spain during the Spanish Civil War on the basis of his successful achievements in the world of espionage. I recall asking him once how it had been possible for him to have been given such a high-level appointment in Spain from a desk job at the KGB Centre in Moscow. Orlov didn't give me a direct answer but grinned, as if to confirm that he had held more than a routine position at the KGB Centre.

Deadly Illusions credits Orlov with the recruitment of the British traitors Kim Philby, Donald Maclean and Guy Burgess, as well as a number of others, while they were students at Cambridge University in England during the mid-1930s. These notorious Communist idealists betrayed their country and went on to become the most productive spies in the modern history of the KGB. The book records that Orlov was the chief of the illegal *rezidentura* in London for a time in the mid-1930s and that he was ably assisted by the veteran KGB officers Theodore Mally, Arnold Deutsch and Ignaty Reif. Orlov spoke well of these KGB officers but never in the context of England. In time I was convinced, in part by the book, that Orlov had had a role in the recruitment of the Cambridge spies but more so by my recollection of one of our conversations in 1972 regarding the KGB's policy of recruiting spies.

At the time, Orlov directed me to a section in his 1963 book, *Handbook of Intelligence and Guerrilla Warfare*, which dealt with one of the aspects under discussion. He specifically pointed to the following paragraphs, which he credited for the KGB's success in the field of spy recruitment:

However, in spite of all the efforts expended by Soviet intelligence officers to help their informants attain promotions in government service, the results were spotty and far from satisfactory. Only in the early 1930s did one of the Chiefs of the NKVD intelligence hit upon an idea which solved this most difficult problem as if by magic. He succeeded because he approached the problem not only as an intelligent man, but as a sociologist as well. This officer took account of the fact that in capitalistic countries lucrative appointments and quick promotion are usually assured to young men who belong to the upper class, especially to sons of political leaders, high government officials, influential members of parliament, etc. To them promotion is almost automatic, and it does not surprise anyone if a young man of this background, fresh from college, passes the civil service examinations with the greatest of ease and is suddenly appointed private secretary to a cabinet member and in a few short years assistant to a member of the government.

Accordingly, in the early 1930s, the NKVD *rezidenturas* concentrated their energy on recruitment of young men of influential families. The political climate of that period was very favorable for such an undertaking, and the young generation was receptive to libertarian theories and to the sublime ideas of making the world safe from the menace of Fascism and of abolishing the exploitation of man. This was the main theme on which NKVD *rezidenturas* based their appeal to young men who were tired of a tedious life in the stifling atmosphere of their privileged class. And when the young men reached the stage when their thinking made them ripe for joining the Communist Party, they were told that they could be much more useful to the movement if they stayed away from the Party, concealed their political views, and entered the 'revolutionary background'. The idea of joining a 'secret society' held a strong appeal for the young people who dreamed of a better world and of heroic deeds.

A very important part in influencing the young men was played by idealistic young women of various nationalities who already had a smattering of Marxian theory and who acted as a powerful stimulus which spurred the young converts to action. Having been brought up first by governesses as sissies and later sent to exclusive private schools, they were charmed by the daring Amazons, and their intellectual association with them often blossomed into romances, which frequently culminated in marriages. These young men hardly regarded themselves as spies or intelligence agents. They did not want anything for themselves – least of all money. What they wanted was a purpose in life, and it seemed to them that they had found it. By their mental make-up and outlook they reminded one very much of the young Russian Decembrists of the past century, and they brought into the Soviet intelligence the true fervor of new converts and the idealism which their intelligence chiefs had lost long ago.

The NKVD intelligence no longer worried about attaining promotions for their charges. The promotions came automatically, and the NKVD chiefs looked forward with great anticipation to seeing some of the new recruits in ambassadorial posts a few years hence.

In Orlov's *Handbook*, he purposely omitted in some instances the names of the people he mentioned, as in the above case. In those instances, I only had to ask and he would reveal the identity. I was more than curious about the identity of the Chief of the NKVD who had promulgated the KGB's 1930s' policy for the recruitment of spies and suspected that the man in question was in fact Orlov; however, as this was only a hunch, I asked him for the man's identity. Without the slightest hesitation, he replied that he was the KGB Chief who had instigated the policy. At the time, I assumed he was just being modest, but today feel it was his way of concealing his role in the Cambridge spy network. Any historian who has studied the Cambridge Group can attest that Philby, Maclean and Burgess, as well as the other members of this particular spy network, fit precisely Orlov's 1930s' profile for recruitment. At the time that Orlov revealed he was the author of the policy, I never connected it with the Cambridge Group, although, had I been more astute, I should have.

The closest I ever got to discussing the Cambridge spy network with Orlov was one evening when we were talking about the British spy Sydney Reilly. Somehow the conversation led to Kim Philby. Orlov informed me that he held Reilly in high esteem because of his courage and willingness to take excessive risks to carry out an assignment. He felt that Reilly was a hero in the true sense of the word and a model of the British tradition. He observed that Reilly's daring judgement at times was obscured from reality but that this idiosyncrasy might also have been the factor that made for a successful mission. Orlov insisted that, notwithstanding certain frailties in Reilly's character, he was indeed the mould for and the standard by which intelligence personnel should be selected.

Orlov observed that Philby was the opposite of Reilly in that he took up a cause against his own country thus becoming a traitor rather than a hero. Orlov related that Philby had caused considerable damage to his own country as well as to the West, although, from the Soviet perspective, he was probably the best asset the KGB had ever developed to penetrate the Western intelligence establishment. In retrospect, I would have to say that Orlov knew what he was talking about based on his probable personal knowledge of Philby's recruitment.

There was yet another factor that came to my attention which led me to believe that Orlov may have had some connection with the recruitment of the Cambridge Group, or at least some degree of personal knowledge. When Orlov died, I donated most of his large collection of hardback books to the Cleveland Public Library. However, I did keep his books on espionage and the Spanish Civil War for my own personal collection. After I learned of his possible connection with the Cambridge Group through *Deadly Illusions*, I recalled that one of the books I had claimed was Orlov's personal copy of *PHILBY: The Spy Who Betrayed a Generation* by Bruce Page et al (André Deutsch, London, 1968). It was then I noticed that throughout this book the margins contained a system of pencilled notations of one dot, two dots and three dots, as well as horizontal and vertical lines in a variety of combinations, which appeared to be some sort of personal code. I reviewed Orlov's other personal books and could not find the same type of coded entries. I attempted to analyse the coded paragraphs by correlating the information in the paragraphs with what information I knew about Orlov in the concurrent time frame but never came to any definite conclusions. What did not escape me was the fact that Orlov had more than a passing interest in the Philby book.

While on the topic of the Cambridge spy cell, there is yet another myth that should be laid to rest. This one deals with supposed meetings that Orlov had with Philby in France during the Spanish Civil War. *Deadly Illusions* relates that,

Philby was scheduled to leave London by 4 June [1937], but it was not until 4 September that [Arnold] Deutsch eventually received specific instructions from the Centre for SONNCHEN [Philby's code name] personally to re-establish contact with Orlov. The arrangements were made through the NKVD's 'legal' *rezident* in Paris, Georgy Niklaevich Kosenko, whose code name was FIN. Ten days later Philby travelled to Biarritz, the elegant spa on the French Atlantic coast, to make his first rendezvous in two years with Orlov. In the café of the Miramar Hotel they arranged that they would meet at least twice a month at Narbonne to exchange military and political intelligence according to a prearranged schedule.

The episode indicates that Narbonne was chosen for the meeting site as it was convenient for Orlov and would not arouse any suspicion if Philby made the trip. There, Orlov and Philby would hold their regular meetings.

However, Orlov's Soviet diplomatic passport, which I retrieved from his safe-deposit box shortly after he died in 1973 and which the KGB did not know was still in existence, recorded Orlov's travels between Spain and France. The passport contains the dated stamped ink impressions for each time he crossed the border with the city of departure and the city of entry noted in both directions. What he told me during his lifetime concerning his travels between Spain and France coincided exactly with the dates that were reflected in his passport. This supported my belief that he had always been truthful with me.

Orlov's passport does not indicate that he made any trips outside of Spain during the month of September 1937, when the KGB contends that Orlov met Philby in Biarritz for the first time in two years. Orlov did make two trips to France in November 1937 and one in December 1937, but these trips were in conjunction with making arrangements to hide his wife and daughter in France. However, it is conceivable that he could have made time to meet Philby as the route he took could have taken him near to Narbonne. Orlov made six trips into France during 1938 before he defected, one of which was a business trip to Paris during June. The other five journeys were short overnight trips to his family's secret hiding place in France, which was far away from Narbonne. The stamped border entries verify the route to the secret hiding place.

The twice-a-month meetings between Orlov and Philby that the KGB contends took place are not supported by the official record. Orlov would not have travelled to France to meet Philby using a false passport as he would have lost his diplomatic immunity if he were caught in a compromising situation. There was no valid reason for him to have resorted to false documentation under any circumstances. In addition, he could not afford to use false documentation as by 1937 he was well known to the border-crossing officials in both Spain and France. This is not to suggest that Philby was not used by the KGB, but it seems unbelievable that a twenty-five-year-old spy on the level of a reporter would have been handled by the chief of the organisation rather than by someone on Orlov's staff.

To my personal knowledge, Orlov never made his connection to the Cambridge Group known to the American authorities and, on the surface, this would appear to substantiate the KGB's claim that by withholding this information he had not been completely honest with the US Government. What has to be understood is the fact that Orlov made a pact with the devil and had to hold up his end of the bargain to keep his and his family's lives intact. His defection letter to Stalin and Yezhov was his insurance for survival, his promise not to divulge any of the KGB's operations and spies in exchange for the KGB not retaliating against him, his family or his relatives living in Russia. As long as he held his silence, everyone was safe, as witnessed by the fact that the KGB did not make its first contact with Orlov until 1969. At this juncture, there were only two possibilities why this contact occurred: either the KGB had never given up its search for the recalcitrant defector but had not been able to locate him until 1969, or else it had abided by its end of the bargain until there was a very special need to find him in 1969.

During his years in hiding, Orlov could never know for certain which of these two scenarios was in operation. Under these conditions, he had to be totally committed to safeguarding his and his family's lives by remaining in hiding and not revealing any of the KGB's secrets. Not knowing how effective his 'insurance' was, he lived in constant fear of his life.

By 1953, Orlov felt that he had paid enough premiums on his 'life insurance' and reasoned that his relatives in Russia must have died of old age by this time, so he felt secure enough to surface, but not out of hiding, for the purpose of denouncing Stalin. From that day forward, he furnished invaluable information to the FBI, the CIA and the US Senate Judiciary Committee investigating internal security, and gave a picture of KGB operations never before known. However, he still did not disclose his alleged work in England.

Perhaps he felt that he had nothing to disclose as there was no way he could have known how far his recruits had travelled on the path to top positions within the British Government. In time, Philby, Burgess and Maclean had all achieved brilliant careers in positions of trust, where they were privy to many secrets of the Western establishment; however, there was no way Orlov would have known this from his hiding place in the United States. After all, they were mere college students in the 1930s and after

Orlov defected in 1938 he had no way of following their careers. Even if Orlov had been in contact with Philby several years later in Spain during the Spanish Civil War, Philby was still only a foreign correspondent and his prospects for the future did not look bright. Orlov was probably first aware of Guy Burgess and Donald Maclean after their highly publicised escape to Moscow in May 1951, when they were about to be arrested for treason. At that point, Orlov had not yet surfaced and, for fear for his own safety, probably felt that the damage was already done; what little he could add to the matter was of questionable value as compared to the greater risk that would have been imposed on his own longevity. I suspect that he used the same reasoning when the world became aware that Philby was also a Russian spy after he fled to Moscow in January 1963 and subsequently boldly admitted working for the KGB.

Notwithstanding my own conjecture as stated above, there was another factor that more than likely impacted on his decision not to disclose his connection with the Cambridge Group to the American authorities: 'loyalty', not to the KGB or the Soviet Government, but to the spies he may have recruited or been responsible for recruiting. From my own experiences, I know that a strong bond exists between an agent and his informant with the underlying tacit understanding that the agent will never breach this trust and confidentiality by revealing the identity of the informant. Orlov understood that I had to be running informants on behalf of the FBI and on several occasions casually asked what my policy would be if I were placed in a position where I was forced to divulge the identity of a source. I told him that this would never happen as my only priority was my loyalty to the informant. He agreed with my assessment and related that this would be his position.

On one occasion he even pointed out several paragraphs in his handbook on intelligence that were relevant to our topic of discussion concerning loyalty to informants. These paragraphs reflected his strong belief that loyalty towards informants had to be maintained. In particular, he noted the following paragraph from his book: 'Unlike Western intelligence services, Soviet intelligence treats its informants with genuine solicitude. It never violates its promise not to divulge their identity or services in behalf of the Soviet Union, and it rushes to their aid whenever they are in trouble.' In retrospect, the following sentence pointed out by Orlov seems to be most applicable to Orlov's probable relationship with the Cambridge spies: 'The dangers to which the informants and the officer expose themselves and the joys they share as a result of successful exploits bind them into a bond of genuine friendship, and I have seen many manifestations of sincere devotion and affection on the part of the officers towards the informants.' Perhaps Orlov was trying to tell me something.

However, I do know that if Orlov had had to choose between his loyalty to the US Government and any loyalty he might have had towards Philby and the others, when it came to be a matter of US national security he would have come down on the side of the United States. This is not speculation on my part but based on his co-operation with the FBI, when he did reveal the identities of KGB officers and gave the most in-depth picture of the KGB that was available up to that time. Had he known at the time what had become of the Cambridge Group, he would not have hesitated to furnish that information to the FBI. He kept his silence, although, had I had the least inkling he was somehow connected to the Cambridge spy network, my asking him about it would have resolved the matter. Of course, I am assuming that, unlike other claims put forward by the KGB, the information to this effect is not a fabrication.

There is one other area that I must address which would be a dereliction of my duty if I did not bring the matter to the reader's attention. In the spirit of the post-Cold War period, the Soviets released information in 1992 as to how they were able to steal US atom bomb secrets during the Second World War, which enabled them to develop their own nuclear weapon. They credit a vital link to this end to Morris Cohen, an idealistic member of the Abraham Lincoln Battalion who fought on the side of the Republicans during the Spanish Civil War. They claim that Cohen was recruited into Soviet intelligence in 1938, when he was recuperating from an injury in Barcelona. In 1941 or 1942, Cohen came in contact with a physicist who was working on the Manhattan Project and this information was passed on to Soviet intelligence. The physicist was recruited by the Soviets and the rest is history. In 1950, Morris Cohen and his wife Lona escaped the FBI dragnet, which rounded up the members of the Soviet spy ring involved in stealing US atomic secrets and fled to England under their new identities of Peter and Helen Kroger. There they became members of another KGB spy network that operated under the leadership of a KGB illegal by the pseudonym of Gordon Lonsdale. The Lonsdale spy network succeeded in penetrating the British naval base at Portland and stole British secrets on submarine warfare. In 1961, the CIA came into possession of information that led to the downfall of the Lonsdale spy ring and the members of the network, including Lonsdale, were arrested and convicted of espionage. The Cohens were imprisoned in England for a number of years until they were repatriated to Moscow in 1964 in exchange for Greville Wynne, the British businessman who had acted as a courier for British intelligence and was caught by the KGB and tried.

In *Deadly Illusions*, it states that,

> Orlov's NKVD file reveals that it was he who personally selected, trained and recruited Morris Cohen. . . . A dedicated Communist and former high school football star, Cohen was selected for training at the secret spy school, where he demonstrated a special aptitude for undercover work. His NKVD file shows that in terms of resourcefulness and longevity, Cohen's active career rivalled that of Philby. 'In April 1938,' Cohen recalled in his KGB autobiography, 'I was one of a group of various nationalities sent to a conspiratorial school in Barcelona. Our chief commissar and leaders were Soviets.'

It is important to note that Cohen in his 'KGB autobiography' does not mention Orlov by name; had he done so, *Deadly Illusions* would not have ignored this fact. The KGB certainly could not alter Cohen's autobiography as it was already in print by that time. The 'chief commissar' that Cohen mentions may be Colonel Kotov, Orlov's deputy in charge of all the KGB's guerrilla warfare training centres in Spain during the Spanish Civil War; however, even this possibility is somewhat remote. Orlov set the policy and his deputy enforced it. Kotov handled the day-to-day operations at all the guerrilla warfare camps, including the specialised training schools within the camps. It would have been highly unlikely for Kotov to have had any direct contact with Cohen as he operated from KGB headquarters through his staff, who were stationed at each guerrilla training camp. As to the term 'commissar', it seems that everyone above a relatively minor rank was called a commissar in the Soviet political and military structure of the time and in this instance the 'chief commissar' was probably a reference to the camp's commandant.

From the time of Cohen's self-admitted recruitment in April 1938 to Orlov's defection on 11 July 1938, there is only a period of about three months in which Orlov and Cohen could have interacted. By early 1938, Orlov's entire concentration was on his efforts to safeguard his family by hiding them in France and on his contingency plans to defect. Over 3,000 recruits passed through the various schools at his guerrilla camps during the period he was in Spain and it was highly unlikely that he even concerned himself with the names on the personnel lists. To say that Orlov 'personally selected, trained and recruited Morris Cohen' during this crucial period in his life is grossly exaggerated and falls into the category of KGB disinformation, which Costello then honestly reported.

I believe that the key to unlocking all these mysteries – and the question-mark surrounding Orlov's and Costello's death – is the appendix to the defection letter that Orlov wrote to Stalin and Yezhov in 1938, in which he outlined all of the KGB's secret operations that he was privy to. It would seem that by 1973 the appendix contained few secrets of present-day value to the KGB. If the KGB assertion was correct that Orlov was the mastermind behind the recruitment of the Cambridge Group of spies, they had all been exposed by 1973 and the appendix would therefore have little value today. However, at this point we must stop and reconsider the facts.

My contention is that there was one more espionage operation or spy mentioned in the appendix that had not surfaced by 1973 and probably has never surfaced to this day. Possibly it was the information regarding the KGB's spy cell that was recruited at Oxford University in the 1930s. Orlov was an old man by 1973 and actually had little to fear from the KGB. He had twice turned down the KGB's proposal for him to return to the Soviet Union and it was evident that his loyalty and trust lay with the US Government. It was therefore conceivable that he might expose the secret he carried with him to the FBI or the CIA before his death. Perhaps this was the 'sensational' information that he wanted to tell me just before he died.

Whatever the KGB was seeking had to be of the highest priority considering the extraordinary efforts it went to to put its elaborate plan into effect before Orlov died. To my personal knowledge, Orlov's defection letter and its appendix were never found, which would strongly indicate that the letter and appendix were the motive for the burglary. My guess is that the person or persons the KGB wanted to shield were well-respected and prominent official(s) with the British or American Governments. Perhaps another member of the Cambridge Group that had never been exposed, or possibly someone from the Oxford Group, or perhaps even the unidentified individual from Harvard University that the KGB had asked Orlov to seek a dead-drop accommodation for in Boston on his 1932 trip to the United States. Whoever or whatever it was, Orlov's 'sensational' secret went to the grave with him in 1973.

POSTSCRIPT

KGB General Alexander Orlov was laid to rest in Cambridge, Massachusetts, following his death in April 1973. As already related, prior to his death the KGB twice made strong overtures to him to return to the Soviet Union for their own political agenda or possibly worse. However, Orlov vehemently rejected the KGB's offer and vowed that he would never return to the Soviet Union while the Communists and the KGB were in power. He never rejected the possibility of visiting his homeland but only when conditions changed in Russia.

Orlov did in fact return to the Soviet Union by a roundabout way shortly after he died. At the time of his death, I discussed with one of my colleagues in the US intelligence community the possibility of having some of Orlov's ashes shipped to the Soviet Union and secretly deposited at an appropriate location in Moscow. My colleague agreed that this would be a fitting accolade to the man who had assisted the US Government in the fight against the spread of Communism at the risk of his own life. Like myself, he was aware of Orlov's strong bonds to Russia and his passionate aversion to the KGB and Communism and felt the gesture was appropriate. My personal motivation was sentimental attachment to the old KGB General as well as giving him the opportunity to have the last laugh on the KGB. I am positive he would have approved the gesture with his usual grin.

At the time Orlov was cremated, I asked Tommy Corrigan to separate and box a small portion of Orlov's ashes from the bulk of ashes that were in the process of being prepared for shipment to Mount Auburn Cemetery. In turn, I gave the small box of ashes to my colleague, who agreed to make the shipping arrangements to the USSR and final burial. Several months later, I was assured by my colleague that Orlov's ashes had made their way to Gorky Park, not too far from the Kremlin and the old KGB Centre, in Moscow, where they had been deposited clandestinely. He knew how much Orlov and his family had enjoyed the park when he was assigned to the KGB Centre and felt this venue would be a fitting place for their final disposal. I agreed.

I have often wondered what the official KGB reaction would be if it knew that its archenemy's ashes were buried in Moscow right under its nose. I would venture that it would be really riled to know that in spite of its very best efforts to lure its master spy to the Soviet Union, it was its staunchest adversaries who accomplished the feat.

INDEX